CONTROVERSIAL ISSUES
CONFRONTING SPECIAL EDUCATION

CONTROVERSIAL ISSUES CONFRONTING SPECIAL EDUCATION

DIVERGENT PERSPECTIVES

SECOND EDITION

WILLIAM STAINBACK
SUSAN STAINBACK
University of Northern Iowa

ALLYN AND BACON
Boston   London   Toronto   Sydney   Tokyo   Singapore

Senior Editor: Ray Short
Editorial Assistant: Christine M. Shaw
Executive Marketing Manager: Steve Dragin
Production Administrator: Annette Joseph
Production Coordinator: Holly Crawford
Editorial-Production Service: Connie Leavitt, Camden Type 'n Graphics
Composition Buyer: Linda Cox
Manufacturing Buyer: Megan Cochran
Cover Administrator: Suzanne Harbison
Cover Designer: Susan Paradise

Copyright ©1996, 1992 by Allyn & Bacon
A Simon & Schuster Company
Needham Heights, Mass. 02194

Library of Congress Cataloging-in-Publication Data

Controversial issues confronting special education : divergent
    perspectives / [edited by] William Stainback, Susan Stainback. —
2nd ed.
        p. cm.
    Includes bibliographical references.
    ISBN 0-205-18266-6
    1. Special education—United States.   I. Stainback, William C.
II. Stainback, Susan Bray.
LC3981.C67   1995
371.9'0973—dc20   95-12622
                                                          CIP

Printed in the United States of America
10 9 8 7 6 5 4 3 2 1 00 99 98 97 96 95

*This book is dedicated to
Gabriella Bray Stainback,
our smiling, supportive other,
who is responsible for us
maintaining our priorities in
perspective on a daily basis*

Contents

Few, if any, people would advocate that their field never change, that lack of growth and stagnation serve as the norm. Change, however, along with potentially providing benefits, is also fraught with potential dangers. Change without direction or in ill-conceived directions can create difficulties and problems sometimes beyond those encountered with traditional theories, perspectives, and practices. Thus it is essential to approach change cautiously, with careful thought and analysis of the major issues. Discussion and debate of current and emerging theories, perspectives, processes, and procedures can help provide an impetus for carefully thought out experimentation and prudent change. This is as true in education as it is in any other field.

As we approach the twenty-first century, a number of critical issues or questions confront the field of special education that could potentially profoundly change the nature of the field in ways never before considered possible. For example, should all children, including those classified as having profound and multiple disabilities, be included in the mainstream of general education classrooms? Should selected students be labeled gifted and talented and given special programs to meet their unique needs, or should we instead identify and foster the gifts and talents of all students? Should there be a de-emphasis on behavioral, directive approaches to teaching and a corresponding increase in the holistic, constructivistic perspective? Is it realistic to advocate for increased collaboration among school personnel and students with so little time in the schools for this to occur? What about research—is the field dominated by quantitative research methodologies based on a positivistic scientific theory to the extent that it stifles understanding, critical thought, creativity, and progress in the field?

This book draws together divergent perspectives on these and other controversial issues in general and special education. Each contributing author was requested to outline his or her position about a particular issue and to provide the strongest supporting arguments and evidence available.

There are a number of changes and updates in this revised edition of *Controversial Issues Confronting Special Education*. The book reflects the most recent knowledge, thought, and ideas of the authors regarding the topics presented. All of the original chapters included in the first edition have been rewritten. Most have been almost completely changed; all contain updated references and discussion of recent changes in the field. In addition, totally new chapters on holistic, constructivistic, and critical thought regarding instruction, assessment, and classroom discipline are now an integral part of the book along with new chapters on the pros and limitations of the movement toward competitive employment for adults with disabilities.

The book is divided into twelve sections. Each addresses a major issue in education. The reader will find that the perspectives presented in each section are divergent. They are often conflicting, but not always; sometimes they are simply different. That is, the book is designed to provide the reader with different and often conflicting perspectives about the most hotly debated issues in the field.

A number of people need to be thanked. We are grateful to the contributors who provided excellent and progressive information in a timely fashion. They deserve special thanks for their willingness to adjust their busy professional and personal agendas to meet the time lines of the production schedule. We also are grateful to Dr. Sandy Alper who has provided encouragement and support for all of our scholarly endeavors, including this book. Finally, Ray Short, Senior Editor at Allyn and Bacon, contributed significantly to the impetus for the development of the book as well as this revised edition.

CONTRIBUTORS

Howard S. Adelman is professor of psychology and codirector of the School of the Mental Health Project at the University of California, Los Angeles. He began his professional career as a remedial classroom teacher in 1960 and received his Ph.D. in psychology from UCLA in 1966. From 1966 to the present, he has been involved in research and teaching focused on youngsters in school settings who manifest learning, behavior, and emotional problems. He and his colleagues have published a variety of works relevant to the fields of education and mental health. In keeping with a reciprocal deterministic understanding of human behavior, one emphasis in much of his work has been on delineating sequential intervention models that address the need first for system changes and then, if needed, individual remediation. Another focus has been on clarifying the role of intrinsic motivation in relation to the causes and correction of learning and behavior problems.

M. L. Anderegg holds a doctorate in behavioral disorders from Georgia State University with a cognate area in psychology. Dr. Anderegg is executive director of the Cobb Education Consortium, a collaborative of six public education entities. The Consortium has won widespread acclaim for its innovative initiatives in public education. In her fourteen-year involvement in education, she has taught students with mild to moderate disabilities in both general and special education settings, and she continues to move between general and special education settings.

Dr. Anderegg is well known for more than twenty years of advocacy for individuals with special needs. Her main interests are children and survivors from abusive backgrounds and children with aggressive and violent behaviors. She has served as an expert witness in legal cases to preserve the rights of children to a free appropriate education. She has had more than thirty articles published by professional journals, coauthored five textbook chapters and a curriculum guide, and coedited a dictionary of special education and rehabilitation. She has also served as an associate editor with professional journals such as *Exceptional Children, Remedial and Special Education, Teacher Education and Special Education, Journal of Teacher Education,* and *Beyond Behavior.*

Barbara Ayres is currently an assistant professor of special education at Montana State University, Billings. She received her Ph.D. from Syracuse University in 1993. In addition to teaching undergraduate- and graduate-level courses in special education, she spends time working alongside educators and parents in Montana around issues such as school inclusion, cooperative learning, adult teaming, and positive behavioral support.

Douglas Biklen is a professor of cultural foundations of education in the School of Education at Syracuse University. He has published numerous books on educational issues, including *Schooling Without Labels: Parents, Educators and Inclusive Education* (Temple University Press, 1992) and *Achieving the Complete School* (Teacher College Press, 1985, coauthored with Robert Bogdan, Dianne L. Ferguson, Stanford J. Searl, and Steven J. Taylor), and *Communication Unbound* (Teacher College Press, 1993). For over twenty years he has been an outspoken advocate of full inclusion of children with disabilities in America's schools. He has received leadership awards for his work from such diverse organizations as the National Parent Network on Disabilities and the Association for Persons with Severe Disabilities. He was executive producer of the nationally acclaimed documentary *Regular Lives,* which aired on PBS stations nationally in 1988. He is also the educational advisor to HBO's Academy Award–nominated documentary *Educating Peter,* the story of one child's inclusion in a regular class.

Dr. Biklen teaches and does research on the sociology of disability, educational mainstreaming, and most recently, communication. His latest articles have appeared in the *Harvard Educational Review, Journal of the Association for Persons with Severe Handicaps,* and *Topics in Language Disorders.* News accounts of his work have appeared in the *New York Times Magazine, Newsweek, U.S. News and World Report,* the *Washington Post Magazine,* and on *CBS Evening News,* ABC's *Primetime Live,* NPR's *Talk of the Nation,* and the nationally syndicated *Larry King Live Radio.* Dr. Biklen has been a member of the faculty at Syracuse since 1973.

Robert Bogdan received his Ph.D. in sociology from Syracuse University in 1971. He is a professor of education and sociology at Syracuse University where he directs the interdisciplinary doctoral program in the social services. He has published widely in qualitative research methods and disability studies.

Barbara Clark is a professor in the Division of Special Education at California State University, Los Angeles, where she is coordinator for graduate programs in the area of gifted education. Dr. Clark is the author of the widely used text, *Growing Up Gifted,* now in its fourth edition, published by Charles E. Merrill in 1979, 1983, 1988, and 1992, and *Optimizing Learning,* published by the same company in 1986. She has chapters in several books, including "Early Development of Cognitive Abilities and Giftedness" in J. Whitmore (Ed.), *Intellectual Giftedness in Young Children* (Hawthorne Press, 1986), and "Educating Gifted Students in a Multicultural Society" in J. Banks (Ed.), *Multicultural Education* (Allyn & Bacon, 1993). In addition, she has published many articles in a variety of professional journals and serves as a review editor for the *Gifted Child Quarterly,* the *Journal of Gifted Education,* and the *Roeper Review,* and a consulting editor for *Gifted International.* Dr. Clark has served as the president of the California Association for Gifted Children, the National Association for Gifted Children, and is the vice-president of the World Council for Gifted and Talented Children.

Curt Dudley-Marling is professor of education at York University in Toronto, Canada, where he teaches courses in language and literacy. His books published by Heinemann include *Readers and Writers with a Difference* (1988 with Lynn Rhodes), *When School Is a Struggle (1990), When Students Have Time to Talk* (1991 with Dennis Searle), and *Who Owns Learning?* (1995 with Dennis Searle).

Marjorie V. Fields is professor of early childhood education at the University of Alaska Southeast. She coordinates graduate and undergraduate early childhood teacher education programs on campus and offers early childhood endorsement courses throughout the state of Alaska. A former kindergarten and first grade teacher, she teaches courses in beginning literacy, guidance and discipline, and classroom management, as well as general early childhood topics. She is the primary author of the textbook *Emergent Literacy: Let's Begin*

Reading Right, Developmentally Appropriate Beginning Literacy (Charles E. Merrill, 1995). In addition, she has published several articles in professional journals and chapters in edited books on the topic of emergent literacy, has written a book for parents on that topic, and has recently written *Constructive Guidance and Discipline: Preschool and Primary Education* (Macmillan, 1994). She is active in professional associations at the local and national levels, having just completed a term as vice-president of the National Association of Early Childhood Teacher Educators. Marjorie has also served on the governing board of the National Association for the Education of Young Children. In her spare time she has raised two sons: Michael, who is currently in law school, and David, who is just completing a degree in engineering.

Alan Gartner (see biographical information included with Dorothy Kerzner Lipsky)

Thomas G. Haring, Ph.D., received his doctorate from the University of California at Berkeley and San Francisco State University. At the time of his death in 1993, he was a professor of educational psychology at the University of California, Santa Barbara. His research interests, within which he contributed over fifty articles and books, included skill generalization, social development, methods to promote school integration, and instructional planning for persons with severe disabilities. A major focus of his research was on structuring peer support groups to facilitate the integration of students with severe disabilities into regular classes and friendship formation.

H. William Heller, Ed.D., is currently campus executive officer and dean at the University of South Florida, Saint Petersburg. He received his doctorate in special education and school psychology from the University of Northern Colorado. He has taught children with mental and emotional disabilities in the public schools, directed several programs at the federal level preparing personnel for special education, and administered a 2,000-bed hospital for people who are mentally ill. He has written extensively in the area of professional standards and ethical practice and is a strong advocate for national standards of personnel preparation in special education as well as for national accreditation of teacher education programs.

Dr. Heller's primary research and scholarly interests are in teacher education and the effective administration of preparation programs in higher education with an emphasis on organizational and interpersonal dynamics. He serves as coeditor for the *Journal for Teaching Exceptional Children,* chairs the Florida Comprehensive System for Personnel Development, and is a member of the Exceptional Needs Standards Committee of the National Board for Exceptional Teaching Standards. Dr. Heller has served as a department chair of special education and as a dean of a college of education.

Lawrence J. Johnson received his Ph.D. from the University of Illinois in 1984. He currently serves as associate dean and director of the Arlitt Child and Family Research and Development Center in the College of Education at the University of Cincinnati. Dr. Johnson has been an active scholar and has published over sixty articles and made numerous presentations at national conferences on issues related to special education. Currently he serves as chairperson of research of the Early Childhood Division of the International Council for Exceptional Children (CEC), and serves as the publication chair for the Teacher Education Division of the CEC. Dr. Johnson also serves on numerous editorial boards and is currently editor of *Focus on Research,* associate editor of the

Journal of Early Intervention, and consulting editor for *Teacher Education in Special Education,* the *Journal of Teacher Education, Remedial and Special Education,* and the *Journal of Education for the Gifted.* Dr. Johnson's current interests revolve around the provision of services to young children with special needs, innovative methods of assessing children, and ways to foster collaborative relationships among professionals within school districts.

Craig H. Kennedy, Ph.D., received his doctorate from the University of California at Santa Barbara, and is currently an assistant professor in the College of Education at the University of Hawaii. His research interests include students with severe intellectual disabilities, functional analyses of problem behavior, and the analysis and facilitation of social relationships between people with and without disabilities. To date, he has coauthored over forty research articles and related publications. He currently serves as an associate editor for the *Journal of Behavioral Education* and is a member of the board of editors for the *Journal of Applied Behavior Analysis, Behavioral Disorders,* and the *Journal of the Association for Persons with Severe Handicaps.*

Chris Kliewer, M.S., is a Ph.D. candidate in the Department of Teaching and Leadership at Syracuse University. His areas of interest include early childhood literacy and the social construction of disability.

Chow S. Lam, Ph.D., is professor in the Department of Psychology at the Illinois Institute of Technology (IIT). He is also director of the Rehabilitation Psychology Program and Center for Vocational and Psychological Services at IIT. He is a recipient of the 1994 Distinguished Research Fellowship from the National Institute on Disabilities and Rehabilitation Research and the 1993 Rehabilitation Educator of the Year award from the National Council on Rehabilitation Education.

Laurence M. Lieberman received his doctorate in special education from Teachers College, Columbia University, in 1972. He has been a teacher of disabled children in the New York City public schools; learning disabilities coordinator in the U.S. Office of Education, Washington, D.C.; and the chairman of the Special Education Doctoral Program at Boston College. For the past sixteen years, he has been a self-employed consultant to school systems throughout the United States, Canada, Europe, and Asia. He has authored three books titled *Preventing Special Education . . . For Those Who Don't Need It* (Glo Worm Press, 1984), *Special Educator's Guide . . . To Regular Education* (Glo Worm Press, 1986), and *Preserving Special Education . . . For Those Who Need It* (Glo Worm Press, 1988).

Dorothy Kerzner Lipsky is director of the National Center on Educational Restructuring and Inclusion of the Graduate School and University Center of the City University of New York, where **Alan Gartner** is dean for research. Together they are editors of *Beyond Separate Education: Quality Education for All* (Paul H. Brookes, 1989) and authors of *Supporting Families with a Child with a Disability* (Paul H. Brookes, 1991), as well as authors of more than a score of book chapters and journal articles concerning educational restructuring and inclusion. Dr. Lipsky has served as a school superintendent, as well as chief administrator in the Division of Special Education of the New York City public schools, where Dr. Gartner was executive director.

Zana Marie Lutfiyya, Ph.D., received her doctorate from Syracuse University. She worked as a research associate at the Center on Human Policy, where she coordinated a long-term qualitative research study looking at the social networks and personal relationships of individuals with developmental disabilities. She is currently an assistant professor in the Department of Educational Psychology, Faculty of Education, at the University of Manitoba. As well as helping to prepare preservice teachers, she conducts a graduate-level course in qualitative research methods.

Ann Nevin has a Ph.D. in educational psychology from the University of Minnesota and is currently a professor in the education unit at Arizona State University West in Phoenix. Dr. Nevin has been involved with experimental education programs for the past twenty years and has field tested the collaborative consultation model described in this book. She coauthored two other books: *Collaborative Consultation* (Pro-Ed, 1986) and *Practices in Curriculum Based Assessment* (Pro-Ed, 1995). Her current areas of interest include the analysis of teacher behaviors and administrative variables for effective integration of learners with and without disabilities, and the analysis of intercultural/international variables that affect collaborative consultation.

Phyllis Paolucci-Whitcomb, Ed.D., is currently professor in the Department of Social Work at the University of Vermont, Burlington. She earned her Ed.D. from Boston University. She was among the first regular classroom teachers in the state of Vermont selected for M.Ed. degree training in special education as a consulting teacher. She has provided consultation training to over seventy different organizations in twenty different states and several different countries. Her current research interests are in the areas of collaborative consultation, leadership, and human services. She is the coauthor of *Collaborative Consultation* (Pro-Ed, 1986).

Mary Poplin, Ph.D., a native of northern Texas, taught for several years in special education before receiving her Ph.D. degree from the University of Texas in 1978. From 1978 until 1981 she taught at the University of Kansas. She was the editor of the *Learning Disability Quarterly* from 1980 to 1984 and is published widely in the field of special education. Her publication topics range from contemporary learning theories applied to special education to *Voices From the Inside: A Report on Schooling From Inside the Classroom* (Institute for Education and Transformation at Claremont Graduate School, 1992). Since 1981, Poplin has been on the faculty in education at the Claremont Graduate School in California. She is currently professor and director of teacher education at the Institute for Education in Transformation. Her current scholarly interests include the development of a practical theory of learning appropriate for our nation of diverse learners. Poplin draws heavily on theories of constructivism, multicultural and critical pedagogies, feminine pedagogy, and her close associations with "transformative" educators.

Marleen C. Pugach is associate professor in the Department of Curriculum and Instruction at the University of Wisconsin, Milwaukee, where she has been a faculty member since 1986. She received her Ph.D. in special education and teacher education from the University of Illinois at Urbana-Champaign, in 1983. Her interests include developing strong collaborative relationships between special and general educators in the schools, at the level of higher education in programs of teacher preparation, and in the realm of educational policy.

Specifically in urban settings, Dr. Pugach's work is focused on how educational practice can be conducted collaboratively so that labels associated with disability, race, ethnicity, language, or gender do not interfere with a teacher's commitment to educate all students. She has published widely in the special education and teacher education literature and is the coauthor, with Lawrence Johnson, of *Collaborative Practitioners, Collaborative Schools* (Love, 1995); coeditor (with R. Clift and W. R. Houston) of *Encouraging Reflective Practice in Education: An Examination of Issues and Programs* (Teachers College Press, 1990); and coeditor (with C. Warger) of a forthcoming book on the relationship between curriculum reform and the reform of special education.

Julie Ann Racino, M.A.P.A., is principal of Community and Policy Studies and has previously served as deputy director of the National Research and Training Center on Community Integration at the Center on Human Policy at Syracuse University. She has taught at the university and college levels and has held diverse roles in management, research, and training. She has consulted throughout the United States and in Great Britain in community integration, particularly in the areas of policy, practices, and change strategies. She received her master's degree in public administration from the Maxwell Program at Syracuse University, while developing and administering community services at a private nonprofit agency.

Her major research interests include social policy and disability; community services and systems change; and the relationships among individuals, communities, and systems. She is currently working on cross-disability issues in support services. She includes among her numerous publications a community participation book series, which includes a book on community living for adults with disabilities.

Daniel J. Reschly is professor and director of the School Psychology Program at Iowa State University in the Department of Psychology and Professional Studies in Education. Reschly earned graduate degrees at the University of Iowa (M.A., 1968) and the University of Oregon (Ph.D., 1971). He has served as a school psychologist in Iowa, Oregon, and Arizona, and was an assistant professor for four years at the University of Arizona. Reschly has published widely on the topics of school psychology, professional practices, mild mental retardation, litigation concerning the rights of students with disabilities, behavioral consultation, adaptive behavior, and assessment of minority students. He has been active in national and state school psychology leadership roles, including serving as president of the National Association of School Psychologists, editor of the *School Psychology Review,* and chair of NASP program approval. He has received three NASP Distinguished Service Awards, the Stroud Award, and appointment to Fellow of the American Psychological Association.

David M. Rice received his Ph.D. from the University of Pittsburgh in 1979. He is president of Melmark, Inc., in Berwyn, Pennsylvania. He has previously held administrative positions with Devereux Foundation and Elwyn, Inc. He has also served as associate professor at Edinboro University (Pennsylvania) in the Department of Psychology and Rehabilitation Counseling. He is currently researching the development of training programs designed to prepare direct care service delivery workers to assist clients with disabilities.

Marvin Rosen received a doctorate in clinical psychology from the University of Pennsylvania in 1961. He has served in various clinical and administrative positions at Elwyn, Inc., Elwyn, Pennsylvania, since 1963, including director of psychology, clinical director, assistant to the president, and vice-president for research and development. He has authored over seventy-five papers and been the author or editor of five books on mental retardation, rehabilitation, and psychology. Dr. Rosen now coordinates clinical services for Elwyn's Children's Division and is a consultant for the training of psychology interns at the Devereux Foundation.

Mara Sapon-Shevin, Ed.D., is professor of education in the Teaching and Leadership Division of the School of Education at Syracuse University. She teaches in the university's new Inclusive Elementary and Special Education Teacher Education Program, which prepares teachers for inclusive, heterogeneous classrooms. She is active in working with schools to promote the full inclusion of all students and the creation of cooperative school communities. She is a board member of the International Association for the Study of Cooperation in Education and gives workshops on cooperative learning and cooperative games for the classroom. She is the author of many articles and book chapters on cooperative learning, full inclusion, diversity education, and the politics of gifted education. Her most recent book is *Playing Favorites: Gifted Education and the Disruption of Community* (SUNY Press, 1994).

Robert G. Simpson, Ph.D., is professor of special education in the Department of Rehabilitation and Special Education, Auburn University, Alabama. He earned his doctorate from the University of Florida in 1977. Dr. Simpson has published numerous scholarly articles concerning assessment of disabled children. His publication research has addressed the use and validity of various assessment instruments in special education. He has also investigated inter-rater reliability associated with the use of behavior rating scales and checklists to identify deviant behavior in children. Most recently he has published a proposed nonformula discrepancy model to identify children with learning disabilities, and has examined the relative effectiveness of techniques used to teach children with learning disabilities. Presently, Dr. Simpson is one of two coeditors of *Diagnostique,* the official journal of the Council for Educational Diagnostic Services.

Susan Stainback (see biographical information under William Stainback)

William and Susan Stainback received their doctorates from the University of Virginia, Charlottesville, in the early 1970s. Their professional experiences involve elementary-, secondary-, and university-level teaching. The Stainbacks have coauthored and edited numerous publications including books, monographs and chapters in books, and articles in professional journals. The publishing rights to several of their writings have been extended to republication in a number of foreign countries including Australia, Spain, Germany, and Israel. They have also served in a visiting scholar capacity to several universities and have served on the editorial/consulting boards of a large number of national journals and organizations.

Among recent recognitions, the Stainbacks were selected to fill the Matthew J. Guglielmo Endowed Chair Professorship for Distinguished Scholars at California State University; received the Outstanding Publication Award from the National Teacher Education and Special Education Association and the Award for Outstanding Scholarship from the College of Education at the University of Northern Iowa; and were cited in a number of professional resource books such as *Who's Who in American Education, Who's Where Among Writers,* and *Contemporary Authors.* The Stainbacks' current professional interests involve how to address the educational needs of all students in regular schools and classrooms.

Mary-Claire Tarlow is an assistant professor of elementary education at the University of Alaska Southeast. She teaches courses in reading and writing education, classroom discipline and management, and classroom research. She also coordinates the graduate and undergraduate elementary education programs at UAS. Dr. Tarlow has public school teaching experience with diverse populations and a Ph.D. from the University of California, Berkeley, in language and literacy education. Dr. Tarlow served as the assistant coordinator of the Alaska State Writing Consortium. She has served as a consultant throughout the state as well, traveling to remote villages to support the professional development of teachers. Dr. Tarlow is currently involved with the Alaska Teacher Researcher Network, a group of teachers throughout Alaska doing and promoting classroom research.

Sara G. Tarver is a professor and director of the Learning Disabilities Program in the Department of Rehabilitation Psychology and Special Education at the University of Wisconsin, Madison. She received her Ph.D. in education from the University of Virginia. She has conducted research and written extensively about the attention and memory problems of students with learning disabilities. Currently, she is interested in the design of instruction that is effective with all types of students who are at risk of failure in school. She is particularly interested in using Direct Instruction techniques and materials in the regular classroom to accomplish the objectives of the Regular Education Initiative.

Steven J. Taylor, Ph.D., is director of the Center on Human Policy and its Research and Training Center on Community Integration. He is a professor of education and sociology at Syracuse University. His interests include social policy, qualitative research methods, the sociology of disability, advocacy, and community integration. He is the author or editor of numerous published articles and books, including *Life in the Community* (Paul H. Brookes, 1991), *Introduction to Qualitative Research Methods* (Wiley, 1984), *The Social Meaning of Mental Retardation* (Teacher College Press, 1994), and *Community Integration for People with Severe Disabilities* (Teacher College Press, 1987). He is currently the editor of the journal *Mental Retardation,* which is published by the American Association of Mental Retardation.

Sue Thorson is a doctoral student and assistant director of the Teacher Education Program at the Claremont Graduate School in Claremont, California. She previously taught a secondary learning disabilities resource room program near Philadelphia, Pennsylvania. Her research interests include student understandings of discipline procedures, teacher research projects, in-service education, and transcultural interactions.

Since 1986, **Jacqueline S. Thousand** has coordinated a graduate training program at the University of Vermont, Burlington, that prepares integration facilitators, advanced educational leadership personnel who work with administrators, teachers, and families to redesign the delivery of special education services. This enables learners with extensive educational and psychological challenges to experience quality educational and social opportunities within their local general education and community environments. Dr. Thousand's most recent research is in the areas of collaborative consultation and teaming, school-based systems change strategies, cooperative group learning and partner learning, transition planning, attitudinal change strategies, and international educational exchange.

Glenn A. Vergason is professor emeritus of the Educational Psychology and Special Education Department at Georgia State University after twenty-seven years of service. He spent eleven years at Georgia State as chair of the Special Education Department, building extensive programs from the bachelor's through the doctoral level. He has produced ten textbooks, nine chapters in books, five monographs, and more than fifty articles. He has also been active as an associate editor with professional journals in the field, including *Exceptional Children, Focus on Exceptional Children, Teaching Exceptional Children, Teacher Education and Special Education, Education and Training of the Mentally Retarded,* and the *British Columbia Journal of Special Education.*

Since his retirement, Dr. Vergason has intensified his nationally known advocacy for individuals with special needs, especially abused children. He has gained wide acclaim for his involvement in special education and childhood abuse litigation.

Richard A. Villa's primary field of expertise is the development of administrative support systems for educating all students within general education settings. Dr. Villa has taught a number of subjects at both the middle and secondary school levels, including biology, chemistry, physics, government, and special education. His administrative experiences include serving as a special education administrator, pupil personnel services director, and director of instructional services. Dr. Villa is currently president of the Bayridge Educational Consortium and an adjunct professor at the University of Vermont, Trinity College, and St. Michael's College. He teaches courses and supervises practica in the development of effective administrative and instructional skills for accommodating all students within general education classrooms.

Pamela M. Walker is a research associate at the Human Policy, Research, and Training Center on Community Integration. She is a doctoral candidate in the Special Education Program at Syracuse University. Her research interests include family supports, residential supports for adults, and social integration into neighborhoods and communities.

Kevin K. Walsh, Ph.D., received his M.A. and Ph.D. degrees in life-span developmental psychology from the University of Akron in Ohio. He has held a variety of positions in both facility-based and community settings for people with mental retardation and developmental disabilities. Currently Dr. Walsh is director of research at the Center for Human Development of the Morristown Memorial Hospital in New Jersey. Dr. Walsh is on the board of the American Association of Mental Retardation (AAMR) and has also served as chair of the Mideastern Region (Region IX) of that association. He is currently a consulting editor of the journal *Mental Retardation* and regularly publishes in the field.

In addition, he was a member of the health care reform work group of the National Reform Agenda of the President's Committee on Mental Retardation and serves on several statewide committees of the New Jersey Division of Developmental Disabilities including the Interdisciplinary Research Committee, the Behavioral Review Committee, the Quality Assurance Work Group, and the Long Range Planning Advisory Committee.

Paul Wehman is professor at the Department of Physical Medicine and Rehabilitation, Medical College of Virginia, and director of the Rehabilitation Research and Training Center, Virginia Commonwealth University. Internationally recognized for his service and scholarly contributions in the fields of special education, psychology, and vocational rehabilitation, Dr. Wehman is the recipient of the 1990 Joseph P. Kennedy, Jr. Foundation Award in Mental Retardation and received the Distinguished Service Award from the President's Committee on Employment for Persons with Disabilities in October, 1992. He is the author or editor of over one hundred books, research monographs, journal articles, and chapters in the areas of traumatic brain injury, mental retardation, supported employment, and special education. Specific research interests include transition from school to work and supported employment.

Dudley J. Wiest is associate professor of educational counseling at California State University, San Bernardino. He received his Ph.D. from Claremont Graduate School. His writing and research address the topics of system transformation, service delivery for school psychology, school counseling, intrinsic motivation for adolescents, and bereavement. Dr. Wiest has been a teacher, school counselor, and school psychologist, both in public and parochial school settings. He is a licensed psychotherapist and consults to parents and schools.

SECTION ONE

ORGANIZATIONAL STRATEGIES

Educational reform movements are changing the face of school structures. What should the organization of a school look like to maximize learning benefits for each of the student members? In Chapter 1, Lipsky and Gartner critique current educational structures and practices, including special education placements, and show that there are limited benefits to students. They challenge the very nature of the special and regular education dichotomy. They propose fundamental educational restructuring and inclusive education as ways to improve educational benefits and outcomes for students. Lipsky and Gartner point out that real reform will *not* be achieved by simply letting students with disabilities into the current mainstream of general education, but instead will require a basic restructuring, a transformation of the schools.

Lieberman, in Chapter 2, maps out a perspective of school organization that maintains a dual system of special and regular education as requisite to providing maximum learning benefits to all students. Lieberman discusses how disabling conditions alter the course of human life and argues for the preservation and maintenance of a special education system to meet the needs of students with disabilities.

CHAPTER 1

Inclusive Education and School Restructuring

DOROTHY KERZNER LIPSKY
ALAN GARTNER

Outcomes of youth with disabilities exiting public schools have not improved significantly during the last decade. Both historical and current data indicate that this population of individuals continues to drop out of school at a rate ranging from 30–80% and to experience low levels of full-time employment. (Kohler, 1993, p. 107)

EDUCATIONAL REFORM

Increasingly, policy advocates have come to recognize that what is needed to change public education rather than "fixing" the current dual system of general and special education is broad educational restructuring. The future work in educational reform remains extensive; yet there is hope of creating a better society for all. If the handicap is a function of a disabling environment (physical or attitudinal), and if disability is a social construct, then the changes must come in both the physical environment and in the social relationships. Both of these are an integral part of the work of remaking U.S. society. As Barton and Landman (1993) point out, this raises even more fundamental matters: "The issue of integration is an important one. It provides an opportunity for raising serious questions about the kind of society we desire and the nature and functions of schooling" (p. 41).

Skrtic (1991) describes the nature of postindustrial society, with its emphasis on collaboration, mutual adjustment, developing a community of interests among the organizations' members, consumers, and host community. Educational equity, Skrtic asserts,

is a precondition for excellence in the post-industrial era, for collaboration means learning collaboratively with and from persons with varying interests, abilities, skills, and cultural perspectives, and taking responsibility for learning means taking responsibility for one's own learning and that of others. Ability grouping and tracking have no place in such a system. (p. 181)

The issues go beyond preparation for work in the future. They extend to the nature of society—to who is to be included and who is not. In the course of U.S. history, participation in the polity has been limited by race, gender, religion, class, and intellectual capability. In the public schools, historically, educational enrollment has been limited by race, gender, religion, class, and physical and intellectual capacity.

In both the polity and the education system, these formal exclusions have been progressively removed. For the most part, all adult U.S. citizens are eligible to vote and all children can be enrolled in the public schools. What has not been settled in either system—the polity or the schools—is the nature, implications, and consequences of that participation, both for the individuals and the institutions.

In terms of students with disabilities, the critical future challenge will be how we view and treat difference—as abnormality or as an aspect of the human condition. Hahn (1994) points out that as with other disadvantaged groups, people with disabilities are striving to translate previously devalued personal characteristics into a positive sense of self-identity. He says, "a consciousness that disability simply signifies another human difference instead of functional restrictions might form the basis . . . to promote an increased appreciation of diversity and heterogeneity in everyday life" (p. 18).

THE CURRENT STATE OF SPECIAL EDUCATION

Since the passage of P.L. 94-142 in 1975, there have been two major developments in terms of numbers and placement of students:

- First, the number of students served has increased to more than 1.3 million additional students. This is an extraordinary achievement in terms of access.
- Second, despite this substantial change in numbers—and the greatest increase has been among those labeled "learning disabled"—the placement pattern has remained nearly identical: About a third of the students are served in regular classes, a third in resource rooms, and a third in special classes and more restrictive settings.

Student Population

The most recent federal report, for the 1992–93 school year, reports 5,170,242 students served per IDEA, Part B, and Chapter I (*Sixteenth Annual Report*, 1994, Table 1.1). After limited year-to-year percentage increases during most of the 1980s, the percentage increase from 1990–91 to 1991–92 was 3.7 percent, followed by another 3.7 percent increase from 1991–92 to 1992–93; these were the largest two-year increases in the law's history.

Four categories continue to encompass nearly 95 percent of all students served: specific learning disabilities, speech or language impairments, mental retardation, and serious emotional disturbance.

Placement Patterns

Placement issues involve the pattern of placement of students, as well as variability among categories and across the states. The 1992–93 school year marked the first time the proportion of students with disabilities who attended mostly regular classes outpaced those in resource rooms, separate classes, or more restrictive settings. Slightly more than a third of the students were served in regular classes (35.7 percent), a third (34.4 percent) in resource rooms, and somewhat fewer than a third (29.9 percent) in separate classes and other more restrictive placements (*Sixteenth Annual Report*, 1994, Figure 1.3).

Within these overall figures, there were wide ranges in placement patterns based upon student age, disability condition, and differing state practices. The most striking differences were among the states. For example, for students with specific learning disabilities, the range among the states of those placed in regular classes was from 2.37 percent in California to 93.59 percent in Vermont. For students with speech or language impairments, the range among the states of those placed in regular classes was from 4.25 percent in West Virginia to 99.87 percent in Indiana. For students with mental retardation, the range among the states of those placed in regular classes was from 0.30 percent in Iowa to 65.95 percent in Vermont. For students with serious emotional disturbance, the range among the states of those placed in regular classes was from 0.90 percent in Arizona to 69.90 percent in Vermont (*Fifteenth Annual Report*, 1993, Table AB2). These variations exist despite a single federal law that defines the categories and imposes on all the states a common requirement for placement of students in the least restrictive environment (LRE).

The biased views of and low expectations for students in special education are reflected not only in their separation from general education classes and students but also from broader educational efforts: Program innovations, designed to improve education for all students, for the most part leave out students with disabilities. For example, a recent U.S. Department of Education study of magnet schools found that students with disabilities are underrepresented in such programs (*Educational innovation*, 1994). Compared with their percentage in the district as a whole, approximately a third fewer special education students are enrolled in magnet programs, according to the study conducted by the American Institutes on Research.

Racial and Language Minorities and Gender Bias

Race, language, and gender biases interact in special education. Nationwide, blacks are twice as likely as whites to be in special education programs. "In 39 states, according to a *U.S. News [& World Report]* analysis of Department of Education data, black students are overrepresented in special education programs, compared with their percentage of the overall student population" ("Separate and unequal," 1993, p. 48). Wide disparities occur when one examines nationally the percentage of racial groups by disability category:

- Retarded: black, 26%; white, 11%; Hispanic, 18%
- Learning disabled: black, 43%; white, 51%; Hispanic; 55%
- Emotionally disturbed: black, 8%; white, 8%; Hispanic, 4%
- Speech impaired: black, 23%; white, 30%; Hispanic, 23% ("Separate and unequal," 1993, p. 54)

Wide discrepancies occur in states' labeling of black students with retardation. For example, five states label more than a third of their black special education students as retarded: Alabama, 47 percent; Ohio, 41 percent; Arkansas, 37 percent; Indiana, 37 percent, and Georgia, 36 percent. On the other hand, five states label fewer than a tenth of their black special education students as retarded: Nevada, 9 percent; Connecticut, 7 percent; Maryland, 8 percent; New Jersey, 6 percent; and Alaska, 3 percent ("Separate and unequal," 1993, p. 55).

The disparities in national data reflect the reality in local districts. Indeed, the disparities are magnified as minority special education students are overrepresented in placement in more restrictive settings, producing—in effect—double segregation. In the New York City public schools, for example, 84 percent of students in separate special education classes were black and Hispanic, while 73 percent of the overall student population was comprised of these two groups. On the other hand, white students, who comprised 20 percent of the school system's population, accounted for 37 percent of the special education students placed in general education settings while receiving support services (Richardson, 1993, p. B7).

While issues of gender have not been extensively addressed in studies of special education referral and placement, some data suggest over-referral and overcertification of males (Haigh & Malever, 1993–94; Weinstein, 1993–94). At the same time, the National Longitudinal Transition Study (NLTS) of special education students reports that

> females in secondary special education represented a different combination of abilities and disabilities than males. As a group, females were more seriously impaired; even among males and females with the same disability category, females had marginally greater functional deficits than males. (Wagner, 1992, pp. 33, f.)

Outcomes

Nationally, some one-quarter of the students with disabilities who exited school in the 1990–91 school year dropped out. In addition to the 23.3 percent reported as having dropped out, it is likely that a significant portion of the 15.8 percent for whom the exiting basis is reported as "status unknown" are likely to have dropped out (*Fifteenth Annual Report,* 1993, Figure 1.5).

According to the National Longitudinal Transition Study of special education students, "During secondary school, poorer school performance was noted for students with disabilities that were male, African American, or from low-income or single-parent households" (*The transition experiences,* 1993, pp. 1–4).

Comparisons with the general education student population are confounded by differences in the outcome categories used by the Office of Special Education Programs (OSEP) and those used generally. Based on a pilot study, "29 percent of all students in the NCES pilot test will drop out over the course of their high school careers, [while] the percentage of students with disabilities who will drop out, based on the same definition of a dropout, will be 38 percent" (*Fifteenth Annual Report,* 1993, p. 35).

Fewer than half of the students with disabilities (45.7 percent) exited the educational system with a regular diploma. An additional 13.3 percent exited with a certificate of completion, certificate of attendance, modified diploma, or completion of an IEP. The range among disability conditions varied greatly. For the four largest categories of students, the percentages of those who graduated with a regular diploma were specific learning disabilities, 51.7 percent; speech or language impairments, 41.3 percent; mental retardation, 38.7 percent; and serious emotional disturbance, 30.8 percent (*Fifteenth Annual Report,* 1993, Table 1.9).

Demographic factors also influence postschool outcomes. Recent research has provided striking evidence of how schools shortchange girls. Although that research concerned the general population of girls, NLTS data demonstrate similar experiences for girls with disabilities. This shortchanging of girls in their school experiences has consequences for postschool outcomes (Wagner, 1992).

The rate of unemployment for persons with disabilities is the highest among any population subgroup. Two-thirds of persons with disabilities are not working, while 20 percent work full time and 13 percent work part time. Eight out of ten who do not work say they would like to work; this is up from two out of three in 1986 (*Persons with disabilities,* 1994).

Looked at comprehensively, young people with disabilities are not doing as well as their counterparts in the general population along a number of axes. According to the National Longitudinal Transition Study of special education students (1992), a comparison of 15- through 20-year-old youth with disabilities with youth in the general population who were in secondary

school or who had been out of school for less than two years indicates that:

- more exiters with disabilities left secondary school by dropping out;
- fewer dropouts with disabilities completed GEDs;
- fewer graduates with disabilities attended postsecondary schools, although about the same percentage attended postsecondary vocational schools;
- fewer youth with disabilities had paid jobs, both during and after secondary school;
- more employed youth with disabilities worked part-time and in low-status jobs;
- fewer out-of-school youth with disabilities achieved residential independence; and
- more youth with disabilities were arrested. (p. 47)

These failures are not ones of the school system alone. We live in a society in which barriers for persons with disabilities, both physical and attitudinal, continue to exist. While the Americans with Disabilities Act is a major step forward, there is yet much to be done to assure that the United States is a country of openness and opportunity for persons with disabilities.

A CRITICAL ANALYSIS OF LIMITED BENEFITS

Several reasons may account for the limited benefits of the current special education design for its students. Possible reasons include: inadequacies in practice, prejudice and discrimination, and conceptual limitations.

Inadequacies in Educational Practice

The adequacy of educational practice is difficult to measure. Public Law 94-142 requires that states develop personnel preparation programs that require "state-of-the-art" practices (Gilhool, 1989); however, there are no reliable overall data as to the usage of "best practices" in special education across the country. For example, Williams et al. (1990) report that while Vermont teachers express a high level of acceptance of "best practices," there was a marked gap between that level of acceptance and the level of implementation. While there have been improvements in special education practice—both in their design[1] and their implementation—there is a substantial inadequacy in educational practices in the current system, which accounts for the failures in student outcomes.

Prejudice and Discrimination

Special education plays a role in the broad sorting function that characterizes schools, both for those consigned to special education and for those students who remain in general education.

> Children of Special Education are children of Small Expectations, not great ones. Little is expected and little is demanded. Gradually, these children—no matter their IQ level—learn to be cozy in the category of being 'special.' They learn to be less than they are. (Granger & Granger, 1986, p. 26)

> Every time a child is called mentally defective and sent off to special education for some trivial defect, the children who are left in the regular classroom receive a message: No one is above suspicion; everyone is being watched by the authorities; nonconformity is dangerous. (Granger & Granger, 1986, p. xii)

The mother of a nondisabled kindergarten student provides another perspective ("Beyond normal," 1993). At a conference with her son's teacher, the mother was told that two students with physical disabilities would be in his class. The teacher "quickly added that there would be a full-time paraprofessional so their presence would not take away time from other students. This statement was made with the best of intentions—for my son" (p. 4). When the mother picked up her son at the end of the first day, he pointed to an adult, and said, "That lady is for the wheelchair people."

> Today I thought, "What was Charlie going to learn about people with physical disabilities and other differences that carry the perception of not normal?" He could learn that people with disabilities are not competent and need another person to be with them, that they cannot communicate for themselves, that they remain together as a subculture within a larger

community, that they are always the recipients of help from caregivers. (p. 4)

> The presence of children with physical disabilities in my son's class represents just one of many kinds of diversity in today's classrooms and schools. Physical proximity is the start of what could be invaluable and positive learning about and appreciating differences. I believe that children with disabilities do not take away from other children. They do not diminish the community. I believe, instead, that these two children, currently known as the "wheelchair people," have the potential to contribute enormously to my son's learning and growth—but only if the environment and people take advantage of this opportunity. (p. 5)

The consequences of such factors in educational practice are documented by Podell and Soodak (1993).

> [W]hen a child with mild learning problems is from a low-SES family, teachers with low personal efficacy are less likely than teachers with high personal efficacy to consider regular education to be an appropriate placement for the child. Personal efficacy did not, however, influence placement judgments about high-SES children. Thus, low-SES students may be at greatest risk for referral because of teacher, rather than student, factors. In other words, teachers' decisions about poor children are susceptible to bias when teachers perceive themselves as ineffectual. That finding may be important in understanding the overrepresentation of low-SES children in special education. (p. 251)

Current student assessment practice performs a pernicious function, and its premises implicate racial and ethnic discrimination; using IQ tests for special education certification is based on an erroneous understanding of intelligence, as a fixed and largely heritable characteristic, that can be precisely measured and provide an accurate predictor as to future school—and life—course.

Conceptual Limitations

Skrtic (1991) presents a far-ranging and incisive critique of the current design and conceptualization of special education. Of the critics of the present system, he says, "their criticism stops at the level of special education practices . . . [without] questioning the assumptions in which these practices are grounded" (p. 150). He summarizes these presuppositions as follows:

- Disabilities are pathological conditions that students have.
- Differential diagnosis is objective and useful.
- Special education is a rationally conceived and coordinated system of services that benefits diagnosed students.
- Progress results from rational technological improvements in diagnostic and instructional practices. (p. 152)

The current design of special education is one of programs largely separate from, sometimes parallel to, and occasionally intersecting with the mainstream of education. Presently, it is the inappropriate product of an earlier period, when students with disabilities were excluded from public education. Public Law 94-142, the Education of All Handicapped Children Act, enacted in 1975, was designed to rectify that policy of exclusion. At the same time, it sought to provide both uniformity of response in the midst of a growing number of court decisions that held that such exclusion was unconstitutional, and due process rights to parents of children with disabilities, who had been largely ignored in the education of their children. (See especially Walker, 1987.)

In many ways, P.L. 94-142 has been an extraordinary success. It (and its successor, the Individuals with Disabilities Education Act) has assured that with few exceptions all eligible students with disabilities are provided with access to publicly supported education. While well-meaning and an advance over prior practices, the law's concept of least restrictive environment (LRE) is inherently flawed. As Taylor (1988) has pointed out, the LRE principle:

- legitimates restrictive environments. While it incorporates a presumption favoring less restriction, it also implies the acceptability of a more restricted and segregated setting for at least some students.

- confuses segregation and integration on the one hand with the intensity of services on the other. The clear implication is that students who need more intensive services must receive them in more restrictive settings. As Brown et al. (1983) noted more than a decade ago, "Any developmentally meaningful skill, attitude, or experience that can be developed or offered in a segregated school can also be developed or offered in a chronologically age appropriate regular school" (p. 17).
- is based on a "readiness" model. That is, students must prove their readiness for an integrated setting, rather than presuming such a setting as the norm. Not only is this morally unacceptable, the evidence is that more restrictive settings do not prepare people for less restrictive ones.
- directs attention to the physical settings rather than to the services and supports people need to be integrated into the community.

The law's assurance to all eligible students of a free appropriate public education (FAPE) suggests a pathway for educational improvement.

FORCES FOR EDUCATIONAL IMPROVEMENT

At the present time, there are at least six factors that conduce toward educational improvement for all students.

1. Growing concern as to the limited outcomes for all students, particularly those in special education
2. The broader education reform movement, which calls attention to higher standards for all students
3. Recent court cases which have supported inclusion
4. Increasing insistence by the disability rights movement for full participation, as well as the effects of attention to the Americans with Disabilities Act and its implementation
5. Costs of special education

6. Increased parental advocacy and involvement in school reform efforts

Limited Outcomes

The outcomes in education for general and special education students have been limited. This is especially significant in special education where whatever the metric used—student learning, drop-out rates, graduation rates, post-secondary training and education, subsequent employment, or community living—the current design as a whole has failed these students. These failures come at a cost—in students' lives and the nation's resources. And, these costs increasingly are less acceptable, among students, their parents, and taxpayers alike.

Broader Educational Reform Movement

To a large extent, the national attention to educational reform has ignored students with disabilities. In its report to the president and Congress, the National Council on Disability (NCD, 1994) stated, "A review of eight major federal initiatives [put forward between 1990 and 1992] involving school-age children and youth shows that six did not include specific provisions for students with disabilities" (p. 9). This makes the attention to students with disabilities in Goals 2000: Educate America Act (P.L. 103-227) all the more significant. At the same time, however, the continuing debate as to the use of resources under the Carl D. Perkins Vocational and Applied Technology Education Act (P.L. 101-392) for students with disabilities makes clear the continuing struggle for their inclusion.

Recent Court Cases

In the past several years, four federal district courts have issued similar decisions supporting inclusion. The cases involve an eleven year old with Down syndrome, a nine year old labeled mentally retarded, a kindergarten student with severe behavior problems, and a student with severe mental retardation and physical disabilities.[2]

(See Lipton, 1994, for a comprehensive review of these decisions.) Affirming the decision, the 3rd Circuit Court of Appeals stated, "Inclusion is a right, not a privilege of a select few." It went on to note:

> We construe IDEA's mainstreaming requirement to prohibit a school from placing a child with disabilities outside of a regular classroom if educating the child in the regular classroom, with supplementary aids and support services, can be achieved satisfactorily. (Lipton, 1994)

On behalf of the Office of Special Education of the U.S. Department of Education, the Justice Department filed an *amicus* brief in *Holland,* stating that IDEA:

> prohibits a school from placing a child with disabilities outside the regular classroom if educating the child in the regular classroom, with supplementary aids and support services, can be achieved satisfactorily. (Lipton, 1994)

The denial by the U.S. Supreme Court to review the circuit court's decision in *Holland* suggests that with circuits in agreement, these decisions are likely to stand as the law of the land. However, two 1994 district court decisions have reaffirmed that each case will be decided based upon its factual circumstances.

Disability Rights Movement

Hahn (1994), a theorist of the disability rights movement, argues for "the need to alter the educational environment rather than to pursue continuous efforts to modify the functional characteristics of disabled students" (p. 9). Echoing the language of race relations, he goes on to state, "Since separation on the basis of disability is apt to leave an enduring imprint on the hearts and minds of disabled young people, desegregation or inclusion is a fundamental component of this process" (p. 9). Morris (1990) makes a similar point.

> People's expectations of us are informed by their previous experience of disabled people. If disabled

people are segregated, are treated as alien, as different in a fundamental way, then we will never be accepted as full members of society. This is the strongest argument against special schools and against separate provision. (p. 53)

While some argue that the special education legislation (IDEA) is not a matter of civil rights (for example, Shanker, 1994), there is no question that the Americans with Disabilities Act (ADA) is a civil rights law. In a recent case, *Peterson v. Hastings (Neb.) Public Schools,* the court accepted the argument that the ADA supplements IDEA ("*Peterson* ruling," 1994). And as the ADA requirements in some areas go beyond those of IDEA, the civil rights perspective concerning inclusion gains added impetus. A further factor is that under ADA, private schools are included as public accommodations and are thus bound by its provisions (42 *U.S.C.* Sec. 1218(7)(J)).

Costs of Special Education

The high costs of current special education programs have been previously noted. Also noted is that, over time, inclusive education is less expensive than a separate design. Some have charged that districts may be adopting inclusion for the sole purpose of cutting costs. However, in light of the high costs of the current design and the evidence as to its ineffectiveness, both the lower costs and the greater benefits of inclusive education warrant its adoption.

Parental Involvement

Increasingly, many families of children with disabilities are insisting on placement for their children in general education settings, with the necessary supplementary aids and support services. Especially active are families of young children, who benefited from IDEA's preschool programs in integrated settings. They are active in demanding that such options be made available for their children in the public schools. Furthermore, parent organizations and advocacy groups are becoming increasingly active in

their support for inclusion and the training of parents in their rights.

INCLUSIVE EDUCATION AND EDUCATIONAL RESTRUCTURING

Educational restructuring does not require the "fixing" of special education nor moving it closer to nor even into the "mainstream." Rather, it is a challenge to the very nature of this dual system, which utilizes mainstream education for partial integration of some special education students. This cannot be achieved merely by bringing students with disabilities into the current system.

As Biklen has pointed out, "How schools see integration is crucial: Is integration understood as an outsider coming in, or as creating a school culture so that it accepts all comers?" (cited in Slee, 1993, p. 3). Biklen's use of the word *integration,* with its connotation of race relations, is significant. It reminds us that real integration can be achieved not by "allowing" persons of color into the existing white society but only as that society is transformed, a process of politics involving both the distribution of power and the culture of power.

Some have seen tension between the drive for school reform—with its emphasis on upgrading standards—and inclusion of all students. It is well to remember, however, that Edmonds's work in school effectiveness was driven by a concern to narrow the gap between the learning of minority and white students, a gap that he argued could be reduced by raising the floor (Edmonds, 1979).

In testimony before the House Subcommittee on Select Education and Civil Rights, the National Council on Disability has challenged the least restrictive environment (LRE) conceptualization as the basis for special education programs. The council pointed out that LRE conceptualization derived from prisoners' rights issues and is not appropriate to the education of students with disabilities. Instead of the concept of a continuum, which at least on some occasions requires students to be separated from their age peers to receive the services they require (see Taylor, 1988), the council favored the concept of an array of services.

Special education, the council urged, "needs to evolve as a support to typical education, not as a way of supplanting it. Inclusion is the most promising way to achieve this end" (NCD, 1994).

Inclusive education programs are being implemented across the nation. The National Center on Educational Restructuring and Inclusion has recently reported on inclusion programs nationally (National Center, 1994). The study reported:

- Inclusion programs are taking place in every state.
- Inclusion programs are taking place in a wide range of locations—urban, suburban, and rural school districts, and in large and small school districts.
- Inclusion programs are occurring at all grade levels, involving students across the entire range of diabilities.
- Inclusion programs are being initiated by administrators, teachers, parents, university faculty, and state departments of education, and as a result of court orders.
- The evaluation of inclusion programs is addressing issues of implementation, outcomes, and financing.

Based upon the National Center's survey and review of the research, seven factors are necessary for inclusion to succeed.

1. *Visionary leadership*: Illustrative of this is the statement of a Vermont special education director.

Some years ago we came to view inclusion as a subset of the restructuring of the entire educational system. From this perspective we no longer view special education as a means to help students meet the demands of the classroom, but as a part of the classroom services that must be available to accommodate the learning needs of all children in a restructured school.

2. *Collaboration*: Reports from school districts indicate that the achievement of inclusive education presumes that no one teacher can—or ought to—be expected to have all the expertise required to meet the educational needs of all the students in the classroom. Rather, individual teachers must have available to them the support systems that provide collaborative assistance and which enable them to engage in cooperative problem solving. Building planning teams, scheduling time for teachers to work together, recognizing teachers as problem solvers, conceptualizing teachers as front-line researchers—each of these are tools reported as necessary for collaboration.

3. *Refocused use of assessment*: Traditionally, student assessments have been used as screening devices—to determine who gets into which slot. In special education, a myriad of studies have addressed the inadequacy of this screening. Inclusive education schools and districts report moving toward more "authentic assessment" designs, including the use of portfolios of students' work and performances, and generally working to refocus assessment.

4. *Supports for staff and students*: Two factors are essential for successful inclusive education programs: systematic staff development and flexible planning time for special education and general education teachers to meet and work together. And from the vantage point of students, supports for inclusion often mean supplementary aids and support services. Districts report that these include assignment of school aides, full- or part-time, short- or long-term; provision of needed therapy services integrated into the regular school program; peer support; "buddy systems" or "circles of friends"; and effective use of computer-aided technology and other assistive devices.

5. *Funding*: Current special education funding formulas often encourage separation placements. Changes in funding, so that funds follow the students, are essential to the success of inclusive education. When this occurs, inclusive education programs are no more costly overall than segregated models ("Does inclusion cost more?", 1994; McLaughlin & Warren, 1994).

6. *Effective parental involvement*: Inclusive schools report encouraging parental participation through family support services, as well as the development of educational programs that engage parents as co-learners with their children.

Programs that bring a wide array of services to children in the school settings report at least two sets of benefits: the direct benefits to the children, and the opportunities for parents and other family members to become involved in school-based activities.

7. *Curricula adaptation and adopting of effective instructional practices*: Classroom practices that have been reported as supporting inclusive education include multilevel instruction, cooperative learning, activity-based learning, mastery learning, use of instructional technology, peer support, and tutoring programs.

Given the limited time period in which inclusive education programs have been implemented, there have been relatively few full-scale evaluations of outcomes (Rossman & Salzman, 1994). A number of statewide studies are under way, including Massachusetts (Rossman & Anthony, 1992), Vermont (Hasazi, Furney, & Johnstone, 1994), Oregon (Arrick et al., ND), Michigan (Christmas, 1992), and Utah (McDonnel, McDonnel, Hardman, & McCune, 1991). Among the findings from initial studies are:

- Where students came from separate classes, there was a substantial increase in time spent on learning activities in general education classrooms (Chase & Pope, 1993).
- Students with learning disabilities made academic gains as reflected in scores on criterion-referenced tests and report cards (Chase & Pope, 1993).
- Students with significant disabilities had greater success in achieving IEP goals than matched students in traditional programs (Ferguson, Meyer, Jeanchild, Juniper, & Zingo, 1992).
- Benefits to students with disabilities occurred without curtailing the educational program available to students without disabilities (*Co-teaching,* 1991).
- Gains occurred in student self-esteem (Burello & Wright, 1993), acceptance by classmates (Christmas, 1992; Marwell, 1990), and social skills (McDonnel, McDonnel, Hardman, & McCune, 1991).

- Support from parents of students with disabilities was found to be positive (Chase & Pope, 1993; Michigan State Department of Education, 1991; Marwell, 1990).
- Support from students was generally positive (Chase & Pope, 1993; *Co-teaching,* 1991), although not uniform (Rossman & Anthony, 1992).
- Among school staff, support ranged from very enthusiastic (Burello & Wright, 1993; *Co-teaching,* 1991; Rogan & Davern, 1992) to more moderate support (Chase & Pope, 1993; Christmas, 1992; McDonnel, McDonnel, Hardman, & McCune, 1991; Rossman & Anthony, 1992).

A multiyear study of the implementation of inclusion in Vermont (*Vermont's Act 230,* 1993), reports:

- Grades for special education students served in general education settings were not significantly different than their grades had been when in special education classes.
- General education teachers, special educators, parents, and the students themselves judged students to have comparable performance in the general education class settings in all of the categories measured: behavior, social interaction, classroom performance, and overall success. For example, 92 percent of the general education teachers, 95 percent of the special educators, 91 percent of the parents, and 94 percent of the students responded affirmatively to the question, "Overall, do you feel the student was successful in school?"

SPECIAL EDUCATION AND EQUITY

The term *equity in education* is commonly used to discuss racial and language minorities, women, and the poor. Generally, it has not been used in conjunction with students with disabilities. In part, this reflects the general societal attitude toward issues of disability, that disabilities are simply medical conditions and that students with impairments require special treatment. Part of that special treatment is a special and separate education system.

While there are a number of aspects to the debate about inclusion, a critical question is whether the inclusion is a civil rights matter. AFT president Al Shanker demurs. "I see no basis for the civil rights [analogy]. Black youngsters were eager to learn. That's different from a youngster who is yelling and screaming and so forth." At the heart of the segregation issue was merely the color of a child's skin, Shanker noted, which "was totally irrelevant of their education. These are two very, very different motivations" ("Teachers union president," 1994, p. 174).

A leading special education litigator and acting executive director of TASH (The Association of Persons with Severe Handicaps), Frank Laski, challenges Shanker's viewpoint. In an article commemorating the fortieth anniversary of *Brown v. Board of Education,* he argues the common ground people with disabilities have with African Americans and other oppressed minorities. He cites the argument made by John Davis, in response to Thurgood Marshall in *Brown*:

> I think if [Marshall's construction of the Fourteenth Amendment] should prevail here, there is no doubt in my mind that it would catch the Indian within its grasp as much as the Negro. If it should prevail, I

am unable to see why a state would have any further right to segregate its pupils on the ground of . . . mental capacity. (Cited in Laski, 1994, p. 4)

Laski goes on to cite Justice Marshall, who after surveying the extensive record of social exclusion of persons with disabilities, concluded that a regime of state-mandated segregation of persons with disabilities had emerged that "in its virulence and bigotry rivaled and indeed parallelled the worst excesses of Jim Crow" (cited in Laski, 1994, p. 4).

The issues of social justice and equity encapsulated in inclusion are powerfully stated by Branson and Miller (1989).

> [I]ntegration must be . . . oriented toward its own destruction, aiming to destroy the very categories which are seen as needing to be "integrated" into the "normal" world. If the disabled are "normal," so much an accepted part of our world that we take their presence, their humanity, their special qualities for granted, then there can be no "integration" for there is no "segregation," either conceptually, in terms of categories, taxonomies, or actually, in terms of institutional separation. (p. 161)

As it has been throughout the course of U.S. history, the education system is both a means for advancement of its students in the society and a forum for debate about the nature of that society.

NOTES

1. Pertinent here, for example, is a reconceptualization of dyslexia. A report from the Center on Molecular and Neuroscience, Rutgers University, in the proceedings of the National Academy of Sciences, suggests that dyslexia is at root not a visual or ordinary hearing problem, but a flaw in a specific brain circuit that handles rapidly flowing auditory information (Blakeslee, 1994). If this is correct, the design of pedagogical programs to teach reading to students correctly identified as dyslexic would require a major shift.

2. The cases are *Daniel R.R. v. State Board of Education* in the 5th Circuit, *Greer v. Rome City School* in the 11th Circuit, *Oberti v. Board of Education of the Borough of Clementon School District* in the 3rd Circuit, and *Sacramento City Unified School District v. Rachel Holland,* 9th Circuit. See Lipton (1994) for a comprehensive review of these decisions.

REFERENCES

Arrick, J., Krug, D., Falco, R., Jackson, P., Anderson, N., & Brazeau, K. (ND). *Supported education in Oregon summary of findings: Elementary school report.* Portland, OR: Portland State University.

Barton, L., & Landman, M. (1993). The politics of integration: Observations on the Warnock Report. In R. Slee (Ed.), *Is there a desk with my name on it? The politics of integration.* (pp. 41–49). London: The Falmer Press.

Beyond normal: Will our children learn to value diverse community members? (1993). *Inclusive Education in Minnesota: What's Working?, 1,* pp. 4–5.

Branson, J., & Miller, D. (1989). Beyond policy: The deconstruction of disability. In L. Barton (Ed.), *Integration: Myth or reality?* London: The Falmer Press.

Brown, L., Ford, A., Nisbet, J., Sweet, M., Donnilhan, A., & Gruenewald, L. (1983). Opportunities available when severely handicapped students attend age appropriate regular schools. *Journal of the Association for the Severely Handicapped, 8*(1), 16–24.

Burello, L. C., & Wright, P. T. (Eds.) (1993, Winter). Strategies for inclusion of behaviorally challenged students. *The Principal Letters, 10.*

Chase, V., & Pope, E. (1993, February 24). *Model for mainstreaming: The synergistic approach.* Paper presented at the Learning Disabilities of America Conference, San Francisco.

Christmas, O. L. (1992). *The Michigan non-mandated aide pilot project.* Lansing: Michigan State Department of Education.

Co-teaching: Regular education/special education and co-teaching reference guide. (1991). Lansing: Michigan State Department of Education.

Does inclusion cost more? (1994). *Inclusive Education Programs, 1*(5), 4–5.

Educational innovation in multiracial contexts: The growth of magnet schools in American education. (1994). Washington, DC: U.S. Department of Education.

Edmonds, R. (1979). Effective schools for the urban poor. *Educational leadership, 37,* 15–18, 20–24.

Ferguson, D. L., Meyer, G., Jeanchild, L., Juniper, L., & Zingo, J. (1992). Figuring out what to do with the grownups: How teachers make inclusion "work" for students with disabilities. *Journal of the Association for Persons with Severe Handicaps, 17*(4), 218–226.

Fifteenth Annual Report to Congress on the Implementation of the Individuals with Disabilities Education Act. (1993). Washington, DC: U.S. Department of Education.

Granger, L., & Granger, B. (1986). *The magic feather.* New York: E.P. Dutton.

Hahn, H. (1994). *New trends in disability studies: Implications for educational policy.* Paper prepared for the National Center on Educational Restructuring and Inclusion invitational conference on inclusive education, Wingspread (WI) Conference Center.

Haigh, J. A., & Malever, M. C. (1993–94). Special education referral practices by gender, ethnicity, and comparison to state and district enrollments. *CASE in Point, 8*(1), 13–24.

Hasazi, S. B., Furney, K. S., & Johnstone, A. P. (1994). A study of the implementation of Vermont's Act 230. Unpublished manuscript. Burlington, VT: University of Vermont.

Kohler, P. D. (1993). Best practices in transition: Substantiated or implied? *Career Development for Exceptional Individuals, 16*(2), 107–121.

Laski, F. (1994). On the 40th anniversary of *Brown v. Board of Education*: Footnotes for the historically impaired. *TASH Newsletter, 20*(5), 3–4.

Lipton, D. (1994). The state of the law. *NCERI Bulletin, 2.*

Marwell, B. E. (1990). *Integration of students with mental retardation.* Madison, WI: Madison Public Schools.

McDonnel, A., McDonnel, J., Hardman, M., & McCune, G. (1991). Educating students with severe disabilities in their neighborhood school: The Utah elementary model. *Remedial and Special Education, 12*(6), 34–45.

McLaughlin, M. J., & Warren, S. H. (1994). *Resource implications of inclusion: Impressions of special education administrators at selected sites.* Palo Alto, CA: Center for Special Education Finance.

Morris, J. (1990). Progress with humanity? The experience of a disabled lecturer. In R. Rieser & M. Mason (Eds.), *Disability, equality in the classroom: A human rights issue* (pp. 45–63). London: ILEA.

National Center on Educational Restructuring and Inclusion. (1994). *National study of inclusive education.* New York: The Graduate School and University Center, The City University of New York.

National Council on Disability. (1993). *Serving the Nation's students with disabilities: Progress and prospects. A report to the President and the Congress of the United States.* Washington, DC.

National Longitudinal Transition Study of special education students. (1992). *How well are youth with disabilities really doing? A comparison of youth with disabilities and youth in general.* Menlo Park, CA: SRI International.

National Organization on Disability. (1994). *Persons with disabilities lag behind other Americans in employment, education, and income.* Washington, DC.

NCD calls for end of special education as you know it. (1994). *The Special Educator, 10*(1), 5.

Peterson ruling raises troubling questions on ADA. (1994). *The Special Educator, 10*(4), 49, 59–60.

Podell, D. M., & Soodak, L. C. (1993). Teacher efficacy and bias in special education referrals. *Journal of Educational Research, 86*(4), 247–253.

Richardson, L. (1993, April 6). Minority students languish in special education system. *The New York Times*, A1, B7.

Rogan, P., & Davern, L. (1992). *Inclusive education project: A building-based approach to developing classroom and school models that include students with severe handicaps.* Syracuse, NY: Syracuse City School District.

Rossman, G. B., & Anthony, P. G. (1992) Restructuring from within: The Massachusetts experiment with integrating all students in the classroom. Unpublished manuscript.

Rossman, G. B., & Salzman, J. (1994). *Evaluating inclusive education programs: A survey of current practice.* Paper prepared for the National Center on Educational Restructuring and Inclusion invitational conference on inclusive education, Wingspread (WI) Conference Center.

Separate and unequal. (1993, December 13). *U.S. News & World Report,* pp. 46–60.

Shanker, A. (1994, February 6). Inclusion and ideology. *The New York Times*, E28.

Sixteenth Annual Report to Congress on the Implementation of The Individuals with Disabilities Education Act. (1994). Washington, DC: U.S. Department of Education.

Skrtic, T. M. (1991). The special education paradox: Equity as the way to excellence. *Harvard Educational Review, 61*(2), 148–207.

Slee, R. (1993). Introduction. In R. Slee (Ed.), *Is there a desk with my name on it? The politics of integration* (pp. 1–3). London: The Falmer Press.

Taylor, S. (1988). Caught in the continuum: A critical analysis of the principle of least restrictive environment. *Journal of the Association for Persons with Severe Handicaps, 13*(1), 41–53.

Teachers union president calls inclusion "fad." (1994). *The Special Educator, 9*(12), 173–174.

The transition experiences of young people with disabilities. (1993). Menlo Park, CA: SRI International.

Vermont's Act 230: Three years later, A report on the impact of Act 230. (1993). Montpelier: Vermont Department of Education.

Wagner, M. (1992. April). *Being female—A secondary disability? Gender differences in the transition experiences of young people with disabilities.* Paper presented at the American Educational Research annual meeting, San Francisco.

Walker, L. (1987). Procedural rights in the wrong system: Special education is not enough. In A. Gartner & T. Joe (Eds.), *Images of the disabled, disabling images* (pp. 97–116). New York: Praeger.

Weinstein, D. F. (1993–94). Special education referral and classification practices by gender, family status and terms used: A case study. *CASE in Point, 8*(1), 25–36.

CHAPTER 2

Preserving Special Education . . .
For Those Who Need It

LAURENCE M. LIEBERMAN

INTRODUCTION

When the devil comes to tempt you, he will not be cloaked in fire, nor will he try to roast you with the hot coals of his eyes. He will soothe you with words of human kindness and play your emotions like a banjo.

The suggestion is not that people who espouse full inclusion in regular classrooms should be associated with the devil. Nor is it proper to associate anyone who speaks in words of humaneness and caring with anything other than the purist intent. "The road to hell is paved with good intentions" is not necessarily a fact. However, it may be a warning. *Caveat emptor*. Let the buyer beware.

The purpose of this chapter is to provide a counterpoint, not only to the preceding chapter, but to the fundamental ideas and statements provided by all those who would plunge children with severe disabilities full time into regular classrooms. To deliver wake-up calls to dreamers is not a task relished by this author. For that is what much of this is all about—dreaming. Yet much of my own career to date has been founded on dreaming of what could be, rather than what is. To be on the other side of a profound issue from a dreamer is to be in a very awkward and agonizing position. As a result, the reader may find some equivocation in this chapter. There will be a tendency toward not rejecting the validity or the truthfulness of those authors cited for their full inclusionist position. Rather the overall tone will reflect a conciliatory position while presenting issues that will never go away, at least not in the foreseeable future.

The fundamental questions remain. Are the dreamers dreaming at the expense of others? Are educational change agents about to start using children to effect educational change? Are professionals preying on the emotions of parents who should be wrenched free from denial and helped to get on with their lives, instead of being jerked back into hoping for possibilities that are minutely feasible? The purpose is not to suggest a priori limitations on what is possible. However, the potential price of a shattered fantasy rather than reality must be pointed out. There may be greater problems and potential abuses inherent in full inclusion than in any separate special education program.

Aristotle saw every attempt at persuasion to comprise three elements: logos (intellectual content), pathos (emotional content), and ethos (authority based on personal charisma). The selling points for full inclusion are emotionally powerful. They do not lend themselves to being easily challenged, nor can they always be rationally addressed. The arguments speak in ideals for all humanity. Images are presented that show friendship, loyalty, togetherness, unity, helpfulness without monetary compensation, caregiving from the heart, and building a society based on mutuality of interest. As my fellow man goes, so go I. Only a cynic would take this on: to puncture the balloons with pins, and to even enjoy the sound of the popping.

The purpose is not to question the ideals, but to question the strategy. Shall children with profound retardation be the standard bearers for the millennium? Shall they be the ones to lead us to that higher form of ourselves that might make us truly human? We know who gets killed first in battle—the ones who can be seen most easily—the ones carrying the flags. Shall we send the children to change the world and then stand by and watch the carnage? There will be individual victories. They will not be sufficient to overcome the carnage. The goals are wonderful. Sending the children cannot be the strategy.

LARGER CONTEXT

Strategies for inclusion into regular classrooms are found in all current movements toward educational reform. Effective schools, direct instruction, and curriculum-based assessment are all woven through the fabric of models or programs like the Adaptive Learning Environments Model (Wang, 1981), the Integrated Classroom Model (Affleck, Madge, Adams, & Lowenbraun, 1988), and the Consulting Teacher Model (Egner & Lates, 1975).

It is perhaps an oversimplification to suggest that what all these reforms have in common is a sense of child-centeredness, of getting back to the nature of children, of holistic thought, of loftier educational goals than mere standardized achievement test scores on isolated subskills. Alas, the real trend seems hardly to take notice of such pinings for the 1960s. We are testing more, not less. We are locking teachers into constrained curricula and syllabi more, not less. The imprint of statewide accountability and government spending based on tangible, measurable, tabulatable, numerical results is no longer a thumbprint. It is a footprint and fast becoming a whole body indentation.

The flexibility demanded by full inclusion is rarely encountered. When figures are reported on television telling us that more African American males are in prison than in college, or that the school drop-out rate in inner cities approaches 40 percent, is this due to flexibility and an educational system organized to meet the needs of individuals? The school system is not for individuals.

Individuals drop out. Students who respond to the system succeed. Educational reformers suggest that there are no unique methods for use with students labeled exceptional that differ in kind from those used with normal children. In other words, all the students are individuals, but teach them all the same. It is abundantly clear that large numbers of so-called normal students do not succeed in school for the primary reason that they are not treated or taught differently.

If students are different, they all learn differently. If they learn differently, they need to be taught differently. In accordance with Kerzner Lipsky and Gartner's statement, exceptional children should be taught like normal children. But under current practices, many normal children are doomed to failure. The obvious concern must be for the nature of schooling for all children. Until success is assured for the majority, can the minority really have a chance? Doubtful.

Strully and Strully (1989) candidly discuss the nature of their severely disabled daughter and her successful inclusion. However, public policy, or determining what is good or fair or just for every human being, cannot be built on the success of individuals. What can be built on the success of individuals is the choice to fully include more individuals. Let each case be judged on its own merits. To do otherwise suggests the following syllogistic arguments:

> Stevie Wonder is a musical genius.
> Stevie Wonder is blind.
> All blind people can be musical geniuses.

or by analogy:

> Shawntell (Strully & Strully, 1989, p. 60) is severely disabled.
> Shawntell is fully included in regular classrooms and having a successful educational experience.
> All severely disabled children can be fully included in regular classrooms and have a successful educational experience.

To be against full inclusion as public policy, or educational or school policy, is not to be for exclusion. To be against the pro-life position is not to be for abortion. It is to be for choice. People advocating for the placement of a severely disabled student in a regular class are one thing. Talking about shutting down all special services if they are in some way separate is something else. Full inclusionists seem to reject choice or any continuum of service delivery (Biklen, Bogdan, Ferguson, Searl, & Taylor, 1985). This posture certainly raises the suspicion that full inclusion is a subset of the abortion issue. Pro-life or pro-choice? Full inclusion or continuum of special services? The major argument seems to be that choice leads to abortion and choice leads to exclusion. Therefore, eliminate choice.

Another interesting dichotomy shaping up in the field, especially among parents, is between the mentally retarded and the learning disabled. It appears that many parents of children with retardation have grabbed hold of full inclusion in a regular classroom as an extremely important goal to enhance the lives of their children. The parents of children with learning disabilities seem not to want to touch it with the proverbial ten-foot pole. The field of learning disabilities is apparently so distraught over this discussion that it is continuously confusing the regular education initiative (REI) (Will, 1986) and full inclusion and railing against REI (Lieberman, 1990).

REI suggests that regular classroom teachers be more accommodating and responsive to those students with disabilities who are already included for all or part of their day in regular classrooms. This is not something to be against. It is to be applauded. Full inclusion is another matter. The following is an excerpt from a statement of the National Joint Committee on Learning Disabilities (January, 1993).

> The National Joint Committee on Learning Disabilities (NJCLD) (1993) supports many aspects of school reform. However, one aspect of school reform that NJCLD cannot support is the idea that *all* students with learning disabilities must be served only in regular education classrooms, frequently referred to as *full inclusion.* The Committee believes that *full inclusion,* when defined this way, violates the rights of parents and students with disabilities as

mandated by the Individuals with Disabilities Education Act (IDEA). (p. 3)

Stainback, Stainback, and Forest (1989, p. ix) stress "the importance of regarding all students as unique and whole individuals." Full inclusion implies that this is true in regular classrooms or can be more easily found in regular classrooms, or can be more easily engineered in regular classrooms, which is probably quite the reverse of reality. One could base this on nothing more than a comparison of pupil–teacher ratios in special and regular classrooms. This does not imply that class size is the sole criterion for individualization, but it is certainly of major importance, if not to researchers, then to the teachers themselves, as noted by groups such as the New Brunswick Teachers Association (1988, February).

SPECIFIC CONTEXT

A handicap is a limitation of choice that prevents a quality of life commensurate with one's personal desires. Handicapping conditions alter the course of human life. Some would argue that these alterations could be life enhancing. Even persons with handicaps themselves might suggest that they are better off (perhaps characterwise) for having undergone the ordeal of a physical or mental challenge. While there may be some subjective validity to this position, it is invariable that a handicap imposes a limitation of choice. The negative effect of this limitation will almost always outweigh the potential benefits of striving to overcome it. For this reason, this author purposely avoids terms like exceptional, special, or challenged. They seem to suggest a direct benefit from being handicapped. Handicaps are not beneficial to anyone.

Portraying the meaning of being handicapped requires that the limitation in question is understandable. Also, it is reasonable and realistic to assume that it, and it alone, is responsible for fewer choices and a diminished quality of life. This is where personal desire is important. Two people can have the same disability (e.g., blindness). Yet, one will be handicapped due to a personal desire that cannot be fulfilled (e.g., to become a mechanical engineer). The other, not having a desire that would require normal vision, is not handicapped by definition. Thus, there are no handicapping conditions per se, except for profound retardation, severe autism/schizophrenia, or total immobility. These conditions render choice itself meaningless. Barring these conditions, a handicap is really an individual phenomenon. The question becomes: What does the person really want to do in life that he or she cannot do? What quality of life does the person aspire to that cannot be attained?

Another important aspect of being handicapped is that it is mostly relative. It depends on the environmental context, cultural mores, and social norms, as well as personal choice. Handicaps are subjective. Even being deaf and blind, as Helen Keller demonstrated for the world, is a subjective handicap. It depends on personal desire and quality of life.

The most dramatic stories of overcoming disability are generally found in the realm of physical disability such as blindness, deafness, or loss of limbs. Mental disabilities are usually expressed in the form of mental retardation, learning disabilities, and emotional disorders. It may be argued that these conditions are also physical from the standpoint of damage, inadequate development of physical structure (i.e., brain), or biochemical imbalance. They are referred to as mental because they mostly have to do with cognition and ideational processes rather than acquiring information (sensory input), movement, and physical response. This is another important distinction to consider when discussing handicaps and the limitation of choice, and especially, full inclusion in regular classrooms.

The intention is not to rank certain conditions according to their potential to become handicaps. However, limitations of choice are considerably more severe for the mentally disabled than the physically disabled. This is especially true when it comes to choices that involve academic pursuits and/or powerful thought processes. People with physical handicaps can choose to aspire to almost any profession or any activity involving mental competence. Blind people have become physicians, deaf people have become lawyers, and so forth. The list of professions that include people with physical disabilities is as long as the list of professions. This is not true in the case of people with mental disabilities.

People with retardation who are less mentally competent than the norm cannot aspire to academic and professional choice. A huge chunk of the potential for a higher quality of life has been removed. This is not to say that a high quality of life cannot be achieved outside the realm of academics or professions. After all, quality of life is not absolute. It is relative to individual desire. It is only that a major avenue for this achievement in our society has been eliminated. The same is true for the chronically mentally ill or emotionally disturbed. Their illness usually interferes with the acquisition of ideational flexibility, coherent thought processes, logical problem solving, and a varied response repertoire. This leads to fewer choices and a potentially diminished life style.

The definition of learning disabilities is more vague because the people who make up this population are quite different in the manifestations of their problems. Like people with physical disabilities, individuals with learning disabilities show up in all the professions and in all academic pursuits. The individuals who succeed in these realms are usually exceptional in ways that enable them to override their difficulties and compensate for them. They generally have great perseverance and an abundance of overall ability. People with learning disabilities who do not possess this measure of ability are not usually found in academic or professional pursuits.

To fail in an academic curriculum undoubtedly limits choice and will affect one's quality of life. Therefore, academic failure results in being handicapped. There are children with mental disabilities. They will become adults with mental disabilities, and they will be handicapped by their lack of academic success. This is mostly unavoidable. Most people with mental disabilities are not competent in academic pursuits and even if they muddle through an academic curriculum in school, their endeavors in life more likely than not, will not require academic competence. However, a mental disability that results in academic weakness, and consequently a handicap, is obviously relative and very far from any absolute limitation. In fact, many people overcome limitations imposed by academic failure. There are many significant ways to achieve a quality of life commensurate with personal desires that have nothing or very little to do with academic performance.

School failure is another matter. It has much greater potential to result in a significant handicap. The ability to perform well in school is an important road to self-esteem, self-confidence, and the acquisition of the basic skills one needs to live effectively in our society. School failure may render an individual incapable of responding to almost any choice. What makes it even worse, from both a moral and societal view, is that it is preventable or at least avoidable in most cases. To think otherwise is to presuppose that the power and responsibility to succeed in school resides solely within the student and that the school system is not mandated or even morally obligated to provide an effective educational experience. There are too many factors beyond the control of the students to hold them totally responsible for their own successes or failures.

The most potent reason why children cannot be allowed to experience school failure is because it has the potential to create lifelong handicaps. Unfortunately, school failure occurs because school has become synonymous with academics. It is easy to trace the progression. People with mental disabilities are less able in academic performance. They are held accountable for academics anyway and academic failure is synonymous with school failure. Self-esteem and self-confidence are severely diminished, and the consequences of school failure may indeed continue through adulthood to old age. School failure becomes life failure.

For the people with physical disabilities, this discussion is almost meaningless. Their ability to function in an academic curriculum is generally unaffected. By definition, people with mental disabilities are at risk of failure in an academic curriculum that demands mental competence. Therefore, the potential for an academic handicap to become a school handicap increases manyfold for those with mental disabilities.

School does not have to be solely about academics. It can include a multitude of other things. If students are successful in nonacademic ways, their self-esteem, motivation, ambition, and striving for personal choices will remain intact. They can be successful in school, but not necessarily in academic schooling.

Changing the nature of school for these students by providing alternative curricula and building success would go very far toward minimizing the impact of an academic handicap. By definition, the regular classroom is where the academic curriculum rules. Consequently, full inclusion into regular classrooms for students with severe mental disabilities imposes both academic and school failure on them.

The vast majority of special education students do not spend most of their day in regular classrooms. They are pulled out throughout the day for all manner of special services. The plain truth is that these pull-out models do not necessarily work to the benefit of the children who experience them. The reason is not that the continuum of services is conceptually faulty, nor is it a commentary on pull-out models. It is not working because the interface segment of the continuum has never been adequately defined. What does exist in terms of defined practice is the all-or-nothing circumstance: maximum separation of services or full-time regular classroom placement. Both situations usually have well-defined purposes. The special placement (class or school) evolves its own curriculum based on the needs of its population. The regular class responds to the dictates of the curriculum as established by state and local guidelines and standards. The middle ground (partial time spent out of the regular classroom and in special education services) has not been defined. A primary reason is that special educators have been seduced by the pressures of academic schooling and have lost what was special about special education. Special education pull-out programs have become a form of regular education in small groups. What is the purpose of the pull-out? What should be taught? What should be learned? Who should teach what? How should it be taught? How should it be measured and graded and evaluated? When should the pull-out occur? What can and should be sacrificed? What can be compromised? What is the overall goal?

The problem with the continuum of services is that these questions as applied to the middle ground, the interface, the circumstance of having children who exist simultaneously in regular and special education, have not been answered. In many places, the questions haven't even been asked. There is an old quip that goes something like, "If you don't know where you are going, you will never get there."

Pull-out programs should be cut back. If professionals determine that a child needs to be pulled out of a regular classroom for an hour a day, most of the time they are wrong. The focus must be on the place where the failure is occurring. If Herculean efforts are made to provide an appropriate, effective education in the regular classroom, and success is still not assured, then the student must be removed in order to ensure his or her success. Of course the student might return for classes like music, art, and gym, but only if he or she can be successful in music, art, and gym. In other words, it is more important to prevent the handicap of school failure than to expose children with handicaps to their peers without handicaps.

Pull-out models, as the middle ground between full-time special class and full-time regular class, are also the middle ground for academics. This is the essential decision behind pull-out programs. It is determined that the child can learn, perform, and participate in an academic curriculum . . . sometimes. It is expressly at those times that the student should be part of regular classroom attendance. This becomes murky again when one realizes that many children, even children with mental disabilities, can benefit both at the moment and in future life, from academic learning. In this sense, special

educators who want to abolish separate facilities are not wrong. They have realized that many of the special school or special class students are learning academics anyway at some time during the day, and at those times they might be better off in regular classrooms for the reasons cited earlier. The important point here is not necessarily to do away with all separate programming. The point is to make the middle ground work effectively. This is where the vast majority of students with mental disabilities will be found.

Twenty years ago the philosophy of special education was to maximize the potential of children with handicaps. Today the philosophy of special education is to return those children to regular education classrooms. To maximize their potential? (Lieberman, 1988, p. iv)

Maximizing potential is a philosophy. Full inclusion is a strategy, not a philosophy. It has been presented as the way to accomplish the goal of maximizing potential. The argument goes something like this: A child can learn to live in the "mainstream" of society only by participating in the "mainstream" of school. It is only through this process that his or her potential can be maximized. Also, children with disabilities change the attitudes and stereotypes held by their "normal" peers primarily through exposure and experience. When these normal children grow up and take their place in society, their previous exposure and presumed positive attitudes will translate into a society that will allow for greater participation by people with handicaps. There is a sense that if all children were in the same classrooms, ultimately we wouldn't need large monetary fines to keep people without handicaps out of handicapped parking zones. They would stay away out of respect and a sense of compassion for people in wheelchairs.

The other side of the argument begs the question of the validity of this position. Would an elderly person with pain in the joints stay out of the closest parking spot (handicapped zone) because he or she went to an inclusive school as a child? Are racial bigots created by never having interacted with the racial group in question? To know one is to love all of them? Experience suggests that having experience with others is not the issue. It is the quality of the experience one has.

The primary difference between elementary and secondary school must be considered. This difference may be conceptualized along the lines of skills (elementary level) and content (secondary level). The mission of elementary school programs, both regular and special, should be to teach basic skills. Some would define these skills as reading, writing, spelling, and arithmetic. Others would define them more broadly and include any tool needed to learn higher-order academics. This would include memory training, reasoning, problem solving, thinking, and so on, in addition to the three Rs plus spelling. Some would make basic skills synonymous with life skills and add socialization, cooperation, sharing, competing, and emotional well-being.

Many children with mental disabilities can learn these skills to some acceptable degree of independent competence by the time they leave sixth grade. Some would benefit from a continuation of this skill emphasis through junior high school and possibly beyond.

Every program prior to junior high school should be defined in relation to skills. Special education and regular education must make a commitment to teaching skills a priority. Some students will need more intensive, one-on-one tutoring in order to learn them. Some might require a smaller group. Others can function in regular classes with the selected basal texts. Certain skills can be taught by different teachers at certain times in different places. These decisions must be made on an individual basis. Evaluation for success is done daily and weekly, even on a lesson-by-lesson basis. If success is questionable, let that student be taught differently by the same teacher or by someone else, using different materials and different strategies, in a different place, and possibly at a different time. If the goal is the same for everyone, then the number of strategies used to attain the goal is limited only by the available resources.

The secondary level is more complicated. Basic skills, particularly the three Rs plus spelling,

are only one aspect of life skills. This is why special education at the secondary level plays an important role. At this time, perhaps beginning in ninth grade, the decision to forgo academics comes into focus. The curriculum shifts into high gear in the form of bodies of knowledge, usually referred to as content-area courses. Students are expected to digest the material and through their skills demonstrate the ability to use the information for ever-increasing abstract purposes. These purposes are only occasionally practical in the sense of everyday use.

The choice for special education at the secondary level should be a choice for life skills. For some students with mental disabilities, it is a decision that implies, "You are academically handicapped. You will always be academically handicapped. Special education will help you overcome it and simultaneously prevent you from having the lifelong handicap of school failure."

A candidate for special education is any student with a disability who requires specialized or individualized teaching approaches in order to succeed in school at that particular point in time. It may be momentary or it may be for the duration of the individual's schooling. Special services may be required for the duration of the individual's life (special education might be thought of as one component of special services).

Herein lies a great problem. Who gets tracked for academics and who doesn't? For whom is academics the key to the future? In the context of junior and senior high school, academics means content courses. Basic skills should be everybody's emphasis in elementary school. Unfortunately, the full inclusionists' answer to the question of who gets tracked for academics in the secondary school is also everybody.

If not for special programs, who will teach the people with mental disabilities how to manage their lives, how to eat, how to cook, how to socialize, how to manage money, how to acquire information, how to be a consumer, how to spend leisure time, how to pursue happiness? It is all a question of priorities. Many students with mental disabilities require special training in life skills, a continued focus on literacy skills, and relegate academic content to a low-priority status.

Decisions must be made on behalf of each student with mental disabilities (in junior–senior high). He or she may or may not be best served in an academic track. Educators and parents are going to make these decisions with the student's assistance and with the student's best interest in mind.

The choices available at the secondary level are full-time placement in either regular or special education, or some combination of the two. It is the middle ground that again needs definition, but it is a more complicated process in high school. The same principles hold. If the student is to be "mainstreamed" for some academic subjects, he or she must have a decent opportunity to succeed in whatever tier or track he or she is placed in. Even then, a significant question arises as to whether it is important anyway. Will world history or biology make that much of a difference in his or her life, or would that time be better spent on life skills development? What about the social–emotional benefits to be gained from participating in a regular class? These questions cannot be answered here. Answers are provided through decisions made by professionals, who analyze individual profiles and develop programs to meet individual needs.

Most students with physical disabilities and many with mental disabilities can and should pursue school success through the academic curriculum. It behooves the secondary schools to provide different academic tracks to accommodate the range of students who can respond successfully to an academic curriculum. In this manner, even academic handicaps can be minimized.

Defining needs is the essence of what is special about special education. Yet when special education is chosen to meet the academic needs of students with disabilities and/or handicaps, it is a contradiction. A choice for academics is a choice for regular education. Defining needs for special education purposes requires looking beyond academic content to the nature of the individual student.

The use of special education as a service delivery system is predicated on two things: the needs of the student and the probability that the intervention requires a special set of circumstances that are generally unavailable in regular classroom settings. Most important of all is the allowable shift of emphasis or curriculum priority, from academic skills in the regular classroom to student-based needs in the special classroom.

In other words, the meaning of special education itself seems to be linked to defining needs that are essentially nonacademic in nature. Defined needs are sometimes not critical for academic success but are critical for the prevention of a handicap or for life success. An example would be teaching blind people cane travel. Therefore, special education is warranted for many needs that people with disabilities have that may or may not be required for the pursuit of academic success. Using special education exclusively for direct academic instruction destroys the need for special educators to effectively define student needs.

From a special educator's perspective, defining needs means determining those activities, strategies, and interventions that will prevent a handicap from developing in an individual with a disability.

THE NEED FOR SPECIAL SERVICES

There are children who, at some point in their lives, may need a special education program that is completely outside the purview of the regular classroom. Here are the reasons.

• Some children with disabilities need highly specialized skills taught by specially trained teachers in order not to become handicapped.
• Some children with disabilities might never respond to the demands of an academic curriculum and will require alternatives.
• Some children with disabilities could participate in an academic curriculum but would require an inordinate amount of time and attention from a regular class teacher, such that it would be inequitable for the other children in the class.

• Some children with disabilities need the support of a peer group that is more like they are, rather than being thrust out into the "mainstream" and left to fend for themselves.

• Some children with disabilities might experience school failure without a special education curriculum tailored to their needs.

• Some children with disabilities need a pipeline of services that begins with special education and proceeds through all manner of social agencies and support services that may extend throughout life.

• Some children with disabilities have greater opportunities to succeed in special education because there is a greater emphasis on parental partnerships, parental cooperation, and active parental participation in the education of the child.

• Some children with disabilities need special education because without the quasi-legal support of IEPs, regular class teachers will not allow for different ways of responding to the dictates of a standardized curriculum. (Lieberman, 1988, pp. 115–116)

Full inclusionists seem to have forgotten who the children are. They seem to negate the reasons special education is needed or the fact that many of these children could not be accommodated in regular classrooms in the first place.

As long as there are people with disabilities, there will be a need for special services that goes beyond anything a regular classroom teacher can ordinarily provide. For example, a teacher of people with mental retardation is so much more than a teacher. He or she is a member of a medical management team, a social worker's team, a psychologist's team. He or she must be an expert on mental retardation in order to participate. Being mentally retarded is a bigger concept than being mentally retarded in school. It is the fact of being mentally retarded in life that must be addressed. Regular classroom teachers attempt to meet physical–motor, cognitive–intellectual, and social–emotional needs just as special educators do. Yet their focus tends to be different. Regular class teachers are given an agenda called the cur-

riculum. They are provided with it prior to seeing any student. They are told that this is what they have to teach, and sometimes what book to use and even how to use it. This more standardized approach to education for the masses generally succeeds . . . for the masses. It misses some individual children by a mile, children who may be normal and a little bit different, or who may have a disability and be a lot different. The greater the difference, the greater the chance that the student will fall through the cracks of any standard way of doing something, especially in an educational setting.

CONCLUSION

There seem to be two different camps of full inclusion advocates. One group does not attempt to justify its position in logical, pragmatic, or curricular terms. When asked what has to be done in order to make full inclusion work successfully, they generally reply that nothing has to be done. Just doing it will make it happen. They seem to think that the task of preventing handicaps, overcoming academic handicaps, and promoting successful school experiences will be accomplished merely by declaration. It is not so. Regular classroom placement is an important strategy, but not at the expense of creating handicapped children.

Some children with disabilities should not be in regular classrooms. Placing them there handicaps them even more. To have children with disabilities failing in the regular classroom is unacceptable. If the students with mental disabilities in question are smart enough to know they have friends and are socializing and being part of everything, they are smart enough to know that they have absolutely no idea of what the teacher is talking about or what the other students are doing. To expose children with disabilities to the pressures of stringent assignments, time frames, grades, standards, competency testing, and so on, is unacceptable, unless the children can be successful.

This is analogous to closing institutions for people with mental disabilities with the intended purpose of forcing the issue onto community-based housing. Without proper preparation, this has become a disaster that adds to homelessness, crime, degradation, and more human misery. If the institution is a snake pit, let's make it a humane place to live. Turning the people loose is no solution. This analogy is enough of an argument against this basically nonsensical position as to render further discussion superfluous.

The second group of full inclusionists recognizes that full inclusion requires a great deal of fundamental change in education practices. There is a need for different school structures. There is a need for the development of new ways of thinking, such as establishing regular classroom teachers as ultimately responsible for all children assigned to them, regardless of severity of disability. In effect, they would be case managers, supported by all manner of professionals to implement instructional programs in or out of the regular classroom.

> Under the REI [Author's note: Full Inclusion], teachers are given authority over all instruction in their classrooms. In a sense this is a heavy burden. However, classroom teachers should not be (and cannot reasonably be) made responsible for students who follow non-traditional curricula. There are limits to the demands that can be placed on classroom teachers. (Jenkins, Pious, & Jewell, 1990, p. 490)

There are advocates for "more sophisticated partnerships" between regular and special educators, which would presumably lead to determining strengths and weaknesses and appropriate placement along a restructured continuum. "Thus, no one group would bear the major responsibility for students who do not learn at the same rate or with the same instructional materials as the majority of their peers." (Trent, 1989, p. 24.) Responses suggest that the result would be that "no group will bear responsibility for these students" (Carnine & Kameenui, 1990, p. 141).

Full inclusionists are advocating for a program, while the more important issue continues to be the needs of individual children. According to full inclusionists, the fundamental need all children with disabilities have, no matter what, is to be in a regular classroom. This notion seems to be based on some idealistic sense of socialization, normalization, and friendship, and assumes that there is no price to pay for such a placement.

The resolution is choice. It is the ability to choose full inclusion in a regular classroom as a viable and appropriate placement for some students with disabilities, even some with severe disabilities. The continuum of services must be preserved. A range of service options is needed because of the range of people with a wide range of needs, many of which cannot possibly be met in the regular classroom. Full inclusionists seek to destroy this range. Their position is that everyone is in—no decision making, no choice. Everyone is in. This fundamental denial of reality plays well with some budget-cutting bureaucrats and some fanatical parents.

The resolution is based on the fundamental ability to choose, to decide what is an appropriate educational placement for the specific child in question, to determine what is most advantageous to the future of the individual. It is public policy based on options. Hopefully, the choices that school personnel and parents make on behalf of children will evolve out of consensus. If not, these choices will ultimately be made by judges in courtrooms. (See *Daniel R. v. El Paso Independent School District,* 1989). The following quotes are excerpts from this case.

> Ultimately, our task is to balance competing requirements of the EHA's dual mandate: a free appropriate public education that is provided, to the maximum extent appropriate, in the regular education classroom.

> Our analysis is an individualized, fact specific inquiry that requires us to examine carefully the nature and severity of the child's handicapping condition, his needs and abilities, and the schools' response to the child's needs.

> Mainstreaming would be pointless if we forced instructors to modify the regular education curriculum to the extent that the handicapped child is not required to learn any of the skills normally taught in regular education.

We examine whether the child will receive an educational benefit from regular education. We also must examine the child's overall educational experience in the mainstreamed environment, balancing the benefits of regular and special education for each individual child.

We ask what effect the handicapped child's presence has on the regular classroom environment and thus, on the education that the other students are receiving.

If we determine that education in the regular classroom cannot be achieved satisfactorily, we next ask whether the child has been mainstreamed to the maximum extent appropriate. The EHA and its regulations do not contemplate an all-or-nothing educational system in which handicapped children attend either regular or special education. Rather, the Act and its regulations require schools to offer a continuum of services.

After sincere attempts were made to fully integrate Daniel, the appeals court affirmed the previous court's ruling that in this particular case, Daniel's full-time placement in special education was warranted, appropriate, and beneficial to both him and his nonhandicapped peers in the regular classroom.

Can full inclusion work in individual cases? Can full inclusion be beneficial to all concerned? Yes. One can envision an idyllic community in which everyone is a neighbor, where it is all for one and one for all, where people know their neighbors and truly care about one another in ac-tions rather than just words. This would be a place where all the children know one another and grow up in each other's homes, a place where the sense of community prevails above all else.

The seeds of failure for full inclusion are in diversity. The larger the city, the more diverse the population, and the sense of community suffers. Small-town North America is where full inclusion is possible. Can a child with a severe mental disability be fully included in regular classrooms, in the school, in the community, on the street, in all manner of social gathering? Yes. Absolutely yes. It must be given careful consideration by thoughtful committed people who are making decisions based on the best interests of individuals. This is what public policy must be, not extremist, fanatical rhetoric that deals in a reality that exists only in the minds of its subscribers.

The day the standard for education becomes meeting the individual needs of all children, all children with disabilities can be in regular classrooms. This statement comes at a time when the movement in education is away from the individual and toward preservation of the system in terms of arbitrary standards and competencies and excellence of achievement in a set curriculum or course of study. Perhaps the pendulum will swing back. It usually does. But for now, we had better fight to preserve special education.

REFERENCES

Affleck, J. Q., Madge, S., Adams, A., & Lowenbraun, S. (1988). Integrated classroom vs. resource model: Academic viability and effectiveness. *Exceptional Children, 54*(4), 339–348.

Biklen, D., Bogdan, R., Ferguson, D. L., Searl, S. J., & Taylor, S. J. (1985). *Achieving the complete school: Strategies for effective mainstreaming.* New York: Teachers College Press.

Carnine, D. W., & Kameenui, E. J. (1990). The general education initiative and children with special needs: A false dilemma in the face of true problems. *Journal of Learning Disabilities, 23*(3), 141–144.

Daniel R. v. El Paso Independent School District, 874 F.2d 1036 (5th Cir. 1989).

Egner, A. N., & Lates, B. J. (1975). The Vermont consulting teacher program: A case presentation. In M. C. Parker (Ed.), *Psychological consultation: Helping teachers meet special needs* (pp. 31–53). Reston, VA: The Council for Exceptional Children.

Jenkins, J. R., Pious, C. G., & Jewell, M. (1990). Special education and the regular education initiative: Basic assumptions. *Exceptional Children, 56*(6), 479–491.

Lieberman, L. M. (1988). *Preserving special education . . . For Those Who Need it.* Newtonville, MA: Glo Worm Publications.

Lieberman, L. M. (1990). REI: Revisited . . . again. *Exceptional Children, 56*(6), 561–562.

National Joint Committee on Learning Disabilities (1993, March/April). A reaction to Full Inclusion: A reaffirmation of the right of students with learning disabilities to a continuum of services. *LDA Newsbriefs,* p. 3.

New Brunswick Teachers Association. (1988, February). *Report on a survey of classroom teachers on the integration of special needs/exceptional pupils.*

Stainback, S., Stainback, W., & Forest, M. (1989). *Educating all students in the mainstream of regular education.* Baltimore: Paul H. Brookes.

Strully, J. L., & Strully, C. F. (1989). Friendships as an educational goal. In S. Stainback, W. Stainback, & M. Forest (Eds.). *Educating all students in the mainstream of regular education* (pp. 59–68), Baltimore: Paul H. Brookes.

Trent, S. (1989). Much to do about nothing: A clarification of issues on the regular education initiative. *Journal of Learning Disabilities, 22*(1), 23–25, 45.

Wang, M. C. (1981). Mainstreaming exceptional children: Some instructional design and implementation considerations. *Elementary School Journal, 81,* 195–221.

Will, M. C. (1986). Educating children with learning problems: A shared responsibility. *Exceptional Children, 52,* 411–415.

SECTION TWO

SCHOOL SERVICE
DELIVERY APPROACHES

Can all students, including those traditionally classified as having severe, profound, and multiple disabilities, be educated in the mainstream of general education classrooms? Ayres and the Stainbacks spell out in Chapter 3 why it is important to do so and outline how it is being done in increasing numbers of schools throughout the United States, Canada, Italy, Australia, and a number of other countries. In Chapter 4, Vergason and Anderegg explain that it is unrealistic to think general education classes can meet the needs of all students. They provide a rationale for maintaining a continuum of special education service delivery options.

CHAPTER 3

Schools as Inclusive Communities

SUSAN STAINBACK
WILLIAM STAINBACK
BARBARA AYRES

INTRODUCTION

Hansen Elementary in Cedar Falls, Iowa; Winooski High in Winooski, Vermont; Brook Forest School in Oak Brook, Illinois; Gilbert Linkous Elementary in Blacksburg, Virginia; St. Francis in Waterloo County, Ontario; Chapparal in Albuquerque, New Mexico; and O'Hearn School in Boston, Massachusetts, are just a few of the schools that have recently had the attention of parents, educators, and community members focused on them. These schools are examples of a new breed of schools developing across North America.

What these and a growing number of other schools have in common is a desire to develop educational settings that are inclusive, supportive communities. The goal in such schools is to be sure that all students, regardless of any individual differences they might have (be they classified disabled, at-risk, homeless, or gifted), are fully included in the mainstream of school life. This goal incorporates the idea that all students deserve to be safe, happy, secure, and successful learners within the mainstream.

Before discussing the characteristics of schools that are in the process of becoming inclusive communities, it is useful to review background information about why full inclusion of all students into the education mainstream is an important goal.

RATIONALE FOR FULL INCLUSION

Benefits to Students

Numerous investigations have demonstrated the gains that can be achieved by students when they are provided appropriate educational experiences and support in inclusive settings. While many of the academic gains are reported for students labeled as having mild disabilities (Jenkins et al., 1994; Madden & Slavin, 1983; Wang, 1989), recent studies conducted with students labeled as having more significant disabilities illustrate gains in the areas of social competence, communication, engaged time, and acquisition of IEP objectives (Brinker & Thorpe, 1984; Cole & Meyer, 1991; Hunt, Alwell, Goetz, & Sailor, 1990; Hunt, Farron-Davis, Beckstead, Curtis, & Goetz, 1994; Kennedy & Itkonen, 1994; York, Vandercook, Caughey, & Heise-Neff, 1990). In addition, the results of preliminary studies focusing on the academic performance of students who do not have disability labels indicate that there are no adverse effects of inclusion, and anecdotal comments from general education teachers support the positive gains experienced by these students.

> Inclusion has had an effect on the other children's academic learning by increasing awareness of their own capabilities and respect for themselves and others, which affects the learning climate and susceptibility to learning. (Vandercook et al., 1991, p. 1)

As with learning, attitude change toward students with disabilities can positively develop when appropriate guidance and direction from adults is provided in inclusive settings. That is, in inclusive settings students can learn to understand, respect, be sensitive to, and grow comfortable with individual differences and similarities among their peers (Murray-Seegert, 1989; Peck, Donaldson, & Pezzoli, 1990; Stainback, Stainback, Moravec, & Jackson, 1992; Voeltz, 1980, 1982). Students also can learn to interact, communicate, develop friendships, work together, and assist one another based on their individual strengths and needs (Forest, 1987; Harris, 1994; Hedeen, 1994; Stainback & Stainback, 1988; Strully, 1986, 1987). As noted by Vandercook, Fleetham, Sinclair, and Tettie (1988): "In integrated classrooms all children are enriched by having the opportunity to learn from one another, grow to care for one another, and gain the attitudes, skills, and values necessary for our communities to support the inclusion of all citizens" (p. 15).

Another major benefit that can occur as a result of school inclusion is that it prepares students for integrated community living. The 1982 report of the Disability Rights, Education, and Defense Fund found "that regardless of race, class, gender, type of disability, or age at its onset, the more time spent in integrated public school classes as children, the more people achieved educationally and occupationally as adults" (Ferguson & Asch, 1989, p. 124). In a series of studies, Wehman (1990) found the same thing. He concluded: "Segregated classes do not lead to independence and competence, but instead foster an unrealistic sense of insulation" (p. 43). A recent National Longitudinal Transition Study of Special Education Students (NLTS) also supports these findings reporting that students with physical disabilities "were 43 percent more likely to be competitively employed after graduation than their peers who spent only half their class time in regular education" (Staff, 1994, p. 3). Some parents intuitively know this. One parent commented on her daughter's integrated education.

> When she's finished with school, she'll be able to be in some sort of integrated situation. She'll have social skills she wouldn't have had and an ability to function in more complex situations than she would've been able to do if she'd stayed segregated. (cited in Hanline & Halvorsen, 1989, p. 490)

To be accepted in the work place and the community at large, people with disabilities need to learn how to function and perform in the "real, regular" world and interact with their peers, and equally important, their peers need to learn how to interact and function with them. This cannot occur if educators place students with disabilities into segregated, special classes and, in effect, separate students with and without disabilities during their school years. As noted by Flynn and Kowalczyk-McPhee (1989): "To be excluded from an ordinary educational career and placed in a special education system probably means the person is destined for a special life style and special employment" (p. 30).

Avoiding the Ill Effects of Segregation

A second reason for including all students in the mainstream is to avoid the ill effects of segregation inherent when students are placed in separate, special schools and classes. Lack of self-confidence, lack of motivation, and lack of positive expectations for achievement are all products of segregated learning environments. As noted by Chief Justice Warren in the 1954 *Brown v. Board of Education* decision, separateness in education can "generate a feeling of inferiority as to [children's] status in the community that may affect their hearts and minds in a way unlikely ever to be undone. This sense of inferiority . . . affects the motivation of the child to learn . . . [and] has a tendency to retard . . . educational and mental development" (Warren, 1954, p. 493).

This concern voiced by Warren was confirmed by a statement of a student who attended separate, special classes throughout his school years.

> The only contact we had with the "normal" children was visual. We stared at each other. On those occasions, I can report my own feelings: embarrassment. . . . I can also report their feelings: YECH! We, the children in the "handicapped" class, were internalizing the "yech" message—plus a couple of others. We were in school because children go to school, but we were outcasts with no future and no expectation of one. (Massachusetts Advocacy Center, 1987, pp. 4–5)

Equality

The third and by far the most important reason for including all students in the mainstream is that it is the fair, ethical, and equitable thing to do. It deals with the value of *equality*. As was decided in the *Brown v. Board of Education* decision, *separate is not equal*. All children should be a part of the educational and community mainstream.

It is discriminatory that some students, such as those labeled disabled, must earn the right or be gotten ready to be in the general education mainstream or have to wait for educational researchers to prove that they can profit from the mainstream, whereas other students are allowed unrestricted access simply because they have no label. No one should have to pass anyone's test or prove anything in a research study to live and learn in the mainstream of school and community life. It is a basic right, not something one has to earn.

The basic premise of equality inherent in inclusive schooling was summarized on the floor of the U. S. Congress by former Senator Lowell Weicker.

> Authorities on disabilities have often said, and I have quoted them on this floor before, that the history of society's formal methods of dealing with people with disabilities can be summed up in two words: SEGREGATION and INEQUALITY. Psychologist Kenneth Clark, whose testimony about the damaging effects of segregation provided pivotal evidence in the landmark case of *Brown versus Board of Education,* stated that "segregation is the way in which a society tells a group of human beings that they are inferior to other groups of human beings in the society." As a society, we have treated people with disabilities as inferiors and made them unwelcome in many activities and opportunities generally available to other Americans. (Senator Lowell Weicker, 1988, p. 1)

It is not very comforting to think that in the past we have actually decided that some children or adults should be excluded from our regular lives, classrooms, and communities. This exclusion has *not* been done maliciously, but rather with good intentions to help students; however, we cannot continue to ignore the effects of this segregation. If we truly want a fair, egalitarian society in which all people are considered to have equal worth and equal rights, we need to reevaluate how we operate our schools. If we want integration and equality for all people in our society, segregation in schools cannot be justified. When a single person, who has not broken any laws, is excluded from the mainstream of school and community life, we all become vulnerable.

Before closing this section, it should be clarified that at issue is not whether students should receive appropriate educational experiences geared to their unique needs, and the specialized tools and techniques they need, from highly qualified school personnel and specialists in order to fulfill their potential. That this should occur is accepted by both those who advocate for restructuring and those who do not. At issue is whether students should receive these services in integrated or segregated settings.

PARADIGM SHIFT IN EDUCATION

The rationale just outlined and the trend toward including all students in the mainstream of general education has resulted from a paradigm shift regarding how people think about and view the education of students with disabilities. In the past, educators have assumed a "functional limitations" approach to services (Hahn, 1989). This old paradigm places the problems on the students with disabilities when they experience problems with learning or adapting in general education classrooms. From this perspective, the primary task of educators is to remediate these students' functional deficits to the maximum extent possible. That is, educators attempt to fix, improve, or make ready the students who are being unsuccessful by providing them with the skills to be able to succeed in a mainstreamed educational environment that is *not* adapted to meet their particular needs, interests, or capabilities. And if this is not possible, they must be relegated to special, separate learning settings. In the functional limitations paradigm the student is expected to fit into the existing program or educational environment.

This paradigm is gradually being replaced by a "minority group" paradigm (Hahn, 1989). The minority group paradigm of school operation places the principle difficulties of students with disabilities not with the student, but rather with the organization of the general education environment. That is, school failure is the result of such things as educational programs, settings, and criteria for performance that do not meet the diverse needs of the students. From this perspective, the problem is with the educational organization or environment that needs to be modified in order to address the diverse needs of all students.

According to Hahn and other disability rights advocates (e.g., Ferguson & Asch, 1989; Snow, 1989; Worth, 1988), as well as a growing number of parents and professional educators (e.g., Biklen, 1985; Buswell & Schaffner, 1990; Forest, 1987; Gartner & Lipsky, 1987; Strully, 1986, 1987), people with disabilities are a minority group and should be afforded the same rights as other minority groups, including educational programs that meet their needs in the mainstream. The U.S. Congress apparently agrees. Although not focused directly on education issues, the Senate recently approved the *Americans with Disabilities Act* which "is to provide a clear and comprehensive national mandate to end discrimination against individuals with disabilities giving them the same protection in our society available to other individuals protected by civil rights laws" ("Senate Overwhelmingly Approves," 1989, p. 1). In the Senate debate on the act, proponents

> likened it to the Civil Rights Act of 1964, which prohibited racial or religious discrimination. Some turned the clock back further: to the freeing of the slaves. Senator Tom Harkin, D-Iowa, one of the measure's chief sponsors, calls it a "20th century Emancipation Proclamation for people with disabilities." ("Congress on Verge," 1989, p. B1)

In a recent interview, Tom Hehir, the director of the Office of Special Education Programs for the U.S. Department of Education, said:

> Disabled people are no longer viewed as the objects of charity, but as a distinct minority who have been historically subject to discrimination and have now gained full civil rights through the passage of the Americans with Disabilities Act. The ADA seeks nothing less than full participation and integration of disabled people in all aspects of American society. (Miller, 1994, p. 5)

Thus, the minority group paradigm is gaining recognition. It creates a different world view for the future in regard to disability.

In regard to education per se it should be stressed here that Hahn (1989), Daniels (1990), and other disability rights advocates are not calling for the simple dumping of students with disabilities into general education classes, but rather integration *coupled* with a restructuring of general education classes to meet the unique needs of all students, including those with disabilities. That is, disability rights advocates are not arguing that people with disabilities do not sometimes need specialized instructions, tools, techniques, and equipment, but they are saying that the major difficulty faced is the negative attitudes and "let's fix it" approach held by many people, along with a lack of real opportunities to participate in the mainstream of schools and communities *designed to accommodate everyone* (e.g., lifts on buses, curriculum and teaching methods in mainstreamed classes geared to the learning characteristics of students with disabilities).

Recent court cases have supported the accommodation of students with disability labels within general education settings. In *Oberti v. Board of Education of the Borough of Clementon School District* (1993), the federal district court and the Third Circuit Court of Appeals ruled that Rafael Oberti, a student with Down syndrome and difficult behaviors, be provided with supplementary supports and services within the general education classroom. The ruling in this case has been described as "a controversial decision that may have ushered in a new era of judicial activism in LRE cases. . . ." (Osborne & Dimattia, 1994, p. 6) and as ". . . a mandate for inclusion . . ." (Webb, 1994, p. 1). Similarly, in *Board of Education, Sacra-*

mento City Unified School District v. Holland (1992), the Ninth Circuit Court of Appeals determined that a student should be placed in a special education classroom only when he or she "cannot receive a satisfactory education in the general education class with appropriate support services" (Osborne & Dimattia, 1994, p. 11). According to Osborne and Dimattia (1994) the recent court decisions illustrate a movement toward supporting the inclusion of students with disability labels and "indicate that an inclusionary placement must be the placement of choice and that a student with disabilities may be excluded from a general education setting only in the face of strong evidence that the student cannot be satisfactorily educated in that setting" (p. 12).

Finally, contrary to popular opinion, research has indicated that many general educators are willing to join special educators in making general education classes more flexible and conducive to the needs of students with disabilities, *if* they are involved in the planning process and have choices about the design and types of support and assistance they will receive (Ferguson, Meyer, Jeanchild, Juniper, & Zingo, 1992; Myles & Simpson, 1989; Rankin et al., 1994). While general educators are often apprehensive about these efforts in the beginning, actual experience in inclusive classrooms facilitates attitude change and allows teachers to move forward in accommodating the needs of all their students (Giangreco, Baumgart, & Doyle, in press; Giangreco, Dennis, Cloninger, Edelman, & Schattman, 1993; Hedeen, 1994; Stainback et al., 1992).

INCLUSIVE SCHOOLS

Only a few short years ago, it was considered "unrealistic" by most people to even discuss the possibility of educating all students, including those classified as having severe and profound disabilities, in general education classes. However, this is changing. The reason is that it is now being done successfully in a growing number of schools in Canada, Italy, Australia, the United States, and other countries (Berrigan, 1988; Bik-

len, 1988; Blackman & Peterson, 1989; Conn, 1992; Cross & Villa, 1992; Forest, 1987; Jackson, 1992; Jakupcak, 1993; Porter & Collicott, 1992; Schattman, 1992). It is being accomplished by the establishment of what has been termed *inclusive schools*. In this section, what is meant by the term *inclusive school* is defined, and the characteristics of such schools are outlined.

An inclusive school or classroom educates all students in the mainstream. This means that all students, including students with learning and physical disabilities, and those who are at risk, homeless, and gifted, are included in integrated, general education classes. It also means providing all students within the mainstream with (1) appropriate education experiences that are challenging yet geared to their capabilities and needs; and (2) any support and assistance they or their teachers require.

While inclusive schools are not identical to each other, they tend to share a number of similar characteristics.

All Children Belong

Inclusive schools generally start with a philosophy that all children can learn and belong in the mainstream of school and community life. That is, most establish a philosophy that, based on egalitarian and democratic principles, integration is to be valued; it is not an experiment to be tested (Ferguson & Asch, 1989). In these schools no students, including those with disabilities, are relegated to the fringes of the school by placement in segregated wings, trailers, or special classes.

A Sense of Community

Inclusive schools and classrooms do *not* focus on how to help any particular category of students—such as those classified as disabled—fit into the mainstream. Instead, the focus is on how to operate classrooms and schools as supportive communities that include and meet the needs of everyone (Sapon-Shevin, 1992). Personnel in such schools and classrooms purposefully foster community—a sense that everyone belongs, is accepted, and supports and is supported by his or her peers and other members of the school community in the course of having his or her educational needs met. There is a great deal of emphasis on students as well as staff caring about and accepting responsibility for each other.

Diversity Is Valued

In inclusive schools, diversity is valued and is believed to strengthen the school or classroom while offering all of its members greater opportunities for learning.

Robert Barth (1990), a Harvard professor, described the value of diversity.

> I would prefer my children to be in a school in which differences are looked for, attended to, and celebrated as good news, as opportunities for learning. The question with which so many school people are preoccupied is, "What are the limits of diversity beyond which behavior is unacceptable?" . . . But the question I would like to see asked more often is, "How can we make conscious, deliberate use of differences in social class, gender, age, ability, race, and interest as resources for learning?" . . . Differences hold great opportunities for learning. Differences offer a free, abundant, and renewable resource. I would like to see our compulsion for eliminating differences replaced by an equally compelling focus on making use of these differences to improve schools. What is important about people—and about schools—is what is different, not what is the same. (pp. 514–515)

Natural Proportions

Inclusive schools have a natural or normal proportion of students with disabilities. They avoid serving as "centers" or "cluster sites" for any category of students. This is important since placement of a disproportionately large number of students with disabilities or other characteristics into any one general education class reduces the diversity in the class and can result in enclaves or segregated sub-

sets of students within the class, negating many of the benefits inherent in integrated, inclusive classrooms (Stainback & Stainback, 1990).

Services Based on Need Rather than Labels

In inclusive schools and classrooms, students are viewed and approached as individuals rather than as members of categorical groups. This makes it much more likely that educators will focus on the specific needs, interests, and capabilities of the students. As noted by Lilly (1979), once we begin looking at students as individuals, the data available concerning their instructional needs is far more specific and precise than what is implied from any categorical label.

Support Provided in General Education Classrooms

Another characteristic of an inclusive school is that it delivers specialized services and supports in general education settings to anyone who requires them. If a student is experiencing difficulty or needs certain types of curricular or instructional modifications or special tools and techniques to succeed educationally or socially, the inclusive school works out ways to get those services and supports to the student where he or she naturally is placed with his or her age peers.

When students are referred, they are referred for support and assistance in the general education class; they are not referred for educational placement into a special, segregated setting outside of the mainstream. That is, the student is *not* taken to the service or support, rather the service or support is taken to the student. The focus is on determining ways students can get their educational and related needs met within the existing, natural settings.

Interdependence and Support Networks

Inclusive schools tend to foster interdependence and natural support networks. The staff as well as the students encourage such support. There is an emphasis on peer tutoring, buddy systems, circles of friends, cooperative learning, and other ways of connecting students together in natural, ongoing supportive relationships (Jorgensen, 1992; Sapon-Shevin, Ayres, & Duncan, 1994). There also is an emphasis on teachers and other school personnel working together and supporting each other through professional peer collaboration, team teaching, teacher and student assistance teams, and other cooperative arrangements. Cooperation and collaboration with peers rather than competitive or independent activities are generally fostered among students and staff (Villa & Thousand,1988; 1994). It is assumed that natural supportive relationships in which individuals within the classroom or school assist and support one another as peers, friends, or colleagues are as important as providing professional support from "experts." Focusing on natural supports within the school helps connect students and staff together in ongoing peer and collegial relationships which facilitates the development of a supportive community (Strully & Strully, 1985).

Support Facilitators or Collaborating Teachers

In inclusive schools, special educators generally integrate themselves into general education. Although some become classroom teachers or consulting specialists, others may assume a role of encouraging and helping to organize support in general education classrooms. Special educators have been referred to as collaborating teachers, support facilitators, methods and resource teachers, or inclusion facilitators (Ferguson et al., 1992; Porter, 1989; Stainback & Stainback, 1990; Thousand & Villa, 1989). Regardless of what they have been called, they work in collaboration with other school personnel to help ensure that students' needs are met in the mainstream. *Collaboration* means that the support facilitator, teacher, students, and other school personnel work together cooperatively with no one assuming an expert, supervisory, or evaluator role. In this way, everyone (not just support facilitators) is involved in

facilitating support systems and adapting instruction to individual needs.

> The collaborative process is multi-directional, since all members are considered to have unique and needed expertise. At any point in time a member of the collaborative relationship may be the giver or receiver of consultation . . . [or] any member of a group may become a leader by taking actions that help the group complete its tasks and maintain effective collaborative relationships. (Nevin, Thousand, Paolucci-Whitcomb, & Villa, 1990, p. 21)

A major aim of support facilitators is to work side by side with classroom teachers and other school personnel to *encourage natural support networks.* They place particular emphasis on promoting peer interdependence through buddy systems, peer tutoring, cooperative learning, and friendship development, wherein students want to and learn how to assist each other (Jorgensen, 1992; Stainback & Stainback, 1990).

The support facilitator or collaborating teacher also frequently functions as a *resource locator,* since a classroom teacher cannot be expected to have expertise in every possible assessment, curricular, or behavior management area needed by all students in inclusive, heterogeneous classrooms. The role may involve locating appropriate materials, equipment, or specialists, consultants, teachers, and other school personnel who have expertise in a particular area(s) needed by a classroom teacher and/or student.

These collaborating teachers or support personnel can also provide direct help as *team teachers,* facilitating learning in their expertise area(s) (Bauwens, Hourcade, & Friend, 1989; Bauwens & Hourcade, 1995). In addition they often work side by side with classroom teachers providing support to enable or empower teachers to adapt and individualize instruction to meet the unique needs of all class members. It is crucial to note that the general education teacher maintains responsibility for the education and support of *all* students in the class. The collaborating teacher or support facilitator acts as a resource to the teacher, family, principal, and the class as a whole in building support networks and adapting instruction to individual needs.

Curriculum Adapted When Needed

In inclusive schools, the focus is not exclusively on how to help some students, such as those with disabilities, fit into the existing, standard curriculum of the school. Rather the curriculum is adapted, when necessary, to meet the needs of any students for whom the standard curriculum is inappropriate or who could be better served through adaptation.

As classroom teachers have increased exposure to and experience with diversity in their classrooms, they are learning in collaboration with special educators and others how to offer curricular content appropriate for a wide range of students, in addition to learning about delivering their instruction through the use of approaches that are designed to accommodate diversity (Ford, Davern, & Schnorr, 1992; Giangreco et al., in press; Jorgensen, 1992; Rankin et al., 1994). There are possibilities for students classified as having severe and profound mental disabilities to participate in meaningful ways in history, math, English literature, science, and other classes at the high school level as well as the elementary level. It is also possible for students to learn self-care and daily life skills in inclusive, integrated schools.

Resources Combined

Through the use of waivers (Will, 1986) or by other means (Salisbury & Chambers, 1994), resources—including personnel, curriculum, and instructional procedures—from special and regular education are combined to design educational experiences to meet diverse student needs in integrated classrooms. Teachers and other school personnel are empowered to make decisions as to how the combined resources will be used. The only stipulation on how resources can be used is that *no student can be left out;* that is, all students' unique educational and related needs must be met. In this way, resources and expertise in

special and general education, from classroom instruction, counseling, administration, school psychology, consultative services, occupational therapy, behavior management personnel, speech therapy, and other sources, are employed in flexible ways to assist any student, including those with disabilities, according to his or her unique needs. It should be stressed that accountability and data collection procedures are designed to be sure that students traditionally under-served or ill-served, such as those with disabilities, receive the services they need to progress in school (Lipsky & Gartner, 1989).

Finally, is it idealistic to think that schools and classrooms can become inclusive communities where students and teachers care about and support each other? Yes, it is idealistic! But as Forest (1985) stated: "We create our tomorrows by what we dream today" (p. 40). Fortunately, some parents and educators have established the vision or dream of inclusive classroom communities and are diligently working toward making it a reality. As increasing numbers of schools demonstrate success, others will follow.

DISCUSSION

When racial integration in the schools began in the late 1950s and early 1960s there were numerous rationales given as to why it was not a good idea and/or why it would not work: "the quality of instruction is what is most important, not the place," "research shows that black students will be rejected by white teachers and students," "it's not in their best interest," "the schools are not ready," "it's too idealistic," "we need more analysis and study," and " it is a communist plot." The justifications that have been offered in this book and elsewhere (e.g., Fuchs & Fuchs, 1994; Kauffman, 1989; Vergason & Anderegg, 1989) for continuing to place students with disabilities into segregated, special classes and schools are also numerous. A few examples include: "regular education is not prepared," "integration is a Reagan–Bush plot to reduce funds to students with disabilities," "university professors and administrators do not want to do it," "there is a need for further analysis and study," "we need to maintain a continuum of services," "students with disabilities need special treatment and interventions," "educational achievement is more important than placement."

But none of these arguments can really justify segregating students with disabilities or any other students from the mainstream of school and community life. An analogy may clarify this point.

At the time of the American Civil War, should Abraham Lincoln have asked to see the scientific evidence on the benefits of ending slavery? Should he have consulted "the experts," perhaps a sociologist, an economist, a political scientist? . . . Slavery is not now and was not then an issue for science. It is a moral issue. But, just for a moment, suppose that an economist had been able to demonstrate that blacks would suffer economically, as would the entire South, from emancipation. Would that justify keeping slavery? And suppose a political scientist had argued that blacks had no experience with democracy, they were not ready for it. Would that have justified extending slavery? Or imagine that a sociologist could have advised Lincoln against abolishing slavery on the grounds that it would destroy the basic social structure of southern plantations, towns, and cities. All these arguments might have seemed "true." But could that really justify slavery? Of course not. Slavery has no justification. (Biklen, 1985, pp. 16–17)

Although arguments can be made about Lincoln's motivations, and about the fact that the abolishment of slavery did not actually occur until the Thirteenth Amendment became law, the above analogy nevertheless points out that some things are simply morally and ethically wrong.

Those parents, professionals, politicians, and community members who have entered the struggle for the inclusion of all students into the mainstream have made a value judgment that integrated education is the best and most humane way to proceed. From their perspective, the point just made about slavery applies also to current segregationist practices in the schools throughout America. If we want an integrated society in which all persons are considered of equal worth and as having equal rights, segregation in the schools cannot be justified. That is, no defensible excuses or rationales can be offered, and no amount of scientific research can be conducted that will in the final analysis justify segregation. Segregation has no justification.

Separation is repugnant to our constitutional tradition. Integration is a central constitutional value—not integration that denies difference but, rather, integration that accommodates difference; appreciates it and celebrates it. (Gilhool, 1976, p. 8)

Cathy Heizman (1990), a parent of a child with severe disabilities, has clearly communicated the above point.

On a hot, sunny day in 1955, Miss Rosa Parks refused to take her place at the back of the bus in Montgomery, Alabama. That one simple act of defiance and courage changed the face of America forever.

Somebody asked me once why I was so adamant about integration. "Kids with disabilities don't learn any better or any easier in an integrated class," he said. "Their education isn't any better." Maybe not.

And the ride in the first seat of the bus isn't any smoother than in the back. But Miss Rosa Parks knew just how important it was to be in the front in 1955.

And so do I. (p. 1)

A few years ago, only some parents and educators were saying that they thought it might be possible to educate all students in the mainstream of America's schools. Now, growing numbers of people are convinced that it can be done, given that the mainstream is sensitive to individual differences, and teachers and students are provided adequate support and assistance. The reason is that, as noted earlier, it is beginning to be done successfully in schools in the United States, Canada, Italy, and a number of other countries. Basically, these schools have identified appropriate but challenging goals within the mainstream for students with diverse needs rather than requiring them all to learn the exact same thing or always function at the same level of proficiency as their peers. They also have worked to provide teachers and students with the support and assistance they need to make successful inclusive education a reality.

But it will be difficult to achieve success on a widespread basis if, as a society, we are unwilling to (1) provide each student the support necessary for him or her to be in the mainstream, and (2) adapt and adjust the mainstream, when necessary, to accommodate all students. The key is our willingness to visualize, work for, and achieve a mainstream that is adaptive and supportive of everyone. Few people, including those classified as disabled, want to be in a mainstream that does not meet their needs and make them feel welcome and secure. Thus it is essential that we make the mainstream flexible and sensitive to the unique needs of all students and that we foster friendships for students in the mainstream. This is why restructuring is so critical. With restructuring, the literally billions of dollars now spent on segregated, special education programs and the hundreds of thousands of educators currently working in segregated, special settings could be integrated into general education to help make the mainstream supportive, flexible, and adaptive to the individual needs of all students.

Finally, it should be emphasized that to say it can be done is not the same as saying it will be easy. Segregation has been practiced for centuries and there are entrenched attitudes, laws, policies, and educational structures that work against achieving full inclusion of all students on a widespread basis. In addition, because a second system of education (i.e., "special" education) has operated for so long, many schools unfortunately do not know at the present time how to adapt and modify the curriculum and instructional programs to meet diverse student needs, deal with behavioral difficulties, and/or provide the specialized tools, techniques, and supports some students need to be successful in the mainstream. Thus, achieving full inclusion of all students is likely to be a very challenging undertaking. But the goal of having inclusive schools where everyone belongs, has friends, and is provided appropriate education experiences and supports is far too important not to accept the challenge.

If integration is valued, as Bogdan (1983) states, " 'does mainstreaming work' is a silly question. . . . Where it is not working, we should be asking what is preventing it from working and what can be done about it?" (p. 427).

REFERENCES

Barth, R. (1990). A personal vision of a good school. *Phi Delta Kappan, 71,* 512–571.

Bauwens, J., Hourcade, J. (1995). *Cooperative teaching: Rebuilding the schoolhouse for all students.* Austin, TX: Pro-Ed.

Bauwens, J., Hourcade, J., & Friend, M. (1989). Cooperative teaching. A model for general and special education integration. *Remedial and Special Education, 10*(2), 17–22.

Berrigan, C. (1988, February). Integration in Italy: A dynamic movement. *TASH Newsletter,* 6–7.

Biklen, D. (1985). *Achieving the complete school.* New York: Columbia University Press.

Biklen, D. (1988). (Producer). *Regular Lives.* [Video]. Washington, DC: State of the Art (WETA, P.O. Box 2226, Washington, DC 20013).

Blackman, H., & Peterson, D. (1989). *Total integration neighborhood schools.* LaGrange, IL: LaGrange Department of Special Education.

Board of Education Sacramento City Unified School District v. Holland, 786 R. Supp. 874 (E. D. Cal. 1992).

Bogdan, R. (1983). 'Does Mainstreaming Work?' is a silly question. *Phi Delta Kappan, 64,* 427–428.

Brinker, R., & Thorpe, M. (1984). Integration of severely handicapped students and the proportion of IEP objectives achieved. *Exceptional Children, 51,* 168–175.

Buswell, B., & Schaffner, B. (1990). Families supporting inclusive schooling. In W. Stainback & S. Stainback (Eds.), *Support networks for inclusive schooling: Interdependent integrated education* (pp. 219–230). Baltimore: Paul H. Brookes.

Cole, D., & Meyer, L. (1991). Social integration and severe disabilities: A longitudinal analysis of child outcomes. *Journal of Special Education, 25,* 340–351.

Congress on verge of passing landmark disabilities act. (1989, December). *Waterloo Courier,* p. B1.

Conn, M. (1992). Aligning our beliefs with action. *The School Administrator, 2(49),* 22–24.

Cross, G., & Villa, R. (1992). The Winooski School System: An evolutionary perspective of a school restructuring for diversity. In R. Villa, J. Thousand, W. Stainback, & S. Stainback (Eds.), *Restructuring for caring and effective education* (pp. 219–237). Baltimore: Paul H. Brookes.

Daniels, S. (1990). Disability in America: An evolving concept, a new paradigm. *Policy Network Newsletter, 3,* 1–3.

Ferguson, P., & Asch, A. (1989). Lessons from life: Personal and parental perspectives on school, childhood, and disability. In D. Biklen, A. Ford, & D. Ferguson (Eds.), *Disability and society* (pp. 108–140). Chicago: National Society for the Study of Education.

Ferguson, D., Meyer, G., Jeanchild, L., Juniper, L., & Zingo, J. (1992). Figuring out what to do with the grownups: How teachers make inclusion "work" for students with disabilities. *Journal of the Association for Persons with Severe Handicaps, 17,* 218–226.

Flynn, G., & Kowalczyk-McPhee, B. (1989). A school system in transition. In S. Stainback, W. Stainback, & M. Forest (Eds.), *Educating all students in the mainstream of regular education* (pp. 29–42). Baltimore: Paul H. Brookes.

Ford, A., Davern, L., & Schnorr, R. (1992). Inclusive education: "Making sense" of the curriculum. In S. Stainback & W. Stainback (Eds.), *Curriculum considerations in inclusive classrooms: Facilitating learning for all students* (pp. 37–61). Baltimore: Paul H. Brookes.

Forest, M. (1985). Education update. *Canadian Journal of Mental Retardation, 35,* 37–40.

Forest, M. (1987). *More education integration.* Downsview, Ont: G. Allan Roeher Institute.

Fuchs, D., & Fuchs, L. (1994). Inclusive schools movement and the radicalization of special education reform. *Exceptional Children, 60,* 294–309.

Gartner, A., & Lipsky, D. (1987). Beyond special education. *Harvard Educational Review, 57,* 367–395.

Giangreco, M., Baumgart, D., & Doyle, M. B. (in press). Including students with disabilities in general education classrooms: How it can facilitate teaching and learning. *Intervention in School and Clinic.*

Giangreco, M., Dennis, R., Cloninger, C., Edelman, S., & Schattman, R. (1993). "I've counted Jon": Transformational experiences of teachers educating students with disabilities. *Exceptional Children, 59,* 359–372.

Gilhool, T. (1976). Changing public policies: Roots and forces. In M. Reynolds (Ed.), *Mainstreaming: Origins and implications* (pp. 8–13). Reston, VA: Council for Exceptional Children.

Hahn, H. (1989). The politics of special education. In D. Lipsky & A. Gartner (Eds.), *Beyond Special Education* (pp. 225–242). Baltimore: Paul H. Brookes.

Hanline, M., & Halvorsen, A. (1989). Parent perceptions of the integration transition process: Overcoming artificial barriers. *Exceptional Children, 55,* 487–493.

Harris, T. (1994). Christine's inclusion: An example of peers supporting one another. In J. Thousand, R. Villa, & A. Nevin (Eds.), *Creativity and collaborative learning* (pp. 293–301). Baltimore: Paul H. Brookes.

Hedeen, D. (1994). *The interwoven relationship of teaching, learning, and supporting in inclusive classrooms.* Unpublished doctoral dissertation, Syracuse University.

Heizman, C. (1990). The need to belong. *Iowa News, 90,* 1.

Hunt, P., Alwell, M., Goetz, L., & Sailor, W. (1990). Generalized effects of conversation skills training. *Journal of the Association for Persons with Severe Handicaps, 15,* 250–260.

Hunt, P., Farron-Davis, F., Beckstead, S., Curtis, D., & Goetz, L. (1994). Evaluating the effects of placement of students with severe disabilities in general education versus special classes. *Journal of the Association for Persons with Severe Handicaps, 19,* 200–214.

Jackson, H. J. (1992). Full inclusion at Helen Hansen Elementary School: It happened because we value all children. In R. Villa, J. Thousand, W. Stainback, & S. Stainback (Eds.), *Restructuring for caring and effective education* (pp. 161–168). Baltimore: Paul H. Brookes.

Jakupcak, J. (1993). Innovative classroom programs for full inclusion. In J.W. Putnam (Ed.), *Cooperative learning and strategies for inclusion: Celebrating diversity in the classroom* (pp. 163–179). Baltimore: Paul H. Brookes.

Jenkins, J., Jewell, M., Leicester, N., O'Connor, R., Jenkins, L., & Troutner, N. (1994). Accommodations for individual differences without classroom ability groups: An experiment in school restructuring. *Exceptional Children, 60,* 344–358.

Jorgensen, C. (1992). Natural supports in inclusive schools. In J. Nisbet (Ed.), *Natural supports in school, at work, and in the community for people with severe disabilities* (pp. 179–215). Baltimore: Paul H. Brookes.

Kauffman, J. (1989). The regular education initiative as Reagan–Bush education policy: A trickle down theory of the hard-to-teach. *The Journal of Special Education, 23,* 256–279.

Kennedy, C., & Itkonen, T. (1994). Some effects of regular class placement on the social contacts and social networks of high school students with severe disabilities. *Journal of the Association for Persons with Severe Handicaps, 19,* 1–10.

Lilly, S. (1979). *Children with exceptional needs.* New York: Holt, Rinehart & Winston.

Lipsky, D., & Gartner, A. (1989). School administration and financial arrangements. In S. Stainbank, W. Stainback, & M. Forest (Eds.), *Educating all students in the mainstream of regular education* (pp. 105–129). Baltimore: Paul H. Brookes.

Madden, N., & Slavin, R. (1983). Mainstreaming students with mild academic handicaps: Academic and social outcomes. *Review of Educational Research 53,* 519–569.

Massachusetts Advocacy Center. (1987). *Out of the mainstream.* Boston: Author.

Miller, E. (1994). Changing the way we think about kids with disabilities: A conversation with Tom Hehir. *The Harvard Education Letter, 10*(4), 5–7.

Murray-Seegert, C. (1989). *Nasty girls, thugs, and humans like us: Social relations between severely disabled and nondisabled students in high school.* Baltimore: Paul H. Brookes.

Myles, B., & Simpson, R. (1989). Regular educators' modification preferences for mainstreaming mildly handicapped children. *Journal of Special Education, 22,* 479–489.

Nevin, A., Thousand, J., Paolucci-Whitcomb, P., & Villa, R. (1990). Collaborative consultation: Empowering public school personnel to provide heterogeneous schooling for all. *Journal of Educational and Psychological Consultation, 1*(1), 41–67.

Oberti v. Board of Education of the Borough of Clementon School District, 19IDELR423 (original) and (appeal) 19IDELR903 (1993) (D.N.J. 1992).

Osborne, A., & Dimattia, P. (1994). The IDEA's least restrictive environment mandate: Legal implications. *Exceptional Children, 61,* 6–14.

Peck, C., Donaldson, J., & Pezzoli, M. (1990). Some benefits nonhandicapped adolescents perceive for themselves from their social relationships with peers who have severe handicaps. *Journal of the Association for Persons with Severe Handicaps, 15,* 241–249.

Porter, G. (Producer). (1989). *A chance to belong* [Video]. Downsview, Ont.: (Canadian Association for Community Living, Kingsman Building, 4700 Keele St., Downsview, Ontario M3J IPE Canada).

Porter, G., & Collicott, J. (1992). New Brunswick School Districts 28 and 29: Mandates and strategies that promote inclusive schooling. In R. Villa, J. Thousand, W. Stainback, & S. Stainback (Eds.), *Restructuring for caring and effective education* (pp. 187–200). Baltimore: Paul H. Brookes.

Rankin, D., Hallick, A., Ban, S., Hartley, P., Bost, C., & Uggla, N. (1994). Who's dreaming?—A general education perspective on inclusion. *Journal of the Association for Persons with Severe Handicaps, 19,* 235–237.

Salisbury, C., & Chambers, A. (1994). Instructional costs of inclusive schooling. *Journal of the Association for Persons with Severe Handicaps, 19,* 215–222.

Sapon-Shevin, M. (1992). Inclusive thinking about inclusive schools. In R. Villa, J. Thousand, W. Stainback, & S. Stainback (Eds.), *Restructuring for caring and effective education* (pp. 335–346). Baltimore: Paul H. Brookes.

Sapon-Shevin, M., Ayres, B., & Duncan, J. (1994). Cooperative learning and inclusion. In J. Thousand, R. Villa, & A. Nevin (Eds.), *Creativity and collaborative learning* (pp. 45–58). Baltimore: Paul H. Brookes.

Schattman, R. (1992). The Franklin Northwest Supervisory Union: A case study of an inclusive school system. In R. Villa, J. Thousand, W. Stainback, & S. Stainback (Eds.), *Restructuring for caring and effective education* (pp. 143–159). Baltimore: Paul H. Brookes.

Senate overwhelmingly approves Americans with Disabilities Act (1989). D.C. Update. *TASH Newsletter, 4,* 1–2.

Senator Lowell Weicker on the Americans with Disability Act (1988, July). *D.C.Update,* p. 1.

Snow, J. (1989). Systems of support: A new vision. In S. Stainback, W. Stainback, & M. Forest (Eds.), *Educating all students in the mainstream of regular education* (pp. 221–234). Baltimore: Paul H. Brookes.

Staff. (1994). New research supports inclusion for physically disabled; vocational ed prevents dropping out. *The Harvard Education Letter, 10*(4), 3.

Stainback, S., & Stainback, W. (1988). Educating students with severe disabilities in regular classes. *Teaching Exceptional Children, 21,* 16–19.

Stainback, W., & Stainback, S. (1990). *Support networking for inclusive schooling: Interdependent, integrated education.* Baltimore: Paul H. Brookes.

Stainback, W., Stainback, S., Moravec, J., & Jackson, H. J. (1992). Concerns about full inclusion: An ethnographic investigation. In R. Villa, J. Thousand, W. Stainback & S. Stainback (Eds.), *Restructuring for caring and effective education* (pp. 305–324). Baltimore: Paul H. Brookes.

Strully, J. (1986). *Our children and the regular education classroom: Or why settle for anything less than the best?* Paper presented to the 1986 annual conference of the Association for Persons with Severe Handicaps, San Francisco, CA.

Strully, J. (1987, October). *What's really important in life anyway? Parents sharing the vision.* Paper presented at the 14th Annual TASH Conference, Chicago, IL.

Strully J., & Strully, C. (1985). Teach your children. *Canadian Journal of Mental Retardation, 35,* 3–11.

Thousand, J., & Villa, R. (1989). Enhancing success in heterogeneous schools. In S. Stainback, W. Stainback, & M. Forest (Eds.), *Educating all students in the maintream of regular education* (pp. 89–103). Baltimore: Paul H. Brookes.

Vandercook, T., Fleetham, D., Sinclair, S., & Tettie, R. (1988). Cath, Jess, Jules, and Ames . . . A story of friendship. *IMPACT, 2,* 18–19.

Vandercook, T., York, J., Sharpe, M., Knight, J., Salisbury, C., LeRoy, B., & Kozleski, E. (1991). The million dollar question. . . . *IMPACT, 4,* 1, 20–21.

Vergason, G., & Anderegg, M. (1989). Bah, Humbug, an answer to Stainback & Stainback. *TASH Newsletter, 15*(11), 8–10.

Villa, R., & Thousand, J. (1988). Enhancing success in heterogeneous classrooms and schools: The power of partnership. *Teacher Education and Special Education, 11,* 144–153.

Villa, R., & Thousand, J. (1994). One divided by two or more: Redefining the role of a cooperative education team. In J. Thousand, R. Villa, & A. Nevin (Eds.), *Creativity and collaborative learning* (pp. 79–101). Baltimore: Paul H. Brookes.

Voeltz, L. (1980). Children's attitudes toward handicapped peers. *American Journal of Mental Deficiency, 84,* 455–464.

Voeltz, L. (1982). Effects of structured interactions with severely handicapped peers on children's attitudes. *American Journal of Mental Deficiency, 86,* 380–390.

Wang, M. (1989). Accommodating student diversity through adaptive instruction. In S. Stainback & W. Stainback (Eds.), *Educating all students in the mainstream of regular education* (pp. 183–197). Baltimore: Paul H. Brookes.

Webb, N. (1994). With new court decisions backing them, advocates see inclusion as a question of values. *The Harvard Education Letter, 10*(4), 1–3.

Wehman, P. (1990). School to work: Elements of successful programs. *Teaching Exceptional Children, 23,* 40–43.

Will, M. (1986). Educating children with learning problems: A shared responsibility. *Exceptional Children, 51,* 33–51.

Worth, P. (1988, December). *Empowerment: Choices and change.* Paper presented at the 15th Annual TASH Conference, Washington, DC.

York, J., Vandercook, T., Caughey, E., & Heise-Neff, C. (1990). Regular class integration: Beyond socialization. *The Association for Persons with Severe Handicaps Newsletter, 16*(5), 3.

CHAPTER 4

Preserving the Least Restrictive Environment: Revisited

M. L. ANDEREGG
GLENN A. VERGASON

INTRODUCTION

The past three years have been exciting for advocates for individuals with disabilities. This period has produced some interesting twists on the concept of least restrictive environment. In a misplaced zeal for total inclusion, some special educators have lost touch with the historical struggle involved in educating students with disabilities. These professionals have misinterpreted the philosophy of least restrictive environment (Langone, 1990). The intent of this chapter is to restate the intent of the law and show how it has been misinterpreted. We will also show how recent court decisions have begun to rewrite rather than interpret the law.

In Turnbull's (1979, 1990) discussions of the history of least restrictive environment in education, he traced the development of the concept of least restrictive alternative. State governments had applied restrictive regulations (or alternatives) to control interstate commerce. The gist of these cases was that, to preserve individual freedoms, the least restrictive alternative (or minimal rules and regulations) should always be applied. Out of the concept of least restrictive alternative grew the term *least restrictive environment*. The substitution of the word *environment* for *alternative* has misled some people to assume that the placement of least restriction is a physical location.

The original focus of the Education for All Handicapped Children Act (P.L. 94-142) was never to place more children in one specific physical location (the general education classroom). "The act [P.L. 94-142] and its regulations [and subsequence renewal] require schools to offer a continuum of services," according to the *Daniel R. R.* ruling (1989).

Until the regular education initiative, the central focus of advocacy for children with disabilities was to provide instruction in the environment which least restricted the student's potential for benefiting from instruction. This purpose was clearly stated in P.L. 94-142:

> It is the purpose of this Act to assure that all handicapped children have available to them, within the time periods specified, a **free appropriate public education which emphasizes special education and related services** designed to meet their unique needs, to assure that the rights of handicapped children and their parents are protected. . . . (Education for All Handicapped Children, Section 1400 (c)) [emphasis added]

The Individuals with Disabilities Education Act (IDEA), passed in 1992, includes this wording with the only language change being from "handicapped children" to "individuals with disabilities."

Neither legislators nor parents have forgotten the purpose of an individualized education program and the right to a free appropriate public education. However, some special educators, either seduced by the siren of inclusion or influenced by Madeline Will's requirement of failure in the mainstream ("Davila to head," 1990), have forgotten the purpose of a placement decision for a student with disabilities.

Among the advocates of reducing the role of special education and the service delivery system, in addition to the Stainbacks (1992), are Gartner and Lipsky (1987); and Reynolds, Wang, and Walberg (1987). Our discussion here, however, centers on the importance of preserving the least restrictive environment (LRE) so the purpose of P.L. 94-142 and IDEA can be fully realized. The least restrictive environment is still an instructional climate designed to provide free appropriate public education, and to teach the skills needed to facilitate participation in society by individuals as adults. Some educators believe the use of the consultative model with inclusion will produce that instructional climate. However, Gredler (1990), who discussed a large-scale implementation of the consultative model, found such is not the case. We agree with Gredler. States investing heavily in such models to implement total inclusion should take note of these results so that history does not repeat itself.

HISTORICAL DEVELOPMENT OF LRE

Intent of the Education for All Handicapped Children Act

Prior to the enactment of the Education for All Handicapped Children Act, the right of a student with a disability to be included in the educational process had been tested in the courts. The judicial tests highlighted the "functional exclusion" of millions of children from educational benefits. Four million children with disabilities in this country had been provided an inadequate experience in general education and one million had been provided no education (Turnbull, 1990). The hearings preceding passage of the Education for All Handicapped Children Act focused on the failure of public education to provide opportunities for appropriate education for students with disabilities equal to the opportunities available for

children without disabilities. The legislators had a clear picture of the civil rights issues involved, establishing in those hearings that education which avoided the provision of appropriate services failed to meet the requirements or the spirit of earlier legislation. During the proceedings which culminated in the law's passage, discussions returned repeatedly to violations of the Fifth and Fourteenth Amendment freedoms of individuals with disabilities.

Wording of the Education for All Handicapped Children Act

The framers of P.L. 94-142 carefully included two provisions supporting their intent to provide for the protection of the civil rights of individuals with disabilities. The first provision (see Federal Regulations, Sections 300.550–300.556), least restrictive environment, referred to instruction which provided a reasonable expectation of benefit from instruction and which was based on the student's individual needs. The individual states were required to establish procedures assuring that removal from general education

> occurs only **when** the nature or severity of the handicap is such that education in regular classes with the use of supplementary aids and services cannot be achieved satisfactorily. (P.L. 94-142, Section 1412 (5b), p. 169) [emphasis added]

Use of the word *when* in the law clearly demonstrates, for us, that Congress recognized that there would be children whose disabilities would preclude a general education placement.

Abe Abeson (1977), one of the principal authors of P.L. 94-142, specifically addressed this issue. He called determination of the educational placement, in which the appropriate program for each child can be provided, a key element.

> Thus, some handicapped children will, in order to receive an appropriate education, need a program in a special class setting. Others will need a combination of a part time special class/regular class pro-

gram. And still others will require other settings. (Abeson, 1977, p. 39)

That intent is further underscored by the continuum of alternative placements which provides the means by which the goal of LRE is reached (*Code of Federal Regulations,* 1989, p. 54). The goal of LRE should be the degree to which "clients reach specific goals rather than how well they embody a particular approach" (Epstein, 1982, p. 155). This thesis has driven the Swedish approach to educating children with disabilities. Normalization, the Swedish term for educating children with disabilities in a manner as much as possible like that of other children, is the ultimate goal of the LRE. The term *normalization* is frequently misused in this country to describe inclusion. Unlike inclusion, normalization aims at the mastery of basic adaptive behaviors which will permit the individual to "be considered a fully functioning member of society" (Epstein, 1982, p. 155), whatever those adaptive behavior needs may be. Thus, normalization, focusing on the end and not on the means, is a better reflection of LRE than of inclusion. That difference demands clarification of the term *inclusion.*

Discussions in the professional literature (Reynolds, Wang, & Walberg, 1987) have focused on the setting of the general classroom in a placement known as mainstreaming or inclusion. Bender (1986) says some professionals have worked from the assumption that mainstreaming and inclusion were "legally mandated" (p. 475). In such discussions *mainstreaming* and *inclusion* are used as though they were synonymous with least restrictive environment. They are not synonymous now, nor have they ever been. Nowhere in the law, nor in the discussions culminating in its passage, were the terms *mainstreaming* or *inclusion* ever used. The term *mainstreaming* originated during the application of LRE regulations when administrative decisions were made to place students with mild disabilities in the general education classroom as the most feasible learning environment.

The second provision included protection of the civil rights of students with disabilities through requirements that each child be provided a free appropriate public education (FAPE). Except for a few authors (Turnbull, 1990), the interactive requirement of free appropriate public education has been largely overlooked in discussions of the LRE as the latter has been falsely equated with inclusion. But P.L. 94-142 expressly defined the meaning of free appropriate public education.

> The term "free appropriate public education" means special education and related services which (a) have been provided at public expense, under public supervision and direction, and without charge, (b) meet the standards of the State educational agency, (c) include an appropriate preschool, elementary, or secondary school education in the State involved, and (d) are **provided in conformity with the individualized education program** required under section 1414(a)(5) of this title. [emphasis added]

The astute reader will note that the special education and related services are to conform, not to boundaries of setting, but rather to the boundaries of the individualized education program developed specifically to meet each learner's needs, Abeson's (1977) "key element" (p. 39). Grouping learners with similar individual needs in the same setting is an administrative decision made to maximize the use of available resources, not an instructional decision made to meet the specific child's needs.

In sum, the concept of least restrictive environment is inextricably bound up in the concept of free appropriate public education. Turnbull (1990) calls LRE "a method for assuring an appropriate education" (p. 153) and notes that implementation of LRE entails "an obligation of educational benefit" (Turnbull & Turnbull, 1990). Earlier, in 1979, Turnbull warned that one of the risks to be faced in judicial and administrative interpretations would be the loss of the concept of enhancement in determining least restrictive environment.

> What is enhancing is sometimes necessarily more restrictive [in geographical proximity to nondisabled children] than "normal" (e.g., a classroom for seriously emotionally disturbed children or severely

retarded children may be highly "restrictive" and separated from "regular" programs but also highly enhancing of their abilities to learn). (p. 44)

Least restrictive should refer not to location but, instead, to appropriateness or enhancement of the instruction offered if the full meaning of the law is to be understood. As Turnbull (1990) points out, "The right to placement in an integrated or regular educational environment is not an absolute right but is secondary to the primary purpose of education in the public schools—namely, an appropriate education" (p. 147). Stewart (1990) also objected to the emphasis on LRE when it was a secondary provision of the main intent of the law. The same objection is reflected by Osborne and DeMattia (1994).

REGULATIONS DESIGNED TO PROMOTE LRE

The federal agency charged with the responsibility of overseeing the implementation of P.L. 94-142 (Office of Special Education and Rehabilitation

Services) developed specific regulations, including those to promote LRE, as published in the *Code of Federal Regulations* (1984). The sections relevant to our discussion here, and their provisions, are shown in Table 4.1.

In each of the five sections (Sections 300.550 through 300.555), the common focus is on the individual child's needs and potential to benefit from special education and related services. The general classroom has been the preferred option, but these regulations explicitly recognized the probability of and the need for other placements as well. Judicial decisions, both pre- and post- P.L. 94-142, have demonstrated strong adherence to both the letter and the spirit of the legislation and the regulations developed to implement the concept of least restrictive environment.

JUDICIAL COMMITMENT TO LRE

Two major issues are reflected in the judicial commitment to the LRE provision of P.L. 94-142. The first is the protection of the right to a free

TABLE 4.1 Federal Regulations Sections 300.550–300.555 and the Provisions of Each Applicable to P.L. 94-142 and its Renewal (IDEA)

SECTION	REGULATION
General (300.550)	1. Provide education with nondisabled peers "to maximum extent appropriate" 2. Remove only when use of "supplementary aids and services" fails to compensate in regular classroom
Continuum of alternative placements (300.551)	Mandated seven alternative placements to be available to choose from 1. Annual review 2. Direct link to child's IEP 3. As near child's home as possible
Nonacademic settings (300.553)	Student availability to counseling, transportation, sports, physical education, and extracurricular activities as alternative to academic mainstreaming
Children in public or private institutions (300.554)	Where institutionalization due to nonacademic factors, access to regular public school setting still applies
Technical assistance and training activities (300.555)	Training for all who might be involved in implementing P.L. 94-142

appropriate public education (FAPE). Central to the protection of FAPE is the protection of the civil rights of the parent and child alike under constitutional requirements of due process and equal protection under the law. The second issue is the provision of instructional placement in the least restrictive environment. LRE is the outcome of the preservation of due process and equal protection rights. Ironically, proponents of wholesale inclusion who have called least restrictive environment a civil rights issue have missed the crux of the matter.

Protecting the Right to FAPE

Instrumental to the protection of FAPE in the courts has been the preservation of due process and equal protection rights. These two issues provided the foundation for the hearings preceding passage of P.L. 94-142 and are at the base of FAPE in the federal law. The judicial decisions listed at the end of this chapter (Legal Bibliography) each reflect the ongoing support of the preservation of FAPE through protection of due process and equal opportunity rights.

In the *Daniel R. R.* case (1989), FAPE was called the "cornerstone of the EHA [Education of All Handicapped Children Act]" (p. 1043). The guardian of that cornerstone has been the protection of the constitutional right to due process.

Due Process. More than sixty cases involving due process violations as primary complaints are synopsized in *Handicapped Students and Special Education* (1989). Additional cases have been added since that date demonstrating that due process continues to be an important issue in the determination of appropriate placement.

Thus the due process right is a kindred provision to equal protection under the law, and both are linked to the appropriateness of the education. Many of the judicial decisions are the result of noncompliance with the due process and equal protection requirements of P.L. 94-142.

Equal Protection. The New York Association for Retarded Citizens decision (*Jessup v. Family Court of New York,* 1975) set the standard for applying the equal protection principle to educational placements. It directly linked Fourteenth Amendment rights to the concept of appropriateness of education. The plaintiffs had asserted that

> they have not been provided with a free public education **suited to their needs and capabilities,** although their need for such an education is no different from that of other children who are given such an education. This disparate treatment ... denies them the equal protection of the law guaranteed by the Fourteenth Amendment. (p. 762) [emphasis added]

From these two constitutional rights, due process and equal protection of the law, emerged the concept of free appropriate public education as provided for in P.L. 94-142. Thus the application of procedural requirements of the law, equally administered to all students, results in the provision of instruction in the least restrictive environment.

Culmination of the Least Restrictive Environment

As both Turnbull (1990), and Osborne and DeMattia (1994) note, determination of least restrictive environment hinges primarily on appropriateness of the instruction—not on proximity—that can be offered in that setting. Each court decision has shown a preference for proximity to peers without disabilities, but the decisive factor has been the provision of instruction which has a reasonable expectation to benefit the learner. To provide the reasonable expectation of benefit, instruction must be tailored to the learner's needs. A Georgia report (Georgia Department of Education, 1990) has shown that setting-driven decisions have resulted in the use of local public schools over residential facilities to the detriment of learners. Less proximity, therefore, can actually result in greater expectation of benefit. As Turnbull and Turnbull (1990) believe, "There is a paradox (less restriction in settings often results in more restriction in programs because the setting lacks sufficient programming) that can be overcome if children are placed into segregated settings" (p. 27). Even Davila, the head of the Office of Special Education and Rehabilitation, has been quoted as saying, "For some children, special schools will provide placement in the least restrictive environment" ("Davila," 1990). This was recently restated by Secretary Richard Riley (1994). Although the preference in legislation, regulation, and litigation is clearly in favor of placement with or near children without disabilities, that placement can be, and has been, overturned.

Overturning the expectancy for a general education placement is dependent on preserving due process and equal protection of the law. As we have pointed out in previous sections and in prior writings, appropriateness of the educational setting relies on an individualized education program (IEP). That program can be implemented in any of seven settings prescribed by law as the continuum of services. To limit the continuum is to violate both the spirit and the letter of the law (as in *Daniel R. R., 1989*) and providing the opportunity to socialize is no excuse for restricting the available services. Availability of services or cost of services is accepted only if the continuum is preserved (see *Roncker v. Walters,* 1983; *Statum v. Birmingham,* 1993).

Maintaining the continuum of services does not require giving up the benefits of inclusion or the benefits of appropriate education. A careful reading of the Regulations (Section 300.553) and an examination of the parent accommodation reached following *Daniel R. R.* offer a way to have our cake and eat it too (Martin, 1990).

Daniel was a child with Down syndrome whose parents requested a 100 percent inclusion placement at the local school. A temporary enrollment in a general education setting resulted in Daniel's requiring the majority of the general education teacher's time. The parents were offered a part-time inclusive placement rather than total enrollment in the general education class. They rejected that placement. They then sued and lost their suit for full-time inclusion because of the negative effect that placement had on the other students' opportunity to learn.

Daniel R. R. was later given "mingling" opportunities with his peers without disabilities in unstructured, nonacademic settings such as the playground before school, art, and music. Admittedly, these opportunities will likely result in only parallel play types of activities such as are common in children like Daniel who function at preschool levels. The ability of students like Daniel for generalization is known to be very low without specific, intensive interventions. Some researchers (Haring & Liberty, 1990) say that only about 20 percent generalization can be expected without systematic implementation in a special education setting. However, for children with disabilities whose "severity and nature" (P.L. 94-142) may preclude inclusive educational placements, "mingling" might provide programmatic ways to interact with peers without disabilities. No one's rights under law to an appropriate education in the least restrictive environment will be endangered and the intent of P.L. 94-142/IDEA may actually be enhanced.

RELEVANT STUDIES AND FUTURE PROJECTIONS

The tide of professional debate appeared to turn in 1990 more toward the intent of Congress. *Daniel R. R. v. El Paso* (1990) clearly made this point. The court rejected a cookie-cutter approach, carefully reviewing the intent of Congress, federal rules and regulations, and previous cases. In reviewing the facts before making a decision, the *Daniel* court demonstrated the need for individualizing placement decisions. In their deliberations, they specifically showcased the *Rowley* (1982) decision in arriving at the *Daniel R. R.* decision. The *Rowley* decision supported the expectation of academic benefit.

The decision in the *Daniel R. R.* case is so carefully drawn that it may well be considered a landmark case. In the process of the examination, the court reviewed the case of *Roncker v. Walters* (1983), in which another Down syndrome child sought enrollment in general education. In *Roncker,* much of the discussion dealt with whether an appropriate education could be provided in the general education class, with an aide and specialized instructors bringing education and therapy to the child. In *Daniel R. R.,* that argument was rejected and, in fact, the justices believed some harm would accrue to Daniel in academic courses.

Another development involves a new advocacy by some groups to maintain the continuum of services for individuals with sensory impairments. Stewart (1990) discusses being educated in the elementary grades in what is now referred to as an inclusive environment, and later receiving an education in a residential school for hearing-impaired students. His experience in the residential school was the highlight of his educational career. This same advocacy showed less opposition to residential placements in a study conducted in Georgia by a team of six outside national consultants (Georgia Department of Education, 1990). The study found that the three state schools for sensory-impaired children were greatly underused, and that this underuse had resulted from local school systems' refusal to write IEPs for the state schools except as a last resort.

The report indicates a strong need for the state Department of Education to reeducate administrators concerning the federal requirements for least restrictive environment. This panel recognized that students should not be denied services they need simply so they can go to school close to home or with hearing or sighted peers. The study quotes a report by Sy DuBow in 1989, legal director of Gallaudet University Center for Law and the Deaf, as saying the preference for placing children with disabilities with students without disabilities has always been secondary to the "paramount goal of the Act," the provision of an appropriate education that meets the needs of each child with disabilities. Werner Rogers, state school superintendent of Georgia has said that one reason for the continued focus on location of instruction is that "it is easier to determine whether a child has been mainstreamed than whether the educational program provided is appropriate" (W. Rogers, personal communication, June 12, 1990).

Recent Developments

A recent *Special Education Report* ("Courts perched," 1994) summarizes cases and conclusions drawn, and Osborne and DiMattia (1994) have also described the state of the art in litigation on LRE. Osborne and DiMattia believe that school districts have not included students with disabilities to the fullest extent possible and that the courts are becoming impatient with the perceived delay. Based on some of the higher profile cases so often quoted by some advocates, we realize this may be true. Those cases usually involve young students with severe disabilities, but are beginning increasingly to involve high school students. The common element is that students with more and more severe disabilities are being placed in general education settings. Some of these have disabilities that are even more severe than those of children that Abeson (1977) said would rarely be placed in general education. He even called it alarmist to suggest such placements. Ironically, students with milder disabilities sometimes have less access to general education settings.

In *Greer v. Rome City School* (1990), a nine-year-old student with Down Syndrome was retained in a general education first grade. Now, four years later, she receives about half her instruction in special education. In *Greer v. Rome,* the *Daniel R. R.* case was used as the primary precedent but the judge ruled for an inclusive setting which was an interesting juxtaposition to the *Daniel R. R.* ruling.

In a Birmingham case (*Statum v. Birmingham City Schools*) a mother sought to have her daughter (with severe retardation) maintained full time in a general education setting. This expectation flew in the face of the fact that the child was grossly out of place academically, not toilet trained, and severely language impaired. Interestingly enough, a Nebraska court (*French v. Omaha Public Schools,* 1991) found a similar level of language impairments to those of Anna Statum to be sufficient cause to question the efficacy of a mainstream placement. A Pennsylvania district court also chose to refuse a general education setting because of the social isolation of oral communication deficits (*Johnson v. Lancaster-Lebanon,* 1991).

Anna Statum remains in general education with what we believe is little hope of success or the likelihood that she will receive an appropriate, much less enhanced, education. As Lynch and Beau (1990) have indicated in their study of IEPs of children in general education settings, the deficits are largely academic and behavioral. Further, they stated, "Students with mild handicaps are receiving a remedial general education curriculum as demonstrated on IEPs and observations" (p. 54). In spite of court decisions, this is what we expect to see happen in Anna Statum's program in the future. We do not anticipate much functional emphasis.

Another recent case, *Oberti v. Board of Education of Clemonton School District* (1992) also mirrored the courts' recent decisions. These favor an affirmative obligation for students with disabilities to be placed in general education settings. The actions of the school systems heavily influenced the considerations in arriving at the *Oberti* decision. Systems which provide insufficient evidence that the first placement consideration was other than the general education classroom with supplementary aids and services usually find themselves losing.

The *Oberti* decision was followed by the *Holland* case which is the latest decision and one which was won on appeal and may well go to the Supreme Court (*Board of Education, Sacramento City District v. Holland,* 1992). The court relied heavily on the *Greer* and *Daniel R. R.* decisions. The court supported the placement in inclusive settings in general education classrooms "if students can receive a satisfactory education there even if it is not the best academic setting for the students" (Osborne & DiMattia, 1994, p. 11). The Ninth Circuit Court of Appeals upheld the deci-

sion indicating that four factors should be considered in LRE decisions: (1) the educational benefit a student will derive from placement in a general education environment, (2) the nonacademic benefits of placement in a general education setting, (3) the effect the student will have on other students in the class, and (4) the cost of supplementary aids and services. See Table 4.2.

Notice how few of these factors really address appropriate education or whether the instruction will prepare the student for adult life. In our estimation, the courts have laid out guidelines on LRE and then violated their own rules. Certainly, in *Greer, Statum, Oberti,* and *Holland,* academic benefits will be extremely limited and social benefits will be questionable.

While we note the high visibility of the above cases, we do not believe anything has really changed. Certainly P.L. 94-142 and IDEA haven't changed. Also, as Perry Zirkel, a law professor at Lehigh University, has noted, there have been two dozen decisions in the past three years (mostly in federal courts) supporting school decisions to place students in special education as often as they have in inclusive settings ("Courts perched," 1994). Without great elaboration, we note just a few decisions.

A hearing officer ruled that a special day class was appropriate placement for a student with specific learning disabilities (Sequoia Union HS District, (1994). In *Carter v. Florence Co. School District* (1991), the court accepted placement in a private school in lieu of public school placement. In *Briggs v. Board of Education of Connecticut* (1989), the Second Circuit Court of Appeals ruled that mainstreaming was not appropriate when the nature or severity of the student's disabilities was such that education in a typical classroom could not be achieved satisfactorily. There are still other examples.

The best decisions, however, are still based on an individual determination of where the students have the strongest hope for developing the skills needed to maximize their individual capability for independent adulthood. We expect a backlash as

TABLE 4.2   Four Factors in LRE Decisions

1. Education benefit available in general education setting	
a. Preparation for mainstream adult life	*Oberti*, 1992
b. Degree of education benefit (reasonable expectation)	*Holland v. Board*, 1992; *Greer*, 1991; *Rowley*, 1982
c. Balance between social and educational benefit	*Oberti*, 1992; *Holland*, 1994
2. Nonacademic benefits from general education	
a. Sufficient socialization	*French*, 1991; *Johnson*, 1991
b. Preparation for adult socialization	*Greer*, 1991
c. Judging nonacademic benefits	*Greer*, 1991; *Statum*, 1993
d. Impact of severity on choice between nonacademic and academic	*Johnson*, 1991
3. Effect on nondisabled peers	
a. Teacher time	*Daniel R. R.*, 1989; *Gillette*, 1991
b. Disruption	*Liscio*, 1989
c. Curricular modifications	*Oberti*, 1992
d. Nature and severity of disability	*French*, 1991
4. Cost	
a. Centralization to provide language	*Barnett*, 1991
b. Centralization to benefit all children	*Schuldt*, 1991

parents who sought and won inappropriate placements begin to recognize the limited value of their winnings.

SUMMARY

Judgment of free appropriate public education and least restrictive environment is dependent on a three-pronged test, as discussed in *Daniel R. R.* An important part of that test is to determine whether procedural requirements incorporated to protect individual rights are being followed. Waivers of regulations governing implementation of P.L. 94-142 and IDEA are not enough to legalize 100 percent inclusion as a programmatic policy for every child regardless of what the courts have said.

To legalize uniform placement by programmatic policy, such as is envisioned in wholesale inclusion placements of students with disabilities, would require that P.L. 94-142 (IDEA) be repealed, the court cases overturned, and the Fifth and Fourteenth Amendments revoked as they apply to education as a property right of children.

The law, judicial history, and constitutional rights all reject programmatic placement decisions. The presumption has been in favor of general education if the child can receive an appropriate education there. The first question for special educators should be, Can this student be best educated in an inclusive setting? The next consideration should be, What would it take for the general education setting to be responsive to the student's needs?

There are those who believe that 100 percent inclusion is a civil rights issue. Where tension has existed between the child's right to an appropriate education and the child's need for social interactions with peers, the courts have, in recent cases, been supportive of general education placements. The legislative and judicial histories of education for children with disabilities, except in a few cases, make incomprehensible the support of 100 percent inclusion as the least restrictive environment. But such a discussion belongs more appropriately in judicial circles. As educators, we need to continue our legal responsibilities under the law.

Even if legislative changes should occur legalizing the mandated inclusion of all children with disabilities (which is highly unlikely given current court decisions) such a change would hardly legitimize a return to the pre-P.L. 94-142 days. Specific exclusion from any level of a full continuum of services constitutes functional exclusion as much in the 1990s as it did in the 1950s and 1960s.

REFERENCES

Abeson, A. (June, 1977). The educational least restrictive alternative. *AMICUS,* 38–40.

Bender, W. N. (1986). Effective educational practices in the mainstream setting: Recommended model for evaluation of mainstream teacher classes. *Journal of Special Education, 20*(4), 475–587.

Code of Federal Regulations (1984). Washington, D C: U.S. Government Printing Office. Vol. 34.

Courts perched to speed schools' inclusion pace, researchers say. (1994, September 7) *Special Education Report, 20*(18), 1, 3.

Davila to head OSERS. (1990). *CAID-News 'N' Notes* p. 5.

Epstein, H. R. (1982). Means, ends, and the principle of normalization: A closer look. *Education and Training of the Mentally Retarded, 17*(2), 153–156.

Gartner, A., & Lipsky, D. K. (1987). Beyond special education: Toward a quality system for all students. *Harvard Educational Review, 57,* 367–395.

Georgia Department of Education (1990, May). *Partners in education: The role, scope, and function of state-operated schools in the education of Georgia's sensory impaired students.* Atlanta, GA.

Gredler, G. R. (1990, Fall). Brief highlights from the TSP meeting: School psychology: Status of the field 1990. *Trainers' Forum.* Stockton, CA, 2–4.

Handicapped Students and Special Education, (1989). Rosemount, MN: Data Research.

Haring, N. G., & Liberty, K. A. (1990). Matching strategies with performance in facilitating generalization. *Focus on Exceptional Children, 22*(8), 1–16.

Langone, J. (1990). *Teaching students with mild and moderate learning problems.* Boston: Allyn and Bacon.

Lynch, E. C., & Beau, P. C. (1990). The quality of IEP objectives and their relevance to instruction for students with mental retardation and behavior disorders. *Remedial and Special Education, 11,* 48–55.

Martin, R. (1990, April 2–3). *Review of recent court decisions.* Costa Mesa, CA: California Institute on Special Education Law and Practice.

Osborne, A. G., Jr., & DiMattia, P. (1994), The IDEA's least restrictive environment mandate: Legal implications. *Exceptional Children, 61*(1), 6–14.

Reynolds, M. C., Wang, M. C., & Walberg, H. C. (1987). The necessary restructuring for special and regular education. *Exceptional Children, 53*(5), 391-398.

Riley, R. (1994). Memorandum on maninstreaming. Washington, DC: U.S. Department of Education.

Stainback, S., & Stainback, W. (1992). Schools as inclusive communities. In W. Stainback & S. Stainback (Eds.), *Controversial Issues Confronting Special Education: Divergent Perspectives* (pp. 29–44). Boston: Allyn and Bacon.

Stewart, L. G. (1990, Fall). Deaf children and the regular education initiative: A view from within. *Illinois CEC Quarterly, 39*(3).

Teacher survey shows surge in special education new hires. (1990, September 12). *Education of the Handicapped,* Vol. 16, No. 19. Alexandria, VA: Capitol Pubications.

Turnbull, H. R., III. (1979). The past and future impact of court decisions on special education. *Educating Exceptional Children, 1979/80* (pp. 41–45). Guildford, CT: Dushkin Group.

Turnbull, H. R., III. (1990). *Free appropriate public education: The law and children with disabilities.* Denver: Love.

Turnbull, H. R., III, & Turnbull, A. P. (1990). The unfulfilled promise of integration: Does Part H ensure different rights than Part B of the Education of the Handicapped Act? *Topics in Early Childhood Special Education, 10*(2), 33–47.

Wagner, M. (1989). *The school programs and school performance of secondary school students classified as learning disabled: Findings from the National Longitudinal Transition Study of Special Education Students.* Menlo Park, CA: SRI.

LEGAL BIBLIOGRAPHY

Abella et al. v. Riverside, App. 135 Cal. Rptr. 177 (1976).

Barnett v. Fairfax County School Board, 927 F.2d 146, 66 Ed. Law Rep. 64 (4th Cir. 1991).

Armstrong v. Kline, 513 F. Supp. 425 (E. D. Pa. 1980).

Board of Education, Sacramento City Unified School District v. Rachel Holland (9th Cir. 1992).

Briggs v. Board of Education of Connecticut, 882 F.2d 688, 55 Ed.Law Rep. 423 (2d Cir. 1989).

Brown v. Board of Education, 347 U S. 483, 74 S. Ct. 686, 98 L. Ed. 873 (1954).

Carter v. Florence Co. School District, 950 F.2d 156, 71 Ed.Law Rep. 633 (4th Cir. 1991); affirmed on other grounds sub nom. Florence County School District v. Carter, 114 S. Ct. 361, 86 Ed.Law Rep. 41 (1993).

Crowder v. Riles, No. CA 00384 (Super. Ct. Los Angeles Co., filed December 20, 1976).

Cuyahoga Association for Retarded Children v. Essex, No. C-74–587 (N. D. Ohio, 1976).

Daniel R. R. v. El Paso, 874 F. 2d 1036 (5th Cir. 1989)

Diana v. State Board of Education, Dist Crt N. CA (1970).

Fialkowski v. Shapp, 405 F. Supp. 946 (E. D. Pa. 1977).

Frederick v. Thomas, 557 F. Supp. 2d 373 (3d. Cir. 1977).

French v. Omaha Public Schools, 766 F. Supp. 765, 68 Ed.Law Rep. 630 (D. Neb. 1991).

Gillette v. Wayne Local School District (SEA, OH) 16 EHLR 1031 (1991).

Greer v. Rome City School District 17 EHLR 881, 762 F. Supp. 936 (1991).

Irving v. Tatro, 82 L. Ed. 2d 664 (1984).

ISD 623 Roseville, MN v. Digre, 893 F 2d 987 (8 Cir. 1990)

Jessup v. Family Court of New York, 379 N. Y. S. 2d 626 (1975).

Johns, 21 *IDELR* 571 (OSERS 1994).

Johnson v. Lancaster-Lebanon Intermediate Unit 13, 757 F. Supp. 606, 66 Ed.Law Rep. 227 (E.D. Pa. 1991).

Kruse v. Campbell, 434 U. S. 808 (1977).

Lebanks v. Spears, 417 F. Supp. 169 (1976).

Liscio v. Woodland Hills, 862 W.D. PA., 20 IDELR 1324 843 F. Supp. 1236 (1989).

Mills v. D. C. Board of Education, 348 F. Supp. 866 (1972).

New York Association of Retarded Children v. Carey, 393 F. Supp. 715 (E. D. N. Y., 1975), 612 F. 2d 644 (2d Cir. 1979), EHLR 551:687 (2d Cir. 1980).

New York Association of Retarded Children v. Rockefeller, 357 F. Supp. 752 (1973).

Oberti v. Board of Education of Clementon School District, 19 IDELR 423 (original) and (appeal) 19 IDELR 903 (1993) (D.N.J. 1992).

Pennsylvania Association for Retarded Children (PARC), Nancy Beth Bowman et al. v. Commonwealth of Pennsylvania, David H. Kurtzman, et al., E. D. Pa., 334 F. Supp. 1253 (1971).

Rhode Island Society for Autistic Children v. Board of Regents, Civ. Act. No. 5081 (DRI Sept 15, 1975).

Rodriquez v. San Antonio, 337 F. Supp. 280 (W. D. Texas 1971).

Roncker v. Walters, 464 U. S. 864, 104 S. Ct. 196, 78. L. Ed. 2d 171 (1983).

Rowley v. Board of Education, 483 F. Supp. (1982).

Schuldt v. Mankato Indep. School, 18 IDELR 16, 937 F. 2d 1357 (1991).

Sequoia Union HS Dist., 21 IDELR 495 (SEA CA 1994).

Springdale v. Grace, 693 F. 2d 4 (8th Cir. 1982).

Statum v. Birmingham City Schools, CV-92-P2054-F (N. U. S. Dist. AL 1993).

Wyatt v. Stickney, 344 F. Supp. 373, 387, 396 (M. D. Ala. 1972).

SECTION THREE

MAXIMIZING THE TALENTS AND GIFTS OF STUDENTS

Should selected students be classified as gifted and talented and given special programs that meet their unique needs? Clark provides a rationale in Chapter 5 for the identification of selected students as gifted and talented and the provision of special classes and programs for them. She states that there is a need for a range of program options for these students, including special classes for highly gifted students, if we are to provide them with opportunities to maximize their potential.

In Chapter 6, Sapon-Shevin points out that all children need to be recognized as having gifts and talents and challenged to be the best they can be, and that until this happens, charges of elitism will be leveled at those who defend special programs only for selected students. She stresses that to achieve true equality in our schools, all children, not just a few selected students, need an education that meets their unique needs and capitalizes on their gifts. Finally, Sapon-Shevin provides a rationale for meeting the needs of all students within "regular" education classrooms, including those identified as gifted and talented.

CHAPTER 5

The Need for a Range of Program Options for Gifted and Talented Students

BARBARA CLARK

INTRODUCTION

If you have in your classroom several children who have already mastered a part or even most of the content of the subjects you will be teaching during the year, learn very rapidly and remember ideas very well, tend to monopolize the discussions and often diverge into related but more complex ideas that the other students do not understand, and produce work quickly and at a level that causes other children to feel that their work is inferior, what would you do? Some of these same students soon begin to lack motivation when they see the type of work other students are doing, and begin to produce similar work. They move easily at a level of the top group of the grade and do not learn good study skills, complain that they always have to do the work for their group, find no challenges, and generally seem uninterested in ever "doing their best." This is often the experience of gifted students in the regular classroom that is typical in the United States today, a classroom that uses traditional approaches and organization (Goodlad, 1984). When we add to this group of gifted students an increasing diversity of students of varying languages, abilities, disabilities, beliefs, backgrounds, and experiences we can see the need for a wide range of materials, strategies, structures, programs, and opportunities so that all children can have their needs met and learn at their highest level of potential. In this chapter we will discuss the group first mentioned, gifted children, and how a wider range of programming can best meet their needs. Happily, such provisions will better meet the needs of all students, and most happily, of the teachers as well.

In any discussion of appropriate programming for gifted and talented students there must be an understanding of several issues: who the students are to whom this label is generally assigned, how giftedness is developed and nurtured, what unique educational needs are commonly found in this population, and in what organizational configurations provision for these unique needs can best be made. It is the purpose of this chapter to provide background information that will allow for an understanding of these issues and to establish a rationale for the necessity of providing a range of program options as the most appropriate means of optimizing the learning of gifted and talented students.

BACKGROUND INFORMATION

Who Are the Gifted and Talented Students?

The federal definition is that gifted and talented students are those "who give evidence of high performance capability in areas such as intellectual, creative, artistic, leadership capacity, or specific academic fields, and who require services or activities not ordinarily provided by the school in order to fully develop such capabilities" (P.L. 97–35, Section 582, 1981). This definition allows identification by observation and other evaluative means and refers to a variety of ways in which to express intellectual ability.

In recent years an understanding of intelligence has become available from research in the neurosciences. This research must be considered as we seek to define high levels of intelligence and identify those who perform at such levels. While much has been made of the possibility that the construct of intelligence is separable into specific types of intelligences according to the characteristics of brain function (Gardner, 1983), intelligence would be more appropriately seen as a unified process that can be expressed in a variety of ways depending on the genetic structure and the environmental opportunities of the individual.

An acceptance of the variety of possible expressions of intelligence (Clark, 1979, 1988, 1992; Gardner, 1983) is important for appropriate identification of gifted and talented individuals. The universe of intelligence must include at least four functional areas as seen in the organization of brain function: cognitive abilities, both rational linear and spatial gestalt; affective abilities, both emotional and social; physical abilities, those involved in sensing and those involved in movement; and intuitive abilities, including those involved in prediction, futurism, creativity, and altruistic and global concerns.

It is obvious from just this brief description of the many facets of intelligence that identification of high levels or giftedness cannot simply be made based on samples of school-related tasks or rational, linear ability such as is measured in an intelligence test. If the highly intelligent individual is to be identified, all of the areas of possible expression must be honored as examples of intellectual achievement. Many school programs still use only achievement on school-related tasks or some form of testing that measures only rational, linear ability as measures of intelligence. Most of the programs provided for gifted individuals are also focused on these abilities. However, much work has been done in the past few years, with the support of grants made possible by the Javits Act Program as administered by the Office of Educational Research and Improvement, of the U.S. Department of Education, to enlarge the scope of identification of gifted individuals by including more types of abilities from a wider range of cultures beginning at younger ages. In most states, any public money for identifying and serving gifted learners is given according to the federal definition and depends on several methods of identification of talents and abilities that may include: academic records and tests; portfolio material of the student's work; information from teachers, parents, and peers; intelligence tests; creativity tests; and any other appropriate information.

Two features of brain function that are particularly important to any discussion of the origin and nurture of giftedness are the mutable nature of the brain, resulting in a concept of intelligence that must be seen as dynamic rather than static, and the interactive nature of the development of the brain, in which both genetic and environmental factors must be considered interdependent. Those in the past who considered the development of intelligence static often claimed that a child is born gifted. This has resulted in misunderstandings about the importance of challenging an individual at his or her level of performance.

From the early work of brain researchers such as Rosenzweig (1966) and Krech (1969, 1970) in the 1960s and early 1970s it became apparent that the nature of intelligence is dynamic. This leaves no doubt that if appropriate challenges are not included in education planning for students, they will not progress; rather they will regress. These features resulted in a new view of the learning environment and the opportunities it provides as critical to the development of high levels of intelligence and to the development and maintenance of giftedness. From this view, not only must the environment provide experiences that challenge and stimulate the level of development of each learner, but it must do this on a consistent and continuing basis (Conlan, 1993; Diamond, 1988; Kandel & Schwartz, 1991; Krech, 1969, 1970).

A most commonly held premise from neuroscience research related to talent and ability can be summed up in the phrase "use it or lose it." Education can no longer be comfortable with environments or policies that treat all learners as age normed, nor can schools offer heterogeneously grouped classes the same experiences presented from the same materials and expect that appropriate learning is being provided.

Giftedness is now understood to be a biologically rooted phenomenon wherein genetic patterns and environmental opportunities interact to produce a variety of physical results. These include: areas of advanced or increased brain growth (such as an increase in neuroglial cell production) allowing for more support for the neurons and a more effective and efficient neural system (Diamond, 1993; Rosenzweig, 1984; Thompson, Berger, & Berry, 1980); growth of dendrites and biochemical changes within the neural cell allowing for more advanced and complex patterns of thought and an increase in the potential for interconnections between neurons (Hutchinson, 1986; Kandel & Schwartz, 1991); and an increase in the number of synapses and in the size of the synaptic contact, allowing more accelerated and complex thought processes within the system (Hutchinson, 1986; Thompson, Berger, & Berry, 1980).

Regardless of how this power, acceleration, complexity, and effectiveness of intellectual function are expressed, whether creatively, artistically, or through academics or leadership ability, the need for appropriate stimulation for students with these abilities is critical if growth is to continue. Students who have developed their abilities to the extent that we call them gifted and talented cannot maintain their abilities if their education experiences are not challenging and appropriately paced: If they cannot progress, they will unfortunately regress.

How Is Giftedness Developed and Nurtured?

Children are not born gifted; they are only born with the potential for giftedness. The amount of potential for intellectual development within the brain and each genetic program is awesome; however, only those children who are fortunate enough to have opportunities to develop their uniqueness in an environment that responds to their own patterns and needs will be able to de-

velop to a level of intelligence at which they will be identified as gifted individuals. Restriction of either nature or nurture inhibits high levels of intellectual development (Berg & Singer, 1992; Bouchard & McGue, 1990; Grunwald, 1993; Lewontin, 1982).

From conception throughout the fetal period, the environment interacting with the genetic structure of the individual enhances or inhibits the development of intelligence (Restak, 1986; Verny, 1981). Nutrition and learning opportunities during infancy and early childhood will continue to enhance or inhibit this development until observable differences in performance begin to appear as high levels (giftedness) or lesser levels of ability (Kagan, 1971; Slavkin, 1987; White, 1975). It is unfortunately all too often that a child born with potential that might have been virtually unlimited is so inhibited by the opportunities of the environment that the result is far lower ability than could have been actualized. At present the ability of education to reverse this loss of potential is not commendable. Although some economically disadvantaged children have profited from early intervention, through programs such as Head Start, most parents are as yet unaware of the strategies and experiences they could provide to enhance the intelligence of their children. Unreasonably large numbers of children perform at average levels or below, and society accepts this as a proper and expected condition. Little is yet done to change this deplorable waste of talent and ability. If anything, our society tends to prefer the average and is uncomfortable and suspicious of the advanced or highly intelligent among us. To keep from having to face the lack of opportunities for a large part of our population, it has become popular to suggest that all children are gifted and ignore the need for and results of appropriate challenge and stimulation during the early years.

The environment that is responsive to each individual child, providing rich and varied experiences with the child's pace and interests in focus seems to be the best for optimal development. The responsive learning environment is the single most important component in the development of potential resulting in giftedness, at home and at school. As early as 1969, Dubos suggested that human potential has a better chance of developing when the social environment is sufficiently diversified to provide a variety of stimulating experiences.

> The total environment affects individuality through the influences it exerts on the organism during the crucial phases of development, including the intra-uterine phase. These early influences affect lastingly and often irreversibly practically all anatomical, physiological, and behavioral characteristics throughout the whole life span. (p. 6)

Bloom (1964) provides additional validation that gifts and talents are created. He interviewed individuals who had attained "world class" status in a variety of fields, inquiring about their parents, their teachers, and the conditions and determinants of their success. These gifts and talents could not have been actualized without the encouragement, support, and environmental opportunities provided by the parents and teachers. Genius indeed cannot "win out" in spite of circumstance, but must be developed, perhaps even created. Whatever the original "gifts," without extremely favorable supporting and teaching circumstances over more than a decade, these individuals would not have been likely to reach the levels of attainment for which they became known. Bloom found evidence that learning rates can be altered by appropriate educational and environmental conditions, which suggests that very favorable learning conditions provided in the early years can markedly influence learning rates. As the rate of learning is an expression of advanced and accelerated brain development, this evidence relates to the discussion of developing intelligence.

Unique Educational Needs of Gifted and Talented Learners

The literature on gifted education lists many characteristics commonly observed among gifted learners. These characteristics are important to the educator because they provide the basis for adapt-ing the curriculum and learning experiences to meet the individual needs of gifted and talented students. For example, knowing that most gifted students show a pattern of fast-paced learning, educators can modify a curriculum to allow for that characteristic. Also, knowing that gifted students often can be two to eight years ahead of the curriculum content provided to their age-grouped classmates, educators can provide more advanced content to an individual student when needed. Students of gifted education study these lists of characteristics for the purpose of providing the variety and complexity of materials and strategies that will be needed by the gifted learners they serve. Individualizing the delivery of the curriculum to meet the needs of gifted students is made far easier when the curriculum materials have been extended and supplemented with accelerated, complex, advanced, and in-depth content.

Gifted and talented students have more complex needs than average and below-average learners. A need for variety in pacing, content, and complexity are but a few. If these needs are not met we now know that ability cannot be maintained; indeed, brain researchers tell us that ability will be lost. To compound this issue, the higher the level of intelligence that students have attained, the more unique are their needs and the greater is the risk of loss. Highly gifted students, those whose pace of learning, energy, vocabulary, concept development, and complexity of thought are significantly beyond advanced students, gain little from the content and learning experiences found in the regular classroom. Often they become either isolates or underachievers when no appropriate programs are provided. When no programs are available to this group of learners a disservice is done not only to these students but to all of society, as our finest minds not only lack nurture, they are wasted.

PROGRAM OPTIONS

One could argue that it is not where students are educated that matters, but rather how they are educated. In a perfect world such a statement might have merit; however, in the schooling structure of today, even with the most enlightened restructuring, the two concerns must go together. The organization of schools has basic flaws that provide barriers to any attempt to meet the needs of atypical learners. One could even suggest that these organizational problems prevent any student from reaching optimum levels of education. But for the atypical, the problem is awesome.

Of major concern is the fact that classes are organized by age grouping. Long ago it was found that age has nothing to do with learning; experience does, but not age. Most recently we have seen this information validated by neuroscience; however, the grouping by age continues with all curriculum decisions based on this irrelevant attribute. For students whose experiences have allowed them to develop advanced and acceleration information and processing skills, this type of grouping has been a nearly insurmountable barrier. Attempts to overcome this problem such as acceleration (in any form), compacting the curriculum, cross-grade grouping, and grouping by ability or need have all been discouraged by administrative decision makers, although the literature consistently shows very positive results both educationally and emotionally from any of these approaches (Kulik, 1992; Reis et al., 1993; Rogers, 1991).

There are other barriers such as inadequate time allowed for learning, especially evident in the forty-five-minute blocks provided by secondary schools. While short-term memory can take place in seconds, time for analysis, organization, synthesis, and practical application of the new information is needed for long-term memory to take place. Most students need far more time to accomplish these tasks and assure retention of new concepts; however, gifted students often pursue ideas in depth and to a level of complexity that makes time flexibility even more of a necessity.

The use of vocabulary in the average classroom is inappropriate for advanced learners. A common characteristic of such learners is early and fluent use of complex language and concepts. Much of the business of schooling is carried on by the language of the classroom. Most classrooms use language and concepts leveled just below the average. By consistently having to oversimplify ideas and use language below their rate of development, the advanced students are not challenged to grow and, worse, lose the ability to think at higher levels.

Within the past few years attempts have been made to move the practices of critical thinking into the regular classroom. While this is long overdue and of great benefit to all students, such practices are usually carried out at an introductory level and do not incorporate the advanced concept development needed by gifted learners. If we learn nothing else from the brain research, we must note the reference often made to the dynamic nature of the brain. Unless we challenge the students at the level at which they are functioning they will *lose function*. Some gifted students continue to use advanced vocabulary in the average classroom with the result that their classmates register disapproval by isolating the children or making fun of their thoughts and expression of ideas.

Texts and materials in regular classrooms are too often limited in range and complexity. Again the challenge needed by the advanced student is missing; conformity is expected. Students who are two to eight grade levels beyond the age-leveled curriculum are expected to use the same material as those working closer to the norm with the rationale that if they move beyond this artificial range they will have nothing to do the following year and will be bored, making it difficult for the next year's teacher. The solutions offered range from tutoring other students who are not as advanced, as in cooperative learning groups or age-peer tutoring, or to pursue a concept "in depth" whether or not the student is interested in the topic or area of study. Such "in-depth study" can be especially difficult to plan in skill areas and often means that the student will be assigned twice as much work *at the same level* as the average learner. Another way this excess time is used is to allow the advanced student to do "independent study." While well-planned independent study programs should always be one of the options in the range of programs provided to advanced learners, the type of independent study assigned to fill the student's time seldom follows the guidelines needed to assure a quality experience with this provision (see Independent Study Programs discussed later in this chapter).

Another barrier to growth found in most regular classrooms is the inflexible pacing the classroom structure requires. Gifted students learn faster; it is one of their most common traits and is a direct outcome of the increase in neuroglial cells in the brain commonly found in people with high levels of intelligence. Flexible pacing and continuous progress must be addressed within the planning for gifted learners.

Advanced learners need opportunities to interact with their intellectual peers. Such opportunities provide challenge, a more realistic view of their abilities, and the opportunity for understanding and social interaction with those who entertain many of the same concerns and enthusiasms. If the reason for keeping advanced students with age peers is to prevent "feelings of superiority" or "elitism," research shows that advanced students who are grouped with their age peers are more likely to feel superior than those who are grouped with their intellectual peers.

Not the least of the concerns, when planning appropriate experiences for gifted learners, is the regular education teacher's frequent lack of information and training in gifted education. Such lack of information is through no fault of the regular classroom teacher. In most teacher education programs little mention is made of the needs of gifted learners. With the advent of mainstreaming, many programs have included other areas of exceptionality in the scope of the teacher education curriculum even if in a limited way. Even for those who are especially interested in specializing in the education of gifted students there are all too few universities that offer such specialization opportunities. In one state an independent study was made of the state's programs for gifted learners at the request of the legislature to evaluate the programs, presumably as a basis for deciding an appropriate funding level. The report asked teachers who were

engaged in the education of gifted learners where they had received their training to meet these students' special needs. The response showed that a large majority of those few who had had any training had received it from attendance at annual professional conferences and infrequent district inservices. The problem is not found in only one state. In a study (Archambault, 1993) of regular classroom practices with gifted students, it was found that such a lack of knowledge of needs and strategies appropriate for advanced learners is true across the country. This lack on the part of most teachers makes it necessary for trained, knowledgeable teachers to be in charge of gifted programs if the needs of this population are to be addressed.

The movement in regular education for increased class size and diversity places heavier demands on regular classroom teachers. As this happens, the need for a range of programs based on the educational needs of the learner becomes clearly evident.

Suggested Program Options

The Responsive Learning Environment. The range of services suggested by this author begins with a regular classroom that consciously attempts to empower students, meets the needs of each student through differentiation of curriculum and individualization of instruction, and builds trust and self-esteem among students and teachers. It is a classroom that uses flexible grouping, cross-grading, team teaching, and thematic instruction as part of the organizational pattern, and provides a choice of a wide variety of materials and strategies that cover many styles, modalities, and levels of learning. Ideally this classroom uses the community as an integral part of the learning environment, has teachers with training in the education of gifted learners, and has resources available when the needs of the students require additional support. Anything less than the classroom described will not be adequate to meet the needs of mildly to moderately gifted and talented students and would only minimally be able to provide instruction to average and below-average students. Although data to support the high productivity of such classrooms have been available for over a decade, few such classrooms exist in regular education settings (Clark, 1986; Goodlad, 1984).

Because of their importance in providing appropriate educational experiences for gifted learners, flexible grouping, differentiated curriculum, and individualized instruction are discussed in more detail than other components of the classroom using the responsive learning environment model. Although important for all students, these provisions become uniquely appropriate for gifted learners as they center on the characteristics and needs of this population.

Flexible Ability Grouping.   This is a provision that allows some students to be separated from the students working closer to the grade level norm based on some given criterion—in this case, needs, measured academic abilities or performing talents, or interest. Flexible ability grouping may be implemented within class groupings, special classes or schools, magnet programs, special groups meeting prior to or after school hours, or summer programs. Interestingly, such provisions have never been questioned if the ability in question is musical (such as found in orchestras, bands, or choruses) or in the visual and performing arts, which are provided for in drama and art classes, clubs, and competitions. This is especially true of physical performance talents, such as those needed for varsity teams or athletic events, where special coaching and intramural challenges are provided. The question of inappropriateness is only raised in the case of academically or intellectually gifted students.

Flexible ability grouping, as opposed to rigid tracking (the mindless assignment of students to one level of experience without regard to their different needs in different areas of the curriculum) has many advantages. Such temporary grouping allows teachers to more efficiently and effectively meet the needs of each student. Students have different strengths in different curricular areas and flexible grouping allows differ-

entiated experiences for different areas. Even the most advanced students are not equally able in every subject. However, education decision makers are often concerned that removing gifted students from the regular classroom will be detrimental to the other students. Teachers are concerned that slower children will have no incentive, no "spark." Goldberg and Passow (Passow, 1988) found that when achievement gains were compared between classes heterogeneously grouped with gifted students and classes comprising nongifted students, only in math was there a downgrading effect in the heterogeneously grouped classes. No effect was evident when gifted students were removed from any of the other subject areas.

The evidence is clear that neither grouping, enrichment, or acceleration should be used alone in programming for gifted learners, because each provides for a different need exhibited by this population. Each provision requires the presence of the others if it is to bring about the desired outcome.

Grouping in any form does not solve the problem of poor teaching or an inappropriate curriculum, but without grouping, good teaching and the delivery of an appropriate curriculum can be limited. There is a current trend that encourages the use of only heterogeneous grouping in all classrooms. This situation has been brought about by sincere concerns that some children are not receiving quality educational experiences and are being penalized by the practices of the educational system. There is no denying that the system as it is now organized fails to serve all students equally well. Students who enter the schooling process without the skills that will allow them to operate as successful learners—those who have little support from home, those whose families are part of the culture of poverty, those who have limited language ability in either their native language or in the dominant language of the classroom, and those who are significantly ahead of the designated grade-level curriculum—will find learning in the current schooling system difficult. Many will fall further and further behind. Others who began ahead will find no way to realize the extent of their abilities and they too will not reach their potential. A simplistic notion has been advanced to account for the failure of these children: the practice of grouping in classrooms (Goodlad, 1984; Johnson & Johnson, 1987; Oakes, 1985). It is interesting to note that in all of this discussion there is little mention of age grouping, which is the most inappropriate of any form of grouping.

There can be no doubt that there have been abuses in the practice of grouping. Grouping students from test scores recorded in their files without any observation of the students or their specific needs is an abuse. Tracking learners into all advanced classes without consideration for where their talents need advancement is an abuse. Keeping students rigidly in one of three groups for the entire year and sometimes year after year is an abuse. Using grouping without assessment of ability, interest, or pace of learning is an abuse. The answer is not to discontinue the benefits of grouping but to reveal the abuses and suggest better grouping practices and more alternatives to help students succeed.

There have been many reviews in the literature of the effects of grouping on learning and self-concept. Among the most recent are Kulik (1992), Kulik and Kulik (1992), and Rogers (1991). Of those reviews, Rogers investigates grouping as it affects the gifted student. Older studies (Kulik & Kulik, 1982; Slavin, 1987) used disclaimers at the beginning of their reviews stating that studies of special classes for the gifted and for low achievers would be excluded as they were "fundamentally different from comprehensive ability grouping plans" (Slavin, 1987, p. 297). Kulik (1992) reports that programs that make only minor adjustments of course content for differing ability usually have little or no effect on student achievement. However, grouping programs that make more substantial adjustments of curriculum for ability have clearly positive effects on children. Students in such grouping programs outperform equivalent control students from heterogeneously grouped classes. Programs that include enrichment and acceleration, when appropriate, have the largest effects on student learning, and gifted students from such classes outperform equivalent students from conventional classes by almost one full year on achievement tests when acceleration is used, and four to six months when enrichment is evident. Another review (Kulik & Kulik, 1982) has shown that the effect of grouping on the achievement of average and below-average learners is insignificant. Students of all abilities liked their school subjects more when they studied with peers of similar ability, and some students in grouped classes developed more positive attitudes about themselves and about school.

When gifted students in regular classrooms learn more quickly and complete their assignments more rapidly, their teachers usually respond by (1) giving them more of the same type of problem or assignment to complete; (2) having them do nonrelated recreational reading; or (3) asking them to teach another student who does not yet understand the material. None of these approaches challenges the gifted student and several of these provisions create problems for the student and often for the class. Cushenberry and Howell as far back as 1974 criticized the use of gifted students as teachers' aides, demonstrators, tutors, or record-keepers. Today criticism comes from not only researchers, but from the students themselves as they are increasingly used as tutors in cooperative learning groups, and put in the position of risking their scholastic record if they do not bring the other members of their group up to their standards.

The following are results most often noted in the research when classes were appropriately grouped using flexible ability grouping.

- Significant academic gains result when programs are adjusted to student abilities. Grouping alone is insufficient to show differences in achievement.
- Positive development in self-concept and a sense of well-being result from special group placement.

- There is more opportunity for individual expression, in-depth study, acceleration, and freedom from regimentation in ability-grouped classes.
- There are more high achievers and fewer underachievers reported in ability-grouped classes.
- More learning takes place in ability-grouped classes.
- There is a lack of cliquishness and friction among students in ability-grouped classes.
- Interest in subject matter increased in ability-grouped classes (Findley & Bryan, 1971: Goldberg, Passow, Justman, & Hage, 1965; Kulik,1992; Kulik & Kulik, 1982; McDermott, 1977; Moos, cited in Contenta, 1988; Rogers, 1991; Walburg & Anderson, 1972).

Homogeneous and heterogeneous grouping practices have important contributions to make to teaching and learning. The realization that students may be highly able in different areas and may have needs that differ one from the other forces us to conclude that *equity of opportunity does not mean the same opportunity.* To assure that student needs are met, we must provide differentiated curricula and individualized instruction.

Differentiated Curricula and Individualized Instruction.   The curriculum planning must take into account the characteristics and needs of the population the curriculum is to serve, and the planning of the child's program must account for his or her unique needs. Such a plan for providing both a differentiated curriculum and individualized instruction would ask several things of the teacher.

1. To develop a responsive environment that will allow flexibility of structure and pacing, a variety of levels and types of materials, choice, a range of grouping and methods of teaching, and safety and support
2. To plan how to extend and enhance the age-leveled curriculum to include activities that will provide appropriately for the characteristics and needs of gifted learners
3. To assess the functional level of all students
4. To determine the skills and learning experiences within the age-leveled curriculum that have been mastered and should be eliminated, those that should be reinforced, and those that should be extended for each student
5. To translate these skills and learning experiences into strategies in the areas of content, process, and product providing opportunities appropriate to the principles of the differentiated curriculum for gifted learners.

Mentor Programs.   Mentors are older students from higher grades, parents, other teachers, or people from the community who are successful in their field willing to share their expertise with learners who are interested in the same field and who are at a point of development in that field that they can benefit from involvement with an expert. Such programs provide advanced learners with challenging and complex ideas and guidance in advanced study in their area of interest.

Independent Study Programs.   These programs can include acceleration of material and concepts, and can be carried out in a variety of settings. Doherty and Evans (1981) suggest a three-phase process for using independent study. Phase 1 is teacher-led and incorporates learning centers, experimentation, and simulation as the student explores the depth and breadth of the academic area. Phase 2 is the independent study and involves a nine-step process of locating and using data, producing new ideas, and developing a product that is examined by experts.

The independent student:

1. Selects a topic that is issue oriented
2. Establishes a schedule
3. Develops five or more questions (first objectives) to direct the research
4. Secures references and seeks sources or raw data

TABLE 5.1.   Gifted Programming Alternatives

Gifted Needs Met by Program

Programs for Delivery of Services	Abstract Concepts	Accelerated Pace	Advanced Content	Complex Processes	Continuity	Continuous Progress	Flexible Grouping	Flexible Time	Independence	Individualization	Interdisciplinary	Peer Interaction	Varied Products	Variety of Material
Regular Classroom														
with cluster												✓		
with pullout	✓		✓	✓						✓		✓	✓	✓
with cluster and pullout	✓		✓	✓						✓		✓✓	✓	✓
Individualized Classroom														
with cluster	✓	✓	✓	✓	✓	✓	✓	✓	✓	✓	✓	✓✓	✓	✓
with cluster and pullout	✓	✓	✓	✓	✓	✓	✓	✓	✓	✓	✓	✓✓	✓	✓
with cross-grading	✓	✓	✓✓	✓	✓✓	✓✓	✓✓	✓	✓✓	✓✓	✓	✓✓	✓	✓✓
Adjunct Programs														
Mentors, tutorials, and internships	✓	✓	✓	✓					✓	✓		✓	✓	
Independent study	✓	✓	✓	✓				✓	✓✓	✓			✓	✓
Resource rooms	✓	✓	✓	✓		✓			✓	✓	✓	✓	✓	✓
Special Class Scheduled With Some Heterogeneous Classes	✓✓	✓✓	✓✓	✓✓	✓	✓	✓	✓	✓	✓	✓	✓	✓	✓✓
Special Classes	✓✓	✓✓	✓✓	✓✓	✓✓	✓✓	✓✓	✓✓	✓✓	✓✓	✓✓	✓✓	✓✓	✓✓

Levels of Involvement: Level 1 Mildly Gifted; Level 2 Moderately Gifted; Level 3 Highly Gifted

Source: Adapted from B. Clark, *Growing Up Gifted*, 3rd ed. Columbus, OH: Merrill. Used by permission of the author.

5. Researches the topic, collects raw data, and takes notes
6. Develops five final objectives using Bloom's taxonomy
7. Has a conference with the teacher, who evaluates the depth of knowledge and the idea production
8. Makes a product showing some of his or her new ideas
9. Displays the product, which is evaluated with a friend and examined by an expert

The final phase is a culminating seminar. This process allows students to build the skills necessary to carry out an investigation that will satisfy their intellectual curiosity and truly enrich their academic lives.

Special Classes.   Special classes in a more intensified form are recommended for highly gifted or talented students. Governor's schools, high schools for the performing arts, and residential schools for math and sciences are some of the types of schools that represent this model. A summary of alternative program options for gifted students can be found in Table 5.1.

CONCLUSION

Our sociopolitical system is based on democratic principles. The school as an extension of those principles must not refuse gifted students the right to educational experiences appropriate to their level of development. As noted, the more intelligent the individual, the more rapid will be the processing of the brain, and the more complex will be the thought processes. A range of program options must be available to provide for all areas of ability; therefore, an array-of-services model should be used. All programs should allow differentiation of curriculum, individualization of instruction, building of trust and self-esteem, flexibility of grouping, choice, a variety of materials, continuous progress, and pacing appropriate to the individual student's needs, interests, and abilities. In a perfect world the ideal classroom would make this range of programs unnecessary. However, with the barriers now commonly found in regular education classrooms, we must provide alternatives when they are needed. Appropriate educational experiences must be available to all students and they must include those who least fit the present schooling system and who now are the largest body of underachievers in that system—those learners known as gifted and talented students.

REFERENCES

Archambault, F. X., Jr. (1993). *Regular classroom practices with gifted students: Results of a national survey of classroom teachers.* Research Monograph 93101. Storrs, CN: National Research Center on the Gifted and Talented, University of Connecticut.

Berg, P., & Singer, M. (1992). *Dealing with genes: The language of heredity.* Mill Valley, CA: University Science Books.

Bloom, B. (1964). *Stability and change in human characteristics.* New York: John Wiley & Sons.

Bouchard, T. J., Jr., & McGue, M. (1990, March). Genetic and rearing environmental influences on adult personality. *Journal of Personality.*

Clark, B. (1979). *Growing up gifted,* Columbus, OH: Merrill.

Clark, B. (1986). *Optimizing learning.* Columbus, OH: Merrill.

Clark, B. (1988). *Growing up gifted* (3rd ed.). Columbus, OH: Merrill.

Clark, B. (1992). *Growing up gifted* (4th ed.). New York: Merrill/Macmillan.

Conlan, R., (Ed.). (1993). *Journey through the mind and body: Blueprint for life.* Alexandria, VA: Time–Life Books.

Contenta, S. (1988, February). Working class kids short-changed: High schools need complete overhaul Ontario study says. *The Toronto Star,* p. 1.

Cushenberry, D., & Howell, H. (1974). *Reading and the gifted child.* Champaign, IL: Research Press.

Diamond, M. (1988). *Enriching heredity: The impact of the environment on the anatomy of the brain.* New York: The Free Press.

Diamond, M. (1993, July). Lecture on brain development, presented at The Developing Brain: New Frontiers of Research Conference, University of California, Los Angeles.

Doherty, E., & Evans, L. (1981). Independent study process: They can think, can't they? *Journal for the Education of the Gifted, 4*(2), 106–111.

Dubos, R. (1969). Biological individuality. *The Columbia Forum, 12*(1), 5–9.

Findley, W., & Bryan, M. (1971). *Ability grouping 1970: Status import, and alternatives.* Athens,

GA: Center for Educational Improvement, University of Georgia.

Gardner, H. (1983). *Frames of mind.* New York: Basic Books.

Goldberg, M., Passow, A., Justman, J., & Hage, G. (1965). *The effects of ability grouping.* New York: Bureau of Publications, Columbia University.

Goodlad, J. (1984). *A place called school.* New York: McGraw-Hill.

Grunwald, L. (1993, July). The amazing minds of infants. *Life,* pp. 47–60.

Hutchinson, M. (1986). *Megabrain.* New York: Simon & Schuster.

Johnson, R., & Johnson, D. (1987). *The achieving student in heterogeneous cooperative learning groups.* Paper developed for a workshop at the University of Minnesota.

Kagan, J. (1971). *Change and continuity in infancy.* New York: John Wiley & Sons.

Kandel, E., & Schwartz, J. (1991). *Principles of Neural Science* (3rd ed.). New York: Elsevier.

Krech, D. (1969). Psychoneurobiochemeducation. *Phi Delta Kappan, L,* 370–375.

Krech, D. (1970). Don't use the kitchen sink approach to enrichment. *Today's Education, 59,* 30–32.

Kulik, J. (1992, February). *Analysis of the Research on Ability Grouping.* Storrs, CN: National Research Center on the Gifted and Talented.

Kulik, J., & Kulik, C. (1982). Effects of ability grouping on secondary school students: A meta-analysis of evaluation findings. *American Educational Research Journal, 19,* 415–428.

Kulik, J., & Kulik, C. (1992, Spring). Meta-analytic findings on grouping programs. *Gifted Child Quarterly.*

Lewontin, R. (1982). *Human diversity.* New York: Scientific American Books.

McDermott, R. (1977). Social relations as contexts for learning in schools. *Harvard Educational Review, 47*(2), 191.

Oakes, J. (1985). *Keeping track: How schools structure inequality.* New Haven: Yale University Press.

Passow, H. (1988). Issues to knowledge: Grouping and tracking. In *Critical issues in curriculum: The National Society of Education yearbook.* (pp. 205–225). Chicago: University of Chicago Press.

Reis, S., Westberg, K., Kulikowich, J., Cailard, F., Hebert, T., Plucker, J., Purcell, J., Rogers, J., & Smist, J. (1993). *Why not let high ability students start school in January? The curriculum compacting study.* Research Monograph 93106. Storrs, CN: National Research Center on the Gifted and Talented, University of Connecticut.

Restak, R. (1986). *The infant mind.* Garden City, NY: Doubleday.

Rogers, K. (1991). *The relationship of grouping practices to the education of the gifted and talented learner.* Storrs, CN: National Research Center on the Gifted and Talented, University of Connecticut.

Rosenzweig, M. (1966). Environmental complexity, cerebral change and behavior. *American Psychologist, 21,* 321–332.

Rosenzweig, M. (1984). Experience, memory and the brain. *American Psychologist, 39*(4), 365–376.

Slavin, R. (1987). Ability grouping and student achievement in elementary schools: A best-evidence synthesis. *Review of Educational Research, 57*(3), 293–336.

Slavkin, H. (1987, February). *Science in the 21st century.* Speech presented at the 25th Annual Conference of the California Association for the Gifted, Los Angeles.

Thompson, R., Berger, T., & Berry, S. (1980). An introduction to the anatomy, physiology, and chemistry of the brain. In M. Wittrock (Ed.), *The brain and psychology,* New York: Academic.

Verny, T. (1981). *The secret life of the unborn child.* New York: Summit Books.

Walberg, H., & Anderson, G. (1972). Properties of the achieving urban classes. *Journal of Educational Psychology, 63,* 381–385.

White, B. (1975). *The first three years of life.* Englewood Cliffs, NJ: Prentice-Hall.

CHAPTER 6

Including All Students and Their Gifts within Regular Classrooms

MARA SAPON-SHEVIN

INTRODUCTION

In many school districts, a small group of children is selected for inclusion in special programming designated as "gifted and talented." In some cases, this programming is provided in segregated, full-time placements, but in the majority of the cases, students identified as "gifted and talented" are served in part-time, pull-out programs, leaving their regular classrooms for part of the day (or week) to receive special services elsewhere in the building or the district.

This chapter will: (1) briefly describe the typical reasons for segregating children who are identified as gifted and talented; (2) explore some of the logical fallacies and pedagogical flaws which underlie those assumptions; (3) discuss the consequences for all students, teachers, parents, and society of segregating children for special services; and (4) develop a rationale for meeting the needs of all students, including those identified as gifted and talented, within "regular" education classrooms.

Rationales for Segregating Gifted and Talented Students

At a basic level, there are gifted programs because the educational community (as a reflection of the broader society) typically sorts and identifies different "kinds" of students and provides for them differentially. Programs of bilingual education, remedial reading, and accelerated math all stem from the belief that different children have differ-

ent educational needs, and that it is the responsibility of schools to provide appropriate education to meet the needs of different learners. The following are the typical educational arguments in support of identifying and providing special programming for gifted and talented students.

1. Gifted children represent a unique group of students, members of an objectively definable population that can and must be "found" and labeled in order for their needs to be met.

> A gifted child is not a normal child whose differences are secondary—interesting decorative frills that can for the most part be ignored. . . . To deal with the gifted child in exactly the same way one deals with a normal child is to deal inappropriately and so to cause harm, as it would cause harm to give a person with pneumonia only aspirin simply because colds are so much more common. (Tolan, 1987, pp. 186–187)

2. Gifted children require qualitatively different kinds of educational experiences from those provided to "average" or "typical" students within the regular classroom. Since regular classrooms are conceptualized as being geared to the "norm," some gifted educators like Steinbach (1981) argue that "a good program for everyone else, by definition couldn't be good for the gifted." (p. 5)

3. The unique needs of gifted students cannot be met within the regular classroom; gifted children must be grouped together in order to receive appropriate education.

Only through ability grouping can the gifted student engage in discourse and debate with his intellectual peers. This needed high-level engagement of like minds cannot be carried on effectively or efficiently in the typically heterogeneous classroom. (Ward, 1975, p. 296)

Gifted education proponents argue that the regular classroom as currently organized and implemented is largely not amenable to change, and many teachers and students are hostile to gifted students, thus necessitating the removal of gifted students to a "safe haven" where they can be with other students like themselves.

Because regular classes group students according to chronological age, not mental age, gifted students often find themselves in situations which meet neither their social not their intellectual needs. They may develop poor social skills from their inability to find "true peers" with similar abilities, interests and needs. Many experience feelings of isolation and social frustration. . . . As a solution to problems of social isolation and lack of academic stimulation, one dependable strategy is to bring gifted students together. . . . because they are experiencing many of the same problems, gifted peers offer strong understanding and social and academic support for each other. (Davis & Rimm, 1989, pp. 136–137)

Why Else Are There Gifted Programs?

In order to understand the renewed interest in gifted education and the increasing number of programs available, we must look beyond educational rhetoric to some of the social, political, and economic factors contributing to concern for "our Nation's best and brightest" (Sapon-Shevin, 1987b). One reason schools and school districts have gifted programs is that there is often parental demand for such services. When an adjacent school district has a gifted program, other districts feel considerable pressure to implement some kind of differential programming or risk the departure of those familes whose children might have been served in such a program. Within large urban districts,

particularly those characterized by impoverished, struggling schools and large ethnically diverse populations, gifted programs (including gifted magnet programs) have served (and sometimes been promoted) as a way of stemming "white flight." By providing segregated programming for gifted students, school districts can keep some white parents—whose children are in the gifted program—within the district (and the tax assessment area). The Massachusetts Advocacy Center (1990) describes the situation in Boston.

One middle school principal tried to entice a parent . . . into enrolling his daughter into the school's Advanced Work Class by assuring the parent that the program would be located in an isolated wing of the building and that his daughter would rarely mix with "regular" students. Obviously, the use of segregation as a selling point for any high-status program conveys more than just the value placed on the learning of selected students; it also transmits a negative message about the rest of the school. (p. 25)

Having one's child identified as "gifted and talented" is an important source of parental pride, largely due to the assumption that gifted children are often the products of gifted or exceptional parents. Unlike other labels that children acquire in school ("slow learner," "learning disabled," "emotionally disturbed"), the "gifted" label is usually welcomed by parents, and sometimes actively solicited.

At a broader level, recent national concerns about the United States' loss of preeminence in the economic and political world have led to pressure to reorder educational priorities. Some education leaders have strongly supported the need to "invest" in gifted children as a way of insuring the United States' recovery of economic and political prominence. A changing political climate which attributes many of the nation's educational problems to overinvestment in poor, disadvantaged, and minority students (at the expense of those who are more academically talented) also provides impetus for increased gifted programming (Sapon-Shevin, 1987b).

Challenging Assumptions Underlying Gifted Education

I will now discuss each of the above frequently cited arguments in support of gifted education.

There Is Such a Thing as a Gifted Child. Children (and all human beings) vary along many dimensions: height, eye and skin color, musical skills, and tested IQ. When we decide to label a group of children who differ along a specific continuum "gifted," we have made a decision; we have decided that certain characteristics are of special interest or importance and that educational and placement choices appropriately stem from these characteristics. The literature on gifted education is full of questions like, "What proportion of the population is truly gifted? Is it 3 percent or 5 percent? Csikszentmihalyi and Robinson (1986) respond to that question.

> The naturalistic assumption is that giftedness is a natural fact, and therefore the number of gifted children can be counted, as one might count white herons or panda bears. If this is the sense in which people are asking the question, the question is meaningless. The attributional assumption recognizes that giftedness is not an objective fact but a result jointly constituted by social expectations and individual abilities. From this perspective, it is obvious that the question "What proportion of the population is gifted?" means "What proportion of the population have we agreed to call gifted?" (p. 266)

I am not arguing that there are not differences in children, simply that the decision to attend to specific differences as the most salient is not natural or inevitable, but represents a social and educational policy and practice. While most children's differences are not treated as educationally relevant, we do act as though IQ scores (still the predominant method for identifying gifted children) are objective, empirical measures of an educationally significant difference.

An understanding of *other* special education categories such as "retarded" and "learning disabled" as social constructions has altered our way of looking at children whose performances are deemed deficient. In particular, we now challenge the assumption that such students are different enough from "typical" students to warrant their labeling and removal (see Mercer, 1973; Sleeter, 1986; Stainback & Stainback, 1984). Similarly, we need to ask: If IQ scores are recognized as culturally biased, subjective, uni-dimensional and largely educationally irrelevant when they are applied to the "low end" of the educational spectrum, how can they be seen as objective, clear, legitimate sources of educational decision making when applied to the "high end" of the same educational spectrum?

Gifted Children Need "Special Education." While the gifted literature is full of descriptions of "what gifted children need"—process education, mentors in the community, learning activities at an appropriate level and pace, experience in creative thinking and problem solving—there is no evidence that this is not what *all* children require (Sapon-Shevin, 1987b). At a recent meeting to inform parents that their children had been selected for a gifted and talented pull-out program, the teacher explained that the "gifted" third graders would be pursuing a unit on animals; they would study and build animal habitats, learn to identify animals by their tracks and markings, write stories about animals, and learn about endangered species. This raises the obvious question: Why weren't all third-grade students involved in such a unit? What was so unique about these activities that they were appropriate only for children whose IQs were over 120 (the entrance requirement for the gifted program)? Ironically, some of the same activities that are described as being especially appropriate for gifted children are *also* those described as being appropriate for children who are "educationally handicapped," "at risk," and "underachieving." *All* of these groups of children are described as benefiting from educational activities that are hands-on, relevant to their lives and experience, child-centered, and which promote positive self-awareness and self-esteem. If this is the case, and no one's educational needs are best met by endless worksheets and dittos, then why are enriched learning activities only advisable for and available to a small group of students?

The Needs of Gifted Children Cannot Be Met in the Regular Classroom / Regular Education Won't Change. This argument is perhaps the most important and the most complex. There is little doubt that regular education classrooms *as currently constituted and organized* do not meet the educational needs of many students identified as gifted and talented. Much of the curriculum in general education is boring and rigid, students are often lock-stepped through texts and instruction, and many teachers are not comfortable responding to individual differences within a whole-class setting. But to assume that these characteristics are only problematic for gifted students is to deny that our educational system is currently failing to meet the needs of large numbers of students! While many negative characterizations of current schools' structures and organizational models are true, the leap to assuming that removing gifted children from such an environment constitutes the best or the only solution should not be automatic.

As many schools move toward full inclusion of students with disabilities, there has been increasing attention paid to the need to restructure schools to better meet the needs of a wide range of learners within a common context. Many of what are now considered "best practices" in education—whole language, cooperative learning, critical problem solving, thematic instruction, multiple intelligences programming, and portfolio assessment—are practices wholly consistent with the inclusion of students identified as "gifted" within "regular" classrooms. Pull-out models of gifted education cannot be justified on the grounds that regular classrooms are "no good" for certain children, without examining whether these same classrooms are actually good for the majority of children. Instead of removing children who don't fit, why don't we change classrooms so that all children can be welcomed, accommodated, and well educated?

The removal of gifted children is also advocated in response to the often hostile, unaccepting,

sometimes even scornful treatment such students receive in some regular classrooms. If, in fact, teachers and other students are often or even sometimes hostile to students who are "different," either in terms of their physical characteristics or their intellectual skills, removing certain children to a "safe haven" does little to address this bleak picture of unaccepting, intolerant classrooms. It is hard to believe that the same children who mock a child who reads exceptionally well would respond positively to the child who reads more slowly, lives with two same-sex parents, speaks Spanish at home, or is in some other way identified as "different" or marginal. While removing any students who are experiencing failure or who are miserable in the regular classroom may constitute an emergency, stop-gap solution, to glorify such solutions as best educational practice is to doom educational reform before it begins.

Consequences of Segregated Gifted Programs

Labeling and removing a small group of children from the regular classroom has implications and consequences which go far beyond the effects on those identified, labeled, and removed.

Consequences for Students Identified as Gifted. While "gifted" is generally considered a more positive, sought-after label than, say, "retarded," there are striking parallels; labels tend to change the behavior of those who interact with the labeled individual. Children identified as gifted are often lumped together in a category, although their individual gifts may be quite different; the expectations of those around them tend to be elevated (often inappropriately so); and the gifted label may stigmatize and isolate children, making it difficult for them to fit in. While some argue that children's *differences* lead to these results, and not the label per se, labels and differential treatment tend to reify differences, making them appear more real or more salient than they might be. Rigid school structures which classify and rank children also increase the likelihood that labeled children will be responded to more in terms of their differences from other children than in term of their similarities.

Children who are chosen to be included in the gifted program must adjust to an altered classroom position. If they express pride in the work they do in the gifted program or return eager and anxious to talk about their latest project or accomplishment, then they may be viewed as showing off, an "egghead," a "brain," the "teacher's pet," snotty, or arrogant. If they wish to avoid this kind of response, they may feel that they have to "keep quiet" or play down what they have done during their time away from the classroom (Sapon-Shevin, 1994). One administrator, in describing the gifted program in his district, explained that the gifted children are "coached" how to re-enter the room with a minimum of disruption so that they won't call attention to themselves in any way or incur the resentment of the teacher or other students. How can children feel good about their abilities, skills, and interests if these differences become the source of social isolation or friction with classmates or teachers? Some students choose not to be in gifted programs so that they won't have to feel alien, different, isolated, or strange. Children who are academically advanced sometimes feel that they must choose between scholastic excellence and having friends, between doing well and fitting in, between their teacher's approval and that of their friends. Having to leave the classroom, being singled out, bearing the label of "gifted," all affect how children see themselves.

Some children respond by minimizing their achievements and negating their differences; one first grade boy, a fluent reader, said "I found out that if I make mistakes, everybody likes me more—the teacher and the kids." Even without articulating or expressing such feelings, students may yield to subtle and direct pressure *not* to do well. The pressure on girls to hide their accomplishments and talents is particularly strong (Silverman, 1986: Wolleat, 1979): "never beat a boy"; "it's not good to be too smart"; "the boys won't like you if you do better than they do"—these and other messages often discourage high achievement.

Some students are relieved to be identified as "gifted" since that label leads to their removal from a learning environment which may be painful or inappropriate. Undifferentiated, boring classroom settings in which academic excellence is not encouraged and is sometimes punished or resented makes many students grateful for the opportunity to work in academic settings in which their full participation and achievement is appreciated and validated. Some students feel guilty about the opportunities they are having that are not afforded their classmates; others become scornful or resentful of classmates who are not "as smart" and are grateful to be removed (Fetterman, 1988).

It is undeniable that the ways in which our classrooms and schools are currently structured and the ways in which some teachers now respond to individual differences leave many academically advanced students unhappy and ill served. But removing children who are different will *not* create classrooms and schools which are responsive to individual differences, will *not* force schools to create inclusive classroom communities in which all children feel valued and comfortable, and will *not* guarantee that society benefits from all students' skills and abilities. Given the philosophy and commitment of the inclusion movement, which talks about the value of having diverse groups of students come to know, understand, and appreciate one another, it seems ironic and self-defeating to integrate students with disabilities and simultaneously remove those identified as gifted (Sapon-Shevin, 1984).

Consequences for "Nongifted" Students. When some students are labeled "gifted," the rest of the students in the class are implicitly identified as "nongifted." What are some of the consequences of this non-label? Beyond the formal school curriculum presented in schools, students also learn about themselves, their place in the world, and their relationship with other people. They learn how they are viewed and evaluated by others, and they internalize a set of beliefs and assumptions about how schools work and how the world is structured.

When a small group of students is selected for special treatment, many children are curious about who those children are, why they were selected, and what they are doing that is different. The ways in which teachers respond to children's explicit questions about these areas and the explanations teachers give—or fail to give—about the gifted program in general, all help to shape children's beliefs, understandings, and values related to differences in human beings and the appropriate response to those differences.

Students are often painfully aware of the opportunities afforded to some of their classmates, especially as those compare to their own. Just as students know that the bluebird reading group is "higher" than the robins, students are aware that some students receive different treatment. Children learn who is "smart," who isn't, and which category *they* fit into; their notions of classroom and societal justice are also impacted, as they learn who "deserves" what, and whether or not *they* are worthy.

In a book entitled *Locked In/Locked Out: Tracking and Placement Practices in Boston Public Schools* (Massachusetts Advocacy Center, 1990), a third-grade boy describes what he knows about the Advanced Work Classes that exist in his school.

> My friend's in Advanced. He's smart, so he's got the hardest teacher in school. They do maps a lot—and dictionary work. He gets books that are real big—as big as dictionaries. He let me hold his book bag, and it was really heavy. His books are real big and hard. (p. 21)

Other students noted that only some children got to go on field trips or are offered foreign language classes. Another student explained:

> Students in the high cluster go [to the library], I think, last period every Monday for the whole period. We don't go to the library now; we go to word processing. It's o.k., but I'd like to go to the library. (p. 27)

Not only are children's self-esteem and self-concept affected by differential labeling and instruction, the nature and quality of the curriculum and instruction offered in gifted classes are generally different from that provided in the regular classroom. Certain opportunities become designated as "for the gifted class," and "only appropriate for the gifted"; districts sometimes allocate their "best" teachers to the gifted program and the educational opportunities of regular, "nongifted" students are often curtailed in direct relation to the differentiated, enriched curriculum provided to gifted students. In my daughter's school, for example, students in the gifted English program went to the theater to see a Shakespeare production, while other students did not. And yet, seeing literature "come alive" might have been just the educational opportunity to encourage reluctant readers or students with limited English skills to aspire to increased literacy and participation.

In many cases, teachers do not address issues of selection, placement, and differential programming directly; children learn quickly that differences in ability, how children were selected for the program, and their own desire to be included are not appropriate topics of conversation (Sapon-Shevin, 1994). This creates a situation in which questions of justice, fairness, and differential treatment are never subjected to critical analysis, never become part of the overt curriculum, but remain both hidden and powerful.

Consequences for Teachers.   How do teachers feel about gifted education within their school or school district? Given the constraints which many teachers experience in their own classrooms—too many students, lack of materials, inadequate planning and preparation time, and chronic exhaustion—some teachers are relieved to have students removed from their purview and responsibility. Some teachers voice relief that something is being done to help the students they feel they often neglect while attending to the pressing needs of struggling and disruptive children. Frustrated by the sense that there is much more that academically advanced children could be doing, some teachers are grateful that these needs are being met elsewhere, thus freeing up their time and energy to work with poorly achieving or underachieving students.

Other teachers, however, are resentful at the removal of the students they sometimes see as "spark plugs." Using language such as "a brain drain" and "creaming off the top," these teachers are angry and annoyed at having their classroom depleted of students who offer them and other students support, ideas, and encouragement. As one teacher said, "Sometimes it's a child like Michael that really keeps you going, especially on the tough days." Teachers express frustration with the removal of gifted students for a variety of reasons: they are sorry to see less advanced students deprived of the peer models and enrichment which more advanced students provide, and they often resent the resources, energy, and attention being poured into special, segregated programs at a time when they themselves are feeling unsupported and under-resourced. Removing gifted children in order to provide for them adequately also implies that the regular classroom teacher is somehow inadequate for that task, either because he or she isn't smart enough or creative enough, or because he or she is already overloaded with responsibilities (which confirms teachers' own perceptions of that overload).

There is also evidence that the existence of separate gifted programs contributes to the *de-skilling* of regular classroom teachers. By removing those students whose educational needs are perceived as divergent from the rest of the class (often a false perception), teachers are discouraged from finding multiple, diverse, innovative ways of structuring their teaching and curriculum. The belief that "their needs are met *out there*" can keep teachers from recognizing the limitations in their own curriculum and classroom structure and from seeing the diversity that exists among *all* the students in the class (Sapon-Shevin, 1990). Removing children who are identified as "different" contributes to the inclination to see such students as more different than they actually are (teachers look for signs of difference) and to see other ("nongifted") students as more similar than they actually are (the ones that are left are seen as a homogeneous group). Teachers' beliefs in the concept of an "average student" and the appropriateness of "teaching to the middle" are perpetuated by removing students who are seen as different.

Teaching strategies which depend on student diversity and heterogeneity, such as cooperative learning and peer teaching, are jeopardized by narrowing the real or imagined range of skills, interests, and abilities in the "regular classroom." The impetus and the apparent necessity of engaging in multilevel, multimodality teaching for *all* children is diminished by the belief that "special" needs are met elsewhere. And, many of the special strategies used for students identified as "gifted," such as curriculum compacting and acceleration, are very appropriate to a wide range of students. Wouldn't it be beneficial if *every* student's educational programming was the result of a careful consideration of goals and objectives, strengths and weaknesses, and included attention to diverse teaching strategies and authentic assessment?

Consequences for Parents. When some children are labeled "gifted" and removed from the regular classroom, the parents of these children also acquire a label, "parents of gifted children." This label is generally a source of pride and satisfaction to parents as it attests to their child's precocity or high performance. Previous research has indicated that parents often change their behavior, expectations, and attitudes toward their child after he or she has been labeled "gifted" (Sapon-Shevin, 1987a). What varies, however, is the nature and magnitude of this change. Some parents, relieved that their child's "difference" is labeled in a positive way, relax the rigidity of their expectations, confident that the child will do well and be appreciated: "If he wants to spend all his time playing with dinosaurs, I guess that's just his area of talent, so it's okay." Other parents interpret the label differently, demanding that their child do well in all areas and live up to the label: "If you're so gifted, how come you failed your math test and leave your dirty socks on the floor?"

Parents' relationships with the schools may also shift. If the parents have actively lobbied for their child's identification and labeling, then they are likely to be pleased to see their high regard for their child confirmed publicly and officially. If the parents have not been aware of the identification and labeling process (or possibility), their response may be less clear; they may wonder what the label means, and what it means for *their* child. Having a child in the gifted program may make parents eligible for membership in gifted parents' organizations, may lead them to subscribe to *Gifted Children's Monthly* or to order toys from the *Gifted Children's Catalogue.* Parents who were not previously involved with the organization of the school may now come to that effort with the label of "parent of a gifted child," and may be solicited for lobbying efforts on behalf of gifted children. If the parents are not familiar with the school culture or organization, their child's acquisition of the label may be confusing; they may wonder what they should be doing differently, whether or not they have the education or resources to adequately provide for a gifted child, or they may even be resentful of the child's school success. Many parents also worry about the effect on other children in the family of having one of their children labeled as gifted and eligible for special programs (Cornell, 1983).

In the same way that students try to make sense of being labeled and removed (or not labeled and maintained in the regular classroom), parents also wrestle with finding meaning in their new status and the status of their child. What does it mean to have a "gifted child"? What should I as a parent be doing for/with such a child? Will it damage my other "nongifted" children for Kristi to be in the gifted program? Will Ari become alienated from his peer group? Is my parenting adequate to such a challenge? How will I explain my child's giftedness when I am asked why she is like that? Will I be seen as "overly proud" and become alienated from my friends whose children were *not* chosen?

At the same time that some parents are acquiring the label of "parent of a gifted child," most parents implicitly (though certainly not formally) acquire the label of "parent of a nongifted child." If the parents are aware of the identification and labeling process, they may be resentful of children and parents who are chosen to participate, or they may simply accept that their child did not, at some level, pass muster for entrance into the gifted program. Some parents may be unaware of the existence of the program per se and thus may not react to the labeling event in the same way (Sapon-Shevin, 1994).

Conversely, parents of children not selected may wonder why their child wasn't chosen. They may ask: Will my child be disadvantaged in the future by not participating in such a program? Does my child's "nongiftedness" reflect on my parenting, resources, or skills? If I had had the money to send my child to preschool would he or she have gotten labeled as "gifted"?

Parents of children identified as gifted must also make decisions about their involvement in school programming and the extent to which they will become advocates for gifted education (as opposed to lobbying for schoolwide change). Parents of gifted children may find themselves in active opposition to parents of (for example) students with disabilities who are also lobbying for limited school resources, and they must decide what their relationship to such other groups will be, adversarial or coalitional. In the same way that gifted programs can disrupt the classroom community, creating rifts or divisions among students, such programs can create similar divisions among parents.

Consequences for Schools.   The two major barriers to creating inclusive school communities are labeling/segregation and competitive structures and orientations. When children are labeled and segregated—"resource room" or "gifted"—and when teachers are similarly labeled and separated—the "gifted teacher," the "learning disabilities teacher"—it is difficult to create a school climate in which all students and teachers feel that they belong and in which all teachers feel responsible for all students. Schools become fragmented, subdivided groups of teachers and students who pursue discrete educational and social agendas.

Developing, organizing, and implementing gifted programs contribute to competitive, hierarchical ways of viewing both students and teachers. Decisions about selection, resource and space allocation, and teacher assignment to gifted programs all can create situations in which individuals must compete for scarce resources, often justifying their need in contrast to that of other groups, i.e., which program is more worthy of the new computer, the resource room or the gifted program? Which students should be selected to attend a special theater program, go on field trips, or participate in a writing workshop? Which teacher should be assigned the gifted program, the highly competent veteran teacher or the new teacher struggling with classroom management? In some ways, these decisions are also the result of a scarcity of resources; since there's not enough to go around, to whom shall we give? And competition for scarce resources keeps us from asking the more fundamental question: Why is there such a scarcity of resources for schools and education? All of these decisions are both based on and communicate the values of the participants, mirroring beliefs about individual worth, ability, merit, diversity, fairness, justice, and democracy.

Consequences for Society.   The effects on society of providing a different education for a small group of students, usually those who are economically and socially advantaged, are powerful. At one level, schools mirror the social and economic inequalities which exist within society; children who come to school advantaged by family background, money, and membership in certain ethnic groups are much more likely to be placed in upper-level programs or to be identified as gifted. But schools not only mirror these inequalities; they also perpetuate them by providing differential education for students from different backgrounds. The number of poor and minority students served in gifted programs is in no way proportionate to their representation in society as a whole. In racially diverse cities, gifted programs

are often explicitly used as a way of stemming white flight and of resegregating students racially within theoretically integrated schools and classrooms (Sapon-Shevin, 1994). In some upper-middle-class districts, nearly 25 percent of the children in the district are identified as "gifted and talented" while in other districts, such designation is rare. Those who come to school advantaged maintain or increase that advantage. Those who come to school disadvantaged receive preparation and education consistent with maintaining their low economic and social status in the wider world. In times of economic crisis, when programs for poor and minority students are being cut (including aid to pregnant mothers, Head Start preschool programs, and child care services), these discrepancies become even more pronounced.

How can such glaring inequities continue to exist? We would certainly be uncomfortable with a rationale that said, "We give rich children a better education because they deserve it more." But we are quite comfortable characterizing gifted programs as "appropriately differentiated learning experiences for children with unique learning needs, or with special skills and abilities." The end result, however, is likely to be the same. Although we are uncomfortable with a meritocracy based on wealth, we have grown inured to one based on evaluations of ability or talent, even though those differences may come as the result of middle-class economic privilege.

In many ways, we have given up our hope for a society in which all children are well educated and well cared for. In our despair about ever having the kind of society we would like, we have invented elaborate rationales to explain why providing well for only some students is rational and reasonable.

One of the most devastating effects of gifted programs is that they have functioned as *escape valves* for the schools; by removing the pressure of those parents (often very vocal, as well as politically and economically empowered) to provide a better education for *their* children, many current, dysfunctional practices of the system have remained untouched and unreformed. By developing gifted programs, schools engage in a kind of *educational triage* whereby they provide exemplary, enriched programming for some (those chosen to be worthy) and continue to provide the majority of students with mediocre, unstimulating education. And, saddest of all, such programming also socializes students, teachers, and parents to accept what has been called "the justice of unjust outcomes" (Fine, 1987), teaches them that it is their fault and their deficiency which keep them from further opportunities and education, and deprives them of any critical understanding of the political and economic forces which support the sorting and selection mechanism of schooling.

Toward New Models of Inclusive Schools

In addressing these issues, some educators propose creating more egalitarian gifted programs, admitting more children of color to such programs and providing gifted education that is more culturally appropriate. But such attempts are limited at best since they address only a small proportion of the nation's students. While a gifted program that has proportionate numbers of Hispanic, African American, and Native American students is clearly better than one that does not, such programs do little to address the majority of students who are left in inappropriate, uncreative, boring school settings.

All children, regardless of how or what they have been labeled, have gifts and talents that must be nurtured, supported, stretched, and encouraged. Identifying the gifts and talents of only a small group of students is inherently unfair, and it is easy to see why the charge of elitism has been leveled at special gifted programs that recognize and reward the gifts and talents of only a few select students. Adding categories like "handicapped gifted" and "economically disadvantaged gifted" does not address the fact that *all children* have unique skills and abilities which must be responded to if our schools are to achieve true equality. Global labels that identify only some children as "gifted"—just like labels that identify certain

children as "handicapped"—are educationally irrelevant and politically indefensible when they result in different qualities of instruction.

Even exemplary gifted programs may impede whole-school reform that is solidly grounded in broader economic and social concerns because they give the illusion that "something is being done." By siphoning off the efforts and commitment of concerned parents, teachers, and administrators, such stop-gap or partial measures may keep schools from hitting "rock bottom" and thus facing the magnitude and embeddedness of their problems. Eliminating gifted programs will not solve school or societal problems, because the problems do not result from the gifted programs. Rather, gifted programs are a response to the inappropriateness and inflexibility of schools—a response that creates as many problems as it solves—and to an economic system that depends on the schools to maintain social, educational, and economic stratification. Even exemplary gifted education programs do little to address the place of schools in redressing societal and economic inequities, to force people to understand the connections between school inequalities and inequalities in housing, jobs, and the distribution of other societal resources. The promotional brochure from a gifted and talented program in a small midwestern city begins with this quote:

> Equal education is the foundation of the right to be a human being. . . . This does not mean that any child or any other gifted child having a greater capacity to learn may or shall be deprived of his or her opportunity of learning more. It does mean that every child shall have the equal opportunity to learn to the best of his or her ability. That opportunity must be made available to all on equal terms.
>
> Alfred Gitelson, Judge
> County of Los Angeles
> Superior Court Case 822854

But this statement in no way addresses the fact that all children do not have and are not given equal opportunities to excel; making the opportunity available "on equal terms" must mean not just allowing all students to take and be judged by the same entrance exam, but assuring that all infants and children receive adequate food, housing, care, stimulation, and nurturing so that they can profit from an enriched education designed to support their special gifts.

While eliminating or challenging gifted programs may not be the solution, such a bold step may force those with a controlling interest in their children's education and welfare to seriously examine the consequences of prejudicial differentiation and work to create just and equitable schools and societies. Neither improving nor eliminating gifted programs will automatically lead us to new solutions or help us to develop new models. The alternative to gifted programs is *not* undifferentiated education or the denial of individual differences or needs. The alternative is the creation of school programs that meet individual needs within the context of heterogeneity, respect for diversity, and high expectations for all.

Recent efforts to create "inclusive schools" and to "detrack" are surely steps in this direction. Chapter 3 of this book provides some specific examples of the kinds of schools and classrooms necessary to meet the needs of all students. An excellent example of such a school is provided by Central Park East in New York City which has figured out ways of providing high-quality education for all children without segregating children by race, IQ, or native language (Bensman, 1987; Meier, 1989).

Schools that attempt to meet the needs of all children within the context of newly organized, newly structured "regular schools" and "regular classrooms" will require changes in school structures, curriculum, staff allocation, and teacher education. These changes are the same as those required for the full-time integration of other children previously segregated in special education classrooms. Such schools might make extensive use of cooperative learning models, peer tutoring, multilevel teaching, and integrated curricula.

Similarly, existing divisions between staff and students would disappear with multi-age, multi-ability, and flexible grouping becoming normative. There are also implications for class size, staff assignments, and teacher education. (Other chapters in this text address these issues in more detail than possible here.) But it is critical to note that these changes will not necessarily be met by widespread acceptance and acclaim, because they do embody a different set of beliefs about pedagogy, about what schools are for, and about the value of teaching students to take responsibility for one another's education. Columnist Joan Beck (1990) decries the use of cooperative learning techniques and others in which "bright" students must work with "slow students."

> Bright children already know most of what they are expected to learn during an average school year. . . . To expect them . . . to spend much of their class time helping slower learners is an inexcusable waste of their irreplaceable learning time. They need the challenge of new ideas and new material and opportunities to learn at the accelerated speed most comfortable for them. (Beck, 1990)

Challenges such as Beck's illuminate the highly political nature of schooling and the tracking debate: Is helping others a waste of time? What about the "irreplaceable learning time" of students who are left with boring, low-level teaching and curricula? We must decide whom the schools are for, and whether we really believe that all children require and deserve a quality education. It has been argued that gifted education represents some of the best current pedagogical thinking and can revitalize the entire educational system, acting as a "beacon" and a model for the educational community (Fetterman, 1988). If that is to happen, we must think critically about the values and practices that gifted programs embody and ensure that *all* students get an education of equal quality. Only then will we be able to move our schools and our society toward educational excellence *and* social justice.

REFERENCES

Beck, J. (1990. June 9). Tracking debate threatens to harm the bright children. *Grand Forks Herald*. B1, 3.

Bensman, D. (1987). *Quality education in the inner city: The story of Central Park East schools*. New York: Central Park East School.

Cornell, D. (1983). Gifted children: The impact of positive labeling on the family system. *American Journal of Orthopsychiatry, 53*, 322–335.

Csikszentmihalyi, M., & Robinson, R. E. (1986). Culture, time and the development of talent. In R. J. Sternberg & J. E. Davidson (Eds.), *Conceptions of giftedness* (pp. 264–284). New York: Cambridge University Press.

Davis. G. A., & Rimm, S. B. (1989). *Education of the gifted and talented* (2nd ed.). Englewood Cliffs: Prentice Hall.

Fetterman, D. (1988). *Excellence and equality: A qualitatively different perspective*. New York: State University of New York Press.

Fine, M. (1987). Expert testimony for Englewood School District Case.

Massachusetts Advocacy Center (1990). *Locked in/locked out: Tracking and placement practices in Boston public schools*. Boston, MA: Author.

Meier, D. (1989, May). Success in East Harlem: Question the content. *High Strides. 1*(2).

Mercer, J. R. (1973). *Labeling the mentally retarded*. Berkeley: University of California Press.

Sapon-Shevin, M. (1984). The tug of war nobody wins: Allocation of educational resources for handicapped, gifted and "typical" students. *Curriculum Inquiry, 14*(1), 57–81.

Sapon-Shevin, M. (1987a). Explaining giftedness to parents: Why it matters what professionals say. *Roeper Review, 9* (3), 180–183.

Sapon-Shevin, M. (1987b). Giftedness as a social construct. *Teachers College Record, 89*(1), 39–53.

Sapon-Shevin, M. (1990). Gifted education and the deskilling of classroom teachers. *Journal of Teacher Education, 41* (1), 39–48.

Sapon-Shevin, M. (1994). *Playing favorites: Gifted education and the disruption of community*. Albany, NY: State University of New York Press.

Silverman, L. K. (1986). What happens to the gifted girl? In C. J. Maker (Ed.), *Critical issues in gifted education: Defensible programs for the gifted*. Rockville, MD: Aspen.

Sleeter, C. E. (1986). Learning disabilities: The social construction of a special education category. *Exceptional Children, 53* (1), 46–54.

Stainback, W., & Stainback, S. (1984). A rationale for the merger of special and regular education. *Exceptional Children, 51*, 102–111.

Steinbach, T. (1981). *Parents, power, politics and your gifted child*. Chicago: Illinois Council for the Gifted.

Tolan, S. (1987). Parents and "professionals": A question of priorities. *Roeper Review, 9*(3), 184–187.

Ward, V. S. (1975). Basic Concepts. In W. B. Barbe & J. S. Renzulli (Eds.), *Psychology and education of the gifted*. New York: Irvington.

Wolleat, P. (1979). Guiding the career development of gifted females. In N. Colangelo & R. Zaffrann (Eds.), *New voices in counseling the gifted* (pp. 331–345). Dubuque, Iowa: Kendall/Hunt.

SECTION FOUR

CLASSIFICATION AND LABELING

Is classification and labeling some children in their best interest? In Chapter 7, Kliewer and Biklen point out that disability labels are ideas not facts. We create or construct them and we do so within particular cultural contexts. As a consequence, definitions of disabilities are always in flux, constantly being redefined or modified, and certainly not static, objective, natural, or a given. Kliewer and Biklen also point out a number of serious problems with disability labeling such as fostering stereotyping attitudes and actually blocking the essential agenda of good teaching.

In Chapter 8, Adelman explains that classification is necessary in terms of advancing knowledge about human problems and their amelioration. But he does note that the current system is fraught with a number of problems and suggests some possible future directions for those individuals who may want to work toward improving classification in special education.

CHAPTER 7

Labeling: Who Wants to Be Called Retarded?

CHRIS KLIEWER
DOUGLAS BIKLEN

EVERYDAY LABELS

Labels are ways people have of thinking about others. We assign many labels—athlete, musician, mother-in-law, college student, Deadhead, and ballet dancer—that locate people in relation to ourselves. Each conjures up associated group stereotypes that we use in considering who we are as individuals.

These stereotypes, often embedded deep in our culture, have a tremendous influence over how we react to people around us. For instance, to be described as a "girl" results in radically different expectations than to be described as a "boy" in our society. These differences may be assumed to be natural, or inherent, based on biological distinctions between the sexes. However, an alternative perspective recognizes that gender is a social construction: we are socialized into behaving within the constraints of traditional sex roles (Britzman, 1993; Weiler, 1988).

These different expectations are very apparent in the schooling experiences of children. Earlier in the twentieth century, home economics classes were developed as the legitimate path toward an appropriate education for girls (Hansot, 1993). Today, home economics remains associated with female gender roles while numerous other subjects remain outside the stereotype of activities believed appropriate for girls.

Mathematics is an area of study related more to boys than girls. However, this attitude is not based on ability in the content area. Girls' performance in mathematics may be equal to that of boys', demonstrating girls' active resistance to discriminatory attitudes, yet teachers have been shown to relegate girls' ability to factors other than intelligence (Walkerdine, 1990). For instance, a boy who is struggling with algebra is likely to be described as "intelligent and has potential, but needs time to develop," while a girl who is succeeding in math class may have her ability dismissed as a "tendency to follow rules well; hard work gets her by."

What is understood to be a natural distinction between the sexes in a conceptual area of schooling, with "boys" as the ideal, is actually a product of social expectations. Girls can struggle against these expectations, but the struggle itself may be misinterpreted. This chapter explores these same forces at work in the area of disability. Just as stereotyping attitudes marginalize girls from some ideal in certain areas of education, people with certain differences come to be known within various categories of the idea of disability, dramatically affecting both the way people think of them and the opportunities that are accessible to them.

DISABILITY LABELS: IDEAS NOT FACTS

Disability labels are ideas not facts. When we create or construct them, we do so within particular cultural contexts. That is, someone observes particular behaviors or ways of being and then describes these as a classification with a label. For example, the idea of autism as a particular and distinct label was first proposed by the physician Leo Kanner in 1943. He described as "autistic" children who exhibited certain behaviors, including breakdowns in communication, inability to play with other children in a typical fashion, repetitive and stereotyped actions, a desire for sameness, and a *seeming* lack of awareness or concern for the feelings and desires of people around them. Kanner lumped these observable behaviors together and called the resulting diagnosis autism.

Related descriptions are a part of current definitions of autism. Disability researcher Uta Frith (1989) contends that a primary defining point of autism is a "lack of empathy" (p. 154). She claims that "Autistic people are noted for their indifference to other people's distress, their inability to offer comfort, even to receive comfort themselves" (p. 154).

The term *autism* was introduced into the Individuals with Disabilities Education Act (Department of Education, 1992) as one of the official disability classifications.

> "Autism" means a developmental disability significantly affecting verbal and nonverbal communication and social interaction, generally evident before age 3, that adversely affects a child's educational performance. Other characteristics often associated with autism are engagement in repetitive activities and stereotyped movements, resistance to environmental change or change in daily routines, and unusual responses to sensory experiences. The term does not apply if a child's educational performance is adversely affected primarily because the child has a serious emotional disturbance. (Department of Education, 1992, p. 44801)

Interestingly, the emergence of autism as an officially recognized disability in education law occurred even as debates continued to rage about what the term really meant, who fit within the category, and whether the central elements of the category made any sense. In 1987 the prevailing

definition of autism (American Psychiatric Association, 1987) included the characteristic,

> marked lack of awareness of the existence or feelings of others (e.g., . . . does not notice another person's distress; apparently has no concept of the need of others for privacy). (p. 38)

This was a particularly interesting "characteristic" inasmuch as it was a metaphor stated as fact. Certainly an observer of an individual might interpret various actions to indicate a lack of awareness, but equally certain is the fact that the observer cannot actually know what the person is aware of. How can anyone really know what another is thinking? Clearly, this definition is an example of a hypothesis treated as if it were a fact. A few years later, that same association deleted that element of the definition but included another similar item: "lack of social and emotional reciprocity" (American Psychiatric Association, 1994).

Frith (1989) ties this seeming lack of empathy on the part of people with autism to an inability to recognize different mental states in themselves or others. She explains that people with autism lack a basic "theory of mind": They have an "inability to realize fully what it means to have a mind and to think, know, believe and feel differently from others" (p. 173).

However, autobiographical accounts by people classified as autistic, including those of individuals judged to be both "high functioning" (see Barron & Barron, 1992; Grandin & Scariano, 1986; Williams, 1992, 1994b) and "low functioning" (see Eastham, 1985; Eastham, 1992; and Sellin, 1995) challenge this presumption of aloofness and lack of concern for others. Barron and Grandin both credit their successes in part to their experiences with inclusive schooling and to the love and perseverance of family, friends, and teachers. They speak in glowing, personal terms of individuals who helped them. In her autobiography, Grandin quotes from a letter her mother sent to her camp, noting that "when Temple is in secure surroundings where she feels love above all, an appreciation, her compulsive behavior dwindles. Her voice loses its curious stress and she is in control of herself" (Grandin & Scariano, 1986, p. 48). She found that Temple's difficulties mounted when she was tired and in new circumstances, such as returning to school after a vacation.

> She wants someone near her in whom she has confidence. Her improvement is tied in, I'm sure, with appreciation and love. Until she is secure in her surroundings, knows the boundaries and feels accepted and actively appreciated, her behavior is erratic. (p. 48)

This account describes Temple's performance in a way that directly contradicts the notion that she might be aloof or unaware. Temple herself reveals deep sensitivity over and over again. For example, she once threw a book at a student who called her "Retard! You're nothing but a retard!" (p. 64).

We can see similar connectedness (as opposed to aloofness) in the words of Birger Sellin who says he longs to be "one with the ordinary people who lead lives without any confusion," "to be respected," "a person with dignity, to be loved, to know joy," "like anybody else," "functioning okay" (Sellin, 1995, p. 115).

Firsthand accounts as well as research studies, definition manuals, and theoretical commentaries suggest that the very definitions of disabilities are always in flux, constantly being redefined or modified, and certainly not static, objective, natural, or a given. We have already seen how definitions of autism are being challenged. Williams (1994a), noted author of *Nobody Nowhere* (1992) and *Somebody Somewhere* (1994b), suggests that any theorizing about autism by people without autism is born to be problematic, essentially because it is by definition ill informed. "When people without autism assume that people with autism are merely 'slow' or 'broken' versions of themselves, they may not only insult, but additionally confuse and frustrate the person with autism

with behavior that naturally stems from these arrogant and ignorant assumptions" (Williams, 1994a, p. 197).

THE CASE OF MENTAL RETARDATION

A good example of how our understanding of disability changes can be found in the case of mental retardation. The term itself is a metaphor. It might be stated thus: Some people score poorly on tests, including intelligence tests, and have difficulty with particular tasks (e.g., adaptive behavior activities such as self-care). Compared to their age peers, it is theorized that it is *as if* these individuals cannot comprehend how to answer the test questions or what has been asked of them in terms of adaptive behavior. It is *as if* their thinking is in some way held back, poorly developed, limited, retarded.

Over time the term mental retardation has come to be considered something real within the culture. This occurs as the term becomes applied to real people; is thought of as describing particular behavior; becomes associated with particular associations and vocations (e.g., American Association of Mental Retardation); is an official category written into law (e.g., mental retardation appears in the Individuals with Disabilities Education Act); is used in humor (e.g., moron jokes); has institutions and agencies to monitor, serve, and house people so labeled; and is "found" through testing (i.e., intelligence testing). As these institutional processes develop, rarely do users of the term think of it as a metaphor. Rather it is treated as something real. It has been reified.

Yet, even though it is thought to be real, it keeps changing! Mental retardation has been redefined regularly, at least every decade, typically in response to changes in ideas about testing and education, but also in response to the perceived social consequences of labeling. In the middle part of the twentieth century, there was a category of mental retardation called "borderline" that was assigned to people who scored between one and two standard deviations from the mean on intelligence tests. In 1973, the American Association on Mental Deficiency published a new classification system that erased this group from the ranks of the retarded. Apparently, a principal reason for the change was protest from lower-class and otherwise discriminated-against groups who tended to test in this category more than did other segments of the population (see p. vii, AAMD, 1973).

Similarly, the presumptions about the capabilities and futures of people with particular disability labels change regularly. In 1952 the American Psychiatric Association defined people with severe retardation as needing total restriction: "Severe refers to the functional impairment requiring custodial or complete protective care, as would be expected with IQs below 50" (cited in Biklen, 1982, p. 128). Today, half of those individuals who in 1952 would have been presumed to be severely retarded are classified as moderately retarded. And neither those with the classification of severe retardation nor those considered as having moderate retardation are seen as requiring custodial treatment. Rather, they have the right to live in and partake of community life.

Such adjustments occur for many groups whose conditions have been thought linked to retardation. In the 1960s it was commonly presumed that three-quarters of all people with cerebral palsy were retarded. With the advent of alternative communication methods (e.g., pointing, gesturing, typing on electronic and other typing devices) (Brown, 1970; Nolan, 1987; Sienkiewicz-Mercer & Kaplan, 1989), the presumption of incompetence in so many diminished. Clearly, the nature of the disabling condition had not changed. Rather, perceptions, assumptions, and opportunities had.

Similarly, note the changing assessment of Down syndrome. The example of Down syndrome is particularly instructive, for although mental retardation has not been ruled out for people with Down syndrome, presumptions of incompetence in association with Down syndrome have

undergone regular adjustment in the direction of normalcy.

> Up to the early 1900s people with Down syndrome were typically viewed as being *profoundly* mentally retarded. Surveys of children and adults during the first half of this century classified most people with Down syndrome in the severely mentally retarded category. Kirman's ... review suggested that the majority of Down syndrome children fell in the *moderately to severely* retarded range, with 2–3% achieving at the *mildly* retarded level. In the 1960s there were reports of up to 10% of cases being *educable* or *mildly* retarded. By the mid-70s it was suggested that perhaps as many as 20–50% of older children and adults with Down syndrome were in the *mild* range, with a small number even achieving within the normal range. (Clunies-Ross, 1990)

It is unlikely that Down syndrome is changing; but the demonstration and/or assessment of greater competence in people with Down syndrome must be: hence the changes in how people with Down syndrome are evaluated vis-à-vis retardation and the opportunities now made available to them. For instance, in a recent autobiographical account of two young men with Down syndrome, *Count Us In: Growing Up With Down Syndrome* (Kingsley & Levitz, 1994), Jason's and Mitchell's mothers, writing about the breaking of stereotypes, comment: "Jason and Mitchell thrived in public school. In an environment of encouragement and optimism they constantly surprised and delighted us—and their teachers—with accomplishments we'd never dreamed of" (p. 6). Jason described certain of his high school grades received in the regular classroom: "Some other grades that I had: I got 88 on my shop test, 89 on my history test, 76 on my math test—that's kind of a good grade, but I don't like it very much. Math was algebra" (p. 46). Mitchell, also included in regular education, noted: "I took U.S. government and economy. . . . It was very difficult at times. But to me it was easy to understand because I keep up in the world, what's been happening in the world and what's happening in the newspaper" (p. 53).

THE POLITICS OF LABELING: THE MYTH OF CLINICAL JUDGMENT

Lest we paint a particularly linear picture of progress toward greater and greater competence and acceptance, it is noteworthy that the twentieth century has been characterized by ever-burgeoning ranks of those classified as disabled. This development has occurred in concert with the growth of the testing movement (Gould, 1981) and with bureaucratization of the welfare state (Tomlinson, 1981). As old classifications have been altered, new ones have emerged, for example the classifications of learning disability and attention deficit disorder (Department of Education, 1992).

We might presume that once definitions of particular disabilities have been agreed upon, they would be applied in careful, objective ways, with the outcome that one's label would reflect the latest scientific knowledge. In other words, clinical judgment, derived from a meeting of specialists from fields such as psychology, social work, education, and speech communication, would determine one's program and placement. That appears to be a false assumption. In fact, the label one wears appears dependent more on where one lives than on any other factor. A government report found that in excess of 50 percent of all students with disabilities in the states of Alaska and California were identified learning disabled, while Wisconsin and South Carolina had less than one-third of their students with disabilities classified with that designation. A student classified as disabled is six times more likely to be classified as emotionally disturbed in New York as in California. A student labeled disabled in Ohio is 2.5 percent more likely to be classified as mentally retarded than a student in Wisconsin or Texas (see Biklen, 1992, pp. 101–102). To make matters even more baffling and elusive, researchers have not been able to discover differences between those students labeled and served separately and those students regarded simply as low achievers in regular classes (Ysseldyke, Algozzine, Shin, & McAve, 1982).

Contrary to popular myth, the decision as to whether a child receives a particular classification or a particular placement or program type does not often depend primarily on clinical evidence or an objective judgment about what is best for a child but on other factors. Funding and specialized programming are among the most influential factors in placement and classification. If a state provides additional funding for educating particular categories of students, educators and their districts are likely to take advantage of the perceived windfall. Similarly, funds for construction of separate buildings historically led to extensive segregated school services in Illinois, New York, New Jersey, Missouri, and Ohio (Biklen, 1992, p. 102). Also, funding patterns to individual districts can influence the percentages of students labeled disabled, as well as the proportional representation of "minorities" in special programs (Magnetti, 1982). Other factors that may supersede the mythical clinical judgment (for an elaboration of this critique, see Biklen, 1988) include the following:

> past practice of segregating students, the prior existence of separate schools, lack of experience with regular school and classroom placement of students with severe disabilities, parent advocacy, and regulatory limitation on out-of-school and out-of-district placement. (Biklen, 1992, pp. 102–103)

PROBLEMS OF BEING LABELED: HANDICAPISM AND CREATION OF THE "OTHER"

The problems with being labeled have to do with the place of disability within the culture. Disability is not a neutral term. In most quarters it is not a valued status. Rather, disability has been a perceived basis for stereotyping, prejudice, and discrimination (i.e., handicapism).

> Disabled people are scapegoats. It is not just that disabled people are different, expensive, incon-

venient, or odd: it is that they represent a threat—either . . . to order, or, to the self-conception of western human beings—who, since the Enlightenment, have viewed themselves as perfectible, as all-knowing, as god-like: able, over and above all other beings, to conquer the limitations of their nature through the victories of their culture. (Shakespeare, 1994, p. 298)

In this framework, people with disabilities are seen as being objectified, the object of the dominant culture's gaze, made into the "other." This occurs, Shakespeare argues,

> by reducing ambiguity; by physically controlling it; by avoiding it; by labeling it dangerous; by adopting it in ritual. Historical experiences—such as the freakshow, the court jester, the asylum, the Nazi extermination and so forth—can be conceptualized straightforwardly using such categories, and it is in this way that disability can be usefully regarded as anomalous, as ambiguous.
>
> Disabled people are seen to be ambiguous because they hover between humanity and animality, life and death, subjectivity and objectivity. (Shakespeare, p. 295)

People with disabilities are controlled, contained, and made into the "other" through classification and labeling, and through special programming, including special education. The dominant society exercises a persistent campaign of exclusion against them: exclusion from competency; exclusion from central location and therefore presence; exclusion from opportunity; exclusion from acceptance and valued status; and exclusion from power and self-determination.

In the next parts of this section of the chapter, we will explore the meaning of labeling to individuals who endure it, first by looking at autobiographical literature and then by examining several classroom incidents.

FIRSTHAND UNDERSTANDINGS OF LABELING

The official view of mental retardation emphasizes deficit or departure from the norm. For example, in defining retardation, the American Association of Mental Retardation (Luckasson et al., 1992) refers to individuals as having substantial limitation in present functioning as measured by:

1. Significantly subaverage intellectual functioning. This is defined as an IQ standard score of approximately 70 to 75 or below.
2. Existing concurrently . . . with limitations in adaptive skills . . . in two or more of the applicable areas (including) communication, self-care, home living, social skills, community use, self-direction, health and safety, functional academics, leisure, and work.

The idea that in being labeled retarded one is the object of a search for inadequacy or deviation from the norm is not lost on people so labeled. A self-advocacy group in Australia found itself so stereotyped by the label that it published a poster to counter the effect of being seen as nonthinkers, saying: "Don't Think That We Don't Think" (Center on Human Policy, n.d.). Bogdan concluded from his interviews of those diagnosed retarded that they say they are not retarded "because they have never really thought of . . . [themselves] as bad" (Bogdan, 1980, p. 78).

This is a good example of the cultural construction of labels. While mental retardation might be seen as a clinical term applied to people who score poorly on certain tests, its has broader meanings derived from the cultural context in which testing, categorizing, and placing people is common practice. An individual's actions are treated as "bad" or deviant by some individuals with whom the person interacts. Typically, the person with a disability does not deny the behavior, only the interpretation of it as "bad" or deviant.

In the book *The Social Meaning of Mental Retardation*, Bogdan and Taylor (1994) interview two individuals labeled retarded about their lives. They describe the institutional processes of exclusion, a process of being treated as "bad." This first example is from a man who describes the testing process that landed him in a state institution.

Tests really don't tell about the person. This is the real sad part. The guy who is doing the test, you can't really blame him—he's doing a job. He's making a living at it. The sad part of it is he fails, too, because he fails to see I am an individual, a person. The system fails because it only tells you that we have someone that we have to be responsible for and we send them off. You know, it took them three months to get me to Empire (a state institution). It's not like they put you in for three years or something. But at a state school, you're just in. You don't realize how far away these places are. It's much easier to get in than it is to get out. You lose so much. They take the human character—you've heard of raping a girl—they rape the character until by the time you get in, you feel so low you don't know what's happening. Then one day you wake up and you say, "What the fuck am I doing here?" It tears you down. (pp. 88–89)

What is retardation? It's hard to say. I guess it's having problems thinking. Some people think that you can tell if a person is retarded by looking at them. If you think that way you don't give people the benefit of the doubt. You judge a person by how they look or how they talk or what the tests show, but you can never really tell what is inside the person. (pp. 90–91)

In a second example from Bogdan and Taylor (1994) we see a young woman decrying certain human service labels as masks for exclusion.

They call it a training school. Now they call it a developmental center. Those names don't hit no bell. Developmental sounded to me like they were really trying to get kids developed. That's not what really goes on there. They try to make a name for it, but the names they are using is not what they are doing at all. They should name it for what they are doing, but they don't want anybody to know. I would name it "prison." A prison home. That is really what it was. (p. 137)

Not surprisingly, people labeled retarded often try to escape (i.e., disaffiliate with) their diagnosis because being labeled retarded results in their lack of access to the opportunities enjoyed by non-labeled people. Patrick Worth, president of People First Ontario levied a national campaign to change the name of the Canadian Association for Retarded Citizens to the Canadian Association for Community Living. Worth has elaborated on why he does not accept his diagnosis: "Nobody has the right to label someone retarded." He pointed out that the label acted as a kind of punishment, keeping people from getting jobs and prohibiting them from living where they wanted. "It is demoralizing to see someone as a label instead of [as] somebody. I am somebody. My name is Patrick Worth. I am not retarded. I don't think anyone is. I think labels are unnecessary" (Worth, 1988, p. 48).

Mitchell Levitz, in *Count Us In*, is asked if he ever thinks about being considered someone without Down syndrome. He responds: "Yes. . . . I don't know how to say this—but I'd rather think of myself as normal than as a disability" (p. 48). Jason Kingsley explains that being considered mentally retarded has been a source of harassment in certain classrooms. He feels dehumanized: "People who do the teasing don't know that I have feelings. My feelings get hurt" (p. 46). When asked if he's strong enough to tell those teasing him to stop, Jason replies: "I think I'm strong enough to tell them, 'Hey stop it you bastard' " (p. 49).

Clearly, certain labels have more pejorative connotations within the culture than others. We have chosen to focus mainly on mental retardation because it is the disability category in which we can see the most extreme effects of exclusionary practice. A prevailing theme in the accounts of labeled people about the label of mental retardation is that it should not be applied to anyone.

Recently, alternative and augmentative communication approaches have given a voice to many who have previously been diagnosed retarded. A common message typed out by those individuals armed with a new means of communication is the desire to escape the label of mental retardation.

Lucy (age 17 and previously identified as having an intelligence score of 42) frequently types about "intelligence," rendering it as a feeling of competence from someone "inside," and describing how relieved she is that facilitation (the method by which she learned to type her thoughts) has allowed others to see that inside intelligence:

THIS HAS CHANGED MY WHOLE LIFE. I CAN NOW TELL PEOPLE HOW INTELLIGENT I AM INSIDE. I CAN TELL PEOPLE WHAT I LIKE AND DISLIKE. I AM ME AND EVERYONE CAN LOVE ME NOW BECAUSE I AM A GOOD AND VALUABLE PERSON. . .

Learning to type has been my rebirti as a nosrmal person . . . someone who does anything tieh want with their life. people understand that i am an intelligent person e very one wants to be treated with respect. (Biklen & Duchan, 1994)

Describing what it was like before she had such a means of expression, she explained that it was as if "i was a clown in a world that was not a circus" (McClellan, 1991).

Sharisa Kochmeister is a fifteen year old who now can communicate by typing on a computer. When she began to learn to type, she required facilitation in the form of a communication partner (e.g., a family member, teacher, or friend) holding her hand or arm as she hunted for letters on a keyboard. She has since progressed to where she can type independently (i.e., with no physical support). Prior to learning to type, she had a measured intelligence quotient of 15; upon retesting after she learned to type, her intelligence quotient was measured at 142 (see Watts & Wurzburg, 1994). When asked what has made the biggest difference in her life now that she can type with no direct physical support, Sharisa responded: "OTHER PEOPLE KNOWING I'M SMART AND SELF CONTROL AND ESTEEM." Sharisa explained that she had to overcome others' "DISBELIEF IN MY INTELLECT AND INTEGRITY [and] MY OWN DOUBTS ABOUT BEING READY TO GIVE UP SUPPORT AND CONTACT" (Watts & Wurzburg, 1994).

Lucy and Sharisa do not consider themselves mentally retarded. To them, the label was something unwanted, something imposed on them, a terrible misunderstanding, a wall between the people they knew themselves to be and the world. It was something that stood between them and the chance to be seen as valuable.

We can further surmise that even had they not developed their newfound means of communication, the treatment they received when labeled retarded was demoralizing. In this regard their comments parallel those of Worth, Levitz, and Kingsley and of the two individuals interviewed by Bogdan and Taylor. They would rather have been regarded as competent than as incompetent (i.e., excluded from the ranks of the able).

In stark contrast to the reject-the-label approach to challenging society's exclusionary practices, some people and groups have adopted the label as a kind of badge of solidarity, taking it on with pride, as an affront to the dominant culture. This is most apparent in the Deaf pride movement and among people with physical disabilities. Biklen (1992) characterized this approach in an earlier account.

Nancy Mairs adopts "crippled" as her label of preference, with the intent to shock; "People—crippled or not—wince at the word 'cripple,' as they do not at 'handicapped' or 'disabled.' Perhaps I want them to wince. I want them to see me as a tough customer, one to whom the fates/gods/viruses have not been kind, but who can face the brutal truth or her existence squarely. As a cripple, I swagger." She selects "cripple" as a way of saying, "I accept myself for who I am, and I am going to force you to accept me on the same terms." (p. 11)

Mairs accepts herself as a full person and does not accept less from others. She will force society to admit its practice of labeling and to live with the knowledge of what it does in labeling people (Mairs, 1986).

CASE EXAMPLES OF LABELING IN SCHOOLS

A disability category applied to an individual has a profound effect on how we understand that person. Though we easily may recognize people without disabilities as complex and multifaceted, when a label is applied to a person, that often becomes central to our understanding of who she or he is. For instance, instead of understanding someone with autism as having varied interests and passions, we may tend to dismiss, ignore, or misinterpret any behavior other than what supports the stereotypes we have come to associate with autism. As an example, an elementary school psychologist, echoing Frith's (1989) contention that people with autism lacked a "theory of mind," recently told a group of student interns in the field of social work that they should expect to "get nothing back" from their work with the children in the school labeled autistic. He suggested that the children lacked any emotional investment in the people who cared for them most. Accepting this psychologist's belief, one of the student social workers later questioned whether a particular child was autistic because she saw him hug his mother. Such a behavior, common to all children including those considered autistic, assaulted her understanding of the label. However, rather than changing her definition of autism, she chose to retain her stereotypes and dismiss the child as someone who mistakenly was added to the category.

Labels have a way of drawing our attention away from understanding the individual as a complex and competent person. Rather, what we see is reinterpreted within the stereotypes associated with the particular disability category. Just as girls may not be expected to participate in and do well in academic subjects, people with disabilities may also find themselves excluded from particular contexts. Mark was an eleven-year-old boy with Down syndrome in a classroom described as self-contained for "mildly" disabled children with learning disabilities. Mark's teacher considered him to be one of his more capable students in various subjects including reading. However, due to the appearance of Down syndrome, people's expectations for Mark were limited.

In one field research observation, a substitute teacher was seen leading the class through a reading activity on "drawing conclusions." After reading a paragraph out loud, she would ask a student to respond to a question about the paragraph. The substitute teacher did not call on Mark until the final question. By this time, most students' attention, including Mark's, had wandered. However,

at hearing his name he sat up and looked in the direction of the teacher, calling out, "What?" Several students laughed and jeered at Mark, often a focus of their teasing. The substitute teacher asked, "Where might Mr. Jones find what he's looking for?" Mark responded without hesitation, "He should go to grocery store."

The substitute teacher said, "Wow! Very good!" It was one of the few correct responses she had received. Several of the students snickered and hooted. The teacher asked Mark a follow-up question, something she had not done with any other student. It was difficult to hear her above the noise of the class. Mark laid his head down on his desk and covered it with his hands. The substitute teacher shouted her question again over the noise, calling out, "Mark! I'm talking to you, Mark!" Mark remained with his head down. The substitute teacher cried out above the fray, "Quiet! Even if he could respond I couldn't hear him."

When later questioned about how she thought the lesson had gone for Mark, the substitute teacher responded: "Oh, it was tough. You know? I think it's great he's given this chance. I mean to be in a class like this, but really. Is it for him? It's tough. Could he really do it?" Mark's correct response was seemingly forgotten. The teacher's focus was on his covered head and the fact that he didn't answer her second question, which made her doubt whether a child with Down syndrome should even be in a self-contained classroom for children with learning disabilities (i.e., a classification not associated with mental retardation).

SCHOOLING WITHOUT LABELS: WHAT WOULD IT LOOK LIKE?

Questioning the assumptions associated with disability labels does not mean we believe all people are equally capable in all areas. Clearly, we are different from one another. The important consideration, though, is how we come to understand what those differences mean. What is the meaning of scoring at least two standard deviations below some presumed norm on what is described as an intelligence test? Traditionally, it has meant that an individual will receive a label of mental retardation resulting in his or her exclusion from regular classrooms and from the community.

Differences do not inherently or naturally result in labels or forced segregation. Rather, those things are reactions created by society at a given point in history. Currently, the inclusive schooling movement, in which children are not segregated from regular classrooms based on the idea of disability, is a central challenge to the idea that labels are helpful in the education and life of a person who carries the label. Biklen (1992) described the various facets involved in purposeful inclusion of all people with disabilities: the idea of inclusive education recognized that people not trained in special education can learn the skills of working with individual children in regular classrooms; purposeful inclusion was unconditional, and took place in an atmosphere in which diversity was accepted as having a positive impact on all people within the context; labels were avoided, and the person with disabilities was thought of as a unique individual with gifts and needs as complex as those of people not considered disabled.

Such observations are supported by regular education teachers who have children with severe disabilities as a part of their classroom (Giangreco, Dennis, Cloninger, Edelman, & Schattman, 1993). Giangreco et al. (1993) quote several elementary and junior high school teachers with inclusive classrooms who were a part of their research project. Of the nineteen teachers described, seventeen suggested they had gone through a transformation process: when the students with disabilities entered their rooms, they were thought of as outsiders, in some cases as not quite human. Over time these perceptions dramatically changed.

> I started seeing him as a little boy. I started feeling that he's a person too. He's a student. Why should I not teach him? He's in my class. That's my responsibility, I'm a teacher. (p. 365)

> Now that I've dealt with her, I have rolled her down the hill and I've taken her sliding with the other kids and stuff. She's a little girl like everyone else. (p. 365)

The idea that children with disabilities are complete and unique members of inclusive classrooms is a dramatic part of our own on-going research. Many teachers recognize that they must see beyond the label or, ideally, set aside the label, to understand the child. One second-grade teacher, whose inclusive classroom included three children with disability labels, two described as autistic and one considered mentally retarded due to Down syndrome, bristled at the idea that those children did not fit into her classroom. In describing Lee, the child with Down syndrome, she said,

> If you came into the room and were told there's a retarded child in the class, a child with special needs, I don't think you would pick Lee out. The (other) kids seem to really believe that he's as capable as they are, intellectually the same.

Lee has extremely limited spoken language. He communicates through the use of several hand signs, and through typing on a letterboard. He was observed taking a test with the other children in his reading group. Lee would point to the multiple choice response he felt best fit the question asked by the teacher. As the test progressed, Lee became more and more agitated between his responses, twisting his body around and making loud growling sounds. His teacher, after asking him to remain quiet, said to the group, "I think Lee is telling us that we're going too slowly for him. I'm going to pick up the pace, and if any of you need to slow down we'll work that out." Lee immediately calmed down and focused on the remaining portion of the test. Later, while reflecting on the test, the teacher said,

> See, I think we're at a ceiling in terms of him being at a real comfortable level. A lot of the other kids are actually going too slow for him. He gets frustrated—That's the feeling I get. Yeah—so we let him work ahead, and make sure he's ready when it's his turn to be called on.

Clearly, this teacher's expectations do not fit the traditional assumptions associated with the labels of Down syndrome or mental retardation. In the inclusive classroom, he is seen as a competent member of the group working at a level beyond many of his peers. In order to understand him in this way, though, the teacher had to confront stereotypes she held about what it means to be a person with Down syndrome. Initially, these stereotypes were seemingly affirmed in some ways by Lee's aggressive tantrums. This teacher came to recognize those behaviors as manifestations of frustration that occurred when his intellect was not taken seriously.

Another teacher in an inclusive preschool setting described her resistance to a school psychologist's interpretation of one of her toddlers with Down syndrome. The psychologist was giving the child a formal cognitive assessment in which one item called for the child to separate blocks and spoons, placing the blocks in a container, and the spoons in the container's lid. She said,

> Have you ever seen this (assessment) item? Well, toddlers don't do that. Isaac picked up every spoon, pretended to taste from them, then threw them on the floor, and put all the blocks over here. And he didn't get credit for it! He didn't do it right, but he clearly knew which was the block and which was the spoon. Also, we'd been working all year—his family is really into pretending . . . so of course he was going to eat with those spoons. He wasn't going to put them in the lid which is not what you do with spoons.

The psychologist used Isaac's behavior to further ideas of his incompetence. The teacher resisted this interpretation, understanding Isaac's response to the test item as a normal toddler response to the situation.

In another preschool situation, in a class of three- and four-year-old children, we observed a close relationship between Abraham, a child with Down syndrome, and Benny, a child considered nondisabled. Both were described by their teacher as "readers," a label given to those children who are known to be able to read text from children's literature. Most of their preschool peers were not described as readers. When asked what seemed to be the foundation of the two children's relationship, the teacher replied without hesitation,

"Books. A lot of what they talk about is books. They would spend all day together flipping through books." Abraham's spoken language was extremely difficult to decipher, and in fact was clearest when reciting a story. In this example, a child with Down syndrome has exciting literacy skills that might remain unseen if traditional expectations were placed over him, and those skills served in part to develop friendships based on shared interests.

Biklen (1992, p. 161) describes a fourth-grade inclusive classroom in which Tammy, considered to have a disability, was socially isolated. Rather than assuming this was inherently a part of her disability label, several of her peers began writing her notes. Tammy was a prolific reader, and the notes became an important social connection between her and her classmates. The teacher, seeing the importance of the notes, instituted a mail system in the class so all the children could write to one another. The children in the class did not see Tammy as naturally separated from them. Rather, they altered the way they approached her in order to build friendships demonstrating that limitations associated with disabilities may have more to do with the mindset of people without disabilities than with the minds of people with disabilities.

CONCLUSION

Labels block the essential agenda of good teaching, namely inquiry through dialogue and interaction, teacher with student. Vivian Gussin Paley (1989) describes the problem well when she notes that in college, teachers often were alienated from the complexity of children when they would study " 'faceless' children and were given maps that promised to tell us where every child lives. Yet we felt anonymous and were unable to locate ourselves on the maps" (p. vii). She reminds us that we typically learn the language and customs of the profession outside of classrooms, disconnected from students. Yet when we meet a child, or for that matter anyone, "the script must be rewritten," that is, if we want to know the person in his or her complexity. And for this to work, she argues, we must learn to study ourselves, asking, "What really is going on here? What do my words mean? What am I missing?" (p. vii). Labels are words for us to question. What do we intend by them? What do we really think we learn from them? Whose interests do they serve?

Who wants to be called retarded? Does assigning a particular disability label to a person help that individual in any way? Earlier in this century, researchers interested in disability described people as idiots, imbeciles, or morons depending on their assumed level of handicap (Blatt, 1987). Were these labels really any more pejorative than the terms we use today? Traditionally, the social meaning of mental retardation has been forced segregation from one's own community, and the stigmatization that goes along with the notion that the labeled person is somehow defective, less than human. Norman Kunc (1994), a disability rights advocate who himself is considered to have cerebral palsy, told a hushed audience, "I am not broken! I am not broken! I am a representative of the diversity of the human race!" The use of disability labels by professionals in the various fields associated with special education and rehabilitation highlight an individual's supposed weaknesses, her or his assumed defects. Often, this practice hides the complexity and uniqueness of the person labeled. Recognition of the gifts and abilities of people occurs in places and circumstances in which labels and the stereotypes they elicit, are cast aside.

REFERENCES

American Association of Mental Deficiency. (1973). *Manual on Terminology and Classification in Mental Retardation.* Washington, DC: Author.

American Psychiatric Association. (1987). *Diagnostic and Statistical Manual of Mental Disorders,* (3rd ed.). Washington, DC: Author.

American Psychiatric Association. (1994). *Diagnostic and Statistical Manual of Mental Disorders* (4th ed.). Washington, DC: Author.

Barron, J., & Barron, S. (1992). *There's a boy in here.* New York: Simon & Schuster.

Biklen, D., & Duchan, J. (1994). "I am intelligent": The social construction of mental retardation. *Journal of the Association for Persons with Severe Handicaps, 19* (3), 173–184.

Biklen, D. (1982). The least restrictive environment: Its application to education. In G. B. Melton (Ed.), *Legal reforms affecting child & youth services.* New York: Haworth.

Biklen, D. (1988). The myth of clinical judgement. *Journal of Social Issues, 44*(1), 127–140.

Biklen, D. (1992). *Schooling without labels.* Philadelphia: Temple University Press.

Blatt, B. (1987). *The conquest of mental retardation.* Austin, TX: Pro-Ed.

Bogdan, R. (1980). What does it mean when a person says, 'I am not retarded'? *Education and training of the mentally retarded, 15*(1), 74–79.

Bogdan, R., & Taylor, S. (1994). *The social meaning of mental retardation: Two life stories.* New York: Teachers College Press.

Britzman, D. P. (1993). Beyond rolling models: Gender and multicultural education. In S. K. Biklen & D. Pollard (Eds.), *Gender and education* (pp. 25–42). Chicago: National Society for the Study of Education.

Brown, C. (1970). *Down all the days.* London: Mandarin.

Center on Human Policy. (n.d.) Don't Think That We Don't Think. (Poster). Syracuse, NY: Human Policy Press.

Clunies-Ross, G. (1990). *The right to read: Publishing for people with reading disabilities.* Canberra: National Library of Australia.

Department of Education (1992, September 29) *Assistance to States for the Education of Children with Disabilities Program and Preschool Grants for Children with Disabilities; Final Rule.* 34 CFR Parts 300 & 301. Washington DC: Federal Register (Vol. 57, No. 189, 44794–45852).

Eastham, D. (1985). *Understand.* Ottawa: Oliver & Pate.

Eastham, M. (1992). *Silent words.* Ottawa: Oliver & Pate.

Frith, U. (1989). *Autism: Explaining the enigma.* Cambridge, MA: Basil Blackwell.

Giangreco, M., Dennis, R., Cloninger, C., Edelman, S., & Schattman, R. (1993). "I've counted Jon": Transformational experiences of teachers educating students with disabilities. *Exceptional Children, 59* 359–372.

Gould, S. J. (1981). *The mismeasure of man.* New York: W. W. Norton.

Grandin, T., & Scariano, M. M. (1986). *Emergence: Labeled autistic.* Novato, CA: Arena.

Hansot, E. (1993). Historical and contemporary views of gender and education. In S. K. Biklen & D. Pollard (Eds.), *Gender and education* (pp. 12–24). Chicago: National Society for the Study of Education.

Kanner, L. (1943). Autistic disturbances of affective contact. *Nervous Child, 2,* 217–250.

Kingsley, J., & Levitz, M. (1994). *Count us in: Growing up with Down syndrome.* San Diego: Harcourt Brace & Co.

Kunc, N. (1994). *Hell-bent on helping: Benevolence, friendship, and the politics of help.* Keynote presented at the 4th Annual Facilitated Communication Conference, Syracuse, NY.

Luckasson, R., Coulter, D. L. Polloway, E. A., Reiss, S., Schalock, R. L., Snell, M. E., Spitalnick, D. M., & Stark, J. A. (1992). *Mental retardation: Definition, classification, and systems of supports* (9th ed.). Washington, DC: American Association of Mental Retardation.

Mairs, N. (1986). *Plaintext: Deciphering a woman's life.* New York: Harper & Row.

Magnetti, S. S. (1982). Some potential incentives of special education funding practices. In K. A. Heller, W. H. Hotzman, & S. S. Messick (Eds.), *Placing children in special education: A strategy for equity* (pp. 300–321). Washington, DC: National Academy Press.

McClellan, A. (1991). Breaking the silence. (Television segment). Sydney, Australia: 60 Minutes Australia.

Nolan, C. (1987). *Under the eye of the clock.* New York: St. Martin's Press.

Paley, V. G. (1989). Preface. In W. A. Ayers, *The good preschool teacher.* New York: Teachers College Press.

Sellin, B. (1995) *I don't want to be inside me anymore.* New York: Basic Books.

Shakespeare, T. (1994). Cultural representation of disabled people: Dustbins for disavowal? *Disability & Society, 9*(3), 283–300.

Sienkiewicz-Mercer, R., & Kaplan, S. B. (1989). *I raise my eyes to say yes.* Boston: Houghton Mifflin.

Tomlinson, S. 1981. *Educational subnormality: A study in decision-making.* London: Routledge & Kegan Paul.

Walkerdine, V. (1990). *Schoolgirl fictions.* New York: Verso.

Watts, G., & Wurzburg (1994). (Videotape). *Every Step of the Way: Toward Independent Communication.* Syracuse NY: Syracuse University, Facilitated Communication Institute.

Weiler, K. (1988). *Women teaching for change: Gender, class, and power.* New York: Bergin & Garvey.

Williams, D. (1994a). In the real world, *Journal of the Association of Persons with Severe Handicaps, 19*(3) 196–199.

Williams, D. (1992). *Nobody Nowhere.* New York: Times Books.

Williams, D. (1994b). *Somebody Somewhere.* New York: Times Books.

Worth, P. (1988). You've got a friend. In D. Gold & J. McGill (Eds.), *The pursuit of leisure* (pp. 47–52). Downsview, Ont.: G. Allan Roeher Institute.

Ysseldyke, J., Algozzine, B., Shinn, M., & McAve, M. (1982). Similarities and differences between low achievers and students classified learning disabled. *Journal of Special Education, 16,* 73–84.

CHAPTER 8

Appreciating the Classification Dilemma

HOWARD S. ADELMAN

Nothing less than the futures of children is at stake.
—(Hobbs, 1975, p. 1)

"What's the use of their having names," the Gnat said, "if they won't answer to them?"

"No use to them," said Alice, "but it is useful to people who name them, I suppose. If not, why do things have names at all?" (Lewis Carroll, *Through the Looking Glass*)

What's in a name? Assignment of a label plays a major role in decisions to intervene and can profoundly shape a person's future. In education and psychology, for example, particular attention is paid to labeling problems in human functioning (i.e., diagnostic classification) with a view to doing something about such problems. People associate strong images with specific diagnostic labels and tend to act upon these images. Sometimes the images are useful generalizations; sometimes they are harmful stereotypes. Because of the potential harm caused by diagnostic classification, the practice of labeling individuals is widely criticized. Attacks range from critiques of specific labels to arguments against all diagnostic categorizing.

Those who study diagnostic classification are especially concerned about the role labeling plays in segregating individuals with physical, cognitive, social, and emotional differences—including a disproportionate number from minority groups. In this regard, many writers discuss how society's interests shape decisions about which psychological and educational phenomena are given primary attention. It is commonplace to use political processes in establishing guidelines that define problems, differentiate one phenomenon from another, and shape the planning, implementation, and evaluation of intervention (see Adelman & Taylor, 1994).

With respect to diagnostic classification of children, cautions about potential abuses of labeling provide a window for understanding society's role and interests.

> Categories and labels are powerful instruments for social regulation and control, and they are often employed for obscure, covert, or hurtful purposes: to degrade people, to deny them access to opportunity, to exclude "undesirables" whose presence in some way offends, disturbs familiar custom, or demands extraordinary effort.... Society defines what is exceptional or deviant, and appropriate treatments are designed quite as much to protect society as they are to help the child.... "To take care of them" can and should be read with two meanings: to give children help and to exclude them from the community. (Hobbs, 1975)

Few would deny that labeling can have negative effects. And awareness of this possibility is a good reason for care in how labels are used. Moreover, evidence that negative effects outweigh benefits is a good reason to do away with a particular label. But such concerns are not sufficient reasons to stop classifying phenomena. They simply underscore that diagnostic labeling, like all classification in science, is a flawed enterprise.

Scientists know that distinguishing among phenomena is a practical necessity and an ethical imperative in advancing knowledge. As Aristotle, the father of all classificationists, stated: "To think is to order." Ultimately, conceptual and methodological schemes for differentiating people, places, problems, programs, actions, outcomes, and so forth provide the terminology to facilitate communication related to describing and understanding phenomena (permitting parsimony without simplicity and aiding recognition of fundamental structures and relationships). Thus, classification schemes play a key role in improving and providing new directions for theory, research, and practice (e.g., Adelman & Taylor, 1994; Cantwell & Rutter, 1994; Blashfield, 1993; McReynolds, 1989; Reynolds, 1991; Widiger & Ford-Black, 1994; Widiger & Trull, 1991).

Even writers who challenge the tenets of logical positivism and those who stress the holistic nature of phenomena find it necessary to conceive parts of the whole to advance understanding. Despite the dilemmas involved in breaking phenomena apart, classification remains an indispensable tool. As Neisser (1976) notes: "We cannot perceive unless we anticipate"; he cautions, however, "we must not see only what we anticipate" (p. 43).

Given the many concerns about classification, the search continues for the most useful labels and for ways to minimize negative effects. One criterion of a "good" label is that the designation helps more than it hurts. This, of course, raises the question: Who is the label supposed to help? Researchers? Practitioners? Clients? Client advocates? Society? Each may have a different vested interest; each may have a different motivation or need for using a label; each may use different labels; and each may use different criteria in weighing benefits and costs. Thus, how "good" a particular label is usually depends on whose interests and needs are referenced in making the judgment.

To provide a fundamental appreciation of classification as it affects special education, this chapter briefly (1) reviews concerns about special education labeling, (2) highlights fundamentals related to diagnostic classification, (3) illustrates the potential value of broadening the bases for such classification, (4) outlines ways to minimize negative effects, and (5) underscores the degree to which a chosen classification scheme shapes the essence of the field.

CONCERNS ABOUT SPECIAL EDUCATION LABELING

The history of special education is marked by frequent changes in diagnostic terminology (e.g., terms such as *idiot* and *feebleminded* have been replaced by terms designating degree of mental retardation). In addition, new categories are added (e.g., learning disabilities), and efforts are made to differentiate subgroups within existing ones (e.g., to distinguish between blindness and partial sightedness). Paralleling this activity over the last thirty-five years have been calls for radical shifts away from traditional special education categories (e.g., Adelman, 1992; Dunn, 1968; Hobbs, 1975, 1980; Johnson, 1962; Lilly, 1992; Reynolds, 1984; Reynolds, Zetlin, & Wang, 1993; Ysseldyke, 1987).

Throughout the field's history, concerns about diagnostic labels and identification practices have been legion. For example, in recommending development of a new "comprehensive diagnostic and classification system for handicapped, disadvantaged, and delinquent children," the conclusion of the influential *Report of the Project on Classification of Exceptional Children* (Hobbs, 1975) was that

> available classification systems are gross and inadequate. They obscure both the uniqueness of individual children and the similarities of children assigned to various categories. Gross classification leads to gross and inadequate solutions to problems at every level of concern. Federal, state, and local governments are organized on the basis of outmoded classification concepts. . . . The familiar categories of exceptionality have limited value in planning education or treatment programs for most exceptional children. (pp. 233, 236)

Prevailing technical criticisms of diagnostic procedures are that they lack reliability and validity, do not validly indicate specific treatment needs, and lead to fragmentation of services and training (cf. Adelman, 1971; Adelman & Taylor, 1983, 1993, 1994; Hobbs, 1975; Jenkins, Pious, & Peterson, 1988; Macmann, Barnett, Lombard, Belton-Kocher, & Sharp, 1989; Reynolds, 1984; Reynolds, Wang, & Walberg, 1987). Critics also stress ethical and legal concerns. Some refer to a growing "bounty hunter" mentality. Others emphasize how categories lead to segregating children (e.g., Adelman & Taylor, 1984; Heller, Holtzman, & Messick, 1982; Lipsky & Gartner, 1989). Such concerns are bolstered by the view that current forms of special programming produce insufficient benefits to warrant labeling and special placements (e.g., see Gartner & Lipsky, 1987; Glass, 1983; Jenkins et al., 1988; Leinhardt & Pallay, 1982; Stainback & Stainback, 1984) and by a desire to change attitudes toward individuals with handicapping conditions (Hobbs, 1975). Many of these concerns also find support in "the principle of normalization" (Bank-Mikkelsen, 1976; Wolfensberger, 1972). This principle is associated with antilabeling, mainstreaming, and deinstitutionalization policies, and what in the United States has been dubbed the regular or general education initiative and the movement toward inclusion (i.e., educational integration).

In addition, present labeling practices are criticized for colluding with the presumptive tendency toward viewing learning and behavior problems as caused by pathology within the individual (e.g., Adelman, 1971, 1992; Hobbs, 1975). This tendency downplays the possibility that many persons assigned labels have problems initially caused (and perhaps maintained) by environmental factors. Downplaying the environment's role when making a diagnosis keeps intervention narrowly focused on individuals. That is, interventions to alter environmental systems that cause problems for individuals are de facto deemphasized, and strategies to increase individual coping and adaptation are overemphasized.

And, of course, assigning a label to an individual raises concern about negative consequences (e.g., harmful stereotyping and stigmatization, undermining self-esteem, generating negative expectations, misidentification, and misprescription). The hope is that the benefits the individual accrues will be greater than the costs. However, with respect to special education labels, research is equivocal regarding how often good outweighs harm and vice versa (cf. MacMillan & Hendrick, 1993; MacMillan & Meyers, 1979). Thus, it is not surprising that changes in diagnostic labels stem as much from socio-political-economic considerations and rational analyses as from scientific activity (e.g., see Reid, Maag, & Vasa [1994] on the move to make attention deficit hyperactivity disorder a disability category).

The above concerns characterize the state of the art now and for the near future. Some use the concerns to support the position that all diagnostic classification is so flawed as to warrant noncategorical identification of individuals with educational and psychosocial problems and physically handicapping conditions (see discussions by Hobbs, 1980; Jenkins et al., 1988; Morsink, Thomas, & Smith-Davis, 1987; National Association of School Psychologists, 1986; Reynolds, 1984; Reynolds et al., 1993).

Given the deficiencies and negative impact of differential diagnostic labels, procedures, and policies, dissatisfaction with current special education labels and diagnostic procedures is quite understandable and appropriate. Calls for improvement in classification and identification systems certainly are warranted and timely; calls for eliminating all classification and identification are premature. As suggested above, when it comes to advancing knowledge about human problems and their amelioration, some form of classification and identification is both a practical necessity and an ethical imperative. At this time, addressing the classification problem means finding better ways to categorize phenomena, rather than finding ways to do away with classification. In this respect, it should be stressed that not all critics of categorical special education programs are against classification in some form (e.g., Reynolds et al., 1993; Wang & Walberg, 1988). The interest of many is in replacing current categories with a system that identifies special individual needs (1) only as such needs become relevant to providing an appropriate education and (2) through a process and terminology that have direct relevance to intervention and that minimize negative consequences.

It also should be pointed out that opponents of radical efforts to do away with special education classification and revamp special education warn of resultant inequities (e.g., Fuchs & Fuchs, 1994; Kauffman, 1989, 1993). Specifically, they argue that many students will suffer because teachers will lack the competence and time required to deal with the diversity of educational needs in their classrooms. In addition, they stress that support for special education will be jeopardized because the general public, elected officials, policy makers, judges, administrators, and so forth will not appreciate special individual needs. To bolster their argument, the experience in England and Wales is cited as evidence that negative consequences result when categories of handicap are abolished (Feniak, 1988).

In sum, even after all the concerns are laid out, there remains the problem of classifying problems in ways that maximize the benefits for science and practice, and minimize the negative consequences to individuals and society. I hasten to add that to argue for classification is not to argue that provision of all forms of special help should be tied to formal diagnoses. The point simply is that classification is essential to scientific advances and basic to efforts to improve intervention efficacy in applied fields such as special education. Indeed, the classification problem is one of four fundamental problems associated with intervention theory (Adelman & Taylor, 1988, 1994). Ultimately, the nature of intervention planning, implementation, and evaluation is inextricably intertwined with how the classification problem is handled.

SOME FUNDAMENTALS RELATED TO DIAGNOSTIC CLASSIFICATION

The importance of and difficulty in dealing with the classification problem is reflected in the continuous debates over how to define and differentiate educational and psychosocial problems and psychopathology (cf. Adelman, 1994, in press; Adelman & Taylor, 1986, 1994; Kazdin & Kagan, 1994; Reynolds, 1984). Considering all the discussion, it is surprising how little attention has been paid to classification per se. Any argument for or against diagnostic classification should be based first and foremost on a fundamental appreciation of the nature of diagnostic classification.

Conceptually, the task of defining and differentiating educational and psychosocial problems and psychopathology is tantamount to the general task of classification or taxonomic sorting. Wojciechowski (1974) nicely places the task into philosophical and empirical perspective: "To take the problem of classification seriously is, and has always been, a sign of intellectual maturity and a prerequisite for effective investigation of reality. [The problem is] as old as philosophy and as open and unsettled as a philosophical system." He argues that the problem remains unsettled because two opposing factors are at play and counterbalance each other: "the imperative desire of the intellect to understand the overwhelming richness of the phenomena . . . and the varied and varying, seemingly endless multiplicity of data." Given this, our choice is to attempt to formulate a global and exhaustive classification ("reach for the apparently supreme intellectual ideal of the total conceptual horizon") or to be less grandiose and opt for what is more attainable and less controversial—partial classification. The two choices, of course, are complementary (but this is not to say that total classifications result from combining partial ones).

Providing a psychological perspective, Datta and Farradane (1974) postulate that the desire to find order is a basic human "drive." As a cognitive activity, classification involves more than ordering entities, activities, or other elements of external reality; it is an "organization of our mental concepts or constructs of external entities and elements." Moreover, they see classification as not just concerned with grouping concepts by selected characteristics, but focused on the relationships between concepts or groups of concepts.

Theoretically generated classification begins with a definition of the domain to be described, decisions about level of generality, and creation of categories into which phenomena will be ordered. Categories are formed along vertical (i.e., hierarchical) and horizontal dimensions. The process of constructing categories may be inductive, deductive, or both. How many class categories are created depends essentially on one's ability to abstract from one's experience (including statistical analyses). The categories may range in level of abstraction from highly descriptive to extremely abstract.

Principles used in constructing such classes usually are closely related to the purposes for which the classification scheme is developed. In this regard, researchers may adopt different principles from practitioners, and both may prefer to classify phenomena differently from advocates, policy makers, and administrators.

Classification, of course, involves more than developing a conceptual scheme; it requires reliable procedures for differentiating (e.g., operationally identifying) phenomena of interest. Differentiations may be of a qualitative (i.e., different kinds) or quantitative nature (i.e., differences in degree) and are meant to reduce heterogeneity (i.e., partition out variance) in desired ways. A constant problem, however, is the graduated rather than discrete nature of so much phenomena that are of interest (see Widiger & Trull, 1991).

A great deal of criticism aimed at special education and psychiatric classification activity stems from the fact that current identification procedures result in heterogeneous groupings. That is, individuals assigned the same diagnostic label may differ with reference to symptoms, causes, current performance, and prognosis. At the simplest level, this criticism raises the point that a group assigned a particular label encompasses important subgroups. At a more complex level, this criticism suggests that the diagnostic label does not capture the essence of an important class of phenomena.

To clarify this crucial matter: Homogeneity is not a quality inherent in a phenomenon, but a construction of the observer and classifier. Take, for example, the delineation in biological classification of a genus and the species it encompasses. If a particular diagnostic label (e.g., depression, learning disabilities) is like a genus, it cannot be criticized for not designating the significant subgroups (species) within it. However, if the label is more akin to a species than a genus, the group of which it is a subgroup should be clarified. In either case, the problem is not heterogeneity per se. From this perspective, Zigler and Phillips (1961) conclude "it would perhaps be more fruitful to dispense entirely with the homogeneity–heterogeneity distinction . . . allowing us to direct our attention to the underlying problem of the relative merits of different classificatory principles."

Heterogeneity aside, efforts to classify psychological and educational problems use taxonomies and typologies defined in terms of current dysfunctioning, causal factors, intervention implications, or some combination of all of these. (For our purposes here, the debate that distinguishes taxonomies from typologies is ignored.) General strategies for developing classification schemes include the use of (1) prototype, (2) dichotomous grouping, (3) monothetic, (4) polythetic, and (5) dimensional approaches (Blashfield, 1993).

Taxonomy building generally is based on observation or multivariate statistical techniques. The specific variables and criteria used in defining a category usually are chosen because they have immediate relevance for research, intervention, or administrative or policy matters. For many labels, however, the difficulty in validly identifying cause precludes doing more than grouping by symptoms and handicapping condition. Special education and psychiatric classifications, for example, use a polythetic approach whereby those persons who share a number of attributes usually are assigned the same label. It should be noted, however, that designated symptoms have constituted a relatively limited range of the potentially important correlates, and the classification schemes have not adequately dealt with the dimensions of severity and pervasiveness or with causality.

In general, controversy rages over what constitutes a symptom and how symptoms relate to etiology and intervention. And the controversy will continue as long as (1) the primary focus of research is on a limited range of correlates seen as symptomatic of special education problems and (2) demonstrating the important relationship of such functioning to problem cause and remediation remains a relatively intractable research problem.

Efforts to improve classification of problems involve an interplay of conceptual and empirical activity. Progress has accelerated with advances in methodology (especially measurement and sequential decision making) and research using multiple approaches (Achenbach, 1988; Adelman & Taylor, 1991). However, the consensus among reviewers in this area is that considerable problems remain, especially with respect to validating taxonomies (Achenbach & Edelbrock, 1983; Cantwell & Rutter, 1994; Quay, Routh, & Shapiro, 1987; Rutter & Tuma, 1988). As Quay et al. (1987) stress in discussing classification of childhood problems, the field needs "categories or dimensions that: (a) can be discriminated from other syndromes and thus reliably diagnosed or measured; and also meet one or more of the following criteria: (b) are associated with different causes, (c) have different outcomes, or (d) respond to different interventions."

When the emphasis is on current dysfunctioning, both severity (mild–profound) and pervasiveness (narrow–broad) are of concern. This is so because these two basic dimensions have profound implications for planning, implementing, and evaluating intervention. Controversy arises around how to define severity and pervasiveness. Severity might be defined as intensity and frequency of specified deviant and devious behavior and/or nonoccurrence of adaptive skills and behavior. Pervasiveness might be defined as the range of developmental areas and/or situations affected. Satisfactorily operationalizing these dimensions is a major problem confronting classification researchers. Specific criteria used in judging severity and pervasiveness, of course, depend on prevailing contextual norms and standards surrounding an individual's development (e.g., expectations related to age, sex, subculture, social status). Deviance, after all, is defined by social groups (Becker, 1963).

As graphically presented in Figure 8.1, the combination of pervasiveness and severity, treated here for discussion purposes as discrete categories rather than continuous variables, yields nine classification groups. When the *paradigmatic* cause of the dysfunction is added as a third dimension, the schema jumps to twenty-seven groups. If duration (e.g., recent onset to long-standing chronic condition) is added, another large leap in the number of categories results.

One simple fact underscored by the relatively straightforward nine-group classification of severity and pervasiveness is that differentiations made with respect to such basic dimensions are *minimally* essential for planning, implementation, and evaluation (including accountability demands). For example, in evaluating intervention efficacy for groups, one must control for severity given comparably pervasive problems and vice versa. More specifically, with respect to prognosis and evaluation of intervention efficacy, there are groups for whom it is reasonable to predict that amelioration of problems will be easier to achieve. In general, realistic planning and evaluation of outcomes requires a recognition that comprehensive improvements for two *groups* manifesting an equally broad range of learning and behavior problems should be easier to demonstrate for the group whose severity is rated mild (X''') as contrasted to profound (X').

Causal classification demonstrates other complexities. Classification by cause may be done *broadly* with reference to paradigmatic cause or specifically with regard to primary instigators, secondary contributing factors, or both. To illus-

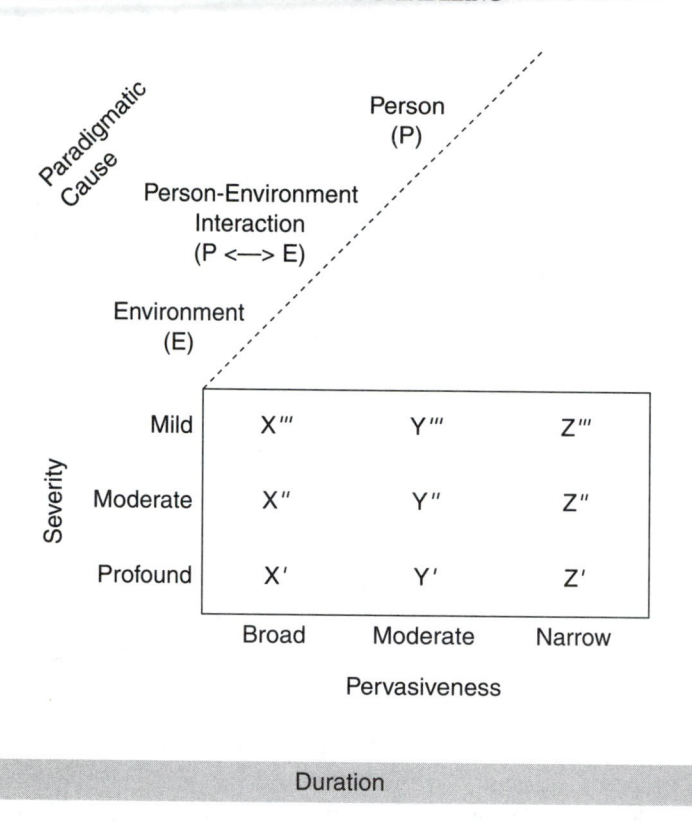

FIGURE 8.1   Four Key Dimensions of Concern in Classifying Educational and Psycholosocial Problems

Source: Reprinted from *Clinical Psychology Review, 8*(6); H. S. Adelman and L. Taylor, "Clinical Child Psychology: Fundamental Intervention Questions and Problems," pp. 637–665 (1988), with kind permission from Elsevier Science Ltd., The Boulevard, Langford Lane, Kidlington 0X5 1GB, U.K.

trate the empirical and conceptual problems of using cause in classification, Table 8.1 elaborates on a reciprocal deterministic paradigm for understanding human behavior to outline major factors hypothesized as causing learning and behavior problems. Note that secondary causal factors interact with primary instigators. In general, the degree to which secondary factors exacerbate problems is determined by the type of primary instigator and the degree of dysfunction produced by it. This is exemplified when a genetic anomaly or physiological "insult" causes a major CNS disorder and the effect on behavior is so severe and

pervasive that resultant dysfunctioning cannot be significantly worsened. In contrast, when CNS disorders are minor, a great many secondary variables can aggravate existing dysfunctions and create other problems. As this analysis suggests, there are times when causal factors and their effects are logically important indicators for intervention decisions and are potential predictors of outcome. That is, outcomes should differ for groups who differ in the degree to which the pathological impact of causal factors can be compensated for or reversed. Thus, classification of causal factors and their immediate effects and current manifestations

TABLE 8.1   Factors Instigating Learning and Behavior Problems

ENVIRONMENT (E)	PERSON (P)	INTERACTIONS AND TRANSACTIONS BETWEEN E AND P*
1. Insufficient stimuli (e.g., prolonged periods in impoverished environs; deprivation of learning opportunities at home or school such as lack of play and practice situations and poor instruction; inadequate diet) 2. Excessive stimuli (e.g., overly demanding home or school experience, such as overwhelming pressure to achieve and contradictory expectations) 3. Intrusive and hostile stimuli (e.g., medical practices, especially at birth, leading to physiological impairments; conflict in home or faulty child-rearing practices, such as long-standing abuse and rejection; migratory family; language used in school is a second language; social prejudices related to race, sex, age, physical characteristics, and behavior)	1. Physiological "insult" (e.g., cerebral trauma, such as accident or stroke, endocrine dysfunctions and chemical imbalances; illness affecting brain or sensory functioning) 2. Genetic anomaly (e.g., genes which limit, slow down, or lead to any atypical development 3. Cognitive activity and affective states experienced by self as deviant (e.g., lack of knowledge or skills such as basic cognitive strategies; lack of ability to cope effectively with emotions, such as low self-esteem) 4. Physical characteristics shaping contact with environment and/or experienced by self as deviant (e.g., visual, auditory, or motoric deficits; excessive or reduced sensitivity to stimuli; easily fatigued; factors such as race, sex, age, unusual appearance which produce stereotypical responses) 5. Deviant actions of the individual (e.g., performance problems, such as excessive errors in reading and speaking; high or low levels of activity)	1. Severe to moderate personal vulnerabilities and environmental defects and differences (e.g., person with extremely slow development in a highly demanding, understaffed classroom, all of which equally and simultaneously instigate the problem) 2. Minor personal vulnerabilities not accommodated by the situation (e.g., person with minimal CNS disorders resulting in auditory perceptual disability enrolled in a reading program based on phonics; very active student assigned to classroom which does not tolerate this level of activity) 3. Minor environmental defects and differences not accommodated by the individual (e.g., student is in the minority racially or culturally and is not participating in many school social activities and class discussions because he or she thinks others may be unreceptive)

*May involve only one P and one E variable or may involve multiple combinations.

Source: Adapted from *Learning Disabilities in Perspective,* by H. Adelman and L. Taylor (1983), p. 35. Glenview, IL: Scott, Foresman and Company. Reprinted with permission of Scott, Foresman and Company.

could be of great significance in evaluating outcomes (e.g., for research purposes and in response to accountability demands). The problem, of course, is that for many individuals seen by special educators, hypotheses about cause must be made tenuously and available methodology for assessing cause(s) has major limitations.

TOWARD BROADENING SPECIAL EDUCATION CLASSIFICATION

Ultimately, it may be necessary to accept the idea that special education practitioners, other practitioners who serve the same populations, researchers, and policy makers require different classification schemes. Even so, it seems essential, at the very least, to have classification systems that give equal emphasis to (1) major pathological conditions and (2) problems of daily living—including those caused primarily or partially by environmental factors. Without the latter, people are unlikely to maintain a fair perspective about when interventions focused on changing persons are inappropriate.

A clear indication of the need to address a wider range of variables in labeling problems is seen in efforts to develop multifaceted classification schemes. The dominant approach in this respect is the multiaxial classification system developed by the American Psychiatric Association (American Psychiatric Association, 1994). This might be seen as a step in the right direction. However, although the system includes a dimension acknowledging "psychosocial stressors," this dimension is used mostly to deal with environmental factors as a contributing factor to a person's disorder (i.e., such stressors are not usually specified as primary causes).

The following conceptual example is offered to illustrate one type of broad classification scheme that might be useful. After fundamental hearing, visual, speech, and physical impairments are identified and accounted for, the dominant concern in special education is for amelioration of learning and behavior problems. In this regard, efforts to improve intervention might benefit from identification of individuals manifesting similar symptoms with respect to *learning* problems (e.g., deficiencies in readiness skills, reading and writing problems) or *behavior* problems (e.g., acting out, withdrawn, reactively or proactively motivated) or both. Such identification could draw on data from interview schedules, observation measures, and psychometric instruments; from rating scales and other reports provided by family members, teachers, employers; and from physical (biological/neurological) assessments reported by other professionals.

Because of data limitations and comorbidity (two of the more frustrating problems confronting classification researchers), some individuals, of course, will not fall readily into a group (Rutter, 1994). However, those whose symptoms can be differentiated then can be placed along a continuum that separates problems caused by internal factors, environmental variables, or a combination of both with reference to the dimensions discussed.

As can be seen in Figure 8.2, problems caused by the environment can be placed at one end of such a continuum and referred to as Type I problems. At the other end are problems caused primarily by pathology within the person and designated as Type III problems. In the middle are problems stemming from a relatively equal contribution of environmental and person sources, labeled Type II problems.

To be more specific: In this scheme, diagnostic labels connoting *extreme* problems of dysfunction caused by pathological conditions within a person are most appropriate for individuals whose problems fit the cluster designated as Type III problems. Obviously, some problems caused by pathological conditions within a person are not manifested in severe, pervasive ways, and there are persons without such pathology whose problems do become severe and pervasive. The intent is not to ignore these individuals; as a first categorization step, however, it is essential they not be confused with those seen as having Type III problems.

At the other end of the continuum are individuals with problems arising from outside the person

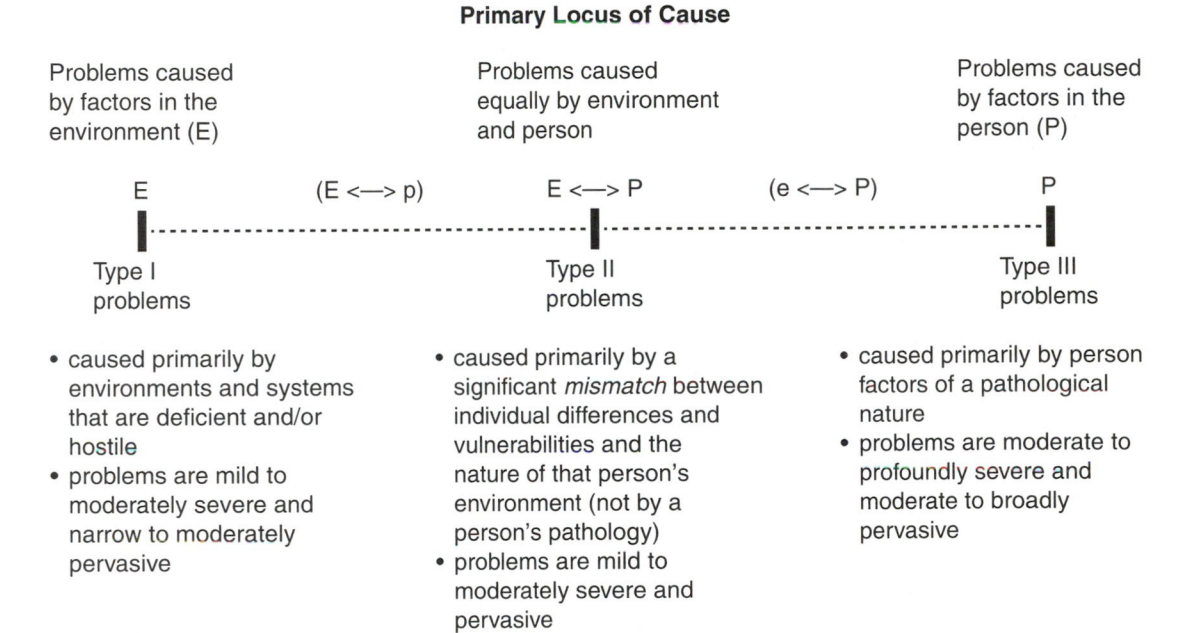

FIGURE 8.2   A Continuum of Problems Reflecting a Transactional View of the Locus of Primary Instigating Factors*
Source: From H. S. Adelman and L. Taylor (1994), *On Understanding Intervention in Psychology and Education,* p. 39. Westport, CT: Praeger, an imprint of Greenwood Publishing Group, Inc., Westport, CT. Reprinted with permission of the publisher.

(i.e., Type I problems). For example, many persons grow up in impoverished and hostile environmental circumstances; based on the best evidence available, such environmental conditions should be considered first in hypothesizing the *primary instigating* causes of the behavioral, emotional, and learning problems these individuals manifest. (Once such conditions are ruled out as the basis for observed problems, hypotheses about within-person causality become more viable.)

To provide a reference point in the middle of the continuum, a Type II category is used. This group consists of persons who do not function well in situations where their individual differences and minor vulnerabilities are poorly accommodated or are responded to hostilely. The problems of an individual in this group are a rela-

tively equal product of person characteristics and failure of the environment to accommodate that individual.

There are, of course, variations along the continuum that do not precisely fit a category. That is, at each point between the extreme ends, environment–person transactions are the cause, but the degree to which each contributes to the problem varies. Toward the environment end of the continuum, environmental factors play a bigger role (represented as E<—>p). Toward the other end, person variables account for more of the problem (thus e<—>P). Where along the continuum an individual falls depends on where one sets cut-off scores on the specific criteria measures used.

After the general groupings have been identified, it becomes relevant to consider the value of differentiating subgroups or subtypes within each major type of problem. For example, subtypes for the Type III category might first differentiate behavioral, emotional, and learning problems arising from serious internal pathology (e.g., structural and functional malfunctioning within the person that causes disorders and disabilities and disrupts development). Then, subtypes might be differentiated within each area. In formulating subtypes, basic dimensions such as problem severity, pervasiveness, and chronicity continue to play a key role, as do considerations about development, gender, culture, and social class.

Clearly, such a simple continuum cannot do justice to the complexity involved in classifying and differentiating individuals manifesting learning and behavior problems (e.g., see Adelman & Taylor, 1990, 1993, 1994). However, as an example, the above conceptual scheme illustrates the value of initially using a broad, paradigmatic conception of causality. Specifically, the approach minimizes the presumptive tendency toward viewing all such problems as caused by deficiencies or pathology within the individual. In doing so, it helps avoid tendencies toward "blaming the victim." It also helps broaden the focus of intervention by highlighting that a prerequisite and sometimes sufficient approach for some problems involves improving the environment's accommodation of individual differences.

For instance, based on the above typology, my colleagues and I are evolving the concept of a personalized classroom environment as the first step in a sequential and hierarchical model for ameliorating (including preventing) learning and behavior problems (Adelman, 1971, 1989b, 1994; Adelman & Taylor, 1993, 1994). Personalization, whether carried out in regular or special education classrooms, is seen as essential in enabling teachers to account for an increased range of individual differences in developmental capability and, as importantly, in intrinsic motivation.[1] Moreover, work to date suggests that personalizing classroom instruction should be a sufficient strategy for most Type I and some Type II problems. Thus, it should reduce the number of students labeled as

needing remediation. It also should facilitate identification of those in the classroom (including Type III problems) with specific remedial needs.

MINIMIZING NEGATIVE EFFECTS

As the discussion to this point suggests, the potential negatives related to classification activity go beyond the impact of labeling. Decisions about which phenomena to categorize have potential negative consequences both for what is labeled and what isn't. Moreover, in fields such as psychology and special education, the deficiencies of current labeling practices limit progress and often generate public censure, both of which affect a field's reputation and support. Thus, the classification problem encompasses concerns about how to minimize negative consequences. As briefly described below, consequences can be minimized (1) by improving existing classification schemes and methodology and (2) by anticipating and addressing negative effects arising from labeling practices.

Improving Classification Schemes and Methodology

Many difficulties involved in devising classification schemes are rooted in complex problems of an epistemological, philosophical, theoretical, and methodological nature. Nevertheless, some directions are emerging with promise for improving classification schemes relevant to intervention. One is continued refinement of the multiaxial approach, paired with efforts to view pathology from a reciprocal determinist perspective. This should lead to improved schemes for multidimensional classifications of psychosocial, environmental/organizational, and transactional problems. Another promising direction involves adding a focus on classifying nonproblem functioning and strengths.

Methodologically, the path to improvement remains one of enhancing reliability and demonstrating the differential validity of each category in a scheme. This involves not only development of precise criteria and readily applied operations, but effective training procedures for those who do the labeling (including error reduction strategies).[2]

In terms of general guidelines, those suggested by Jablensky (1988) are readily adapted. He states that good classification is designed for a clearly stated purpose and that it (1) divides the universe of observations into heuristic units leading to action (e.g., research, intervention), (2) generates new observations and questions, (3) is reliable, (4) satisfies the cognitive needs of users (i.e., is in "accord with their 'world maps'," avoids jargon, and is easy to learn and internalize), (5) is adaptable and meaningful in a large number of cultural settings, and (6) can be related to previous and other current classification systems.

Guidelines for Minimizing Negative Consequences

No agreement exists about processes or criteria for assessing and weighing the benefits and negative consequences of current labeling practices. There is consensus, however, that intervention ethics require steps be taken to minimize negative effects. The following guidelines illustrate the minimal requirements that should be expected of those involved in labeling others.

First, persons responsible for assigning labels must acquire a fundamental awareness of potential immediate and long-term negative impacts on individuals, groups, and society. Based on this awareness, proactive steps must be taken to (1) provide those potentially affected with information about possible negative consequences (e.g., indicate risks during the consent process); (2) maximize the valid application of assessment practices and decision processes used in arriving at a label (e.g., actively seek both confirmatory and disconfirmatory data in arriving at a differential diagnosis); (3) prevent inappropriate communication and use of labels (e.g., protect privacy through confidentiality procedures, clarify limitations of a label with respect to its valid applications); and (4) take specific actions to counter reactive effects (e.g., prepare those potentially affected to use protective strategies and encourage others not to react in harmful ways).

As steps are taken to minimize negative consequences, a shift should occur in the cost–benefit equation related to a particular label and classification scheme. How to gather and weight the data used in such an equation, however, remains a problem.

CLASSIFICATION DETERMINES THE ESSENCE OF SPECIAL EDUCATION

Special education is a concept. As with all abstract constructs, its operationalization is difficult and fraught with complex problems and issues. Consequently, any current operationalization (e.g., classification schema, procedures for identifying special needs, approaches to service delivery) is controversial and an easy target for criticism. Such critiques cut two ways. They can hurt a field's image by laying out its deficiencies. At the same time, the criticism can be a stimulus for improving the unsatisfactory status quo.

A particular danger with respect to contemporary approaches to classification of problems is that the widespread criticism may be misinterpreted. That is, the general public may see the criticism as evidence that the concept of special education is invalid or that there is no need for a field to improve the state of the art related to the concept.

Hopefully, the extensive criticism of current practices will counter the tendency of many to ignore the fundamentals that tie general and special education and different groups of special educators together. Piecemeal and uncoordinated approaches to improving education waste resources, have limited efficacy, and contribute to the false impression that the concerns of various groups of educators are mutually exclusive.

Efforts to improve special education classification can play a central role in improving all education. In choosing a classification scheme, a field profoundly shapes its very essence. Thus, discussion of change in the special education classification system raises major theoretical, practical, legal, and ethical matters of profound concern to policy makers, practitioners, and researchers. Any fundamental change affects the ways individuals are described, served, and studied; alters funding and intervention practices; and requires major revision of general and special education training and certification. It is not surprising, therefore, that debates about classification schemes, specific diagnostic procedures, and the very act of labeling are so heated.

The field of special education began with a focus on individual pathology. In daily practice, it has been necessary to go well beyond this focus (Adelman & Taylor, 1993; Davis, 1989; Gartner & Lipsky, 1987; Heshusius, 1989; Jenkins et al., 1988; Stainback & Stainback, 1984). As a result, the field's tenets and practices are applied to matters probably better served by a broader set of ideas and approaches.

A fundamental example is seen in existing labels. Initially created to account for special needs of individuals with pathological conditions, some labels increasingly have been assigned to individuals whose learning and behavior problems are not caused by such conditions. In part, this inappropriate generalization is the product of sociopolitical-economic considerations. However, the trend also reflects the inadequacy of existing classification schema and differential diagnostic procedures. I would suggest that reversal of this trend is unlikely to occur within the constraints of theory and practice focused on individual pathology.

Fortunately, special educators are reaching out for new paradigms and models (e.g., Heshusius, 1989, 1994). In particular, there are signs of increasing appreciation of reciprocal deterministic, cognitive–affective, and sequential and hierarchical models for understanding and correcting learning/behavior problems (cf. Adelman, 1989a;

Adelman & Taylor, 1993, 1994; Deci & Ryan, 1985). Such models hold great promise for guiding the development of broad classification systems—that is, schemes that encompass and contrast performance problems caused primarily by (different) pathological conditions within an individual and those caused primarily by (different) environmental factors.

These models also hold promise with regard to guiding both general and special education beyond their current piecemeal approaches to ameliorating problems. Increased efficacy depends on comprehensive approaches to creating an accurate conceptualization of the range of individual differences in motivation and capability found among persons manifesting learning and behavior problems (cf. Adelman, 1989b; Adelman & Taylor, 1993, 1994).

CONCLUSION

In concluding, I reiterate that the nature of intervention is inextricably intertwined with how the classification problem is handled. At a time when so many disciplines have the potential to make outstanding advances related to educational and psychological interventions, the classification problem continues to plague practitioners, researchers, and policy makers. There is no more fundamental problem than that of refining existing and developing new classification systems. Indeed, the roots of much of the backlash against special education probably can be traced to the inadequate state of the art with respect to assigning differential diagnostic labels. Until there is a better conceived classification scheme and valid procedures for making differential diagnoses, the efforts of researchers and practitioners alike will continue to raise concerns. And they should.

NOTES

1. Adelman and Taylor (cf. 1993; 1994) use the term *personalization* to differentiate their approach from individualized interventions (e.g., individualized instruction) that do *not* systematically account for differences

in *both* motivation (especially intrinsic motivation) and development. Furthermore, they stress that, in planning and implementing a personalized intervention, primary consideration is given to the intervenee's perceptions.

Because it is the intervenee's perceptions that are used to define whether the intervention is appropriately responsive to his or her interests and abilities, personalization is viewed as a psychological construct. This approach to intervention (e.g., classroom instruction) represents a theoretically based effort to operationalize the concept of establishing an optimal match between person and environment as advocated by leading scholars such as Piaget, Bruner, Vygotsky, J. McV. Hunt, and so many others. It is a much broader approach than has been pursued by aptitude X treatment researchers.

2. Error detection studies are essential to the development of error reduction strategies (e.g., see Adelman, Lauber, Nelson, & Smith, 1989; McKenzie, 1991).

REFERENCES

Achenbach, T. M. (1988). Integrating assessment and taxonomy. In M. Rutter, A. H. Tuma, & I. S. Lann (Eds.), *Assessment and diagnosis in child psychopathology* (pp. 28–41). New York: Guilford.

Achenbach, T. M., & Edelbrock, C. S. (1983). Taxonomic issues in child psychopathology. In T. H. Ollendick & M. Hersen (Eds.), *Handbook of child psychopathology* (pp. 65–93). New York: Plenum.

Adelman, H. S. (1971). The not so specific learning disability population. *Exceptional Children, 37,* 528–533.

Adelman, H. S. (1989a). Beyond the Learning Mystique: An interactional perspective on learning disabilities. *Journal of Learning Disabilities, 22,* 301–304, 328.

Adelman, H. S. (1989b). Toward solving the problems of misidentification and limited intervention efficacy. *Journal of Learning Disabilities, 22,* 608–612, 620.

Adelman, H. S. (1992). LD: The next 25 years. *Journal of Learning Disabilities, 25,* 17–21.

Adelman, H. S. (1994). Learning disabilities: On interpreting research translations. In N. C. Jordan & J. Goldsmith-Phillips (Eds.), *Learning disabilities: New directions for assessment and intervention* (pp. 1–19). Boston: Allyn and Bacon.

Adelman, H. S. (in press). Clinical psychology: Beyond psychopathology and clinical interventions. *Clinical Psychology: Science and Practice.*

Adelman, H. S., Lauber, B. A., Nelson, P., & Smith, D. C. (1989). Minimizing and detecting false positive diagnoses of learning disabilities. *Journal of Learning Disabilities, 22,* 234–244.

Adelman, H. S., & Taylor, L. (1983). *Learning disabilities in perspective.* Glenview, IL: Scott, Foresman.

Adelman, H. S., & Taylor, L. (1984). Ethical concerns and identification of psychoeducational problems. *Journal of Clinical Child Psychology, 13,* 16–23.

Adelman, H. S., & Taylor, L. (1986). The problems of definition and differentiation and the need for a classification schema. *Journal of Learning Disabilities, 19,* 514–520.

Adelman, H. S., & Taylor, L. (1988). Clinical child psychology: Fundamental intervention questions and problems. *Clinical Psychology Review, 8,* 637–665.

Adelman, H. S., & Taylor, L. (1990). Intrinsic motivation and school misbehavior. *Journal of Learning Disabilities. 23*(9), 541–550.

Adelman, H. S., & Taylor, L. (1991). Issues and problems related to the assessment of learning disabilities. In H. L. Swanson (Ed.), *Handbook on the assessment of learning disabilities.* Boston:College-Hill Press.

Adelman, H. S., & Taylor, L. (1993). *Learning problems and learning disabilities: Moving forward.* Pacific Grove, CA: Brooks/Cole.

Adelman, H. S., & Taylor, L. (1994). *On understanding intervention in psychology and education.* Westport, CT: Praeger.

American Psychiatric Association (1994). *Diagnostic and statistical manual of mental disorders* (4th ed./revised). Washington, DC: American Psychiatric Association.

Bank-Mikkelsen, N. E. (1976). Administrative normalizing. *S.A.-Nyt, 14,* 3–6.

Becker, H. S. (1963). *Outsiders: Studies in the sociology of deviance.* Glencoe, IL: Free Press.

Blashfield, R. K. (1993). Models of classification as related to a taxonomy of learning disabilities. In G. R. Lyon, D. B. Gray, J. F. Kavanagh, & N. A. Krasnegor (Eds.), *Better understanding learning disabilities: New views from research and their implications for education.* Baltimore: Paul H. Brooks.

Cantwell, D. P., & Rutter, M. (1994). Classification: Conceptual issues and substantive findings. In M.

Rutter, E. Taylor, & L. Hersov (Eds.), *Child and adolescent psychiatry: Modern approaches* (3rd ed., pp. 3–21). Oxford: Blackwell Scientific.

Datta, S., & Farradane, J. E. L. (1974). A psychological basis for general classification. In J. Wojciechowski (Ed.). *Conceptual Basis of the Classification of Knowledge: Proceedings of the Ottawa Conference* (pp. 320–321). Pullach/Munchen: Werlag Dokumentation.

Davis, W. E. (1989). The regular education initiative debate: Its promise and problems. *Exceptional Children, 55,* 440–446.

Deci, E. L., & Ryan, R. M. (1985). *Intrinsic motivation and self-determination in human behavior.* New York: Plenum.

Dunn, L. M. (1968). Special education for the mildly retarded—Is much of it justifiable? *Exceptional Children, 35,* 5–22.

Feniak, C. A. (1988). Labelling in special education: A problematic issue in England and Wales. *International Journal of Special Education, 3,* 117–124.

Fuchs, D., & Fuchs, L. S. (1994). Inclusive schools movement and the radicalization of special education reform. *Exceptional Children, 60,* 294–309.

Gartner, A., & Lipsky, D. K. (1987). Beyond special education: Toward a quality system for all students. *Harvard Educational Review, 57,* 367–395.

Glass, G. V. (1983). Effectiveness of special education. *Policy Studies Review, 2,* 65–78.

Heller, K., Holtzman, W., & Messick, S. (1982). *Placing children in special education: A strategy for equity.* Report of the National Academy of Sciences' Panel on Selection and Placement of Students in Programs for the Mentally Retarded. Washington, DC: National Academy Press.

Heshusius, L. (1989). The Newtonian mechanistic paradigm, special education, and contours of alternatives: An overview. *Journal of Learning Disabilities, 22,* 403–415.

Heshusius, L. (1994). Freeing ourselves from objectivity: Managing subjectivity or turning toward a participatory mode of consciousness? *Educational Researcher, 23,* 15–22.

Hobbs, N. (1975). *The future of children: Categories, labels, and their consequences.* San Francisco: Jossey-Bass.

Hobbs, N. (1980). An ecologically oriented, service-based system for the classification of handicapped children. In S. Salzinger, J. Antrobus, & J. Glick (Eds.), *The ecosystem of the "sick" child* (pp. 271–290). New York: Academic.

Jablensky, A. (1988). Methodological issues in psychiatric classification. *British Journal of Psychiatry, 152* (Suppl. 1), 15–20.

Jenkins, J. R., Pious, C. G., & Peterson, D. L. (1988). Categorical programs for remedial and handicapped students: Issues of validity. *Exceptional Children, 55,* 147–158.

Johnson, G. O. (1962). Special education for the mentally handicapped—A paradox. *Exceptional Children, 29,* 62–69.

Kauffman, J. M. (1989). The Regular Education Initiative as Reagan–Bush education policy: A trickle-down theory of education of the hard-to-teach. *Journal of Special Education, 23,* 256–277.

Kauffman, J. M. (1993). How we might achieve the radical reform of special education. *Exceptional Children, 60,* 6–16.

Kazdin, A. E., & Kagan, J. (1994). Models of dysfunction in developmental psychopathology. *Clinical Psychology: Science and Practice, 1,* 35–52.

Leinhardt, G., & Pallay, A. (1982). Restrictive educational settings: Exile or haven? *Review of Educational Research, 52,* 557–578.

Lilly, M. S. (1992). Labeling: A tired, overworked, yet unresolved issue in special education. In W. Stainback & S. Stainback (Eds.), *Controversial issues confronting special education* (pp. 85–95). Boston: Allyn and Bacon.

Lipsky, D., & Gartner, A. (1989). *Beyond separate education.* Baltimore: Paul H. Brooks.

Macmann, G. M., Barnett, D. W., Lombard, T. J., Belton-Kocher, E., & Sharp, M. N. (1989). On the actuarial classification of children: Fundamental studies of classification agreement. *Journal of Special Education, 23,* 127–149.

MacMillan, D. L., & Hendrick, I. G. (1993). Evolution and legacies. In J. I. Goodlad & T. C. Lovitt (Eds.), *Integrating general and special education* (pp. 23–48). Columbus, OH: Merrill/Macmillan.

MacMillan, D. L., & Meyers, C. E. (1979). Educational labeling of handicapped learners. In D. Berliner (Ed.), *Review of research in education* (Vol. 7). Washington, DC: American Educational Research Association.

McKenzie, D. A. (1991). A proposed prototype for identifying and correcting sources of measurement error in classification systems. *Medical Care, 29,* 521–530.

McReynolds, P. (1989). Diagnosis and clinical assessment: Current status and major issues. *Annual Review of Psychology, 40,* 83–103.

Morsink, C. V., Thomas, C. C., & Smith-Davis, J. (1987). Noncategorical special education programs: Process and outcomes. In M. C. Wang, M. C. Reynolds, & H. J. Walberg (Eds.), *The handbook of special education: Research and practice.* (Vol. 2, 287–309). Oxford, England: Pergamon.

National Association of School Psychologists. (1986). *Rights without labels.* Washington, DC: Author (Reprinted in *School Psychology Review, 18,* 1989).

Neisser, U. (1976). *Cognition and reality: Principles and implications of cognitive psychology.* San Francisco: W. H. Freeman.

Quay, H. C., Routh, D. K., & Shapiro, S. K. (1987). Psychopathology of childhood: From description to validation. In *Annual Review of Psychology, 38,* 491–532.

Reid, R., Maag, J. W., & Vasa, S. F. (1994). Attention deficit hyperactivity disorder as a disability category: A critique. *Exceptional Children, 60,* 198–214.

Reynolds, M. C. (1984). Classification of students with handicaps. In E. W. Gordon (Ed.), *Review of research in education* (Vol. 11, 63–92). Washington, DC: American Educational Research Association.

Reynolds, M. C. (1991). Classification and labeling. In J. W. Lloyd, N. N. Singh, & A. C. Repp (Eds.), *The regular education initiative: Alternative perspectives on concepts, issues, and models* (pp. 29–41). Sycamore, IL: Sycamore Publishing.

Reynolds, M. C., Wang, M. C., & Walberg, H. J. (1987). The necessary restructuring of special and regular education. *Exceptional Children, 53,* 391–398.

Reynolds, M. C., Zetlin, A. G., & Wang, M. C. (1993). 20/20 analysis: Taking a close look at the margins. *Exceptional Children, 59,* 294–300.

Rutter, M. (1994). Comorbidity: Meanings and mechanisms. *Clinical Psychology: Science and Practice, 1,* 100–103.

Rutter, M., & Tuma, A. H. (1988). Diagnosis and classification: Some outstanding issues. In M. Rutter & A. H. Tuma (Eds.), *Assessment and diagnosis in child psychopathology.* New York: Guilford.

Stainback, S., & Stainback, W. (1984). A rationale for the merger of special and regular education. *Exceptional Children, 51,* 102–111.

Wang, M. C., & Walberg, H. J. (1988). Four fallacies of segregationism. *Exceptional Children, 55,* 128–137.

Widiger, T. A., & Ford-Black, M. M. (1994). Diagnoses and disorders. *Clinical psychology: Science and practice, 1,* 84–87.

Widiger, T. A., & Trull, T. J. (1991). Diagnosis and clinical assessment. *Annual Review of Psychology, 42,* 109–133.

Wojciechowski, J. (1974). The philosophical relevance of the problem of the classification of knowledge. In J. Wojciechowski (Ed.), *Conceptual Basis of the Classification of Knowledge: Proceedings of the Ottawa Conference* (p. 13). Pullach/Munchen: Werlag Dokumentation.

Wolfensberger, W. (1972). *The principle of normalization in human services.* Toronto: National Institute on Mental Retardation.

Ysseldyke, J. E. (1987). Classification of handicapped students. In M. C. Wang, M. C. Reynolds, & H. J. Walberg (Eds.), *The handbook of special education: Research and practice.* (Vol. 1, 253–271). Oxford, England: Pergamon.

Zigler, E., & Phillips, L. (1961). Psychiatric diagnosis: A critique. *Journal of Abnormal and Social Psychology, 63,* 607–618.

SECTION FIVE

ASSESSMENT

A great deal of controversy has surrounded the assessment of children's abilities and achievements in recent years. In Chapter 9, Reschly outlines why past and alternative assessment approaches based on normative data and psychological constructs have failed to provide meaningful data. He proposes a direct, functional assessment approach and outlines why it is a better alternative.

In Chapter 10, Dudley-Marling offers a political critique of the trend toward curriculum-based assessment (CBA), one of the primary forms of the direct, functional assessment approach. He believes that while many educators portray CBA as an equitable alternative to culturally and racially biased standardized achievement tests, CBA offers little in regard to remedies for the inequities of U.S. schooling in which disability, race, class, and gender play a significant role in the quality of children's educational opportunities. Dudley-Marling suggests some possible alternatives to CBA.

CHAPTER 9

Functional Assessment and Special Education Decision Making

DANIEL J. RESCHLY

INTRODUCTION

A change in the current delivery system in education is much needed in order to improve special education and related services for children and youth with mild disabilities. Changes in assessment are fundamental to the delivery system change; indeed, it is impossible to implement changes in one without changes in the other. The delivery system changes involve a paradigm shift, from emphasis on internal child attributes and deficits to a method of short-run empiricism in which there is a close relationship between assessment and instruction or intervention. This chapter will proceed from a discussion of the paradigm shift, to delivery system reform, and then to contrasts between traditional and alternative assessment procedures.

THE TRADITIONAL SPECIAL EDUCATION PARADIGM

The dimensions of the paradigm shift include assumptions and theories about the etiology of disabilities and approaches to assessment and interventions. Delivery system reform involves shifts away from medical model conceptions of disabilities and presumed aptitude by treatment interactions between internal cognitive or neuropsychological status and intervention methodology. Social system conceptions of disability, short-run empiricism, and functional/behavioral assessment replace the traditional approaches to defining and treating educationally related disabilities (Reschly, 1987).

Traditional Assessment Models

Traditional assessment practices in school psychology and special education reflected the medical model conception of disabilities and the inherently attractive idea that disorders in underlying cognitive styles, abilities, or neuropsychological characteristics were both the causes of disorders and the key to effective intervention or remediation efforts. This idea has several variations that produce quite different methods of designing interventions for students with learning or behavioral problems (see later section "Advances in Assessment and Intervention"). All of the variations were to a large degree dependent on Cronbach's (1957) application of the correlational discipline of scientific psychology or his aptitude-by-treatment interaction methodology.

The correlational discipline emphasizes assessment of the natural variations among people in cognitive, physical, and social–emotional domains. These variations are then related to actual performance in academic or employment settings. If there are significant relationships (correlations) between these natural variations and performance, increased efficiency in the use of resources and enhanced overall performance can be produced by differential selection or placement. The correlational discipline attempts to enhance opportunities and improve educational performance by selection and placement of students in programs from which they will derive optimum benefits. The assessment of overall intellectual ability and the placement of students into special programs such as special classes for students with mild mental retardation (MMR) or an accelerated curriculum for gifted students are prime examples of applications of the correlational science.

In contrast, the fundamental aim of the experimental discipline of scientific psychology according to Cronbach (1957) is to create higher levels of performance through first discovering the best interventions and then disseminating and implementing them. Different treatments or interventions are carefully contrasted so that causal statements can be made about which had the highest average effects for groups of participants or, in single-subject designs, for individuals. Careful control of experimental conditions was extremely important so that valid comparisons could be made between experimental conditions (i.e., treatments).

Aptitude-by-Treatment Interaction Theory

In 1957 Cronbach suggested that a merger of the two disciplines of scientific psychology would produce maximum benefits in human services such as the education of children and youth. The use of aptitude-by-treatment interactions (ATI) was seen by Cronbach as the means to use the strengths of each of the two disciplines to maximize human welfare. "For any potential problem, there is some best group of treatments to use and some best allocation of persons to treatments" (p. 680). The ATI approach involves the study of: a) differences among treatments; b) aptitude differences among persons; *and* c) the interaction of aptitudes and treatments. Based on the interactions, individuals are assigned to the treatments that would produce the best results. The educational applications suggested by Cronbach (greater emphasis on individual prescriptions) continue to be the basis for much of special education and school psychology. "We should *design* treatments, not to fit the average person, but to fit groups of students with particular aptitude patterns. . . . we should seek out the aptitudes which correspond to (interact with) modifiable aspects of the treatment" (Cronbach, 1957, p. 681).

ATI is one of the most attractive ideas in all of basic and applied psychology (Arter & Jenkins, 1977, 1979). It is an idea that "should" work in the laboratory and in practice. The idea of matching treatment to naturally occurring characteristics of the person makes inherently good sense; clearly, it is consistent with our humanistic commitments of individualizing instruction and psychological treatments in order to maximize opportunities. ATI is especially attractive in special education settings in which most of the work traditionally has been with individual children referred for learning and behavior problems. However, what "should" work, what is inherently appealing, is not always a sound basis for practice. Such was the case with the efforts to use ATI as the foundation for special education and applied psychology.

ATI Failure and Short-Run Empiricism

In less than two decades, Cronbach's frustration with ATI as a basis for applied psychology was palpable in another *American Psychologist* article: "Once we attend to interactions, we enter a hall of mirrors that extends to infinity." (Cronbach, 1975, p. 119). In the years between 1957 and 1975, Cronbach and colleagues conducted many studies in which attempts were made to identify interactions of aptitudes and treatments. Unfortunately, the hypothesized interactions often did not occur, were extremely weak when they did appear, and often were entangled in intractable and hopelessly complex higher-order interactions that were virtually impossible to study in laboratory settings let alone use in practical situations. Furthermore, potent interaction effects, when they did exist, were for prior achievement or skill levels within the domain(s) of behavior that was/were the dependent variable(s) in the ATI experiments. Indeed, the current level of knowledge or skills is an important variable in designing instructional interventions; however, the effect of prior knowledge was not the kind of aptitude envisioned in Cronbach's grand design or in the school psychology and special education applications of ATI.

In the 1975 article, Cronbach abandoned ATI as the basis for applied psychology. The strategy he suggested to replace ATI was remarkably similar to the outcomes criteria and problem-solving strategies that will be discussed in more detail later in this chapter and in the system reform literature of the past decade. In place of ATI, Cronbach suggested context-specific evaluation and short-run empiricism; "One monitors responses to the treatment and adjusts it" (p. 126). Two realistic goals were proposed by Cronbach for applied psychology: "One reasonable aspiration is to assess local events accurately, to improve short-run control. The other reasonable aspiration is to develop explanatory concepts, concepts that will help people use their heads" (1975, p. 126). The use of short-run empiricism (problem solving), and the selection of behavior change or instructional design principles from the available literature (selecting explanatory concepts and "using our heads") is the contemporary application of Cronbach's suggestions for moving beyond the rigidity and insufficiency of the two disciplines of scientific psychology.

Applications of Cronbach's Two Disciplines

Most school psychology and special education services have been dominated by the correlation or aptitude-by-treatment interaction approaches to designing interventions. The correlational parallel occurs with traditional placement services in which referred children are assessed to determine if they meet the criteria for classification as disabled. Children with low scores on measures of current intellectual functioning and academic achievement, or large discrepancies between the scores on intellectual and achievement measures, are often placed in different educational programs for part or all of their school day. The differential placement is seen as necessary to allow children to benefit educationally because the general education program is inappropriate to their naturally occurring level of abilities or their pattern of aptitudes, applications of the

correlational discipline described in 1957 by Cronbach. The experimental discipline described by Cronbach was used infrequently in school psychology and special education during the first eight decades of this century. Recently described methods of special education instruction guided by formative evaluation (Fuchs & Fuchs, 1986) and single-subject designs are the clearest applications of the experimental discipline (Sulzer-Azaroff & Mayer, 1991).

FAILURE OF TRADITIONAL MODELS

Empirical evidence does not support the traditional model of providing special education services to students with mild disabilities through differential placement in self-contained classes, or matching aptitudes (e.g., learning styles, modality strengths, or neuropsychologically intact functions) to treatments (teaching methodology). Recent evidence provides little confidence in the utility of current diagnostic categories or in treatments based on aptitudes (Kavale, 1990).

Special Education Outcomes

In Table 9.1 the outcomes of program placement and aptitude-based treatments are summarized based on Kavale's 1990 review. The first two items contain the average effect of being classified in the categories of MMR or SLD and placed in traditional special education programs. These meta-analyses are consistent with the interpretation that classification as MMR or SLD and special education placement produces negligible effects in the former case and weak effects in the latter case. Traditional aptitude-based treatments also fare poorly in the meta-analyses (see the third and fourth items in Table 9.1). Matching instructional methodology to visually based or auditorially based aptitudes has no identifiable positive effects. The disappointing outcomes associated with traditional diagnoses such as MMR and SLD and with matching intervention methodology to aptitudes is part of the push toward system reform (Reschly & Ysseldyke, 1995).

TABLE 9.1   Summary of Effect Sizes in Meta-Analyses of Placements and Interventions[a]

PLACEMENT/INTERVENTION	EFFECT SIZE[b]
Traditional diagnoses:	
MMR diagnosis/special education placement	−.14
SLD diagnosis/special education placement	.29
Traditional ATI applications:	
Modality matched instruction (auditory strength)	.03
Modality matched instruction (visual strength)	.04
Behavioral interventions with functional assessment:	
Behavior modification/behavior therapy (social behavior goals)	.93
Curriculum-based progress monitoring with formative evaluation	.70
Curriculum-based progress monitoring with formative evaluation and systematic use of reinforcement	1.00

[a]The results in this table are abstracted from results reported by Fuchs and Fuchs (1986) and Kavale (1990). Interested readers are referred to those sources for more information.

[b]Effect size expresses in standard deviation units the average results of interventions, placements, or treatments from many studies.

Concerns about and alternatives to the traditional conceptions of disabilities and special education interventions have become increasingly prominent in the literature over the past twenty years. These problems and suggested solutions closely parallel the different applications of the two disciplines of scientific psychology—the ATI movement, and Cronbach's endorsement of practice, informed by theory and research and guided by a methodology of short-run empiricism.

Problems in Current Practice

Survey studies of the practice of school psychology and special education yield results (Reschly & Wilson, in press) suggesting the continued reliance on norm-referenced standardized tests that are used to diagnose disabilities such as MMR and SLD and place students in different special education programs. The value of these current assessment practices depends heavily on the benefits to students classified as disabled and placed in special education programs. Do differential diagnoses of MMR or SLD lead to different treatments, and are those treatments differentially effective depending on the student's diagnosis?

Nonfunctional and Stigmatizing Labels. In most states, a specific disability must be designated as part of a classification and placement process whereby children and youth with learning and behavior problems receive special education and related services. The critical question is, "Do the mild disability categories make any difference to treatment?" (Reschly, 1987).

Substantial evidence indicates that the same treatment goals and teaching strategies are adopted regardless of the category of mild disability (Reynolds & Lakin, 1987). For example, the top IEP goals typically are reading, then math, then written expression, regardless of whether the disability is MMR, SLD, or behavior disorder (BD), and the same teaching strategies are used regardless of disability category. Furthermore, programs for low-achieving students (e.g., Chapter I) and special education for students with mild disabilities are highly similar in terms of the needs of the students served and the intervention methodology used. Despite these similarities, markedly different levels of financial support are provided in special education and Chapter I, often on the basis of a few points on a test or a pair of tests. Some students are called disabled (and much more money is spent on their education) while others remain in regular education with little assistance. Do these distinctions make sense? It is difficult to justify the labeling process if program benefits are not clearly documented and if differential treatment is not related to the category assigned (Cromwell, Blashfield, & Strauss, 1975; Heller, Holtzman, & Messick, 1982). System reform efforts often involve noncategorical special education, with less emphasis on finding the right category, or differential diagnosis among disabilities, and more emphasis on the determination of programming needs and the design of interventions (Reynolds & Lakin, 1987; Ysseldyke, 1988).

The Special Problem of Specific Learning Disabilities. Nearly every system reform discussion focuses more attention on SLD than any other area. The reason is that although SLD is only one of thirteen categories of disability recognized in federal legislation, slightly over half of all students with disabilities are classified as SLD (*Sixteenth Annual Report,* 1994). Although there are many tantalizing findings in the SLD research, few generalizations can be made beyond the observation that students with SLD have low achievement, most often in reading. The same conclusion applies to students in Chapter I programs. Notably absent in the SLD research and practice is evidence for validated differential treatment based on the SLD diagnosis or the identification of reliable subtypes of SLD for whom matching treatment to subtype produces better outcomes (Shinn, Ysseldyke, Deno, & Tindal, 1986; Sleeter, 1986; Ysseldyke, Algozzine, & Epps, 1983; Ysseldyke et al., 1983).

Quality of Interventions. One of the greatest concerns about current practice is the quality of interventions at the prereferral level and within special education (Flugum & Reschly, 1994; Gresham 1989). Basic intervention principles often are not implemented in IEPs, special education programs, and prereferral interventions, and these interventions typically are not evaluated using individualized, treatment-sensitive meas-

ures. An absence of high-quality interventions coupled with poor evaluation of individual progress may alone account for the undocumented benefits of special education.

Treatment Validity of Assessment Procedures

In Table 9.2 some of the most frequently used assessment procedures in special education and school psychology from a 1991–1992 survey are listed. Two conclusions are apparent from an examination of this list. First, many of the instruments have mediocre to poor technical characteristics (Christenson & Ysseldyke, 1989; Reschly, 1980; Salvia & Ysseldyke, 1995; Witt, 1986). Second, the instruments with strong technical characteristics (Wechsler Scales and Woodcock-Johnson Achievement) have relatively little application in the determination of specific treatment needs or in monitoring and evaluating the effects of treatments. As noted in a Buros Mental Measurements Yearbook review, the Wechsler Scales have excellent technical characteristics related to determining relative standing in a normative group, information that is useful for classification, but are largely irrelevant to treatment. "In short, the WISC-R lacks treatment validity in that its use does not enhance remedial interventions for children who show specific academic skill deficiencies" (Witt & Gresham, 1985, p. 1717).

Current Ability Training and Aptitude-by-Treatment Approaches

The original ATI applications in school psychology and special education involved *training* weak areas in perceptual–motor or psycholinguistic domains, or *matching* instructional methodology to strong areas in these domains. By the early 1980s these approaches generally were viewed as ineffective (Arter & Jenkins, 1977, 1979; Hammill & Larsen, 1974, 1978; Kavale, 1981; Kavale & Mattson, 1983; Ysseldyke & Mirkin, 1982). Recent work by Das and Naglieri (in press) represents an effort to revive the practice of training

TABLE 9.2   School Psychologists' Self-Report of Assessment Instrument Use per Month

INSTRUMENT	TIMES USED PER MONTH
Structured Observation Procedures[a]	10.64
Wechsler Scales[b]	10.08
Bender Motor Gestalt Test	7.06
Draw-A-Person	5.30
Anecdotal or Unstructured Observation	4.84
House–Tree–Person	4.13
Developmental Test of Visual-Motor Integration	3.71
Kinetic Family Drawings	3.65
Woodcock-Johnson Achievement	3.59
Wide Range Achievement	2.59

[a]Includes the sum of duration, event, interval, and time sampling observations.

[b]Includes the sum of the following Wechsler scales: Wechsler Preschool and Primary Scale of Intelligence, Wechsler Intelligence Scale for Children, and Weschsler Adult Intelligence Scale.

Source: Data from *The Times They Are A'Changing': Assessment Training and Practice Are Not,* by M. S. Wilson and D. J. Reschly (1994). Manuscript submitted for publication. Reprinted with permission from the authors.

weak cognitive skills. The usefulness of this approach remains to be seen and there is ample reason for skepticism (Reynolds, 1986); however, the criteria to evaluate training weak areas were stated well by Hammill and Larsen (1974, 1978).

Despite this negative evidence and the more general complications of ATI research (Cronbach, 1975), the practice of attempting to match instruction to aptitude strengths continues to be prominent. Recent aptitude constructs used in the matching process involve cognitive processing strengths such as successive or simultaneous processing of neuropsychologically intact areas (Hartlage & Reynolds, 1981; Hartlage & Telzrow, 1986; Kaufman, Goldsmith, & Kaufman, 1984; Kaufman & Kaufman, 1983; Reynolds, 1981, 1986, 1992). These aptitude-by-treatment constructs have been no more successful than their modality-processing predecessors (Ayers & Cooley, 1986; Ayers, Cooley, & Severson, 1988; Good, Vollmer, Creek, Katz, & Chowdhri, 1993). Indeed, the major barrier to the use of these more recent aptitude constructs in school psychology is the near total absence of treatment outcome results wherein the aptitudes are assessed, intervention

methodology is matched and mismatched to these aptitudes, interventions are implemented, and results carefully examined (Teeter, 1987, 1989). Whether we conceptualize aptitude as cognitive processes, information-processing modalities, or intact neurological areas, Cronbach's (1975) characterization of ATI is still accurate: "Once we attend to interactions, we enter a hall of mirrors that extends to infinity" (p. 119).

PARADIGM SHIFT AND SYSTEM REFORM

System reform themes prominent in the current literature address the critical shortcomings in the current delivery system (*Advocacy for Appropriate Educational Services for All Children,* 1985; Heller et al., 1982; Reschly, 1980, 1988; Reynolds & Lakin, 1987; Reynolds, Wang, & Walberg, 1987; Wang, Reynolds, & Walberg, 1987, 1988, 1990; Will, 1986; Ysseldyke, Reynolds, & Weinberg, 1984). The reforms address problems such as the undocumented effectiveness of special education programs, nonfunctional and stigmatizing classification of students with mild disabilities, failure of aptitude-by-treatment interaction approaches in assessment and interventions, poor treatment validity of most current assessment measures, overlapping and poorly coordinated special programs, and poor quality of interventions.

The system reform principles involve a) the adoption of an outcomes criterion to determine the effectiveness of services; b) the use of functional assessment procedures that are directly related to defining problems in natural settings, monitoring progress, and evaluating outcomes; c) systematic problem solving; d) direct measures of academic and social–behavioral performance in natural settings; e) frequent progress monitoring with changes in interventions when progress toward goals fails to meet expectations; and f) the systematic implementation of principles of instructional design and behavior change (Reschly, 1988; Reschly & Tilly, 1993). System reforms may also involve: a) noncategorical classification schemes for students now classified in mild disability categories such as SLD and MMR; b) combining remedial and special education programs such as Chapter I and resource pull-out programs; and c) attempts to prevent disability classification through the provision of services in general education, and the delivery of special education to general education classrooms (Reynolds & Lakin, 1987; Reynolds et al., 1987).

Several system reform statements have been approved by professional and scientific organizations: a) *School Psychology: A Blueprint for Training and Practice* (Ysseldyke et al., 1984); b) *Advocacy for Appropriate Educational Services for All Children* (1985); c) *Rights Without Labels* (1986); and d) NASP-NASDE-OSEP (1994). The recent NASP-NASDE-OSEP statement describes the system changes needed including the use of more appropriate and effective assessment practices. Delivery system change is seen as a crucial prerequisite to changes in assessment practices. The first step emphasized is to change the categorical classification system and to fund services and supports needed by children and youth without disability categories. This statement estab-

lishes the context for applying the knowledge base of system reform and principles of instructional design and behavior change through describing a comprehensive problem-solving approach that would be used to determine eligibility for services, to organize and provide those services, to monitor progress and change programs as needed, and to evaluate outcomes. All of the system reform statements have the common elements of: a) rejecting traditional methods of classifying children as disabled in order to provide services; b) strongly advocating for the development of systems that provided services and supports needed by children and youth without labeling them disabled; c) establishing experimental system-change programs that would investigate ways to provide services without labeling and at the same time maintain rigorous protection of the rights of parents and students.

The knowledge base for these system reforms includes monographs directed to a discussion of traditional categories and alternative conceptions of disabilities (Wang et al., 1987, 1988, 1990), alternative delivery system conceptions and principles (Graden, Zins, & Curtis, 1988), and intervention principles that are fundamental to effective programs (Stoner, Shinn, & Walker, 1991).

ADVANCES IN ASSESSMENT AND INTERVENTION

We are drawn to delivery system alternatives by advances in assessment and intervention techniques that have the promise to substantially improve the outcomes of special education. Implementation of these alternatives has the potential for creating a revolution in the use of assessment procedures with children experiencing learning and behavioral problems (Reschly, 1988; Ysseldyke et al., 1984).

Individual assessment has been, and will continue to be, prominent in school psychology and special education; however, vast changes will occur with system reform in assessment purposes, techniques, and outcomes (Christenson &

Ysseldyke, 1989; Reschly, 1980, 1986; Ysseldyke & Christenson, 1988). Purposes will focus more on interventions, specifically, what can be changed in environments to produce improved learning and behavior. Techniques will increasingly involve gathering information in natural environments with direct measures of behaviors that can be used frequently as interventions are implemented. These measures will be used to define problems, to establish intervention goals, to monitor progress, and to evaluate outcomes. These measures also will be used as the basis for classification of students as eligible for more intensive instructional or social–emotional intervention programs, including special education (Deno, 1985, Germann & Tindal, 1985; Marston & Magnusson, 1988; Shapiro & Kratochwill, 1988; Shinn, Tindal, & Stein, 1988).

Outcomes Criteria

A major shift to a focus on outcomes rather than intervention inputs or processes is apparent in the reform literature. An outcomes orientation has been applied to analyses of overrepresentation of minority students in special education (Reschly, 1979; Reschly & Tilly, 1993). Greater recent attention to documentation of outcomes is pervasive in general and special education (Ysseldyke, Thurlow, & Bruininks, 1992).

The quality of special education services can be examined from a number of perspectives. Since the enactment of mandatory special education legislation, inputs related to programs were the principal methods for judging quality. Inputs include factors such as the rigorous implementation of the procedural safeguards, involvement of a team of persons in the IEP design, delivery of special education services according to the IEP, timely annual reviews, and triennial reevaluations. Although these input factors are important to ensuring the rights of parents and students, perhaps too much emphasis has been placed on *who* made decisions and *where* services were provided at the expense of focusing on the actual outcomes of these services. In the future there is likely to be a greater

emphasis on the outcomes of services (Thurlow & Ysseldyke, 1994).

Increasingly, special education will be viewed as a range of services that are brought to natural settings rather than as a *place* where children with disabilities receive educational services. The question of *where* will become less important than questions related to what progress occurs in the acquisition of critical social and academic skills as a result of special education services. With outcomes criteria, treatment validity becomes the most important characteristic of assessment instruments or procedures.

Problem Solving

Several problem-solving approaches have appeared in the literature, with slight variations related to intended population or type of problem (Bergan & Kratochwill, 1990; Knoff & Batsche, 1991; Rosenfield, 1987). All have common features involving problem definition, direct measures of behaviors, design of interventions, monitoring progress with intervention revisions as necessary, and evaluating outcomes. All are consistent with the experimental tradition in psychology as well as the short-run empiricism described by Cronbach (1975) as a promising replacement for interventions guided by aptitude-by-treatment interactions.

Problem solving is an essential component of implementing advances in assessment and interventions. I caution against superficial versions of problem solving, particularly those that do not involve precisely defined problems, direct measures of behavior, pre-intervention data collection, intentional application of instructional design and behavioral change principles, frequent progress monitoring with program changes as needed, and evaluation of outcomes through comparisons to initial levels of performance. As Fuchs and Fuchs (1992) noted, "feel good" consultation is likely to make the participants feel good, with little benefit to students.

Problem solving provides the overall structure for an alternative delivery system and the associ-

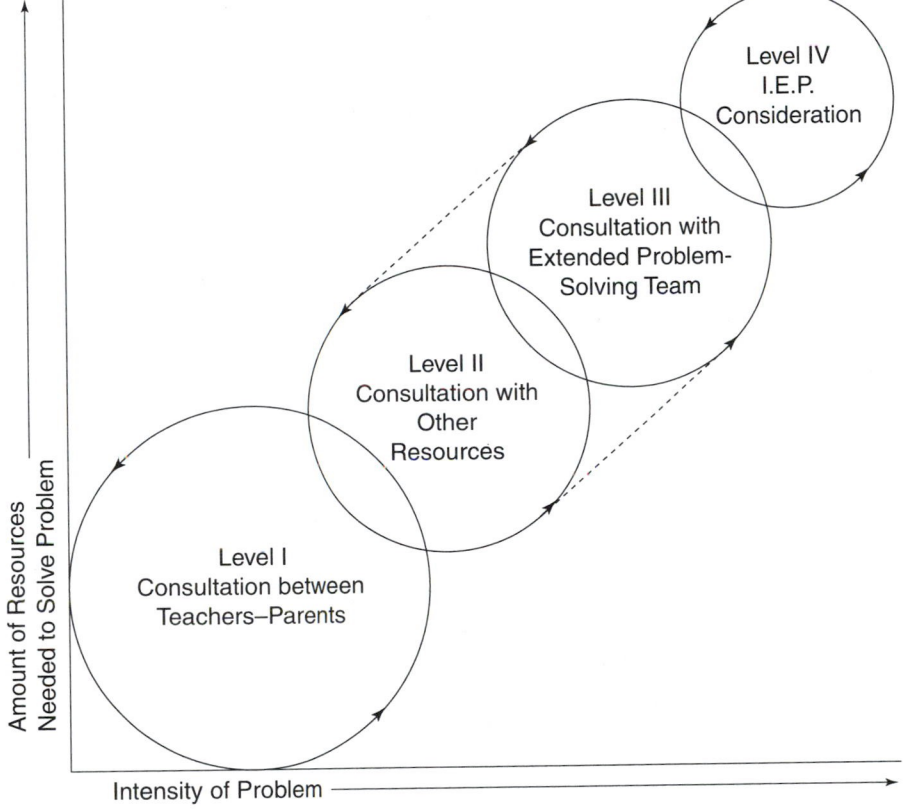

FIGURE 9.1   Heartland Area Education Agency Levels of Problem Solving

Source: Program Manual for Special Education. Johnston, IA: Heartland Education Agency, p. 17. Used with permission.

ated changes in assessment. Different levels of problem solving are illustrated in Figure 9.1, which reflects an alternative delivery system developed by the Heartland Area Education Agency in Iowa. The four levels of problem solving involve different degrees of intensity and different levels of special education and support services involvement. The first two levels occur entirely within general education with the occasional involvement of related services providers such as psychologists. Level III problem solving, involving related services personnel, is a rigorous, data-driven intervention effort that must meet exacting standards for parental involvement, problem definition, systematic data collection, problem analysis, goals, intervention plan development,

intervention plan implementation, progress monitoring, and decision making. Detailed standards have been developed for each of these problem-solving components (*Professional Practices in Problem Solving,* 1994). Interventions meeting these quality indices must be implemented for a reasonable period of time and found to be insufficient according to progress-monitoring data before Level IV problem solving is initiated.

In Level IV problem solving, classification of the student as needing special education may be considered based on documentation of substantial discrepancies from average levels of classroom performance that are not resolved to a sufficient degree by high-quality interventions in general education, or behavioral discrepancies that require programming elements or instructional intensity beyond the resources that reasonably can be provided in general education. This system depends heavily on problem solving, curriculum-based and behavioral assessment, and high-quality interentions. A critical eligibility criterion is resistance to intervention (Gresham, 1991), with rigorous standards established for quality of interventions.

Assessment Technology and Decision Making

Significant advances in assessment technology permit greater emphasis on measures functionally related to interventions. Most of these advances can be classified as behavioral assessment procedures (Shapiro & Kratochwill, 1988). The knowledge base for practice has improved substantially with the development of curriculum-based assessment and curriculum-based measurement (Deno, 1985; Howell, Fox, & Morehead, 1993; Shapiro, 1989; Shinn, 1989). Advances in the assessment of instructional environments provide further technological support to academic and behavioral interventions (Ysseldyke & Christenson, 1993). Parallel advances in behavioral assessment of social and emotional phenomena have led to equally substantial improvements in practice in these areas (Shapiro & Kratochwill, 1988). Technologically sophisticated assessment methods (e.g., Ecobehavioral Assessment Systems Software [EBASS] [Greenwood, Carta, Kamps, Terry, & Delquadri, 1994]) have been developed to aid in the detailed collection of observational data in classrooms.

The assessment technology to support practice guided by an outcomes criterion is now available for the first time in the history of special education. Behavioral assessment measures also can be used in decisions about eligibility for various special programs and in decisions about placement (Gresham 1991; Shinn, 1988). It appears that virtually the same students will be identified as needing specialized instruction and social–emotional interventions using behavioral assessment procedures; however, the behavioral assessment procedures yield information useful for intervention planning and evaluation as well as eligibility determination.

Instructional Design.   Behavior assessment and instructional analysis are inextricably related in the functional assessment of academic behaviors. The marriage of instructional design principles (e.g., Englemann & Carnine, 1982) with behavioral intervention technologies have produced impressive outcomes for students (Becker & Carnine, 1980; Kavale, 1990). As noted in the last three items of Table 9.1, the effects of interventions based on behavior therapy principles, combined with progress monitoring and changes in programming based on rate of progress (Fuchs & Fuchs, 1986) (recall Cronbach's short-run empiricism) produce strong effects according to the meta-analysis evidence.Use of this knowledge base produces results that are markedly superior to traditional special education programs or instruction based on matching teaching methods to presumed strengths in cognitive style, information processing, or neuropsychological status. Much of system reform is driven by the desire to implement more effective interventions.

Behavior Change.   Behavior change principles and characteristics of effective schools are well established in the literature (Bickel, 1990; Stoner et al., 1991; Sulzer-Azaroff & Mayer, 1991). There is a solid knowledge base for assessment and intervention; however, the remedial programs for most children and youth do not apply all, or even most, of this knowledge base.

SUMMARY

One of the main themes in system reform is improved application of the available knowledge on assessment, instruction, learning, and behavior change. Improved application of this knowledge base may be facilitated by the movement toward noncategorical classification and integration of diverse programs intended to serve children and youth. Reductions in the amount of time devoted to standardized testing to determine eligibility will permit greater opportunities for school psychologists and special educators to be involved in new roles involving functional assessment, intervention implementation, and evaluation of student progress.

A paradigm shift is occurring at different rates and in varying forms throughout the United States. There are, however, few states that have not been involved in special education reform and the pace of change is anticipated to quicken in the latter part of the 1990s. Admittedly, a paradigm shift does not occur quickly or easily; indeed, many unanticipated barriers have been encountered and will be encountered in the future. Despite the necessity to acknowledge significant impediments to reform, there are many reasons for optimism about the delivery system and role changes described in this chapter. This faith is based on a conviction that these changes are in the best interests of children, youth, and families, and that application of the outcomes criterion will increasingly invigorate and strengthen the support for a paradigm shift from the correlational science of prediction and placement to an experimental science of interventions designed to maximize learning guided by short-run empiricism. This paradigm shift will make a difference in, rather than predictions about, students' lives.

REFERENCES

Advocacy for Appropriate Educational Services for All Children (1985). Washington DC: National Association of School Psychologists. (Reprinted in *School Psychology Review, 19*[4].)

Arter, J. A., & Jenkins, J. R. (1977). Examining the benefits and prevalence of modality considerations in special education. *Journal of Special Education, 11*, 281–298.

Arter, J. A., & Jenkins, J. R. (1979). Differential diagnosis—prescriptive teaching: A critical appraisal. *Review of Education Research, 49*, 517–555.

Ayers, R., & Cooley, E. J. (1986). Sequential versus simultaneous processing on the K-ABC: Validity in predicting learning success. *Journal of Psychoeducational Assessment, 4*, 211–220.

Ayers, R. R., Cooley, E. J., & Severson, H. H. (1988). Educational translation of the Kaufman Assessment Battery for Children: A construct validity study. *School Psychology Review, 17*, 113–124.

Becker, W. C., & Carnine, D. W. (1980). Direct instruction: An effective approach to educational intervention with the disadvantaged and low performers. In B. B. Lahey & A. K. Kazdin (Eds.), *Advances in clinical and child psychology* (Vol. 3, pp. 429–473). New York: Plenum.

Bergan, J. R., & Kratochwill, T. R. (1990). *Behavioral consultation and therapy.* New York: Plenum.

Bickel, W. E. (1990). The effective schools literature: Implications for research and practice. In T. B. Gutkin & C. R. Reynolds (Eds.), *The handbook of school psychology* (2nd ed.), (pp. 847–867). New York: Wiley.

Christenson, S. L., & Ysseldyke, J. E. (1989). Assessing student performance . . . An important change is needed. *Journal of School Psychology, 27*, 409–426.

Cromwell, R., Blashfield, R., & Strauss, J. (1975). Criteria for classification systems. In N. Hobbs (Ed.), *Issues in the classification of children* (pp. 4–25). San Francisco: Jossey-Bass.

Cronbach, L. J. (1957). The two disciplines of scientific psychology. *American Psychologist, 12*, 671–684.

Cronbach, L. J. (1975). Beyond the two disciplines of scientific psychology. *American Psychologist, 30*, 116–127.

Das, J. P., & Naglieri, J. A. (in press). *Das-Naglieri: Cognitive Assessment System.* Chicago: Riverside.

Deno, S. L. (1985). Curriculum-based measurement: The emerging alternative. *Exceptional Children, 52*, 219–232.

Englemann, S., & Carnine, D. (1982). *Theory of instruction: Principles and applications.* New York: Irvington.

Flugum, K. R., & Reschly, D. J. (1994). Pre-referral interventions: Quality indices and outcomes. *Journal of School Psychology, 32*, 1–14.

Fuchs, D., & Fuchs, L. S. (1992). Limitations of a feel-good approach to consultation. *Journal of Educational and Psychological Consultation, 3*, 93–97.

Fuchs, L. S., & Fuchs, D. (1986). Effects of systematic formative evaluation: A meta-analysis. *Exceptional Children, 53,* 199–208.

Germann, G., & Tindal, G. (1985). An application of curriculum-based measurement: The use of direct and repeated measurement. *Exceptional Children, 52,* 244–265.

Good, R. H., Vollmer, M., Creek, R. J., Katz, L., & Chowdhri, S. (1993). Treatment utility of the Kaufman Assessment Battery for Children: Effects of matching instruction and student processing strength. *School Psychology Review, 22,* 8–26.

Graden, J. L., Zins, J. E., & Curtis, M. J. (Eds.). (1988). *Alternative educational delivery systems: Enhancing instructional options for all students.* Washington, DC: National Association of School Psychologists.

Greenwood, C. R., Carta, J. J., Kamps, K., Terry, B., & Delquadri, J. (1994). Development and validation of standard classroom observation systems for school practitioners: Ecobehavioral Assessment Systems Software (EBASS). *Exceptional Children, 61,* 197–209.

Gresham, F. M. (1989). Assessment of treatment integrity in school consultation and prereferral intervention. *School Psychology Review, 18,* 37–50.

Gresham, F. M. (1991). Conceptualizing behavior disorders in terms of resistance to intervention. *School Psychology Review, 20,* 23–36.

Hammill, D., & Larsen, S. (1974). The effectiveness of psycholinguistic training. *Exceptional Children, 41,* 5–14.

Hammill, D., & Larsen, S. (1978). The effectiveness of psycholinguistic training: A reaffirmation of position. *Exceptional Children, 44,* 402–414.

Hartlage, L. C., & Reynolds, C. R. (1981). Neuropsychological assessment and the individualization of instruction. In G. W. Hynd & J. E. Obrzut (Eds.), *Neurological assessment and the school age child: Issues and procedures.* New York: Grune & Stratton.

Hartlage, L. C., & Telzrow, C. E. (1986). *Neurological assessment and intervention with children and adolescents.* Sarasota, FL: Professional Resource Exchange.

Heller, K., Holtzman, W., & Messick, S. (Eds.). (1982). *Placing children in special education: A strategy for equity.* Washington D.C.: National Academy Press.

Howell, K. W., Fox, S. L., & Morehead, M. K. (1993). *Curriculum-based evaluation teaching and decision making* (2nd ed.). Columbus, OH: Charles E. Merrill.

Kaufman, A., Goldsmith, B. Z., & Kaufman, N. L. (1984). *K-SOS: Kaufman sequential or simultaneous.* Circle Pines, MN: American Guidance Service.

Kaufman, A., & Kaufman, N. (1983). *Kaufman Assessment Battery for Children* (K-ABC). Circle Pines, MN: American Guidance Service.

Kavale, K. A. (1981). Functions of the Illinois Test of Psycholinguistic Abilities: Are they trainable? *Exceptional Children, 47,* 496–510.

Kavale, K. (1990) The effectiveness of special education. In T. B. Gutkin & C. R. Reynolds (Eds.), *The handbook of school psychology* (2nd ed., pp. 868–898). New York: Wiley.

Kavale, K. A., & Mattson, P. D. (1983). "One jumped off the balance beam": Meta-analysis of perceptual-motor training. *Journal of Learning Disabilities, 16,* 165–173.

Knoff, H. M. & Batsche, G. M. (1991). Integrating school and educational psychology to meet the educational and mental health needs of all children. *Educational Psychologist, 26,* 167–183.

Marston, D., & Magnusson, D. (1988). Curriculum based measurement: District level implementation. In J. L. Graden, J. E. Zins, & M. J. Curtis (Eds.), *Alternative educational delivery systems: Enhancing instructional options for all students* (pp. 137–172). Washington, DC: National Association of School Psychologists.

NASP/NASDE/OSEP (1994). *Assessment and eligibility in special education: An examination of policy and practice with proposals for change.* Alexandria, VA: National Association of State Directors of Special Education.

Professional Practices in Problem Solving (1994). Des Moines, IA: Bureau of Special Education, Iowa Department of Education.

Program Manual for Special Education. Johnston, IA: Heartland Area Education Agency.

Reschly, D. J. (1979). Nonbiased assessment. In G. Phye & D. Reschly (Eds.), *School Psychology: Perspectives and issues* (pp. 215–253). New York: Academic.

Reschly, D. J. (1980). School psychologists and assessment in the future. *Professional Psychology, 11,* 841–848.

Reschly, D. J. (1986). Functional psychoeducational assessment: Trends and issues. *Special Services in the Schools* (Special Issue on Emerging Perspectives on Assessment of Exceptional Children), *2*, 57–69.

Reschly, D. J. (1987). Learning characteristics of mildly handicapped students: Implications for classification, placement, and programming. In M. C. Wang, M. C. Reynolds, & H. J. Walberg (Eds.), *The handbook of special education: Research and practice* (Vol. I, pp. 35–58). Oxford, England: Pergamon.

Reschly, D. J. (1988). Special education reform: School psychology revolution. *School Psychology Review, 17,* 459–475.

Reschly, D. J., & Tilly, W. D. (1993). The WHY of system reform. *Communique, 22*(1), 1, 4–6.

Reschly, D. J., & Wilson, M. S. (In press). School psychology faculty and practitioners: 1986 to 1991 trends in demographic characteristics, roles, satisfaction, and system reform. *School Psychology Review.*

Reschly, D. J., & Ysseldyke, J. E. (1995). School psychology paradigm shift. In A. Thomas & J. Grimes (Eds.), *Best practices in school psychology III* (pp. 17–31). Washington DC: National Association of School Psychologists.

Reynolds, C. R. (1981). Neuropsychological assessment and the habilitation learning: Considerations in the search for aptitude x treatment interaction. *School Psychology Review, 10,* 343–349.

Reynolds, C. R. (1986). Transactional models of intellectual development, Yes. Deficit models of process remediation, No. *School Psychology Review, 15,* 256–260.

Reynolds, C. R. (1992). Two key concepts in the diagnosis of learning disabilities and the habilitation of learning. *Learning Disability Quarterly, 15,* 2–12.

Reynolds, M. C., & Lakin, K. C. (1987). Noncategorical special education for mildly handicapped students. A system for the future. In M. C. Wang, M. C. Reynolds, & H. J. Walberg (Eds.), *The handbook of special education: Research and practice* (Vol. I, pp. 331–356). Oxford, England: Pergamon.

Reynolds, M. C., Wang, M. C., & Walberg, H. J. (1987). The necessary restructuring of special and regular education. *Exceptional Children, 53,* 391–398.

Rights Without Labels. (1986). Washington, DC: National Association of School Psychologists. (Reprinted in the *School Psychology Review,* 1989, *18*[4].)

Rosenfield, S. A. (1987). *Instructional consultation.* Hillsdale, NJ: Erlbaum.

Salvia, J., & Ysseldyke, J. E. (1995). *Assessment* (6th ed.). Boston: Houghton Mifflin.

Shapiro, E. S. (Ed.). (1989). *Academic skills problems: Direct assessment and intervention.* New York: Guilford.

Shapiro, E. S., & Kratochwill, T. R. (Eds.). (1988). *Behavioral assessment in schools: Conceptual foundations and practical applications.* New York: Guilford.

Shinn, M. R. (1988). Development of curriculum-based norms for use in special education decision-making. *School Psychology Review, 17,* 61–80.

Shinn, M. R. (Ed.). (1989). *Curriculum-based measurement: Assessing special children.* New York: Guilford.

Shinn, M. R., Tindal, G. A., & Stein, S. (1988).Curriculum based measurement and the identification of mildly handicapped students. *Professional School Psychology, 3,* 69–85.

Shinn, M. R., Ysseldyke, J. E., Deno, S. L., & Tindal, G. A. (1986). A comparison of differences between students labeled learning disabled and low achieving on measures of classroom performance. *Journal of Learning Disabilities, 19,* 545–552.

Sixteenth Annual Report to Congress on the Implementation of the Individuals with Disabilities Education Act. (1994). Washington DC: United States Department of Education, Office of Special Education Programs.

Sleeter, C. (1986). Learning disabilities: The social construction of a special education category. *Exceptional Children, 53,* 46–54.

Stoner, G., Shinn, M. R., & Walker, H. M. (1991). *Interventions for achievement and behavior problems.* Washington DC: National Association of School Psychologists.

Sulzer-Azaroff, B., & Mayer, G. R. (1991). *Behavior analysis for lasting change.* New York: Holt, Rinehart, & Winston.

Teeter, P. A. (1987). Review of neuropsychological assessment and intervention with children and adolescents. *School Psychology Review, 16,* 582–583.

Teeter, P. A. (1989). Neuropsychological approaches to the remediation of educational deficits. In C. R. Reynolds & E. Fletcher-Janzen (Eds.), *Handbook of clinical child neuropsychology* (pp. 357–376). New York: Plenum.

Thurlow, M. L., & Ysseldyke, J. E. (1994). Focusing on outcomes: Challenges for special education personnel. *Special Services in the Schools, 8,* 167–184.

Wang, M. C., Reynolds, M. C., & Walberg, H. J. (Eds.). (1987, 1988). *The handbook of special education: Research and practice* (Vols. 1–3). Oxford, England: Pergamon.

Wang, M. C., Reynolds, M. C., & Walberg, H. J. (Eds.). (1990). *Special education research and practice: Synthesis of findings.* Oxford, England: Pergamon.

Will, M. C. (1986) Educating children with learning problems: A shared responsibility. *Exceptional Children, 52,* 411–415.

Wilson, M. S., & Reschly, D. J. (1994). The times they are a'changin': Assessment training and practice are not. Manuscript submitted for publication.

Witt, J. C. (1986). Review of the Wide Range Achievement Test-Revised. *Journal of Psychoeducational Assessment, 4,* 87–90.

Witt, J. C., & Gresham, F. M. (1985). Review of the Wechsler Intelligence Scale for Children Revised. In J. Mitchell (Ed.), *Ninth mental measurements yearbook* (pp. 1716–1719). Lincoln, NE: Buros Institute.

Ysseldyke, J. E. (1988). Classification of handicapped students. In M. C. Wang, M. C. Reynolds, & H. J. Walberg (Eds.), *The handbook of special education: Research and practice* (Vol. I, pp. 253–271). Oxford, England: Pergamon.

Ysseldyke, J. E., Algozzine, B., & Epps, S. (1983). A logical and empirical analysis of current practice in classifying students as handicapped. *Exceptional Children, 50,* 160–166.

Ysseldyke, J. E., & Christenson, S. L. (1988). *Linking assessment to intervention.* In J. L. Graden, J. E. Zins, & M. J. Curtis (Eds.), *Alternative educational delivery systems: Enhancing instructional options for all students* (pp. 91–110). Washington, DC: National Association of School Psychologists.

Ysseldyke, J. E., & Christenson, S. L. (1993). *The Instructional Environment System-II.* Longmont, CO: SOPRIS West.

Ysseldyke, J. E., & Mirkin, P. K. (1982). The use of assessment information to plan instructional interventions: A review of the research. In C. R. Reynolds & T. B. Gutkin (Eds.), *The Handbook of School Psychology.* New York: Wiley.

Ysseldyke, J. E., Reynolds, M. C., & Weinberg, R. A. (1984). *School psychology: A blueprint for training and practice.* Minneapolis, MN: National School Psychology Inservice Training Network, University of Minnesota.

Ysseldyke, J. E., Thurlow, M. L., & Bruininks, R. H. (1992). Expected educational outcomes for students with disabilities. *Remedial and Special Education, 13*(6), 19–30.

Ysseldyke, J. E., Thurlow, M., Graden, J., Wesson, C., Algozzine, B., & Deno, S. (1983). Generalizations from five years of research on assessment and decision making: The University of Minnesota Institute. *Exceptional Education Quarterly, 4,* 75–93.

CHAPTER 10

Curriculum-Based Assessment and Literacy Instruction: A Political Critique

CURT DUDLEY-MARLING

INTRODUCTION

Critique is a means of bringing to bear various perspectives from which we can view a problem, an event, a field of study, or a community. By challenging what is taken for granted or by illuminating relationships that were previously unrecognized, critique enriches human understanding. The social criticism of Chomsky (1989), for example, challenges the independence of modern journalism by demonstrating the symbiotic relationship between the media and elected government officials. Gilligan's (1982) feminist critique of the social sciences exposes the patriarchal assumptions which underpin much of what passes for knowledge in Western society. In education, Marxist criticism clarifies the role of schools in reproducing social inequities (Apple, 1979; Bowles & Gintis, 1975).

Critical lenses have often been brought to bear on the field of special education. Heshusius (1982), Iano (1986), Poplin (1984, 1988), and Skrtic (1991), for example, have used critique to challenge the behavioral theory that underlies much of the work in special education. The analyses of Carrier (1986) and Sleeter (1987) illustrated how special education participates in the practice of sorting students on the basis of race, culture, and ethnicity. Fulcher (1989) used discourse theory to examine the role "disability" plays in government efforts to exert more control over the lives of its citizens. It is difficult to gauge the effect of these critiques, but there is little evidence that these critiques have affected the way special educators view themselves, their field, or the people they serve.[1]

Critical analysis is not always welcome, but it may be crucial to ensuring a diversity of ideas as a means of protecting a field of study from intellectual and moral isolation and decay. The ability of a field like special education to shield itself from criticism may seem reaffirming, but the skill with which a field of study deflects criticism in the short term may seal its fate in the long term. The health of any field of study depends upon persistent and penetrating criticism.

In this paper I offer a political critique of the trend toward curriculum-based assessment (CBA) in special education. It is my intention to examine the potential of CBA to either sustain or to remedy the inequities of American schooling in which race, class, and gender play a significant role in the quality of children's educational opportunities (Apple, 1979; Bowles & Gintis, 1975; Kozol, 1991; Swann, 1992). Many CBA proponents portray CBA as an equitable alternative to culturally and racially biased standardized achievement tests (Cohen & Spruill, 1990; Galagan, 1985; Marston, 1989), but is CBA necessarily a more equitable form of assessment? I focus on the political implications of CBA for literacy instruction because of the role literacy instruction can play in perpetuating inequities (Allington, 1994; Collins, 1991; Shannon, 1993) and because my own work focuses on literacy. After examining the political implications of CBA I briefly consider a holistic alternative to CBA. I begin, however, by offering a brief overview of CBA as I understand it.

A BRIEF OVERVIEW OF CBA

Tucker (1985) observed that "curriculum-based assessment includes any procedure that directly assesses student performance within the course content for the purpose of determining that student's instructional needs" (p. 200). Depending on how *directly* is interpreted, assessing almost any student performance deriving from or related to the classroom curriculum, including portfolio assessment, could be an example of CBA. More often, however, discussions of CBA have been limited to measures which are quantifiable, reliable, and efficient (Fuchs & Deno, 1991).

Fuchs and Deno (1991) describe two types of measurement-driven CBA: *specific subskill mastery measurement* and *general outcome measurement.* Specific subskill mastery measurement derives measurable outcomes directly from the curriculum to assess students' progress. Blankenship (1985), for example, recommends that teachers "list the skills presented in the material selected; examine the list to see if all important skills are presented; decide if the resulting, edited list has skills in the logical order; write an objective for each skill on the list; prepare items to test each listed objective . . ." (p. 236). The close link between the curriculum and assessment enables teachers to determine the need for curricular adaptations quickly and then initiate targeted instruction (Gickling & Thompson, 1985). Focusing assessment and therefore instruction on the curriculum also facilitates collaboration between regular and special education. Specific subskill mastery measurement has been criticized, however, for its uncertain reliability and validity and its relative inability to assess the long-term effectiveness of instruction or to compare the relative effectiveness of various instructional strategies (Fuchs & Deno, 1991). As an alternative to specific subskill mastery measurement, Fuchs & Deno (1991) recommend general outcome measurement (see also Deno, 1985; Marston & Magnusson, 1985).

General outcome measurement, or curriculum-based measurement, assesses global performance outcomes toward which the curriculum is directed (Fuchs & Deno, 1991). For example, the effectiveness of reading instruction may be assessed by measuring the number of words a student reads correctly in one minute, perhaps drawing reading passages from students' basal reading program (Deno, 1985). Similarly, writing growth may be assessed by measuring the number of words a student writes in three minutes in response to a story starter prompt (Deno, 1985). From a classical psychometric perspective this approach has the advantage of enabling users to make explicit statements about the reliability and validity of outcome measures. The validity evidence for these measures derives from their relationship to "socially important indexes of achievement" such as achievement tests and teacher judgments (Fuchs & Deno, 1991).

Despite differences between these two approaches to CBA, they share an implicit assumption about the meaning of literacy, an assumption that has important political implications. To the extent that CBA is tied to a prescribed curriculum (i.e., specific subskill mastery measurement) CBA users "define" literacy development in terms of a finite set of discrete skills identified by curriculum developers. The nature of these skills isn't at issue here. What is at issue, however, is the tacit assumption that people learn to read or to write *once and for all* by mastering a set of autonomous skills that presumably generalize across a range of social and cultural contexts. Proponents of general outcome measurement commit themselves to a similar principle by assuming that reading and writing development can be measured by a single measure or set of measures. The willingness to apply these measures across a range of contexts further assumes that general outcome measures are context-neutral.

The assumption that people learn to read or write by mastering a set of autonomous skills contrasts with views of literacy as social practice

(Bloome & Egan-Robertson, 1993; Bloome, Harris, & Ludlum, 1991; Fairclough, 1989; Gee, 1990, 1992; Myers, 1992).

LITERACY AS SOCIAL PRACTICE

As social practices, reading and writing are viewed as transactive, socio-psycholinguistic processes in which readers and writers use a variety of sense-making strategies as they interact with print (Rosenblatt, 1978; Shanklin, 1981; Weaver, 1994). Reading and writing are transactive in the sense that both readers and writers contribute something to the act of making meaning. As Rosenblatt (1978) put it: "Transaction designates . . . an ongoing process in which the elements or factors are . . . aspects of a total situation, each conditioned by and conditioning the other" (p. 17).

Reading and writing are sociolinguistic processes in that they are always used and understood in a sociocultural context that shapes the meaning of any text. Halliday (1978) observed that

> language comes to life only when functioning in some environment. We do not experience language in isolation—if we did we would not recognize it as language—but always in relation to a scenario, some background of persons and actions and events from which the things are said to derive their meaning. (p. 28)

The meaning of language, written or oral, derives not so much from the content of words, as from the social and cultural context within which it is used, including the "interplay of what went before and what will come later" (Bloome & Egan-Robertson, 1993, p. 309). From this perspective, words can have meanings independent of the intentions of writers or speakers (see Gee, 1990). A text may have racist or sexist implications, for example, regardless of the writer's intentions.

Each instance of written language behavior is a complex socio-psycholinguistic event requiring the simultaneous orchestration of phonetic, syntactic, and semantic cues within a language context in order to construct meaning (Harste & Burke, 1978). These cueing systems interact with each other to facilitate the production or reception of other language cues. Edelsky (1984) observed that language systems "not only operate in context; they also are interdependent, each one having consequences for the other. In any instance of genuine . . . language use, a choice in one system has ramifications for what choices or interpretations are possible in another" (p. 9). Because available cues and processing requirements vary according to the context of use, each composition–comprehension transaction between writer and reader is unique. We would not, therefore, expect a reader to assign precisely the same meaning to subsequent readings of the same text, for example, given changes in setting, the reader's background knowledge (which is changed by each reading of the text), and purpose.

Processing requirements also vary according to the sociocultural context. Certain religious rituals, for example, require people to *read* texts in languages they do not understand, relying on phonetic cues almost to the exclusion of semantic and syntactic cues. In this example people read without comprehension, but not without meaning. The sociocultural context also affects how people process texts by assigning more or less authority to the text itself. When I was teaching third grade, for example, a picture of a gravestone in a book we were reading stimulated a discussion of how long people lived. After much discussion, we seemed to agree that few people lived beyond one hundred years. The following day Ali sternly told me, "My dad said Noah lived to be 950 years old." Ali's cultural background indicated that certain texts are to be taken literally. My background suggests a different reading of such texts, but, in either case, the process by which we used our background knowledge as readers depended on a set of culturally determined beliefs.

Viewing reading and writing as social practices has a number of important implications for a discussion of CBA. First of all, literacy as social practice indicates that people do not learn to read *once and for all*. Linguist James Gee (1990) argues that the verb *read* can never be used intransitively (the same can be said of *write*). Instead, people learn to read and to write particular texts in particular ways appropriate to the social and cultural context. As Gee (1990) put it, people do not learn to read, but learn to read texts of type X in way Y and "one does not learn to read texts of type X in way Y unless one has had experience in settings where texts of type X are read in way Y. . . . One has to be socialized in a *practice* to learn to read texts of type X in way Y, a practice other people have already mastered" (Gee, 1990, p. 43).

As social and cultural practices, reading and writing "involve specific ways of interacting with people, specific ways of using language (including written language), specific sets of values for various kinds of behaviors, and specific sets of interpretations for understanding and guiding behavior" (Bloome et al., 1991, p. 22). A Gospel read to a congregation and reading bits from the newspaper at the breakfast table, for example, involve people in different ways of talking, interacting, thinking, valuing, and believing. Similarly, school reading lessons often require that students display behaviors appropriate in school—acting, thinking, and talking like a student (Bloome et al., 1991). Wortham (1993), for example, described how students in high school English classes learned to display reading comprehension to their teachers by relating assigned reading to their personal experience during class discussions. In this context reading *meant* summoning personal experiences to signal comprehension independent of whether students understood the story in the conventional sense. As social practices, reading and writing involve people in different ways of being in the world (e.g., social relationships, values, beliefs) (Gee, 1990; Heath, 1983; Sola & Bennett, 1991) as well as different ways with words.

From the perspective of reading and writing as social practices, "number of words read correctly in one minute" or "number of correctly spelled words written in three minutes" (as in CBA) are not so much general measures of reading and writing development as they are displays of literate behaviors associated with a particular context, in this case the context of traditional schooling. Similarly, a specific subskill measurement approach to CBA does not assess requisite reading skills as much as it assesses what counts as reading in schools. In other contexts, contexts that involve people in different ways with words and of being in the world, the skills assessed either by specific subskill mastery measurement or general outcome measurement may or may not *count* as reading or writing. The skills involved in an authoritative reading of a passage from a basal reader, for example, are not the same as a "critical" reading of a political campaign poster (Fairclough, 1989). It is uncertain, therefore, whether the literacy skills acquired in the context of schooling generalize to out-of-school literacy contexts (Allington, 1994; Gee, 1990; Myers, 1992; Nespor, 1991). Myers (1992) concludes:

> Defining literacy skill as a collection of socially constructed practices . . . suggests that the traditional skill-based school instruction cannot transfer to literacy use in other contexts. The skills of exercises are not the same as the skills of literacy in other social contexts. (p. 302)

In summary, viewing literacy as social practice suggests that traditional literacy instruction does not teach students to read and write *once and for all* as much as it teaches students a literacy practice associated with schooling (Gee, 1990). From this perspective, there are a range of culturally defined literacies, and school literacy, understood as a set of skills or general outcome measures, is merely one type of literacy that involves people in processes and conventions associated with that practice. It is uncertain that the processes and practices of school literacy transfer to literacy in other contexts (Myers, 1992). This is not to suggest that mastering school literacy is unimportant. The constraints of "essayist" school literacy offer powerful forms of understanding (Bennett, 1991) and the failure to master school literacy can limit students' educational and occupational opportunities. Lisa Delpit (1988) is persuasive when she argues that teachers who do not explicitly teach the skills of school literacy to minority students, students overrepresented among struggling readers and writers, may condemn these students to failure. However, a school literacy "that seeks itself as the model for what should be," viewing itself "as a universal form of reading, writing, and language use" (Mitchell, 1991, p. xviii) creates an exclusionary literacy that favors the literacy practices and the associated ways of being in the world of particular cultural groups. Assessment and instructional practices that portray literacy as a set of autonomous skills mask the possibility that school literacy privileges middle-class "ways with words" (Heath, 1983). In this sense, defining literacy is political since it raises questions about the equitable distribution of "social goods" ("anything that the people in the society generally believe are beneficial to have or harmful not to have . . . including life, space, time, 'good' schools, 'good' jobs, wealth, status, power or control" [Gee, 1990, p. 23]) in American society.

THE MEANING OF EQUITY

Curriculum-based assessment has been portrayed as an equitable alternative to biased standardized achievement tests (Cohen & Spruill, 1990; Galagan, 1985; Marston, 1989). Galagan (1985) observed that CBA's "emphasis on curriculum performance and the development of instructional interventions render them more racially and culturally neutral than most psychometric instruments" (p. 294). Claims for the equity of CBA depend, however, upon the assumption that the curriculum itself is unbiased. Presumably, an equitable curriculum is achieved by developing a set of instructional objectives common to all students, thereby creating a "level playing field" (Holmes, 1980) where all children have an equal opportunity to learn regardless of their background. This assumption underlies much of the thinking around school reform and, indeed, the common school movement of the early nineteenth century was founded on the belief that equality of educational opportunity could be created through a common curriculum for children of all social and economic classes (Pullin, 1994). CBA strengthens claims

that curricula are fair by enabling teachers to make needed adjustments to the curriculum and instructional practices in accordance with students' needs.

Ultimately, achieving equity through common curricular objectives augmented by instructionally relevant assessment rests on accepting that the content of school curricula is or even can be socially and culturally neutral. It is doubtful, however, that reading and writing instruction, for example, can ever be "socially or culturally neutral." From the perspective of literacy as social practice every reading and writing practice, including school literacy, entails a set of culturally determined conventions embodying certain attitudes, values, norms, and beliefs (Gee, 1990) particular to the sociocultural context. Bennett (1991) observes that "there is a growing body of research on literacy from the perspective of anthropology, cognitive science, sociolinguistics, and the humanities that makes it difficult to view literacy any longer as . . . neutral to the social, political, and cultural conditions within which literacy takes its particular forms (p. 14).

School literacy, like any literacy practice, is not about learning to read and write as much as it is about learning to read and write in certain ways (and, by implication, curriculum-based literacy assessment assesses students' ability to read and write *in certain ways.*) Traditional school literacy emphasizes, for example, reading and writing fictional stories, distancing oneself from texts, being able to talk about language conventions (i.e., meta-knowledge), being overly explicit, writing and speaking like storybooks, and treating "chunks" of text as autonomous wholes. Importantly, the schools' "ways with words" closely resemble literacy practices in middle-class homes (Gee, 1990; Heath, 1983; Michaels, 1981). The schools' valuing of "essay-texts" literacy, for example, which assumes that one should ignore what the hearer knows and explicitly say it anyway mirrors practices in many middle-class homes such as having children repeat back an often read book or rehearse at the dinner table events that everyone already knows about (Gee, 1990). "In other social groups, and, indeed, on other occasions for middle-class groups, such explicitness may be seen as rude because it is distancing, blunt, or condescending to the hearer's intelligence or relation to the speaker" (Gee, 1990, p. 60).

Privileging the literacy practices of middle-class families provides a significant advantage to the children of those homes. When many middle-class children enter school they do not so much learn school literacy practices as they practice what they already know, making many of them appear to be quick studies compared to their less privileged peers (Gee, 1990). Common reading and writing curricula may provide a "level playing field," but the children most likely to "win the game" (i.e., children from middle-class homes) enjoy a significant "home field advantage." It is, after all, *their* game. As Collins (1991) put it:

> I would like to suggest that schooled literacy achieves a "social magic" of definition and deception. It uses yet disguises biases of text, curriculum, and classroom practice by evoking the literate tradition in ways which discriminate against those who have the least exposure to that tradition. It does so by treating aspects of the tradition which are most tied to particular class-based varieties of language as symptomatic indices of skill, ability, or proficiency in general. (p. 237)

Curricula that advantage some groups of children—and disadvantage others—merely because the values, norms, attitudes, and beliefs of their families happen to match the values, norms, attitudes, and beliefs of teachers, school administrators, and curricula developers can never be fair. Nor can assessment practices that are bound to those curricula no matter how reliable, efficient, easy to administer, or well intentioned ever be fair.

Since various literacy practices engage people both in different "ways with words" and different "ways of being in the world," the privileging of the literacy practices of middle-class families not only disadvantages students from nondominant groups by denying *their* literacy experiences, but also has the effect of effacing the cultural values, beliefs, and attitudes in which these students' literacy practices are embedded. "The written texts children are taught to produce in U.S. schools today are used to carry certain kinds of social relationships and to construct certain kinds of cultural knowledge. Schools use writing instruction not only to inculcate certain skills, but to shape their students into particular kinds of social beings" (Sola & Bennett, 1991, p. 35). Even if CBA technology is able to help students from nondominant groups master school discourse practices—and Gee (1990) argues this will always be difficult—these students' ability to succeed in school may be linked to their willingness to be shaped into particular kinds of social (and cultural) beings. Linking success in school to the mastery of particular literacy practices risks denying many students their social and cultural identities.

Finally, equality of opportunity to learn in school also depends on an equitable distribution of resources. No teaching practice or assessment technology can overcome the "savage inequalities" in which the advantages enjoyed by middle- and upper-class students are augmented by better schools, better teachers, better health care, safer neighborhoods, and teachers who expect more of them (Kozol, 1991). CBA cannot overcome the powerful effects of disadvantage and discrimination that make it difficult for many people to achieve a measure of social and occupational success no matter how literate they become. The nation cannot assess its way out of its problems (Madaus, 1994). Nor can we create a more just and democratic society by linking testing to curricula that seek to level the social, cultural, and linguistic differences that make students interesting people. Bellah, Madsen, Sullivan, Swidler, and Tipton (1991) observe that "the real danger is that America, in the form of the great society, continuously undermines pluralism and diversity, that it implacably subverts bilingualism and biculturalism (not to mention multilingualism and multiculturalism), that the great society is an agent of homogenization, not diversity" (p. 304). I do not doubt the ability of CBA to help struggling students master common curricular objectives. There is, however, good reason to question the role of common curricular outcomes in perpetuating the unequal distribution of social goods in American society.

LITERACY ASSESSMENT: A HOLISTIC ALTERNATIVE

As a "procedure that . . . assesses student performance within the course content for the purpose of determining that student's instructional needs" (Tucker, 1985, p. 200), holistic literacy assessment is a type of CBA. However, holistic assessment differs from measurement-driven forms of CBA in several important ways. First of all, holistic assessment is not constrained by traditional notions of reliability that restrict teachers' focus to behaviors that are stable and quantifiable. Holistic educators are especially interested in reading and writing behaviors that are neither stable nor quantifiable (but are assessable) including, for example, writers' "voice," readers' emotional response to text, the ability of readers and writers to use print for introspection and critical reflection, students' ability to use background knowledge and experience to construct meaning, and how students orchestrate various cueing systems (phonics, syntax, and semantics) as they read and write according to their purposes and the demands of the sociocultural context. From a holistic perspective, valid assessment does not require reliable measures (see Moss, 1994 for an interesting discussion of validity without reliability).

Holistic assessment is also informed by a different notion of curriculum. Holistic curricula are not prescribed, but emerge from tacit "negotiations" between students and teachers (Boomer, 1982) which honor broad curricular objectives without effacing the interests, values, beliefs, attitudes, and knowledge students bring with them to school. Holistic curricula describe what teachers and students do, not what distant curriculum developers expect them to do.

A different sense of assessment and curriculum leads holistic educators to ask different sorts of questions. Instead of examining students' reading and writing development relative to a scope and sequence of curricular outcomes, a holistic educator might ask, for example, How do students use various cueing systems to make sense of texts? or Have students discovered the power of literacy to affect their lives in and out of school? Instead of seeking global measures of reading and writing effectiveness, holistic educators are more likely to ask, What sorts of literacy activities do students engage in? or How can I expand the purposes for which and sociocultural contexts within which students read and write?

The theoretical underpinnings of holistic literacy assessment, informed by work on literacy as social practice, also lead to a different sense of equity. Holistic educators believe that the standardization of learning outcomes will always disadvantage students from nonmainstream homes by disregarding or devaluing the literacy practices and associated ways of being in the world that differ from a standard that equates middle-class reading and writing practices with a generic literacy. Holistic educators endeavor to create an equitable learning environment by working collaboratively with students to create a space that is congenial to the widest possible range of literacy practices. Therefore, holistic assessment does not gauge students' literacy development by comparing students' reading and writing behaviors to a curricular or normative standard. Instead, holistic literacy assessment seeks to identify the range of purposes for which students use reading and writing and the social and cultural settings in which they are able to fulfill these intentions. Holistic educators use this assessment data to help them expand the range of purposes for which students use reading and writing and the social and cultural settings within which students attempt to fulfill their intentions.

Holistic assessment (and instruction), because of its ability to make room for a range of culturally embedded literacy practices, has the potential to create more equitable schools. But this potential is not always realized. Holistic educators themselves often focus on a narrow range of literacy practices (e.g., reading and writing fictional stories) at the expense of other ways with words as Ali reminded me when he insisted that Noah lived to be 950 years old. The holistic stance that rejects the skills of school literacy as inauthentic—not *real* reading and writing—may especially disadvantage non-mainstream students for whom the learning of these skills will be difficult without explicit instruction (Delpit, 1988; Gee, 1990). To provide an equitable alternative to measurement-driven CBA, holistic educators must acknowledge that school literacy is a kind of literacy and that the mastery of this literacy can affect students' educational and occupational opportunities.

To illustrate the nature of holistic literacy assessment, I offer a summary of my assessment of Lila, a struggling third-grade student with whom I worked.[2] (For a comprehensive description of holistic assessment see, for example, Barrs, 1988; Rhodes & Shanklin, 1993; Taylor, 1990).

When I listened to Lila on the first day of school, she read slowly and haltingly, pointing to each word with her finger as she read. She recognized few words on sight and when she encountered an unknown word her preferred strategy was to sound it out—no matter how long it took. Because Lila's phonics skills were weak, this was rarely a successful strategy. The following excerpts from her reading of *Clifford the Big Red Dog* (Bridwell, 1985) are illustrative.

Text	Lila
My dog is a big red dog.	My dog is a big r- red dog.
I have the biggest,	I have the biggest,
reddest dog on our street.	reddest dog on our str— (10 sec.) street.
We play games.	We play ga, We play gums, We play agums, We play gums, gu—mz, We play gu—mz (over 30 sec.), games.
I throw a stick.	I thr—, I thr— (over and over for more than 1 min. before I gave her the word) a stick.
and he brings	and he br-, br-, br—ing—z (after 30 sec. I gave her the word)
it back to me.	it back to me.

In general, Lila rarely used contextual information to make sense of text and her oral reading miscues (errors) often resulted in significant changes of meaning. There were rare exceptions, however. For example, from my notes on October 1st:

> Lila read *The House that Jack Built* with the class, a book she'd read with her mother . . . One interesting miscue: "cock awoke" for the "cock crowed" which resulted in little change in meaning.

Throughout the year Lila's reading became increasingly fluent as she began to use a variety of cues to make sense of text. Still, late in the year she would sometimes sound out relatively easy words like *no*. As Lila increased the range of cues she used as a reader her reading comprehension—as indicated by retellings and her participation in literature-sharing groups—improved dramatically. More importantly however, reading went from being a chore for Lila to a preferred activity. When asked about her progress as a reader she said, "I'm a lots better reader now (because) I can read harder books. I love to read and it's all because of you."

Lila wrote willingly at the beginning of the school year but she wrote very slowly, laboriously sounding out most words as she wrote. Because she wrote so slowly her pieces were usually short. Also, Lila rarely used punctuation and usually capitalized only the first word of any piece of writing. Her writing typically contained numerous spelling errors, but her spellings usually included most of the sounds (e.g., *dactrr* for doctor) even if she wasn't able to represent them conventionally. In early September she wrote a piece about her grandmother's cat.

> My gamoow has a cat the cat has a bookun boon me and my bagg brradr want to the dactrr he had to stae in the hospital for to days
>
> (My grandma has a cat. The cat has a broken bone. Me and my big brother went to the doctor. He had to stay in the hospital for two days.)

The length of Lila's pieces increased throughout the year. Sometimes she worked on a single piece of writing for up to two weeks, eventually illustrating and publishing a lengthy piece about babysitting her nephew. Lila generally preferred to write about her experiences but she did write a few fictional pieces later in the year. Lila was able to do some minor editing of her pieces by the end of the year but was able to undertake significant revision (deletions, movement of text) only with my support. Lila learned to capitalize the first word of sentences and proper names and to use periods in her writing. Her writing continued to be marked by frequent misspellings but her (mis)spellings gradually took on more and more features of conventional English orthography (see Wilde, 1992).

My initial and ongoing assessment of Lila was based on anecdotal notes—derived from regular, intensive observation of Lila as she read (books, directions, chart stories, environmental print) and wrote (stories, notes, record-keeping, classroom assignments), as she responded to reading and writing instruction, and as she talked about her reading and writing (interviews, literature-sharing groups, class discussions)—, routine analysis of her oral reading miscues (i.e., Reading Miscue Analysis; see Goodman, Watson, & Burke, 1987), and a careful analysis of her writing samples. In general, every effort was made to learn about her reading and writing for a range of purposes in a variety of instructional and social settings.

Like measurement-driven CBA, my holistic literacy assessment led directly to instructional strategies. In order to encourage Lila to increase the range of cues she used to make sense of texts, for example, I provided lots of time for Lila (and other struggling readers) to read and made available predictable reading materials that encouraged her to use text patterns to make sense of text. I also used repeated reading, assisted reading, reading partners, choral reading, cloze, and the strategic use of environmental print to reduce her reliance on phonics and increase her sight vocabulary (Rhodes & Dudley-Marling, 1988). Unlike measurement-driven CBA, however, the open-ended definition of literacy that informed assessment and instruction in my classroom honored the range of culturally determined literacy practices my students brought with them to school.

SUMMARY

Special education seeks to improve the educational opportunities of students deemed exceptional by virtue of special needs. Since the pool of exceptional students includes disproportionate numbers of individuals disadvantaged by poverty and discrimination, special educators are naturally concerned with equity issues. If equity is defined in terms of "equal opportunity to learn," curriculum-based assessment, by enabling teachers to effectively and efficiently adjust instruction to students' learning needs, seems to reinforce special education's commitment to fair and effective instruction for *all* students.

This view accepts the curriculum as unproblematic, however. The assumption that CBA by its very nature is an equitable form of assessment depends on the fairness of the curriculum to which CBA is linked. I have used the example of literacy to show how traditional, school-based literacy instruction privileges the reading and writing practices associated with middle-class American families. Literacy instruction that favors some students and disadvantages others on the basis of who their parents are is not fair nor are assessment practices that are linked to such instruction.

Holistic instruction (and assessment), because it is not constrained by curricula that reify official versions of what counts as valid knowledge, has at least the potential to create more equitable, democratic schools. Still, as I learned from Ali, this potential is not always realized.

The strength of CBA, and here I include holistic assessment as a type of CBA, lies in its close link to the curriculum, but this can also be its greatest weakness. If the content of the curriculum is unfair, as it often is, then assessment practices tied to that curriculum are no more or less fair than the curriculum itself. Ultimately, the development of equitable assessment practices is an ideological and not a technological issue. Equitable instruction and equitable assessment depend upon a willingness to accept the possibility that the content of school instruction is based on our own culturally determined notions of what counts as valid knowledge regardless of the theoretical positions that inform our assessment practices. Unless we are willing and able to critically examine the ideological meaning of schooling as part of our efforts to create more inclusive schools, tests of schooling will always carry the risk that they are really tests of culture.

NOTES

1. To be fair, the polemic tone of these critiques has not always been conducive to establishing a meaningful dialogue.

2. During the 1991–1992 academic year I took a leave from my university duties to teach third grade.

REFERENCES

Allington, R. L. (1994). The schools we have. The schools we need. *Reading Teacher, 48,* 14–29.

Apple, M. W. (1979). *Ideology and curriculum.* Boston: Routledge & Kegan Paul.

Barrs, M. (1988). *The primary language record.* Portsmouth, NH: Heinemann.

Bellah, R. N., Madsen, R., Sullivan, W. M., Swidler, A., & Tipton, S. M. (1991). *The good society.* New York: Knopf.

Bennett, A. T. (1991). Discourses of power, the dialectics of understanding, the power of literacy. In C. Mitchell & K. Weiler (Eds.), *Rewriting literacy* (pp. 13–33). Toronto: OISE Press.

Blankenship, C. S. (1985). Using curriculum-based assessment data to make instructional decisions. *Exceptional Children, 52,* 233–238.

Bloome, D., Harris, L. H., & Ludlum, D. E. (1991). Reading and writing as sociocultural activities: Politics and pedagogy in the classroom. *Topics in Language Disorders, 11,* 14–27.

Bloome, D., & Egan-Robertson, A. (1993). The social construction of intertextuality in classroom reading and writing lessons. *Reading Research Quarterly, 28,* 305–332.

Boomer, G. (1982). *Negotiating the curriculum.* Sydney: Ashton Scholastic.

Bowles, S., & Gintis, H. (1975). *Schooling in capitalist America.* New York: Basic Books.

Bridwell, N. (1985). *Clifford the big red dog.* New York: Scholastic.

Carrier, J. G. (1986). *Learning disability: Social class and the construction of inequality in American education.* New York: Greenwood.

Chomsky, N. (1989). *Necessary illusions: Thought control in democratic societies.* Boston: South End Press.

Cohen, L. G., & Spruill, J. A. (1990). *A practical guide to curriculum-based assessment for special educators.* Springfield, IL: Charles C. Thomas.

Collins, J. (1991). Hegemonic practice: Literacy and standard language in public education. In C. Mitchell & K. Weiler (Eds.), *Rewriting literacy* (pp. 229–254). Toronto: OISE Press.

Delpit, L. (1988). The silenced dialogue: Power and pedagogy in educating other people's children. *Harvard Educational Review, 58,* 280–298.

Deno, S. L. (1985). Curriculum-based measurement: The emerging alternative. *Exceptional Children, 52,* 219–232.

Edelsky, C. (1984). The content of language arts software: A criticism. *Computers, Reading, and Language Arts, 1,* 8–11.

Fairclough, N. (1989). *Language and power.* New York: Longman.

Fuchs, L. S., & Deno, S. L. (1991). Paradigmatic distinctions between instructionally relevant measurement models. *Exceptional Children, 57,* 488–500.

Fulcher, G. (1989). *Disabling policies? A comparative approach to education policy and disability.* Philadelphia: Falmer.

Galagan, J. E. (1985). Psychoeducational testing: Turn out the lights, the party's over. *Exceptional Children, 52,* 288–299.

Gee, J. P. (1990). *Social linguistics and literacies.* Philadelphia: Falmer.

Gee, J. P. (1992). *The social mind: Language, ideology, and social practice.* New York: Bergin & Garvey.

Gickling, E. E., & Thompson, V. P. (1985). A personal view of curriculum-based assessment. *Exceptional Children, 52,* 205–218.

Gilligan, C. (1982). *In a different voice.* Cambridge, MA: Harvard University Press.

Goodman, Y. M., Watson, D. J., & Burke, C. L. (1987). *Reading miscue inventory.* New York: Richard C. Owen.

Halliday, M. A. K. (1978). *Language as social semiotic.* Baltimore: University Park Press.

Harste, J., & Burke, C. (1978). Toward a socio-psycholinguistic model of reading comprehension. *Viewpoints in Teaching and Learning, 54,* 9–34.

Heath, S. B. (1983). *Ways with words.* Cambridge, England: Cambridge University Press.

Heshusius, L. (1982). At the heart of the advocacy dilemma: A mechanistic world view. *Exceptional Children, 49,* 6–13.

Holmes, M. (1980). Forward to the basics: A radical conservative reconstruction. *Curriculum Inquiry, 10,* 383–412.

Iano, R. P. (1986). The study and development of teaching: With implications for the advancement of special education. *Remedial and Special Education, 7,* 50–61.

Kozol, J. (1991). *Savage inequalities.* New York: Harper Perennial.

Madaus, G. F. (1994). A technological and historical consideration of equity issues associated with proposals to change the nation's testing policy. *Harvard Educational Review, 64,* 76–95.

Marston, D. (1989). A curriculum-based measurement approach to assessing academic performance: What is it and why do it? In M. R. Shinn (Ed.), *Curriculum-based measurement: Assessing special children* (pp. 18–78). New York: Guilford.

Marston, D., & Magnusson, D. (1985). Implementing curriculum-based measurement in special and regular education settings. *Exceptional Children, 52,* 266–276.

Michaels, S. (1981). "Sharing time": Children's narrative styles and differential access to literacy. *Language in Society, 10,* 423–442.

Mitchell, C. (1991). Preface. In C. Mitchell & K. Weiler (Eds.), *Rewriting literacy* (pp. xvii–xxvii). Toronto: OISE Press.

Moss, P. A. (1994). Can there be validity without reliability? *Educational Researcher, 23,* 5–12.

Myers, J. (1992). The social contexts of school and personal literacy. *Reading Research Quarterly, 27,* 297–333.

Nespor, J. (1991). The construction of school knowledge: A case study. In C. Mitchell & K. Weiler (Eds.), *Rewriting literacy* (pp. 169–188). Toronto: OISE Press.

Poplin, M. S. (1984). Toward an holistic view of persons with learning disabilities. *Learning Disability Quarterly, 7,* 290–94.

Poplin, M. S. (1988). The reductionist fallacy in learning disabilities: Replicating the past by reducing the present. *Journal of Learning Disabilities, 21,* 389–400.

Pullin, D. C. (1994). Learning to work: The impact of curriculum and assessment standards on educational opportunity. *Harvard Educational Review, 64,* 31–54.

Rhodes, L. K., & Dudley-Marling, C. (1988). *Readers and writers with a difference.* Portsmouth, NH: Heinemann.

Rhodes, L. K., & Shanklin, N. (1993). *Windows into literacy.* Portsmouth, NH: Heinemann.

Rosenblatt, L. M. (1978). *The reader, the text, the poem.* Carbondale, IL: Southern Illinois Press.

Shanklin, N. K. (1981). *Relating reading and writing: Developing a transactional theory of the writing process.* Bloomington, IN: Monographs in Teaching and Learning, School of Education, Indiana University.

Shannon, P. (1993). Developing democratic voices. *The Reading Teacher, 47,* 86–94.

Skrtic, T. M. (1991). *Behind Special Education.* Denver, CO: Love.

Sleeter, C. E. (1987). Why is there learning disabilities? A critical analysis of the birth of the field in its social context. In T. S. Popkewitz (Ed.), *The formation of school subjects.* (pp. 210–237). Philadelphia: Falmer.

Sola, M., & Bennett, A. T. (1991). The struggle for voice: Narrative, literacy, and consciousness in an East Harlem school. In C. Mitchell & K. Weiler (Eds.), *Rewriting literacy* (pp. 35–55). Toronto: OISE Press.

Swann, J. (1992). *Girls, boys, and language.* Cambridge, MA: Blackwell.

Taylor, D. (1990). Teaching without testing. *English Education, 22,* 4–74.

Tucker, J.A. (1985). Curriculum-based assessment: An introduction. *Exceptional Children, 52,* 199–204.

Weaver, C. (1994). *Reading process and practice.* Portsmouth, NH: Heinemann.

Wilde, S. (1992). *You kan red this!* Portsmouth, NH: Heinemann.

Wortham, S. (1993, February). *The reification of classroom discourse.* Paper presented at the annual Ethnography in Education Forum, Graduate School of Education, University of Pennsylvania, Philadelphia.

SECTION SIX

INSTRUCTIONAL STRATEGIES

Has the field of special education been dominated by a reductionistic view toward teaching and learning such as is found in current medical, behavioral, and metacognitive models? Would students in special education benefit from a move away from a reductionistic paradigm and toward the ideas and thoughts embedded in constructive, multicultural, feminine, and critical pedagogues? These views are currently gaining ground in general education and to a lesser degree in special education. In Chapter 11 Tarver clearly outlines the reasons and evidence for maintaining and improving present-day models of direct instruction, which include specific objectives, task analysis, behavioral principles, and knowledge and communication analyses. In her view, direct instruction is concerned with the how and what of teaching and is much more holistic than many critics want to acknowledge. She further notes that there is an impressive body of research supporting the benefits to students that includes but is not limited to behavioral principles.

In Chapter 12, Poplin, Weist, and Thorson point out a need for a major paradigm shift in the way schooling and instruction is viewed. They review the major problems with reductionistic perspectives and practices. As an alternative they outline the principles and strategies inherent in constructive, critical, multicultural, and feminine pedagogies. They discuss how meaning is constructed by the learner and how passion, interest, and personal involvement in the subject and activities are directly related to what is learned.

CHAPTER 11

Direct Instruction

SARA G. TARVER

INTRODUCTION

Direct Instruction or constructive/holistic approaches to teaching? This is the instructional question of the day. Although the issue is current, it is deeply rooted in age-old debates in which empiricism or behaviorism has been pitted against gestaltism or holism. Many educators espouse a rapprochement of these two opposing world views; others contend that a meaningful rapprochement is neither possible nor desirable. In this chapter I attempt to make the case that principles of both behaviorism and holism are incorporated into the theory underlying Direct Instruction and that the practices derived from that theory constitute our best approximation of a long-sought rapprochement. In the first edition of this book, I attempted to dispel myths and misconceptions about Direct Instruction by using a series of positive and negative examples. In this second edition, those examples have been revised to provide more direct responses to some of the criticisms of Direct Instruction often raised by those who advocate holism/constructivism (e.g., Poplin and Stone, 1992). The negative examples show that Direct Instruction is not what holists/constructivists portray it to be and that many of the criticisms of reductionistic approaches are not applicable to Direct Instruction. The positive examples show that Direct Instruction is consistent with some of the principles of holism/constructivism and that Direct Instruction, in practice, may actually be more holistic than the so-called holistic approaches of the day.

DIRECT INSTRUCTION IS NEITHER A PURE BEHAVIORAL NOR A GENERIC DIRECT INSTRUCTION APPROACH

Included in Direct Instruction programs are many components of the "pure" behavioral approaches that were so popular in special education in the early to mid 1970s (e.g., specification of objectives, feedback, reinforcement) and most of the components of generic direct instruction approaches that followed in the late 1970s and early 1980s (e.g., academic engaged time, guided practice and review, frequent verbal responding, correction procedures). Because these components are the more easily observed components of Direct Instruction, they have often been portrayed mistakenly as the only components of Direct Instruction. This has resulted in the common practice of classifying Direct Instruction as a behavioral/reductionistic approach with no mention of important features that make it distinctly different. Accordingly, it has been commonly assumed that limitations of other reductionistic approaches are applicable to Direct Instruction also. I will attempt to show how Direct Instruction differs from reductionistic approaches, including the pure behavioral and generic direct instruction approaches, and why the limitations of those approaches are not applicable to Direct Instruction. (The reader should note that *d*irect *i*nstruction (not capitalized) signifies generic direct instruction and *Direct In*struction (capitalized) signifies the particular Direct Instruction approach that is advocated in this chapter.

This particular Direct Instruction approach has been developed by Engelmann and his colleagues over the last quarter-century (Engelmann, 1992). Defined briefly, it is a comprehensive system in which curriculum design is integrated with teaching techniques and methods to produce instructional programs in language, reading, writing, spelling, mathematics, reasoning, and science. For more detailed descriptions of the curriculum components and teaching techniques/methods, the reader is referred to Carnine, Granzin, and Becker (1988), and Kinder and Carnine (1991). In keeping with the topic of this book, this chapter is focused on controversial issues about instructional matters.

Direct Instruction differs from both pure behavioral approaches and generic direct instruction approaches in theory and in practice. Perhaps the most important distinction is that specially designed curricula form the core of Direct Instruction, whereas the other two approaches are curriculum neutral. Neither the direct instructionist nor the behavior analyst specifies the content to be learned or the way that content is to be organized to form a whole curriculum. Instead, they focus on specific methods of teaching any isolated skill (in the case of pure behavioral approaches) or on generic teaching methods thought to be applicable to all of the skills and strategies contained in any curriculum (in the case of generic direct instruction). To state this distinction another way, direct instructionists and behavior analysts specify the *how* but not the *what* of teaching, while Direct Instructionists specify both the *how* and the *what* of teaching. Direct Instruction is not easily distinguished from other behavioral and direct instruction approaches on the basis of teaching techniques (the *how*); it is easily distinguishable on the basis of curriculum components (the *what*).

Separation of curriculum from the system of delivering it (or, separation of the *what* and the *how*) has been considered to be a serious limitation of both direct instruction (Gersten, Woodward, & Darch, 1986; Putnam, Lambert, & Peterson, 1990) and the behavioral approaches (Kazdin, 1981). This limitation is not applicable to Direct Instruc-

tion. In Direct Instruction programs, both curriculum content and techniques/methods of delivering the content are specified and, most important, the techniques/methods are carefully tailored to the content. In this sense, Direct Instruction is a much more complete approach to teaching than are pure behavioral and generic direct instruction approaches.

As will be explained in the following section, it is the curriculum components of Direct Instruction that account for its success in demonstrating the kind of generalization that is involved in higher-order thinking. By the same token, it is the absence of these curriculum components that accounts for behaviorists' and direct instructionists' failure to demonstrate acquisition and generalization of higher-order thinking skills and strategies.

DIRECT INSTRUCTION IS HOLISTIC

Advocates of constructivism (e.g., Poplin & Stone, 1992) often described reductionistic approaches as part-whole and holistic approaches as whole-part-whole. In this section I will attempt to show that Direct Instruction is more accurately described as a whole-part-whole rather than a part-whole approach and that criticisms of part-whole, reductionistic approaches are not applicable to Direct Instruction. In so doing, I will attempt to show also that some of the merits generally attributed to holistic approaches are more applicable to Direct Instruction than they are to so-called holistic approaches

To understand the whole-part-whole nature of Direct Instruction, it is necessary to know (a) the three analyses that constitute Engelmann and Carnine's (1982) theory of cognitive learning and (b) how published Direct Instruction programs are derived from those analyses. The first analysis is an analysis of the knowledge system of concern (e.g., reading, mathematics, spelling, etc.). That analysis is conducted to determine the structure of the knowledge system—its elements, connections among the elements, and how the elements are organized to constitute the whole. The knowledge system analysis is followed by a communications analysis that is conducted to determine ways of communicating the elements, their connections, and the organizational structure. The products of these two analyses are scripted lessons that contain clear explanations and/or dynamic presentations of the elements and their connections. During field testing of the lessons in classrooms, a third analysis—a behavior analysis—is conducted to determine how teachers can deliver the lessons most effectively and efficiently. The behavior analysis yields numerous presentation techniques and methods, including methods of observing, monitoring, and correcting student responses. The methods/techniques derived from the behavior analysis are combined with the curricular materials derived from the knowledge system and communications analyses to produce complete instructional programs.

To show how elements are presented and then combined or integrated with other elements in Direct Instruction programs, an example from the comprehension strand of the *Corrective Reading* program (Engelmann, Osborn, & Hanner, 1989) is presented here. In that program, series of exercises are devoted to teaching the thinking operations of analogies, deductions, classifications, similarities, and inferences. As instruction progresses, the bits of information presented within a given series are integrated into other series. For example, after the student has learned to complete analogies in analogies exercises (e.g., a bear is to a paw as a man is to a _____; birds are to flying as fish are to_____) and has learned that bears, men, birds, and fish are all in the class of animals in classification exercises, then the two kinds of information are integrated to teach students that both parts of an analogy tell about things from the same class. For example, after presenting the analogy that "birds are to flying as fish are to swimming," the teacher asks, "What class are birds and fish in?" (animals). Still later the teacher teaches that flying tells how a bird moves and swimming tells how a fish moves and asks the students "So, what does this analogy tell?" (how animals move). Gradually analogies exercises are expanded to include

classes other than the class of animals—the class of colors, the class of objects, the class of vehicles, and so on.

Much later in the program, after definitions of words such as *reside* and *construct* have been taught in definitions exercises, definitions are incorporated into analogies exercises to yield analogies such as:

> reside:live somewhere::construct:build

Still later, after parts of speech have been taught, that information is integrated into analogies exercises such as:

> reside:verb::residence:noun

and

> reside:residence::construct:construction

Students are taught not only to fill in missing elements, but also to tell what an analogy tells (e.g., the definition or the part of speech). Students are also taught directly that if one part of the analogy tells the definition, then the other part must also tell the definition; if one part of the analogy tells the part of speech, then the other part must also tell the part of speech.

In this kind of instruction, a general strategy for constructing analogies is communicated: begin with two things from the same class (any class) and tell the same thing (anything) about both of them. This kind of instruction enables students to construct a huge number and wide array of analogies. In other words, it enables students to construct new analogies by generalizing what they learned in structured presentations of carefully selected examples. It also enables students to apply their understanding of analogies to construct meaning from the writings of others when that meaning is not stated explicitly. To illustrate how that might occur, consider the following reading comprehension exercise from Snider (1989):

> Alan was a writer. He had written a book but now he had to get a copyright. A copyright would protect him from people who might copy parts of his book and say that they wrote it.

Leonard was a great inventor. He had a model of his invention and that model worked. Now he had to get a patent. An inventor gets a patent and a writer gets a copyright.

Question: How would a patent help Leonard?

a. It would let other people know about his invention.
b. It would help him remember how to make his invention.
c. It would make him famous.
d. It would protect him from other people who might copy his invention.

The analogy, inventor:patent::writer:copyright, is given in the last sentence of the passage, but it does not provide all of the information needed to answer the question. It does not provide a literal link with *protect*. To form that link, the reader could use analogical reasoning that might go something like this:

I know that Alan and Leonard are both in the class of persons. I know that a copyright protects Alan because that is stated in the first paragraph. And I know that if one part of an analogy tells what protects, the other part must also tell what protects. So if a copyright protects Alan, then a patent must protect Leonard. Bingo, item (d) is the correct answer.

In deductions exercises such as the following, students learn to use evidence to draw conclusions:

All planets orbit around a sun.
Pluto is a planet.
So _____ .

Students read the evidence (the first two statements) and then respond to the teacher's questions: "So, what's the conclusion about Pluto?" (Pluto orbits around a sun.) and "How do you know that Pluto orbits around a sun?" (Because all planets orbit around a sun.) Later, students are required to use deductive reasoning to answer comprehension questions. For example, they might be expected to deduce that Mercury orbits around a sun after having been given the information that Mercury is a planet.

Just as simple analogies exercises lay a foundation for teaching complex analogical reasoning, simple deductions exercises lay a foundation for teaching complex logical reasoning. Students can be taught, for example, to solve syllogisms such as "All A are B, C is A, so_____ " by applying the same kind of deductive reasoning that they learned earlier in structured deductions exercises.

Analogical and logical reasoning are important components of general intelligence as well as reading comprehension (Sternberg, 1985; Wagner & Sternberg, 1984). Direct Instruction's emphasis on the teaching of cognitive strategies that are involved in higher-order cognitive processes should be evident from the examples provided here. The contention that what students learn from Direct Instruction programs actually does add up to higher cognitive thinking is supported by research showing significant IQ and reading comprehension gains for students taught with Direct Instruction (Becker, Engelmann, Carnine, & Rhine, 1981; Gersten, Becker, Heiry, & White, 1981). Moreover, a comprehensive review of empirical evaluations of interventions for teaching logical and analogical reasoning led Grossen and Carnine (in preparation) to challenge the common hypothesis that discovery methods are more likely to lead to generalization than are methods that teach explicit strategies directly.

It is hoped that the analogies and deductions examples will help to dispel the myth that Direct Instruction is designed to teach rudimentary skills only. It is hoped that they will also make clear that Direct Instruction is not simply a reductionistic, atomistic, part-whole approach as implied by some constructivism advocates (e.g., Poplin & Stone, 1992). Direct Instruction is more accurately described as combinative, integrative, and holistic. Direct Instruction curriculum developers begin with an analysis of a whole knowledge system. That analysis yields many parts. Those parts are then recombined to reconstitute the whole.

The contention by some constructivists that reductionistic models create generalization and maintenance problems may be applicable, to some extent, to pure behavioral and direct instruction approaches, but it is not applicable to Direct Instruction. In Direct Instruction, generalization is not treated as an add-on to learning, as claimed by Poplin, but as a natural outcome of well-designed instruction. As shown by the analogies examples, it is the examples and the ways in which they are combined that enable the learner to acquire general strategies and construct more and more complex cognitive understandings.

At the theoretical level, Direct Instruction is not inconsistent with Gestalt theory, the theory from which many holistic principles have been derived. As explained by Marx and Hillix (1963), Gestaltists are not opposed to the analysis of psychological phenomena; they do insist, however, that the psychologist who analyzes psychological phenomena must specify the principles by which the parts are combined to constitute the whole. Direct Instructionists have done that. Principles of combining elements to communicate the whole are inherent outcomes of the knowledge system and communications analyses. Furthermore, Direct Instructionists have applied those principles in numerous published Direct Instruction programs.

To fully appreciate the holistic nature of Direct Instruction, it is necessary to know that Engelmann and Carnine's (1982) knowledge system analysis is very different from traditional task analysis. As claimed by some constructivists (e.g., Poplin & Stone, 1992), traditional task analysis usually takes the form of reducing isolated academic skills and strategies into smaller and smaller elements. In contrast, Engelmann and Carnine's (1982) analysis is aimed at the detection of *samenesses* among seemingly disparate elements (e.g., that all analogies are the same in that they tell the same thing about things from the same class). Samenesses define the connections among the elements; without an understanding of these connections, there can be no understanding of the whole system. Detection of relevant samenesses/connections is essential to the learner's generalization of cognitive learning. Unless a body of knowledge is structured to communicate relevant samenesses clearly, two unfortunate re-

sults are likely: (1) the learner will not detect the relevant samenesses/connections which are essential to appropriate generalization, and/or (2) the learner will focus on irrelevant samenesses which lead to inappropriate overgeneralizations or misconceptions. Most important, detection of *numerous* relevant samenesses and their interconnections is essential to the learner's acquisition of a holistic understanding of complex academic knowledge systems.

DIRECT INSTRUCTION IS CONSTRUCTIVE, BUT IT IS INCONSISTENT WITH CONSTRUCTIVISM AS IT IS CONCEPTUALIZED IN EDUCATION TODAY

Is the learner more likely to acquire a deep understanding of knowledge when the structure of that knowledge is communicated directly via instruction or when provided with opportunities to discover/construct the knowledge in the absence of explicit instruction? This is a question of great import in today's debate. Bruner (1960) addressed that question many years ago when he wrote:

> To aid the learner in making connections, a body of knowledge must be structured in a way that a learner can use the propositions acquired to generate new knowledge, conclusions, or propositions. In other words, in learning how to make connections, the learner "learns how to learn." . . . To learn structure, in short, is to learn how things are related. (pp. 6–7)

Although Bruner's theory has long been recognized as a leading cognitive theory, too few educators are aware that Direct Instruction is the epitome of that theory in practice.

Instruction, by definition, is information about a structure or structures. Academic instruction is information about cognitive structures. As pointed out by Kameenui and Simmons (1990), information comes in many different forms.

> Every reading skill or language concept is a piece of information. Information, whether in the form of a skill, concept, fact, rule, operation, algorithm, or a set of relationships and facts in a content area, can be taught. (p. 16)

In contrast to the Direct Instructionists' belief that the teacher should and can present information directly is the constructivists' belief that the learner should and can construct/discover that information in the absence of explicit instruction. The constructivist teacher does not present informational elements of the system to be learned, but, instead, "supports" or "guides" the learner as she discovers the elements and constructs the whole. Constructivists have provided little detail about the forms that such support and guidance might take. Articles written by whole language teachers suggest that what they actually do is (1) provide the learner with opportunities to demonstrate what she already knows, (2) observe those demonstrations, and (3) describe what she has done or what they believe she knows.

Although constructivists' attempt to describe the cognitive structures that the learner has already constructed (i.e., what the learner already knows), they do little or nothing that might enable the learner to construct new cognitive structures. In contrast, Direct Instruction is designed to communicate information that will enable the learner to build new cognitive structures. As expressed by Kameenui and Simmons (1990):

> Teachers are ultimately responsible for taking a child from a state of "unknowing" to a state of "knowing"; that is, a state in which a child can read basic CVC (consonant, vowel, consonant) words (e.g., cat, cot, sit) or interpret the fourth soliloquy of Hamlet in ways that weren't possible before. The teaching process should involve more than merely providing children with an opportunity to demonstrate what they already know. Teaching involves enabling the learner to do things that could not be done before. (p. 10)

In Direct Instruction, information that was previously unknown is presented before the student is expected to demonstrate a working knowledge of that information. This proactive approach sets the stage for student success. Remember that the information presented by the Direct Instruction teacher comes in many forms and communicates the complex samenesses/connections that enable the student to construct new knowledge by generalizing. So, setting the stage for student success means setting the stage for successful demonstrations of deeper understandings and more complex constructions than the student was able to demonstrate previously. To put it another way, Direct Instruction enables students to construct what they had not previously constructed. It is in this sense that Direct Instruction is constructive.

In contrast, so-called constructive approaches are reactive; they set the stage for student failure when they expect the student to demonstrate new understandings and meanings but provide none of the information from which those understandings/meanings can be constructed. Only those students who have already acquired such information elsewhere can be successful in this situation. Perhaps that is why constructive/holistic approaches have such a poor track record with students who are likely to have limited stores of preexisting background knowledge (e.g., students who are disadvantaged and/or have learning disabilities). Less advantaged and less abled students are in greater need of Direct Instruction than are their more advantaged and abled peers. This is not to say that advantaged and abled students don't benefit from explicit instruction; they do. It is to say that some students benefit more than others.

I once heard a constructivist criticize Direct Instruction on the grounds that it teaches only that which is known. That is true; it is not possible to communicate that which is unknown. It must first become known. Where the constructivists are wrong is in their contention that communicating the known explicitly prohibits, or at least interferes with, the construction of new knowledge which was previously unknown. In conflict with this contention are the many accounts of discoverers creating new understandings or knowledge by identifying connections among the elements of the known (Carnine, 1990). New cognitive structures, like new physical structures, are constructed of known elements; the newness is attributable to a unique combination or organization of the elements. NO THING has ever been constructed of NOTHING and NO THING will ever be constructed of NOTHING.

In our advanced society, the probability that one will create/discover significant unknowns without first acquiring a large store of knowns is considerably lower than the probability that one will win the lottery. To fail to teach what is known directly so that students will have opportunities to detect previously undetected connections among the elements of the known is to reduce the chances that new knowledge will be created. To expect young students to create unknowns in some domain in which they have acquired few of the elements of what is known (mathematics, for example) is to play a terrible trick on the minds of those students. So-called *con*structive practices can, and often do, have *des*tructive effects on the lives of students.

DIRECT INSTRUCTION DOES NOT PLACE THE ONUS OF RESPONSIBILITY FOR CAUSE AND CURE ON THE STUDENT; CONSTRUCTIVE APPROACHES DO

Charges by some constructivists (Poplin & Stone, 1992) that reductionistic models place the onus of responsibility for cause and cure of failure on the student clearly is not applicable to Direct Instruction. If there is a single Direct Instruction motto, it is this: "If the student hasn't learned, the teacher hasn't taught." It follows that the "cure" lies in the teaching/instruction and not in the student.

There is a great deal of hypocrisy in the constructivists' claims that others "blame the child," when it is they who do just that. How else can one interpret the constructivists' well-known practice of explaining a young child's failure to learn to read with the simple statement, "the *child* isn't ready." Constructivists fail to consider the possibility that the teacher may not have been ready to teach the skills and strategies that constitute reading readiness and/or the likelihood that the reading curriculum was devoid of information from which the student might discover or construct such skills and strategies.

DIRECT INSTRUCTION IS EFFECTIVE

Direct Instruction is supported by an impressive body of research. It is the most research-based and research-supported approach to teaching that has ever been developed (Gersten et al., 1986). No attempt will be made to review that large body of research in the space allotted here. However, concluding comments of several reviewers will be mentioned.

Elliott and Shapiro (1990) reviewed research regarding intervention techniques and programs for academic performance problems and concluded:

> Future research issues related to Direct Instruction do not need to center upon demonstrations of its effectiveness. These data exist and are convincing. (p. 654)

Kinder and Carnine (1991) reviewed the findings of Project Follow Through (a large-scale, national, longitudinal-evaluation study of over twenty approaches to teaching economically disadvantaged students in kindergarten through third grade); a variety of experimental and quasi-experimental studies; single-subject studies with learners with more severe disabilities; and a meta-analysis by White (1988). Among their conclusions were: (a) research establishes a strong case both for the use of published Direct Instruction programs and for the application of Direct Instruction principles in teaching basic and higher-order skills, (b) experimental and quasi-experimental studies strongly support the use of Direct Instruction with special education populations, and (c) recently developed programs in which technology is employed to assist instruction are promising. Most important in the context of this chapter are Kinder and Carnine's (1991) findings regarding Follow Through comparisons:

> Low-income students, who were taught with materials carefully designed to present information, made statistically and educationally significant gains when their test scores were compared to students' in the other Follow Through models. These initial effects endured with fifth- and sixth-graders

maintaining their academic advantages but also achieving higher college acceptance rates than comparison groups. (p. 210)

In Project Follow Through, the Direct Instruction model produced greater gains than other educational models in basic skills, cognitive problem solving, and affective learning (Abt Associates, 1976–77; Watkins, 1988). Among the educational models found to be less effective than Direct Instruction were several that are included, today, in the rubric of constructive approaches—an Open Classroom Model, a Piagetian Cognitive-Oriented Curriculum Model, A Tucson Early Education Model that emphasized use of the language experience approach, and a Bank Street Model.

Recent reviews of research on beginning reading are consistent with the Follow Through findings. Reviews by Stahl and Miller (1989) and Adams (1990) revealed little support for language experience and whole language approaches. A synthesis of research with low-income children led Chall, Jacobs, and Baldwin (1990) to conclude that (a) low-income students, like other students, benefit most from early and direct teaching of word recognition skills, including phonics, and (b) the use of enriched, literature-based beginning reading programs may be less effective.

DIRECT INSTRUCTION IS HUMANISTIC

A strong case for the contention that Direct Instruction is humanistic can be made on the basis of its effectiveness with the least privileged students in our schools—students who are economically disadvantaged. As expressed so eloquently by Delpit (1988), to fail to teach minority and poor students how to read and write is to ensure that they remain outside our "culture of power" and that the power status quo is perpetuated. Delpit recommends that teachers "teach all students the explicit and implicit rules of power as a first step toward a more just society" (p. 289). Included among those rules of power are the linguistic rules or codes of our spoken and written language systems—the grammar of written language, the phonetic code that links our written language system to our spoken language system. Direct Instruction communicates those linguistic rules of power clearly and effectively.

SUMMARY

The most important thing that can be said about Direct Instruction is this: IT WORKS! It is the most effective approach to the teaching of academic skills and strategies—higher-order as well as basic skills and strategies—that has ever been developed. As expressed by Elliott and Shapiro (1990), "It is unfortunate that the technology and resources exist for accelerating the academic performance of low-achieving youngsters, but continue to go relatively untapped" (p. 654).

As stated at the beginning of this chapter, principles of both behaviorism and holism are incorporated into the theory underlying Direct Instruction. The teaching approach derived from that theory communicates both whole knowledge systems and the parts that compose those systems. Pure behavioral approaches are limited by a focus on parts to the exclusion of the whole, while pure holistic approaches are limited by a focus on the whole to the exclusion of the parts. The question, Should we teach parts *or* wholes? should be replaced by the question, How can we teach both parts *and* wholes effectively? No other instructional approach has been shown to communicate both parts *and* wholes as effectively as Direct Instruction.

The question of who constructs meaning—the student or the teacher—should also be reconceptualized as, How can teachers present information in such a way that students will be more likely to discover/construct new knowledge? Furthermore, the related question—Should curricula be determined by the teacher or predetermined by curriculum developers (or the authors of textbooks)—should also be reconceptualized as, How can teachers evaluate curriculum materials and textbooks to ensure selection of the most well-designed instructional materials?

Teachers know that they are likely to be more successful at promoting their students' discoveries and constructions if they have access to instructional materials that are well designed for the purpose of communicating relevant samenesses or connections among the elements of the academic domain of concern. Because new knowledge is constructed of previously known elements, it is essential that known elements and their connections be communicated clearly. To expect teachers to analyze complex knowledge systems and devise effective ways of communicating the elements and their connections as they are working with students in the classroom is to expect the impossible. Students, teachers, *and* curriculum developers are essential contributors to effective instruction. Either–or questions (e.g., the student *or* the teacher?, the teacher or curriculum developers?) should be replaced with a question that encompass the student *and* the teacher *and* curriculum developers. That question might be: How

can teachers deliver well-designed curricula that will enable their students to acquire information from which new knowledge can be constructed or discovered?

To fail to recognize that Direct Instruction provides our most promising answer to that question is to continue to tolerate unnecessary school failure. The International Institute of Advocacy for School Children defines academic child abuse as the use of practices that cause unnecessary failure (Engelmann, 1992). Our nation can no longer afford to tolerate so-called constructive, holistic, humanistic approaches that are shrouded in positive-sounding rhetoric but nonetheless have the negative effect of causing unnecessary failure. Let's replace the currently popular holistic/constructive approaches with an approach that has been demonstrated to cause school success and have positive effects on students. That approach is known as Direct Instruction.

REFERENCES

Abt Associates. (1976–77). *Education as experimentation: A planned variation model.* (Vols. 3A and 4). Cambridge, MA: Author.

Adams, M. J. (1990). *Beginning to read: Thinking and learning about print.* Cambridge, MA: MIT Press.

Becker, W. C., Engelmann, S., Carnine, D. W., & Rhine, W. R. (1981). Direct Instruction model. In W. R. Rhine (Ed.), *Making schools more effective.* New York: Academic.

Bruner, J. S. (1960). *The process of education.* Cambridge, MA: Harvard University Press.

Carnine, D. (1990). Beyond technique—Direct Instruction and higher order skills. *Association for Direct Instruction News, 10*(1).

Carnine, D., Granzin, A., & Becker, W. (1988). Direct Instruction. In J. Braden, J. Zino, & M. Curtis (Eds.), *Alternative educational delivery systems: Enhancing instructional options for all students* (pp. 327–349). Washington, DC: National Association for School Psychologists.

Chall, J. S., Jacobs, V. A., & Baldwin, L. E. (1990). *The reading crisis: Why poor children fall behind.* Cambridge, MA: Harvard University Press.

Delpit, L. D. (1988). The silenced dialogue: Power and pedagogy in educating other people's children. *Harvard Educational Review, 58,* 280–298.

Elliott, S. N., & Shapiro, E. S. (1990). Intervention techniques and programs for academic performance problems. In T. B. Gutkin & C. R. Reynolds (Eds.), *The handbook of school psychology.* New York: John Wiley & Sons.

Engelmann, S. (1992). *War against the schools' academic child abuse.* Portland, OR: Halcyon House.

Engelmann, S., & Carnine, D. (1982). *Theory of instruction: Principles and applications.* New York: Irvington.

Engelmann, S., Osborn, S., & Hanner, S. (1989). *Corrective reading.* Chicago: Science Research Associates.

Gersten, R., Becker, W. R., Heiry, T. J., & White, W. A. (1981, April). *Relationship between entry IQ and yearly academic gains in a direct instruction model.* Paper presented at the meeting of the American Educational Research Association, Boston.

Gersten, R., Woodward, J., & Darch, C. (1986). Direct Instruction: A research-based approach to curriculum and teaching. *Exceptional Children, 53,* 17–31.

Grossen, B., & Carnine, D. (in preparation). Review of empirical evaluations of interventions for teaching logical and analogical reasoning.

Kameenui, E. J., & Simmons, D. C. (1990). *Designing instructional strategies.* Columbus, OH: Merrill.

Kazdin, A. E. (1981). Behavior modification in education: Contributions and limitations. *Development Review, 1,* 34–57.

Kinder, D., & Carnine, D. (1991) Direct Instruction: What it is and what it is becoming. *Journal of Behavioral Education, 1,* 193–213.

Marx, M. H., & Hillix, W. A. (1963). *Systems and theories in psychology.* New York: McGraw-Hill.

Poplin, M. S., & Stone, S. (1992). Paradigm shifts in instructional strategies: From reductionism to holistic/constructivism. In W. Stainback & S. Stainback (Eds.), *Controversial issues in special education* (pp. 153–179). Boston: Allyn and Bacon.

Putnam, R. T., Lambert, M., & Peterson, P. L. (1990). Alternative perspectives on knowing mathematics in elementary schools. In C. B. Cazden (Ed.), *Review of research in education* (pp. 57–150). Washington, DC: American Educational Research Association.

Snider, V. E. (1989). Reading comprehension performance of adolescents with learning disabilities. *Learning Disability Quarterly, 12,* 87–96.

Stahl, S. A., & Miller, P. D. (1989). Whole language and language experience approaches for beginning reading: A quantitative research synthesis. *Review of Educational Research, 59,* 87–116.

Sternberg, R. J. (1985). *Beyond IQ: A triarchic theory of human intelligence.* New York: Cambridge University Press.

Wagner, R. K., & Sternberg, R. J. (1984). Alternative conceptions of intelligence and their implications for education. *Review of Educational Research, 54,* 179–223.

Watkins, C. L. (1988, July). Project Follow Through: A story of the identification and neglect of effective instruction. *Youth Policy,* 7–11.

White, W. A. T. (1988). A meta-analysis of the effects of direct instruction in special education. *Education and Treatment of Children, 11,* 354–374.

CHAPTER 12

Alternative Instructional Strategies to Reductionism: Constructive, Critical, Multicultural, and Feminine Pedagogies

MARY POPLIN
DUDLEY J. WIEST
SUE THORSON

INTRODUCTION

Most instructional strategies in the field of special education have been based on models of learning that are more, rather than less, reductionistic. These include the medical, behavioral, and psychological processes, and metacognitive or strategy models. Within all of these models there is an underlying assumption that students with disabilities have discrete deficits that can be specifically and accurately diagnosed and remediated. Concomitant to this assumption, though often unstated, is the belief that this diagnosis and remediation of specific, sometimes minute, deficits will ultimately improve larger student achievement goals.

Contrary to these assumptions are principles of less reductionistic learning theories that seek to assist students in the creation of meaning around larger and more relevant tasks. These theories start with the assumption that all people are always learning and are constantly creating new meanings in ways that fit their own individual needs, interests, sociocultural contexts, developmental levels, and previous and current experiences. Although both reductionistic and less reductionistic proponents offer direct instruction, less reductionistic or more holistic educators seek to do so by engaging the student in whole tasks relevant to their development, experiences, interests, and sociocultural contexts. It is the task of the student, through

various experiences and assistance, to break down the whole and put it back together. Reductionists choose predetermined sets of skills or strategies that have already been broken down into parts and then instruct the students in these parts. The purpose of this chapter will be to present briefly the limitations of reductionistic methods and their assumptions and then to present four alternative models of instruction and their assumptions which lie on the more holistic end of the continuum of learning theory. These include constructivism, critical pedagogy, multicultural education, and feminine pedagogy. There are still critical issues in each of these pedagogies that remain to be solved but this will not be the purpose of this chapter. (For more information on these issues, see Rivera & Poplin, 1995.)

REDUCTIONISM IN SPECIAL EDUCATION

In the field of special education, we have used various models of instruction drawn largely from our inherent assumptions about disability. These models have included (1) the medical model whereby medical knowledge of the disability is seen as critical to educational planning, (2) the psychological processing model whereby we have looked at the prerequisite psychological phenomenon that is supposed to underlie learning, (3) the behavioral model whereby disability and remediation is directed at specific behaviors whose presence or absence denote the disability, and (4) the strategic or metacognitive models that emphasize the diagnosis and instruction of strategic behaviors associated with learners without disabilities.

Even though these models look substantively different from one another in terms of method or content of instruction, we argue that they differ only superficially from one another. Each one shares what Koch (1981) calls the reductionistic fallacy, the fallacy of believing that a complex whole is the same as its parts and that the whole can be explained entirely by describing the parts (e.g., mental states are nothing but neural processes). This fallacy encourages us to view the explanation of a phenomenon as real rather than the phenomenon being explained (Angeles, 1981). So the hypothesized cause of a problem becomes the diagnosis and remediation as well. Koch also posits even more serious problems with reductionistic views. He suggests these views so narrow the range of admissible questions that educators and psychologists can no longer engage in the larger, more meaningful, and critical questions raised by human beings, such as the purpose of one's life and the larger view of what it means to be human.

The methods we currently apply in special education exemplify this failure to consider bigger pictures as well as mirror the erroneous belief that complex wholes such as human learning and behavior can be broken down (reduced) into component parts (e.g., neural processing, hypothetical psychological processes such as long- and short-term memory, prerequisite cognitive skills, observable academic and social behaviors, or cognitive or learning strategies). We use these predetermined component parts to design what we hope will be more effective practice in assessment and instruction. However, our success rates defy this notion. For all their apparent differences, the four models under which we most frequently operate in special education share powerful funda-

mental assumptions. We believe these shared beliefs are exemplary of the reductionistic fallacy that emerges as a result of our adherence to reductionistic theories about learning. Some of the common assumptions follow. (For other and more detailed discussion of these, see Poplin, 1987, 1988a; 1988b; Poplin & Stone, 1992; Heshusius, 1984, 1989.)

1. A reductionistic diagnosis of problems seeks to *discover deficits within the student.* This view limits the degree to which other possible contributions to the problem can be taken into consideration. For example, how do institutional racism, second language issues, poor instruction, and the previous experiences and interests of the child get figured into our understanding of a problem a student is experiencing in school?

2. Reductionistic models form a *diagnosis around the hypothesized cause* of the disability. The theory regarding the cause of the disabling condition drives the selection of the diagnostic instruments which further narrows the range of possible explanations and solutions. If one believes the problem is caused by memory deficits, memory deficits will be measured.

3. *Diagnosis drives instruction.* Whatever has been determined to be wrong, whether it be memory functions or pieces of academic skills or cognitive strategies, these become the target for instruction. Thus the whole process of theorizing, diagnosing, instructing, and researching merely reifies the basic assumptions made in the first place about students with disabilities.

4. Reductionistic models *segment learning into parts,* either parts leading to an academic or social behavior, parts of cognitive or learning strategies, or parts of mental processes. This breaking down of skills is done outside the student and then delivered to the student in a logically ordered sequence, logical from the standpoint of adults without disabilities who designed the sequence based on their own experiences and knowledge.

5. Reductionistic models *tightly control instruction,* leaving the learner in a basically passive, responsive role. The student's primary choice in instruction is whether or not to be compliant.

6. *Instruction is deficit-driven.* Because theory about cause drives diagnosis and assessments, and diagnosis drives instruction, the majority of students' time in school becomes focused on things that are difficult for them to do. Very little, if any, time is devoted to locating or supporting activities in which students have talent.

7. *Instruction is viewed as unidirectional.* The teacher is to deliver instruction, the teacher knows, the student receives. This is often referred to as the "banking system of education" (Freire, 1970).

8. Reductionistic assessment and instruction promotes almost exclusively *school goals rather than life goals.* Because the view of the problem and context is so limited in reductionistic instructional settings, goals for students become truncated and expectations lowered because of the constant focus on deficits.

REDUCTIONISM RECONSIDERED

Increasingly, serious questions are being raised about the reductionistic assumptions used across special education (as has been the case for many years in general education). These questions have permeated every aspect of special education from teacher education to research methods. The *Journal of Special Education* (1994) recently published a special issue on the alternative pedagogy of constructivism. The *Journal of Learning Disabilities* (1995) will publish a series of articles on alternatives to reductionistic theories and methods in special education.

The call for more qualitative research in special education is another such manifestation of concern over reductionistic thinking in the field (Iano, 1986; Poplin, 1987; Stainback and Stainback, 1984). SooHoo's (1990) ethnography of a day in the life of a child receiving special services is critical to an understanding from a child's point of view of the effects of the reductionistic division of the instructional day for many special education students. Heshusius's (1978) powerful qualitative study of the real lives of adults with mental retar-

dation reveals the similarities of life goals that go unnoticed in our exclusive attention to the details of disability.

Qualitative research by Gleason (1990) documents two residents with multiple and profound developmental disabilities who exhibit the very grasping behaviors in play situations that are diagnosed as deficits and used for therapy in the instructional setting. Additionally, the playing of the two residents with a plastic lawn mower which results in grasping is defined by professionals as fighting. Gleason perfectly describes the problem of reductionism.

> The reduction of their experience to clinical facts, characteristics, and skills foreshortens professional understanding of their experience and in turn limits the effectiveness of intervention. The reliance on the clinical model to interpret their experience points to the fundamental flaw in our knowledge, inquiry and practice. In the eyes of the staff, the residents only do what the program is designed to teach them to do. A fuller human understanding and appreciation of their ability and potential are possible only through awareness of the meaning and significance of the disability for the individual. In the case of persons with severe and profound levels of retardation and multiple disabilities this is achieved through an appreciation of their performance in the context of their everyday life. (p. 61)

Denny Taylor (1990) reveals how reductionism narrows our ability to assess and diagnose children and their work. Taylor carefully documents a child's development in written and oral language while simultaneously detailing the attempts of special education professionals to diagnose and place the same child in a learning disability setting despite parent desires to the contrary. The formal diagnostic process for ascertaining language skills misses the fact that this child is actually writing his own books. Five (1991), a fifth-grade teacher, carefully documents the progress of several special learners in her regular classroom in which she employs the writing process. Her text is critical reading for any special education teacher who desires to move away from reductionistic methodologies, as is the book by

Rhodes and Dudley-Marling (1988) detailing the writing process with special learners. Cousin's (1989, 1993) dissertation details the use of a constructivistic intervention with a student with mild disabilities, and Palincsar (1992) has demonstrated that less reductionistic methods are more viable for a group of youngsters with learning disabilities.

Serious examination of the multitude of problems in transmitting behavioristic practices from research to education settings to teacher education settings in the field of the severely handicapped reflects the rising discontent with reductionistic practices (Guess, 1988; Guess & Thompson, 1990). Sleeter (1986), using critical anaylsis, reinterpreted the history of the field of learning disabilities in the larger context of education after Sputnik. She concludes that *learning disability* is a socially constructed category that met larger sociocultural demands. All of these are merely examples of the growing disillusionment with reductionistic explanations and methods in the field of special education. We do not doubt the viability of reductionistic methods to answer very specific questions or to teach very specific mechanical tasks, or its role in the evolution of such inventions as technology (Poplin, 1995). What we do challenge is its ability to provide significant direction overall in the larger issues that plague special educators and their students. We quite forcefully then challenge its current privileged position in the field in terms of policy, diagnosis, assessment, instruction, and theory.

FOUR DEVELOPING PEDAGOGICAL ALTERNATIVES

Within the larger context of education, several alternatives to reductionistic pedagogies have been developed over the past several decades. More than other areas of education, special education has clung to reductionistic pedagogies. However, as we have shown, special educators exhibit a growing interest in exploring new opportunities to educate students with disabilities. Some of these alternatives include constructivistic, critical, multicultural, and feminine pedagogy.

Constructivism

Constructivism is the best known of the alternative pedagogies in special education. The special issue of the *Journal of Special Education* (1994) attests to its increased popularity in the field. Contructivism emphasizes that learning is the process of creating new meanings from experience. This is opposed to more reductionistic theories that presume the transmission of predetermined knowledge from one person to the next, the teacher or text to the student. In constructivism, the teacher is to develop experiences for students in the classroom that will spark their interest, connect to previous knowledge, and thus stimulate students to become actively involved in constructing new meanings for themselves. This is the way we go about learning even as adults. We come in contact with an experience that sparks our interest and connects to something we already know and care about. This sends us into a headlong search to learn more. This activity yields enough energy to hold our interest while we sort through the details of the new phenomenon and integrate the new experience with what is already known.

Constructivists point out that this meaning-making happens in a sequence that goes from whole to part to whole, or as Whitehead (1929) called it: romance, precision, and wisdom. First we see the whole of the new experience, be it organic gardening, golfing, or a new theory, and we are attracted to that whole experience. Then we begin to study the subject and experiment with it ourselves. Gradually we find that we must get more precise in order to master our new area and we begin to seek help to break down the task. We begin to have enough failed experiences, for example, in organic gardening with faulty carbon-to-nitrogen ratios, that we find we must master the specifics of composting. We begin to work on specific strokes in golf or we begin to search for various authors' explanations of the principles of our newly found theory. This breaking down is done by the learner and is driven by the energy of the romance, the first whole.

So it is with a young child who, finding his or her first storybook, romances it, listens to it over and over, and pours over its pages and pictures. Gradually the child begins to tell the story, becoming more and more accurate as the experience progresses until one day the child locates a word and "knows" it. At this point, the student will begin to drop in fluency in reading and writing because the period of seeking and attending to detail, the parts or precision aspect of learning, is a slow and tedious one. But it is naturally one that is driven by interest, the child's own interest. This is a very different sequence from having teachers break down phonetic knowledge and teach it absent from any initiative on the students' part. When reading is taught in this reductionistic way, teachers stand in danger of teaching parts and pieces of things that students cannot integrate into their own schemas or systems of making sense or meaning. Using writing to teach reading allows students with disabilities to learn text qualities on words and ideas they care about. Infusing classrooms with real literature allows students to become attracted to and curious about text. Constructivism is best known in the language arts, particularly in special education; however, it is not a theory limited to language development.

Hands-on-science techniques, a derivation of constructivistic theory, allow students to develop important questions for instruction as opposed to using materials that presuppose and preempt student questions, interests, and concerns. The same is true of the constructivistic math techniques which encourage much experimentation with manipulatives so that students can develop concepts, strategies, and questions from within themselves. This allows students easy access to knowledge as opposed to struggling to understand some adult-developed concept or abstract sequence for which they may be neither ready nor interested.

Questions and struggles share dominant places in constructivism as students are to use these to move deeper into understanding. Piaget called this process disequilibrium, a state whereby the learner comes to know something is not right and seeks to right it through an active search with adults and texts and more experiences. Once students have learned something new through this struggle, they can no longer see the problem or issue as they did before. A child who has just learned that the same word looks the same over and over, no longer reads pictures alone. Scribble writing gives way to something that more closely approximates the look of text. (See Rhodes & Dudley Marling, 1988; Five, 1991; Poplin, 1983; DuCharme, Earl, & Poplin, 1989).

In constructivism, it is the learner who regulates learning. It is the teacher who can organize and arrange experiences within the child's grasp (zone of proximal development; see Moll, 1992). The child regulates the actual learning, but is not some lone individual in constructing meaning. Social interactions among peers around content are as critical to learning as interactions with teachers, parents, and the larger community (See Cousin, 1989, 1993). And because it is the child who regulates his or her own learning, it is the child who must be integrally involved in the evaluation of learning. With learners who are and are not challenged, Thomas (1993) details assessments that involve students in the evaluation of learning.

Constructivistic learning theory is primarily concerned with students' cognitive and academic development, especially that development centered around literacy, mathematical, and higher-order analytic thinking skills. Historically, great educators who have devoted their lives to students with various challenges from disability to poverty have exemplified the principles of constructivism. These include Grace Fernald, Salome Urena, Mary Bethune, Maria Montessori, and Sylvia Ashton Warner.

Critical Pedagogy

Critical pedagogists also believe that learners create meanings, but they are more interested in sociopolitical meanings than simply higher-order thinking skills. There is considerable overlap between definitions of multicultural education (Nieto, 1992; Sleeter, 1991) and the assumptions and goals of critical pedagogies (Sleeter & McLaren, 1995). Critical theorists urge us to set up experiences in school in which students can create meanings around larger social issues. Students in our extensive study on schooling echo some of these notions when they asked teachers to help them understand more about life (Poplin & Weeres, 1992). Critical theorists would critique the silence of teachers and students on issues such as disability. Why is it that we have never developed serious dialogues or strategies for raising the issues that children with disabilities think so much about, such as, Why am I different? Why am I excluded? Why am I in this special class? or Why don't I have any say about this? By silencing students, we leave in the dark issues that will plague these students for the rest of their lives. So while the constructivists are happy with using nice texts that students like, critical theorists want schooling to lead to a life of action, not simply higher-order cognition or passive responding.

Critical pedagogy, sometimes referred to as liberatory pedagogy, was first brought to the attention of the world by Paulo Freire (1970) who developed a literacy campaign in Brazil in the 1960s to teach peasants to read. The methods he used encouraged peasants to locate and talk and write about their lives within the larger context of the society. His texts document the way that what the constructivist would call *language experience with phonemic instruction and critical social analysis* was fused in a program to bring adults to voice and literacy (Freire and Macedo, 1987). In Appalachia, Myles Horton ran the Highlander School where adults came together to voice and plan strategies for various social action projects including labor unions and the civil rights movement (Horton and Freire, 1990). Rosa Parks did not, as popular myth would have it, sit in the front of the bus accidentally or because she was too tired. This action, along with much of the early nonviolent civil rights resistance, was developed in the educational setting of Highlander, using

processes that are now commonly referred to as critical or liberatory education (Giroux, 1988; Shor, 1980; Walsh, 1991).

The development of student voice is an important aspect of critical practice. Classroom teachers set up important dialogues with and among students, helping students to voice their opinions and to hear others' voices. To these voices expressed verbally and often in writing as well, the teacher adds texts from outside. Students research the issues that concern them and revise their voices, share with others, and listen again, research and revise. This process of voice and study leads to action and students act and reflect, act and reflect in a continuous cycle. Critical pedagogy is most alive in schools that have worked toward projects such as recycling, environmental action, or political action, such as students who protested the proposition in California that would take social services from undocumented workers. These are examples of critical pedagogy in action. Other examples can be found in the works of Freire (1970, 1985, 1987), Freire & Macedo (1989), McLaren (1989), Shor (1980), Benesch (1988), Walsh (1991), and Park (1993).

It would be appropriate for special educators to assist students in the development of their voices on issues like these and on issues related to special placement, tracking, inclusion, or special classes. In particular, students could study texts about disabilities and come to better understand their own disabilities especially in concert with parents. The number one complaint by students about the teaching and learning process used in the school is that it is boring and irrelevant to their lives. Critical practices, on the other hand, encourage teachers to develop experiences for students that help them see and sort through what is going on in the world and their own place in it.

In a critical education project with illiterate teen mothers, teen mothers came back to school with the help of child care and worked together as a group to come up with a project that would benefit themselves and their community. After discussing their own lives, they decided that one of their most urgent needs was for some medical knowledge outside of formal medicine, since most of them had no medical insurance or access to physicians. These illiterate teen mothers decided to begin by interviewing their mothers and grandmothers on herbal remedies and the like. They compiled the stories and community knowledge into a text for the community complete with directions on where certain herbs grew among the New York City sidewalks. The project offered both a resource for the community and the impetus for these young mothers to learn to read and write (Ada, 1990). This is but one example of how less reductionistic pedagogies unite the learning of skills with the larger interests and needs of life.

Multicultural Pedagogy

Multicultural pedagogies emphasize equity of access, expectations, and opportunities for students of color, as well as issues of institutionalized racism, curriculum revision, increasing teachers of color, linguistic diversity, and biculturalism. All of these issues are relevant for special educators who often find a disproportionate number of students of color in special education programs. Many have revealed and explained this phenomenon (Brosnan, 1983; Hillard, 1992; Maheady, Towne, Algozzine, Mercer, & Ysseldyke, 1983; Ortiz, 1986, 1991; Ortiz and Yates, 1983; Wright & Santa Cruz, 1983). Special education is filled with hegemonic practices in diagnosis and assessment which make it far more likely for students of color and the poor to qualify as having disabilities. Given the numbers of students of color referred and placed in special education, it is critical that special educators come to understand the linguistic and cultural differences that exist in this country. Otherwise, special educators cannot design instruction that will be relevant to students' current experience.

The dominant curriculum is still being taught within special education, with even less attention to cultural inclusiveness than our general education counterparts. Very few special classes exist to promote students' native languages if they are not English, though research shows that literacy is best learned by using the primary language of the child. Bilingual students with disabling conditions are even more at risk in failing to develop competency in either language. Jim Cummins's (1983) work is important here as is his observation that were someone from another planet to look at bilingual programs in North America they would have to conclude that we believe bilingualism to be good for the rich and bad for the poor. One of the most well-developed holistic education programs for students with mild disabilities has been developed for bilingual special education students. The program OLE (Optimal Learning Environment) uses whole language and literature methods, as well as alternative time arrangements to bring bicultural special education students to biliteracy (Ruiz, 1989, in press a; in press b; Ruiz, Rueda, Figureroa, & Boothroyd, in press). Goldstein (1993, in press) uses the writing process, immigration stories, and family stories to draw out the literacy of her bilingual special students, as does Five (1991) in her fifth-grade class in which are both second-language learners and learners with various disabilities. Ada (1988) used the parent as the protagonist of the children's stories to unite family and school in a migrant community in the California Pajaro Valley.

Maria Montano-Harmon (1988), working from Kaplan's (1982) theory, has revealed how educators teaching second languages must not only teach vocabulary and syntax but styles of writing. The preferred style of writing in American English in which authors tell the audience what they are going to tell them (often in three parts), and then tell the audience what they have been told is not only not shared by other cultural/linguistic groups but is considered insulting. Preferred styles of communicating are embedded in individuals from their primary culture, even individuals who have fully learned a second language. As educators we must understand these issues fully in order to guide our students to literacy (see Poplin & Phillips, 1993).

Lisa Delpit (1988, 1991, 1993) critiques the whole language movement as one largely developed by and for Euro-American middle-class children who have been immersed in standard English since birth. For children who have not been immersed in standard English, special attention and instruction in the context of their writing and reading must be provided, for it is unlikely that the standard forms will develop naturally. What emerges naturally comes from one's experience. Like the critical pedagogists, Delpit recommends we teach these children of color the sociopolitical reasons that standard English is dominant. She also critiques the institutionalized racism that allowed this situation to go unnoticed in schools. Special educators who understand these important linguistic and cultural differences can create much richer, more connected experiences for their students as they will have a better picture of the students' current knowledge and linguistic structure upon which to draw. (See also Smith, 1986, for a discussion of the linguistic differences of African American children.)

Special educators must also take advantage of the rich multicultural literature that helps us make our curriculum more relevant, as well as special conferences such as the Cross-Cultural Special Education Conference sponsored each year by the San Diego County Office of Education. These resources help us bring students to biliteracy and to use materials and methods that are culturally appropriate, as well as more holistic. To take the larger view of education, special educators must know the particular sociocultural environments in which we work. Special educators of color often naturally bring this bicultural knowledge to the classroom, but just as in general education, most educators are Euro-American and this knowledge of other cultural and linguistic characteristics is not implicit in their own experience and thus must be explicitly learned.

Feminine Pedagogy

A fourth pedagogy that seeks to avoid the pitfalls of reductionism is feminine pedagogy. This pedagogy is a derivative of feminine theory which has as one of its purposes the study of the feminine side of all of us. Our masculine sides are far more represented in public life while our feminine sides are relegated to private life. Grumet (1988) critiques the effect of this on teachers when she points out that we often teach teachers that when they enter the schoolhouse door each morning they must leave who they are as parents and private people outside. This results in the inclination to do things with "other people's children" that we would never do with our own.

The work of Carol Gilligan (Gilligan, 1982; Gilligan, Ward, & Taylor, 1988; Gilligan, Lyons, & Hammer, 1990) on women's and girls' moral reasoning, as well as her work with men, led her to conclude that there are at least two voices of moral reasoning—justice (identified by Kohlberg & Mayer, 1972) and care. This care voice is more relational and is concerned with preserving connections among people. Gilligan noted that all people have both ways of perceiving and solving moral dilemmas, though women use the care voice more often than men.

Belenky, Clinchy, Goldberger, and Tarule (1986) present ideas for a feminine pedagogy of connection, positing that personal connection spurs learning. Other educators have drawn out other aspects of the feminine in pedagogy. Greene (1988) reminds us that passion for what one is learning is supremely important and that this passion brings into play the larger moral purposes for our work. Noddings (1984; Noddings & Shore, 1984) highlights intuition and caring as overlooked areas in education, areas that we often feel are too unsophisticated to bring into the academic discourse about schools and teaching.

While certainly special educators are caring people, it is often a care that goes both unacknowledged in formal structures and uncritiqued. That is, too much caring that leads to "doing for" students rather than allowing them to learn to "do things for themselves" can be detrimental as it produces learned helplessness. Liberalism is under attack because the care that white liberals often extended to the poor and oppressed embodied an assumption about the inferiority of "other" people. This too can happen in special education where low expectations are rife (Taylor, 1990). Caring too much or in wrong ways often creates struggles for teachers with their own authority and causes them to give up their authority, the opposite of authoritarianism. Freire (Shor & Freire, 1987) speaks of the line we must walk as educators between giving up our authority and falling into authoritarianism. Claiming authority but not becoming authoritarian is critical to the development of nonreductionistic pedagogies.

Relationships central to feminine pedagogists are not the relationships of the humanistic pedagogists. In humanism, which is also prevalent in special education, the teacher develops a relationship through somewhat nondirective means. The teacher or therapist is to know the student but the student is not to know the teacher. In feminine pedagogy there is an emphasis on knowing one another, on the authenticity of the relationship. A young high school student in our study of schooling in America (Poplin & Weeres, 1992) provides the best description of this relationship and its effect on his work in school: "Teachers should get to know their students a little better, not to where they bowl together but at least know if they have brothers and sisters. I have found that if I know my teacher I feel more obliged to do the work so I don't disappoint them. Once my trust is gained I feel I should work for myself and also for the teacher" (p. 21).

These are the issues raised by feminine pedagogists that are critical to special educators' dialogues as well. We need to explore the issues of care in teaching and we need to look at our curriculum and instruction to find the area in which students' passionate interest in learning might be raised. As Paulo Freire aptly notes, "education must be joyous and rigorous" (Horton & Freire, 1990, p. 170). Often special education is not joyous, as the work we prescribe is monotonous and repetitive, disconnected from the lives of learners largely because we have accepted reductionistic notions that big things must be broken into tiny parts. Our work fails to be rigorous because an unexamined liberal care causes us to hold very low expectations of students. Students primarily complain that school is boring and students in remedial and special education tracks complain about this even more so (Poplin & Weeres, 1992).

Feminine pedagogists also encourage greater involvement with caregivers, parents, and the larger community, in order to preserve the important relationships of students. Martin (1985) and Brabeck (1989) show how our disconnections from one another and the disconnections of ourselves from intellectual content mirror one another.

SUMMARY

These four pedagogies, while sharing an attempt to circumvent reductionistic and behavioral assumptions about learners, differ in some substantial ways. The constructivists are primarily concerned with cognition and the development of critical reasoning skills, the critical pedagogists with sociopolitical development, the multicultural educators with broadening sociocultural perspectives and challenging implicit and explicit racism, and the feminine pedagogists with issues of relationship and the desire for learning. While these pedagogies were not developed explicitly for special learners (neither were behavioristic pedagogies) the issues they raise broaden our perspective of what it means to be a teacher and a learner. They encourage us to look outside the narrow confines of the reductionistic diagnosis of very minute school-related tasks and to use strategies that help students take an active role in their own learning. They also encourage us to reexamine our curriculum in light of its meaningfulness to the student and to the larger social environment.

As the spirit of the law in special education sought to provide more and better opportunities for students with disabilities to receive appropriate education, various aspects of the letter of that law actually narrowed our vision of what appropriate education could mean. Within the letter of the law are mandated reductionistic ideologies that keep us from making decisions based on what is best for each child. With the advent of the IEP, reductionistic educational planning was mandated. The option for various special classrooms increases or decreases each year based on the current vogue.

Diagnoses and placements have more to do with test scores and ideologies than with the needs and desires of children and their parents, or the needs of teachers. The law also created a massive special education bureaucracy that insulated the field from innovations and the concerns of general education.

There is much to be learned about putting it all back together again so that students with disabilities can have an education that inspires them to become the best people they can become, not merely to achieve the next little objective on the list. Mother Teresa (1990) tells a story of attending a conference on world hunger. She struggled to find her way to the hotel with a couple of her sisters and just as they found the hotel, they also found a man outside in the gutter dying of hunger. They picked him up, took him to their place, cleaned him, prayed with him, and fed him. He died shortly afterward and she found her way back to the conference. As she walked into the conference area there were screens overhead bearing charts and graphs of food production projections over several years and decades. And she stated, "Sometimes when you look at the numbers, you get lost, while we are looking at the numbers someone dies."

As special educators, we too must be careful that our numbers and our ideologies don't cause us to miss the obvious.

REFERENCES

Ada, A. F. (1988). The Pajaro Valley experience: Working with Spanish-speaking parents to develop children's reading and writing skills through the use of children's literature. In T. Skutnabb-Kangas and J. Cummins (Eds.), *Minority education: From shame to struggle.* (pp. 223–236). Clevedon: Multilingual Matters.

Ada, A. F. (1990). *Panel on critical pedagogy.* California Association of Bilingual Education Conference.

Angeles, P. (1981). *Dictionary of philosophy.* New York: Barnes and Noble.

Belenky, M. F., Clinchy, B. M., Goldberger, N. R., & Tarule, J. M. (1986). *Women's ways of knowing.* New York: Basic Books.

Benesch, S. (1988). *Ending remediation: Linking ESL and content in higher education.* Alexandria, VA: Teachers of English Speakers.

Brabeck, M. M. (Ed.). (1989). *Who cares? Theory, research, and the educational implications of the ethic of care.* New York: Praeger.

Brosnan, F. L. (1983). Overrepresentation of low-socioeconomic minority students in special education programs in California. *Learning Disability Quarterly, 6* (4), 517–525.

Cousin, P. (1989). *Language use in a special education classroom: The social construction of learning success and failure.* Doctoral dissertation, Indiana University, Bloomington.

Cousin, P. (1993). The functional uses of language and literacy by students with severe language and learning problems. *Language Arts, 70* (7), 585–596.

Cummins, J. (1983). Bilingualism and special education: Program and pedagogical issues. *Learning Disability Quarterly, 6* (4), 373–386.

Delpit, L. (1988). The silenced dialogue: Power and pedagogy in educating other people's children. *Harvard Educational Review, 58* (3), 280–298.

Delpit, L. (1991). A conversation with Lisa Delpit. *Language Arts, 68,* 541–547.

Delpit, L. (1993). The politics of teaching literature discourse. In T. Perry & J. W. Fraser (Eds.), *Freedom's plow: Teaching in the multicultural classroom* (pp. 285–295). New York: Routledge.

DuCharme, C., Earl, J., & Poplin, M. (1989). The author model: The constructivist view of the writing process. *Learning Disability Quarterly, 12,* 237–247.

Five, C. L. (1991). *Special voices.* Portsmouth, NH: Heinemann.

Freire, P. (1970). *Pedagogy of the oppressed.* New York: Continuum.

Freire, P. (1985). *The politics of education: Culture, power and liberation.* South Hadley, MA: Bergin & Garvey.

Freire, P. (1987). *Education for critical consciousness.* New York: Continuum.

Freire, P., & Macedo, D. (1987). *Literacy: Reading the word and the world.* South Hadley, MA: Continuum.

Freire, P., & Macedo, D. (1989). *Learning to question: A pedagogy of liberation.* South Hadley, MA: Bergin & Garvey.

Gilligan, C. (1982). *In a different voice.* Cambridge, MA: Harvard University Press.

Gilligan, C., Lyons, N. P., & Hanmer (Eds.), (1990). *Making connections: The relational worlds of adolescent girls at Emma Williard School.* Cambridge, MA: Harvard University Press.

Gilligan, C., Ward., J. V., & Taylor (Eds.), (1988). *Mapping the moral domain.* Cambridge, MA: Harvard University Graduate School of Education.

Giroux, H. (1988). *Teachers as intellectuals: Toward a critical pedagogy of learning.* Granby, MA: Bergin & Garvey.

Gleason, J. J. (1990). Meaning of play: Interpreting patterns of behavior of persons with severe developmental disabilities. *Anthropology and Education Quarterly, 21,* 59–77.

Goldstein, B. (1993). Assessment of oral storytelling abilities of Latino junior high school students with learning handicaps. *Journal of Learning Disabilities, 26* (2), 138–143.

Goldstein, M. (in press). Critical pedagogy in a bilingual special education classroom. *Journal of Learning Disabilities.*

Greene, M. (1988). *The dialectic of freedom.* New York: Teachers College Press.

Grumet, M. (1988). *Bitter milk: Women and teaching.* Amherst, MA: University of Massachusetts Press.

Guess, D. (1988). *Problems and issues pertaining to the transition of behavior management technologies from researchers to practitioners.* Behavior Management and Integration Symposium, Research and Training Center on Community-Referenced Behavior, University of Oregon, Eugene.

Guess, D., & Thompson, B. (1990). Preparation of personnel to educate students with severe and multiple disabilities: A time for change? In L. Meyer, C. Peck, & L. Brown (Eds.), *Critical issues in the lives of people with severe disabilities.* Baltimore: P. and H. Brookes.

Heshusius, L. (1978). *Meaning in the lives of young adults labeled retarded: A participant observation study.* Doctoral dissertation, Indiana University, Bloomington.

Heshusius, L. (1984). Why would they and I want to do it? A phenomenological-theoretical view of special education. *Learning Disability Quarterly, 7,* 363–368.

Heshusius, L. (1989). Holistic principles: Not enhancing the old but seeing a-new: A rejoinder. *Journal of Learning Disabilities, 22* (7), 403–415.

Hillard, A. G. (1992). The promises and pitfalls of special education practice. *Exceptional Children, 59* (2), 168–172.

Horton, M., & Freire, P. (1990). *We make the road by walking: Conversations on education and social change.* Philadelphia: Temple University Press.

Iano, R. P. (1986). The study and development of teaching: With implications for the advancement of special education. *Remedial and Special Education, 7* (5), 50–61.

Journal of Learning Disabilities (1995). August, September, October, November.

Journal of Special Education (1994). Fall 1994, Whole Issue, Vol. 28. No. 3.

Kaplan, R. (1982). An introduction to the study of written texts: The discourse compact. In R. B. Kaplan (Ed.), *Annual Review of Applied Linguistics—1982* (pp. 138–151). Rowley, MA: Newbury House.

Koch, S. (1981). The nature and limits of psychological knowledge. *American Psychologist, 36,* 257–269.

Kohlberg, L., & Mayer, L. (1972). Development as the aim in education. *Harvard Educational Review, 42* (4), 449–496.

Maheady, L., Towne, R., Algozzine, B., Mercer, J., & Ysseldyke, J. (1983). Minority overrepresentation: A case for alternative practices prior to referral. *Learning Disability Quarterly, 6* (4), 448–456.

Martin, J. R. (1985). *Reclaiming a conversation: The ideal of the educated woman.* New Haven CT: Yale University Press.

McLaren, P. (1989). *Life in schools.* New York: Longman.

Moll, L. (Ed.). (1992). *Vygotsky and education: Instructional implications and applications of sociohistorical psychology.* Cambridge, England: Cambridge University Press.

Montano-Harmon, M. (1988). *Discourse features in the compositions of Mexican, English-as-a-second language, Mexican-American/Chicano, and Anglo high school students: Considerations for the formulation of educational policies.* Doctoral dissertation, University of Southern California, Los Angeles.

Noddings, N. (1984). *Caring: A feminine approach to ethics and moral education.* Berkeley: University of California Press.

Noddings, N., & Shore, P. J. (1984). *Awakening the inner eye: Intuition in education.* New York: Teachers College Press.

Ortiz, A. A. (1986). Recognizing learning disabilities in bilingual children: How to lessen inappropriate referrals of language minority students to special education. *Journal of Reading, Writing, and Learning Disabilities International, 2* (1), 43–56.

Ortiz, A. A. (1991). Assessment intervention model for the bilingual exceptional student. *Teacher Education and Special Education, 4* (1), 35–42.

Ortiz, A. A., & Yates, J. R. (1983). Incidence of exceptionality among Hispanics: Implications for manpower training. *National Association of Bilingual Education Journal, 7* (3), 41–53.

Palincsar, A. (1992). Fostering literacy learning in supportive contexts. *Journal of Learning Disabilities, 25* (4), 211–225, 229.

Park, P., Brydon-Miller, M., Hall, B., & Jackson, T. (Eds.), (1993). *Voices of change: Participatory research in the United States and Canada.* Westport, CT: Greenwood.

Poplin, M. (1983). Assessing developmental writing abilities. *Topics in Learning and Learning Disabilities, 3* (3), 63–75.

Poplin, M. (1987). Self-imposed blindness: The scientific method in education. *Remedial and Special Education, 8* (6), 31–37.

Poplin, M. (1988a). The reductionistic fallacy in learning disabilities: Replicating the past by reducing the present. *Journal of Learning Disabilities, 21* (7), 389–400.

Poplin, M. (1988b). Holistic/constructivist principles of the teaching/learning process: Implications for the field of learning disabilities. *Journal of Learning Disabilities, 21* (7), 401–416.

Poplin, M. (1995). The dialectic nature of technology and holism: The use of technology for the liberation of the learning disabled. *Learning Disability Quarterly, 18,* 3.

Poplin, M., & Phillips, L. (1993). Sociocultural aspects of language and literacy: Issues facing educators of students with learning disabilities. *Learning Disability Quarterly, 16,* 245–255.

Poplin, M., & Stone, S. (1992). Paradigm shifts in instructional strategies: From reductionism to holistic/constructivism. In W. Stainback & S. Stainback (Eds.), *Controversial issues confronting special education: Divergent perspectives* (1st ed., pp. 153–179). Boston: Allyn and Bacon.

Poplin, M., & Weeres, J. (1992). *Voices from the inside: A report on schooling from inside the classroom.* Claremont, CA: The Institute for Education and Transformation at the Claremont Graduate School.

Rhodes, L., & Dudley-Marling, C. (1988). *Readers and writers with a difference: A holistic approach to teaching learning disabled and remedial readers.* Portsmouth, NH: Heinemann.

Rivera, J., & Poplin, M. (1995). Multicultural, critical, and constructive pedagogies seen through the lives of youth: A call for the revisioning of these and beyond: Toward a pedagogy for the next century. In C. Sleeter & P. McLaren (Eds.), *Multicultural education, critical pedagogy, and the politics of difference* (pp. 300–338). Albany, NY: SUNY Press.

Ruiz, N. (1989). An optimal learning environment for Rosemary. *Exceptional Children, 56* (2), 130–144.

Ruiz, N. (in press, a). The social construction of ability and disability, I: Profile types of Latino children identified as language learning disabled. *Journal of Learning Disabilities.*

Ruiz, N. (in press, b). The social construction of ability and disability, II: Optimal and at-risk lessons in a bilingual special education classroom. *Journal of Learning Disabilities.*

Ruiz, N., Rueda, R., Figueroa, R., & Boothroyd, M. (in press). Shifting paradigms of bilingual special education teachers: Complex responses to educational reform. *Journal of Learning Disabilities.*

Shor, I. (1980). *Critical teaching in everyday life.* Chicago: University of Chicago Press.

Shor, I., & Freire, P. (1987). *A pedagogy for liberation: Dialogues in transforming education.* Portsmouth, NH: Heinemann.

Sleeter, C. (1986). Learning disabilities: A social construction of a special education category. *Exceptional Children, 53* (1), 46–54.

Sleeter, C. (1991). *Empowerment through multicultural education.* Albany, NY: SUNY Press.

Sleeter, C., & McLaren, P. (1995). *Multicultural education, critical pedagogy, and the politics of difference.* Albany, NY: SUNY Press.

Smith, E. (1986). *Ebonics and the standard English barrier.* Afro-Asiatic and Niger-Congo Linguistics. Occasional Paper, Watts College, Compton, CA.

SooHoo, S. (1990). School renewal: Taking responsibility for providing an education of value. In J. I.

Goodlad & P. Keating (Eds.), *Access to knowledge.* (pp. 205–221). New York: College Entrance Examination Board.

Stainback, W., & Stainback, S. (1984). Broadening the research perspective in special education. *Exceptional Children, 50,* 400–408.

Taylor, D. (1990). *Learning denied.* Portsmouth, NH: Heinemann.

Teresa, M. (1990). *Loving Jesus.* Ann Arbor: Servant Books.

Thomas, S. (1993). Rethinking assessment: Teachers and students helping each other "through the sharp curves of life." *Learning Disability Quarterly, 16* (4), 257–279.

Walsh, C. (1991). *Pedagogy and the struggle for voice: Issues of language, power and schooling for Puerto Ricans.* New York: Bergin & Garvey.

Whitehead, A. N. (1929). *The aims of education.* New York: Basic Books.

Wright, P., & Santa Cruz, R. (1983). Ethnic composition of special education programs in California. *Learning Disability Quarterly, 6* (4), 387–394.

SECTION SEVEN

CLASSROOM MANAGEMENT

What is the most humane and effective approach to discipline? In Chapter 13, Fields and Tarlow advocate a constructivistic approach based on unconditional valuing of the person and expression of genuine caring and reciprocal respect. They outline specific ways of helping students understand and accept behavior limits that are compatible with goals of constructivism.

Haring and Kennedy, in contrast, advocate in Chapter 14 that classroom discipline be based on the principles of applied behavior analysis. They outline the characteristics of behavior analytic interventions and review research that supports its effectiveness. They point out that contrary to claims of critics, behavioral approaches can be humane, flexible, and contextualistic.

CHAPTER 13

Constructivistic Approaches to Classroom Management for Students with Disabilities

MARJORIE V. FIELDS
MARY-CLAIRE TARLOW

INTRODUCTION

Constructivistic approaches to education are based on the theories of Jean Piaget regarding the development of moral and intellectual autonomy. Developing moral and intellectual autonomy means helping children to learn to think clearly, to make wise decisions, and to govern themselves accordingly (Kamii, 1984). Therefore constructivistic education is not compatible with rewards or punishments: the external controls of behavioristic approaches are counterproductive to the goals of intellectual and moral autonomy.

As long as others are making the decisions for a child, solving the child's problems and taking responsibility for control, the child gets no practice in those important skills. The child learns to rely on others to do the thinking and governing instead of learning to do it personally. External controls work on a temporary basis in a sheltered environment but do not prepare for independent living. Rewards and punishment do not help children with behavior disorders to live more productive lives (DeVries and Zan, 1994). Ultimately it is their own ability to govern themselves that will allow them to function effectively in society. For this reason we are convinced that these children, *even more than others,* need education and guidance aimed at developing intellectual and moral autonomy.

Some people become fearful when they hear about teaching for autonomy. They think it means letting children run wild and do whatever they want. Similar fears about academic expectations arise from misunderstandings about developing intellectual autonomy. These fears demonstrate how reliant U.S. culture has become on the behavioristic system of reward and punishment that permeates our schools (DeVries & Zan, 1994). Many educators and parents find it difficult to envision any system other than the coercive one they have known. Many have come to view successful learning as getting good grades. Most have come to view guidance and discipline as something adults *do* to children rather than something they *teach* to children. When told that rewards and punishment are not acceptable, they believe that chaos is the only alternative. Thus, constructivism requires major retraining in guidance approaches as well as significant rethinking of the teaching/learning process.

The field of special education has been involved in significant rethinking of goals, values, and methods. Current practices in special education emphasize that children with disabilities are children first and foremost. This emphasis goes behind the recommended terminology: *children with special needs* rather than *special needs children* (Wolery & Wilbers, 1994). This apparently subtle difference is part of the major reevaluation of special education that led to including children in regular classrooms who previously would have been segregated into special education classrooms. In conjunction with heightened awareness regarding the negative effects of labels and segregation, many educators are questioning the tradition of behavioristic approaches to behavior management for children with special needs. Instead of limiting intervention to adult control of children's undesirable behaviors, the focus is shifting to ways of helping youngsters develop their own controls. Methods are changing to be more congruent with the goals of inclusion of students with disabilities not only in the classroom but in society.

RECIPROCAL RESPECT

If rewards and punishment are out, what is left? Many of the major approaches to guidance are compatible with the goals of constructivism (Fields & Boesser, 1994). The overriding principle of reciprocal respect is common to these approaches. Most people accept that children are supposed to respect their elders, but few seem to consider the importance of adults respecting children. Piaget's studies (1965) emphasize the need for mutual respect in motivating socially desirable behaviors.

Brief introspection by an adult would clearly demonstrate the personal importance of the respect they receive in relation to the cooperation they give. However, this fairly obvious relationship is routinely ignored as adults use coercive measures instead of respectful ones with youngsters. The most efficient way of getting a child's respect is not to demand it but to give that child your respect. Students with disabilities need that respect even more than others.

Piaget also emphasizes the role of caring relationships in helping children to develop moral autonomy (1965). His research points out that such relationships are prerequisite to abandoning an egocentric position. It is imperative that the perspectives of others be considered in coming to just conclusions. Thus any discipline approach compatible with constructivistic goals must be implemented within the context of a caring relationship between the adult and student and must foster caring relationships between youngsters. Obviously, the approach also must not be one that damages these relationships. Caring for others and feeling cared for by them provides a powerful reason for behaving in ways that will continue that goodwill. A person who feels alienated from society or rejected by teachers and peers not only has little motivation to understand the needs or feelings of others but also has little to lose from negative actions. Students with disabilities need assistance in developing caring relationships even more than students without disabilities.

Caring relationships and respect are both based on acceptance of the individual as a person, not on rewards for behaving in a certain way. This may mean accepting that a child in your second-grade classroom exhibits the emotional maturity of a two year old. Your caring and respect for this child means adjusting your expectations to that child's maturational level rather than withholding rewards for not exhibiting "grade-level" behaviors. Accepting that child's current ability does not preclude assistance in growing toward more mature levels any more than it does with an actual toddler. The peer models and teacher guidance that assist development will be effective only if they are part of caring and respectful relationships.

RELATED CONSEQUENCES

With the guidelines of respect and caring in place, we can examine how specific interventions assist youngsters to understand and accept behavior limits. We advocate the use of natural and related consequences as powerful tools for teaching discipline. As children experience the consequences of their actions, they learn cause-and-effect relationships (Curwin & Mendler, 1988). For example: If I don't eat at snack time, I get hungry before lunch. If I hit other kids, they don't want to play with me. If I dump paint on the floor, I don't get to paint.

Consequences are very different from punishment and have very different effects (Dreikurs, 1964). Though depriving a child of using the paints because he purposely dumped the paint may look a lot like punishment, the difference lies in the inherent fairness of the relationship between the act and the result. Children do respond to this fairness and tend to accept the consequences as just. Being kept in from recess for dumping paint would not be a related consequence and is not accepted in the same way. However, if the paint is dumped just prior to recess and the child is asked to stay inside to clean up the mess, missing recess may be a related side-effect of a related consequence.

Teachers who choose to teach discipline by helping youngsters to recognize the consequences of their actions have several types of consequences to choose from. Depriving students of materials misused is one type of consequence; not allowing a child to paint as a result of misusing the paint is an example of a deprivation consequence. Encouraging children to make restitution is another category of consequences (Piaget, 1965), illustrated by asking the child to clean up the paint. Excluding youngsters from situations in which they behave inappropriately is another type of consequence. Sometimes other students impose this consequence, as in the example, If I hit other kids, they don't want to play with me. At other times the teacher imposes an exclusion type of consequence, as when a child who is disrupting the group during storytime is asked to leave the group.

It is important that these consequences don't become a "life sentence," however. Unless children see hope for reprieve, there is little motivation for reformed behavior. We not only want youngsters to have motivation to improve their behavior, we also want to put them in charge of changing their behavior and bringing about better results in their lives. This is related to the goal of personal autonomy. Therefore, when the teacher asks Kelvin to leave the story group and return to his seat, he is told he may rejoin the group when he feels he is able to listen to the story without bothering others. Similarly, when Abigail is told she may not paint because she dumped the paint on the floor, she is only deprived of the paints until *she decides* that she can use them properly.

Of course there will be children who decide to return immediately to the "scene of the crime"

without having reformed and who immediately repeat the same offenses. Often youngsters need teacher assistance in thinking about alternative behaviors to unacceptable ones. Therefore, it is reasonable for exclusion consequences or deprivation consequences to persist at least until the teacher has a chance to confer with the child. However, students always need another chance as they learn; failures must not be permanent but rather must be viewed as part of learning. Students with disabilities may need more chances than others.

When other students reject a youngster who exhibits antisocial behaviors, they sometimes are not willing to give that child another chance. It is all too easy for a child to become labeled socially undesirable at an early age and lose all hope of acceptance. Once a youngster becomes a social outcast, negative behaviors are self-perpetuating and tend to create permanent social disorders (Ramsey, 1991). Therefore, the teacher not only needs to teach more desirable behaviors but also needs to intervene on behalf of the child who is practicing new social skills. If a child is practicing improved social behavior, it is important that there be some positive results in order to demonstrate that the new skills are valuable. This feedback is important to encourage continued efforts.

The three types of consequences just described are all imposed by others. However, there are many important learning experiences that simply require the adult to get out of the way and allow children to experience the natural consequences of their actions. "If I don't eat at snack time, I get hungry before lunch" is an example of this type of consequence. Too often adults get into power struggles with children by trying to keep them from experiencing the consequences of poor choices. Unless the natural results are either dangerous or don't matter to the child, there is rarely good reason for adults to get involved. Often it would be much more effective to let children find out for themselves why coats are needed for recess or why it is a good idea to put away art supplies. Rather than nagging Damion every day about putting his scissors and paste back in his cubby when he is through, his teacher may decide to let him experience the frustration of not being able to find them when he leaves them lying around. Natural consequences allow youngsters to see clearly the results of poor choices and to learn the reasons for making better ones (Dreikurs, Greenwald, & Pepper, 1982). Students with disabilities, even more than others, need many repetitions of this kind of opportunity to learn.

Types of Consequences

Natural

If you don't eat, you get hungry.

Exclusion

If you can't cooperate with the group, leave until you can.

Deprivation

If you misuse materials, you may not use them until you decide to use them appropriately.

Restitution

If you knock over someone's block tower, you must help rebuild it.

As with most learning, experience is a better teacher than a lecture. It is important not to add the lecture, no matter how tempted you are to say I told you so. Children are better able to focus on the behavior that caused the unpleasant result when they don't have to defend themselves or "save face." The adult should be neutral or sympathetic as the consequence is experienced in order to maintain the value of the consequence and keep it from being punitive to the child.

The teacher's attitude plays a large part in the use of related consequences as opposed to punishment: A teacher whose aim is using consequences to help children to learn and understand limits will generally approach the situation with a matter-of-fact calm. The realization that guidance and discipline is a teaching process helps the adult to have patience with the time it takes young people to learn. This attitude eliminates blame or other ways of putting students on the defensive. Instead it addresses the situation with logic in the caring context that accompanies all good teaching. The teacher whose aim is to control through fear of punishment will typically approach the situation with anger. Children respond differently to these

different teacher attitudes (DeVries & Zan, 1994). Anger breeds reciprocal anger, creating more antisocial behaviors (Bettleheim, 1985).

Care must be taken to ensure that consequences do not inadvertently become punishment. The adult's nonpunitive attitude coupled with clear relationships between the behavior and the results are essential for keeping the distinctions between consequences and punishment. The disrespectful aspects of punishment destroy mutual respect, damage relationships, and undermine self-esteem (Miller, 1990), thus eliminating the basis for socially acceptable behavior. In addition, the retaliatory nature of punishment fosters retaliation from the child; therefore, we often see an escalation of negative behaviors with a corresponding escalation of punishment severity.

Some people will protest that students with behavioral disabilities cannot understand cause and effect. We acknowledge that this crucial aspect of self-control is difficult for many such youngsters, but we consider that all the more reason to allow them to experience the results of their behaviors. Children who have difficulty comprehending cause-and-effect relationships need more practice. Even more than other students, they need the effective and relevant teaching that can come from actual experience. If we were to give up hope of their understanding the results of their actions, we would be giving up hope that they could ever become independent adults. Without this understanding, they will require constant lifelong supervision.

EFFECTIVE COMMUNICATION

Another way to help children understand the results of their actions is through clear, nonpunitive communication. Many adults talk to young people in disrespectful, judgmental, and threatening ways, apparently having learned these kinds of interactions from their own parents and teachers. Thomas Gordon (1970) summarizes these ineffective adult–child messages and labels them "roadblocks to communication." Not surprisingly, students don't listen well when teachers are talking in these ways. The roadblocks Gordon describes include lecturing and giving solutions, as well as criticizing, ordering, blaming, and shaming. Even reassuring and praising are listed as roadblocks.

You can probably easily understand why criticizing, blaming, and shaming are unpleasant; they are clearly negative judgments. However, you may be puzzled about lecturing and giving solutions; those are usually perceived as helpful. Gordon points out that the intent is to be helpful, but the implication is that the person with the problem is not capable of figuring out personal answers or solutions. You may totally disagree with the contention that praise or reassurance could have a negative impact. Gordon and others (eg., Hitz & Driscoll, 1988; Shalaway, 1980) point out that praise, albeit positive, is a judgment just as much as blame. What about reassurance? This is a way of trying to make bad feelings go away and can have the effect of denying the strength of a person's feelings (Gordon, 1970). If you doubt these conclusions, watch for your own reactions as people give you reassurance, praise, or solutions when you share a problem with them.

When confronted with Gordon's list of communication roadblocks, many people ask, What's left? It might appear that all common ways of speaking are considered ineffective. Gordon (1970; 1989) offers three alternatives: (1) "I" messages, (2) active listening, and (3) problem solving.

"I" Messages

An "I" message is used to express your feelings when someone is doing something that bothers you. It is careful not to blame or condemn and it contains no put-downs. In addition, an "I" message does not tell the other person what to do. A complete "I" message has three components according to Gordon.

1. It is specific about what the unacceptable behavior is.
2. It states your resultant feelings, reaction, or problem.
3. It explains why the behavior is causing your problem.

It is important to stop right there. Too many people start out with a good "I" message and then ruin it by telling the other person what he or she should be doing differently. If we use only the three recommended components, we are explaining our problem and respecting the other person's ability and willingness to help. Given a mutually caring relationship, this approach usually gets helpful results. However, if we also tell the other person what to do, the message is different. In that case, we are lecturing and using another roadblock. The typical reaction to such a roadblock is to become defensive rather than helpful.

An "I" message would be appropriate when a student is talking while the teacher is trying to give directions to the group. The teacher might say, "Camille, when you talk while I am giving directions, I am afraid that no one will know what to do." That statement meets the criteria given for an "I" message. However, if the teacher continues and adds, "Please be quiet," the solution has been given and the student is no longer allowed to choose more acceptable behavior. Instead the teacher has told Camille what to do; the whole communication has become less respectful and Camille is less likely to feel good about being cooperative.

If you aren't sure whether you are speaking to a student respectfully, you can easily test yourself: Simply pretend you are speaking to an adult friend and ask yourself if you would talk in a similar way. People are often shocked to hear themselves from this perspective (Ginott, 1965). They realize that what sounds reasonable if addressed to a child may sound totally inappropriate if addressed to an adult. This conclusion indicates the common disrespect shown young people. If you want them to listen respectfully to you, you will need to make certain that your communication approach passes this test.

Active Listening

When the problem is the student's rather than the teacher's, the goal is to help the child figure out how to personally solve the problem. Too many well-meaning teachers and parents think they are being helpful when they try to solve the problem *for* the child. Doing things for youngsters that they should learn to do for themselves may be even a greater temptation when they are youngsters with disabilities. But solving problems for young people has the same drawbacks regardless of who the students are. One obvious drawback is that young people usually don't listen to the voice of mature wisdom, they (like many of us) persist in wanting to learn through their own experience instead of through that of the previous generation. That's why Gordon (1989) calls providing solutions a communication roadblock. Another drawback is that young people don't learn how to solve problems if others do it for them.

Therefore the adult role is to listen carefully, reflecting back to the student what you think you are hearing. This approach has a dual purpose: to show the child that you truly care enough to try to understand, and to help the child think the issue through carefully. Your role as a listener is more important than you may think. Often explaining a problem to a caring listener can help the issues become more clear and therefore will generate ideas for a solution. Other times there is no immediate solution, but strength and comfort can come from the empathy and validation of feelings given by someone listening without judging or lecturing. In either case, you will find that students with disabilities, even more than others, benefit from adults who are caring listeners.

Sometimes teachers need to attend to nonverbal communication also. When Mr. Vasquez saw Jaheid crying and sitting alone at a game board, he went over to the boy to help. He didn't know why Jaheid was crying but guessed it must have something to do with the game or a partner in the game. Mr. Vasquez decided to play it safe and not assume anything, only to respond to what he could see; so he merely said, "It looks like you are unhappy." Jaheid kept his face down and nodded through his tears but offered no explanation. Mr. Vasquez tried again, "Are you unhappy about this game?" Finally the boy opened up and sobbed, "Anna won't play with me anymore." The teacher resisted the temptation to fall back on the

communication roadblocks of advising the boy to find someone else to play with or trying to divert Jaheid's attention to another activity. Instead of trying to solve the problem for the student or make the problem go away, Mr. Vasquez demonstrated his confidence in Jaheid's ability to solve his own problem. He merely said, "It looks like you are really sad that Anna left your game." That left an opening for the child to talk further and to reflect on the situation. As Jaheid started talking about the chain of events that ended in Anna quitting their game, the boy began to gain insights into what happened. When Jaheid said, "Anna said I was cheating," Mr. Vasquez continued reflective listening, asking for verification that he understood correctly: "You and Anna couldn't agree on how to play the game?" After agreeing that this was the case, Jaheid apparently had a plan for dealing with the problem. He went in search of another partner to play the game with him. Mr. Vasquez's intervention accepted Jaheid's feelings and encouraged the student to think about the problem.

Negotiated Solutions

Sometimes the problem is a shared one: two or more people who have conflicting needs or desires. Perhaps one group of students is noisily practicing for a play and disturbing another group that needs quiet to concentrate. An exchange of "I" messages may clarify the problem but will not necessarily lead to a solution. The ability to peacefully discuss conflicting needs and to negotiate some compromise is essential to peaceful coexistence.

This ability apparently does not come naturally and must be taught in order to provide alternatives to physical violence. Evidence of this need can be seen in the prevalence of violent conflict in the world and in the frequency of hitting on the playground. If Jeremy gets in Alex's way, Alex shoves Jeremy away instead of asking him to move. Usually Jeremy will retaliate and a fight ensues. Teachers see this sort of scenario repeated day after day. Clearly school would be a safer and more productive place if other approaches were learned and used.

As we said, an "I" message can be a starting place for negotiated solutions. Alex might learn to tell Jeremy that he is in the way. Jeremy might learn to tell Alex why he wants to play where he is. Then what? The steps for solving a problem such as this can be demonstrated by the teacher through helping students to solve in-class problems. For instance, the students who want quiet may be yelling at those practicing the play. This provides a "teachable moment" for helping those involved on both sides to learn a valuable problem-solving skill.

Teacher intervention can calm the situation and lead the two groups in a discussion of their conflicting needs. Once the problem has been clarified—"We need to study" versus "We need to practice"—the next step is to get both sides to generate possible solutions (Gordon, 1970). Both sides can suggest any ideas they want at this point, but in the next step either side can reject any ideas that are unacceptable. The goal is a mutually acceptable solution, not a vote in which the majority wins. There are no winners and no losers in negotiated solutions.

The quiet group may suggest that the play group quit practicing. The actors may suggest that the studiers quit studying. Neither of these ideas is acceptable to the other group. Someone suggests that they could practice the play on the walkway just outside the classroom. Someone else wonders if they could use study carrels in the library for quiet study. Now the two groups have some potentially acceptable proposals. The teacher has a say also, since safety and supervision are factors here. But soon a mutually acceptable plan is agreed upon. Most important, the students have practiced negotiating a conflict. This kind of learning experience can transfer to the playground and help Jeremy and Alex to avoid a fight.

Steps in Problem Solving

- Clarify the problem: what does each side want?
- Generate ideas for solutions.
- Evaluate ideas and eliminate any unacceptable to either side.
- Select a plan from the remaining ideas.
- Implement the plan.
- Evaluate success.
- Start over if needed.

Communication in Action

When Marina lashes out at Brittany, hitting her with both fists, Ms. A. separates the girls and asks what happened. Brittany immediately relates that Marina "just hit me." Ms. A. listens to Brittany and then turns to Marina for her explanation. Ms. A. is aware that Marina's communication skills are not good. Marina often uses physical aggression because she does not have the verbal skills to express her needs and because she does not associate verbal communication with solving her problems. Although Marina is unable to express herself clearly, Ms. A. can ascertain that Brittany was excluding Marina from a group activity and not sharing the supplies needed to accomplish the group task. In front of both girls Ms. A. helps Marina express the hurt and frustration that she feels, providing many of the words that Marina does not have. She explains to Brittany that it is not easy for Marina to express her feelings yet, but that she still has those feelings. She does this to get Brittany to understand Marina's perspective. She has validated Marina's feelings and helped her to learn to express them.

Next she turns to Marina and discusses the reasons why the physical expression of anger is not useful. She also reminds Marina that all students in the classroom need to feel safe and supported, emphasizing that she hurt Brittany. She asks Marina if she really wants to hurt Brittany. She wonders aloud if Brittany might not want to be around Marina in the future, if she gets hurt. She acknowledges that Marina felt angry and frustrated, but asks Marina to think about how she could use words to express those feelings and satisfy her needs. Later, after both girls have had time to cool down and think about the situation, Ms. A. asks both girls to make a statement about what they learned and how they could act differently in the future.

This kind of talk may seem time-consuming and certainly will not produce a quick fix of behavior. It will, however, accomplish a great deal over time. Both respect and communication are evident here. The teacher is dealing with Marina's lack of communication skills and resulting frustration as well as teaching the behaviors needed to change the cause of the problem. She helps both students reframe the situation to understand more of the forces at work. She shows them respect as important individuals by acknowledging their views of the situation. She also helps them to see that each of them can have a different perspective that seems valid. When Ms. A. gives them respect, they return that respect because she accepts them as valued individuals. She treats each of them as she would a good friend.

THE CLASSROOM ENVIRONMENT

Ms. A.'s intervention is done in a classroom where children are encouraged to think for themselves, solve problems, make decisions, and care about each other. This doesn't happen by accident. Ms. A. begins her year teaching children the necessary skills to be part of a productive, caring community. Students have generated their own rules for behavior and talked about why those rules are needed. Ms. A. mixes discussions about sharing and cooperating and what that means with discussions of the students' own interactions. At the end of the day, Ray reports that he shared with Tim in the block area. "How did you know you were sharing?" Ms. A. asks Ray. Ray reports that he didn't take all the big blocks away from Tim because he knew Tim needed them, and when he wanted a wedge block, instead of just taking it, he asked Tim if he could have it.

Teachers like Ms. A. allow time during the instructional day to learn about behavior problem solving as well as academic problem solving. They use a class meeting (as outlined by Glasser, 1969) or similar structure for students to reflect on their interactions and notice both positive and negative aspects of them. Using logic and taking everyone's perspective into consideration, students discuss and reflect on those interactions that were not productive as well as those that were. Students who are still developing perspective-taking abilities need this exchange of ideas to appreciate others' viewpoints and hear how their behaviors affect others. By discussing behavior in this way, students are treated as capable human beings who can think reasonably and learn to interact in positive ways. This spells respect: respect for the students' abilities and for their capacity to construct appropriate behaviors.

In a classroom like this, students will generate their own systems for helping students with disabilities. Bobby circulates a paper and the kids sign up for their day to wheel Katrina around the playground at recess, or to be with Edward who cannot run with the rest of the children. Doing for each other is valued in the classroom, and children are eager to help. The teacher sets the tone by being kind, respectful, and accepting. The teacher also actively generates these values as a part of the class community.

To be truly successful at building a community in which students care about each other, students must have an academic atmosphere that matches the social one (Devries & Zan, 1994). If students are to feel respected and valued, then they must be given respect academically as competent learners. They must be allowed to make decisions and choices, to find a purpose for their learning, and to actively engage in learning that interests them. Constructivistic learning approaches give students a greater sense of their ability to make meaning of their learning and their environment. Aspects of such learning might include creative and critical thinking, problem solving, cooperative learning, student choice, or peer tutoring. Constructivist teachers plan for generalization and transfer of learning, whole-task instruction, and the integration of real life issues and tasks into the curriculum. Students that engage in these activities find learning so meaningful that they want to direct their own behaviors in order to pursue the learning. When students' construction of knowledge is acknowledged in the classroom through active learning, each student is accepted as a competent thinker who can be trusted to learn. Feeling accepted and trusted, students are better able to accept and trust others. Likewise, if we want to create intellectual independence and critical thinking skills, we should simultaneously be applying those same skills toward behavior, not subverting our academic goals through behavioristic management systems.

LINKS BETWEEN ACADEMICS AND BEHAVIOR

Intellectual autonomy and moral autonomy are intertwined. Students taught to think about their actions instead of merely being given rewards for obedience are more likely to think analytically about academic subjects rather than merely memorize information needed for a test grade (Kamii & DeVries, 1993). Not only do we want students to be able to think independently and logically when making decisions about desirable behaviors, we also want them to exhibit these critical thinking skills when confronting intellectual issues.

The theory underlying the most current instructional approaches is the constructivistic perspective. National associations of language arts education, math education, early childhood education, and others (National Council for Teacher Education, National Association for the Education of Young Children, National Council of Teachers of Mathematics) recognize that students should be seen as able, active learners who engage in a process that is meaningful and purposeful. Leading educators (e.g., Graves, 1983; Kamii, 1989; Smith, 1983) are observing that students want to construct their own knowledge when given choices and responsibilities, appropriate models, and a role in setting goals. Students enjoy solving math problems when they are relevant to their lives. Students like to read books of their choosing, to experience reading as truly pleasurable and relevant to understanding themselves and the world. Students also want to write for real purposes—to communicate with others, to inform others, to express themselves—rather than merely to be evaluated by the teacher. Students are willing to engage in learning by taking intellectual risks in a constructivistic classroom because they do not face a penalty for being wrong. Thinking is at the core of learning. The quality of students' hypotheses, how they evaluate a hypothesis or decide to generate a new hypothesis, is valued more than quickly achieving a "correct" result.

In constructivistic learning environments, students practice a skill through the meaningful use of the whole process; for example, they practice recognizing words within a context of reading a story of interest, or they practice proper punctuation by editing a personal story for classroom publication. The process itself is meaningful, so students want to learn and are willing to practice and improve the process in order to achieve a more advanced product. Students with disabilities need the motivation of meaningful learning even more than most students since they generally need to work even harder and longer to learn. The more personally meaningful the goal, the harder the student will work to achieve it.

The message to students behind this approach to learning is that they are capable of self-direction, already have some knowledge that can be applied to any task, have the ability to work appropriately, and can seek help when necessary. Students are respected intellectually. The control can no longer be solely in the hands of the teacher, for this creates either passive or resistant students. The control must be held jointly by student and teacher, engendering reciprocal respect. It is a cooperative venture, emphasizing mutual respect between teacher and student rather than merely demanding that students respect the teacher.

The constructivistic focus, therefore, is consistent in both intellectual and social development

(Kamii, 1994). The process of learning in either area is one of taking risks as the students try out current theories, analyze results, test new ideas, and exchange viewpoints. A more careful inspection of the similarities between intellectual and social development is instructive.

Purpose

Students need to see a purpose in their learning, just as students need to see a purpose in their behavior. Why do students see the need to cooperate in the classroom? If they have participated in forming class rules, they have heard the reasoning for having them. If they have experienced the benefits of cooperative behavior, they will personally value such behavior. For instance, as students experience a meaningful exchange of ideas within a discussion, they will perceive a purpose in following the conventions associated with such discussion (DeVries & Zan, 1994). If they realize the need for safety to pursue learning activities in the classroom, they will understand the purpose of controlling their bodies to keep others safe. In traditionally behavioristic classrooms, the purpose of good behavior is merely to please the teacher. This purpose has failed in curricular areas as well as behavioral areas. Pleasing the teacher is not a strong enough purpose for most students. That is why grades or rewards are usually utilized. If learning is interesting to students, they will see the purpose in helping to create a classroom that supports learning.

If the classroom is set up so that students help each other to learn and are taught to support each other academically and emotionally, then a student has reason to care about the needs and feelings of others in the group. This caring encourages the consideration of all viewpoints, which is the goal of education for autonomy. Students with disabilities who do not have the requisite skills to function in the classroom community must have the same reasons for cooperative behaviors as other students. They need to care for their classmates and feel cared for by them. When a caring

environment is coupled with purposeful learning, students want to behave in ways that best allow learning to occur.

Meaning and Relevance

Academic learning, in a constructivistic model, is meaningful and relevant (DeVries & Kohlberg, 1990). Content has some bearing on the student's life, or captures the student's imagination or interest. Behavior has meaning and relevance as well. Cooperating with others brings results that are not achieved individually. Communicating one's needs allows the person to get those needs met.

When problems do exist between students, solutions to those problems must also be seen as meaningful and relevant. Punishments carry no relevance to the actions they are intended to correct, whereas consequences are directly related to the action. Effective communication can be understood as a meaningful method of negotiating for the satisfaction of one's needs. Classroom management policies that are consistent with academic approaches make learning meaningful and cooperation relevant to the task of learning. If students see the reason behind an action, they are more likely to initiate it on their own rather than to require external rewards.

Risk Taking

In a constructivistic setting the emphasis is removed from questions that have right answers (Duckworth, 1972). Students do not have to fear that they will fail if they don't develop the one correct answer. The emphasis is placed on the student—the constructor of knowledge—developing the best thinking, and the teacher asking the right question at the right time to elicit progress in the student's thinking. In this context, students with disabilities are able to use their own pace and direction to achieve an end. Accepting variation in pace and direction means allowing for a multitude of differences in student activities. Diversity is accepted as normal under these circumstances. We can apply this philosophy to both academic and social learning.

Models

Constructivistic learning theory acknowledges the value of adult and peer models as students construct understanding. Often learners extract what they need from demonstrations of the process by others as well as from their own personal experiences. For example, students read or hear good literature as part of learning how to write good literature. Students benefit from hearing good readers think aloud about their process of understanding a text, or from seeing their teacher or other students go through the writing process to produce an effective piece of writing. Just as teachers display the appropriate behaviors for an academic learning process, teachers must also display appropriate social behaviors. If teachers manage their classrooms through manipulation, then students will use manipulation when constructing their own social interaction patterns (DeVries & Zan, 1994). If teachers want students to respect others, effectively communicate needs, and use problem-solving techniques, then they must model respect for students, effective communication, and the use of problem-solving techniques in their management style.

The essential quality of the constructivistic learning process for both academics and behavior is thinking. Students are encouraged to create, discuss, compare, and defend ideas, and to construct their understandings through this type of independent thinking. Students actively engage in creating understandings rather than passively accept someone else's information. They then take responsibility for their ideas with a feeling of ownership, since they recognize that they initiated their own understandings. Students with disabilities will develop these same attributes of ownership and responsibility if allowed the same opportunities in actively creating their understanding.

THE TEACHER

Teachers who have been able to shift their paradigm of learning to accept that emphasis on the process of learning is essential to a quality product will be able to shift their paradigm in discipline similarly. In a traditional classroom, behavior is merely treated as a product and students are punished until they figure out on their own how to achieve the product. In a constructivistic classroom, learning communication, respect, and problem solving is valued as a necessary process in achieving the final product of working together to learn.

Students engaged in active learning require active teaching to support them. Constructivist teachers are actively engaged in careful consideration and adjustment of teaching procedures to accommodate varied learning and response opportunities, so students experience less frustration in learning. When students are less frustrated academically, they have more energy to bring to learning and to positive social interaction, especially when the interaction is seen as supportive to their construction of knowledge. For example, Leah may explore her ideas with Jenny concerning a way to produce a graph showing classroom color preferences. While all students in the class have conducted surveys, the type of information and resulting graph may vary in complexity according to the levels of student abilities. Since there is no correct way to display her information, Leah may choose to accept or reject Jenny's opinion, but will think about Jenny's reasoning, and must carefully consider her own reasoning as she defends her position. Mr. S. may contribute to the discussion to reiterate the possibilities and ask questions that will help Leah to determine her choice of graphs. Mr. S. supports the thinking process, but does not make the decision or tell Leah how to proceed (Gordon, 1989; DeVries & Zan, 1994).

Students with disabilities may need similar support in making behavioral decisions. While some students may be able to generate the necessary steps to negotiation after one class discussion, an active teacher must recognize that most children may require help to determine those steps, or may benefit from more practice in meaningful problem solving. Mr. S. may overhear Leah confronting another student about who will use the ruler. He may intervene to remind Leah of possible ways to solve the conflict. Then he steps back, but is available to both students as needed, while they practice negotiating a solution. The constructivist teacher considers the special needs of each student and adjusts the environment or teaching so that all students can benefit from an activity and participate in the learning process. The teacher is constantly tuned to providing on-the-spot coaching where helpful, and also enlists the assistance of the classroom community—other students or aides.

An active teacher also works toward preventing situations that will unnecessarily frustrate students academically or socially. Sometimes this means looking at ways in which classroom "expectations, demands, and interactions" can be modified to increase success for a student (Weaver, 1994 p. xi). Sometimes this means building strong communication skills, establishing shared control with lots of student decision making, and planning effective instruction, which considers the needs of all students in advance of problems. When a conflict arises the teacher may merely remind the student of possible options. Since those skills have been built, the students have them in a repertoire.

Just as the changes in instructional focus require the teacher to develop a different role in the classroom, so too does a constructivistic approach to classroom management require a shift in traditional interactions between teacher and student. Because our own teaching experience has been with authority figures and behavioral control, it is difficult to imagine ourselves doing anything else, even when we agree with the principles of constructivism. As Poplin argues elsewhere in this book, these principles shake the foundation of what was previously held as true in special education. It is difficult to actualize something you cannot visualize. Change to constructivistic teaching requires extensive efforts on the part of the teacher, support by administrators and fellow teachers, as well as specialized training to help teachers to view teaching differently.

Changing one's behavior can be a slow process for both student and teacher. If special education children are included in a regular classroom, then support for these children is needed both academically and behaviorally. In some cases this involves massive support for an extended period of time. The alternative is to give up on these students. When students can learn to govern their own behavior through rational thought and decision making, they can be productive members of a group (Kamii, 1984). Then students will not be passive, helpless "clients," but competent, active participants.

ADDRESSING THE CAUSE

When students make errors in mathematics or in reading, teachers don't use punishment to force correction of mistakes. Instead teachers try to figure out what caused the mistakes: what information or skill is missing for each learner. Knowing what a student needs to learn in order to proceed successfully tells the teacher what to teach. Many discipline problems are caused by a lack of information or skill and can be solved by teaching that provides the missing information or assists with the needed skills (Fields & Boesser, 1994).

Related consequences offer one way to provide missing information that will end some discipline problems. Teaching effective communication and negotiation are ways of giving students useful skills that will solve some discipline problems. However, sometimes the problem is caused by a need for other kinds of information or skills.

Many youngsters behave inappropriately because they do not know productive ways of making contact with their peers; in other words, they have not learned how to make a friend or to be a friend (Ramsey, 1991). They continually "pester" other students in an effort to make social contact. Typically, this annoying behavior is met with rejection from peers and punishment or banishment from adults. Though the rejection and banishment consequences may provide information about lack of acceptability, they do not provide information about alternative ways of behaving. It isn't helpful to teach what *not* to do unless you also teach what *to* do. Without alternative strategies, we see youngsters repeating the destructive patterns over and over.

Coaching in social skills is an important discipline approach. Some teachers will say this isn't what they are hired to do; but unless they do that, they are wasting their time attempting to teach reading or arithmetic. Students who lack friends or positive social contact have basic unmet needs that take priority over learning academics (Rizzo, 1989). They are too focused on meeting their emotional needs to be able to learn school subjects. It is not only those who lack the social skills whose learning is disrupted, but also the others in the group. The child who is crying out for social contact by acting out takes everyone's attention away from learning academics. Therefore, teaching productive ways of making contact is time well spent. This approach is effective because it addresses the cause of the problem.

Some youngsters behave inappropriately because they are less capable than others of conforming to traditional school practices (Weaver, 1994). For instance, while most students find it difficult to sit still and be quiet as passive recipients of information, children with Attention Deficit Hyperactivity Disorder (ADHD) find it impossible. While most students are bored with rote memorization tasks and worksheets, those with ADHD cannot cope with them at all. There is growing conviction among educators that "ADHD is not a disorder located solely within the individual, but rather a set of dysfunctional relationships between an individual with certain neurological predispositions and an environment that generates certain expectations and demands" (Weaver, 1994, p. xi). Teachers can easily observe which situations and activities elicit negative reactions from these youngsters, but most persist in futile and punitive efforts to change the student rather than changing the learning environment. Denny

Taylor (1990) and other education ethnographers have provided sad evidence of how children are damaged when schools refuse to look for the cause of behavior and learning difficulties in the school situation; instead they assume that the cause exists solely in the learner. The types of change recommended to enhance success for students with ADHD are changes from practices reflecting the behavioristic educational theory to those reflecting the constructivistic theory. Once again, the message is clear: Students with disabilities need what other students need; and they need it *more*.

Severe Problems

For some students, neither changes in the classroom nor in their own understanding and skills are enough. Some discipline problems are caused by unmet emotional needs too severe to be solved by teaching social skills. Some students' inappropriate behaviors are the result of severe trauma or deprivation. These youngsters need much more than a "tougher" discipline approach. They and their families typically require massive intervention, which is not the domain of the classroom teacher. Schools placing these youngsters in classrooms with twenty or twenty-five other students must provide strong support systems to the families and to the teacher. The inappropriate behaviors of children with emotional problems cannot accurately be called discipline problems; they are counseling problems (Fields & Boesser, 1994). Discipline approaches are not designed to address these problems: discipline is teaching appropriate behavior. Teaching information and skills is not an effective way of providing for unmet emotional needs. Helping the child to get his or her needs met is the most effective way of matching the intervention to the cause of the problem.

Extreme behavior problems generally have serious causes beyond the scope of classroom discipline (Stroul & Friedman, 1986). Schools must provide resources to determine these causes and then to find the appropriate help for the child. Why does Jessica break down in tears if asked to participate in school in any way? Why does Arden constantly hit others and destroy things? What do these children need in order to be productive in school and in life?

Behavior modification approaches have attempted to control inappropriate behavior caused by emotional problems, chemical imbalances, learning disabilities, and other serious problems. These approaches are designed to control the symptoms of the problem and keep everyone safe while the underlying causes are explored and addressed. Though we accept this intent, we see that too often behavior modification strategies become a permanent rather than temporary solution. This means that the symptoms of serious problems are submerged through coercive measures. The cause of the problem remains and the student becomes dependent upon external controls rather than developing personal discipline. The result is a person unable to function in society without constant supervision and continued behavior modification. Therefore we maintain that students with disabilities deserve the same kinds of teaching as other youngsters and that they, even more than most, need the sophisticated approaches designed to enhance construction of knowledge (Weaver, 1994; Poplin & Stone, 1992).

Yet too many teachers have little or no help as they struggle to meet the needs of all of their students, including those with disabilities of all sorts. The problems, sources, and cures are so diverse that no one simple recipe approach can possibly yield real results. Yet classroom teachers have neither the time nor the training to provide what these children need. Professionals trained in these areas should be in the classroom observing students with problems and then assisting the teacher to respond in useful ways (Bruder, 1994). Since this is rarely the case, it is no wonder that teachers resort to behavioristic systems of reward and punishment as a survival mode. That simple response is all that most have the time to consider. Without understanding the child and the problem, that is all that is possible. It is clearly not enough. Long-term goals of preparing productive citizens for a peaceful society demand much more.

CONCLUSION

Teachers can be guided by remembering that the small children in their classrooms will one day be large adults. When society does not invest in its future citizens, society pays dearly later on. Teachers must also be guided by remembering that the student with disabilities is a person first and foremost. Though unique in certain respects, students with disabilities are more like other students than they are unlike them. We assert that *all* students benefit from constructivistic classroom management that allows them to solve their own problems and take responsibility for directing their own behavior. Helping children to learn effective ways of interacting with others must be viewed as an education issue rather than a control issue. When all students with or without disabilities are helped to develop their own reasons for productive behavior, they have a much better chance of becoming productive, thinking citizens. The moral and intellectual autonomy we foster in our classrooms today is an investment in our society's social structure of tomorrow.

REFERENCES

Bettleheim, B. (1985, November). Punishment versus discipline. *The Atlantic Monthly,* pp. 51–59.

Bruder, M. B., (1994) Working with members of other disciplines: Collaboration for success. In M. Wolery & J. Wilbers, (Eds.), *Including children with special needs in early childhood programs* (pp. 46–70). Washington, DC: National Association for the Education of Young Children.

Curwin, R. L., & Mendler, A. N. (1988). *Discipline with dignity.* Alexandria, VA: Association for Supervision and Curriculum Development.

DeVries, R., & Zan, B. (1994). *Moral classrooms: Moral children.* New York: Teachers College Press.

DeVries, R., & Kohlberg, L. (1990). *Constructivist early education: Overview and comparison with other programs.* Washington, DC: National Association for the Education of Young Children.

Dreikurs, R. (1964). *Children: The challenge.* New York: Hawthorn.

Dreikurs, R., Greenwald, B., & Pepper, F. (1982). *Maintaining sanity in the classroom: Classroom management techniques.* New York: Harper & Row.

Duckworth, E. (1972). The having of wonderful ideas, *Harvard Educational Review, 42,* 217–231.

Fields, M., & Boesser, C. (1994). *Constructive guidance and discipline, preschool and primary education.* New York: Macmillan.

Ginott, H. (1965). *Between parent and child: New solutions to old problems.* New York: Macmillan.

Glasser, W. (1969). *Schools without failure.* New York: Harper & Row.

Gordon, T. (1970). *Parent effectiveness training.* New York: Wyden.

Gordon, T. (1989). *Teaching children self-discipline: At home and at school.* New York: Random House.

Graves, D. H. (1983). *Writing: Teachers and children at work.* London: Heinemann.

Hitz, R., & Driscoll, A. (1988). Praise or encouragement? New insights into praise: Implications for early childhood teachers. *Young Children, 43*(5), 6–13.

Kamii, C. (1984). Autonomy: The aim of education envisioned by Piaget. *Phi Delta Kappan, 65,* 410–415.

Kamii, C. (1989). *Young children continue to reinvent arithmetic–2nd Grade.* New York: Teachers College Press.

Kamii, C. (1994). *Autonomy, drug prevention & math education.* Paper presented at meeting of National Association for the Education of Young Children, Southeast Alaska.

Kamii, C., & DeVries, R. (1993). *Physical knowledge in preschool education: Implications of Piaget's theory.* New York: Teachers College Press.

Miller, D. F. (1990). *Positive child guidance.* Albany: Delmar.

Piaget, J. (1965). *The moral judgment of the child.* New York: The Free Press.

Poplin, M., & Stone, S. (1992). Paradigm shifts in instructional strategies: From reductionism to holistic/constructivism. In S. Stainback & W. Stainback (Eds.), *Controversial issues confronting special education, Divergent perspectives* (pp. 153–179). Boston: Allyn & Bacon.

Ramsey, P. G. (1991). *Making friends in school: Promoting peer relationships in early childhood.* New York: Teachers College Press.

Rizzo, T. A. (1989). *Friendship development among children in school.* Norwood, NJ: Ablex.

Shalaway, L. (1980, October). Are your students addicted to praise? *Instructor,* pp. 61–62.

Smith, F. (1983). *Essays into literacy.* London: Heinemann.

Stroul, B., & Friedman, R. (1986). *A system of care for severely emotionally disturbed children and youth.* Washington, DC: Child and Adolescent Service System Program, Georgetown University Child Development Center.

Taylor, D. (1990). *Learning denied.* Portsmouth, NH: Heinemann.

Weaver, C. (1994). *Success at last! Helping students with attention deficit (hyperactivity) disorders achieve their potential.* Portsmouth NH: Heinemann.

Wolery, M., & Wilbers, J. (1994). *Including children with special needs in early childhood programs.* Washington, DC: National Association for the Education of Young Children.

CHAPTER 14

Behavior-Analytic Foundations
of Classroom Management

THOMAS G. HARING
CRAIG H. KENNEDY

INTRODUCTION

Challenging classroom behavior remains one of the greatest concerns in U.S. education. It is among the most important factors in the referral of students for special education support and the isolation of students with disabilities from their peers, neighborhood schools, and communities. Difficulties in understanding and managing problem behavior are also a major factor in the decision of many otherwise qualified teachers to leave the teaching profession. Research from applied behavior analysts has touched widely on this concern and has provided a systematic foundation on which to build future technologies for effective classroom management. Current research in classroom management from a behavior-analytic perspective is driven by three fundamental principles.

1. *Behavior is functional.* All behavior is effective in accomplishing certain outcomes for the individual. Based on this principle, the key to understanding and reducing problem behavior is to identify its purpose. Once the function of behavior is determined within a given context, socially acceptable behavior can be taught to replace the inappropriate behavior.

2. *Behavior is part of a larger environment of events.* The basic behavioral unit used in behavior analysis is discriminative stimulus–response–reinforcing stimulus (Morris, 1992); behavior and environment are not separable elements in this model. The response stripped of its environment, or the environment without a person acting upon it, has no independent meaning in behavior analy-

sis (Barnes, 1989; Sidman, 1986; Zeiler, 1986). Thus, behavior analysis (contrary to claims made by its critics) is fundamentally contextualistic and nonreductionistic (cf. Hayes, Hayes, & Reese, 1988). Understanding the function of problem behavior entails understanding the relation between behavior and environment (e.g., Haring & Kennedy, 1990; Day, Horner, & O'Neill, 1994).

This principle also means that problem behavior cannot be defined using topographical definitions. That is, problem behavior cannot be understood by merely specifying the physical attributes of a response (e.g., hitting others, property destruction, or screaming). Instead, the behavioral unit is the relationship among the behavior and the situations under which it occurs and the events that follow. For most problem behavior this means that the behavior of teachers and peers must be studied in order to understand the functional control of the problem behavior in terms of the interrelationships between a student's behavior and the behavior of others.

3. *Behavior can be systematically studied using methods of the natural sciences.* Dimensions of students' behavior and peers' and teachers' reactions to that behavior can be quantified and analyzed. Quantifiable information regarding responding can guide efforts to develop procedures and solve problems. Such efforts are then used to make data-based decisions regarding intervention efficacy. Although the impact of intervention is guided by data, the ultimate decisions as to the success of an effort is judged not by those data in isolation, but with consideration of the subjective judgments of people who are part of a student's environment. (The subjective judgments of people who interact with a student can be quantified; this is often referred to as social validity). (Wolf, 1978)

The purpose of this chapter is to describe the effects of these three principles on the development of classroom management procedures. We will review what we believe to be the most important characteristics of interventions espoused by educators who explicitly adopt a world view consistent with behavior analysis. In doing so, we will review several types of interventions that are currently being researched by behavior analysts.

CHARACTERISTICS OF BEHAVIOR-ANALYTIC INTERVENTIONS

A Dynamic and Flexible System for Problem Solving

Behavior analysis is a conceptual system, not just a set of intervention techniques. This conceptual system includes the principles discussed earlier (that behavior is functional, environmentally based, and quantifiable), as well as a host of relations that are synthesized from these basic principles (e.g., how reinforcement operates, how schedules of reinforcement influence behavior, how to establish and promote stimulus control, and how broader socially determined environments promote or inhibit responding). This conceptual system has been employed to generate effective technologies as special education has progressively moved into new areas of concern that reflect current societal values.

The development of instructional technologies in the area of supported employment is a good example of new strategies to achieve societally valued outcomes through the application of behavioral principles. Until recently, students with moderate and severe disabilities (as well as many with mild disabilities) were employed predominantly within segregated special centers and sheltered workshops. As a result of demonstrating the power of applied behavior-analytic techniques in teaching job skills to people who were presumed

to be unemployable (e.g., Rusch, 1992; Wehman, 1992), policy makers and advocates began to create new types of administrative and social supports that would allow the entry of all persons into typical workplaces. *Task analysis* was a significant instructional procedure developed through these efforts (Gold, 1976). According to Rusch and Hughes (1989), behavior analysis also contributed social validation techniques and strategies for promoting generalized and durable, competent performance in the workplace. As these procedures were extended to the supported employment, new instruments, variables, and interventions were developed in order to be sensitive to the requirements of the workplace and the expectations of employers. Thus, behavior-analytic theory and procedures were not simply rotely applied but extensively developed for the unique characteristics of specific jobs and people.

Designing interventions for problem behavior in school settings poses similar challenges. In the past, most students with severe disabilities were served in segregated settings and had little contact with peers without disabilities. Our evolving values system in special education has rejected these earlier programs and insists on complete inclusion into general education classrooms. Because behavior analysis is a flexible conceptual system that guides the creation of new technologies, considerable experimental efforts have been expended to adapt interventions (and develop new interventions) that are sensitive and appropriate to these new settings (e.g., Kennedy & Itkonen, 1994).

There have been several procedures developed to address the need for interventions in inclusive settings. Three areas of current research will serve to exemplify the ability of behavior analysts to generate new procedures given recent changes in special education support environments.

1. Several researchers have demonstrated that specific aspects of social interactions with teachers (e.g., prompts and task demands) accurately predict problem behavior (e.g., Kennedy, 1994). As an example, altering task demands and teaching students to request help under these conditions can substantially reduce problem behavior (Carr & Durand, 1985).

2. As instruction for students with disabilities occurs in general education settings, special educators take on the role of consulting to general educators, rather than providing direct support. Peck, Killen, and Baumgart (1989) provided a behavior-analytic demonstration of a consulting model for integrating preschoolers with disabilities into typical preschool settings. Similarly, Miltenberger and Fuqua (1985) developed a training manual for teaching behavioral assessment interviewing skills that can be used to increase behavior-analytic skills for direct support providers.

3. Another area of current research that has been developed in response to the need for effective behavior management strategies in general education settings is self-management. Self-management is a process that includes (a) discriminating appropriate versus inappropriate examples of a person's own target behavior, (b) evaluating that behavior against a standard, (c) self-recording the performance, and (d) receiving a preferred outcome for achieving set goals (Koegel & Koegel, 1988). Self-management techniques are important because they are linked to how most students monitor their own behavior, and can be used to mediate responding without direct contact with a teacher.

These examples of current research efforts were selected to demonstrate the flexibility of behavior analysis as a conceptual system in adapting to the evolving demands placed on students receiving special education support. Behavior analysis offers a conceptual approach to the analysis of behavior change that allows for the attainment of goals that other processes (e.g., political advocacy, philosophical or ethical analysis, and surveys of best practices) identify as important (Baer, 1993).

Reinforcement Based

Most professionals believe that because inappropriate behavior is learned behavior, the challenge is to identify powerful positive intervention procedures that teach new socially acceptable behaviors

based on behavioral function (Iwata, Dorsey, Slifer, Bauman, & Richman, 1982; O'Neill, Horner, Albin, Storey, & Sprague, 1994). Procedures such as scatter-plot analyses (Touchette, MacDonald, & Langer, 1985) allow for the rapid identification and reduction of even the most extreme inappropriate behavior by identifying the cause of responding. However, it remains an important challenge to continue research examining the processes used to replace problem behaviors that have long histories of reinforcement with more desirable behaviors, and to program the maintenance of these new behaviors under typical conditions.

Another challenge that requires further research is to develop procedures to ensure that new skills that are taught are as effective as or more effective than the challenging behavior in accessing rewards in the environment (e.g., Carr et al., 1994). Empirical laws such as those derived from matching theory predict that when two responses are in competition with each other (the initial inappropriate response and the new socially acceptable response) the response that prevails will be the one that most reliably and efficiently occasions rewards (e.g., Horner & Day, 1991; Mace, McCurdy, & Quigley, 1990). Matching theory forces us to examine the social characteristics of a natural setting in order to understand how appropriate and inappropriate behavior is responded to by those who are important in a student's life. Dunlap, Johnson, and Robbins (1990) argue that the most effective approach to problem behavior is to initiate comprehensive early intervention programs with a focus on the instruction of communication skills, functional curriculum objectives, and parent training as primary proactive support measures. Although few data can be offered to substantiate this position, it is consistent with the principles we have discussed.

Problem Behavior as Socially Meaningful Behavior

All behavior occurs for a reason. For behavior analysts, the causes of behavior are derived from the environment in which they occur (Catania,

1994; Skinner, 1974). The behavior–environment relation, not the student, is viewed as the source of the problem. In many nonscientific approaches, when a student engages in problem behavior, the cause is often attributed to drives, needs, schemas, or emotions within the student. Behavior analysts often refer to these specious approaches to causality as explanatory fictions (Skinner, 1977). For instance, if a student is nonattentive during instruction, some educators might label the student as having a "poor attitude." The locus of the problem is viewed as residing within the student. Because a behavior-analytic approach seeks the cause of problem behavior in the environment, specific aspects of the classroom situation are scrutinized to identify what may be the cause of the problem. For example, it could be that the material is too difficult or that something more interesting is occurring in another part of the classroom.

When a behavior problem occurs, it has meaning. The problem behavior could be said to be informing the teacher that some aspect of the instructional environment needs to be altered. Because behavior occurs within an environment, not in a vacuum, there must be a reason for its occurrence. The teacher's challenge is to effectively analyze the environment in order to understand why a student is acting in a manner that is viewed as inappropriate.

The efficacy of defining problem behavior as a characteristic of a student's interaction with his or her environment, and not as a characteristic of a student in a pathological sense, became clear early in the development of applied behavior analysis (Bijou, 1970; Goldiamond, 1974). For example, the ground-breaking work with children with autism who engaged in self-injury by Lovaas and colleagues demonstrated the applied power of a behavior-analytic approach (e.g., Lovaas, Freitag, Gold, & Kassorla, 1965). When working with a child who spent the majority of her day in physical restraints because of severe self-injury, Lovaas et al. (1965) assessed the antecedent and consequent events that occurred around the problem behavior. Previous attempts by nonbehavior analysts to deal with the problem behavior focused upon the child's need for a closer "bond" with others in her environment. Unfortunately, these previous efforts had failed to decrease the problem behavior. What Lovaas et al. found was that the self-injury tended to be followed by attention from teachers (e.g., hugs, cuddling). When attention was given following self-injury, it actually increased the rate of problem behavior. Conversely, if staff attention was withdrawn when self-injury occurred, and provided when it did not occur, the problem behavior was virtually eliminated. It appeared as if the child, who had no formal communication system, was engaging in self-injury because it was the only reliable means of getting attention from adults. By understanding why various behavior problems occur, Lovaas and his colleagues were able to develop instructive and habilitative settings for children who previously appeared unteachable.

Over the course of the last thirty years numerous environmental variables have been identified as being possible causes for problem behavior. These include variables regarding teachers' instructional behavior, in addition to task-related aspects of instruction. In regard to what teachers do during instruction, the type and frequency of teacher attention provided to students has been identified as an important variable (Carr & Durand, 1985; Durand & Carr, 1987; Kennedy, 1994; Repp, Felce, & Barton, 1988). Other variables related to teacher behavior include the clarity of rules regarding appropriate and inappropriate conduct during instruction (Madsen, Becker, & Thomas, 1968), the style of requests used with students (Berg, Robson, & Wacker, 1990), the timing of requests (Mace et al., 1988; Singer, Singer, & Horner, 1987), and the rate of question presentation (Carnine, 1976).

Task difficulty is also a major factor in occasioning behavior problems. When instructional materials become more difficult, problem behavior can increase (Carr, Newsom, & Binkoff, 1980; Iwata et al., 1982; Steege, Wacker, Berg, Cigrand, & Cooper, 1989; Weeks & Gaylord-Ross, 1981). This area of research has also shown that problem behavior is more likely to occur when greater physical effort is required for correct task completion (Billingsley & Neal, 1985; Carr, 1988; Horner, Sprague, O'Brien, & Heathfield, 1990). These types of variables have been demonstrated to apply to students with behavior disorders, learning disabilities, developmental disabilities, dual sensory impairments, as well as to general education students.

The conceptualization that problem behavior needs to be understood in regard to reasons for it occurring has clearly affected how behavior analysts deal with problem behavior (e.g., Carr et al., 1994; Horner, Dunlap et al., 1991; Sidman, 1989). As the causes of problem behavior continue to be revealed through empirical demonstration, teachers become more effective in understanding the meaning of behavior problems.

The Individualistic Nature of Behavioral Supports

The antecedents of a behavior management technology clearly come from an idiographic (individualistic), rather than a nomothetic (normative), approach to understanding human action. The emphasis on the individual as the focus of analysis has been ubiquitous from the onset of both basic (*Journal of the Experimental Analysis of Behavior,* 1958 to the present) and applied analyses of behavior (*Journal of Applied Behavior Analysis,* 1968 to the present). Given the personalized nature of special education support, individualization of instruction across all aspects of a student's curriculum has been critical in achieving successful outcomes (Haring & Scheifelbusch, 1976; Rusch, Rose, & Greenwood, 1988; Snell, 1992). The assessment of problem behavior as an individual process has allowed for the development of technologies that can accurately and efficiently identify when and why behavior problems occur and what interventions will be effective.

Identifying when and why behavior problems occur provides critical information for teachers in implementing effective programming. Analyzing the commonalities among those circumstances that occasion a student's inappropriate behavior provides initial information for forming hypotheses about why problem behavior is occurring

(O'Neill et al., 1994; Touchette et al., 1985). For example, the presence of a certain teacher, the type of activity, the difficulty of activities, or the specific location might reliably predict behavior. The functional analysis of events allows teachers and others to assess whether problem behavior is functioning to gain social attention, tangible rewards, escape from instruction, or to serve other functions. The reason(s) why a student is producing inappropriate behavior can then be used to structure behavior support programs prior to program development (e.g., Carr & Durand, 1985; Iwata et al., 1982; Mace & Knight, 1986; O'Neill et al., 1994).

Effective strategies for providing a data-based analysis of intervention effectiveness act in concert with assessment strategies for identifying problem behavior functions. This is crucial because problem behavior has been demonstrated (for some students) to occur only within specific settings (Touchette et al., 1985) and for different reasons for individual students across settings (Haring & Kennedy, 1990). Thus, interventions require not only individualization across students, but also across settings. A student may produce problem behavior for one reason during instruction (e.g., to escape tasks) and for another reason during recess (e.g., to obtain attention from peers). The approach to behavioral support would then be changed according to the setting and behavioral function.

As an illustration, Repp et al. (1988) demonstrated the use of an assessment strategy for identifying the most effective intervention for individual students. Their approach uses an intervention design that allows a comparison of interventions used with a single student to assess the comparative effectiveness of each intervention. The individualization of assessing the settings and causes of problem behavior, as well as the effectiveness of interventions is a basic component of behavior analysis.

The Development of Adaptive Repertoires

An implicit theme running throughout this chapter has been the suppression of problem behavior by increasing adaptive alternative behaviors. By focusing on the behavior that teachers, parents, the person with disabilities, and others would like to see increased (e.g., communication), it is possible to reduce problem behavior. This approach has a long history in behavior analysis (Goldiamond, 1974) and is a focal aspect in most, if not all, major texts addressing the reduction of inappropriate behavior (Carr et al., 1994; Durand, 1990; Koegel, Koegel, & Dunlap, in press; LaVigna & Donnellan, 1986; Meyer & Evans, 1989; O' Neill et al., 1994; Reichle & Wacker, 1993; Snell, 1992).

The conceptual basis for focusing on adaptive behavior comes from basic research demonstrating that different forms of behavior can "compete" to obtain similar reinforcers (Catania, 1966). What this implies is that problem behavior that is used to escape from instruction (e.g., screaming) can be replaced by alternative forms of behavior (e.g., requesting a break) if they serve similar functions. This can be done without directly targeting problem behavior, through teaching alternative forms of adaptive behavior (Carr, 1988; Horner & Billingsley, 1988; Kazdin, 1982).

The current research literature in applied behavior analysis is replete with demonstrations of adaptive behavior replacing problem behavior. Typically, researchers have targeted the instruction of academic or task-related behavior (Billingsley & Neal, 1985; Carr & Durand, 1985; Russo, Cataldo, & Cushing, 1981; Wacker et al., 1990). Instructors teach students new skills, reinforce for correct completion or sustained on-task performance, and ignore problem behavior when it occurs. Typically, the results are decreased levels of problem behavior and increases in communication.

Although academic and daily living skills have often been targeted as desirable adaptive behavior, recent research is taking this approach a step further. Increasingly, the communicative functions that problem behaviors serve are being used as the basis for selecting adaptive alternatives. For example, Carr and Durand (1985) began by analyzing the functions that problem behavior served for several students (e.g., gaining access to social attention or avoiding difficult tasks). Once the

specific functions were identified for individuals, an alternative behavior was identified that would serve a similar function as the problem behavior. For instance, for a young girl whose problem behavior served to gain her social attention during instructional sessions, asking "Am I doing good work?" was selected as the adaptive alternative behavior. Carr and Durand's results showed that the alternative behavior rapidly and consistently replaced the problem behavior. This demonstration of the communicative functions that problem behavior can serve has been followed up by additional research aimed at expanding and refining this approach (Durand, 1986; Durand & Carr, 1987; Durand & Crimmins, 1987; Durand & Kishi, 1988; Horner et al., 1990; Wacker et al., 1990).

The Social Validity of Behavior Change

Behavior change occurs within highly complex social environments that react to the alterations of behavior in an equally complex manner. How teachers, parents, related support personnel, students with and without disabilities, and administrators react to the effects of interventions is critical for the continued success of behavior change (Baer, Wolf, & Risley, 1987). For example, an intervention program that is elaborate and difficult to implement is likely to be discontinued or abbreviated when problem behavior is no longer present. Unfortunately, the withdrawal of the intervention may very well occasion the recurrence of the problem behavior. Pragmatically, this is an intervention failure.

The continued success over time of a behavior change intervention is the critical test of its effectiveness and social validity. When the goals of a behavior support program have been achieved (i.e., when certain behavior has increased and other behavior has decreased), how a student's social/educational environment supports and maintains the intervention reveals a great deal about the acceptability of the goals, procedures, and outcomes. This goes beyond individuals' subjective evaluation of the effects of the intervention (e.g., Kazdin, 1977; Wolf, 1978). It causes behavior analysts to focus on behavior change as a function of the behavior of people working in social service systems (e.g., Yeaton & Sechrest, 1981).

The Generality of Behavior Change

A criterion that any intervention must be judged against is the generality of effects across settings, people, and time. For example, a problem behavior that is changed within a classroom setting may still be present within other settings such as the home, community, or playground, when specific people associated with the learning and reinforcement of prosocial behavior are not present. Fortunately, a variety of strategies and models to create generalization have been investigated since the landmark review by Stokes & Baer (1977). Techniques to build generalized responding include exemplar training (e.g., Gaylord-Ross, Haring, Breen, & Pitts-Conway, 1984), general case programming (e.g., Horner, McDonnell, & Bellamy, 1986), recombinative generalization training (e.g., Goldstein & Mousetis, 1989), self-management strategies (e.g., Koegel & Koegel, 1988), and analysis of behavioral variation (Haring, Breen, & Laitinen, 1989).

One of the major difficulties in promoting generalization and maintenance of behavior reduction is that some settings or people within a student's life serve to maintain and support inappropriate behaviors (e.g., Stokes & Osnes, 1988). This stresses the importance of viewing behavior change not as an isolated set of treatment variables that are under the sole control of a teacher or behavioral consultant, but as strategies that need to be discussed and extended throughout the settings in which students live. Interventions should be viewed as embedded within a complex sociologic structure of the school, classroom, home, and community settings. Clearly, more people within these complex systems need to be involved in the identification of problems, planning of interventions, implementation of strategies, and evaluation of outcomes than are currently typical (Kennedy & Itkonen, 1993).

One approach that we are investigating is the use of networks of friends without disabilities to support interactions and normalized behavior for students with disabilities in integrated schools and classrooms (Haring & Breen, 1992). Within this model, networks of peers are recruited, based on common interests, current acquaintances, and participation in the same regular education classes, to attend weekly meetings to discuss and plan times and opportunities to interact with the student with disabilities throughout the school day. Specific problems or stigmatizing behaviors are often discussed, and the group generates ideas and suggestions for how to handle these occurrences. The group is led by an adult facilitator, who guides the discussion but encourages the group members themselves to decelerate inappropriate behavior by facilitating friendship formation and the integration of the student with disabilities into the school. However, for students with autism and other moderate and severe disabilities, alternative behaviors are often discussed, as well as ideas for fuller inclusion of the students with disabilities into typical activities.

Accountability of Behavior Change

A central feature of behavior-analytic interventions is the degree of data-based accountability built into the system. Accountability is an important feature of supports for all students, including those with disabilities, for several reasons.

1. The individualized education program (IEP) is a support plan developed among an educational agency, the person with disabilities, and parents. Data-based accountability allows all those involved to see that the plan is implemented and executed as designed.

2. Data is collected because interventions are rarely initiated without several alterations and modifications to the original procedures. That is, interventions frequently require considerable fine-tuning, and sometimes complete changes in course once they are tried with an individual. Data are needed to identify when an intervention is working and when it is not so that changes can be made. Increased accountability also has the benefit of allowing effective procedures to be more dynamic and reactive to changes in the rate of behavior.

3. The collection of data and progressive refinement of techniques over time leads to more accurate hypotheses regarding how problem behavior functions. This leads to the development of a more complete understanding of behavior–environment interactions.

4. Behavioral interventions are potentially quite effective, and therefore potentially intrusive into a person's social and psychological life. Interventionists thus have an increased responsibility to carefully evaluate and monitor the use of behavioral interventions. Two forms of data are needed to effectively monitor such interventions. First, unambiguous information is necessary to show that the intervention is effectively meeting the goals that were agreed on for the students. Second, social validity information should be collected throughout and after the intervention to ensure that the means as well as the outcomes of the intervention are socially valued and appropriate.

CONCLUSION

Behavior problems and effective classroom management are central challenges to the successful inclusion of students with disabilities into a variety of typical settings. Behavior analysts can provide a flexible conceptual system for providing solutions to these problems. This is not to claim, however, that all solutions are readily at hand. Each student, classroom, school, and community poses a unique configuration of circumstances, history, and social expectations that require creative application of these basic behavioral principles.

Many classroom problems require the development of uniquely tailored procedures to fit the needs of the classroom, teachers, and students. For example, most behavior-analytic procedures deal with solutions that are developed in response to the individual needs of students. However, most interventions are delivered within the complex system of a classroom. This means that a teacher is always responsible for a group of students and that intervention must be realistically usable in a group context. We are only beginning to analyze how a teacher can manage an individual with problem behaviors, while at the same time attend to the instructional needs of an entire class. However, instructional arrangements in general education classes such as classwide peer tutoring (Greenwood et al., 1987) and cooperative learning groups (e.g., Slavin, 1990) indicate the need for embedding intervention within instructional contexts that are radically different from traditional procedures. There is an important need for the development of strategies that the majority of teachers in general education settings can use to promote more adaptive behavior when problems arise.

The strength of behavior analysis can be gauged by its ability to respond to new needs as educational values evolve. The greater appreciation recently of environmental factors and the functions of behavior (though always defining features of behavior analysis) is in large part due to the greater contextualization of special education itself. As the challenges for behavior analysis evolve from facilitating learning that is stripped of social context to learning that occurs based on social context, we must look more closely at how environments affect behavior and how interventions are viewed by people with and without disabilities within those environments.

REFERENCES

Baer, D. M. (1993). Policy and practice, as always. In R. A. Gable & S. F. Warren (Eds.), *Strategies for teaching students with mild to severe retardation.* Baltimore: Paul H. Brookes.

Baer, D. M., Wolf, M. M., & Risley, T. R. (1987). Some still-current dimensions of applied behavior analysis. *Journal of Applied Behavior Analysis 20,* 313–327.

Barnes, D. (1989). Behavior-behavior analysis, human schedule performance and radical behaviorism. *Psychological Record, 39,* 339–350.

Berg, W. K., Robson, K., & Wacker, D. P. (1990, May). *The role of request style on compliance of young children.* Paper presented at the 16th annual meeting of the Association for Behavior Analysis, Nashville, TN.

Billingsley, F. F., & Neal, R. S. (1985). Competing behaviors and their effect on skill generalization and maintenance. *Analysis and Intervention in Developmental Disabilities 5,* 357–372.

Bijou, S. W. (1970). What psychology has to offer education—Now. *Journal of Applied Behavior Analysis, 3,* 65–71.

Carnine, D. W. (1976). Effects of two teacher presentation rates on off-task behavior, answering correctly, and participation. *Journal of Applied Behavior Analysis, 9,* 199–206.

Carr, E. G. (1988). Functional equivalence as a mechanism in response generalization. In R. H. Horner, G. Dunlap, & R. L. Koegel (Eds.), *Generalization and maintenance: Lifestyle changes in applied settings* (pp. 221–241). Baltimore: Paul H. Brookes.

Carr, E. G., & Durand, V. M. (1985). Reducing behavior problems through functional communication training. *Journal of Applied Behavior Analysis, 18,* 111–126.

Carr, E. G., Levin, L., McConnachie, G., Carlson, J. I., Kemp, D., C., & Smith, C. E. (1994). *Communication-based intervention for problem behavior: A user's guide for producing positive change.* Baltimore: Paul H. Brookes.

Carr, E. G., Newsom, C. D., & Binkoff, J. A. (1980). Escape as a factor in the aggressive behavior of two retarded children. *Journal of Applied Behavior Analysis, 13,* 101–117.

Catania, A. C. (1966). Concurrent operants. In W. K. Honing (ed.), *Operant behavior: Areas of research and application* (pp. 213–270). New York: Appleton-Century-Crofts.

Catania, A. C. (1994). *Learning* (4th ed.). Englewood Cliffs, NJ: Prentice Hall.

Day, H. M., Horner, R. H., & O'Neill, R. E. (1994). Multiple functions of problem behaviors: Assessment and intervention. *Journal of Applied Behavior Analysis, 27,* 279–290.

Dunlap, G., Johnson, L. F., & Robbins, F. R. (1990). Preventing serious behavior problems through skill development. In A. C. Repp & N. N. Singh (Eds.), *Current perspective in the use of nonaversive and aversive interventions with the development disabled.* Sycamore, IL: Sycamore Publishing.

Durand, V. M. (1986). Self-injurious behavior as intentional communication. In K. D. Gadow (Ed.), Advances in learning and behavioral disabilities, (Vol. 5, pp. 141–155). Greenwich, CT: JAI Press.

Durand, V. M. (1990). *Severe behavior problems: A functional communication training approach.* New York: Guilford.

Durand, V. M., & Carr, E. G. (1987). Social influences on "self-stimulatory" behavior: Analysis and treatment implications. *Journal of Applied Behavior Analysis, 20,* 119–131.

Durand, V. M., & Crimmins, D. B. (1987). Assessment and treatment of psychotic speech in an autistic child. *Journal of Autism and Development Disorders 18,* 99–117.

Durand, V. M., & Kishi, G. (1988). Reducing severe behavior problems among persons with dual sensory impairments: An evaluation of a technical assistance model. *Journal of the Association for Persons with Severe Handicaps, 12,* 2–10.

Gaylord-Ross, R., Haring, T. G., Breen, C., & Pitts-Conway, V. (1984). The training and generalization of social interaction skills with autistic youth. *Journal of Applied Behavior Analysis, 17,* 229–242.

Gold, M. W. (1976). *Try another way training manual.* Champaign, IL: Research Press.

Goldiamond, I. (1974). Toward a constructional approach to social problems. *Behaviorism 2,* 1–83.

Goldstein, H., & Mousetis, L. (1989). Generalized language learning by children with severe mental retardation: Effects of peers' expressive modeling. *Journal of Applied Behavior Analysis, 22,* 245–260.

Greenwood, C. R., Dinwiddie, G., Bailey, V., Carta, J. J., Dorsey, D., Kohler, F. W., Nelson, C., Rotholz, D., & Schulte, D. (1987). Field replication of classwide peer tutoring. *Journal of Applied Behavior Analysis, 22,* 245–260.

Haring, N. G., & Scheifelbusch, R. L. (1976). *Teaching special children.* New York: McGraw-Hill.

Haring, T. G., & Breen, C. G. (1992). A peer-mediated social network intervention to enhance the social integration of persons with moderate disabilities. *Journal of Applied Behavior Analysis, 25,* 319–333.

Haring, T. G., Breen C., & Laitinen, R. E. (1989). Stimulus class formation and concept learning: Establishment of within- and between-set generalization and transitive relationships via conditional discrimination procedures. *Journal of the Experimental Analysis of Behavior 52,* 13–25.

Haring, T. G., & Kennedy, C. H. (1990). Contextual control of problem behaviors in students with severe disabilities. *Journal of the Applied Behavior Analysis, 23,* 235–243.

Hayes, S. C., Hayes L. J., & Reese, H. W. (1988). Finding the philosophical core: A review of Stephen C. Pepper's *World Hypotheses: A study in evidence. Journal of the Experimental Analysis of Behavior 50,* 97–111.

Horner, R. H., & Billingsley, F. F. (1988). The effect of competing behavior on the generalization and maintenance of adaptive behavior in applied settings. In R. H. Horner, G. Dunlap, & R. L. Koegel (Eds.), *Generalization and maintenance: Lifestyle changes in applied settings* (pp. 197–220). Baltimore: Paul H. Brookes.

Horner, R. H., & Day, H. M. (1991). The effects of response efficiency on functionally equivalent competing behaviors. *Journal of Applied Behavior Analysis, 24,* 719–732.

Horner, R. H., Dunlap, G., Koegel, R. L., Carr, E. G., Sailor, W., Anderson, J., Albin, R. W., & O'Neill, R. E. (1991). Toward a technology of "nonaversive" behavior support. *Journal of the Association for Persons with Severe Handicaps, 15,* 125–132.

Horner, R. H., McDonnell, J. J., & Bellamy, G. T. (1986). Teaching generalized skills: General case instruction in simulation and community settings. In R. H. Horner, L. H. Meyer, & H. D. Fredericks (Eds.), *Education of learners with severe handicaps: Exemplary service strategies* (pp. 289–314). Baltimore: Paul H. Brookes.

Horner, R. H., Sprague, J., O'Brien, M., & Heathfield, L. (1990). The role of response efficiency in the reduction of problem behaviors through functional equivalence training: A case study. *Journal of the Association for Persons with Severe Handicaps, 15,* 91–97.

Iwata, B. A., Dorsey, M. F., Slifer, K. J., Bauman, K. E., & Richman, G. S. (1982). Toward a functional analysis of self-injury. *Analysis and Intervention in Developmental Disabilities, 2,* 3–20.

Kazdin, A. E. (1977). Assessing the clinical or applied importance of behavior change through social validation. *Behavior Modification, 1,* 427–457.

Kazdin, A. E. (1982). Symptom substitution, generalization, and response covariation: Implications for psychotherapy outcome. *Psychological Bulletin, 91,* 349–365.

Kennedy, C. H. (1994). Manipulating antecedent conditions to alter the stimulus control of problem behavior. *Journal of Applied Behavior Analysis, 27,* 161–170.

Kennedy, C. H., & Itkonen, T. (1993). Effects of setting events on the problem behavior of students with severe disabilities. *Journal of Applied Behavior Analysis, 26,* 321–327.

Kennedy, C. H., & Itkonen, T. (1994). Some effects of regular class participation on the social contacts and social networks of high school students with severe disabilities. *Journal of the Association for Persons with Severe Handicaps, 19,* 1–10.

Koegel, L. K., Koegel, R. L., & Dunlap, G. (in press). *Community, school, family, and social inclusion through positive behavioral support.* Baltimore: Paul H. Brookes.

Koegel, R. L., & Koegel, L. K. (1988). Generalized responsivity and pivotal behaviors. In R. H. Horner, G. Dunlap, & R. L. Koegel (Eds.), *Generalization and maintenance: Lifestyle changes in applied settings* (pp. 41–66). Baltimore: Paul H. Brookes.

LaVigna, G. W., & Donnellan, A. M. (1986). *Alternatives to punishment: Solving behavior problems with nonaversive strategies.* New York: Irvington.

Lovaas, O. I., Freitag, G., Gold, U. J., & Kassorla, I. C. (1965). Experimental studies in childhood schizophrenia: Analysis of self-destructive behavior. *Journal of Experimental Child Psychology, 2,* 76–84.

Mace, F. C., & Knight, D. (1986). Functional analysis and treatment of severe pica. *Journal of Applied Behavior Analysis, 19,* 411–416.

Mace, F. C., Hock, M. L., Lalli, J. S., West, B. J., Belfiore, P., Pinter, E., & Brown, D. K. (1988). Behavioral momentum in the treatment of noncompliance. *Journal of Applied Behavior Analysis, 21,* 123–141.

Mace, F. C., McCurdy, B., & Quigley, E. (1990). A collateral effect of reward predicted by matching theory. *Journal of Applied Behavior Analysis, 23,* 197–206.

Madsen, C. H., Becker, W. C., & Thomas, D. R. (1968). Rules, praise, and ignoring: Elements of elementary classroom control. *Journal of Applied Behavior Analysis, 1,* 139–149.

Meyer, L. H., & Evans, I. M. (1989). *Nonaversive interventions for behavior problems: A manual for home and community.* Baltimore: Paul H. Brookes.

Miltenberger, R. G., & Fuqua, W. R. (1985). Evaluation of a training manual for the acquisition of behavioral interviewing skills. *Journal of Applied Behavior Analysis, 18,* 323–328.

Morris, E. K. (1992). The aim, progress, and evolution of behavior analysis. *The Behavior Analyst 15,* 3–30.

O'Neill, R. E., Horner, R. H., Albin, R. W., Storey, K., & Sprague, J. (1994). *Functional analysis: A practical assessment guide* (2nd Ed.). Sycamore, IL: Sycamore Publishing.

Peck, C. A., Killen, C. C., & Baumgart, D. (1989). Increasing implementation of special education instruction in mainstream preschools: Direct and generalized effects of nondirective consultation. *Journal of Applied Behavior Analysis, 22,* 197–210.

Reichle, J., & Wacker, D. P. (1993). *Communicative alternatives to challenging behavior: Integrating functional assessment and intervention strategies.* Baltimore: Paul H. Brookes.

Repp, A. C., Felce, D., & Barton, L. E. (1988). Basing the treatment of stereotypic and self-injurious behavior on hypotheses of their causes. *Journal of Applied Behavior Analysis, 21,* 281–289.

Rusch, F. R. (1992). *Support employment: Models, methods, and issues.* Sycamore, IL: Sycamore Publishing.

Rusch, F. R., & Hughes, C. (1989). Overview of supported employment. *Journal of Applied Behavior Analysis, 22,* 351–364.

Rusch, F. R., Rose, T., & Greenwood, C. R. (1988). *Behavior analysis in special education.* Englewood Cliffs, NJ: Prentice Hall.

Russo, D. C., Cataldo, M. F., & Cushing, P. J. (1981). Compliance training and behavioral convariation in the treatment of multiple behavior problems. *Journal of Applied Behavior Analysis, 14,* 201–222.

Sidman, M. (1986). Analysis of emergent verbal classes. In T. Thompson & M. D. Zeiler (Eds.), *Analysis and integration of behavioral units* (pp. 213–245). Hillsdale, NJ: Lawrence Erlbaum Associates.

Sidman, M. (1989). *Coercion and its fallout.* Boston: Authors Cooperative.

Singer, G. H. S., Singer, J., & Horner, R. H. (1987). Using pretask requests to increase the probability of compliance for students with severe disabilities. *Journal of the Association for Persons with Severe Handicaps, 12,* 287–291.

Skinner, B. F. (1974). *About behaviorism.* New York: Random House.

Skinner, B. F. (1977). Why I am not a cognitive psychologist. *Behaviorism, 5,* 1–10.

Slavin, R. E. (1990). *Cooperative learning: Theory research and practice.* Englewood Cliffs, NJ: Prentice Hall.

Snell, M. E. (1992). *Instruction of persons with severe handicaps* (4th ed.). Columbus, OH: Merrill.

Steege, M. W., Wacker, D. P., Berg, W. K., Cigrand, K. K., & Cooper, L. J. (1989). The use of behavioral assessment to prescribe and evaluate treatments for severely handicapped children. *Journal of Applied Behavior Analysis, 22,* 23–33.

Stokes, T. F., & Baer, D. M. (1977). An implicit technology of generalization. *Journal of Applied Behavior Analysis, 10,* 349–367.

Stokes, T. F., & Osnes, P. G. (1988). The developing applied technology of generalization and maintenance. In R. H. Horner, G. Dunlap, & R. L. Koegel (Eds.), *Generalization and maintenance: Lifestyle changes in applied settings* (pp. 5–20). Baltimore: Paul H. Brookes.

Touchette, P. E., MacDonald, R. F., & Langer, S. N. (1985). A scatter plot for identifying stimulus control of problem behavior. *Journal of Applied Behavior Analysis, 18,* 343–351.

Wacker D. P., Steege, M. W., Northup, J., Sasso, G. M., Berg, W. K., Reimers, T. M., Cooper, L. J., Cigrand, K., & Donn, L. (1990). A component analysis of functional communication training across three topographies of severe behavior problems. *Journal of Applied Behavior Analysis, 23,* 417–430.

Weeks, M., & Gaylord-Ross R. (1981). Task difficulty and aberrant behavior in severely handicapped students. *Journal of Applied Behavior Analysis, 14,* 449–463.

Wehman, P. (1992). *Life beyond the classroom: Transition strategies for young people with disabilities.* Baltimore: Paul H. Brookes.

Wolf, M. M. (1978). Social validation: The case for subjective evaluation, or how applied behavior analysis is finding its heart. *Journal of Applied Behavior Analysis, 11,* 203–214.

Yeaton, W. H., & Sechrest, L. (1981). Critical dimensions in the choice and maintenance of successful treatments: Strengths, integrity, and effectiveness. *Journal of Consulting and Clinical Psychology, 49,* 156–167.

Zeiler, M. D. (1986). Behavioral units: A historical introduction. In T. Thompson & M. D. Zeiler (Eds.), *Analysis and integration of behavioral units* (pp. 1–12). Hillsdale, NJ: Lawrence Erlbaum Associates.

SECTION EIGHT

COLLABORATION/ CONSULTATION

Primarily as a result of the mainstreaming, integration, and full inclusion movements, there has been a heightening interest in collaborative consultation in recent years. In Chapter 15, Johnson and Pugach discuss the importance of collaboration as one way to help achieve the goals of inclusive schools. But they challenge us to move beyond many past and present-day views of collaboration. They suggest a view of collaboration that is characterized by all members of a school and the community working together and supporting each other in a set of multidimensional collegial interactions to provide the highest quality of curriculum and instruction for the diverse students they serve.

In Chapter 16, Thousand, Villa, Paolucci-Whitcomb, and Nevin offer a definition of collaborative consultation that overcomes many of the problems that have plagued consultation in the past. They provide a rationale for their approach to collaborative consultation and point out that collaborative consultation will continue to evolve and that its long-term success is dependent on beliefs held by members of the school and the greater community.

CHAPTER 15

The Emerging Third Wave of Collaboration: Beyond Problem Solving

LAWRENCE J. JOHNSON
MARLEEN C. PUGACH

INTRODUCTION

In the past two decades, special education has participated in the creation of a new form of service delivery, *collaboration.* This has been the central vehicle for enacting a progressive move toward the integration of students with disabilities into general education classrooms nationwide. How best to implement a collaborative philosophy that fosters the joint efforts of special and general education teachers alike has been the focus of much research and debate within the field (Graden, 1989; Pugach & Johnson, 1989a, 1989b), leading to the development of multiple models and various forms of collaborative practice.

Although it is a relatively recent phenomenon, collaboration between special and general education has gone through a rapid evolution over the past two decades. This evolution has occurred in two distinct waves representing two views of collaboration, beginning with an expert consultation model and progressing to a more collaborative, egalitarian problem-solving model—the current view. These first two waves have each been followed by a period of confusion regarding the emerging definition of collaboration. We see this confusion as a product of the progressive interaction between special and general education and the increasingly greater challenges each degree of interaction poses.

Today we are in the midst of a transition to a third view of collaboration, one that is emerging from a context of broad-based schoolwide reform. From this perspective, collaboration is not limited to mutual problem solving to address teachers' concerns about difficulties with learning and behavior. Instead, collaboration is characterized by all members of a school and the community working together and supporting each other in a set of multidimensional collegial interactions to provide the highest quality of curriculum and instruction for the diverse students they serve.

Rather than being defined as a formal, step-by-step approach for addressing problems, collaboration becomes the tacit foundation for good teaching across the school. Problem solving will of course commonly occur as part of collaboration, but what we are suggesting is that collaboration subsumes but is not synonymous with problem solving. Expanding beyond problem solving and toward a broader view of collaboration stands as an important breakthrough that could enable schools to better meet the needs of an increasingly diverse community while also enabling special educators to take a much more prominent role in reaching this goal.

Currently, the view of collaboration as problem solving is well accepted and relatively noncontroversial within the special education community, and it is consistent with the general direction school reform is taking. Thus, its place in a book whose theme is "controversial issues" is slightly problematic. However, we would like to suggest that viewing collaboration as solely problem solving may in fact be limiting because by focusing on individual problems we do not address the broader structural approaches that profoundly impact teachers' abilities to address diverse groups of learners. In order to participate in the larger goal of fundamental school reform, collaboration viewed strictly as problem solving is not a powerful enough definition.

As we move into the next century it is imperative that special educators actively participate in creating an educational system that is responsive to diversity. If we are unsuccessful in creating this system and do not change the role special education plays, we will be left with a continued reliance on special education as a safety valve for those students and families who pose the greatest educational challenges.

Although special educators have long recognized that serving this safety valve function is problematic, the role has been perpetuated largely due to the belief that while placement in special education for many students may in fact be inappropriate, special education can at least meet their individual needs. By helping to confirm that the problem lies in the student and his or her family, such good intentions on the part of special education have done damage at least as problematic as that done by an educational system that is unable or unwilling to meet their needs. So while there does not seem to be controversy about the worth of collaboration as a general process, there may indeed be controversy regarding the role special education will play in creating an educational system responsive to diversity. Are we as special educators going to be participants in reform or will we continue to be passive agents who focus in isolation on those the schools are disinclined to serve adequately.

In this chapter, we begin by offering a brief historical look at the first two waves of collaboration as a way of highlighting their contrast with the emerging, more broad-based third wave. Then, in analyzing this third wave, we address the existing disagreements directly. Finally, we argue that collaboration will be strengthened to the extent that

special education situates itself within a context of diversity, a context that maximizes the potential of the educational system to support a range of individual diversity inclusive of disabilities.

THE FIRST WAVE: EXPERT CONSULTATION

Shortly before the passage of the landmark legislation known as Public Law 94-142, and also shortly after the field of learning disabilities was invented, special educators had already begun to realize that putting their efforts toward improving what went on in general education classrooms was probably a good way to assure the quality of services students with disabilities received (Fox, Egner, Paolucci, Perelman, & McKenzie, 1973; Lilly, 1971). Special education began to take on an indirect service as well as a direct service responsibility; the sole purpose of the consultation portion of this responsibility was to assist classroom teachers in expanding their methodological repertoires.

Defining Problem Solving in the First Wave

Specifically, in these early models, the goal of the relationship between special and general education teachers was to export special education methods into general classrooms; the Vermont program (Fox et al., 1973) stands as perhaps the earliest example of this approach. Other programs that followed adhered strongly to the behavioral model of educational intervention. For example, the Resource Consulting Teacher Program at the University of Illinois stressed mastery learning, data-based instruction, and applied behavior analysis for management problem (Idol-Maestas, 1983). The belief in the power of this class of interventions for students who were having difficulty achieving in school was so strong that rarely was another methodological framework even talked about. Special education teachers were to function as expert consultants who provided requisite know-how in behavioral interventions. Despite this narrowly circumscribed methodological approach, the intent of this early form of interaction between special and regular education teachers, which was always referred to as *consultation,* was nothing short of honorable—to strengthen what went on in the regular classroom.

Three significant problems were associated with this expert model of consultation: (1) the incongruence between the thinking of special and general educators, (2) the difficulty of using instructional or methodological strategies that were far outside of a given teacher's existing repertoire, and (3) the credibility of the consultant in the teacher's eyes (Johnson, Pugach, & Hammitte, 1988). Further complicating matters was the fact that special education teachers were rarely allotted time to engage in the indirect portion of their work such as keeping current in their discipline (Idol-Maestas & Ritter, 1985). Despite the best of intentions, during this first wave classroom teachers did not seem particularly interested in implementing the interventions their special education colleagues created. The interventions were not related to their view of the teaching world. Special education consulting teachers and their counterparts were speaking different languages. What the first wave taught us was that (1) implementing a more interactive model between special and regular education teachers would be hard work, and (2) unless there was a sense of parity among all of the players, the changes special educators wanted to see were not likely to be implemented. This problem quickly led to an interest in finding more collaborative ways of engaging in problem solving.

The Confusing Transition from Consultation to Collaboration

It quickly became apparent that if classroom teachers were going to participate fully in changing their teaching practices for students with disabilities, a far more collaborative model than any yet in use would be required. As the consulting model of service delivery became more commonplace, a new vision of consultation began to emerge that had greater parity between specialists and general classroom teachers at its core. A driving force behind this change was the need to promote ownership of interventions on the part of

classroom teachers. Providing direct prescriptions to classroom teachers came to be seen as increasingly inappropriate, and the term *consultation* also was deemed improper to describe how teachers and other school staff members worked together. The word *collaboration* began to be favored as more descriptive of the ideal relationship among participants in professional interactions.

One tenet of this model of professional interaction was that specialists refrain from prescribing solutions hierarchically. However, because of the model's continued reliance on applied behavioral procedures as an implementation framework, it initially proved to be more a repackaging of the consultation view of interaction and less the radical shift in orientation that real parity demanded. The confusion over the ultimate goal was perhaps best captured in the terminology adopted, namely, *collaborative consultation* (Idol, Paolucci-Whitcomb, & Nevin, 1986).

So at the same time that many special educators were just beginning to understand and take on a part-time consulting role, they were also expected to participate in the transition from a consulting to a newly defined collaborative model of interaction. How to achieve this parity began to dominate the dialogue (for example, Pugach & Johnson, 1988; Friend, 1984). However, the preparation of special educators had not changed radically; methodologically, although they were not to prescribe solutions, what they had to offer was a package of interventions that still were defined largely by the behavioral model. Although parity was the goal, recognizing the limitations of one's own methodological expertise or the strengths of a colleague's expertise was not emphasized in practice or in preparation for practice. This period of confusion gave way to a significant phase of investigation into various approaches to collaborative interaction.

THE SECOND WAVE: EXPERIMENTING WITH COLLABORATION AS JOINT PROBLEM SOLVING

A lively period of experimentation followed the shift from the terminology of consultation to that of collaboration, accompanied by spirited debates over what form collaboration should take. Collaboration unquestionably became the norm for how special education would operate in schools and was endorsed wholeheartedly. The models that were developed to reach this goal were all loosely based on the philosophy that individual teacher change within his or her own classroom was the most expedient way of making necessary accommodations to foster the integration of students with disabilities. What the collaboration models had in common was the goal of solving specific classroom problems through interventions targeted at identified students with disabilities, and then extending outward to students with problems who may not have been formally identified.

These models included a renaissance of teacher assistance teams (Chalfant & Pysh, 1989); the appearance of mainstream assistance teams (Fuchs, Fuchs, & Bahr, 1990), peer collaboration (Johnson & Pugach, 1991), and intervention assistance teams (Zins, Curtis, Graden, & Ponti, 1988); and an expanded version of collaborative consultation (Idol, Paolucci-Whitcomb, & Nevin, 1986). However, despite a common interest in problem solving, in reality these forms of collaboration were often incompatible, differing widely on the issue of parity between special and general education teachers and role definition for special educators as participants in collaborative interactions (Pugach & Johnson, 1995).

Although several important issues were debated during this wave of experimentation, they were not necessarily resolved. Among the most contentious was the degree to which general education teachers needed a specialist present to address the classroom situations that worried them (Pugach & Johnson, 1988). The larger, related issue, and the one that was never settled during this experimental phase with collaboration, was how to define the special expertise of the special education teacher, particularly with respect to students labeled as having mild disabilities. This was the group for whom most of these models were developed, and this was also the group about

which the greatest questions were raised regarding the organization and implementation of the general curriculum and related instructional practices. The failure to deal with this definitional issue head-on left the question of how far special education needed to go to contribute to total school reform unanswered. By setting collaborative practice solely within the classroom and by locating the debate within the domain of situation-specific problem solving, the larger, schoolwide issues were not easily seen as being related in scope.

That special educators and general educators were willing to collaborate was no longer a point of discussion; by this time all debate on the virtues of collaboration had virtually disappeared and, as we observed earlier, today there is little disagreement about its value. In fact, it would be rare to find a special education teacher—either prospective or practicing—who did not mention collaboration as an important part of his or her job. The shift to a collaborative mode of professional interaction was a vitally important and constructive change in the practice of special education. However, the context of education has changed and the situational demands are greater than ever before. In this new setting, the extent to which collaboration is meant to affect more than the classroom alone is the newest question that bears consideration.

A New Transition: Confusion over the Parameters of Collaboration

In a remarkably short period of time, collaboration has become the preferred form of service delivery in special education and special educators have quickly gained proficiency in the various problem-solving models. But today, overlapping with this general, classroom-based approach to collaboration is the implementation of a group of other crucial methods and ideas for improving the capacity of the schools to educate a wider range of students.

Only some of these approaches focus on the classroom level—for example, team teaching between special education/Chapter I and general education teachers (Bauwens, Hourcade, & Friend, 1989; Pugach & Johnson, 1995), cooperative learning (Slavin, 1991), or reciprocal teaching (Palincsar & Brown, 1984). Others focus on schoolwide change and include, for example, building-level decision making or schoolwide Chapter I programs. Still others are designed to contribute directly to the growth and professional development of teachers—action research (Holly, 1991) or peer coaching (Joyce & Showers, 1988). In short, connections other than those specifically between a single special educator and a single general education teacher become crucial as a means of building a strong professional culture among teachers. In contrast to the years during which collaboration first made its appearance specifically in the context of special education and developed into a series of complex ways to solve problems, today special educators and general educators alike find themselves in the midst of a rich menu of defensible choices by which to guide their joint work.

Consequently, the entire educational framework within which collaboration between special and general education takes place has changed dramatically at a time when many special educators have just become skilled in the implementation of one of these many problem-solving models. No longer is collaboration thought of as a unitary strategy for solving specific classroom problems. Instead, how outcomes-based education relates to special education (Shriner, Ysseldyke, Thurlow, & Honetschlager, 1994), how various instructional methods that may be unfamiliar to special educators might be useful (Englert & Palincsar, 1992), how curriculum reform intersects with special education (Pugach & Warger, 1993), in short, all aspects of school reform have a place in the wider scope of collaboration. This has caused confusion about what collaboration between special and general education actually is and how the parameters of this relationship are to be defined.

To make good on the real promise of collaboration, special educators find themselves needing to become active participants in the reform of

education. Some of us worry that becoming involved in the broader educational arena will dilute our efforts with those students traditionally served by special education. However, we believe that the creation of an educational system that is more responsive to individual differences will have a more dramatic impact on these students, particularly those identified as having mild disabilities, than individual problem-solving strategies between teachers. To what extent such an educational system can be created and the role special education will play in moving toward this system is the challenge of the third wave.

THE THIRD WAVE: COLLABORATION AS THE FOUNDATION OF TEACHING

Before we more fully describe the challenges of the third wave of collaboration, we want to make it clear that we are not arguing against individual problem solving between teachers. We believe that such problem solving continues to be an important strategy for facilitating changes directed toward individual student needs and has often resulted in classrooms that are more receptive to differences. But in this new, third wave we believe that special educators must expand their efforts to include reforming the broader educational system so that it is increasingly responsive to diversity. To achieve this end, the current orientation of schooling, which holds individual teachers responsible for student growth, needs to be shifted to a collaborative orientation in which all members of the school work together and are collectively accountable for the progress of all students.

Currently, teaching is an occupation that requires a great deal of interaction with children and youth but demands much less in the way of adult–adult interaction (Pugach & Johnson, 1995). This individualistic orientation can create a sense of isolation and limits how expertise is utilized in the classroom. Generally, the teacher is left alone unless he or she has a problem and is open to the possibility of receiving help from other adults in the school; that is, collaborative relationships are set into motion in direct response to a specific problem and it is the presence of that problem that dictates the collaborative relationship. As a result, the rich intellectual resource the adults in any school represent may be limited to use in only one set of situations—those associated with specific classroom-based problems—rather than the broad array of situations to which a teacher must attend.

On the other hand, if we recognize schools as communities of adult as well as child learners, and define collaboration from this perspective, a more expanded notion of collaboration emerges. Individual accountability for students shifts from isolated classroom teachers to all of the members in the community, and all are held accountable to support the complex work of schools. Thus in the third wave we believe that collaboration can no longer be defined as a unidimensional activity to be used when a problem presents itself. Rather, it becomes a multidimensional set of collegial interactions that occur organically within the day-to-day dynamics of each school according to the situation. In short, we believe that for collaboration to reach its full potential, it must expand beyond isolated or individual problem solving.

Clearly, critical challenges face the field of education as we move toward the twenty-first century. The potential of too many students is not being actualized in our current approach to education. Many students' race, ethnicity, family structure, economic status, language, or disability sets them apart from those for whom school has been a successful experience. The level of preparation for traditional school varies greatly among students and compounds the complex nature of the challenges educators face. Further, most teachers, particularly in urban schools, are not representative of the ethnic, racial, or socioeconomic groups of their students. Teachers who differ from their students in significant ways may view their students' diversity as a deficit requiring remediation, rather than as the asset it might be.

It is unrealistic to expect that a single teacher or pair of teachers engaged in structured problem solving will have the expertise to address these vast differences among students and the complicated responses schools will need to make on their behalf. It is not unrealistic, however, for a school to have the collective expertise to embrace this diversity. To be successful in this effort, teachers will need to support each other as part of a larger community in order to change the culture of their schools.

Although collaboration to solve specific problems is appropriate and beneficial, it was never designed to address these larger problems. If the scope of collaboration between special and general education is limited to this kind of interaction, the potential to achieve these larger changes also is limited. In this third wave of collaboration, efforts at problem solving need to continue, but in addition, the creative energies of teachers must also be directed collectively toward the creation of an educational system that nurtures the development of all children. Unless we are successful in this shift, an increasing number of students will continue to be served inadequately by schools, and special education runs the risk of remaining an overflow program for those the educational system has the most trouble serving.

CONCLUDING THOUGHTS

In many ways, this expanded definition of collaboration is a logical outgrowth of special education's progressive search for integrated classrooms in which the quality of the educational experience is not only acceptable, but exemplary. Although few will argue with the value of collaboration, it is by no means clear how special education will contribute directly to a full reorientation of the educational system, nor indeed whether this level of participation is a good use of resources. This potential difference in perception of the role special education will play, should it emerge, may not be unlike the disagreements we are seeing over the issue of inclusion itself, in which the central issue is not whether integration is a desirable goal, but rather whether there is a high enough degree of confidence in the general education system to make the needed changes (Pugach, in press).

This third wave of increasing general education's responsiveness to diversity is perhaps the one fraught with the most confusion in regard to goals and their accomplishment. That confusion is likely to persist because today it is not only special education practice that is being questioned, but rather educational practice as a whole. Such confusion is threatening because it lacks the stability and security of the past, even if that past—as characterized by specific collaborative problem solving—is relatively recent and is still an effective element for the future. Rethinking the organization and implementation of schooling is difficult, and the specific contribution special educators will make to the collaborative enterprise is as yet unclear. But as a principle to guide special educators, collaboration broadly defined is without question a powerful one to follow.

REFERENCES

Bauwens, J., Hourcade, J., & Friend, M. (1989). Cooperative teaching: A model for general and special education integration. *Remedial and Special Education, 10,* 17–22.

Chalfant, J. C., & Pysh, M. V. (1989). Teacher assistance teams. *Remedial and Special Education, 110*(6), 49–58.

Englert, C. S., & Palincsar, A. S. (1991). Reconsidering instructional research in literacy from a sociocultural perspective. *Learning Disabilities Research and Practice, 6*(4), 225–230.

Fox, W. L., Egner, A. N., Paolucci, P. E., Perelman, P. F., & McKenzie, H. S. (1973). An introduction to a regular classroom approach to special education. In E. Deno (Ed.), *Instructional alternatives for exceptional children.* Minneapolis: University of Minnesota and the National Center for the Improvement of Educational Systems.

Friend, M. (1984). Consultation skills for resource teachers. *Learning Disability Quarterly, 7,* 246–250.

Fuchs, D., Fuchs, L. S., & Bahr, M. W. (1990). Mainstream assistance teams: A scientific basis for the art of consultation. *Exceptional Children, 57*(2), 128–139.

Graden, J. (1989). Redefining "prereferral" intervention as intervention assistance: Collaboration between special and general education. *Exceptional Children, 56,* 227–231.

Holly, P. (1991). Action research: The missing link in the creation of schools as centers of inquiry. In A. Lieberman & L. Miller (Eds.), *Staff development for education in the 90's* (2nd ed., pp. 133–157). New York: Teachers College Press.

Idol, L., Paolucci-Whitcomb, P., & Nevin, A. (1986). *Collaborative consultation.* Austin, TX: Pro-Ed.

Idol-Maestas, L. (1983). *Special educator's consultation handbook.* Rockville, MD: Aspen.

Idol-Maestas, L., & Ritter, S. (1985). A follow-up study of resource/consulting teachers. *Teacher Education and Special Education, 8*(3), 121–131.

Johnson, L. J., & Pugach, M. C. (1991). Peer collaboration: Accommodating the needs of students with mild learning and behavior problems. *Exceptional Children, 57*(5), 454–461.

Johnson, L. J., Pugach, M., & Hammitte, D. (1988). Barriers to effective special education consultation. *Remedial and Special Education, 9*(6), 41–47.

Joyce, B., & Showers, B. (1988). *Student achievement through staff development.* New York: Longman.

Lilly, M. S. (1971). Forum: A training based model for special education. *Exceptional Children, 37*(10), 745–749.

Palincsar, A. S., & Brown, A. L. (1984). Reciprocal teaching of comprehension-fostering and comprehension-monitoring activities. *Cognition and Instruction, 1*(2), 117–175.

Pugach, M. C. (in press). On the failure of imagination in inclusive schooling. *The Journal of Special Education.*

Pugach, M. C., & Johnson, L. J. (1988). Rethinking the relationship between consultation and collaborative problem solving. *Focus on Exceptional Children, 21*(4), 1–8.

Pugach, M. C., & Johnson, L. J. (1989a). Pre-referral interventions: Progress, problems and challenges. *Exceptional Children, 56*(3), 217–226.

Pugach, M. C., & Johnson, L. J. (1989b). The challenge of implementing collaboration between general and special education. *Exceptional Children, 56*(3), 232–235.

Pugach, M. C., & Johnson, L. J. (1995). *Collaborative practitioners: Collaborative schools.* Denver, CO: Love.

Pugach, M. C., & Warger, C. L. (1993). Curriculum considerations. In J. Goodlad & T. Lovitt (Eds.),

Integrating general and special education (pp. 125–148). New York: Macmillan.

Shriner, J. G., Ysseldyke, J. E., Thurlow, M. L., & Honetschlager, D. (1994). "All" means "all"—including students with disabilities. *Educational Leadership, 51*(6), 38–42.

Slavin, R. E. (1991). Synthesis of research on cooperative learning. *Educational Leadership, 48*(5), 71–82.

Zins, J. E., Curtis, M. J., Graden, J. L., & Ponti, C. R. (1988). *Helping students succeed in the regular classroom: A guide for developing intervention assistance programs.* San Francisco: Jossey-Bass.

CHAPTER 16

A Rationale and Vision for Collaborative Consultation

JACQUELINE S. THOUSAND
RICHARD A. VILLA
PHYLLIS PAOLUCCI-WHITCOMB
ANN NEVIN

Today we are faced with the preeminent fact that if civilization is to survive, we must cultivate the science of human relationships—the ability of all peoples, of all kinds, to live together and work together in the same world at peace.
—Franklin Delano Roosevelt, 1945

INTRODUCTION

It has been a scant twenty-five years since a free appropriate public education was ordered for all children who were labeled retarded in Pennsylvania (*PARC v. The Commonwealth of Pennsylvania,* 1971). Public Law 94-142 (1975) was passed shortly after this ruling to extend the right to an education to all U.S. children with special education needs. Embedded in the right to an education mandate was (a) the zero-reject philosophy that established that public schools could not turn away from educating any of their students (Lilly, 1971), (b) the notion that students with special education needs have a civil right to an education with peers who do not have special education needs, and (c) the acknowledgment that school personnel must collaborate with one another and families of children eligible for special education services if they are to meet the unique needs of these children and youth.

It is in this context that collaborative consultation emerged as a process for enabling people with diverse expertise to work together to generate creative solutions for educating students with special education needs in general education classrooms (Idol, Nevin, & Paolucci-Whitcomb,1994). A research base documenting that general and special educators *can* collaborate resourcefully and effectively as equal partners is beginning to emerge (e.g., Thousand, Villa, Meyers, & Nevin, 1994; Villa, Thousand, Meyers, & Nevin, in preparation). Several configurations designed to serve as bridges between the (then) separate general and special education systems have been researched thoroughly: triadic models (Tharp & Note, 1988); teacher assistance teams (Chalfant & Pysh, 1989; Hayek, 1987); consulting teachers (Knight, Meyers, Paolucci-Whitcomb, Hasazi, & Nevin, 1981; McKenzie et al., 1970); and prereferral intervention teams (Graden, Casey, & Christenson, 1985). Knowledge bases, resources, and competencies have been articulated for each of these configurations, all of which were designed to unify the separate general and special educational systems (see S. Stainback & W. Stainback, 1985; W. Stainback & S. Stainback, 1984; Villa, Thousand, & Fox, 1987).

This chapter presents a definition of and rationale for collaborative consultation among school personnel (teachers, students, and administrators) as well as parents and other community members. Descriptions and examples are offered to illustrate how collaborative consultation processes may be employed by ad hoc school-based teams both to address emerging issues and to facilitate school restructuring. We conclude by proposing that the theory and practice of collaborative consultation will continue to evolve, that school personnel no longer have the option of whether or not to collaborate, and that its success is dependent upon beliefs held and actions taken by members of the school and greater community.

AN OPERATIONAL DEFINITION OF COLLABORATIVE CONSULTATION

Various definitions of collaboration and consultation have been forwarded. Among recent definitions is that proposed by Pryzwansky (West, 1990).

> Consultation is a term defined as the process of giving advice or information. . . . The assumption on which it is based is that a professional (the consultee) seeks assistance from a professional resource who is considered an "expert." Collaboration is another type of helping relationship (contrasted with consultation, therapy, education) in which one professional is an active partner with the professional seeking assistance. Collaborative consultation suggests to me that the "expert" is much more involved with the consultee. (p. 1)

We suggest an entirely new mix of these concepts and practices, one in which each participant alternately plays the *consultant/expert* and the *consultee/recipient* role in a forum where solution finding is jointly and equally shared among people with different knowledge and experience.

Idol and colleagues originally defined collaborative consultation as "an interactive process which enables people with diverse expertise to generate creative solutions to mutually defined problems" (Idol, Paolucci-Whitcomb, & Nevin, 1986, p. ix). They later expanded this original conceptualization of collaborative consultation to include the following basic elements (Idol et al., 1994; Nevin, Thousand, Paolucci-Whitcomb, & Villa, 1990).

- Group members agree to view all members, including students, as possessing unique and needed expertise.
- Group members engage in frequent face-to-face interactions.
- Group members distribute leadership responsibilities and hold each other accountable for agreed-upon commitments.
- Group members understand the importance of reciprocity.
- Group members emphasize both task and relationship actions and recognize that these actions will vary based on such variables as the extent to which other members support or have the skill to promote the group goal.
- Group members agree to consciously practice and increase their social interaction and task achievement skills through the process of consensus building.

The outcomes of this type of collaboration are altered and enhanced from the original solutions that group members might produce independently.

This new conceptualization of collaborative consultation avoids several pitfalls of more unidirectional conceptualizations, such as suggesting that the deficit lies with the consultee, failing to promote equity, and often achieving less than satisfactory outcomes (Johnson, Pugach, & Hammitte, 1988). With the new conceptualization, a multidirectional process is experienced; each member of the team has an equal opportunity to be an expert and to serve in the dual role of giver and receiver of information or skills; and all members of the team have opportunities to increase their conceptual and technological knowledge as well as their interpersonal skills. The "expert" collaborative consultant in this new view, then, is both a teacher and a learner.

In this expanded view, collaborative consultation is a process that has been applied to various configurations such as multidisciplinary or child study teams, service delivery options such as teaching teams, and school-based management practices such as staff development and curriculum teams (Idol & West, 1991). Although collaborative consultation is not yet the norm in many North American schools (Phillips & McCullough, 1990), when it has been applied, it has resulted in the improved functioning of school-based programs such as teacher assistance teams (e.g., Chalfant & Pysh, 1989), consulting teacher programs (e.g., Idol, 1993; Paolucci-Whitcomb & Nevin, 1985), and teaching teams (Thousand & Villa, 1990).

Clearly, there are barriers that appear to threaten the widespread implementation of such a process (Johnson et al., 1988; Nevin et al., 1990). Yet the need for effective collaboration among educators could not be more compelling. The student population in general education classrooms has become increasingly more diverse (Reynolds & Birch, 1982; Stainback & Stainback, in press). Teachers successful in educating *all* children in inclusive schools and communities point out that collaboration is a key ingredient to their success (Cross & Villa, 1992; Thousand et al., 1994). In an increasingly complex, international, interdependent world community, there is an information explosion with which no individual teacher is able to keep pace (Benjamin, 1989; Thornburg, 1992). These facts highlight the need for school personnel to collaborate in order to pool their content knowledge and instructional skills so that a more diverse set of instructional methodologies and a broader curriculum can be made available to students. Additionally, for North America's children to be prepared for twenty-first-century society, they need opportunities to collaborate in creating their own educational programs (Villa & Thousand, 1992). This will only occur if teachers and other school personnel fulfill their responsibilities

to model and facilitate opportunities for effective collaborative interactions.

Paula Evans (1994) points out that things are changing in the direction outlined above. There *are* schools that have seriously responded to the need to collaborate and have made collaborative consultation, in its various forms, standard practice.

> There are . . . schools across the country where the culture is changing and nurtures very different habits. Teacher collaboration has become the norm within the school. Teachers can't imagine not teaching with a team of colleagues, not developing and constantly refining their own curriculum. It is expected that they will question themselves and their colleagues, that they will be self-critical. It is understood that everyone will take a serious interest in the well-being of their students and that, of course, teachers will be in touch with parents and guardians. (p. 44)

A RATIONALE FOR COLLABORATIVE CONSULTATION

> At a time when we should be rejoicing in a golden age of plenty, we find ourselves wallowing in conflict—conflict between nations, conflict between races, conflict between management and workers, even conflict between neighbors. These problems that we face cannot be solved by scientific and technical skills alone; they will require social skills. Many of our most critical problems are not in the world of *things,* but in the world of *people.* Our greatest failure as human beings has been the inability to secure cooperation and understanding with others. (Hersey & Blanchard, 1988, p. 3)

Collaborative Consultation Requires and Facilitates the Use of Multiple Intelligences

Multiple intelligences theory originally described by Gardner (1983) and more recently explicated by Armstrong (1994) includes seven areas (linguistic, logical/mathematical, spacial, bodily/kinesthetic, musical, interpersonal, and intrapersonal). The last two—interpersonal and intrapersonal intelligences—are relatively new as identified areas of focus in educational settings. These two areas of intelligence are both requirements and facilitators of collaborative consultation. Interpersonal intelligence has been defined as

> the ability to perceive and make distinctions in the moods, intentions, motivations, and feelings of other people. This can include sensitivity to facial expressions, voice, and gestures; the capacity for discriminating among many different kinds of interpersonal cues; and the ability to respond effectively to those cues in some pragmatic way. (Armstrong, 1994, p. 3)

In contrast, intrapersonal intelligence has been characterized as

> self-knowledge and the ability to act adaptively on the basis of that knowledge. This intelligence includes having an accurate picure of oneself (one's strengths and limitations); awareness of inner moods, intentions, motivations, temperaments, and desires; and the capacity for self-discipline, self-understanding, and self-esteem. (Armstrong, 1994, p. 3)

Idol et al. (1994) have identified interpersonal skills and intrapersonal attitudes as critical components of collaborative consultation. As Armstrong asserts, in current and future times, both interpersonal and intrapersonal intelligences become more important (relative to other intelligences) as we struggle to make choices and to live successfully in an increasingly complex and globally interdependent society.

Peters (1987) suggested several strategies for achieving successful change in business-oriented organizations functioning in a chaotic world. These strategies include (a) creating total responsiveness to the customer (student), (b) pursuing fast-paced innovation, (c) achieving flexibility by empowering people, and (d) learning to love change and embrace chaos. In educational settings, collaborative consultation allows, even demands, the use of the associated skills of inter- and intrapersonal intelligences that mesh with Peters's change strategies. In sum, the knowledge about multiple intelligences helps leaders to value all people and the various gifts that their individual and collective abilities provide in facilitating change.

This notion of individual gifts, also known as a strengths perspective, was described by Saleebey (1992) and recognized as critical knowledge by Schriver (1995) for social work practice. His six assumptions and six key concepts, which presume that all people (i.e., students, families, and co-collaborators) possess multiple intelligences, can and have been adapted and utilized through collaborative consultation. The six assumptions (adapted here for educational settings) related to the strengths perspective are:

1. Respect student strengths
2. Identify and acknowledge that students have many strengths
3. Understand that student motivation is based on fostering student strengths
4. Respond in ways that ensure that the educator is a collaborator *with* the student
5. Avoid the victim mindset
6. Believe that every environment is full of resouces.

The six key concepts (adapted here for educational settings) are:

1. Empowerment
2. Membership
3. Regeneration and healing from within
4. Synergy
5. Dialogue and collaboration
6. Suspension of disbelief

The strengths perspective enables collaborators to identify, value, and enhance (rather than ignore or devalue) every individual's uniqueness.

As previously stated, collaborative consultation requires and facilitates the use of multiple intelligences theory, in that both the collaborative practice and intelligence theory place extensive value on the development of each person's uniqueness. Specifically, key points of multiple intelligences theory are that (a) each person possesses all seven intelligences, (b) most people can develop each intelligence to an adequate level of competency, (c) intelligences usually work together in complex ways, and (d) there are many ways to be intelligent within each category (Armstrong, 1994). The processes of collaborative consultation provide both challenges and opportunities, as teams of people come together to test their courage to change and their willingness to embrace chaos in our collective need to transform a material-based, scarcity-driven world into a spiritual-based, abundance-sharing life.

Collaborative Consultation Enables Schools to Meet Diverse Student Needs through Shared Expertise

Exemplary schooling practices have been researched at the administrative level (Villa, Thousand, Stainback, & Stainback, 1992; Villa & Thousand, in press) and instructional levels (Nevin et al., 1990; Thousand, Villa, & Nevin, 1994; Udvari-Solner & Thousand, in press). These practices empower school personnel to provide heterogeneous learning opportunities for all students (regardless of gender, racial, religious, ethnic, socioeconomic, or intellectual differences). Included among these practices is collaborative consultation, which leads to several benefits.

Shared Ownership of Problem Definitions and Solutions.   There is considerable evidence to suggest that participatory decision-making processes result in (1) increased ownership and commitment to goals (Duke, Showers, & Imber, 1980), (2) more successful implementation of planned interventions (Fullan & Pomfret, 1977), and (3) increased collaboration (Rosenholtz, Bassler, & Hoover-Dempsey, 1985).

Shared Knowledge and Expertise.   As specialists and generalists interact with each other, they are more likely to acquire one another's skills (Thousand, Nevin, & Fox, 1987; Thousand et al., 1986; Villa, Thousand, Meyers, & Nevin, in preparation).

Increased Cohesiveness and Willingness to Work Together on Future Projects.   Group cohesion is defined by D. Johnson and F. Johnson (1987) as the "sum of all the factors influencing

members to stay in the group" (p. 408). Practitioners who predominantly use cooperative and collaborative structures to integrate students with differing abilities report positive outcomes related to cohesiveness (e.g., Thousand et al., 1986, Thousand et al., 1987; Villa et al., in preparation). In a summary of research related to cohesiveness, D. Johnson and F. Johnson (1987) reported a corresponding increase between group cohesiveness and group members' (1) attendance, (2) participation, (3) commitment to the group goal, (4) acceptance of mutually assigned tasks, (5) persistence in working on difficult tasks, and (6) likelihood of goal achievement. Thousand et al. (1986) found that teachers who collaborated to integrate students reported "they have *more say* in what local educational programs look like; [and] they feel *more comfortable* asking for and receiving the material, technical, and emotional support from colleagues to educate more challenging students" (p. 11).

New Conceptualizations and Novel Solutions. Children who learn within heterogeneous cooperative learning groups versus competitive or individualistic learning structures have been found to engage in higher-level thinking processes and to generate more novel solutions (D. Johnson & R. Johnson, 1989). The extant research in this area has yielded the following consistent outcomes.

1. More frequent discovery and development of "higher quality" cognitive reasoning such as category search and retrieval, intersectional classification, metaphoric reasoning, focusing, and elaboration (eleven studies)
2. Transitions to higher levels of cognitive and moral reasoning (twenty-five studies)
3. Increased awareness and use of metacognitive strategies such as detecting errors, noting failures of memory, making judgments about the importance of material being discussed (two studies)
4. Increased evidence of *process gain*—generating new ideas through group interaction that are *not* generated when people work individualistically or *collective induction*—inducing

general principles that none could induce alone (three studies)

The authors have worked extensively in the public schools with adults who practice the proposed new collaborative consultation paradigm (which employs the principles of cooperative learning) and have found that they also experience similar creative thinking and problem-solving outcomes (Thousand & Villa, 1990).

Collaborative Consultation Facilitates a Paradigm Shift to an Adhocratic School

Kuhn (1970), in his discussion of scientific revolutions, described situations in which people who held a particular view (a *paradigm*) of the world experienced a point at which their experience (e.g., unexplained or unexplainable outcomes of experiments) indicated that an old view no longer worked or rang true and a new view had not yet emerged.

> Each of them [Copernicus, Newton, Lavoisier, and Einstein] necessitated the community's rejection of one time-honored scientific theory in favor of another incompatible with it. Each produced a consequent shift in the problems available for scientific scrutiny and in the standards by which the profession determined what should count as an admissible problem or as a legitimate problem solution. And each transformed the scientific imagination in ways that we shall ultimately need to describe as a transformation of the world within which scientific work was done. Such changes, together with the controversies that almost always accompany them, are the defining characteristics of scientific revolutions. (Kuhn, 1970, p. 6)

Skrtic (1991) asserts that professional knowledge and practice also change when the scientific foundational knowledge changes. He (1988, 1991) has described the prevailing organizational paradigm of schooling in North America as a professional bureaucracy and further argues that this paradigm diminishes rather than enhances teachers' abilities to individualize educational services.

The biggest problem is that schools are organized as professional bureaucracies ... a contradiction in terms: professionalization is intended to permit personalization; bureaucratization is intended to assure standardization. To blame the inability to individualize instruction totally on the capacity or will of professionals is misguided in that it blames the teachers for the inadequacies and contradictions of the organizational structure. This is the same kind of distortion of reality we make when we blame particular students for not learning from the existing standardized programs of the school organization. These students are the ones we call "handicapped," which is what I mean when I say that school organizations create "handicapped students." In both cases our tendency is to blame the victims—teachers who fail to individualize and students who fail to learn—for the inadequacies of the system. (Thousand, 1990, p. 31)

To ameliorate the situation created by this organizational paradigm, it has been proposed that school professionals consider making a paradigm shift and organize ad hoc teams (Patterson, Purkey, & Parker, 1986) or an "adhocracy" (Skrtic, 1991, p. 160) where "professionals mutually adjust their collective skills and knowledge to invent unique, personalized programs for each student" (Thousand, 1990, p. 32). In this new paradigm, teachers are inventors who recognize that personalized instruction, by its very nature, will have to be

> continuously invented and reinvented by teachers in actual practice with students who have unique and changing needs. The value of the adhocracy is that it is configured for diversity whereas the professional bureaucracy is configured for homogeneity, and so must remove diversity from the system. (Thousand, 1990, p. 32)

What is suggested here is a revolution in school organization. In the authors' view, this revolution is under way. Ad hoc collaborative instructional and problem-solving arrangements currently are being successfully implemented in inclusion-oriented schools (see Nevin et al., 1990; Thousand & Villa, 1989, 1990; Villa & Thousand, 1992; Villa, Thousand, Stainback, & Stainback, 1992).

Skrtic's conceptualization of an adhocracy has been operationalized and described by Thousand and Villa (1990) as a *teaching team,* "an organizational and instructional arrangement of two or more members of the school and greater community who distribute among themselves planning, instructional, and evaluation responsibilities for the same students on a regular basis for an extended period of time" (p. 152). The reassignment of existing personnel to teaching teams results in a knowledge and skill exchange among team members and higher instructor–learner ratios, outcomes that benefit many students, rather than only the student in need of intensive instructional support. Within this type of dynamic structure, complex work is more likely to be accomplished and novel services are more likely to be crafted to meet unique students' needs (Skrtic, 1989).

Collaborative Consultation Prepares Students for Life in the Twenty-First Century

Educational futurists, forecasting the twenty-first century for which our children must be prepared, describe a highly complex, information-rich society that will require people to value, work with, and cope with an international community of diverse cultures, values, languages, skills, knowledge, and ability (Thornburg, 1992; Villa & Thousand, 1992). To prepare students for this work world and lifestyle, futurists suggest that school curricula emphasize the acquisition of social and communication skills and offer experiences that facilitate the students' abilities to collaborate with others and to cope with adversity and diversity. Futurists also point out that in the next century the amount of available knowledge will increase exponentially, making it essential for schools to concentrate on teaching students *how* to learn—how to be lifelong learners.

Given these projections, what behaviors do the adults of the school community need to demonstrate? At a minimum, they need to model collaboration. They may do this by collaborating with other educators and community members in planning, delivering, and evaluating instruction as members of teaching teams (Thousand & Villa, 1990). They also may do this by sharing their power, decision-making responsibilities, and knowledge of instructional and learning processes with students. Villa & Thousand (1992) describe a number of student–student and student–adult collaboration strategies that offer students experiences as members of instructional teams, advocates for peers and themselves, and partners in decision making. These collaborative strategies are intended to empower students to practice the active learning, advocacy, and collaborative skills needed for adult life in the twenty-first century. In summary, the future world suggests "a new collaborative role for teachers and students in which students accept an active senior partnership role in the learning enterprise" (Benjamin, 1989, p. 9).

Emerging Data Base Yields Positive Outcomes

Idol, Nevin, and Paolucci-Whitcomb (1994) reviewed the various collaborative consultation studies conducted over the past decade and found that collaborative consultation has been studied at the secondary school level (Florida Department of Education, 1989, 1990; Patriarca & Lamb, 1990; Tindal, Shinn, Walz, & Germann, 1987); the elementary school level (Adamson, Cox, & Schuller, 1989; Givens-Ogle, Christ, Colman, King-Streit, & Wilson, 1989; Givens-Ogle, Christ, & Idol, 1991; Saver & Downes, 1991; Schulte, Osborne, & McKinney, 1990; Sumner Elementary School Staff, 1991); the preschool level (Peck, Killen, & Baumgart, 1989); and the adult level (Cross & Villa, 1992; Lutkemeir, 1991; Patriarca & Lamb, 1990; Vlasak, Goldenberg & Idol, 1992). At least three conclusions can be formed from this growing data base (Idol et al., 1994). First, learners with special education needs can be effectively served when their teachers collaborate to generate interventions. Second, school personnel can acquire the related skills and knowledge to collaborate with each other. Third, collaborators can expect positive changes at all three levels— changes in systems, changes in adult collaborators, and changes in student performance.

A "NEW SCHOOL" FOR ENTERING THE TWENTY-FIRST CENTURY

There now are schools that rely on collaborative consultation configurations to invent and reinvent meaningful educational experiences for an increasingly diverse student body (Evans, 1994; Stainback & Stainback, 1990; Thousand, 1990; Villa & Thousand, 1990, 1992; Villa, Thousand, Stainback, & Stainback, 1992). These schools are in the midst of a paradigm shift.

The Ideal School Structure

In the idyllic, futuristic view of a twenty-first-century school that already has undergone the transformation (i.e., paradigm shift), any member of the school and greater community would serve on any number of adhocratic structures within the school, and these structures would employ collaborative consultation processes to creatively solve problems. Patterson et al. (1986) argue that every school needs *many* "flexible, ad hoc problem-solving teams" (p. 74) charged with exploring the problem-solutions that the traditional bureaucratic school structure, to date, has failed to conceptualize or adequately address.

The Structure of a School in Transition

The authors acknowledge that movement toward this conceptualization of a school—one governed by adhocratic structures—will not occur overnight. The change process will be incremental, and people will experience emotional turmoil as they create and experience the paradigm shift from the current bureaucratic to the futuristic adhocratic organizational configuration. The authors also recognize the need to maintain, at least for the short term, a formal, more bureaucratic structure such as that which now exists. Patterson et al. (1986) have clearly articulated this proposition.

> To be effective in this era of change and uncertainty, a school district requires two types of organizational structures. Every school district needs a formal management structure with specified tasks and lines of authority for carrying out the routine business of the day. Every district also needs another structure, one that is not generally shown on the organizational charts. The "other structure" consists of flexible, ad hoc problem solving teams—vehicles for figuring out how to do what the organization doesn't yet know. (p. 74)

A second rationale for maintaining the old structure while creating and recreating the new has been asserted by Skrtic (1989). He has argued that currently the community demands, at least in outward appearance, a traditional (i.e., hierarchical and bureaucratic) school organizational structure. This structure is one that most North American adults have experienced and consider appropriate for well-run businesses, of which education is one. Community members are not likely to accept or fund an educational system with a formal public structure that does not match prevailing perceptions of "good business." Schools in the midst of a paradigm shift need flexible ad hoc structures to combine ideas from unconnected sources (e.g., different departments and specialized programs) and multiple perspectives. But, they also need a publicly accepted organizational structure that has the "power tools" (Patterson et al., 1986, p. 74) to carry out decisions and assignments and to assemble ad hoc solutions into a whole. The good news is that as the business community continues to restructure in order to compete in the world economy, it is relying more and more on collaborative teaming configurations. As more and more community members experience for themselves the benefits of working in collaborative arrangements, they will value and support the implementation of collaborative teaming arrangements among staff, student, and community members within their schools.

A third reason for maintaining the old and familiar structure is that the act of assembling people in adhocratic teams in no way guarantees that team members will behave in a collaborative fashion. Training in collaborative consultation processes (and incentives to support a collaborative culture) are key to a school's evolution toward a creative, adhocratic organization. Yet most educators, administrators, and community members have had little training or experience in functioning in collaborative consultation roles. Some have yet to be convinced of the potential powers of collaboration. Given this state of affairs, if schools were to totally abandon the old structure overnight in favor of ad hoc problem-solving groups, there likely would be more chaos than solution finding. School personnel seriously committed to systems change understand the change process, the incremental nature of change, and the necessity of developing action plans.

An Example of a School in Transition

The school in the midst of a paradigm shift, then, requires both a formal and an informal structure with a fluid and dynamic relationship between the two. The ongoing interaction and communication between people operating within and across the two structures will promote change and lead to the replacement of the bureaucratic paradigm.

A composite example of several Vermont schools that have experienced the suggested paradigm shift illustrates this possibility. Consider the Middletown School District, a school system that has recognized the potential problem-solving capacity of its teachers, support staff, students, and community. Initially, the leadership of the formal structure of the school (i.e., the principal, superintendent, school board) created opportunities and explicit expectations (e.g., redefinition of all job descriptions to include collaborative consultation as an *expected* role) for ad hoc teams to form and function. Table 16.1 identifies some of the actions that formal leadership took to promote adhocratic forums in which staff were able to actively practice collaborative consultation.

As the ad hoc groups of this school system generated and communicated to the formal leadership their solutions to organizational, instructional, and attitudinal issues, the formal school structure itself began to change. For example, the restructuring committee, an ad hoc team representing various programs and departments of the school (e.g., general, special, compensatory, and bilingual education), recommended changing the support program service delivery model from a pull-out to an in-class team teaching configuration. This recommendation, when implemented, clearly represented a fundamental organizational change of the school's formal staffing arrangement. This change, in turn, highlighted the need to make other organizational changes. The reading instruction time in the elementary school had to be restructured so that the primary (grades 1 and 2), middle (grades 3 and 4), and upper (grades 5 and 6) elementary units had different (rather than common) time blocks for reading instruction. Such a change enabled special and compensatory education personnel to join the primary, middle, and upper elementary units as co-instructors during the respective reading blocks. In the middle and high schools, the traditional forty-five-minute instructional blocks were replaced by two-hour time blocks so that interdisciplinary instruction could be provided by teaching teams.

Next, the restructuring committee convinced the formal school leadership to expand the school's curriculum to include student collaboration skills (Villa & Thousand, 1992). As predicted by David and Roger Johnson (Brandt, 1987), the teachers who implemented this curriculum (modeled, coached, and guided students' use of collaborative skills) also became more proficient in the skills needed for functioning as members of collaborative teams.

As the structure of Middletown schools continued to change to reflect solutions generated by ad hoc groups (e.g., ongoing job redefinition, reprioritization of financial and human resources to promote team teaching, expansion of the inservice training agenda to include collaborative and consultative skill building for *all* staff), the direction of influence shifted so that the ad hoc teams themselves were altered. New teams were created for new purposes (e.g., a group was formed to determine how to measure student academic and social progress); some former teams were disbanded (e.g., the restructuring committee was dissolved);

TABLE 16.1   Actions Promoting the Forming and Functioning of Ad Hoc Collaborative Teams

ACTIONS SUPPORTING FORMING OF TEAMS	ACTIONS SUPPORTING FUNCTIONING OF TEAMS
Publicly articulate the rationale for collaborative consultation.	Provide collaborative skill training to all staff, including new members to the organization.
Provide staff with opportunities to visit and/or listen to colleagues who perform the same job as they do.	Educate community members about the accomplishments of collaborative teams.
Allow people to express their concerns about collaboration; provide personal support as they go through the change process.	Periodically provide additional time for teams to meet (e.g., hire substitutes, use scheduled inservice days, provide released time, add a collaboration day per marking period to the school calendar).
School leadership personnel model collaboration.	
Redefine (i.e., in the job description) staff roles so that all are expected to perform the role of collaborative consultant.	Provide incentives for collaboration (e.g., recognize team accomplishments, increase teams' responsibilities, offer additional training, provide release time for teams to attend conferences and make presentations about their accomplishments).
Assess the staff's need for collaboration (e.g., With whom do I need to collaborate to successfully adapt instruction? From which colleagues can I acquire skills through modeling and coaching?)	
Create a master schedule allowing for collaboration (e.g., common planning and lunch periods).	Provide feedback to teams on their collaborative behaviors.
Change the length of the workday or school year (e.g., 220-day instead of 185-day contracts for teachers; early dismissal of students).	

and some were expanded to include students, parents, and other members of the community (e.g., the inservice planning committee and the discipline committee).

The hope for the future is that, as ad hoc teams continue to demonstrate their effectiveness, the school board and the greater community will increase their trust in and value for adhocratic configurations to the extent that they willingly will give up their traditional view of the well-run school as a hierarchical bureaucratic structure. They then will be able to publicly accept, fund, and promote a new twenty-first-century school made up of ad hoc teams that use collaborative consultation processes to solve emerging issues.

CONCLUSION

"Realistically . . . most of us in the education business have finally concluded that change is the most stable thing on which we can depend" (Patterson et al., 1986, p. vii). The conceptualization and practice of collaborative consultation has been evolutionary. Given the current school restructuring movement and the concomitant recognition of collaborative consultation as the preferred process for human interaction within schools, it is likely that collaborative consultation will continue to evolve, undergoing its own paradigm shift as it becomes a part of restructured school organizations.

While some argue that collaboration is and must remain primarily a voluntary activity (Friend

& Cook, 1992; Pugach & Johnson, 1995), the authors contend that school personnel can no longer choose to be isolated professionals. First, for educators to perceive that they have a choice of whether or not to collaborate is analogous to a team of health care professionals thinking they have a choice as to whether or not to collaborate to perform an operation, monitor the patient's progress, or provide follow-up care. As noted earlier in the discussion of the rationale for collaborative consultation, teacher and student success or "survival" literally is contingent upon adults and students collaborating to invent and improve education on a day-to-day basis. Second, as Schlechty (1990) noted, we know what is *respected* in schools by what is *expected* and *inspected.* If we truly respect collaboration, then we must expect it of ourselves and one another and inspect how well we in fact do collaborate and follow through on agreed-upon commitments. Third, some people will never believe in the power of collaborative consultation until they engage in it directly. Contrary to conventional thinking, changes in behavior and beliefs often *follow* experience rather than the reverse (Bennett, Rolheiser-Bennett, & Stevahn, 1991).

Not so long ago, Evelyn Deno questioned whether special education might be a hoax because there was very little evidence as to the effectiveness of the diagnostic–prescriptive model being perpetrated by special educators at the time (Deno, 1978, p. 5). In light of the nascent research in school-based collaborative consultation, the question might be posed again; that is, is collaborative consultation a hoax—an educational intervention process that will not live up to its promise? Or, is it a grand experiment—a continually evolving process through which groups of people identify questions mutually and invent answers, solutions, or choices? As Madeline Hunter (personal communication, August 10, 1986) has instructed, "If you think you can or you think you can't, you're right either way." So it is with collaborative consultation. If we think and act as if it is a hoax, or if we think and act as if it is a grand experiment, we will be right either way.

Collaborative consultation becomes a hoax when we engage in "if only" thinking (Patterson et al., 1986). If only we had more common planning time, then we could collaborate; if only more teachers would volunteer to collaborate, then we could integrate more special education students. "If only" thinking makes it difficult for educators to see beyond the many potential barriers to change. If we as educators choose to think and act in "if only" terms, we most surely will see the barriers to effective collaboration and be tempted to use them to avoid or thwart collaborative consultation opportunities. If, on the other hand, we choose to avoid "if only" thinking, we are more likely to see all that already exists in and for our schools as resources. Also, we are more likely to celebrate the collective wisdom and expertise of students and adults, and to recognize that only when divergence is celebrated, do creative and novel solutions converge. Finally, we will more likely be open to experimenting with collaborative consultation as a wonderfully inventive process for tapping the diversity of human resources for the good of the children. In the end, as Castaneda (1972, p. 184) noted, "The trick is in what one emphasizes. . . . We either make ourselves miserable, or we make ourselves strong. The amount of work is the same."

REFERENCES

Adamson, D., Cox, J., & Schuller, J. (1989). Collaboration/consultation: Bridging the gap from the resource room to the regular classroom. *Teacher Education and Special Education, 12,* 52–55.

Armstrong, T. (1994). *Multiple intelligences in the classroom.* Alexandria, VA: Association for Supervision and Curriculum Development.

Benjamin, S. (1989). An ideascape for education: What futurists recommend. *Educational Leadership, 47*(1), 8–14.

Bennett, B., Rolheiser-Bennett, M., & Stevahn, L. (1991). *Cooperative learning: Where heart meets mind.* Toronto: Educational Connections.

Brandt, R. (1987). On cooperation in schools: A conversation with David and Roger Johnson. *Educational Leadership, 45*(3), 14–19.

Castaneda, C. (1972). *Journey to Ixtlan.* New York: Simon & Schuster.

Chalfant, J., & Pysh, M. (1989). Teacher assistance teams: Five descriptive studies. *Remedial and Special Education, 10*(6), 49–58.

Cross, G., & Villa, R. (1992). The Winooski school system: An evolutionary perspective of a school restructuring for diversity. In R. Villa, J. Thousand, W. Stainback, & S. Stainback (Eds.). *Restructuring for caring and effective education: An administrative guide to creating heterogeneous schools* (pp. 219–242). Baltimore: Paul H. Brookes.

Deno, E. (1978). *Educating children with emotional, learning and behavior problems.* Minneapolis: University of Minnesota, Department of Psychoeducational Studies, National Support Systems Project.

Duke, D., Showers, B., & Imber, M. (1980). Teachers and shared decision-making: The costs and benefits of involvement. *Educational Administration Quarterly, 16,* 93–106.

Evans, P. (1994). Getting beyond chewing gum and book covers: Real professional development begs the question of habit. *Education Week, 14*(7), 44.

Florida Department of Education. (1989). *Evaluating effectiveness, usefulness, practicality of cooperative consultation—1987–1988 pilot study in Florida secondary schools* (Research Report 10). Tallahassee, FL: Author.

Florida Department of Education. (1990, November). *Cooperative consultation regional training 1989–1990* (Research Report 12). Tallahassee, FL: Author.

Friend, M., & Cook, L. (1992). *Interactions: Collaboration skills for school professionals.* White Plains, New York: Longman.

Fullan, M., & Pomfret, A. (1977). Research on curriculum and instruction implementation. *Review of Educational Research, 47,* 335–397.

Gardner, H. (1983). *Frames of mind: The theory of multiple intelligence.* New York: Basic Books.

Givens-Ogle, L., Christ, B., Colman, M., King-Streit, J., & Wilson, L. (1989). Data-based consultation case study: Adaptations of researched best practices. *Teacher Education and Special Education, 12,* 46–52.

Givens-Ogle, L., Christ, B., & Idol, L. (1991). Collaborative consultation: The San Juan Unified School District Project. *Journal of Educational and Psychological Consultation, 2,* 267–284.

Graden, J., Casey, A., & Christenson, S. (1985). Implementing a prereferral intervention system. Part I: The model. *Exceptional Children, 51,* 377–384.

Hayek, R. (1987). The teacher assistance teams: A prereferral support system. *Focus on Exceptional Children, 20*(1), 1–8.

Hersey, P., & Blanchard, K. (1988). *Management of organizational behavior* (5th ed.). Englewood Cliffs, NJ: Prentice Hall.

Idol, L. (1993). *The special educator's consultation handbook* (2nd ed.). Austin, TX: Pro-Ed.

Idol, L., Paolucci-Whitcomb, P., & Nevin, A. (1986). *Collaborative consultation.* Austin, TX: Pro-Ed.

Idol, L., Nevin, A., & Paolucci-Whitcomb, P. (1994). *Collaborative consultation* (2nd ed.). Austin, TX: Pro-Ed.

Idol, L., & West, J. F. (1991). Educational collaboration as a catalyst for effective schooling. *Intervention in School and Clinic, 27*(2), 70–78.

Johnson, D. W., & Johnson, F. (1987). *Joining together: Group theory and group skills.* Englewood Cliffs, NJ: Prentice Hall.

Johnson, D. W., & Johnson, R. T. (1989). *Cooperation and competition: Theory and research.* Edina, MN: Interaction Book Company.

Johnson, L., Pugach, M., & Hammitte, D. (1988). Barriers to effective special education consultation. *Remedial and Special Education, 9*(6), 41–47.

Knight, M., Meyers, H., Paolucci-Whitcomb, P., Hasazi, S., & Nevin, A. (1981). A four-year evaluation of consulting teacher services. *Behavior Disorders, 6,* 92–100.

Kuhn, T. (1970). *The structure of scientific revolutions.* Chicago: University of Chicago Press.

Lilly, M. S . (1971). A training based model for special education. *Exceptional Children, 37,* 745–749.

Lutkemeir, D. (1991). Attitudes and practices regarding the implementation of collaborative educational services. *The Consulting Edge, 3*(2), 1–2.

McKenzie, H., Egner, A., Knight, M., Perelman, P., Schneider, B., & Garvin, J. (1970). Training consulting teachers in the management and education of handicapped children. *Exceptional Children, 37,* 137–143.

Nevin, A., Thousand, J., Paolucci-Whitcomb, P., & Villa, R. (1990). Collaborative consultation: Empowering public school personnel to provide heterogeneous schooling for all or, Who rang that bell?

Journal of Educational and Psychological Consultation, 1(1), 41–67.

Paolucci-Whitcomb, P., & Nevin, A. (1985). Preparing consulting teachers through a collaborative approach between university faculty and field-based consulting teachers. *Teacher Education and Special Education, 8,* 132–143.

PARC v. Commonwealth of Pennsylvania, 344 F. Supp. 1257 (E.D. PA, 1971).

Patriarca, L., & Lamb, M. (1990). Preparing secondary education teachers to be collaborative decision makers and reflective practitioners: A promising model. *Teacher Education and Special Education, 13,* 200–224.

Patterson, J., Purkey, S., & Parker, J. (1986). *Productive school systems for a nonrational world.* Alexandria, VA: Association for Supervision and Curriculum Development.

Peck, C., Killen, C., & Baumgart, D. (1989). Increasing implementation of special education instruction in mainstream preschools: Direct and generalized effects of nondirective consultation. *Journal of Applied Behavior Analysis, 22,* 197–210.

Peters, T. (1987). *Thriving on chaos: Handbook for a management revolution.* New York: Alfred A. Knopf.

Phillips, V., & McCullough, L. (1990). Consultation based programming: Instituting the collaborative ethic in schools. *Exceptional Children, 56,* 291–304.

Public Law 94-142. (1975). *The Education for all Handicapped Children Act.* Washington, DC: U.S. Congress.

Pugach, M., & Johnson, L. (1995). *Collaborative practitioners: Collaborative schools.* Denver: Love.

Reynolds, M., & Birch, J. (1982). *Teaching exceptional children in all America's schools* (2nd ed.). Reston, VA: Council for Exceptional Children.

Rosenholtz, S., Bassler, O., & Hoover-Dempsey, C. (1985). Organizational conditions of teacher learning (NIE-G-83–0041). Urbana: University of Illinois.

Saleebey, D. (1992). *The strengths perspective in social work practice.* White Plains, New York: Longman.

Saver, K., & Downes, B. (1991). PIT Crew: A model for teacher collaboration in an elementary school. *Intervention in School and Clinic, 27,* 116–122.

Schlechty, P. (1990). *Schools for the 21st Century: Leadership imperatives for educational reform.* San Francisco: Jossey Bass.

Schriver, J. (1995). *Human behavior and the social environment: Shifting paradigms in essential knowledge for social work practice.* Boston: Allyn and Bacon.

Schulte, A., Osborne, S., & McKinney, J. (1990). Academic outcomes for students with learning disabilities in consultation anad resource programs. *Exceptional Children, 57,* 162–171.

Skrtic, T. (1988). The crisis in special education knowledge. In E. Meyen & T. Skrtic (Eds.), *Exceptional children and youth: An introduction* (3rd ed., pp. 415–448). Denver: Love.

Skrtic, T. (1989, May). *School organization and service delivery: Are schools capable of change?* Paper presented at Vermont Association of Special Education Administrators Conference, Stowe, VT.

Skrtic, T. (1991). *Behind special education: A critical analysis of professional culture and school organization.* Denver: Love.

Stainback, S., & Stainback, W. (1985) The merger of special and regular education: Can it be done? *Exceptional Children, 51,* 517–522.

Stainback, W., & Stainback, S . (1984). A rationale for the merger of special and regular education. *Exceptional Children, 51,* 102–111.

Stainback, W., & Stainback, S. (1990). *Support networks for inclusive schooling: Interdependent integrated education.* Baltimore: Paul H. Brookes.

Stainback, W., & Stainback, S. (in press). A historical overview. In R. Villa & J. Thousand (Eds.), *Restructuring for diversity: Fitting together the pieces of the inclusion puzzle.* Alexandria, VA: The Association for Supervision and Curriculum Development.

Sumner Elementary School Staff. (1991). Collaborative teaming: Building success for all. *The Consulting Edge, 3*(1), 1–4.

Tharp, R., & Note, M. (1988). The triadic model of consultation: New developments. In F. West (Ed.), *School consultation: Interdisciplinary perspectives on theory, research, training, and practice* (pp. 35–54). Austin, TX: The Association of Educational and Psychological Consultants.

Thornberg, D. (1992). *Edutrends 2010.* San Carlos, CA: Starsong.

Thousand, J. (1990). Organizational perspectives on teacher education and renewal: A conversation with Tom Skrtic. *Teacher Education and Special Education, 13,* 30–35.

Thousand, J., Fox, T., Reid, R., Godek, J., Williams, W., & Fox, W. (1986). *The Homecoming Model:*

Educating students who present intensive educational challenges within regular education environments (Monograph No. 7-1). Burlington, VT: Center for Developmental Disabilities. (ERIC Document Reproduction Service No. ED284 406).

Thousand, J., Nevin, A., & Fox, W. (1987). Inservice training to support education of learners with severe handicaps in their local schools. *Teacher Education and Special Education, 10*(1), 4–14.

Thousand, J., & Villa, R. (1989). Enhancing success in heterogeneous schools. In S. Stainback, W. Stainback, & M. Forest (Eds.), *Educating all students in the mainstream of regular education* (pp. 89–103). Baltimore: Paul H. Brookes.

Thousand, J., & Villa, R. (1990). Sharing expertise and responsibilities through teaching teams. In W. Stainback & S. Stainback (Eds.), *Support networks for inclusive schooling: Interdependent integrated education* (pp. 151–166). Baltimore: Paul H. Brookes.

Thousand, J., Villa, R., Meyers, H., & Nevin, A. (1994, April). *The heterogeneous education teacher survey: A retrospective analysis of heterogeneous (full inclusion) education.* Paper presented at the Annual Convention of the American Education Research Association, New Orleans.

Thousand, J., Villa, R., & Nevin, A. (1994). *Creativity & collaborative learning: A practical guide to empowering students and teachers.* Baltimore: Paul H. Brookes.

Tindal, G., Shinn, M., Walz, L., & Germann, C. (1987). Mainstream consultation in secondary settings: The Pine County model. *The Journal of Special Education, 20*(3), 94–106.

Udvari-Solner, A., & Thousand, J. (in press). Exemplary and promising practices that foster inclusive education. In R. Villa & J. Thousand (Eds.), *Restructuring for diversity: Fitting together the pieces of the inclusion puzzle.* Alexandria, VA: The Association for Supervision and Curriculum Development.

Villa, R., & Thousand, J. (1990). Administrative supports to promote inclusive schooling. In W. Stainback & S. Stainback (Eds.), *Support networks for inclusive schooling: Integrated interdependent education* (pp. 201–218). Baltimore: Paul H. Brookes.

Villa, R., & Thousand, J. (1992). Student collaboration: An essential for curriculum delivery in the 21st century. In S. Stainback & W. Stainback (Eds.), *Curriculum considerations in inclusive classrooms: Facilitating learning for all students* (pp. 117–142). Baltimore: Paul H. Brookes.

Villa, R., & Thousand, J. (in press). *Restructuring for diversity: Fitting together the pieces of the inclusion puzzle.* Alexandria, VA: The Association for Supervision and Curriculum Development.

Villa, R., Thousand, J., & Fox, W. (1987). *The Winooski model: A comprehensive model for providing a quality education for all learners with and without handicaps within an integrated public school setting.* A proposal submitted to U.S. Department of Education, Washington, DC.

Villa, R., Thousand, J., Meyers, H., & Nevin, A. (in preparation). Regular and special educator and administrator perceptions of heterogeneous education.

Villa, R., Thousand, J., Stainback, W., & Stainback, S. (1992). *Restructuring for heterogeneity: An administrative handbook for creating effective schools for everyone.* Baltimore: Paul H. Brookes.

Vlasak, L., Goldenberg, D., & Idol, L. (1992). *Resource/Consultation: A preliminary evaluation of the effects of a multiple district training project.* Unpublished manuscript. Austin, TX: Institute for Learning and Development.

West, J. F. (1990). The nature of consultation vs. collaboration: An interview with Walter O. Pryzwansky. *The Consulting Edge, 2*(1), 1–2.

SECTION NINE

RESEARCH PRACTICES

In recent years, there has been growing interest in the potential contributions of qualitative research to scientific/scholarly inquiry in education. But what role, if any, should qualitative research play in educational research? In Chapter 17, Simpson takes the position that quantitative research should remain the "method of choice." He states that both quantitative and qualitative research have a place in special education, but that whenever possible more quantitative methods are preferable because they lead to decisions about policy and practice that are based on more valid and reliable evidence.

Bogdan and Lutfiyya, in Chapter 18, outline the reasons why qualitative research is both valid and appropriate for use in education. It is the position of Bogdan and Lutfiyya that qualitative research should not be viewed as "soft" or "less preferable" than quantitative research. It has its own merits and can stand alone. They outline a few of the basic misunderstandings that have led some researchers to feel uncomfortable with qualitative research or to want to place it on a continuum of research methods, with quantitative research considered the more valid and reliable.

CHAPTER 17

Quantitative Research as the Method of Choice within a Continuum Model

ROBERT G. SIMPSON

INTRODUCTION

The relative merits of quantitative versus qualitative research is a complicated issue that can be discussed at historical, philosophical, and epistemological levels. Such a comprehensive discussion is obviously beyond the scope of the present chapter. Nevertheless, realizing the diversity of ways in which the topic can be approached has a practical application—that is, that the terms *quantitative research* and *qualitative research* are general descriptors that mean different things to different people (Hedrick, 1994). It is important, then, to present this author's perspective of these two general research approaches prior to discussing their relative merits.

Qualitative research comes in many different varieties, and can include descriptive case studies, interviews, participant observation, and analysis of nonquantifiable information sources (e.g., photo albums, scrapbooks, diaries). It is more subjective than objective in that the researcher views himself or herself as an interactive part of the naturalistic situation under study.

Although some qualitative research can involve intricate designs, typically there is not an emphasis on predetermined data collection and analysis procedures. As Howe (1988) stated, "The qualitative researcher's design consists of some provisional questions to investigate, some data collection sites, and a schedule allocating time for data collection, analysis (typically ongoing), and writing up results" (p. 12). Often, theories, questions, and research design will be allowed to

emerge as the process of data collection proceeds (Jacob, 1988).

In qualitative research, there is not an emphasis on the discovery of truth or laws that would describe reality. Instead, reality is viewed as constantly changing from moment to moment and is a function of the interaction between events and a person's perceptions of those events. Reality (or truth) to one person might not be reality to another person with a different perception. Final products often take the form of rich descriptions of what has been observed over possibly long periods of time. For example, after living with the family of a retarded boy for three months, a researcher might report his findings or perceptions about the daily life and perspectives of the child and his family.

Quantitative research is intended to be more objective in that the researcher attempts to keep from becoming an interactive participant in the situation he or she is studying. Questions to be answered, research design, and method of data analysis are typically established before data collection begins. The researcher's goal is to implement data collection procedures that are as unobtrusive as possible. Once data collection has begun, the researcher strives to remain scientifically "neutral"; that is, he or she strives to prevent his or her own prejudices or opinions from influencing either the data collection or analysis.

In quantitative research the researcher assumes the existence of variables that can be measured. An attempt is made to isolate the variables under

221

study and to control for the possible effects of other confounding variables. Once data collection and analysis have been accomplished, the researcher forms tentative conclusions about probable relationships between variables. The experimental results and conclusions lead to the generation of additional hypotheses and the process is repeated. The researcher is never totally assured that truth has been established; but his or her goal is to be able to predict, with reasonable confidence, what might happen in the future when variables and conditions exist that are similar to those that have been investigated.

COMPATIBILITY OR INCOMPATIBILITY?

A central theme of the present chapter is that quantitative and qualitative procedures should be viewed as part of a research continuum, and that meaningful research should be characterized by both quantitative and qualitative aspects. Nevertheless, there are those who contend that, because of the philosophical foundation upon which they are based, quantitative and qualitative methodologies are incompatible (Bednarz, 1986). Guba & Lincoln (1989) concluded that differences between the two methodologies are irreconcilable because they are based on two very different ways of viewing truth, knowledge, and the nature of reality.

Taking an opposing view are those who contend that quantitative and qualitative methods are not only compatible, but should be combined (House, 1994; Reichardt & Rallis, 1994). Howe (1988) observed that a major difference between quantitative and qualitative research design is that, in quantitative research, the questions, data collection procedures, and analysis are more clearly and precisely specified in an attempt to maintain experimental control. He concluded that the methodology employed depends upon the researcher's purpose; but that quantitative and qualitative methods are inextricably intertwined.

Perhaps at a purely philosophical level, the two "world views" upon which quantitative and qualitative methodologies are based are incompatible.

Nevertheless, at a practical level, assuming an extremist position at either end of the research continuum is not profitable because both quantitative and qualitative procedures, in isolation, have limitations (Reichardt & Rallis, 1994).

LIMITATIONS OF EITHER EXTREME

Subjectivity is an essential characteristic of qualitative research and is often presented as one of its greatest strengths. Nevertheless, subjectivity also presents a significant threat to the validity of qualitative research. The observational skills, prejudices, and integrity of the participant observer are critical to the results of any qualitative study. A researcher's preconceived notions could influence what he or she chooses to observe, whom he or she chooses to interview, and how he or she perceives the information gathered.

The researcher's emphasis is not on objectivity. Rather, in seeking to become an "insider," the researcher subjects himself or herself to the same situational influences and pressures as those he or she is attempting to study. The researcher also cannot know what effect his or her presence has on the behavior of those being studied. For example, the researcher who lives with and observes the family of a retarded child cannot be certain that the family members conduct themselves in the same way in his or her absence.

The final product is the researcher's perceptions of the feelings and perceptions of the observed subjects with whom he or she has interacted. This perceptual filtering of observations, coupled with the human impossibility of any observer being able to observe and record every significant event experienced, represents a serious threat to the validity of obtained conclusions.

Purely qualitative procedures are difficult, if not impossible, to replicate because of the subjective, spontaneous, and interactive nature of data collection procedures, as well as the emergence of unpredictable research questions to be pursued (Bednarz, 1986). Data collection procedures (e.g., what is selected for observation, who is interviewed, what questions are asked, etc.) will vary from one researcher to another. This is not to say that there are no methodologies associated with qualitative procedures; but, given their exploratory and discovery-oriented nature, they are not efficiently replicated. In this day of limited funding for research, efficiency of replication must be considered a significant factor.

Finally, although qualitative investigations can be extensive, they still usually involve the exploration of only one situation (e.g., one class, one school, one family), thereby severely limiting generalizability to other situations. As Rogers (1984) indicated, "Most qualitative research consists of studies of single cases in limited settings and qualitative researchers are constantly faced with the problem of relating their 'micro' studies to the 'macro culture' at large" (p. 93).

To summarize, strictly qualitative procedures tend not to be confirmatory in a way that allows researchers to be confident about the validity, reliability, or generalizability of their conclusions. Nevertheless, by investigating other similar research environments, and by incorporating some quantitative procedures, researchers can become more confident that their results are generally valid. The qualitative researcher who resists the inclusion of any quantitative methodology, citing the imperfection of measurement instruments or the ephemeral nature of truth, will not reach conclusions that will inspire confidence in decision makers who must decide how best to allocate limited dollars for children with disabilities. Hedrick (1994) reported that when members of Congress request evaluation information about programs, they "generally want to know about program compliance, efficiency or effectiveness; they want facts about program impacts as well as relative trade-offs. And the language of these evaluations is . . . quantitative language" (p. 46).

Strictly quantitative procedures, though usually more objective as a result of experimental control, can be somewhat contrived or artificial. There is danger in the belief that complicated issues or concepts in special education can be meaningfully reduced to a number or to a statistically significant difference. Good quantitative research must be characterized by qualitative (i.e., subjective, observational, commonsensical) aspects in formulating research questions and the ensuing hypotheses. It must also be characterized by qualitative aspects in evaluating the answers to those questions once data have been collected and analyzed. As Smith (1994) observed, "Discussions about what to examine, which questions to explore, which indicators to choose, . . . which contrary data to report, what to do with marginally significant statistical results are judgement calls" (p. 38).

The quantitative researcher who resists the inclusion of qualitative aspects runs the risk of asking and answering meaningless questions not grounded in practical reality. One should not take comfort in mindless number-crunching to reach conclusions of dubious validity. At the practical level, the qualitative researcher and the quantitative researcher should acknowledge the valuable features of the "opposing" view and, as appropriate, incorporate some of those features into their own research (Smith, 1994).

A CONTINUUM PERSPECTIVE

Quantitative and qualitative research methodologies are often discussed in professional literature as dichotomous, all-or-none choices. Such a dichotomous viewpoint has more merit at the philosophical level than it has at the practical level. Perhaps a more accurate way to view qualitative and quantitative methodologies would be as points on a research continuum. One can readily acknowledge that there are qualitative procedures and quantitative procedures associated with good research without creating artificial distinctions between the procedures.

Rather than argue for the superiority of one method over the other, a more relevant discussion should be focused on how far toward the quantitative end of the research continuum one should progress before making decisions about policy and practice. The position set forth in the present chapter is that both qualitative and quantitative methodologies have a place in special education.

However, whenever possible, more quantitative methodologies are preferable because they lead to decisions about policy and practice that are based on more valid and reliable evidence.

The continuum view would include relatively unstructured observation of some natural phenomenon at one end of the continuum and pure laboratory research under highly controlled conditions at the other end. Every special education teacher reaches conclusions about his or her students based on qualitative observation of classroom performance. Though this is usually an effective strategy for the insightful teacher, it could hardly be classified as generalizable research.

Conducting research at the opposite (i.e., the quantitative) end of the continuum is often difficult in special education. Highly controlled laboratory conditions are not conducive to the study of what takes place in a classroom. Research in special education involves what children learn, how they learn, the efficiency with which they learn and, often, the behavior they display while they are learning. It also involves teacher behavior, teacher attitudes, and instructional strategies. None of these research activities can be studied appropriately in a sterile laboratory because teaching and learning involve dynamic interactions that occur within a classroom and involve people.

Viewing quantitative and qualitative methodologies as dichotomous tends to encourage the faulty perception that research methodologies are mutually exclusive. For example, if a researcher is viewed as a quantitative researcher, then he or she might be inaccurately perceived as one whose research questions are not grounded in the reality of natural settings, or he or she might stereotypically be presented as one who believes in the unchanging uniformity of nature or human behavior (Hoshmand, 1989). The quantitative researcher's results might be viewed as less relevant because he or she is perceived as one who is not focusing on the complete picture of the research problem. Because he or she focuses on predetermined research questions, the quantitative researcher might be perceived as relatively inflexible, and the research results might be viewed as static rather than dynamic. The quantitative researcher's quest for objectivity renders him or her an outsider rather than an insider. Such perceptions of the good researcher who strives to push to the quantitative end of the research continuum are inaccurate, but are to be expected when one attempts to force an exclusively dichotomous conceptualization of a phenomenon that is better viewed as continuous.

As Howe (1988) suggested, the degree to which one employs qualitative or quantitative methods is a function of the research questions one is attempting to answer. A preliminary or exploratory investigation of a natural situation might dictate the use of a relatively greater number of qualitative procedures. Nevertheless, as one's research questions lend themselves to more quantitative methods of investigation, then those methods are preferred because they lead to greater confidence (not to be confused with total confidence) in the obtained conclusions. As Simpson and Eaves (1985) stated, the guiding principle should be that "good researchers seek to eliminate, control or account for as many of the relevant variables which impinge on the Phenomena under investigation as possible" (p. 328).

Strict experimental control is not always possible in field settings, thereby allowing for the viability of some qualitative procedures. Nevertheless, qualitative procedures should be used only when the use of quantitative procedures is impossible, or when a secondary cross-validating procedure (i.e., a "reality check") is desired. Apparently, Campbell (cited in Bednarz, 1986) agreed with the aforestated conclusion when he said, "I cannot recommend qualitative social science . . . as substitute . . . for the quantitative. But I have strongly recommended [it] as [a] needed cross-validating addition. . ." (pp. 294–295).

QUALITATIVE ASPECTS OF QUANTITATIVE RESEARCH

Researchers typically do not seek to answer meaningless, socially irrelevant questions. Given the desirability of proceeding toward the quantitative end of the continuum, how does one generate theories and determine questions for research? First, the researcher surveys the almost overwhelming array of significant issues that abound in special education.

From the array of researchable topics, he or she selects an area of interest. For example, assume that the researcher decides to investigate the effect of teacher attitude on the success of students with disabilities who have been integrated into the regular classroom. The researcher desires to get a holistic view (or full picture) of the problem. He or she has already theorized that teacher attitudes have some effect on the success of integrated exceptional students, but does not know which attitudes have which effects.

One way to gather information would be to visit an elementary school where exceptional students have been integrated into regular education classes. In addition to observing the activities in various classes, the researcher could interview the teachers, the students with diabilities, and the students without disabilities. He or she could examine bulletin boards, memoranda, and reports from school staffing and eligibility committee meetings. All of the above procedures might be described as qualitative and, certainly, they provide valuable information.

The researcher has observed that some exceptional students seem to learn more than others at the school, and that the teachers of regular education classes seem to display varying levels of acceptance toward exceptional students. Younger teachers seem to be more accepting than older teachers, and female teachers seem to be more accepting than male teachers. The collection of qualitative data, though valuable, has not enabled the researcher to answer confidently the original question because too many other unanswered questions remain. A few of the unanswered questions might be:

1. Are females really more accepting than males, or does the fact that there are only two males in the school prevent one from confidently answering the question?
2. Is there an interaction effect between the attitude, age, and sex of the teacher?
3. How does one assess the academic achievement of exceptional students (e.g., grades, achievement test data, teacher perception)?
4. How does one define and assess an accepting attitude, and how can one know that the assessment procedures are valid and reliable?
5. Is this school typical of other schools?

The keen observer has learned much, and probably has formed some opinions concerning what he or she perceives to be the relationship between teacher attitude and the success of integrated exceptional students. Nevertheless, because he or she desires increased confidence in the validity of his or her conclusions, the researcher proceeds toward the quantitative end of the research continuum. He or she now knows enough to generate specific research questions and hypotheses for further investigation. The researcher might hypothesize, for example, that teacher attitude affects the academic success of integrated exceptional students, but that there is no correlation between attitude and teacher age or sex.

The next step in the investigative process involves operationally defining variables to be examined and determining how best to measure them. Finally, the researcher attempts to implement procedures that will neutralize the effects of confounding variables so that he or she can determine as directly as possible the relationship between the variables selected for study.

The researcher has moved from the qualitative toward the quantitative end of the research continuum, but his or her posing of research questions and hypothesizing have been grounded in reality. Through classroom observation the researcher has entered the "real world," the naturalistic world of education, and has attempted to gain an insider's perspective into the nature of the problem. He or she has observed that some students appear to flourish while others appear to flounder in the integrated classroom. Now he or she is attempting to determine why this apparent difference occurs, so that the research is educationally relevant and socially valid. The perspective is holistic, but he or she realizes that all of the related questions cannot be answered at once. Rather, the researcher will patiently gather evidence in manageable units and attempt to determine the relationship between each new piece of evidence and what is already known about the overall picture.

Once a specific study has been completed and the data have been analyzed, the researcher then reaches a tentative conclusion about whether his or her hypothesis can be accepted or rejected. Though seeking to confirm or to discount the presence of a possible relationship between experimental variables, the researcher does not view his or her experiment as the ultimate discovery of truth. Rather, he or she realizes that, despite the best efforts to control for extraneous variables, some other unconsidered variable might have affected the experimental results.

The researcher also realizes that a certain amount of error is associated with every measurement instrument. No matter how well designed, intelligence tests, achievement tests, rating scales, and questionnaires all suffer from problems with validity and reliability. For example, the researcher can never be totally confident that the teachers who responded to the questionnaire did so honestly and accurately. The researcher would be naive to believe that he or she is measuring some quantity of never-changing truth with a perfectly valid and reliable instrument; but through the use of quantitative (in this case, statistical) methods, the researcher can estimate how much confidence to have in his or her results.

The researcher also realizes that, even if he or she had perfect measurement instruments, "facts" change with time and may vary from one situation to another (e.g., from one teacher to another, from one class to another, or from one school to another). Even if special education "truth" does exist and can be measured at one point in time, there is no guarantee that the same truth will exist at another point in time. Nevertheless, the researcher's purpose is to be able to predict the probability of a relationship between two variables under specified conditions. One way to accomplish this is through statistical analysis with its accompanying probability of error. Another way to strive for predictability is through replication of procedures

and comparison of results of similar experiments in which common variables are analyzed.

Replication of quantitative procedures involves recreating similar experimental conditions and manipulating the same variables as those in an earlier study. Replication of quantitative procedures is often difficult, but replication of qualitative procedures can be even more difficult because of the open-endedness with which research questions are developed and pursued. Valuable information may be gleaned from both efforts, but decision makers with limited dollars must be reasonably confident about the research conclusions on which they base decisions. Although certainly not perfect, replicated quantitative procedures yielding similar results can provide the reasonable assurance that is needed in situations in which time and money are factors.

CONCLUSION

Recent disenchantment with the vulnerabilities of quantitative methodology have led to suggestions that it is artificial, impractical, not grounded in the "real world," and so forth. The contention of the present chapter is that competent researchers are aware of the weaknesses of purely quantitative methods, and employ qualitative methodology both in formulating research questions and in evaluating the answers to those questions. Nevertheless, it has been suggested that research in special education should assume a more qualitative focus (Stainback & Stainback, 1984). To the extent that quantitative research should be grounded in reality, the suggestion is a good one; however, it is not without potential danger. A strong move in the qualitative direction could result in pseudo-research that is used in an attempt to validate socially accepted, yet unproven, concepts.

Stainback and Stainback (1984) presented some of the dangers involved in emphasizing qualitative methodology in special education. In essence, the chief danger is that shoddy, ill-conceived, and poorly conducted research could be legitimized under the guise that it is qualitative. When an individual's pseudo-research is scrutinized and questioned, he or she can respond that the truth he or she discovered is ephemeral and that it is a function of the unique interaction between the participant observer and those who were observed *in situ.* Such "truth" is not only filtered by the preconceived notions, perceptions, and observational abilities of the observer, but it might never be true again because the conditions of the interaction might never occur again. Conveniently, then, replication and verification are impossible.

It is acknowledged, of course, that shoddy, incompetent, and even dishonest research can be conducted and presented as quantitative research. Nevertheless, quantitative methods, by their nature, are better defined and more easily replicated; they are, therefore, more open to independent verification than are qualitative methods .

A second reason why a strong shift in the qualitative direction would be ill advised for research in special education concerns the state of education in general and the state of special education in particular in contemporary U.S. society. Education has been criticized frequently for adopting faddish practices whose merit has been unproven. Sometimes an educational fad, couched in appropriate educational jargon (e.g., "new math"), is subject to public ridicule and/or suspicion because it appears either to be a reinvention of the wheel or to be the needless complication of a relatively simple concept. As a result, there are many people who are skeptical about the quality of public education in the United States.

In the past decade, public education has been blamed (often unfairly) for many of the problems common to U.S. youth (e.g., lower achievement test scores, discipline problems, alcohol and drug abuse, etc.). Panels composed of leaders from government and from private industry have called for "excellence" in education, implying that contemporary U.S. public education is not excellent. There are frequent charges that public education is funded adequately, but that the money is being spent wastefully and inefficiently. Politicians now demand educational "results" in return for tax dollars spent. Political rhetoric is not always valid, but the fact is that public education has an image problem.

Special education, as a part of public education, shares the general image problem, but also has an image problem unique to itself. In addition to those who believe that special education programs are a waste of taxpayers' money, there are also critics, inside and outside of special education, who believe that special education programs are relatively ineffective. Clearly, it is imperative for researchers in special education to investigate and to document the most effective ways to deliver services to students with disabilities. Now is not the time for a shift toward more qualitative research.

To document the most effective strategies in special education requires a research effort that will be convincing to politicians, educators, and a skeptical public. Which delivery systems are most effective in providing services to exceptional children? Which teaching methods result in the greatest academic gains for exceptional children? Which intervention strategies result in the greatest gains in social skills? Which strategies result in the greatest decrease in off-task/disruptive behavior? What social programs are effective in reducing the incidence of school violence or the number of school dropouts?

It is suggested that the questions posed in the preceding paragraph are best answered through the use of quantitative methodology. Rossi (1994) commented that "there is no way that a cost-effective qualitative evaluation can be mounted on a scale large enough to meet the needs of national programs" (p. 32). Sechrest (1992) added that if evaluators want to maximize the likelihood of results being accepted and used, they would do well to ground them "not in theory and hermeneutics, but in the dependable rigor afforded by our best science and accompanying quantitative analyses" (p. 3).

This is not to suggest that qualitative (observational, realistic, commonsensical, human) aspects be ignored by researchers as they formulate research questions and attempt to understand experimental results in the context of the real world, nor is it to suggest the universality or permanence of truth. Rather, this is to propose that, although quantitative research methodology is far from perfect, it remains the best way to document the effectiveness of special education in a manner that provides the greatest degree of confidence in the validity and reliability of conclusions.

REFERENCES

Bednarz, D. (1986). Quantity and quality in evaluation research: A divergent view. *Evaluation and Program Planning, 8,* 289–306.

Guba, E. G., & Lincoln, Y. S. (1989). *Fourth-Generation Evaluation.* Newbury Park, CA: Sage.

Hedrick, T. (1994). The quantitative-qualitative debate: Possibilities for integration. In C. S. Reichardt & S. F. Rallis (Eds.), *The qualitative–quantitative debate: New Perspectives* (pp. 45–52). San Francisco: Jossey-Bass.

Hoshmand, L. (1989). Alternate research paradigms: A review and teaching proposal. *The Counseling Psychologist, 17,* 3–79.

House, E. (1994). Integrating the quantitative and qualitative. In C. S. Reichardt & S. F. Rallis (Eds.), *The qualitative–quantitative debate: New Perspectives* (pp. 13–22). San Francisco: Jossey-Bass .

Howe, K. R. (1988). Against the quantitative-qualitative incompatibility thesis or dogmas die hard. *Educational Researcher, 17,* 10–16.

Jacob, E. (1988). Clarifying qualitative research: A focus on traditions. *Educational Researcher,17,* 16–24.

Reichardt, C., & Rallis, S. (1994). The relationship between the qualitative and quantitative research traditions. In C. S. Reichardt & S. F. Rallis (Eds.), *The qualitative–quantitative debate: New perspectives* (pp. 5–12). San Francisco: Jossey-Bass.

Rogers, V. R. (1984). Qualitative research—Another way of knowing. In P. L. Hosford (Ed.), *Using what we know about teaching* (pp. 85–106). Alexandria, VA: Association for Supervision and Curriculum Development.

Rossi, P. (1994). The war between the quals and the quants: Is a lasting peace possible? In C. S. Reichardt & S. F. Rallis (Eds.), *The qualitative–quantitative debate: New perspectives* (pp. 23–36). San Francisco: Jossey-Bass.

Sechrest, L. (1992). Roots: Back to our first generations. *Evaluation Practice, 13*(1), 1–7.

Simpson, R. G., & Eaves, R. C. (1985). Do we need more qualitative research or more good research? A reaction to Stainback and Stainback. *Exceptional Children. 51,* 325–329.

Smith, M. (1994). Qualitative plus/versus quantitative: The last word. In C. S. Reichardt & S. F. Rallis (Eds.), *The qualitative–quantitative debate: New perspectives* (pp. 37–44). San Francisco: Jossey-Bass.

Stainback, S., & Stainback, W. (1984). Broadening the research perspective in special education. *Exceptional Children, 50,* 400–408.

CHAPTER 18

Standing on Its Own:
Qualitative Research in Special Education

ROBERT BOGDAN
ZANA MARIE LUTFIYYA

INTRODUCTION

Quantitative methods have dominated special education research. A variety of curricular and behavioral interventions have been tested with control groups and single subjects and, along with surveys of attitudes and practices, have formed the bulk of the formal research that has been conducted. The focus of much of this research has been on ascertaining the effect of narrowly defined experiences on specifically defined individuals under certain conditions.

The domination of quantitative research in special education has not served the field well. Our criticism is not so much with the value of the quantitative paradigm as with its monolithic place in the field of special education. Historical, philosophical, as well as sociological and anthropological field research—that is, qualitative research—has been neglected, restricting the field's search for understanding to methods that address only a narrow part of the human experience and take the assumptions of the field of special education for granted (Bogdan, 1986; Bogdan & Kugelmauss, 1984).

In recent years the application of qualitative research methods in special education has been treated with increasing interest (Stainback & Stainback, 1984,1989). Some qualitative studies dealing with disability began appearing in the social science literature in the 1960s (Edgerton, 1967; Goffman, 1963; Scott, 1969). It was not until the 1970s that qualitative research began

making an impact in the special education literature (Blatt, Biklen, & Bogdan, 1977; Bogdan & Taylor, 1976; Edgerton & Bercovici, 1976). We had to wait until the 1980s for qualitative research to become widely known and it wasn't until the 1990s that it became well established (for example, Bercovici, 1983; Bogdan & Taylor, 1982; Bruininks, Meyers, Sigford, & Lakin, 1981; Edgerton, 1984; Ferguson, 1987; Ferguson, Ferguson, & Taylor, 1992; Murray-Seegert, 1989). However, we speculate that even now, the great majority of people in the area of special education research, including those who support the use of qualitative research, have never conducted a qualitative study nor formally studied the approach and hence are not very knowledgeable about this methodology. Special education professionals who are not researchers know even less.

Qualitative research is a long-established and independent research tradition in the social sciences (Bruyn, 1966; Taylor & Bogdan, 1984) built on certain assumptions about how one can learn about human behavior. Qualitative research came out of the phenomenological theoretical perspective. The phenomenologist views what people say and do as a product of how people define their world. It is this very process of definition and understanding that the qualitative researcher wants to document, describe, and analyze. On the other hand, quantitative research comes out of another theoretical perspective, positivism. The positivist seeks the facts or causes of human behavior apart from the subjective states of individuals. For the quantitative researcher rooted in this paradigm, social phenomena are "things" that exercise an external influence on people.

Since positivists and phenomenologists ask different types of questions and seek different kinds of answers, their research demands different methodologies. Adopting a model of research that came from the natural sciences, the positivist searches for causes through methods such as a variety of experimental designs, questionnaires, inventories, and demographics that produce data that are amenable to statistical analysis. Seeking to understand the perspective of a person in a certain situation, the qualitative researcher uses participant observation and in-depth interviewing, which yield descriptive data.

Our task in this chapter, as it was defined to us by the Stainbacks, is to discuss the current controversy in special education over the use and applicability of qualitative research to that field. It is a difficult assignment. People conjure up a raging public battle between those quantitative researchers who do not accept the qualitative paradigm and the qualitative researchers who are irreverent toward experimental design, random sampling, and level of significance. But while there may be competition between quantitative and qualitative researchers over scarce resources (e.g., faculty positions or research funds), a black-and-white controversy does not exist. In fact, we do not remember ever hearing any researcher in the field of special education take a stand against the use of qualitative research. Articles lambasting the method do not appear in the professional journals. However, the lack of blatant opposition does not mean that many quantitatively trained researchers have fully accepted the approach let alone know exactly what it is. There is a norm within all research communities to be skeptical yet also open to different ideas and approaches. Perhaps the lack of expressed concern over qualitative research is an indicator of that norm rather than an accurate tally of how people in special education really think.

Are the Stainbacks creating a controversy by asking us to write about one? Not entirely. We sense that some quantitative researchers reject qualitative research. Whether the opposition arises from a basic lack of understanding, vested interests, tradition, or some combination of these elements is difficult to tell, but the rejection is there. Occasionally there are indications of this rejection during departmental discussions when hiring a new colleague and a choice has to be made between a candidate with a qualitative or one with a quantitative background. When learned scholars are trying to decide whether a particular paper based on qualitative research should be published in the premier journals in the field there may be murmurs of rejection as well. This lack of acceptance is also revealed by governmental requests for proposals that are written in such a way that precludes qualitative research methods. And it is found again in the refereed reports sent to an applicant when her or his proposal is turned down.

There is other evidence that some researchers trained in the quantitative tradition do not feel comfortable with and do not accept qualitative research. The questions that they ask and the assumptions that their questions reveal give them away. At a variety of academic forums, qualitative presenters are asked such questions as: This is interesting, but is it generalizable? Have you thought about the next step—testing your ideas more formally? What about reliability measures? These questions reveal a lack of basic knowledge and understanding of qualitative research. Such questions also reveal basic assumptions by quantitative researchers that get in the way of understanding and accepting qualitative research. These assumptions do not take into account the different theoretical frameworks that underlie the two paradigms. They also inhibit the understanding of qualitative research and its potential for making a contribution to special education.

What follows in this chapter is a list of assumptions that we believe people not familiar with and perhaps even hostile to qualitative research have about the approach, together with our response to them. Our purpose has strayed slightly from the assignment of writing about the controversy between qualitative and quantitative researchers. Our intention is to make overt a controversy that is covert.

Assumption No. 1: Findings from a Qualitative Study Cannot Be Generalized

The strong emphasis quantitative researchers place on selecting subjects, standardizing measurement, and controlling for extraneous variables reflects their concern with the issue of *generalizability*. When they use this term, quantitative researchers are referring to whether the findings of a study hold up beyond the specific research subjects and/or setting being studied. If a particular mainstreamed classroom is being studied, for example, readers want to know whether what is learned can be applied to other mainstreamed classrooms.

Some qualitative researchers are concerned with the question of generalizability as quantitative researchers define it. They may explicitly warn the reader against extrapolating from their work to other subjects and settings. Other qualitative researchers draw upon the results of other studies of similar subjects and/or settings to establish the representativeness of what they have found. Still others may follow an intensive case study with a number of mini-studies to demonstrate the similarity or reveal the differences between the original case study and other settings.

Another way some qualitative researchers approach generalizability is to assume that if they carefully document a given setting or group of subjects, it is then someone else's job to see how it fits into the general scheme of things. Even a description of a deviant or unusual case is considered valuable since theories have to account for all types in the category. These qualitative researchers see their work as having a potential to create anomalies that other researchers might have to explain. Some of these explanations might

entail enlarging or redefining the conception of the phenomenon under study.

Many qualitative researchers do not think about generalizability in the conventional quantitative way. They are often interested in deriving universal statements about general social processes rather than statements of commonality between settings that share the same title, such as mainstreamed classrooms. They may study several different settings (i.e., a mainstreamed classroom, a pool hall, and a community center) in order to study things such as social change, adult socialization, or conflict. Researchers whose goals are to develop sensitizing concepts (Blumer, 1969) and grounded theory (Glaser & Strauss, 1967) embrace this approach to generalizability.

Assumption No. 2: There Is No Reliability in a Qualitative Study

There is some truth to this statement. Quantitative researchers require consistency in the data produced by observations or measurements made by different researchers studying the same phenomena at the same time or by the same researcher over time. Qualitative researchers emphasize validity in their research and use a different definition of reliability in their work. In pursuit of reliability, quantitative researchers attempt to standardize the procedures they use. Whatever happens to the subjects in the research situation should be uniform for each. For example, when they conduct interviews they try to make the research situation the same for all respondents. They are careful to give the questions in the same order each time and to introduce themselves and the task at hand using a set script. Interviewers often dress in a consistent way and use the same venue for all of the interviews.

Qualitative researchers do not accept this standardization as desirable or necessary. Instead, qualitative researchers use a flexible approach to study design which may change over time as the data are analyzed. The collected data dictate the direction of the study. As Taylor & Bogdan (1984,

p. 8) note, "The methods serve the researcher, never is the researcher a slave to procedure and technique." Rather than relying on standardized and rigid procedures that might miss significant data (not yet developed into an hypothesis), the qualitative researcher serves as the research instrument. This allows the researcher to collect and analyze data which, in a different study, might have gone unnoticed.

One reason for this lack of corresponding views between the two methods of research is that people working within the qualitative paradigm tend to see behavior as more situational than people working in the quantitative paradigm. Qualitative researchers think that people do not necessarily act the same in different settings or even in the same situation at different times. But the differences between qualitative and quantitative approaches lie deeper than that.

Special education researchers come from a variety of backgrounds and have divergent interests and training. Some have studied psychology, sociology, child development, anthropology, or social work. The academic training and personal life experience one has had affects the questions one brings to an area of inquiry and what one pays attention to in the field. In the study of special education in a school, for example, social workers might be interested in the social background of the students; sociologists might direct their attention to the school's social structure; developmental psychologists might wish to study the self-concept of pupils in the early grades. Researchers with these different backgrounds and interests may spend more time in some parts of the school than in others, they may speak more to certain people than to others, and they may literally ask different questions of the people in the school. Similarly, theoretical perspectives specific to their fields will result in field notes and interview transcripts varying from one researcher to another.

In qualitative studies, researchers are concerned with the accuracy and comprehensiveness of their data (that field notes contain accurate descriptions of objects and correct renderings of conversation). Qualitative researchers view reliability as a fit between what they record as data (field notes and interview transcripts) and what actually occurs in the setting under study, rather than the literal consistency across different observations or observers. As the preceding discussion indicates, two researchers studying a single setting may come up with different data and produce different findings. The data in both studies can be both reliable and valid.

Reliability is a concept from the quantitative paradigm that does not translate perfectly into the qualitative one. There are other aspects of the data qualitative researchers collect that are not dealt with very well in the quantitative research paradigm. One is *context*. Qualitative researchers are very much concerned with the context within which data are collected. They need to understand context in order to use data. For example, during early studies of institutions for people labeled mentally retarded, staff members changed what they said as they got to know the researchers. These informants first talked about all of the programs that the residents were involved in, and the positive aspects of the residents' lives. Later, staff members said that residents were too retarded to learn from programs and that the staff did not get enough support from the state to do the programming (Bogdan, Taylor, deGrandpre, & Haynes, 1974). Both the preliminary remarks and the later ones were considered data and were valid. But in order for them to be valuable, the researchers had to understand that the earlier remarks were how employees talked to outsiders and the later ones was representative of how they talked among themselves. Even lies make good data if you are aware of the broader context, and you know that they are lies.

Qualitative researchers are concerned with validity. Because the analysis in qualitative research is inductive—that is, the questions, findings, themes, and concepts are developed in the process of collecting data and are derived from the data—the question of whether you are studying what you say you are studying is moot. Quantitative researchers, with their deductive approach replete with preconceived hypotheses, operational definitions, and empirical indicators, have a greater problem in demonstrating validity.

Both quantitative and qualitative researchers are concerned about the significance of their findings. Although quantitative researchers use the word *significance* a great deal, the meaning of the term is a very circumscribed statistical calculation. Qualitative researchers define this concept by referring to the more common use of that word.

Assumption No. 3: Qualitative Research Methods Are Best Used in Combination with Quantitative Approaches

Not only do many researchers trained in the quantitative tradition think that qualitative research should be used with quantitative data but they relegate the use of qualitative research to pilot studies used for deriving hunches. They assume that qualitative research is good for the preliminary work before the more precise scientific quantitative researchers become involved. This is not how qualitative researchers define their role. They see what they do as standing on its own from the beginning to the end of a piece of research, and that it is an important contribution in and of its own right. Qualitative researchers see their quantitative counterparts' view of combining the two paradigms as illustrative of how quantitative researchers do not understand the basic premises of the qualitative research paradigm.

Some researchers suggest combining qualitative and quantitative methods in a single study without relegating the qualitative paradigm to the preliminary work. These people embrace the idea that if one approach to research is effective then two approaches used in combination should be more effective. They call upon the overused and poorly defined concept of triangularization in defending their position. People who think this way do not have a deep understanding of the basic differences in the theoretical underpinnings of the two approaches. Few researchers can successfully combine key elements of both the qualitative and quantitative paradigms into a single study. Rather

than producing a superior hybrid, the result is typically a study that does not meet the criteria for good work in either approach. Qualitative and quantitative research methods are based on different theoretical frameworks that may not be compatible with each other.

We are not saying that qualitative researchers should not use numerical figures and descriptive statistics. It is common for qualitative researchers' reports to contain some numbers. Data reported, for example, might include how many people are working in a particular organization under study and the percentages of women and men. In addition, qualitative researchers often use the quantitative data that are produced by organizations. But rather than taking the data at face value, qualitative researchers often study the way the data were constructed in order to understand the way the members of the organization understand their work and how they use the data in maintaining their definition of the situation (Bogdan & Ksander, 1980).

Assumption No. 4: Qualitative Research Is Not Really Scientific

Special education researchers have modeled their research after that of physical scientists. Measurement and statistics became synonymous with "real science," and anything straying from this approach was suspect. The irony of this is that many scientists in the hard sciences (e.g., physics and chemistry) do not define science as narrowly as some of those who have emulated them. Nobel Prize–winning P. W. Bridgman has this to say of the scientific method: "There is no scientific method as such. . . . The most vital feature of the scientist's procedure has been merely to do his utmost with his mind, no holds barred" (Dalton, 1967, p. 60). Dalton says:

> Many eminent physicists, chemists, and mathematicians question whether there is a reproducible method that all investigators could or should follow, and they have shown in their research that they take diverse, and often unascertainable, steps in discovering and solving problems. (p. 60)

Some people may use an extremely narrow definition of science, calling research only that which is deductive and tests hypotheses in certain ways. For these individuals, Darwin and Piaget were not scientists. But part of the scientific attitude, as we see it, is to be open-minded about method and evidence. For us, scientific research is based on rigorous and systematic empirical inquiry, that is, it is data based. Qualitative research meets these requirements, and there are conventions in this scientific tradition that define what rigorous and systematic investigation entails.

Assumption No. 5: Qualitative Research Methods Are Not Rigorous

Another assumption about qualitative research is that the methods used are so loose and nonrigorous that they really cannot be taught as part of a graduate curriculum. Early qualitative researchers learned to collect, analyze, and write up their field-work from mentors to whom they were apprenticed. Some of this still goes on with graduate students working on funded research projects with their professors. But in conjunction with these experiences, qualitative research methods and theory are taught in graduate courses. Within these courses, students learn the guidelines and conventions of qualitative research that have developed over the years. In addition, most research survey courses include a section on qualitative research methods. This includes extensive consideration of study design, data collection, analysis of the data, and written results.

Assumption No. 6: Qualitative Research Is Impressionistic and Is Not Different from How Others (Nonresearchers) Learn about the World

Many intelligent lay people are astute observers of their world, make systematic inquiries, and come to conclusions. Good teachers, for example, do this constantly. However, this differs from qualitative research in several ways.

First, the researcher's primary focus is the research, not a curriculum, not teaching, and not being with students. Second, qualitative researchers are rigorous about keeping detailed records of what they find. They record data. Third, researchers do not have as much of a personal stake in having the observations come out one way or another. Success is defined by good research. Fourth, qualitative researchers are trained in the use of a set of procedures and techniques developed over the years to collect and analyze data. Finally, qualitative researchers are well grounded in the theory and previous research findings that provide a framework to direct the study and to place what is generated into a broader context.

Assumption No. 7: Qualitative Researchers' Prejudices and Opinions Make Qualitative Research Findings Untrustworthy

Qualitative researchers have wrestled over the years with charges that it is too easy for the prejudices and attitudes of the researcher to bias the data. This worry about subjectivity arises particularly because the data must go through the researcher's mind before it is put to paper. Qualitative researchers are concerned with the effect their own subjectivity may have on the data they record. (It should be noted here that we are talking about limiting a researcher's bias.) Qualitative researchers try to acknowledge and take into account their own biases as a method of dealing with them.

Qualitative researchers try to study objectively the subjective states of their informants. Although the idea that researchers can set aside some of their own biases may be difficult to accept, the methods that qualitative researchers use aid this process. The data must bear the weight of any interpretation, so the researcher must constantly confront his or her own opinions and prejudices with the data. The data that are collected provide a much more detailed rendering of events than even the most prejudiced mind might have imagined prior to conducting the study. Part of the data for qualitative researchers are clearly labeled sections where the role of the researcher is recorded and analyzed. Some qualitative researchers work in teams and have their field notes critiqued by a colleague who pays attention to the potential for researcher bias.

Assumption No. 8: The Presence of the Researcher Changes the Behavior of the People in the Study

Almost all research is confounded by this problem. Because other research approaches suffer from this problem does not mean that qualitative researchers take the issue of "observer effect" lightly. Qualitative researchers try to interact with their informants in a natural, unobtrusive, and nonthreatening manner. The more controlled and obtrusive one's research, the greater the likelihood that one will end up studying the effects of one's methods. If people are treated as research subjects, they will act as research subjects, which is different from how they usually act. Since qualitative researchers are interested in how people act and think in their own settings, they attempt to "blend into the woodwork," or to act so that the activities that occur in their presence do not differ significantly from those that occur in their absence.

No researcher can eliminate all of his or her effects on the informants or obtain a perfect correspondence between what one might wish to study—the natural setting—and what one actually studies, that is, a setting with a researcher present. One can, however, understand one's effect on the informants through an intimate knowledge of the setting and use this understanding to generate additional insights into the nature of social life. Researchers learn to "discount" some of their data, that is, to interpret them in context (Deutscher, 1973).

CONCLUSION

The branches of universities that train practitioners—schools of human development, social work, business, and education—have always shared a feeling of inferiority when comparing their scholarly and research productivity and sophistication to departments that are considered more academic, such as sociology and psychology. This has resulted in a methodological conservatism that inhibits research innovation. In some quarters, this might be thought of as a kind of methodcentrism, or judging other research paradigms using the standards developed to judge one's own work. Whereas a number of the social science disciplines (and indeed other branches of education) have become increasingly eclectic in their research approaches, many special educators have clung to one narrow standard of scientific research. Social scientists are now engaged in discussions of the implications of postmodernism for their craft. Perhaps in the second half of the 1990s we can move beyond the qualitative–quantitative debate.

REFERENCES

Bercovici, S. (1983). *Barriers to normalization.* Baltimore: University Park Press.

Blatt, B., Biklen, D., & Bogdan, R. (Eds.). (1977). *An alternative textbook in special education.* Denver: Love.

Blumer, H. (1969). *Symbolic interactionism.* Englewood Cliffs, NJ: Prentice Hall.

Bogdan, R. (1986). The sociology of special education. In R. J. Morris & B. Blatt (Eds.), *Special education research and trends* (pp. 344–359). Elmsford, NY: Pergamon.

Bodgan, R., and Ksander, M. (1980). Policy data as a social process: A qualitative approach to quantitative data. *Human Organization, 34*(4).

Bogdan, R., & Kugelmauss, J. (1984). Case studies of mainstreaming: A symbolic interactionist approach to special education. In L. Barton & E. Tomlinson (Eds.), *Special education and social interests.* London: Croom Helm.

Bogdan, R., & Taylor, S. (1976). The judged not the judges: An insider's view of mental retardation. *American Psychologist, 31*(1), 47–52.

Bogdan, R., & Taylor, S. (1982). *Inside out.* Toronto, Ontario; University of Toronto Press.

Bogdan, R., Taylor, S., de Grandpre, B., & Haynes, S. (1974, June). Let them eat programs: Attendants and programming on wards in state schools. *Journal of Health and Social Behavior, 15.*

Bruininks, R., Meyers, C., Sigford, B., & Lakin, K. (Eds.). (1981). *Deinstitutionalization and community adjustment of mentally retarded people.* Washington DC: The American Association of Mental Retardation.

Bruyn, S. (1966). *The human perspective in sociology: The methodology of participant observation.* Englewood Cliffs, NJ: Prentice Hall.

Dalton, M. (1967). Preconceptions and methods in "men who manage." In P. Hammond (Ed.), *Sociologists at Work.* New York: Anchor.

Deutscher, I. (1973). *What we say/What we do.* Glenview, IL: Scott, Foresman.

Edgerton, R. (1967). *The cloak of competence.* Berkeley: University of California Press.

Edgerton, R. (1984). *Lives in process.* Washington, DC: American Association on Mental Deficiency.

Edgerton, R., & Bercovici, S. M. (1976). The cloak of competence—years later. *American Journal of Mental Deficiency, 80,* 485–490.

Ferguson, D. (1987). *Curriculum decision making for students with severe handicaps: Policy and practice.* New York: Teachers College Press.

Ferguson, P. M., Ferguson, D. L., & Taylor, S. J. (1992). *Interpreting disability: A qualitative reader.* New York: Teachers College Press.

Glaser, B., & Strauss, A. (1967). *The discovery of grounded theory.* Chicago: Aldine.

Goffman, E. (1963). *Stigma.* Englewood Cliffs, NJ: Prentice Hall.

Murray-Seegert, C. (1989). *Nasty girls, thugs, things and humans like us.* Baltimore: Paul H. Brookes.

Scott, R. (1969). *The making of blind men.* New York: Russell Sage.

Stainback, S., & Stainback, W. (1984). Broadening the research perspective in special education. *Exceptional Children, 80*(5), 400–408.

Stainback, W., & Stainback, S. (1989). Using qualitative data collection procedures to investigate supported education issues. *Journal of the Association for Persons with Severe Handicaps, 14*(4), 271–277.

Taylor, S., & Bogdan, R. (1984). *Introduction to qualitative research methods: The search for meaning* (2nd ed.). New York: Wiley.

SECTION TEN

HIGHER EDUCATION

Should the organizational arrangements of colleges of education be restructured to reflect the changing roles of special educators in the schools? In Chapter 19, Pugach outlines why restructuring is necessary and addresses some of the issues that will need to be considered by those who wish to work toward reform of teacher preparation programs. She does not propose the adoption of any particular organizational structure, but instead urges professors of education to analyze how they are contributing to the reform of the public schools as they attempt to meet the needs of students with diverse needs in mainstream settings. Pugach does suggest that this may require a different conceptualization of what is taught and a change in the organizational patterns that currently exist in colleges of education.

Heller, in Chapter 20, outlines the reasons why special education should remain a separate department or unit within colleges of education. His basic premise is that departments within colleges of education are needed for organizational purposes and thus special education can and should be maintained as a separate department. He points out that maintaining a separate status for special education gives it more visibility and impact within a college of education. Heller also provides data from a survey he conducted that indicates that most deans of education are not, at the present time, in favor of merging special and regular education departments.

CHAPTER 19

Unifying the Preparation
of Prospective Teachers

MARLEEN C. PUGACH

INTRODUCTION

The purpose of this chapter, simply put, is to argue for the unification of teacher education programs whose traditional design separates the preparation of classroom teachers from that of special educators. Given the increasing complexity of the student population, as well as the unprecedented fact that the culture of most novice teachers will differ from those of their students in the years to come (Cazden & Mehan, 1989), such a position should strike no reader as a surprise. The imperative for restructuring is no less pressing for those who prepare the country's new teachers than it is for those who are responsible for the schools themselves. Goodlad's observation that "we are running out of organization and special grouping types of solutions" (1986, p. xi) to the problem of an increasingly diverse and heterogeneous student population applies no less to programs of teacher education than it does to how practitioners respond to the challenges they face in the schools.

If there is to be a counterpart in teacher education to the goal of supporting a diverse student population that includes children and youth with disabilities in the schools, unification at the level of higher education is a requisite condition. In advocating this goal, I do not visualize professors of special education marching en masse into departments of elementary, secondary, or early childhood education and requesting a new departmental "home." Rather, a complete refashioning of teacher education programs is required in which

the expertise of those who are currently aligned with special education or with curriculum and instruction will be blended. How this blending occurs, what forms new teacher education programs will take, and how the new organizational structures to support such programs might look are evolving at different stages in teacher education programs nationwide. But at whatever stage reforms might be, these deliberations are likely to include the issue of teaching children with disabilities only to the extent that special education professors wish to be centrally involved.

The stark realities now facing education require that the concept of the common school undergo fundamental change in this country if it is to survive as a basic means of fostering democracy. The stakes are extremely high and the best thinking of every professional is warranted in all aspects of the educational enterprise. As a way of acting on their stated commitment to the development of schools that routinely and effectively accommodate diverse student populations, among whom are those with disabilities, it is incumbent upon special education professors to be particularly proactive in the redesign of teacher education. This is not an opportunity to forward the traditional special education agenda, which whether intentionally or unintentionally has often tended to be separatist and as a result divisive, but rather it represents a chance for special educators to be explicit about the basic values they want to see promoted for all students. And what better way to promote those values than to participate in designing the new common schools as full partners seeking a common vision?

If professors of special education want to play a substantial role in reconceptualizing what it means to be a teacher in these schools, they cannot do so from the sidelines of departments and programs of special education. Active efforts to overcome the dysfunctional divisions that now exist among departments, and, more important, among competing conceptions of what it means to learn to teach, will have to take place. Fundamentally, this suggests that professors in programs and departments of special education who participate in teacher preparation will have to engage in serious professional soul-searching and ask themselves the following kinds of questions:

What is the function my work and interests represent in preparing teachers to work with diverse classes of students?

What contribution am I qualified to and do I want to make to the preparation of all teachers so that students with disabilities will be better accommodated?

Do I so closely identify with a particular category of disability that I am unsure whether I have a generalizable contribution to make to the preparation of all classroom teachers?

What are my beliefs about the potential competence of general education classroom teachers to meet the needs of students with disabilities, and how do I typically communicate those beliefs to my students?

Is my concern and sense of advocacy limited to how classroom teachers work with students with disabilities, or am I also concerned with how well they are prepared to work with the growing numbers of students who are at the margins of success in school, or who require enrichment?

Am I willing to rethink my professional identity, broadening it to include alliances with professional organizations that represent education more widely? How comfortable am I venturing beyond the relative known of the special education community?

These are by no means easy questions, but they lie at the heart of the process that has to take place in teacher education if we are to meet the challenge of preparing teachers for schooling in the next century. For teacher education reform to proceed, the same kind of internal questioning is required on the part of teacher educators in general education. Given that similar self-appraisal would occur commonly among professors across special education and programs in early childhood, elementary, and secondary education, Lilly (1989) believes we will discover that "we have more goals and interests in common among faculty members in teacher education and special education than we realize" (p. 154). These common goals, once identified, can provide the basis for common action.

The rest of this chapter details three specific aspects of reforming teacher education that must be addressed conceptually and practically to achieve the goal of unified programs for preparing teachers. In the first, the function of professors of special education is addressed. Next, organizational issues are discussed and an approach is presented that supports the deliberation and collaboration needed to accomplish the task of unifying teacher education. The third section is a discussion of curricular issues, with specific suggestions for how a new curriculum for teacher education might look. The chapter concludes with some observations on the preparation of specialists and a commentary on the general issue of reforming teacher education.

TRADITIONAL FUNCTIONS OF TEACHER PREPARATION IN SPECIAL EDUCATION

What role have professors of special education played that in fact differentiates them from their counterparts in general teacher education? More than anything, it is their unique function to prepare teachers *to be accountable for the education of students identified as having disabilities.* That is, they wish to assure the existence of a group of teachers who will advocate for students with disabilities, protect their rights, and provide them with an appropriate education.

The accountability function can play out in two ways. One is to prepare special teachers to protect identified students from what may be considered a dysfunctional system of "regular" education that has previously failed them (Keogh, 1988). Not only is this argument predicated on the belief that what goes on in special education classes is superior to what goes on in general classrooms, it also belies a lack of confidence in the capacity for successful change in general education (Pugach, in press). The second way in which accountability is ensured is by preparing classroom teachers to improve the quality of teaching in general, emphasizing the prevention of school failure, flexibility in working with the natural variation among students, and the accommodation of students whose disabilities are objective and enduring.

Choosing the first approach deprives students with disabilities of opportunities to participate in the mainstream of the classroom and school community. It also deprives classroom teachers of the opportunity to experience the full range of difference in their students (Pugach, 1988). More to the point, as regards teacher education, this option deprives professors of special education of the opportunity to model their commitment to preparing teachers for the broad range of students who are seen as different. Further, it prevents them from placing full attention on how an early childhood, elementary, or secondary classroom teacher would actually create and sustain an instructionally defensible learning environment that is inclusive of the diverse character of the student population. As long as the primary work of professors of special education is the decontextualized preparation of special education teachers, their claims for what should occur in the basic professional education of general education classroom teachers to ensure accountability are likely to lack credibility.

Because it locates their work squarely in the realm of teacher education, selecting the second

option redefines the traditional function of professors of special education. This option is based on their familiarity with the organizational structure and demands of contemporary U.S. classrooms. It further presumes that they have a contribution to make in a specific curricular area such as literacy or mathematics, as a teacher education generalist in instruction and management, or as a specialist in foundational areas of education. In other words, special education professors should be able to make a substantial contribution to the core preparation of all classroom teachers as a way of advancing the agenda they, and many of their counterparts who are not in special education, want to achieve. That agenda is the creation of supportive, inclusive, effective schools for ethnically, racially, linguistically, and academically diverse students, among whom are children with disabilities.

Claims are sometimes made for other unique functions of special education teachers, including, for example, meeting the individual needs of students. Yet despite the commitment to this goal, the promise is not often realized, particularly for students identified as having mild disabilities. What passes for individualization in mild special education is often more likely to be similar IEPs within special education classes (Wesson & Deno, 1989) and an absence of work differentially tailored to individual students (Ysseldyke, O'Sullivan, Thurlow, & Christenson, 1989). Structuring schools to meet individual needs successfully is essentially the same challenge for special and general education.

Further, the idea that it is special education teachers who *really* care about students with learning and behavior problems (see Lilly, 1989) presumes that other teachers do not. By design those who choose a career in special education display their willingness to work with children and youth who have problems. However, the argument that this function belongs singularly to special education loses its cogency when one considers teachers who, under exceedingly difficult working conditions, each day skillfully handle whole classes of students who have complex, multiple needs in our nation's urban schools. Additionally, the nature of the school-aged population is such that children with problems are found everywhere, in urban and suburban schools, in rural and small city schools alike. In other words, although special educators do in fact worry about the education of students labeled as having a disability, they by no means have a monopoly on concern for children who are likely to have problems in school.

Special education continues to subscribe to the philosophy that the general education environment is the most appropriate placement for most, if not all, students with disabilities. This goal has not changed radically for at least the past twenty years since the passage of Public Law 94-142. With this goal in mind, perhaps the most important task for those who are concerned about accountability for educating children and youth with disabilities is to contribute *directly* to the quality of what teachers do in those classrooms for all students. Integrating the functions and expertise of all teacher educators promotes accountability and weaves it directly into the fabric of teacher education programs for all teachers. Conversely, isolating concern for students with disabilities in departments and programs of special education mislocates the energy of those who wish to promote schooling that is inclusive of the wide range of diversity.

ORGANIZATIONAL EFFORTS TO UNIFY TEACHER PREPARATION

In their description of how to facilitate merger at the level of personnel preparation, Stainback and Stainback (1989) suggest a possible professional core of courses appropriate for the basic preparation of all teachers. To assure that such a core integrates knowledge from what they call "regular" and special education, they state:

> Thus, in most cases, it would be *just* a matter of representatives from regular education and what was formerly special education sitting down together to analyze the existing professional core and modifying it, where necessary, to consolidate

best practices from all aspects of education. (p. 125) (emphasis added)

While it would be nice to believe that the process of unification could progress this simply and straightforwardly, in reality the view of the process of change in teacher education represented by the Stainbacks' statement is decidedly optimistic. That programmatic change can and will occur is well within realistic expectations. However, achieving it is "not simply a matter of renegotiating an existing relationship" (Pugach & Lilly, 1984, p. 54), but instead signifies nothing less than recreating the basic culture of schools, colleges, and departments of education within which teacher education takes place. Teacher education has historically occurred as a loose collection of courses across a number of departments. The absence of programmatic coherence has been acknowledged repeatedly in the teacher education reform literature and continues to be cited as one of the major barriers to be overcome (Carnegie Forum on Education and the Economy, 1986; Holmes Group, 1986).

So at the same time that at one level conceptualizing the change process as sitting down and talking is simplistic, at another level it is also an accurate picture of exactly what has to occur—not only between special educators and their colleagues in teacher education, but among teacher educators themselves. Sitting down together to discuss teacher education so that courses and content can be linked sensibly and so that a unified programmatic agenda can be developed is not typical of how faculty members in institutions of higher education operate. In fact, in many places it is still antithetical. The problem is that existing departmental structures work against such communication between professors, leading Lilly (1989) to suggest that "perhaps the best way to set the occasion for increased communication is to create an organizational structure in which communication is necessary in order for all the various parties to have their needs met" (p. 155).

In the 1970s, the Dean's Grants projects (National Support Systems Project, 1980) were generally unsuccessful in achieving truly integrated programs of teacher education, primarily because they failed to attend directly to changing organizational structures or to deal with organizational histories that obstructed communication. And no broad-based context for teacher education reform then existed to support the goals of these projects. As a result, an emphasis on appending special education content seemed to take precedence over the more challenging task, namely, reforming the fundamental nature of teacher education. More recently, calls for the reorganization of teacher education as it relates to special education have emerged from two different perspectives on restructuring: (a) promoting progressively greater inclusion of students with disabilities (Stainback & Stainback, 1989), and (b) relating reform in general teacher education to how teachers generally will be prepared to meet the needs of a diverse student population (Lilly, 1989; Pugach, 1988), which includes those with disabilities.

In reality, the goal of changing organizational norms and the goal of redesigning content must of course be addressed simultaneously. But process goals are likely to be the more difficult and time-consuming of the two, especially in the initial phases of reform. Consider the case of a dysfunctional family that decides to begin family therapy. One does not expect sudden miracles or immediate progress. Many arguments and much emotional stress are likely before progress is made. However, taking the step of agreeing to sit down together can be the most important move of all. The situation in higher education is not altogether dissimilar.

But creating the ongoing dialogue needed to promote reform demands attention itself as a goal for unifying teacher education. It is particularly crucial between special educators and their colleagues in curriculum and instruction in elementary and secondary teacher education due to the disparity in philosophical bases of teaching and learning that has traditionally existed. Moreover, the opportunity for communication, once created, also has to be sanctioned as a regular part of the bureaucratic structure in schools, colleges, and departments of education. Opportunity for ongoing dialogue is where the process of unification

begins. Once common ground exists, such dialogue is needed to sustain interaction among all those who contribute to teacher education to ensure a well-integrated program. This suggests radically new approaches to the governance of teacher education at the level of each institution of higher education, approaches that mandate the need for interaction between formerly isolated faculty members.

Because we are in the midst of a long period of teacher education reform, some alternatives to traditional organizational structures can already be identified. Some universities have experimented with an interdisciplinary structure that exists in conjunction with departments. Others have formed interdisciplinary teams associated with small cohorts of students. Still others have each faculty member belong both to a department and to a permanent working group. The purpose of such interdisciplinary structures is to provide the forum for ongoing collaboration in program and course development, course instruction, programmatic responsibility, and the ongoing study of teacher education. Whether such alternatives stand the test of time is as yet uncertain; at the least, they provide guidance for creating structures that support dialogue and interaction and by design attempt to include all the players in the process of reforming teacher education. Whatever structure is created, it will have to take into account the time needed for people to learn to work together in productive ways. This will be a greater challenge the larger the institution. But by making communication and process changes overt goals in teacher education reform, the task of developing a philosophically sound, thematically unified teacher education program can proceed more effectively.

A UNIFIED CURRICULUM FOR TEACHER EDUCATION

The purpose of describing the functions of special education and dealing with organizational features as described above is to bring teacher educators to a point at which they can design, in an atmosphere of openness and trust, defensible, up-to-date, cohesive programs of teacher education. The issue that remains to be addressed, then, is how a unified teacher education curriculum might look. It is not within the scope of this chapter—nor is it desirable—to prescribe a particular curriculum. That is something each institution of higher education will have to deal with in its own particular context. Rather, what is presented here are some of the basic issues that have to be considered as the curriculum of teacher education is redesigned to prepare teachers to work effectively in diverse classrooms.

It is important to remember that we are not talking about a curriculum that encompasses traditional dual certification in special education and classroom teaching. Instead, we are talking about a singular program designed to prepare all teachers for the current population in our schools. Four aspects related to curriculum deserve attention in this regard: programmatic integrity, the knowledge base for teaching, how teachers learn to teach, and field experiences.

Programmatic Integrity

One goal in curricular reform is defining a theme, or unifying concept, around which teacher education is coherently constructed (Barnes, 1987; Howey & Zimpher, 1989; Kennedy, 1990). By coming to agreement on a unifying philosophy, professors in essence agree to make that idea explicit in each component of the program. There are a number of examples of such programmatic themes. Hollingsworth (1989) describes learning to teach in a program based on constructivistic principles of learning. At Michigan State University, the Academic Learning Program was focused on how to foster conceptual understanding in the various subject areas (Feiman-Nemser, 1990). At the University of Florida, the PROTEACH program focuses on developing reflective teachers (Ross & Krogh, 1988). The developmental orientation at La Salle University specifically was selected to join special education and the preparation of classroom teachers (Feden & Clabaugh, 1986) from a developmental perspective.

Certainly, one option for a theme is the issue of diversity and human variance itself. This is the kind of theme that is implied in the proposed professional core suggested by Stainback and Stainback (1989). In adopting this concept as a unifier, many of the issues of concern to those now affiliated with special education are likely to be addressed. However, the goal of program unification is not to force the issue of which thematic approach is selected. Instead, it is to identify the most effective way of addressing issues related to how teachers deal with the complexities of a diverse student population in every teacher education program in a way that is consistent with the theme selected. Selecting a theme is not easy; it has to be narrow enough to be identified by faculty and identifiable by students, but broad enough to link the important aspects of teaching.

The Knowledge Base for Teaching

Defining and codifying a basic body of knowledge to undergird the preparation of teachers is one means of professionalizing teaching that has received much attention in current reform efforts. Not coincidentally, one of the NCATE standards requires evidence of a knowledge base (National Council for the Accreditation of Teacher Education, 1987). And despite conflicting positions on its role (Floden & Klinzing, 1990; Tom & Valli, 1990), initial attempts to compile a current knowledge base already exist (see Reynolds, 1990).

Many aspects of the identified knowledge base have important implications for equity in educating all students, including those with disabilities. For example, Cazden and Mehan (1989) address the critical effect of teacher expectations on children's learning and self-esteem. Anderson (1989) describes a cognitive-mediational point of view of learning and its implications for equity. When this knowledge base offers guidance for developing teachers who are inclusive of diversity, who are oriented to children's various developmental levels, and who are flexible in meeting student needs, the common interests of special educators and teacher educators can be met. However, it will be important to draw specific linkages between the concept, for example, of teacher expectations and students with enduring disabilities.

The notion of *explicit linkages* comes from recent work in cognitive psychology suggesting that how teachers link main ideas influences how students subsequently construct knowledge in that domain (Anderson, 1989). However, the need for explicit linkages has not traditionally been thought of as applying to the education of teachers. Agreements on what to make explicit, on how to offer particular explanations to preservice students, on what contexts and examples to utilize, all have the power to contribute to raised expectations and consciousness regarding what it means to teach inclusively.

As we consider unifying the preparation of special and general education teachers, making such explicit linkages is a necessary dynamic during the transition. Because special education exists as a structural part of schools, it will not be possible to teach a generalization (e.g., "literacy needs of children can be met with a social constructivistic approach") without showing how and why that works for students who currently are labeled as having a mild disability. If, for example, one talks about raising self-esteem but fails to provide examples involving the most discrepant cases of learners, prospective teachers who never before have encountered pupils with serious self-esteem problems may not make the necessary linkages to help them. These linkages are not likely to happen without care being taken to make them visible to teacher education students. They should serve to stimulate preservice students to stretch the applications of concepts to the most discrepant cases they might expect to find in any given class. Without the presence of special educators to make these linkages during the initial stages of unification, they may not occur.

Developing a professional core will require self-knowledge and understanding on the part of all involved regarding what each believes to be essential to their view of knowledge for teaching. For example, preparation of special education teachers traditionally includes an emphasis on individual difference and adaptation, but is generally less attentive to the content of the academic curriculum. Thus, as discussions of unification take place, the central role of curriculum content may not be adequately appreciated by special educators. Particularly in light of the renewed place of subject matter considerations in teaching (McDiarmid, Ball, & Anderson, 1989; Schulman, 1986), it is crucial for special educators to understand the importance of subject-specific pedagogy as reform moves forward. Alternatively, the emphasis on the teacher as researcher that special education has promoted through practices such as curriculum-based measurement may not be appreciated by general teacher educators as a jumping off point for a much broader interpretation of the teacher as researcher in general teacher education. Such mutual appreciations must be accompanied by an equally mutual willingness—as a result of joint deliberation and an expanded knowledge on the part of all those who prepare teachers—to discard what does not seem to make sense as programs are integrated.

How Teachers Learn to Teach

However, it is certainly not enough to articulate the kind of knowledge base on which a curriculum will be based. The recent and rich research literature on how teachers learn to teach provides invaluable direction for developing effective integrated programs of teacher education (see, for example, Carter, 1990; Hollingsworth, 1989). Such programs should be attentive to preservice students' initial conceptions of teaching, how those conceptions change over time, how novices move toward the kind of complex cognitive structures that characterize expert teachers, how reflection strengthens the teaching act, and so on. The personalistic side of becoming a teacher (Connelly & Clandinin, 1988) is now a viable consideration in teacher education.

Another aspect of the literature on learning to teach involves how teachers use research-based knowledge. As teacher educators work toward building programmatic consensus, different epistemologies may have to be confronted. In the main, special education appears to have subscribed to a relatively scientific view of knowledge for teaching, favoring its direct application to practice. However, competing epistemologies suggest, for example, that research-based knowledge may play a different role, one against which teachers can judge the reasonableness of their actions or with which teachers can be stimulated to attempt new ways of engaging in practice (Fenstermacher, 1986). This epistemological orientation necessitates that teacher education programs be centrally involved in helping novices identify the personal meanings they ascribe to their teaching and classroom, since how teachers will choose to utilize knowledge will depend on their perceptions of those phenomena (Doyle, 1990). This epistemological approach also intersects with the concept of consciously preparing teachers to be reflective practitioners (Clift, Houston, & Pugach, 1990; Schon, 1983) who make deliberate, thoughtful, professional decisions based not on prescription, but certainly tempered by current knowledge. Thus, part of the process of unifying teacher education and special education may entail lengthy discussions and/or arguments to reconcile disparate epistemologies. In sum, developing unified teacher education programs necessitates coming to agreement on what teachers do with research-based knowledge when they teach. As Tom and Valli (1990) remind us, "to have a knowledge base (or bases) for professional education means to have not only knowledge but also insight into how this knowledge is properly related to practice" (p. 389).

Research on learning to teach has much to offer those who have traditionally been aligned with the preparation of special education teachers and in fact represents a body of knowledge that is largely untapped among teacher educators in special education. Its absence in special education prompted the Teacher Education Division of the Council for Exceptional Children to launch an ongoing initiative called the TED Forum to bring current knowledge of research in teacher education to the forefront of its activities (Teacher Education Division, 1990). Research on general teacher education will provide important direction for those who have been more exclusively involved with the preparation of special education teachers.

Field Experience: Linking Study and Practice

What field experiences would best facilitate preparing teachers to work with diverse learners, among them children with disabilities, and where would those experiences best be located? In unified programs of teacher education, field experiences would not be constructed in the traditional mode of dual certification with students working both in special education and general education classrooms (which is the model adopted in the program at La Salle University—see Feden & Clabaugh, 1986). Instead, field experiences for initial certification would take place in multiple classrooms that are inclusive and representative of the range of students one could expect to teach. Ideally they would occur in professional development schools (see Levine, 1992) that are moving toward best practice, collegiality among professionals, and shared study of teaching—schools that would naturally house students with the full range of abilities and disabilities. Further, field experiences would have to be structured to provide regular and consistent opportunities for reflection, since experience alone will not be enough to clarify the knowledge and meanings to be derived from practice (Feiman-Nemser & Buchmann, 1985).

Probably the major issue in field experience is how to assure that prospective teachers gain skills in organizing and sustaining purposeful activity for whole classes as well as the flexibility to adjust for the range of needs that might be encountered in any class. This goal will of necessity be eased by grounding the entire teacher education program in a philosophy of teaching and learning that maximizes learning and more easily permits for the variation required in inclusive schools.

Once basic routines have been mastered and students are no longer consumed with anxiety about whether or not they can successfully manage and instruct large groups in the classroom setting, other forms of clinical experience need to be constructed to focus specifically on the issue of accommodating diversity. This is not to suggest that discussing how to meet the needs of individual students be delayed, but rather refers to the fact that teacher education students are often very concerned with survival issues early on in the field and simply need to get through this stage before they may be able to free up cognitive space for the more challenging task of considering and providing quality instruction within the group context (Hollingsworth, 1989). As they become proficient in the routines associated with guiding the group through activities, cognitive energy can begin to be focused on progressively more complex matters of teaching (Leinhardt & Greeno, 1986).

These subsequent field experiences should focus first on the teachers' responsibility for dealing flexibly with the needs of their students. Along with assuring teachers' instructional competence in a set of child-centered methodologies and structures, among which should be included strategic, learner-centered instruction (Anderson, 1989; Wang & Palincsar, 1989), cooperative approaches to grouping (Cohen, 1986; Slavin, 1983), and flexible grouping (Mason & Good, 1993; Pugach & Wesson, 1995), experiences must be structured so that novice teachers explicitly consider how their conception of their role affects each student.

For example, an experience might be structured specifically around students who appear to be having difficulty in the classroom, requiring the teacher to practice creating and implementing alternative approaches. Prospective teachers could engage in action research projects in which such alternatives are designed and implemented. Pupils who are the focus of such projects might have instructional difficulties or might require specific adaptations due to a physical, visual, or hearing disability. Ideally, projects with a range of individual students would be carried out. This type of experience was utilized in the specialized instruction program at the University of Illinois (Blankenship,

1983); however, the methodology of that program was limited to a behavioral paradigm.

A focused field experience should also address how teachers foster a sense of community among children. How teachers accommodate social difference and how they lessen the distances between children must be a focus of their work, not only as it relates to the use of cooperative grouping techniques, but in all aspects of their work. Finally, as teacher education reform progresses, some programs may institute yearlong internships. Given this approach, mentors working with intern teachers should structure similar projects as the year progresses to ensure that as the intern acquires the habits of teaching, one of those habits is attending to each student.

The twin issues of flexibility in instructional adaptation and community are of course part and parcel of all classroom experiences. However, including them consciously as teaching goals allows prospective teachers to gain confidence in creating a cohesive group within which the needs of individuals can be met. If these issues are not made prominent, novices may be less likely to make the connections between their formal study and the practical challenges of working with children in groups. In other words, attending to individual needs cannot be left to chance, and it is not enough to talk about the importance of making adaptations and being flexible in the classroom. Specific practice in these aspects of teaching is required, but not in a separate special education classroom.

Finally, prospective teachers need experience working collaboratively with other adults in the school to begin to understand the importance of these relationships. Whether they are to be engaged in formal team teaching, in intermittent co-teaching, or in professional development activities, the value of good adult–adult relationships is something that will be required of all future teachers. Although reservations have often been raised regarding the capacity of novice teachers to engage in such collaborative work, if the norm of the school supports this kind of interaction, new teachers can at least get a sense of what it means to work as part of a team.

BEYOND UNIFIED PREPARATION: SPECIALISTS IN THE SCHOOLS

Suggestions for unifying teacher education would not be complete without at least some reference to how various specialists might be prepared. Any discussion of specialization should be predicated on the assumption that in the future the field of teaching is likely to be organized differently than it is today. In general, then, future structures for specialization will also look far different from those we currently know. The question on the minds of special education teachers and teacher educators is whether or not there will be specialists in the future.

Some specific proposals exist for how specializations that currently function within special education might be conceptualized in the future. Elsewhere it has been suggested that all teaching specializations would invariably follow preparation for and experience in classroom teaching (Lilly, 1989; Pugach & Lilly, 1984). Jenkins, Pious, and Jewell (1990) suggest conservatively that special classes will continue to be needed for students with more severe behavioral disorders and for those with severe and profound disabilities. However, they do not specifically describe what preparation those teachers would have. They categorically assert:

> It would not be fair to regular classroom teachers (or their students) to hold them responsible for teaching all possible skills, for example, basic discriminations, mobility, self-care, community living, sign language, speech reading, and Braille reading. Students requiring these services would be placed in special classes. (p. 485)

In contrast, other proposals call for staff with these same skills, as well as a few others, to become part of the regular education curriculum and to be available to all students by teaming with classroom teachers; specializations would parallel specializations in, for example, mathematics or reading (Stainback & Stainback, 1989). Additionally, Stainback and Stainback (1989) promote the role of a specialist in "support facilitation," a specialized teacher whose role is to support the development of student-to-student and teacher-to-teacher networks.

If we accept differentiated staffing in the schools, it is important to consider the levels at which these various specialists might be prepared. For specific support services for students with physical or sensory disabilities or who have severe/profound disabilities, it is clear that specialists will always be needed, even if only for a small population of students. It is unlikely that teachers who now provide services like braille reading or positioning can simply be shifted into regular education and it is also unrealistic to suggest that their specializations become a routine part of the regular curricular offerings.

The picture may be different, however, in relation to competitive and supportive employment. These are areas that affect a substantial number of students in the schools, and the reform of vocational education and its integration with the academic curriculum is fast becoming a national priority with the advent of school-to-work projects (for example, U.S. Department of Labor, 1991). This would indicate that the preparation of teachers who focus on employment would necessarily span students with and without disabilities as a truly integrated effort. This is also an area in which special education may be able to offer much guidance given its long experience with transition programming. Further, in the future this might also represent a new type of position, one which is perhaps based in the business community rather than in the schools. Again, the relationship of this position to serving students with disabilities will have to be an explicit part of teacher preparation.

Perhaps the biggest dilemma facing teacher educators in unified programs of special and general education is how to conceptualize specialists in relationship to the large group of children who are not achieving, who are under the general category of being "at risk for school failure" or having a mild disability. For these children, whatever teaching specialization we have had in the past (for example, Chapter I remedial teachers or special education resource teachers) clearly are not viable options if their jobs continue to be defined in the same separatist way. Conversely, given the degree of diversity teachers are encountering and the demands of new approaches to curriculum and instruction, it is clear that more than a single teacher will be needed to enact teaching in such a way that student achievement can best be supported. Generalists, and plenty of them, will be needed who are comfortable working with other adults and pushing the definition of what it means to teach a diverse group of students. The central professional will be the classroom teacher, and it is groups of classroom teachers that will form the networks needed to support teacher growth and development. Given such a professional norm in schools (see, for example, Rosenholtz, 1989), teachers at a particular building will have to figure out how to utilize their resources to meet the needs of all students responsibly; this includes students with disabilities. As the basic professionals in a school building, teachers are in the best position to determine, through collegial dialogue and a thorough analysis of the population they serve, what types of special services their students may need. Further, as teacher networking and collegial interaction become regular goals for teacher education, the capacity for linking services, specialists, and resources ought to increase.

On the other hand, specialists that have been missing from the equation are teachers who can provide intensive support based on the most credible approaches to instruction possible. A good example is teachers who provide intensive interventions with programs like Reading Recovery (Pinnell, 1989), who are in reality "prevention specialists," teachers whose job it is to assure students of a sound start in literacy education. This represents a completely new concept of what it means to be a specialist, particularly because the motivation is derived from a proactive position of reducing the likelihood of failure, and not from protecting those who have already failed. On the other hand, the underlying philosophy of Reading Recovery would benefit all teachers who applied its principles in literacy teaching. "Specialists" may in fact be well-trained generalists who rotate in and out of a program like Reading Recovery.

Thus, while some specific suggestions for reconceptualizing specializations exist, there certainly is not consensus regarding their form or function. The traditional position of Jenkins et al. (1990) and the alternative conceptualization of specializations to support full inclusion as suggested by Stainback and Stainback (1989) are rooted in a concern for providing services for children and youth with more enduring disabilities. Different specializations are also likely to be needed that support the preventive model so prominent in the minds of many special educators.

Even as concepts of teaching specializations are redesigned, overspecialization in teaching has clearly taken its toll in the schools, and nowhere is this problem as prominent as it is in the field of mild disabilities. As we work toward creating schools in which classroom teachers themselves are intimately involved in the prevention of unnecessary learning problems and are also at the center of a collegial process of teaching, great care needs to be taken in protecting that degree of professionalism among general classroom teachers.

THE CHALLENGE OF REFORM

This chapter should not be misinterpreted simply as arguing for merging departments of special education and teacher education. Departments might be collapsed but no real renegotiation of philosophies might take place. Instead, its purpose is to argue that a completely new conception of teacher education is needed to meet the educational challenges of the coming years, a conception that is anchored in completely new ways of preparing teachers. That teacher education will undergo reform is inevitable (Lilly, 1989). Whether or not those in special education will participate in defining what this new conception will look like will depend on their making the effort to "integrate themselves" (Stainback & Stainback, 1989) into the work of teacher education reform. In many places initial dialogues focused on greater integration in teacher education have already begun. Whether such fledgling efforts will be successful will depend on the degree to which consensus is reached on a basic philosophical framework within which to conduct teacher education.

Teacher education is poised on the brink of major change, change that will build the professionalism of all teachers. The drive for increased professionalism, along with increased knowledge about teaching and learning—as well as knowledge about learning to teach—can finally combine to produce beginning teachers who are ready to accept the challenges of today's schools. What will be most difficult in achieving these changes is not, then, identifying the knowledge to guide the content of this process of reform. Instead, the challenge lies in encouraging change among professionals who heretofore have not necessarily been forced to rethink their work and their philosophies as colleagues in higher education. The current cli-

mate of reform provides an unprecedented opportunity for teacher educators to look carefully and critically at their own work and to engage in collaborative professional self-renewal as a result. This state of affairs should be welcomed.

It would be tragic if this opportunity were squandered because faculty members cannot find ways to come together. If the needs of children and youth are kept at the forefront of the dialogue, the common ground that is needed to redesign teacher education will be forthcoming and change will follow. We really have no choice. The children and youth of this country require teachers who can meet their needs on a daily basis with confidence and skill. Teacher education faculty have a responsibility to work in unison to prepare those teachers—at the highest level of professionalism possible.

REFERENCES

Anderson, L. M. (1989). Classroom instruction. In M. C. Reynolds (Ed.), *Knowledge base for the beginning teacher* (pp. 101–115). New York: Pergamon.

Barnes, H. L. (1987). The conceptual basis for thematic teacher education programs. *Journal of Teacher Education, 38*(4), 13–18.

Blankenship, C. S. (1983). *Specialized instruction program.* Unpublished manuscript. Champaign, IL: Department of Special Education, University of Illinois.

Carnegie Forum on Education and the Economy. (1986). *A nation prepared: Teachers for the 21st century.* New York: Carnegie Corporation.

Carter, K. (1990). Teachers' knowledge and learning to teach. In W. R. Houston (Ed.), *Handbook for research on teacher education* (pp. 291–310). New York: Macmillan.

Cazden, C. B., & Mehan, H. (1989). Principles from sociology and anthropology: Context, code, classroom, and culture. In M. C. Reynolds (Ed.), *Knowledge base for the beginning teacher* (pp. 47–57). New York: Pergamon.

Clift, R. T., Houston, W. R., & Pugach, M. C. (Eds.). (1990). *Encouraging reflective practice in education: An analysis of issues and programs.* New York: Teachers College Press.

Cohen, E. G. (1986). *Designing groupwork: Strategies for the heterogeneous classroom.* New York: Teachers College Press.

Connelly, F. M., & Clandinin, D. J. (1988). *Teachers as curriculum planners: Narratives of experience.* New York: Teachers College Press.

Doyle, W. (1990). Themes in teacher education research. In W. R. Houston (Ed.), *Handbook for research on teacher education* (pp. 3–24). New York: Macmillan.

Feden, P. D., & Clabaugh, G. K. (1986). The "New Breed" educator: A rationale and program for combining elementary and special education teacher preparation. *Teacher Education and Special Education, 9*(4), 180–189.

Feiman-Nemser, S. (1990). Teacher preparation: Structural and conceptual alternatives. In W. R. Houston (Ed.), *Handbook for research on teacher education* (pp. 212–233). New York: Macmillan.

Feiman-Nemser, S., & Buchmann, M. (1985). Pitfalls of experience in teacher preparation. *Teachers College Record, 87*(1), 53–65.

Fenstermacher, G. D. (1986). Philosophy of research on teaching: Three aspects. In M. C. Wittrock (Ed.), *Handbook for research on teaching* (3rd ed., pp. 37–49). New York: Macmillan.

Floden, R. E., & Klinzing, J. G. (1990). What can research on teacher thinking contribute to teacher preparation? A second opinion. *Educational Researcher, 19*(4), 15–20.

Goodlad, J. (1986). Foreword. In E. Cohen, *Designing groupwork: Strategies for the heterogeneous classroom.* New York: Teachers College Press.

Hollingsworth, S. (1989). Prior beliefs and cognitive change in learning to teach. *American Educational Research Journal, 26*(2), 160–189.

Holmes Group. (1986). *Tomorrow's teachers: A report to the Holmes Group.* East Lansing, MI: Author.

Howey, K. R., & Zimpher, N. L. (1989). *Profiles of preservice teacher education: Inquiry into the nature of programs.* Albany, NY: State University of New York Press.

Jenkins, J. R., Pious, C. G., Jewell, M. (1990). Special education and the Regular Education Initiative: Basic assumptions. *Exceptional Children, 56*(6), 479–491.

Kennedy, M. (1990). Choosing a goal for professional education. In W. R. Houston (Ed.), *Handbook for research on teacher education* (pp. 813–825). New York: Macmillan.

Keogh, B. K. (1988). Improving services for problem learners: Rethinking and restructuring. *Journal of Learning Disabilities, 21*(1), 19–22.

Leinhardt, G., & Greeno, J. G. (1986). The cognitive skill of teaching. *Journal of Educational Psychology, 78*(2), 75–95.

Levine, M. (Ed.). (1992). *Professional practice schools: Linking teacher education and school reform.* New York: Teachers College Press.

Lilly, M. S. (1989). Teacher preparation. In D. K. Lipsky & A. Gartner (Eds.), *Beyond separate education: Quality education for all* (pp. 143–157). Baltimore: Paul H. Brookes.

Mason, D. A., & Good, T. L. (1993). Effects of two-group and whole-class teaching on regrouped elementary students' mathematical achievement. *American Education Research Journal, 30,* 328–360.

McDiarmid, G. W., Ball, D. L., & Anderson, C. W. (1989). In M. C. Reynolds (Ed.), *Knowledge base for the beginning teacher* (pp. 193–205). New York: Pergamon.

National Council for Accreditation of Teacher Education. (1987, December). *Standards, procedures, and policies for the accreditation of professional education units.* Washington, DC: Author.

National Support Systems Project. (1980, October). *The Dean's Grant Projects: A descriptive analysis and evaluation.* Minneapolis, MN: Author.

Pinnell, G. S. (1989). Reading Recovery: Helping at-risk children learn to read. *Elementary School Journal, 90*(2), 161–183.

Pugach, M. C. (1988). Special education as a constraint on teacher education reform. *Journal of Teacher Education, 39*(3), 52–59.

Pugach, M. C. (in press). On the failure of imagination in inclusive schooling. *The Journal of Special Education.*

Pugach, M. C., & Lilly, M. S. (1984). Reconceptualizing support services for classroom teachers: Implications for teacher education. *Journal of Teacher Education, 35*(5), 48–55.

Pugach, M. C., & Wesson, C. L. (1995). Teachers' and students' views of team teaching of general education and learning-disabled students in two fifth-grade classes. *Elementary School Journal, 95,* 279–295.

Reynolds, M. C. (Ed.). (1989). *Knowledge base for the beginning teacher.* New York: Pergamon.

Rosenholtz, S. (1989). *Teachers' workplace.* New York: Longman.

Ross, D. D., & Krogh, S. L. (1988, Winter). From paper to program: A story of elementary PROTEACH. *Peabody Journal of Education, 65*(2), 19–34.

Schon, D. A. (1983). *The reflective practitioner: How professionals think in action.* New York: Basic Books.

Schulman, L. S. (1986). Those who understand: Knowledge growth in teaching. *Educational Researcher, 15*(2), 4–14.

Slavin, R. (1983). *Cooperative learning.* New York: Longman.

Stainback, S., & Stainback, W. (1989). Facilitating merger through personnel preparation. In S. Stainback, W. Stainback, & M. Forest (Eds.), *Educating all students in the mainstream of regular education* (pp. 121–128). Baltimore: Paul H. Brookes.

Teacher Education Division. (1990, June). TED Forum. *TED Newsletter, 15*(2), 2.

Tom, A. B., & Valli, L. (1990). Professional knowledge for teachers. In W. R. Houston (Ed.), *Handbook for research on teacher education* (pp. 373–392). New York: Macmillan.

U.S. Department of Labor, Secretary's Commission on Achieving Necessary Skills. (1991). *What work re-*

quires of schools: A SCANS report for America 2000. Washington, DC.

Wang, M. C., & Palincsar, A. S. (1989). Teaching students to assume an active role in their learning. In M. C. Reynolds (Ed.), *Knowledge base for the beginning teacher* (pp. 71–84). New York: Pergamon.

Wesson, C. L., & Deno, S. L. (1989). An analysis of long-term instructional plans in reading for elementary resource room students. *Remedial and Special Education, 10*(1), 21–28.

Ysseldyke, J. E., O'Sullivan, P., Thurlow, M. L., & Christenson, S. L. (1989). Qualitative differences in reading and math instruction received by handicapped students. *Remedial and Special Education, 10*(1), 14–20.

CHAPTER 20

A Rationale for Departmentalization of Special Education

H. WILLIAM HELLER

INTRODUCTION

Before one can discuss the value of separate or merged departments of special and regular education, it is first critical to understand conceptually the organizational contexts within which departments exist. An organization, according to Daft (1986), is a group of people working together to achieve common goals. In an organization, top-level leaders set direction by defining the purpose of the organization, specifying the goals requisite to attaining that purpose, and outlining those strategies to be followed in achieving the delineated goals (Thompson and Strickland, 1984).

Organizations, whether institutions of higher education (IHEs), or schools, college, or departments of education (SCDEs), develop structures as a means of conducting tasks, maintaining accountability and communication, and establishing authority relationships, thereby enabling the work of the organization to be accomplished. Once in place, this structure defines the form and function of the organization's activities and interactive patterns relative to their operation. Structure, as so often depicted on organizational charts, shows how each of the various parts of the organization relate to each other to give it wholeness and unity.

The purpose of organizations and their structures is to delineate and coordinate the activities performed by persons that lead to goal attainment. The basic premise of any organization is that focused group activity can produce more than can persons working individually. The key to successful group effort, however, is coordination, which is the function of structure.

The requirements of structure are reasonably common across organizations whether they are IHEs or major corporations, because the desired outcome is to divide the available labor/expertise according to the tasks to be performed. In addition, structure must seek to engage and coordinate the various tasks to achieve a given objective, whether it is the awarding of degrees or the production of widgets. As the variety of tasks to be performed broadens, the degree of coordination required to facilitate the completion of tasks will increase proportionately. Every organization structures itself to assure an effective division of labor/expertise and a coordination of the tasks or activities undertaken by the organization (Mintzberg, 1983).

The concept of a division of labor/expertise is basic to the differentiation between regular and special education. SCDEs, like other organizational entities, employ persons with differing areas of expertise (specialties) who, collectively and to some extent individually, contribute to one or more of the SCDE's stated purposes. The bureaucratic model, which is the basic organizational model for higher education, relies heavily on the premise of a division of labor in which each position is filled by an expert (Weber, 1947).

According to Mintzberg (1979), there are several forms of bureaucracy, including one referred to as a professional bureaucracy, which represents, in this author's view, most SCDEs. Such a bureaucracy relies on the skills and knowledge of its professionals to function effectively (Hoy and Miskel, 1987). The professionals' expertise is varied and diverse, and consequently they are often given considerable control over their own work and activity. It is possible in a professional bureaucracy for individuals to become entrepreneurs as they pursue interests independently from their colleagues and associate more directly with an external constituency in their specialty area. Deci (1975) describes schools as places where teachers work alone in classrooms, are relatively unobserved by colleagues and superiors, and possess broad discretionary authority over their students. His description of the school setting is very analogous to that of the IHE, where professors have even greater autonomy with regard to schedule, course content, and grading. Professionals in IHEs and SCDEs, for the most part, tend to control themselves and do, to a great extent, develop their own work standards. As Hoy and Miskel (1987) note, "The standards of the professional bureaucracy originate largely from outside its structure, in self-governing associations to which individuals belong. These associations set general standards that are taught by the universities and used by all organizations of the professions" (p. 136). The use of national accreditation standards such as those promulgated by the National Council for Accreditation of Teacher Education (NCATE) and the specialty standards advocated by the Council for Exceptional Children (CEC) are examples of the external structural determinants referred to by Hoy and Miskel.

One clearly distinct characteristic of the professional bureaucracy is its decentralization of power. The power in most professional bureaucracies is vested with the professional at the basic levels of operation. Faculty governance is the rule in IHEs and professionals have not only a great deal to say about what they might do and how they might do it, but also what the organization itself can and might do, not to mention how the organization might do it. It therefore makes much more sense to think in terms of a personal strategy for

each professional in a professional bureaucracy than an integrated organizational strategy (Hoy and Miskel, 1987).

Given the divergency of expertise and the potential for individual autonomy within the professional bureaucracy, the coordination of activities becomes essential. Therefore, the implementation of a structural mechanism that focuses on the grouping of activities in some reasonable manner, on creating work groups of manageable size with common interests, and on establishing a system of reporting and accountability relationships among administrators is critical. Such a structural mechanism is departmentalization.

Departmentalization is the structural process that describes the manner in which divided activities are combined and all personnel are placed into work groups (Miles, 1980). Because the professional bureaucracy model tends to maximize the potential for individual autonomy, it is important that the IHE or SCDE find a way to keep specialized interests focused on the overall goal established for the organization. A maintenance of the stated purpose of the organization is the reason for departmentalization and not a diminution of the professional's autonomy. In a professional bureaucracy it is critical to maintain both if the individual and the organization are each to be maximally effective.

Types of Departments Used to Group Tasks

Moorhead and Griffin (1989) discuss five types of departments commonly used by business and industry as ways of grouping tasks to accomplish goals. The five groupings are by function, process, product, customer, and geography. Interestingly, each grouping can be applied to IHEs and SCDEs, although only three of the five really depict what characterizes most departments in academia.

Function.   Persons associate with peers involved in the same function. This can be as generic as teacher education or as specific as reading education. Functional departments tend to facilitate cooperation and communication among themselves but tend to limit their communications with other organizational groups.

Process.   Process is a structure quite similar to that of the function-oriented structure except that its focus is much more on a specialized activity or type of job performed. This is best typified by departments of counseling, administration, or reading, in which the type of job is reasonably focused. Process groupings facilitate specialization and expertise input among faculty who tend to focus themselves on a single program, which may or may not be related by them to the SCDE's primary purpose. The problem with the process structure, as with the function structure, is one of focus—narrow as opposed to broadly based.

Product.   A structure can be generic, such as the product being a teacher, or specific, such as a teacher of mathematics. The product department usually enhances communication and collaboration among professionals preparing the same type of individual; in fact, the more specific the product, the better the collaboration. Again, as with the process structure, there is a tendency for the professionals to become so engaged in their particular preparation that they fail to see possible applications from other departments to their activities.

Customer.   In the business world the customer grouping would be referred to as departmentalization by market; however, in education this would be more oriented to the educational needs of children. For example, the child with a specific learning impairment would be accommodated by a grouping that prepared persons to deal with this disability. The customer structure is designed to assure that differing needs are served by persons with specialized knowledge and strategies. An example of this structure would be a hospital in which nurses are grouped according to the type of illness they administer to because the differing maladies require different treatment and specialized knowledge (Leatt and Schneck, 1984).

The preceding structural forms for departments do have applicability to SCDEs; however, their application will generally be inclusive of several forms rather than merely one. Teacher education departments are most likely to combine process, product, and customer structural forms. These three forms permit and facilitate the application of specialized expertise to the maximum, a critical imperative for a department as a subunit in an SCDE.

The department as an organizational entity must have several characteristics because it is a unique entity, and it functions as a constellation of human effort. Not only must members of a department have reasonably common areas of expertise, but they must also share terminology, communication patterns, and certain instructional methodologies to be effective as a collective body. This is why merging any two groups within any organization, whether it is an SCDE or General Motors, is such a challenge. Form and structure is of little value if the elements of expertise, terminology, and communicative clarity are too diverse. The most successful administrators (deans/chairs/directors) are those who group their faculty in ways that enhance their commonalities and diminish their differences. As a consequence, departmentalization becomes a management strategy to accomplish commonality.

A quick review of the organizational charts of most SCDEs will confirm the preceding practice, and few will show teacher education as a single entity. Even when the unit is a department of education, it very often is subdivided into programs or various other subunits. Again, the goal is to maximize commonality and minimize differences. Teacher education, not unlike any other educational endeavor, is characterized by differentiation, a differentiation that demands differentiated staffing and programming.

Mergers resulting from a failure to understand the differentiations unique to education will seldom be successful or effective. In merging regular education and special education, the concepts of structure and differentiation must be recognized and addressed. If this does not occur, the end result will be a merged department in perpetual conflict within itself and between its members. The consequences of this result are obvious.

WHAT IS THE STATE OF DEPARTMENTALIZATION IN SPECIAL EDUCATION?

The author in 1989, in an effort to ascertain whether separate special education and regular education departments were the rule rather than the exception, conducted a random review of deans, chairs, and directors of schools, colleges, and departments of education (SCDEs) in 150 institutions of higher education (IHEs) who were members of the American Association of Colleges for Teacher Education (AACTE). The 1989 survey found that special education existed as an organizational entity in the majority of IHEs responding, a finding that based on current data apparently still stands.

As a means of determining the extent to which the 1989 survey results continued to reflect the status of special education within IHEs and their SCDEs, the author conducted a second survey of IHEs. A secondary purpose of this follow-up survey was to ascertain what, if any, impact the movement to promote inclusion was having on the organizational placement of special education within SCDEs. The 1994 survey contacted a random group of 125 deans, chairs, and directors of SCDEs in IHEs whose units held membership in AACTE and which were accredited by the National Council for the Accreditation of Teacher Education (NCATE). The institutions included in the random selection were also listed in the NCATE annual list of accredited programs as having special education programs.

The 1994 survey, like its predecessor in 1989, sought to assess the degree to which special education departments were listed as organizational entities, the major reasons for their departmental status, and whether these were related to factors associated with the merging of special education and regular education.

The response to the survey was quite good, with 101 of the 125 administrators surveyed responding for a return percentage of 81 percent. The institutions responding included comprehensive state institutions, some large, as well as some small producers of educational personnel, and both large and small private institutions, some with very small numbers of graduates. Again, all of the administrators surveyed were in nationally accredited SCDEs and therefore familiar and responsive to meeting the needs of students with exceptionalities. A further indication of the latter is the fact that all responding institutions had special education programs that met the specialty guideline review conducted by the Council for Exceptional Children (CEC). Clearly, the institutions responding to the survey provided a strong national cross section of special education programs in NCATE accredited SCDEs. Consequently, an analysis of their organizational placement serves to present a strong indication of the merits of special education as a separate entity. The current picture likely indicates or reflects a response to the pressures for merger and/or inclusion by forces both within and outside of special education.

Table 20.1 depicts how special education is administered in the SCDEs represented by the 101 respondents. As was reported in the 1989 survey, the majority of SCDEs continue to identify special education as a separate organizational entity. When not a department, the SCDEs identify special education as a program within a department,

TABLE 20.1 Is Special Education a Separate Organizational Entity?

Responses	
Yes	89
No	12
Type	
Department	72
Program	8
Other (center, institute, division)	

usually curriculum and instruction, and/or in an organizational constellation such as an institute or center. Often the latter include related programs such as rehabilitation, related services programs, and speech pathology programs. The frequency of such constellations increased slightly between the 1989 and 1994 surveys.

The identification of special education as an organizational entity seemed at least as strong, if not somewhat stronger, in 1994 than it was in 1989. However, there now appears to be a slight trend toward bringing together other related programs into an organizational entity for purposes of administration, identity, and compatibility This trend is consistent with the departmentalization theory of structure, where attention to product, process, and customer is paramount.

Table 20.2 indicates how many SCDEs previously administered special education as a sepa-

rate organizational entity and indicates that proportionately fewer changes occurred among the 1994 survey group than was true for the 1989 respondents. Table 20.2 presents only three of the 101 SCDEs responding as having changed their organizational structure to remove special education as a separate entity. In one of these cases, a department was renamed to encompass other specialty programs; however, special education remained the largest single program in the new department. The change was made to increase program compatibility as well as to decrease the number of departments within the SCDE surveyed. As in 1989, in those SCDEs in which special education never held a separate organizational identity, nothing changed. There appears to be a slight trend away from diminishing special education's separate status within existing SCDEs at this time.

Table 20.3 summarizes whether or not the deans, chairs, or directors of SCDEs felt that special education is best served by virtue of its organizational status as a separate entity. Of the deans, chairs, and directors responding, 72 percent thought it was best served as a separate entity (up from 5 percent in 1989); 19 percent disagreed with its holding status as a separate

TABLE 20.2   Where Special Education Is Not Now a Separate Entity, Has It Been a Separate Organizational Entity in the Past?

Yes	3
No	9

TABLE 20.3   Is Education Best Served as a Separate Entity? (Responses of Deans, Chairs, Directors)

Yes	73	
No	20	
Undecided	8	
Reasons	*"Yes" Response*	*"No" Response*
Organizational integrity	12	1
Visibility/identity	20	0
Program scope	26	0
Expertise/knowledge base	2	2
State certification	0	0
Federal funding	2	1
Budget/cost	1	9
Size	10	5
Model 4 schools	0	0
Integration w/regular	0	2

entity (down from 32 percent in 1989); and another approximately 8 percent were not certain.

The fact that a greater percentage of deans, chairs, and directors surveyed in 1994 supported special education as a separate organizational entity than was the case in 1989 is even more interesting, given the nature of efforts by many to facilitate inclusion in special education. One might speculate that the deans, chairs, and directors in NCATE accredited institutions were responding to the visibility special education programs receive as a specialty program *or* rejecting as administratively inappropriate the elimination of special education as a separate and identifiable organizational unit. Since the 1989 survey included both NCATE accredited and non-accredited institutions this phenomenon could also account for some of the difference between the responses of the deans, chairs, and directors of SCDEs in 1989 and 1994.

Table 20.3 groups the personal views of those surveyed regarding why they felt special education is best served as a separate organizational entity. First and foremost, they mentioned the scope of the program as a primary reason for organizational separation. Special education has grown across the years and with such growth has come increased scope in programming dimensions, ranging from birth through adulthood. Administrators see departmentalization as a means of accommodating this scope. Fragmentation (placing parts of programs with other entities) is often not feasible or effective because most SCDEs are somewhat more restrictive in scope and focused primarily on school-age populations.

While the concept of identity was not quite as strong in 1994 as in 1989, nonetheless it was the second highest reason given for separate status. This again supports the continued need for individuals in organizations to identify with persons of equal interest, expertise, and common purpose. Administrative interests, which often are not highly related to human factors, are not viewed by deans, chairs, and directors as strong enough to offset the need for special educators to identify with each other in a working situation. Schacter

(1959) in his text *The Psychology of Affiliation* indicates that identity is a need of most individuals. When one loses his or her sense of belonging to a group, positive morale lessens, and effectiveness, both individually and as a group, diminishes.

A further outcome of separation is an elevation of status within the administrative hierarchy. It is clear that any group that does not have access to top administration must rely on others to communicate its needs. For example, in a departmentalized college, the chair has direct contact with the dean and if that chair is of the same discipline as the group he or she represents, all is fine. However, when the chair is of the majority discipline in a department, the minority discipline must still rely on the chair to communicate its needs accurately. If one is a special educator housed in a regular education department, he or she as a minority discipline may well feel unrepresented. Departmentalization permits a rise in the administrative hierarchy and concomitantly, a stronger degree of representation at the higher levels.

One of the surprises in the analysis of the 1994 survey was the number of respondents referring to the "scope" of the special education program as a reason for administrative separation. Thirty-seven respondents noted this as a justification and indeed there is a strong reason for their doing so. Special education training programs exceed the usual parameters of the public school years in terms of the personnel they prepare. Early in its development, special education involved itself in preschool programs for children with disabilities, and likewise it has a long history of involvement with adults who reside in specialized institutions, served by organizations such as the American Foundation for the Blind and highly specialized institutions such as Gallaudet College for the deaf. Special education is definitely concerned with providing an array of services from birth to death for persons with disabilities. In this sense, the merger of special education into a regular education department could actually inhibit rather than facilitate its total programming initiatives. Any proposed merger of special education must consider the element of scope and relate it to the mission of a given department or entity in terms of the population served. If the primary mission of a regular education department is to serve grades K–12, or even if its parameters encompass pre-K and K–12 (as is most often the case), merging special education into it would not be in the best interest of special education, regular education, or the SCDE.

The concept of organizational integrity did arise as the third highest reason by the deans, chairs, and directors for separating special education as an entity within SCDEs. This perhaps accounts for the trend that is occurring to bring all related programs serving persons with disabilities, such as rehabilitation, speech and hearing, adaptive physical education, and so forth, into one organizational context. Again, when one considers that these programs may have been fragmented throughout an SCDE or university, the concept of organizational integrity makes sense. Also, it is highly related to the concept of scope since many of these related programs serve persons beyond the usual parameters of a school-age population.

One management phenomenon clearly evident in the comments related to the separation of special education from other organizational entities, was the element of size. When programs become too large, whether in the numbers of faculty or enrolled students, the scope of the program offerings, research and federal contracts, or diversity of expertise, the tendency of administrators is to departmentalize or form a new entity. This administrative strategy has value in that it may bring new university or college resources to an SCDE, may alleviate a growing-pains problem in another organizational entity, or may serve to give identity and reward to a program within the SCDE that is growing. Any program increasing in size will serve to upset the equilibrium of most host units; therefore, it is often incumbent upon an administrator to consider reorganization as a solution.

Size, or course, can also be associated with being too small. A number of respondents citing size as a reason for not making special education a separate department or entity viewed it as being too small to warrant such an organization designa-

tion. In this case, size certainly has to be considered by an administrator as a matter of both efficiency and management strategy. All of the reasons for making a growing program distinct are also reasons not to make a small program a separate entity. What must be considered is a reasonable retention of both identity and affiliation regardless of the steps taken.

Merging due to size is not a programmatic decision; rather, it is an administrative decision. There have been a number of instances in which the small size of a special education program has resulted in its movement into a larger organizational unit for strictly administrative purposes. Care must be taken not to confuse this action with integration from a program perspective because, while the latter may occur, it is clearly a by-product, not a guaranteed outcome.

Table 20.4 features opinions regarding the possibility of additional departmentalization of special education in those institutions in which it is not now an entity. Given that 88 percent of the deans reporting already noted it as a separate entity, the probability of greater growth is limited. Further, most of those indicating that no department of special education is likely to be created were persons from the smaller IHEs in which the largest administrative unit was itself a department. Size may well have been the determining factor in generating these responses.

Another interesting outcome of the analysis of the 1994 survey, which supports the contention that special education is best served as a department, was the lack of a strong focus on integrating special education with regular education. There is some reason to believe from this that special education can be programmatically supportive and

TABLE 20.4   If Special Education Is Not Now a Separate Entity, Are Plans Underway to Create Such an Entity?

Yes	4
No	5
Possibly	3

collaborative as a separate organizational entity without being physically integrated into a regular education department.

WHAT ABOUT THE ADMINISTRATIVE STATUS OF SPECIAL EDUCATION?

Based on the 1994 survey results, it is clear that special education is more often than not an organizational entity with its own identity. Further, it exists as a separate entity because of the need for identity (affiliation), program scope, and size. Even though there has been a very slight decrease in the number of separate organizational structures for special education in the past ten years, as determined from the 1989 and 1994 surveys, there does not appear to be a clear trend in that direction. In addition, the respondents indicated that there is a distinct tendency to administratively house special education with other specialized groups. Administrative attention to special education as a separate entity appears to be strong among current deans, chairs, and directors. Although some of these administrators do not feel that special education is best served as a separate entity, their appraisal of whether separation is right or not is often based on the context in which special education is housed. For example, locating a program in a department of elementary and secondary education may not serve the needs of special education well at all. Thus, to be a separate entity in that context may have limited value if that separation mitigates against the principles of sound structure for units or programs in a professional bureaucracy.

SHOULD SPECIAL EDUCATION DEPARTMENTS BE SEPARATE?

Schools, colleges, and departments of education (SCDEs) have a primary responsibility to prepare the best persons possible to practice as professionals in U.S. schools. The organization of SCDEs should facilitate this by organizing to maximize the effect of expertise and to diminish dissipation of the latter as a result of barriers to effective collaboration and cooperation. Collaboration can occur between faculty within and/or outside of

TABLE 20.5   Where Are Special Education Programs Located if Not Identified as a Separate Organizational Entity?

Curriculum and Instruction	6
Elementary Education	3
Educational Psychology	1
Specialized Programs	2

departmental configurations. In actuality, there is reason to believe that collaboration, where it does occur, will have considerably more effect when it transpires between individuals from differing administrative units.

Table 20.5 indicates that in those institutions in which special education was not a separate administrative entity, it was most often incorporated into a curriculum and instruction department. In a few instances it was combined with other specialized programs, such as speech and hearing, counseling, and rehabilitation. A number of the respondents indicated that one of the best ways to facilitate collaboration between regular and special education is through an institute or center construct. Although they may exist outside of departments, they do offer an opportunity for a variety of professional disciplines to come together for a joint purpose. Judging from an analysis of organizational structures in some of the institutions, the center construct seems to be a possible strategy to encourage and achieve collaboration in highly departmentalized colleges of education. This may well be a constructive way to offset some of the concerns resulting from the organizational separation of special and regular education programs.

Persons who seek mergers of special education and regular education should pay close attention to a statement made by a departmental chair in a survey conducted by McCarty and Reyes (1987).

> A department is unique. It's somewhat like a family. I don't want to be corny about this, but a department has common goals, a common purpose. The department is where it is at as far as faculty, governance is concerned. That's where the bond is. (p. 5)

A special education department, like a regular education department, can have a uniqueness, it can be like a family, it can have common goals and purposes, and certainly it can be where the real bond is. The fallacies too often generated by persons not familiar with administration include: (1) fewer departments are better than more, (2) specialists will sublimate their specialties to become part of a generic group, and (3) grouping diverse people together in one unit will ultimately lead to their assimilation as a whole. There are a number of former deans, chairs, and directors in SCDEs today who operated on the premise that these fallacies were in fact truths.

Special education can be a partner in the process of preparing teachers without being in a department with elementary or secondary education. Likewise, elementary and secondary education can have a major influence on the preparation of personnel to teach children with special needs without being included in a department with special education. Departments are not mutually exclusive structures designed to keep colleagues out; instead, they are structures designed to maximize the expertise and common interests of a particular group in a particular problem, population, or goal. Although their major interests may be inward, members of most departments also look outside for direction, critique, and support. All departments are influenced by external constituencies, and no department in an SCDE can long operate in a vacuum or in isolation from its colleagues' departments, because interdependence is critical to teacher education. The SCDE must blend the expertise of its diverse faculty through a range of interactions and experiences to be successful, and departmentalization is a way to promote the blend.

But blending occurs in many ways; among them: (1) curriculum and other SCDE committees, (2) team teaching, (3) collaborative research, (4) joint presentations and publications, (5) joint advising of students, and (6) informal and social interactions. No one has to be in a department; he or she can also experience these blends as an individual working within a group context. However, a department will facilitate its occurrence and mitigate the "loner" syndrome.

There is a tendency among persons unfamiliar with administration to assume that one of the ways to achieve reform of various kinds is to orchestrate it through organizational change or mandate. The assumption that the placement of groups together will cause groups to work together is fraught with considerable error and a lack of understanding regarding organizational behavior. Furthermore, there is a basic assumption that combination rather than division is a preferable strategy when, in practice, differentiation is more likely the norm. A good example of the need for departmentalization for persons in education would be the old federal department of Health, Education, and Welfare (HEW). Education certainly shared common goals with its colleague agencies of Health and Welfare; however, its role in establishing what those goals would be was never very clear. Additionally, its share of allocated resources, visibility, impact, and other elements so critical to an organizational identity and sense of purpose were judged to be less than adequate by educators both within and outside of HEW. Moreover, the issue of priority within the larger unit often became a major concern to employees and administrators. Where a group falls in the organizational pecking order does make a difference, and whether its status is real or merely perceived, as it so often is, the results are consistently the same: low morale and a quest for greater identity or autonomy by those affected. It is also important to recognize that those who receive the services of a unit may also be affected by the structural assignment that unit itself has within a department. Those who can remember the arguments for granting departmental status for education in Washington in the late 1970s will also recall clearly that the field (public schools and higher education) thought its identity, its advocacy, and its funding needs were not being met by the HEW organizational structure. The educators in the nation's schools and IHEs considered themselves losers due to the lack of autonomy and identity given education in Washington.

The factor of separation to improve one's place in the administrative hierarchy was clearly an argument for a department of education at the federal level. When education was represented by the

Office of Education in HEW, its head, the commissioner, reported to the secretary of HEW. The commissioner was not a member of the president's cabinet, and therefore, not a regular around the White House table when it came to making budget and program decisions. When the Department of Education was formed in October 1979, its head was elevated to the secretary level; she became a member of the president's cabinet, and had direct access to the president.

As Harold Howe, a former U.S. commissioner of education from 1965 through 1968, noted in March 1980, "a cabinet-level department lends importance to the secretary's voice, which will influence the thinking of many persons about education's goals, practices, results, governance, and costs" (p. 446).

If one would review the arguments for the departmentalization of education at the federal level, he or she would very quickly find arguments analogous to those supporting the retention of special education and regular education as separate organizational entities. All of the arguments are there, not the least of which is a need by the field to have at the federal level a clearly identified group with which to affiliate. Professionals in special education likewise seek a similar identity and affiliations within SCDEs. Separate departments provide them that opportunity.

CONCLUSION

Special education is a specialization, as is elementary education, secondary education, and reading.

There is clear evidence that special education exists as a separate organizational entity in a majority of the schools, colleges, and departments of education in this nation's institutions of higher education. This is further corroborated by a national study conducted by Anderson, Heller, Algozzine, and Audette in 1989 of SCDE organizational structures, and repeated by Heller in 1994. Each national study found special education second only to health and physical education in terms of its frequency as a department. This frequency of occurrence suggests that there is strong support for special education as a separate and identifiable organizational entity. The separation is mirrored at the federal level, where there is an Office of Special Education and Rehabilitative Services, in state education agencies, and in the public schools. Although the frequency of the departmental designation may not in and of itself guarantee that the departmentalization of special education is advantageous, it does suggest that, from an administrative perspective, it has value.

Finally, the issue is not whether separate special education or regular education departments are advantageous. The question is, can they remain organizationally separate and still collaborate to assure that an SCDE attains its stated mission, goals, and objectives? The answer, based on the 1989 and 1994 surveys of deans, chairs, and directors of schools, colleges, and departments of education, is a resounding YES!

REFERENCES

Anderson, R. J., Heller, H. W., Algozzine, B., & Audette, R. H. (1989). *Administrative practices of deans of education in selected United States universities.* Manuscript submitted for publication.

Daft, R. (1986). *Organization theory and design.* St. Paul, MN: West.

Deci, E. L. (1975). *Intrinsic motivation.* New York: Plenum.

Heller, H. W. (1994). *A survey of organizational placement of special education programs within selected NCATE accredited teacher education colleges, departments, and divisions.* Manuscript submitted for publication.

Howe II, H. (1980). Two views of the new department of education and its first secretary. *Phi Delta Kappan, 61,* 446–447.

Hoy, W. K., & Miskel, C. G. (1987). *Educational administration: Theory, research, and practice.* New York: Random House.

Leatt, P., & Schneck, R. (1984). Criteria for grouping nurses in hospitals. *Academy of Management Review, 13,* 150–165.

McCarty, D. J., & Reyes, P. C. (1987). Organizational models of governance: Academic deans' decision making styles. *Journal of Teacher Education, 38,* 2–8.

Miles, R. H. (1980). *Macro organizational behavior.* Santa Monica, CA: Goodyear.

Mintzberg, H. (1979). *The structuring of organizations.* Englewood Cliffs, NJ: Prentice Hall.

Mintzberg, H. (1983). *Structure in fives.* Englewood Cliffs, NJ: Prentice Hall.

Moorhead, G., & Griffin, R. W. (1989). *Organizational behavior.* Boston: Houghton Mifflin.

Schacter, W. (1959). *The psychology of affiliation.* Stanford, CA: Stanford University Press.

Thompson, A., & Strickland, A. (1984). *Strategic management.* Plano, TX: Business Publications.

Weber, M. (1947). *The theory of social and economic organization.* New York: Free Press.

SECTION ELEVEN

ADULT SERVICES—HOUSING

In adult life, what kinds of housing accommodations do persons with disabilities need? In Chapter 21, Walsh, Rice, and Rosen challenge those who advocate for empowerment, choice, and support to remember that real choice means that people with disabilities should have available to them the choice of institutional living along with a wide range of other options. They visualize that during the postschool years persons with disabilities will live in a variety of different housing arrangements, one of which might be small responsive institutions. They believe it is paradoxical that those who have been most vocal in support of empowerment and personal choice have also been the most outspoken critics of maintaining institutions as a choice.

Taylor, Racino, and Walker present the perspective in Chapter 22 that there is a need for a phasing out of the continuum of services and an increased focus on integrated, ordinary work and living situations. They present the position that families should be empowered and supported to keep their children at home and that adults with disabilities should be supported to live in ordinary community housing. They state that people with disabilities should be supported to own their homes when desired, make choices about whom they live with, and create their own living environments reflective of their personal routines, values, and desired lifestyles.

CHAPTER 21

Options and Choices in Residential Service Delivery

KEVIN K. WALSH
DAVID M. RICE
MARVIN ROSEN

INTRODUCTION

The field of developmental disabilities began to change at midcentury from one based largely in institutions to a more broadly dispersed, community-based, and support-oriented system of services. The field now faces a new century with new concepts—replacing terms such as *habilitative treatment, custodial care,* and *programming* with terms such as *empowerment, choice,* and *support.* These changes have been described as a paradigm shift in services for people with developmental disabilities and have become emblematic of efforts to produce wholesale change in the structure of services to people with disabilities nationwide. This shift has found support in legislation, such as the passage of the Americans with Disabilities Act, and has been bolstered by key appointments of people with disabilities to leadership positions within, for example, the federal Administration on Developmental Disabilities (ADD) and the National Institute for Disability Research and Rehabilitation (NIDRR).

While empowerment implies informed personal choice, it also implies that the individual has both options and the control to make choices—of where to go to school, where and how to live, and where to work. In our eagerness to embrace these newer approaches, however, we may ultimately offer individuals little choice given the widespread emphasis on inclusion—it may be that the *only* option will be to live in the family home and

attend regular classes as a child, or to live in a home of your own as an adult and work in supported employment.

In this chapter we focus on one issue in this debate—the possible options for housing. Initially we trace some of the antecedents of the current situation and briefly examine the nature of the shift as it has unfolded during the past thirty years. We trace a number of the options as the field moves into the next century and, finally, we examine some of the problems that may arise and must not be overlooked.

SHIFTS IN EMPHASIS

The depopulation of many large institutional settings has been accomplished, although many remain. Decreases in the numbers of people in large residential facilities that began in the 1960s continue. Conversely, between 1977 and 1987, the number of persons served in facilities housing more than 300 residents decreased from 143,000 to 69,000. Between 1977 and 1988, the number of people in facilities housing six or fewer residents increased from 20,400 to 80,900 (Lakin, Prouty, White, Bruininks, & Hill, 1990; White, Lakin, & Bruininks, 1989). Thus, many institutions have closed; those that remain have drastically reduced numbers and have been revitalized to meet more stringent state and federal regulations and standards of compliance. This trend shows no sign of slowing down. For example, Lakin and his colleagues in numerous reports and publications over the years have tracked changes in the Medicaid Intermediate Care Facility for the Mentally Retarded (ICF/MR) system. They note that in the eleven years between 1960 and 1971, there were only three closures of large Mental Retardation/Developmental Disabilities (MR/DD) institutions nationwide, although in the thirteen-year period between 1980 and 1993 there were seventy-eight such closures with fifty-four of these occurring between 1988 and 1993. Furthermore, they report that twenty-six more such facilities are slated for closure between 1994 and 1996 (Mangan, Blake, Prouty, & Lakin, 1994).

The gains that have been made in affording persons with mental retardation a more normalized living experience should not be underestimated. Legislation, for example, the Americans with Disabilities Act (ADA) and the 1973 Rehabilitation Act as amended, especially Section 504, support a least restrictive environment. Forty years ago the treatment of choice for such persons, endorsed then by the American Association of Mental Deficiency, was institutionalization, shelter from outside influences, spartan settings with low per capita costs being an essential priority for operation, often cruel and dehumanizing conditions, and little hope of return to families or communities. Today there is demand, as perhaps never before, for individual dignity, basic human rights, and quality of life. Segregation of people with developmental disabilities is questioned and inclusion is widely promoted. Certain traditional activities such as classifying and labeling persons, grouping into homogeneous classrooms or work environments, and decision making deemed in the best interests of the person are now subject to criticism and sometimes markedly curtailed. Diagnostic processes and the very definition of mental retardation have been affected in the wake of efforts to maximize inclusion into normal living and work settings. Despite these gains, advocates for persons with developmental disabilities demand even greater degrees of inclusion along with

opportunities for personal choice and personal empowerment for those they represent.

Life in the Community: Fully Integrated?

Limited information exists regarding patterns of social contact between persons with mental retardation and people without disabilities in their local communities. There is also insufficient information about differences in social and leisure time activity among different types of residential facilities. In general, research indicates that persons in small group homes or foster home placements tend to have more contacts with persons without disabilities than those residing within institutions (Conroy & Bradley, 1985; Felice, De Kock, & Repp, 1986; Hill & Bruininks, 1981; Horner, Stoner, & Ferguson, 1988; O'Neil, Brown, Gordon, Schonborn, & Green, 1981). They also tend to participate more in community-based activities. However, individual differences exist both among the different types of residences and among the individuals themselves. While residents in smaller, community-based facilities are more likely to engage in community-based social and leisure time activities, the quality and breadth of these activities may be less than expected or desired (Baker, Seltzer, & Seltzer, 1974; Bjannes & Butler, 1974; Crapps, Langione, & Swaim, 1985; Hayden, Lakin, Hill, Bruininks, & Copher, 1992). People with more severe mental impairments tend to be less active participants in community functions than those with less severe impairments (Bell, Schoenrock, & Bensberg, 1981; Gollay, Freedman, Wyngaarden, & Kurtz, 1978; Hill, Rotegard, & Bruininks, 1984).

Recently Hayden et al. (1992) provided the first national examination of the lifestyles of persons with mental retardation living in foster homes, ICF/MR, or non-ICF/MR, group homes. A total of 9,930 of 10,144 eligible facilities were studied. Children and youth and persons sixty-three years and older were more likely to live in foster homes. Persons with severe or profound mental retardation were more likely to reside in ICF/MR group homes. While increasing numbers of persons are living in the community and participating socially, the majority of persons are still drawing friends from their immediate environments rather than from the community at large. Forty percent of the residents reported that they had no friends. Less than half of all residents were having regular social contact with people without disabilities other than staff or family in their leisure activities. The highest rates were among leisure activities that were generally passive, such as watching television or listening to the radio rather than visiting friends or attending meetings or sporting events. The study concludes that "social integration may require more than the simple physical integration that comes with living in a foster home or small group home . . . social integration needs to be addressed more proactively through staff training, public awareness activities, promotion of volunteer relationships, maintaining preexisting social networks, development of methods to increase or equalize the reciprocity in relationships between people with and without disabilities, and other demonstrably or potentially effective efforts" (pp. 196–197).

The Move to Support Models

At the time this chapter first appeared in a slightly different form (Rosen, Rice, Walsh, Hartman, & McCallion, 1991), there was overwhelming professional agreement that persons with developmental disabilities deserved the opportunity to live in the least restrictive and most normalizing environments possible. Small community-based group homes or other community living arrangements were seen as most advantageous while larger institutional settings were largely viewed as less supportive of typical lifestyles. Although numerous advocates were calling for deinstitutionalization and the subsequent closing of traditional institutional settings, there was not an overwhelming body of research documenting the effectiveness of community settings. Follow-up studies such as those by Conroy and Bradley showed increases in overall levels of adaptive behavior, but better controlled studies of institutionalized

persons moved to smaller group homes, such as the one by Landesman (1986) did not reveal overwhelming improvements. Landesman concluded that professionals must do a better job in identifying the functional aspects of optimal living environments required to substantially improve people's lives. Critics of wholesale deinstitutionalization (Crissey & Rosen, 1986; Walsh, 1992; Walsh & McCallion, 1987; Zigler, Hodapp, & Edison, 1990) have argued for a range of residential options to meet the varying needs of this population at different times of their lives. These authors have suggested that, in certain situations, modest and carefully planned congregate settings may still play a useful role for persons with certain specialized needs such as those with severe challenging behaviors, or people who are medically fragile. At the very least it seems reasonable to preserve what one of us has characterized as resource centers and networks as a means to provide unique functions that were usually centered in the institution in the past (Walsh, 1992).

The field continues to call for greater inclusion of persons with developmental disabilities into the mainstream of society. Integration into normal environments is seen by many in the field as a basic entitlement and not an option to be determined on the basis of empirical findings. The position is consistent with a recent reworking of the basic definition of and classification system for mental retardation by a committee of the American Association of Mental Retardation (Luckasson et al., 1992). The new conceptualization calls for a total shift in the way individuals are identified and classified as having mental retardation, and provides a new focus upon quality of life as the most critical criterion of successful outcome.

The new definition and classification system developed by AAMR represents a significant conceptual change. In this system, mental retardation is not conceived as an absolute trait expressed solely by the individual, but rather as an expression of the interaction of the individual and his or her environment. The individual's strengths and weaknesses are described in relation to four dimensions: (1) intellectual functioning and adaptive skills; (2) psychological and emotional well-being; (3) health, physical well-being, and etiology; and (4) life activity and environments. Exclusively person-centered categories are seen as insufficiently descriptive to fully characterize individuals with mental retardation. Rather than focusing solely upon the strengths and weaknesses of the individual taken in isolation, emphasis is placed upon normalized environments and the types of supports required within environments to optimize functioning. Critical to the approach is an analysis of the nature and extent of supports required to assist the individual in various environments. These supports may be in the form of personal changes to the individual, help from other people, technology, and services. They may involve teaching, befriending, financial planning, employee assistance, behavioral support, in-home living assistance, community and school access and use, and health assistance. If this system were used to evaluate the match between an individual and a particular community living situation, for example, the issue would be what type of supports will be needed to allow the individual to live there, not whether or not the person is capable of living in that situation. Needed resources might include personal maintenance services, homemaker services, home health aides, medical alert devices, and architectural modifications. It is assumed that most persons can live in a variety of environments and that with appropriate supports, their functional level will improve.

Supported living has been defined by Karan, Granfield, & Furey (1992) as "a process that creates opportunities for individuals with disabilities to choose where they live, with whom they live, and how they lead their lives" (p. 5). The tenet of this concept is that living decisions are to be based on the individual's informed choice. These authors elaborate as follows: "Supported living is not something that we as professionals do *for* people with disabilities (i.e., providing supervision), but rather it is something we do *with* them (i.e., support)" (p. 5). This includes ownership or rental of the property in which the individual resides, not

by the service provider, but by the individual him- or herself. This change requires a radical degree of reorienting of staff who work with people with developmental disabilities. Staff play critical and changing roles by serving people, not controlling them. No longer are paid staff the ones who implement programs or enforce consequences; rather, in support models they serve as friend, advocate, broker of services, or counselor.

Racino and Taylor (1993) expand this concept by distinguishing between "facility-based services" and "housing and support approaches." Facility-based residences are those that the agency owns, rents, and staffs, and which provide residential as well as programmatic services. This arrangement, the authors contend, does not adequately meet people's needs or desires. They tend to over- or undersupervise individuals since shift staffing geared toward a group is falsely equated with support. Even group homes, clustered apartments, or other community living arrangements fall into this category since they fail to allow for resident choice. A housing and support approach, on the other hand, provides three major advantages: individuals live within their own homes, personal assistance and other supports are provided depending upon preference and need, and residents shift from being in the community to being part of the community. With this approach, adults, regardless of their ability, have the opportunity to live in a home or apartment of their own in the community, with a choice of neighborhood, selection of housing, and selection of people with whom they live.

Whatever services are rendered must be acceptable to the individual receiving the services. Support providers must understand and respect the values of the individuals they serve. Proponents of this point of view are not oblivious to the difficulties inherent in such a radical change in thinking and philosophy (Smull & Smith, 1994). Yet there is little in the literature that addresses the manner in which those who cannot make informed decisions about where or how they would like to live are to be provided with supported living arrangements. Nor is there significant information regarding how successful the outcomes will be in terms of actual short- and long-term learning and skill development.

Quality of Life

An outgrowth of the philosophy stressing empowerment of and choices by persons with developmental disability has been a new focus upon quality of life (QOL). Quality of life has been studied in nondisabled populations and only recently has become of interest to those who work with people who have developmental disabilities, in recognition of the impact of social environments on an individual's way of life (Edgerton, 1975). Landesman (1986) challenged workers in the field to go beyond adaptive behavior, define the concept of QOL, learn how to measure it, and tease out the factors associated with a high QOL. A number of models and definitions have been offered, one of the broadest being that of Schalock, Keith, Hoffman, & Karan (1989) who view QOL as a criterion of the goodness-of-fit between individuals and their environments. Objective social indicators such as health, friendships, standard of living, education, and neighborhood, as well as psychological indicators, have been suggested as criteria of QOL. Psychological indications are usually defined in terms of personal satisfaction and happiness with a broad range of dimensions including physical and material well-being, relations with other people, social activities, and recreation. Schalock et al. (1989) have suggested that QOL will probably replace deinstitutionalization, normalization, and community adjustment as the issue of the 1990s. Indeed, both Schalock's (1990) and Goode's (1988) edited volumes usher in an era of rigorous research and conceptual development. Goode has argued that the ultimate criterion of QOL, uncontaminated by experimenter bias, is the subjective reaction of the consumer.

Various measures have been developed utilizing both objective and subjective indices. The Quality of Life Questionnaire, for example (Schalock et al., 1989), uses criteria of independence, productivity, and community adjustment for both objective and subjective measurement. Subjective measures have been developed by Cummins (1991), Ouelette-Kuntz (1990), Heal and Chadsey-Rusch (1985), and others. A subjective measure published by Rosen, Simon, and McKinsey (1994) incorporates the four dimensions of perceived stress, affect, loneliness (after Chadsey-Rusch), and satisfaction. Subjective measurement is fraught with problems and is not appropriate for nonverbal individuals. It is of paramount importance, however, in providing individuals with developmental disabilities the opportunity to relate their feelings and opinions concerning the state of their lives. Even for those who can respond reliably, the effort of measurement is meaningless unless the results are translated into effective interventions. Knoll (1990) has pointed out that quality assurance regulations have met their initial goal of providing minimal standards for safety, individual rights, and training but must now address the more difficult issue of what is "the good life." Nowhere is this more true than in the choice of residential settings. Empowerment implies informed choice but choice should be based on what will provide happiness and satisfaction to the person. Furthermore, choice implies that there are several attractive options from which to choose. Insistence upon ownership of residential settings, for example, may be an example of the imposition of standards not necessarily desired by persons with developmental disabilities, that is, a restriction of options, and thereby choice.

RESIDENTIAL OPTIONS

Two Family Stories

Although the names have been changed, these stories reflect real situations. The first, the Damicos, was adapted from a report in the files of the *Waiting List Watch,* a newsletter of the Arc of New Jersey. The Arc of New Jersey publishes information on the growing waiting list for residential services in the state, a list that currently stands at over 4,000 individuals, of whom over

1,000 are categorized as "Category I," needing immediate placement. The story of the second family, the Nunbergs, is drawn from public comments made by Mrs. Nunberg in a statewide planning consortium meeting held by the Department of Mental Retardation and Developmental Disability Services of a large mideastern state.

The Damicos

Teaneck, NJ—Eleanor Damico's sister Jenny Tuso, 34, has Down syndrome and limited use of her left arm, the result of a stroke a number of years ago. Until 1990 Jenny lived with her mother, Dorothy Tuso. When Dorothy unexpectedly passed away, Eleanor received a frantic call from another sister that their mother had been found dead on the kitchen floor. When she arrived, Jenny, who did not understand how to use the telephone or react in an emergency, was crying, upset that her mother would not get up from the floor. Eleanor and her husband Dennis took Jenny to their small home. Four years later, Jenny still sleeps in the front room, a converted porch, of the Damico home. Jenny was finally placed in Category I of the waiting list, which in New Jersey is defined as "Urgently in Need—individual is at risk of harm to self or others or is homeless." Jenny shares this category designation with over 1,000 other individuals, and has waited over four years for a residential placement.

The Nunbergs

Josh Nunberg is 18 and has multiple disabilities—he has both cerebral palsy and mental retardation. Josh cannot walk and uses a wheelchair to get around. Because of his motor and coordination problems, Josh is unable to independently carry out his own physical care or feed himself. In short Josh needs a great deal of physical assistance in all aspects of life. He is nonverbal and expresses his desires through gestures and certain vocal utterances. Regardless, Josh is a bright and happy boy who has lived at home with his parents, Alex and Ellen.

During his school years, Josh received a number of services through his school program. Although resources at home were limited, the Nunbergs managed to provide whatever Josh needed with infrequent respite services available from the state. As Josh has grown physically it has become necessary for the Nunbergs to seek more formal in-home supports including personal assistants to help in caring

for Josh. Finally, the Nunbergs decided to seek a place for Josh in a small, private institutional setting.

Mrs. Nunberg related her experiences to the planning group during a discussion on institutional versus community placement. She was careful to point out that she supported the idea of increased family supports, had wished she had had them with Josh. However, she noted that the intensity of support needed for her son had virtually "turned their home into an institution" and had given rise to stress in their family. At present, Josh is nearby in a safe and supportive environment. The Nunbergs visit regularly and have gotten involved in the parents and friends group of the facility. Josh visits home periodically for vacations and holidays. The Nunbergs relate that everyone appears happier for their decision.

The stories of both the Damicos and the Nunbergs are directly related to questions of public policy facing the field of developmental disabilities. In this section we explore some of the options available to people like Jenny and Josh and their families, and how they came to be.

Public Policy and Housing

Housing as a public policy issue involving people with mental retardation is not a new phenomenon—in fact formal housing policy in states, that is, the allocation of state funds, began in the mid-1800s (Scheerenberger, 1983). As we have noted, for most of the time since then, the *de facto* state housing policy for people with mental retardation and related disabilities has been almost exclusively one of institutional placement. States housed and provided care for people with mental retardation in large centralized public or private institutions. The institution provided not only housing to the individual, but supplied all other needs as well. In short, living in an institution meant living in a protected community, often for long periods of time, if not for life.

Largely in response to widespread abuses in institutions, advocacy efforts resulted in litigation and legislation. The field has shifted to its present position of community support models. It is noteworthy that in institutional models, services were only provided to people who lived in the facility. The earliest housing models (that is, institutions) "packaged" a comprehensive range of services. This meant that the only way an individual with a mental disability could receive services was to live in the institution. As we will see, the legacy of this connection of services to housing is still with us today—and, to some extent, represents a policy barrier to providing certain types of community-based support services. In fact, it is a basic public policy goal of many housing advocates to "unlock" services, or service dollars, from housing resources.

Federal Support

The connection between services and housing was reinforced by the funding of intermediate care facilities for the mentally retarded (ICF/MR) by the federal Health Care Financing Administration (HCVA) as part of the Medicaid Title XX entitlement beginning in the 1970s (see Jacobson, 1991). The ICF/MR program was the first major federal initiative to support housing and services throughout the country and was largely based in institutions. Although the program included provisions for supporting community-based services through special waivers, the initial result was to increase the number of individuals in institutions nationwide. For example, by 1977, which was the high point of the program, 99 percent of all ICF/MR funds supported placements in large facilities, accounting for more than 140,000 certified institutional beds including several thousand in private facilities (Braddock, Hemp, Bachelder, & Fujiura, 1994). In addition to providing federal dollars to support state facilities, the ICF/MR program created standardized services based on active treatment models that carried extensive bodies of physical and programmatic guidelines and standards. Critics have charged that these programs have become rigid, and have actually increased certain negative aspects of institutions (Holburn, 1990, 1992).

As states moved to community-based and support models they turned to housing in typical communities. For example, by 1992, the number of

ICF/MR certified institutional beds had declined to 77,712 (Braddock et al., 1994). Instead, states took advantage of the Medicaid Home and Community-Based Services (HCBS) waiver program to move the federal dollars from institutional placements to community living options. The result is that the number of ICF/MR facilities continues to grow; from June 30, 1977, to the same date in 1993, there was an increase from 574 to 7,611 ICF/MRs nationwide. However, their average size in 1993 was 19.4 residents compared to 186 residents in 1977 (Mangan, Blake, Prouty, & Lakin, 1994).

Community Housing

As large institutions grew smaller and community alternatives increased, the resources formerly supporting institutional placements as well as new funds were more widely dispersed, often to private contract providers in community settings. The first large-scale community development projects for people with disabilities were group homes, typically owned and operated by the provider. As we noted, many of these were developed using HCBS waiver funds, but states and providers developed them without federal funds as well. At present there are between 15,000 and 20,000 such homes in the United States with six or fewer beds in which approximately 70,000 individuals reside (Mangan et al., 1994).

As the responsibility for providing housing shifted from state-controlled facilities to private contract providers, so too did the responsibility for providing all other services required by the individual. That is, the services required by individuals in group homes largely remain linked to housing, as they had been in institutional facilities. Although in some cases different agencies provided different services to individuals, there often were only two—one providing residential services and the other providing some form of day training or programming. It has been argued by some advocates (e.g., O'Brien, 1994) that this is little better than the situation in institutions—that the individual is dependent on one centralized service provider to fulfill all of his or her needs. Put simply, the structure of services (i.e., centralized, single-source) did not change, only the location did.

Regardless, living in the community has expanded and taken many forms in addition to group homes, not the least of which is living in a family. Many people with disabilities who live with their families are children and adolescents. Although this is a prevalent arrangement, little is known about the specific characteristics of such arrangements (Jacobson & Schwartz, 1991). Foster care arrangements continue to be another form of community living that employs private family homes to provide care to between one and six people with disabilities in exchange for a monthly stipend. In the mid-1980s these arrangements increased across the nation due in part to the development of new foster care programs in states to provide community care for people leaving institutions. Foster care continues to be a common form of community living. Mangan et al. (1994) in their nationwide survey identified almost 14,000 family foster care settings in forty-five states responding to the survey and estimate that there are almost 30,000 individuals living in these settings at present. As we described earlier, the concept of supported living has also spread rapidly. These settings provide semi-independent living for people with disabilities and require a concomitant system of personal supports to be effective (Halpern, Close, & Nelson, 1986).

Finally, mention needs to be made of the movement to develop arrangements for home ownership by people with mental retardation and developmental disabilities that is beginning to appear frequently in the literature (Nesbit, 1992; Racino, Walker, O'Connor, & Taylor, 1993). This approach doesn't specify a specific housing type and can be used across models—that is, people with disabilities could jointly own their own group home, or individually own or rent housing.

Funding and Service Needs

It cannot be denied that there has been a paradigm shift and that changes consistent with this conceptual/philosophical change are taking place. However, a philosophical change cannot be equated with the reality of effecting change in a bureaucratic service system. The population to be served *does* have specific needs, yet specialized services, in many instances, are expensive and frequently inaccessible or unavailable. The very act of returning people to the community has created new problems. For example, an unfortunate outcome of the paradigm shift to community and support models is the growth of waiting lists for residential and day services. A housing work group of the President's Committee on Mental Retardation (1994), for example, estimated that about 80,000 people are awaiting residential services nationwide. Waiting lists seem to have grown in direct proportion to recent recessive trends in the national economy and the economies of states. Furthermore, the reductions and cessation of admissions to institutional facilities has exacerbated the problems in finding community housing, giving rise to many stories similar to that of the Damicos and the Nunbergs.

For the most part, the responses to such problems are to advocate for more resources for people with developmental disabilities and to attempt to develop new funding streams and creative housing solutions. As institutions are closed, some resources may be liberated, but these funds are often less than expected. Such funds must follow people leaving facilities and cannot be used to reduce present waiting lists. Unfortunately, none of these solutions has fully solved the problems facing families like the Damicos and the Nunbergs.

Furthermore, the search for more resources often pits groups against each other. Economic analyses do not support the conclusion that community-based residential alternatives are necessarily less expensive. In a Human Services Research Study (HSRI, 1994) prepared for the New Jersey Developmental Disabilities Council, it was concluded that it would be prudent to discontinue large developmental centers. Clearly the fiscal effects will depend on the community services to which the persons with disabilities will move. If the individuals move into current community and day programs, it will create a surplus of $132 million in fiscal year 1997 and a $136 million surplus in fiscal year 2000. However, if people move into specialized group homes and day programs, that is, closing all developmental centers and placing all individuals, even those with the most severe disabilities in such settings, there would be projected deficits of $185 million in fiscal year 1997 and $243 million in fiscal year 2000.

Availability and access to professional services has also been problematic as people with disabilities have moved from centralized facilities to dispersed communities. Paramount among the services that individuals with disabilities living in the community have difficulty in accessing is quality health care (Criscione, Kastner, O'Brien, & Nathanson, 1994; Criscione, Kastner, Walsh, & Nathanson, 1993). Lack of availability and access to psychiatric, behavioral, and rehabilitation services also continues to be problematic for those who live in community settings. These problems may be more intractable than housing since there are more approaches to finding homes than for developing support and professional services.

CONCLUSIONS

As institutions are removed as options for people with developmental disabilities, it is essential that the field not also lose the ability to provide the same services and supports that the older models provided. Strong proponents of support models often contend that all needed services will be available in community settings. Given that people with developmental disabilities often represent a minority, it may not be economically feasible to maintain such services. Yet it is essential to preserve such institutional components as (1) the capacity to deliver highly specialized services; (2) the ability to train future professionals; and (3) the need to preserve and extend the knowledge and research base of the field. In a sense, these elements that once were ensconced in institutions may be better conceptualized as resource networks—perhaps connected through advanced information technology. Ultimately, such systems or networks need to be established on a human scale, in such a way that individuals are provided with opportunities for real choice.

Real choice implies more than the freedom to choose. It also implies that viable options from which to choose exist, that these options are accessible to the individual, and that the individual or his family or representative have full knowledge of the options so that informed consent is possible. If only one option is available to the individual, then choice must be limited to only one decision, that is, whether or not to avail oneself of that option. If many options are available, then real choice exists. Family advocacy organizations for persons with developmental disabilities are not unanimous in supporting community living as the sole or best option for those they represent.

Such a perspective has also found some support in legislative action. For example, the U.S. Congress has given citizens with mental retardation and their families a choice among options. The Social Security Act mandates a "choice option" between home, community, and institutional care. The Developmental Disabilities and Assistance and Bill of Rights Act Amendments of 1994 states that the act "may not be read as a federal policy supporting the closure of institutions." Similarly, parent groups have voiced their concerns in this area. For example, the Voice of the Retarded (VOR), in a position paper revised July 6, 1994, recommends that health care legislation provide "long-term active treatment (birth to death) for citizens with mental retardation in home, community, institution or other specialized settings." They further recommend that "states maintain one or more specialized facilities (numbers based on populations) for evaluation, training, centralized information, and residential treatment to support people with severe/profound disabilities, socially unacceptable or maladaptive behaviors."

It is paradoxical that those who have been most vocal in support of empowerment and personal choice for persons with mental retardation have also been the most outspoken critics of institutions. It is the position of the present authors, all of whom have had a considerable degree of institutional experience, that client choice should be a high priority for change but that choice should be real, based on client wants and needs. Options should be maximized with equal status and availability. All options should ideally be of the highest quality with minimal standards and evaluatory criteria rigorously applied, including objective and subjective criteria for quality of life of residents. Maximum flexibility in the system is necessary, with all components linked and acting in concert to serve the client.

Movement in and out of any component of the system should be easily accomplished so that any given individual may make use of different components at different times in his or her life, depending on need. In this manner, home, community, or institutional options are all available and choice is more than mere illusion and rhetoric.

REFERENCES

Baker, B. L., Seltzer, G. B., & Seltzer, M. M. (1974). *As close as possible: Community residences for retarded adults.* Boston: Little, Brown.

Bell, N. J., Schoenrock, C. J., & Bensberg, G. J. (1981). Change over time in the community: Findings in a longitudinal study. In R. H. Bruininks, C. E. Meyers, B. B. Sigford, & K. C. Lakin (Eds.), *Deinstitutionalization and community adjustment of mentally retarded people* (Monograph No. 4, pp. 195–206). Washington, DC: American Association on Mental Deficiency.

Bjannes, A. T., & Butler, E. W. (1974). Environmental variation in community care facilities for mentally retarded persons. *American Journal of Mental Deficiency, 73,* 429–439.

Braddock, D., Hemp, R., Bachelder, L., & Fujiura, G. (1994). *The state of the states in developmental disabilities: Fourth national study of public spending for mental retardation and developmental disabilities in the United States.* Chicago: The University of Illinois at Chicago, Institute on Disability and Human Development (UAP).

Conroy, J. W., & Bradley, V. J. (1985). *The Pennhurst longitudinal study: A report of five years of research and analysis.* Philadelphia: Temple University, Developmental Disabilities Center.

Crapps, J. M., Langione, J., & Swaim, S. (1985). Quantity and quality of participation in community environments by mentally retarded adults. *Education and Training of the Mentally Retarded, 20,* 123–129.

Criscione, T., Kastner, T. A., O'Brien, D., & Nathanson, R. (1994). Replication of a managed health care initiative for people with mental retardation living in the community. *Mental Retardation, 32,* 43–52.

Criscione, T., Kastner, T. A., Walsh, K. K., & Nathanson, R. (1993). Managed health care services for people with mental retardation: Impact on inpatient utilization. *Mental Retardation, 31,* 297–306.

Crissey, M. S., & Rosen, M. (Eds.). (1986). *Institutions for the Mentally Retarded.* Austin, TX: Pro-Ed.

Cummins, R. A. (1991). A pilot study in the use of the quality of life interview schedule. *Social Indicators Research, 23,* 283–298.

Edgerton, R. B. (1975). Issues relating to quality of life among mentally retarded individuals. In M. J. Begab & S. A. Richardson (Eds.), *The mentally retarded and society: A social science perspective* (pp. 128–142). Baltimore: University Park Press.

Felice, D., De Kock, V., & Repp, A. C. (1986). An eco-behavioral analysis of small community-based houses and traditional large hospitals for severely and profoundly mentally handicapped adults. *Applied Research in Mental Retardation, 7,* 393–408.

Gollay, E., Freedman, R., Wyngaarden, M., & Kurtz, N. R. (1978). *Coming back: The community experiences of deinstitutionalized mentally retarded people.* Cambridge, MA: Apt Books.

Goode, D. A. (Ed.). (1988). *Quality of life: A review and synthesis of the literature.* Valhalla, NY: The Mental Retardation Institute.

Halpern, A. S., Close, D. W., & Nelson, D. J. (1986). *On my own: The impact of semi-independent living programs for adults with mental retardation.* Baltimore: Paul H. Brookes

Hayden, M. F., Lakin, K. C., Hill, B. K., Bruininks, R. H., & Copher, J. I. (1992). Social and leisure integration of people with mental retardation in foster homes and small group homes. *Education and Training in Mental Retardation 27, 187–199.*

Heal, L. W., & Chadsey-Rusch, J. (1985). The Lifestyle Satisfaction Scale (LSS): Assessing individuals' satisfaction with residence, community setting, and associated services. *Applied Research in Mental Retardation, 6,* 475–490.

Hill, B. K., & Bruininks, R. H. (1981). *Family, leisure, and social activities of mentally retarded people in residential facilities*. Minneapolis: University of Minnesota, Department of Educational Psychology.

Hill, B. K., Rotegard, L. L., & Bruininks, R. H. (1984). Quality of life of mentally retarded people in residential care. *Social Work, 2*, 275–281.

Holburn, C. S. (1990). Rules in today's residential environments [Symposium]. *Mental Retardation, 28*(2).

Holburn, C. S. (1992). Symposium: Compliance and quality in residential life. *Mental Retardation, 30*(3).

Horner, R., Stoner, S., & Ferguson, D. (1988). *An activity based analysis of deinstitutionalization: The effects of community re-entry on the lives of residents leaving Oregon's Fairview Training Center*. Salem: Oregon Developmental Disabilities Office.

Human Services Research Institute (1994, June). *The impact of today's fiscal realities and tomorrow's on the system of services for people with developmental disabilities in New Jersey*. New Jersey Developmental Disabilities Council, Trenton, NJ: Author.

Jacobson, J. (1991). Administrative and policy dimensions of developmental disabilities services. In J. L. Matson & J. A. Mulick (Eds.), *Handbook of Mental Retardation* (2nd ed., pp. 3–22). New York: Pergamon.

Jacobson, J., & Schwartz, A. A. (1991). Evaluating living situations of people with developmental disabilities. In J. L. Matson & J. A. Mulick (Eds.), *Handbook of Mental Retardation* (2nd ed., pp. 35–62). New York: Pergamon.

Karan, O. C., Granfield, J. M., & Furey, E. (1992, January/February). Supported living: Rethinking the rules of residential services. *AAMR News & Notes 5*, 5.

Knoll, J. E. (1990). Defining quality in residential services. In V. J. Bradley & H. A. Bersani, Jr. (Eds.), *Quality assurance for individuals with developmental disabilities* (pp. 235–261). Baltimore: Paul H. Brookes.

Lakin, K. C., Prouty, R. W., White, C. C., Bruininks, R. N., & Hill, B. K. (1990). *Intermediate care facilities for persons with mental retardation (ICF/MRs): Program utilization and resident characteristics* (Report No. 31). Minneapolis: University of Minnesota, Center for Residential and Community Services.

Landesman, S. (1986). Quality of life and personal life satisfaction: Definition and measurement issues. *Mental Retardation, 24*, 141–143.

Luckasson, R., Coulter, D. L., Polloway, E. A., Reiss, S., Schalock, R. L., Snell, M. E., Spitalnik, D. M., & Stark, J. A. (1992). *Mental Retardation: Definition, classification, and systems of supports* (9th ed.). Washington, DC: American Association of Mental Retardation.

Mangan, R., Blake, E. M., Prouty, R. W., & Lakin, K. C. (1994). *Residential services for persons with mental retardation and related conditions: Status and trends through 1993*. Minneapolis: University of Minnesota Research and Training Center on Residential Services and Community Living, Institute on Community Integration (UAP).

Nesbit, J. (Ed.). (1992). *Natural supports in school, at work, and in the community for people with severe disabilities*. Baltimore: Paul H. Brookes.

O'Brien, J. (1994). Down stairs that are never your own: Supporting people with developmental disabilities in their own homes. *Mental Retardation, 32*, 1–6.

O'Neil, J., Brown, M., Gordon, W., Schonborn, R., & Green, E. (1981). Activity patterns of mentally retarded adults in institutions and communities—a longitudinal study. *Applied Research in Mental Retardation, 2*, 367–379.

Ouelette-Kuntz, H. (1990). A pilot study in the use of the Quality of Life Interview Schedule. *Social Indicators Research, 23*, 283–298.

President's Committee on Mental Retardation (1994). *The National Reform Agenda and Citizens with Mental Retardation: A Journey of Renewal for All Americans*. Report to the President. Washington, DC: US Department of Health and Human Services, Administration for Children and Families.

Racino, J. A., & Taylor, S. J. (1993). "People first": Approaches to housing and support. In J. A. Racino, P. Walker, S. O'Connor, & S. J. Taylor (Eds.), *Housing, support, and community: Choices and strategies for adults with disabilities*. (Vol. 2, pp. 33–56). Baltimore: Paul H. Brookes.

Racino, J., Walker, P., O'Connor, S., & Taylor, S. (Eds.). (1993). *Housing, support, and community: Choices and strategies for adults with disabilities*. Baltimore: Paul H. Brookes.

Rosen, M., Rice, D. M., Walsh, K. K., Hartman, E., & McCallion, P. (1991). Developmentally disabled people grow up: Needs and resources in the post school years. In W. Stainback & S. Stainback (Eds.), *Controversial issues confronting special education: Divergent perspectives* (pp. 285–298). Boston: Allyn and Bacon.

Rosen, M., Simon, E. W., & McKinsey, L. (in press). A subjective measure of quality of life. *Mental Retardation.*

Schalock, R. L. (Ed.). (1990). *Quality of Life: Perspectives and issues.* Washington, DC: American Association of Mental Retardation.

Schalock, R. L., Keith, K. D., Hoffman, K., & Karan, V. D. (1989). Quality of Life: Its measurement and use. *Mental Retardation, 27,* 25–31.

Scheerenberger, R. C. (1983). *A history of mental retardation.* Baltimore: Paul H. Brookes.

Smull, M. W., & Smith, G. (1994, July/August). Moving to a system of support: Using support brokerage. *AAMR News & Notes, 7,* 4.

Voice of the Retarded (1994, July). *Health care principles vital to VOR.* Rolling Meadows, IL: Author.

Walsh, K. K. (1992). Resource networks for community settings: An alternative view of institutions. *McGill Journal of Education, 27,* 329–341.

Walsh, K., & McCallion, P. (1987). The role of the small institution in the community services continuum. In R. F. Antonak & J. A. Mulick (Eds.) *Transitions in Mental Retardation, Vol. 3: The Community Imperative Revisited* (pp. 216–236). Norwood, NJ: Ablex.

White, C. C., Lakin, K. C., & Bruininks, R. H. (1989, December). *Persons with mental retardation and related conditions in state-operated residential facilities: Year ending June 30, 1988* (Report No. 30). Minneapolis: University of Minnesota, Center for Residential and Community Services.

Zigler, E., Hodapp, R. M., & Edison, M. R. (1990). From theory to practice in the care and education of mentally retarded individuals. *American Journal of Mental Retardation, 95,* 1–12.

CHAPTER 22

Inclusive Community Living

STEVEN J. TAYLOR
JULIE ANN RACINO
PAMELA M. WALKER

INTRODUCTION

During the past decade and a half, our vision of life in the community has changed dramatically as people with disabilities, their families, their friends, professionals, advocates, and citizens examine what it means to live together. Earlier controversies centered on such questions as where people with severe disabilities should live or how the community service system should look. While these remain as controversial issues, we are turning our attention to the community participation and lifestyles of people with disabilities and their families, and to the changes integration implies for society as a whole.

This chapter will trace three major issues that have guided discussion and research on community living during the period starting in the late 1960s until the present.

1. *From institutions to community living.* Should people with developmental disabilities live in the community?

2. *Being in the community.* Should people with disabilities have access to education, employment, housing, transportation, and recreation alongside their nondisabled peers?

3. *Being part of the community.* How can people with developmental disabilities fully and meaningfully participate in community life?

These are simple yet controversial questions that have been answered differently by different people at different times. Since the 1960s we have seen dramatic changes in the quality of lives of people with disabilities, including increased presence and participation in the community, increased social acceptance, and the opportunity for greater self-determination. At the same time, the hidden barriers behind the controversies have remained relatively unchanged, and some would hold, so have the lives of people with the most severe disabilities (Ferguson, 1988). Issues of social justice still lie at the heart of these seemingly different issues. Yet hope lies in the kinds of questions we are now beginning to ask, questions about what integration means, not only for people with disabilities, but for society. As Knoll and Biklen (Lippert, 1987) state,

> We must design schools, homes, workplaces, health care systems, transportation, and other social environments in such a way that they take in everyone.

Preparation of this article was supported in part by the U.S. Department of Education, Office of Special Education and Rehabilitative Services, National Institute on Disability and Rehabilitation Research (NIDRR) through Cooperative Agreement No. H133B00003-90 awarded to the Center on Human Policy, Division of Special Education and Rehabilitation, School of Education, Syracuse University and a subcontract through the University of Minnesota for the Research and Training Center on Community Living through Cooperative Agreement No. H133B80048. The opinions expressed herein are those solely of the authors. No official endorsement by the U.S. Department of Education should be inferred.

Our communities and our societies must be plural-istic rather than exclusionary. (p. 45)

It is important to understand the vestiges of past issues that influence the present in order to better direct our attention to the concepts and societal issues that will guide us to a better society for all.

FROM INSTITUTIONS TO COMMUNITY

Spurred on by lawsuits, federal initiatives, ex-posés, and efforts by parents, people with disabili-ties, and professionals, the 1970s witnessed several dramatic developments that had an impact on the nature of community living for people with disabilities. The first was a shift from a reliance on institutional care to a decline in the use of public institutions for people with developmental dis-abilities from a peak of 194,650 in 1967 to 117,160 in 1982 (Rotegard, Bruininks, & Krantz, 1984). The second major shift, which will be de-scribed in the next section, was the development of the key philosophical and policy con-cepts—normalization, least restrictive environ-ment, and deinstitutionalization—that would continue to provide guidance to the community movement over the next decades. Their wide-spread implementation resulted in an expansion in rights, increased social acceptance, and fuller integration of people with disabilities in society.

Attack and Counterforces on Institutions

In examining the issue of institution versus com-munity, it is important to reflect on four major forces (exposés, organizing by people with dis-abilities and their parents, courts, and federal laws and services) that played a critical role in the at-tack on institutions and on the counterforces (e.g., unions) that, in some states, continue to drain en-ergy, attention, and resources away from improv-ing the lives of people with disabilities in the community (Taylor & Searl, 1987).

The Role of Exposés.   Over the past two dec-ades, hardly an institution in the country has gone unscathed by exposés. Following his unannounced visits to Willowbrook and Rome state schools in New York in 1965, Robert Kennedy was quoted in the *New York Times* as stating: "I was shocked and saddened by what I saw there. . . . There were children slipping into blankness and lifelong de-pendence." The conditions of horror and degrada-tion so vividly described by Kennedy and Blatt and Kaplan (1974) are part of the life heritage of many adults with disabilities who, if they sur-vived, are now living in communities or are still among those confined to institutions.

Organizing by People with Disabilities and Their Parents.   The parent movement of the 1950s, which created a strong local, state, and national force, continued to grow in strength through the 1960s and 1970s. As their advocacy and organiz-ing increased, parents took their demands for bet-ter schooling and services to the nation's courts and legislature. Today, parents remain a powerful voice for change, with those who have experi-enced the benefits of P.L. 94-142 (currently the Individuals with Disabilities Education Act) now beginning to demand the same right to access to adult community services.

At the same time, some parent organizations that emerged in the 1950s have taken on the role of service providers, operating the services some younger parents want to change to better meet the needs of a new generation. In a few states, institu-tional parent groups also remain very active, often encouraged by state and local policies that tend to pit parent against parent in the bureaucracy-cre-ated struggle for resources.

In the 1970s, people with disabilities joined together in groups to confront the societal prejudice and discrimination they faced. In re-cent years, people with mental retardation have founded groups nationally and internationally (e.g., Self Advocates Becoming Empowered and People First) to seek strength from each other, to find common voices, and to demand the same rights and privileges afforded others in society.

The Role of Litigation.   From the 1960s to the 1980s, the courts proved to be a powerful tool for change by attacking institutional practices. A series of class action lawsuits directed at institutional conditions sent shock waves throughout institutions in this country and transformed the face of services for people with developmental disabilities in this country. In less than a fifteen-year span, major lawsuits were filed (usually successfully) against mental retardation and mental health institutions in over twenty states. For a time, at least, these lawsuits put state officials on notice that institutional abuse would not be tolerated, and thus moved entrenched bureaucracies to develop community programs (Taylor & Searl, 1987).

In the 1980s, the federal courts ceased to be an effective tool for institutional change, with the Supreme Court taking a very conservative view of the rights of people with mental retardation confined to institutions. However, state lawsuits targeting institutions, such as *Homeward Bound v. Hissom Memorial Center* (1987) in Oklahoma, have continued to provide the impetus for further change from institutions and other congregate facilities to community living.

Federal Laws and Services.   Beginning in the 1960s, the federal government articulated a national policy toward people with disabilities, with deinstitutionalization being endorsed by President Kennedy and his five successors. Throughout the 1970s, federal involvement in services for and the protection of rights of people with disabilities increased dramatically.

Ironically, one of the major initiatives of this period, the 1971 Amendment of Title XIX of the Social Security Act, Medicaid, became one of the major obstacles to deinstitutionalization nationally. It took nearly ten years for Congress to pass the Omnibus Reconciliation Act of 1981, which included a home and community-based Medicaid waiver option encouraging states to serve people in their natural families and home communities as opposed to placing them in institutions. Today, Medicaid reform and a national health insurance plan, inclusive of an array of community supports for people with disabilities and their families, remain high legislative priorities for the disability community.

In the late 1980s and early 1990s, Congress passed landmark legislation that should change again the face of life in the community for people with disabilities. The first was the Federal Fair Housing Amendments of 1988 which prohibits discriminatory housing provisions against people with disabilities and has already set in motion challenges to site selection laws in this country. The second and by far the most critical legislation is the civil rights bill for people with disabilities, the Americans with Disabilities Act (ADA) (Wehman, 1993).

The Institution–Community Debate

In the 1970s and into the early 1980s, the institution–community debate dominated discussion, framing the political, technical, research, and ethical issues addressed in this society. In the past two decades, a preponderance of research studies have been framed by this debate. Researchers have studied institutions and community settings according to management practices (McCormick, Balla, & Ziegler, 1975), adaptive behavior changes (Conroy, Efthimiou, & Lemanowicz, 1982), size of facility (Landesman-Dwyer, Sackett, & Kleinman, 1980), and a host of other factors.

The preponderance of these studies and experience indicate that life in the community is better than life in institutions in terms of relationships, family contact, frequency and diversity of relationships, individual development, and leisure, recreational, and spiritual resources (Lakin, 1988). Today the field faces more critical issues, and it is time to move on to providing the guidance necessary to solve these new dilemmas.

BEING IN THE COMMUNITY: FROM CONCEPTS TO PRACTICE

The concepts of deinstitutionalization and LRE (least restrictive environment) have made a significant contribution to public policy and the design of services for people with developmental disabilities. However, these concepts have also generated new sets of problems for the community service system and in the lives of people with disabilities.

Deinstitutionalization

Deinstitutionalization primarily refers to efforts to move people with mental disabilities from large, institutional settings into the community. However, the most widely accepted definitions also include the parallel goal of reducing institutional admissions and the competing goal of making the facilities less institutional in nature (National Association for Superintendents, 1974). However, deinstitutionalization in practice has created its own set of problems.

In some states, deinstitutionalization has resulted in what some observers call "transinstitutionalization" (Warren, 1981), the physical movement of people with disabilities from large, public institutions, to smaller, private ones, including large intermediate care facilities, nursing homes, and other congregate group living facilities. Braddock, Hemp, Fujiura, Bachelder, and Mitchell (1989) report that as of 1988 over 45,000 people with mental retardation were living in large (over fifteen-bed) private facilities and over 54,000 were in nursing homes.

In other places, deinstitutionalization has meant the "dumping" or simple "release" of people with disabilities from institutions without the transfer of funding and support services to the community. Thus, as reported in one recent study (Racino, Rothenberg, Shoultz, Taylor, & Traustadottir, 1988), people with disabilities may end up residing in congregate adult room-and-board homes, in single room occupancies (SROs), or on the street, sometimes having "graduated" through the service system.

While the populations of public institutions have declined at a steady pace, states continue to vary dramatically in the degree to which deinstitutionalization has been achieved (Braddock et al.,

1989; Mangan, Blake, Prouty, & Lakin, 1994). Several small states, including New Hampshire, Vermont, Rhode Island, and the District of Columbia have closed their institutions for people with disabilities; others continue to maintain a large number of people in institutions. And, it is commonly acknowledged today that federal funding mechanisms encourage institutionalization and segregated services, despite the existence of federal policies promoting integration (Center on Human Policy, 1989a; Lakin, 1988). Despite these problems, the quality of life of people with disabilities has improved considerably. However, as long ago as 1977, Blatt, Bogdan, Biklen, and Taylor wrote, "Deinstitutionalization—and today we would add community integration—is not a matter of releasing people from institutions; it is a matter of converting from an institutional to a community-based system of services. If we do not reconceptualize deinstitutionalization, it will fail, either by inertia or by backlash."

The Least Restrictive Environment Principle

The principle of the least restrictive environment (LRE) has its roots in both professional writings and the law (Biklen, 1982). Although commonly considered a legal doctrine (see Turnbull, Ellis, Boggs, Brookes, & Biklen, 1981), professional and legal definitions have proceeded hand in hand. As Biklen (1992) notes, the legal principle of LRE is deceptively simple: The government must pursue its ends in a manner that least intrudes or infringes upon individual rights.

As a conceptual and policy framework, LRE emerged in the 1960s when leaders in the field began to advocate for the development of a range of special education placements for students with disabilities. The principle has been implicitly endorsed by Congress (e.g., Developmental Disabilities Act of 1975), federal courts (e.g., *Wyatt v. Stickney,* 1972), and the federal government (e.g., regulations for P.L. 94-142).

As a principle, LRE caught on quickly in the field of special education and services for people with disabilities (Blatt et al., 1977), gaining support from diverse constituencies, including the Council for Exceptional Children, the American Association of Mental Retardation, and the Association for Persons with Severe Handicaps. Despite this widespread endorsement, the meaning of LRE as a principle remains imprecise, although it is commonly associated with the most integrated, normalized setting possible. In the simplest terms, LRE means that services for people with developmental disabilities should be designed according to a range of program options varying in terms of restrictiveness, normalization, independence, and integration, with a presumption in favor of environments that are least restrictive and more normalized (Taylor, 1988).

Since its earliest conceptualization, the LRE principle has been defined operationally as a continuum, an ordered sequence of placements that vary according to the degree of restrictiveness (Taylor, 1988). The most common way of representing the continuum is by a straight line running from the most restrictive (also the most segregated and most intensive) services to the least restrictive (also the most integrated, independent, and least intensive) services. The assumption is that people then move through the continuum, as they gain increasing skills (Hitzing, 1987). This applies whether we are discussing residential services (State of New York, 1987), special education (Zettel & Ballard, 1982), or day/vocational services (Schalock, 1983).

As described in detail by Taylor (1988), the LRE principle and the associated continuum concept are characterized by seven major conceptual flaws.

1. *The LRE principle legitimates restrictive environments.* A principle that contains a presumption in favor of the least restrictive environment implies that there are circumstances under which the most restrictive environment would be appropriate. In other words, to conceptualize services in terms of restrictiveness is to legitimate more restrictive settings. As long as services are conceptualized in this manner, some people will end up in restrictive environments. In most cases,

they will be people with severe disabilities (see Payne & Patton, 1981, p. 219).

2. *The LRE principle confuses segregation and integration on the one hand with intensity of services on the other.* As represented by the continuum, LRE equates segregation with the most intensive services and integration with the least intensive services. The principle assumes that the least restrictive, most integrated settings are incapable of providing the intensive services needed by people with severe disabilities. When viewed from this perspective, it follows that people with severe disabilities will require the most restrictive and segregated settings. However, segregation and integration on the one hand and intensity of services on the other, are separate dimensions.

3. *The LRE principle is based on a readiness model.* Implicit in LRE is the assumption that people with developmental disabilities must earn the right to move to the least restrictive environment. In other words, the person must "get ready" or "be prepared" to live, work, or go to school in integrated settings by passing through "transitional" settings. The irony is that the most restrictive placements do not prepare people for the least restrictive placements (Brown et al., 1983; Wilcox, 1987). Institutions do not prepare people for community living, segregated day programs do not prepare people for competitive work, and segregated schooling does not prepare people for integrated schooling.

4. *The LRE principle supports the primacy of professional decision making.* Integration is ultimately a moral and philosophical issue, not a professional one. Yet LRE invariably is framed in terms of professional judgments regarding individual needs. The phrase *least restrictive environment* is almost always qualified with words such as *appropriate, necessary, feasible,* and *possible* (and never with *desired* or *wanted*). Professionals are left to determine what is appropriate, possible, feasible, or necessary for any particular individual.

5. *The LRE principle sanctions infringements on people's rights.* LRE is a seductive concept; government should act in a manner that least restricts the rights and liberties of individuals. When applied categorically to people with developmental disabilities, however, the LRE principle sanctions infringements on basic rights to freedom and community participation beyond those imposed on people without disabilities. The question implied by LRE is not whether people with developmental disabilities should be restricted, but to what extent (Turnbull et al., 1981, p. 17).

6. *The LRE principle implies that people must move as they develop and change.* As LRE is commonly conceptualized, people with developmental disabilities are expected to move toward increasingly less restrictive environments. Schalock (1983) writes, "The existence of a functioning system of community services would provide a range of living and training environments that facilitate client movement along a series of continua" (p. 22).

Even if people moved smoothly through a continuum, their lives would be a series of stops in transitional placements. Generally, people with developmental disabilities move to "less restrictive environments" ony because new programs open up and space is needed to accommodate people with more severe disabilities. This can destroy any sense of home and may disrupt relationships with roommates, neighbors, and friends.

7. *The LRE principle directs attention to physical settings rather than to the services and supports people need to be integrated in the community.* As Gunnar Dybwad (personal communication, February 1985) stated, "Every time we identify a need in this field, we build a building." By its name, the principle of the least restrictive environment emphasizes facilities and environments designed specifically for people with developmental disabilities. As suggested in the critiques of the traditional continuum model by Hitzing (1980) and Bronston (1980), the field of developmental disabilities has defined its mission in terms of creating facilities, first large ones and now smaller ones, and programs, rather than in terms of providing the services and supports to enable people with developmental disabilities to participate in the same settings as other people.

A failure to critically examine the LRE principle may lead to the development of new community-based continua. While traditional critiques have rightfully rejected the most restrictive and segregated settings and the assumption that segregated settings prepare people to function in integrated settings, it is time to move beyond the notion of the continuum to a more flexible and responsive approach (Racino, Walker, O'Connor, & Taylor, 1992; Smull & Bellamy, 1990). Now we must define the challenge in terms of total integration for people with developmental disabilities, including those with the most severe impairments (Taylor, Biklen, & Knoll, 1987; Taylor, Racino, Knoll, & Lutfiyya, 1987).

The Normalization Principle

Normalization was conceived and developed in Scandinavia by Bengt Nirje (1969) and quickly became one of the most fundamental concepts internationally in the field of mental retardation and human services. According to Nirje, "The normalization principle means making available to all people patterns of life and conditions of everyday living which are as close as possible to the regular circumstances and ways of life of society" (Nirje, 1976, p. 231).

In North America, the normalization principle was popularized by Wolfensberger (1972) through his influential book, *The Principle of Normalization in Human Services.* Wolfensberger defined normalization as follows: "the utilization of means which are as culturally normative as possible, in order to establish and/or maintain personal behaviors and characteristics which are as culturally normative as possible" (Wolfensberger, 1972, p. 28).

Normalization is still widely considered to be the primary guiding principle in the field of mental retardation today. Despite its widespread acceptance, a great deal of unclarity continues to surround the concept. Wolfensberger and others have argued that the concept has been largely misunderstood and misinterpreted. For this reason, Wolfensberger (1983) has proposed a reformulation of normalization as "social role valorization."

In recent publications, Bengt Nirje argues that Wolfensberger's definition of normalization or social role valorization is grounded in a different value base than the original principle. He states that "implicit in the normalization principle is the concept that mentally handicapped people are entitled to the same rights and opportunities as are available to others in their society, including opportunities to exercise freedom and personal choice" (Perrin & Nirje, 1985, p. 69). In contrast to the egalitarian base of this formulation, according to Nirje, Wolfensberger's version tends to emphasize culturally valued social roles and the individual's conformity to values determined by others in the society.

Because the concept of normalization has become subject to so many interpretations, it no longer is as powerful as it once was as a guiding force for change in society's treatment of people with disabilities. While most states and human service agencies endorse normalization, they operate under different definitions and interpretations of what it means.

FROM BEING IN THE COMMUNITY TO BEING PART OF THE COMMUNITY

Being in the community is not the same as being part of the community (Bogdan & Taylor, 1987b). Studies have shown that physical integration alone is not sufficient to guarantee that community participation and relationships will occur (Bercovici, 1983; Bruininks, Thurlow, & Steffans, 1988; Taylor, Bogdan, & Lutfiyya, in press). Today the major challenges revolve around the full participation of people with disabilities and their families in community life, increased personal autonomy and choice, and the development of meaningful community life for all of us.

In order to provide guidance on these issues, the Center on Human Policy, in conjunction with representatives of states, universities, consumer and parent organizations, and agencies from around the country, developed two position statements (see Tables 22.1 and 22.2) regarding community living for children and their families, and for adults.

Supporting Children and Their Families

Families are a key source of integration of children into neighborhoods and communities, and in the development of relationships. The first statement in Table 22.1 is founded on the belief that all children, regardless of ability, belong in families. Although there is a growing recognition and movement to support families to keep their children at home (Center on Human Policy, 1987; Knoll, Covert, Osuch, O'Connor, & Blaney, 1990), children with developmental disabilities continue to be institutionalized in state institutions, private hospitals, facilities on the grounds of institutions, residential schools, nursing homes, and other private, congregate facilities.

The most promising approaches to supporting families include a commitment by professionals to enable all children to live with families and to do "whatever it takes" to support families to maintain quality homelife for all. Permanency planning is the policy expression of the philosophy that all children need permanent homes and enduring relationships with adults (Taylor, Lakin, & Hill, 1989). It provides protection for children at risk of out-of-home placement. In 1980, Congress (P.L. 96-272) mandated that states receiving federal funds for child welfare services comply with these protections, yet these are not routinely applied for children served by developmental disabilities agencies.

The statement in Table 22.1 has been endorsed by individuals and organizations around the country, including the Association for Retarded Citizens–U.S., and has been incorporated into state legislation and policy statements.

Community Living for Adults

The statement in support of adults (Table 22.2) is organized around three themes, any one of which, if fully applied, challenges the service system as it currently exists (Center on Human Policy, 1989b).

TABLE 22.1   A Statement in Support of Families and Their Children (Center on Human Policy, 1987)

These principles should guide public policy toward families of children with developmental disabilities. . . . and the actions of states and agencies when they become involved with them:

All children, regardless of disability, belong with families and need enduring relationships with adults. When states or agencies become involved with families, permanency planning should be a guiding philosophy. As a philosophy, permanency planning endorses children's rights to a nurturing home and consistent relationships with adults. As a guide to state and agency practice, permanency planning requires family support, encouragement of a family's relationship with the child, family reunification for children placed out of home, and the pursuit of adoption for children when family reunification is not possible.

Families should receive the supports necessary to maintain their children at home. Family support services must be based on the principle "whatever it takes." In short, family support services should be flexible, individualized, and designed to meet the diverse needs of families.

Family supports should build on existing social networks and natural sources of support. As a guiding principle, natural sources of support, including neighbors, extended families, friends, and community associations, should be preferred over agency programs and professional services. When states or agencies become involved with families, they should support existing social networks, strengthen natural sources of support, and help build connections to existing community resources. When natural sources of support cannot meet the needs of families, professional or agency-operated support services should be available.

Family supports should maximize the family's control over the services and supports they receive. Family support services must be based on the assumption that families, rather than states and agencies, are in the best position to determine their needs.

Family supports should support the entire family. Family support services should be defined broadly in terms of the needs of the entire family, including children with disabilities, parents, and siblings.

Family support services should encourage the integration of children with disabilities into the community. Family support services should be designed to maximize integration and participation in community life for children with disabilities.

When children cannot remain with their families for whatever reason, out-of-home placement should be viewed initially as a temporary arrangement and efforts should be directed toward reuniting the family. Consistent with the philosophy of permanency planning, children should live with their families whenever possible. When, due to family crisis or other circumstances, children must leave their families, efforts should be directed at encouraging and enabling families to be reunited.

When families cannot be reunited and when active parental involvement is absent, adoption should be aggressively pursued. In fulfillment of each child's right to a stable family and an enduring relationship with one or more adults, adoption should be pursued for children whose ties with their families have been broken. Whenever possible, families should be involved in adoption planning and, in all cases, should be treated with sensitivity and respect. When adoption is pursued, the possibility of "open adoption," whereby families maintain involvement with a child, should be seriously considered.

While a preferred alternative to any group setting or out-of-home placement, foster care should only be pursued when children cannot live with their families or with adoptive families. After families and adoptive families, children should have the opportunity to live with foster families. Foster family care can provide children with a home atmosphere and warm relationships and is preferable to group settings and other placements. As a state- or agency-sponsored program, however, foster care seldom provides children the continuity and stability they need in their lives. While foster families may be called upon to assist, support, and occasionally fill in for families, foster care is not likely to be an acceptable alternative to fulfilling each child's right to a stable home and enduring relationships.

TABLE 22.2 In Support of Adults Living in the Community (Center on Human Policy, December, 1989)

This statement reflects principles to guide states, agencies, and organizations in supporting adults with developmental disabilities in living in homes and participating in community life.

Adults, regardless of ability, should have the right and opportunity to live in a home of their own in the community. Adults should have the right and opportunity to live in typical, decent, safe, accessible, and integrated community housing.

States, agencies, and communities should ensure the availability of such housing for all of its citizens, including adults with disabilities.

Adults, whether married or single, should have choices about the neighborhood they live in, the style of community housing, and the people with whom they will live.

Adults should have the same tenant and ownership rights and opportunities as other citizens, including the option to own or lease their own homes or apartments.

Adults with disabilities should have the opportunity to live in housing free from the conflicting relationship of landlord and service provider.

Adults shall have the opportunity to create a home of their own, reflective of their personal routines, values, and lifestyles.

All individuals should be entitled to the supports and personal assistance needed to live in their own home and participate fully in community life. Adults with disabilities should be entitled to whatever personal assistance and supports they need to live fully in their own home and community with dignity, self-determination, and respect.

Adults should have the option to live in their own home in the community without risking the loss of material or personal assistance support.

Adults shall have maximum control over their personal assistance and other supports, with advocacy and support, independent of service agencies, in making these decisions.

Adults have a right to determine who will provide personal assistance and supports and can choose to hire, train, evaluate, and fire a personal assistance employee.

Adults should have opportunities to participate in community life. Adults with disabilities should have opportunities to be involved with ordinary people on a partnership basis and to develop relationships with neighbors, coworkers, and community members.

Adults with disabilities are entitled to decent, safe, and affordable housing; financial security to meet basic needs; health and medical care; and community transportation, employment, and recreation.

Adults should have opportunities to contribute to the diversity and strength of communities.

The first theme revolves around the central need and right of people to have a place of their own, free of discrimination based on disability, guided by personal and/or shared choices in all aspects, and separate from the provision of services (O'Brien, 1994). While in the 1980s we moved from "homelike" environments to "homes," the next decade should challenge us to examine the meaning of home, including the extension of home ownership strategies to people with disabilities.

Since discrimination and segregation continue in this society based on race, ethnicity, age, and a variety of other characteristics, seeking decent housing and community living for people with disabilities raises critical social justice issues. People with disabilities should have equal access to housing and employment, and the effort to obtain this should be a part, not separate from, the effort to obtain equal access to housing and employment for others as well.

The second theme emphasizes the critical importance of supports, personal assistance services, and self-determination in ensuring the goal of home and community participation. The statement attempts to bridge the gap between the independent living movement philosophy, which defines independence as "the determination of one's own lifestyle" (DeJong, 1979) and self-advocacy efforts on the part of people with developmental disabilities. People with disabilities should be able to exercise the same choices as people without disabilities—nothing more and nothing less.

The statement draws on and broadens the definition of personal assistance services to include whatever is necessary to support individuals to live and participate fully in home, work, and community. Embedded in the statement are substantive issues on the interweaving of informal and formal supports, and the societal goals we are trying to achieve (e.g., shared power or simply a reverse in the pyramid structure of power). On the surface, this section of the statement calls for the availability of personally determined services, unique for each individual.

The third theme begins to move from the narrow view of community living as related to housing and supports, to a broader definition of communities, community issues, and participation in all aspects of community life, including employment, transportation, and recreation. Emphasizing the roles of ordinary citizens and the contributions that people with disabilities make, this part of the statement guides us from disability to "community for all" issues. The statement in support of adults challenges us to reevaluate the role that service systems can or cannot play in the lives of people with disabilities and to examine what we all need to do to reorganize our transportation, employment, schools, housing, recreation, and churches to be more inclusive of all people.

CONCLUSION: FROM BEING PART OF THE COMMUNITY TO BUILDING A BETTER SOCIETY

Many of the exciting developments in the integration of people with disabilities are the repeated discoveries that efforts to create a better, more just society are the same efforts that lead to better lives for people with disabilities. Working toward inclusive community living for people with developmental disabilities implies at the same time working toward inclusive community living for all of us.

This involves recognition that the issues of poverty, housing, food, environment, employment, schooling, transportation, and recreation that affect people with disabilities are the same issues that face, often disproportionately, others in this society who have been traditionally discriminated against. Special solutions, focused only on the needs of people with disabilities, have repeatedly fostered new and different barriers of their own. Community efforts at finding solutions, inclusive of all, hold the greatest promise, not only for the integration of the disenfranchised, but also for the enhancement of communities and society as a whole.

As Bogdan and Taylor (1987a, p. 213) state, "It is exciting to know that people are accomplishing things today that we could not even dream about 15 years ago. We have to realize our dreams are too much a product of what exists today and what we have been through. We can strive for change, but what is down the road is beyond our imagination."

REFERENCES

Bercovici, S. M. (1983). *Barriers to normalization: The restrictive management of mentally retarded persons.* Baltimore: University Park Press.

Biklen, D. (1982). The least restrictive environment: Its application to education. In G. Melton (Ed.), *Child and youth services* (pp. 121–144). New York: Haworth.

Blatt, B., Bogdan, R., Biklen, D., & Taylor, S. (1977). From institution to community: A conversion model. In E. Sontag (Ed.), *Educational programming for the severely and profoundly handicapped* (pp. 40–52). Reston, VA: Council for Exceptional Children.

Blatt, B., & Kaplan, F. (1974). *Christmas in purgatory: A photographic essay on mental retardation.* Syracuse, NY: Human Policy Press.

Bogdan, R., & Taylor, S. J. (1987a). Conclusion: The next wave. In S. J. Taylor, D. Biklen, & J. Knoll

(Eds.), *Community integration for people with severe disabilities* (pp. 209–213). New York: Teacher College Press.

Bogdan, R., & Taylor, S. J. (1987b, Fall). Toward a sociology of acceptance: The other side of the study of deviance. *Social Policy,* 34–39.

Braddock, D., Hemp, R., Fujiura, G., Bachelder, L., & Mitchell, D. (1989). *Third national study of public spending for mental retardation and developmental disabilities* (3rd ed.: FY 1977–1988). Chicago, IL: University Affiliated Facility in Developmental Disabilities.

Bronston, W. (1980). Matters of design. In T. Appoloni, J. Cappuccilli, & T. P. Cooke (Eds.), *Toward excellence: Achievements in residential services for persons with disabilities* (pp. 1–17). Baltimore: University Park Press.

Brown, L., Ford, A., Nisbet, J., Sweet, M., Donnellan, A., & Grunewald, L. (1983). Opportunities available when severely handicapped students attend chronological age appropriate regular schools. *Journal of the Association for the Severely Handicapped,* 8(1), 16–24.

Bruininks, R. H., Thurlow, M., & Steffans, K. (1988). Follow-up of students after school in a suburban special education district: Outcomes for people with moderate to severe handicaps. Minneapolis: University of Minnesota, Institute on Community Integration.

Center on Human Policy. (1987). *Families for all children.* Syracuse, NY: Author.

Center on Human Policy. (1989a). *From being in the community to being part of the community: Summary of the proceedings of a leadership institute on community integration for people with disabilities.* Syracuse, NY: Author.

Center on Human Policy. (1989b). *Summary of proceedings of a national policy institute on community living for adults.* Syracuse, NY: Author.

Conroy, J., Efthimiou, J., & Lemanowicz, J. (1982). A matched comparison of institutionalized and deinstitutionalized mentally retarded clients. *American Journal of Mental Deficiency, 86,* 581–586.

DeJong, D. (1979). *The movement for independence: Origins, ideology and implications for disability research.* East Lansing, MI: University Center for Instructional Rehabilitation, Michigan State University.

Ferguson, P. (1988). *Abandoned to their fate: A history of social policy and practice toward severely retarded people in America, 1820–1920.* Unpublished doctoral dissertation, Syracuse University, Syracuse, New York.

Hitzing, W. (1980). ENCOR and beyond. In T. Appoloni, J. Cappuccilli, & T. P. Cooke (Eds.), *Towards excellence: Achievements in residential services for persons with disabilities* (pp. 71–93). Baltimore: University Park Press.

Hitzing, W. (1987). Community living alternatives for persons with autism and severe behavior problems. In D. J. Cohen & A. Donnellan (Eds.), *Handbook of autism and pervasive developmental disorders* (pp. 396–410). New York: John Wiley & Sons.

Homeward Bound v. Hissom Memorial Center, CA 85-C-437-E (N.D. Okla. 1987).

Knoll, J., Covert, S., Osuch, R., O'Connor, S., & Blaney, B. (1990). *Family support services in the United States: An end of the decade status report.* Cambridge, MA: HSRI.

Lakin, K. C. (1988). *An overview of the concept and research on community living.* Paper presented at the Leadership Institute on Community Integration for People with Developmental Disabilities, Washington, DC.

Landesman-Dwyer, S., Sackett, G. P., & Kleinman, J. A. (1980). Small community residences: The relationship of size to resident and staff behavior. *American Journal on Mental Deficiency, 85,* 6–18.

Lippert, T. (1987). *The case management team: Building community connections.* St. Paul, MN: Metropolitan Council.

Mangan, T., Blake, E. M., Prouty, R. W., & Lakin, K. C. (1994). *Residential services for persons with mental retardation and related conditions: Status and trends through 1993.* Minneapolis: University of Minnesota, Research and Training Center on Residential Services and Community Living, Institute on Community Integration (UAP).

McCormick, M., Balla, D., & Ziegler, E. (1975). Resident-care practices in institutions for retarded persons: A cross-institutional cross-cultural study. *American Journal of Mental Deficiency, 80,* 1–17.

National Association for Superintendents of Public Residential Facilities for the Mentally Retarded (NASPRFMR). (1974). *Contemporary issues in residential programming.* Washington, DC: President's Committee on Mental Retardation.

Nirje, B. (1969). The normalization principle and its human management implications. In R. Kugel & W. Wolfensberger (Eds.), *Changing patterns in resi-*

dential services for the mentally retarded. Washington, DC: President's Committee on Mental Retardation.

Nirje, B. (1976). The normalization principle. In R. Kugel & A. Shearer (Eds.), *Changing patterns in residential services for the mentally retarded* (rev. ed.). Washington, DC: President's Committee on Mental Retardation.

O'Brien, J. (1994). Down stairs that are never your own: Supporting people with developmental disabilities in their own homes. *Mental Retardation, 32*(1), 1–6.

Payne, J. S., & Patton, J. R. (1981). *Mental retardation.* Columbus, OH: Charles E. Merrill.

Perrin, B., & Nirje, B. (1985). Setting the record straight: A critique of some frequent misconceptions of the normalization principle. *Australia and New Zealand Journal of Developmental Disabilities, 11*(2), 69–74.

Racino, J. A., Rothenberg, K., Shoultz, B., Taylor, S. J., Traustadottir, R. (1988). *The service system's hidden places: Adult homes and room and board homes.* Syracuse, NY: Center on Human Policy, Syracuse University.

Racino, J. A., Walker, P., O'Connor, S., & Taylor, S. J. (1992). *Housing, support, and community: Choices and strategies for adults with disabilities.* Baltimore: Paul H. Brookes.

Rotegard, L. L., Bruininks, R. H., & Krantz, G. C. (1984). State operated facilities for people with mental retardation: July 1, 1978–July 30, 1982. *Mental Retardation, 22,* 69–74.

Schalock, R. L. (1983). *Services for developmentally disabled adults.* Baltimore: University Park Press.

Smull, M., & Bellamy, T. (1990). Community services for adults with disabilities. In L. Meyer, C. Peck, & L. Brown (Eds.), *Critical issues in the lives of people with disabilities.* Baltimore: Paul H. Brookes.

State of New York Office of Mental Retardation and Developmental Disabilities. (1987). *Strengthening the continuum 1987–1990.* Albany, NY: Author.

Taylor, S. J. (1988). Caught in the continuum: A critical analysis of the principle of the least restrictive environment. *Journal of the Association for Persons with Severe Handicaps, 13*(1), 45–53.

Taylor, S. J., Biklen, D., & Knoll, J. A. (Eds.). (1987). *Community integration for people with severe disabilities.* New York: Teachers College Press.

Taylor, S. J., Bogdan, R., & Lutfiyya, Z. M. (in press). *The variety of community experience: Qualitative studies of family and community life.* Baltimore: Paul H. Brookes.

Taylor, S. J., Lakin, K. C., & Hill, B. K. (1989). Permanency planning for children and youth: Out-of-home placement decisions. *Exceptional Children, 55*(6), 541–549.

Taylor, S. J., Racino, J. A., Knoll, J. A., & Lutfiyya, Z. (1987). *The nonrestrictive environment: On community integration for people with the most severe disabilities.* Syracuse, NY: Human Policy Press.

Taylor, S. J., & Searl, S. J. (1987). The disabled in America: History, policy, and trends. In P. Knoblock (Ed.), *Understanding exceptional children and youth* (pp. 5–64). New York: Little, Brown.

Turnbull, R., Ellis, J. W., Boggs, E. M., Brookes, P. O., & Biklen, D. P. (Eds.). (1981). *Least restrictive alternatives: Principles and practices.* Washington, DC: American Association on Mental Deficiency.

Warren, C. A. B. (Ed.). (1981). New forms of social control: The myth of deinstitutionalization. *American Behavioral Scientist, 24*(6), 721–846.

Wehman, P. (Ed.). (1993). *The ADA mandate for social change.* Baltimore: Paul H. Brookes.

Wilcox, B. (1987). Why a new curriculum? In B. Wilcox & G. T. Bellamy (Eds.), *A comprehensive guide to the activities catalog* (pp. 1–10). Baltimore: Paul H. Brookes.

Wolfensberger, W. (1972). *The principle of normalization in human services.* Toronto: National Institute on Mental Retardation.

Wolfensberger, W. (1983). Social role valorization: A proposed new term for the principle of normalization. *Mental Retardation, 21,* 234–239.

Wyatt v. Stickney, 344 F. Supp. 373, 387, 396 (M.D. Ala. 1972).

Zettel, J. J., & Ballard, J. (1982). The Education for All Handicapped Children Act of 1985 (P.L. 94–142): Its history, origins, and concepts. In J. Ballard, B. A. Ramirez, & F. J. Weintraub (Eds.), *Special education in America: Its legal and governmental foundations* (pp. 11–22). Reston, VA: Council for Exceptional Children.

SECTION TWELVE

ADULT SERVICES— EMPLOYMENT

An area of concern receiving increasing attention is what happens to the student after the completion of school-based learning. In Chapter 23, Wehman argues forcefully that the goal should be to provide opportunities for competitive employment in real jobs within the mainstream of community life for all persons with disabilities. He reviews the history of the growing movement in the United States to do this. Wehman goes on to discuss supported employment as a way to accomplish the goal of real jobs and work for all. Finally, he provides a review of the research literature and what it tells us about supported employment.

Lam, in Chapter 24, states that offering supported employment to people with disabilities has been one of the most important developments in providing employment options. However, he believes that the question, Is supported employment for everybody? should be seriously considered. He personally advocates for a continuum of service options for employment with supported employment being one option. Lam also states that for persons with severe disabilities who need a more extensive work schedule (more hours), a sheltered workshop program may meet their needs better than supported employment.

CHAPTER 23

Supported Employment:
Inclusion for All in the Workplace

PAUL WEHMAN

INTRODUCTION

There was a time in the not too distant past when people with severe disabilities did not participate in the nation's competitive labor force. Those that did were traditionally involved in sheltered workshops, adult activity centers, or assumed lengthy stays in prevocational training programs. Previous thinking was that people labeled with severe mental retardation, autism, severe cerebral palsy, deafness-blindness, and other severe disabilities could not possibly work in competitive employment. Real work seemed to be outside the realm of possibility for tens of thousands of people who remained at home, lived in institutions, or sat in large segregated day programs of which there are, even today, over 7,000. Beginning in the 1970s, however, behavioral training technologies emerged and began to demonstrate a way in which people with severe intellectual disabilities could achieve vocational competence. Pioneering researchers such as Marc Gold and Tom Bellamy were able to show consistently that intellectually and behaviorally challenged individuals who were nonambulatory could complete challenging vocational tasks such as putting together electronic circuit boards when given systematic training and instruction.

As this behavioral technology developed, a new group of researchers began to investigate ways to expand the range of involvement for people with severe intellectual and physical disabilities in the competitive workplace. This was an important change in thinking since in the 1970s the emphasis was clearly on vocational training, not placement followed by training. Early on it was clear that a nonverbal individual with an IQ of 25 or a person with a high rate of head banging who was labeled autistic could not simply be put alone into a business or industry. This person would obviously fail. In fact, such thinking had never been seriously considered because at face value it appeared ridiculous.

However, as the 1970s drew to a close and the 1980s were ushered in, a new way of providing services began to emerge called *supported employment*. This service technology was as complicated to implement as it was simple in principle. The basic notion that we at Virginia Commonwealth University and others began to develop (Wehman, Sales, & Parent, 1992; Wehman, 1981) was the use of a trained staff person who would accompany the person with severe disability into a paid placement in the workplace. There was no negative outcry from business and industry and individuals with disabilities welcomed the opportunity to try a real job. The greatest challenge, as this technology spread, was to encourage service providers and local programs in the community to critically reexamine their practices and reevaluate what they were doing. It became increasingly clear that many of the dollars that were going to support services for people in segregated day programs would need to be reallocated into supporting job coaches to work with people in the community.

It is important for those of us who work to solve today's problems in supported employment to look carefully at what has been accomplished over the past ten years. The standard of service a decade ago was for a person with a severe disability to enter some type of adult day program; that is, to get off a waiting list and gain day services. There has been a rapid change of philosophy toward placement into competitive employment, which has been enhanced because of and would not have occurred without a supported employment technology.

CHARACTERISTICS OF SUPPORTED EMPLOYMENT

What, then, is supported employment? What features are indigenous to every supported employment program? At a minimum, pay for real work, integrated work settings, and usually some degree of ongoing support are essential. Today, increasing numbers of students with severe disabilities are graduating from school and looking for paid employment. From research, we know that these students can perform jobs that involve difficult tasks.

Encouraged by both current research and experience gained from access to education, parents, advocates, and people with disabilities have raised their expectations for the future. Yet many community programs still only offer to get students "ready" for work, while too few actually provide the assistance students need to get and keep a job.

Supported employment is defined as paid employment for persons with developmental disabilities for whom competitive employment at or above the minimum wage is unlikely and who, because of their disabilities, need ongoing support to perform their work. Support is provided through activities such as training, supervision, and transportation. Supported employment is conducted in a variety of settings, particularly worksites in which persons without disabilities are employed.

Six important features of supported employment programs help to explain how they differ from a traditional service approach.

1. *Employment.* The purpose of these programs is employment with all the regular outcomes of having a job. Wages, working conditions, and job security are key considerations.
2. *Ongoing support.* The focus is on providing the ongoing support required to get and keep a job rather than on getting a person ready for a job sometime in the future.
3. *Jobs not services.* Emphasis is on creating opportunities to work rather than simply providing services to develop skills.
4. *Full participation.* People with severe disabilities are not excluded. The assumption is that all persons, regardless of the degree of their disability, have the capacity to undertake supported employment if appropriate ongoing support services can be provided.
5. *Social integration.* Contact and relationships with people without disabilities who are not paid caregivers are emphasized. Social integration with co-workers, supervisors, and others can occur at work, near work, during lunchtimes or breaks, or during nonwork hours as a result of wages earned.
6. *Variety and flexibility.* Supported employment does not lock people into one or two work options. It is flexible because of the wide range of jobs in the community and the many ways of providing support to individuals in those jobs.

A hallmark in human services during the 1980s and 1990s has been increasing inclusion of children and youths with disabilities into schools and classrooms with nondisabled peers. The underlying philosophy behind this move away from segregation has been to offer opportunities for access to normal activities in environments in which these is no stigma attached.

With the advent of supported employment programs, integration in the workplace and paid work became the gold standard of adult services. Pay levels, work conditions, and amount of hours worked quickly became relatively easy to evaluate in terms of attractiveness. Integration, that is, opportunities to interact with and work with nondisabled co-workers, has not been such an easy aspect to assess. The nature of the work tasks, the work schedule, and difficulty in observing crowded work environments has made vocational integration challenging for job developers and supported employment specialists.

If the 1980s were an exciting and stimulating period of development for supported employment, it is only fair to ask, What do the present and future hold? First, as was noted above, a new standard has been established for adult services. No longer is simply entering and receiving day program services sufficient. These day programs are dead-end psychological ghettos for individuals who are stigmatized by these types of congregated placements. Families, consumers with disabilities, and advocates alike are rightfully asking for real jobs. The second area in which tremendous progress has been made is the amount of participation that has occurred over the short period from 1985 to 1990. This period has witnessed a growth of from less than 10,000 people with severe disabilities in supported employment to now over 75,000 (Wehman, Kregel, & Shafer, 1991). Furthermore, we are finally seeing people with disabilities other than mental retardation being involved.

A third area of growth and progress that we can look back upon favorably is that all fifty states now have established supported employment programs. Families also have a greater likelihood than they did five to ten years ago of helping their adult child with severe disability gain a real job. Finally, there continues to be a growing level of interest in and greater calls for participation, particularly from people with traumatic brain injury, sensory impairment, and physical disabilities, as well as families of young people who are leaving school and are looking for a job for the first time. Also included in this request for services are minorities with disabilities, perhaps the most underserved group of all.

SUPPORTED EMPLOYMENT: MAJOR AREAS OF NEED FOR THE 1990s

What then do we have to look forward to as we come into the 1990s, given the progress that has been made to date? First, fewer than 10 percent of

all individuals currently participating in supported employment have physical disabilities, traumatic brain injury, autism, or sensory impairment. Hence, expanding opportunities for underserved or unserved populations of severe disabilities is one major need.

A second area of need that needs to be further developed is the expansion of alliances with business and industry, particularly in light of the implementation of the Americans with Disabilities Act (Wehman, 1992). Also, business will need to take greater responsibility in establishing reasonable accommodation and nondiscriminatory hiring practices. The need for job coach liaison with natural business support is stronger than ever.

A third area that was discussed heavily in the late 1980s, but in which very little progress has been made, is the area of long-term funding. A major nemesis of many well-established programs, which prevents more people with disabilities from gaining access to services, is the lack of ongoing support dollars to help maintain the covenant that is made with business on initial hiring.

Fourth, we must continue to improve our ways of delivering technical assistance to those local programs converting to supported employment, that are recruiting and training new job coaches, or that need help with new populations. Training and technical assistance is very high on future issue needs since the technology is of little value if it cannot be broadly delivered. Consider comments made at the National Conference of State Legislatures by the Task Force on Developmental Disabilities (National Association of Developmental Disabilities Council, 1990).

Despite the advantages of supported employment, the bulk of state employment funds for persons with disabilities still goes to sheltered workshops and other segregated settings. In 1988, federal and state governments spent between $385 and $582 million to place 109,899 people with developmental disabilities in sheltered workshops at a per capita rate between $3,500 and $5,300. In the same year, only $62 million was spent on 16,458 people in supported employment, at a per capita rate of $3,767. The challenge facing state legislators is to develop methods to transfer people currently in day programs and sheltered workshops into the competitive work force successfully. (p. 28)

Finally, we must reach out to the consumers and their families to study choice and self-determination processes in the context of vocational planning. The need for informal choice in supported employment programs on the part of consumers is a paramount concern.

SUPPORTED EMPLOYMENT: WHAT THE RESEARCH LITERATURE TELLS US

The section that follows reviews the literature on supported employment. One cannot help but be impressed with the tremendous growth of research in the past ten years in this area.

Development and Implementation of Individual Client Interventions

The first category of literature to be reviewed is by far the most substantial. Many papers and articles have been written since the late 1970s about how to provide supported employment intervention for clients with severe disabilities. In developing this review, primarily papers that provided data were included and presented in a chronological time sequence.

Sowers, Thompson, and Connis (1979) developed a Food Service Vocational Training Program at the University of Washington. This program demonstrated clearly that with intensive job training and an extensive on-the-job follow-along, many persons with mental retardation who were currently in workshops could successfully work in competitive employment. The outcome data from this program indicated that not all of the trainees who entered the program were trained and placed successfully. The authors raised the issue of identification of those individuals who are most likely to succeed in a training-for-placement program. Their data indicated that measured intelligence (IQ) was not a useful indicator of success for those whose IQs were above 40 and that poor attitude behaviors were more important.

Concurrent with the Sowers et al. study, Wehman, Hill, and Koehler (1979) reported on a job placement and training program that describes three case studies of individuals with severe developmental disabilities. None of these individuals had worked competitively before. It is in this early paper that the concept of a trainer-advocate being available regularly was outlined as a helpful intervention. In addition to this paper, Wehman and Hill (1980) edited a multi-article volume that reported a number of demonstrations and studies involved with helping put people with severe developmental disabilities into competitive employment using supported employment. The Wehman and Hill volume focused extensively on a "place, train, and follow" along approach.

In 1982, Wehman, Hill, Goodall, Cleveland, Brooke, and Pentecost published one of the first definitive papers documenting three-year outcomes of a supported employment program that focused exclusively on individual placements. This paper described a training and advocacy approach, that is, supported employment that involved client training by the staff at the job site. A total of sixty-three clients were placed, with forty-two working at the time of the report for a placement rate of 67 percent. Wehman et al. reported that clients earned $265,000, and paid over $26,000 in state and federal taxes. The significance of this paper is that it was the first large study that described the follow-along approach of supported employment with clients who had been viewed by professionals and parents alike as "realistically unemployable."

Three years later Wehman, Hill, Hill, Brooke, Ponder, Pentecost, Pendleton, and Brit (1985) published a follow-up paper on individuals with mental retardation that had been working competitively for a six-year period. A total of 167 clients with a median level measure intelligence of 49 had been in competitive employment using the identical model described in the Wehman Hill, Koehler (1979) and the Wehman et al. (1982) paper. Over one million dollars were earned during the six-year period by clients, with the average length of time on a job for all clients being nineteen months. For most clients this was their first real job.

In another study involving the teaching of janitorial skills in a competitive work setting, Test, Grossi, and Keul (1988) examined the use of supported employment in a competitive work environment for a nineteen-year-old student with severe retardation. The job training involved teaching complex janitorial skills and consisted of a combination of total task presentation and an individualized prompting hierarchy. A multiple baseline of cross-behavior design was employed across the three sets of behaviors—emptying trash cans, detail cleaning, and daily cleaning. In yet another report of persons with severe retardation, Wehman, Hill, Wood, and Parent (1987) report the competitive employment experiences of twenty-one individuals with IQs of under 40. Over an eight-year period from 1978 to 1986, twenty-one persons were competitively employed with ongoing or intermittent job sites in competitive employment. A cumulative total of over $230,000 was earned. Significant vocational problems included slow work rate and lack of appropriate social skills (e.g., behavior problems).

It was in this general time frame of 1985 to 1990 that more sophisticated discussion papers began to emerge. For example, Nisbet and Hagner (1988) examined the importance of natural supports in the workplace. They strongly suggested that less intrusive ways of supporting clients at the job should be created; that is to say that the use of agency-sponsored job coaches should not be viewed as the exclusive or primary mode of providing support. Berg, Wacker, and Flynn (1990) wrote extensively on generalization and maintenance of work behavior, particularly in the context of supported employment. They have been major contributors in this area (Wacker, Fromm-Steege, Berg, & Flynn, 1989). In similar fashion to the Nisbet and Hagner (1988) paper, Buckley, Mank, and Sandow (1990) also began, in greater detail, to talk about the varied types of support strategies. For example, they indicated that support strategies could be classified into three categories. The first

involves structurally oriented strategies that directly involve the individual with disabilities. The second set of strategies is aimed at increasing co-worker and supervisor involvement. The third set of strategies is directed toward parent advocates and other service providers.

As a follow-up to the earlier Wehman et al. (1987) article on looking at outcomes for people with severe retardation, Wehman and Kregel (1990) undertook a much larger analysis of 109 persons with severe and profound mental retardation. The mean age of the group was twenty-eight years old and mean intelligence (Standford-Binet) was 30. The data were drawn from over ninety local community programs in the United States, and results indicated that all persons were in supervised residential situations. A total of 93 percent were competitively employed with the mean wage being $3.63 per hour and the mean work week being 22 hours. After twelve months of placement, 81.5 percent of the clients were still employed.

Kregel & Wehman (1989) also undertook perhaps the largest investigation of the characteristics of over 1,400 individuals with severe and profound disabilities who were involved in supported employment in eight states. Results indicated that individuals currently participating in supported employment possessed very limited previous employment experience yet did not possess functional characteristics indicative of individuals with severe or profound disabilities. Persons with severe/profound disabilities were found to be minimally represented in current supported employment efforts representing less than 8 percent of all individuals investigated. When one begins to look carefully at the supported employment outcomes for persons with severe retardation, it becomes abundantly clear that as the 1989 and 1990 papers indicated, the actual participation level in supported employment is much lower than it might be. Undoubtedly this is because of the greater skills required on the part of job coaches to place individuals with severe and profound mental retardation as well as the substantial cost involved.

The late 1980s also showed an increasing interest in studying social integration and the role of co-workers. For example, McNair and Rusch (1992) developed a co-worker instrument to assess levels of friendship and helping in the workplace. At the same time, Parent, Kregal, and Wehman (1992) were validating a Vocational Integration Index.

The above papers, for the most part, are definitely not sophisticated and do not provide stringent experimental controls or even control groups. They are aggregate demonstrations with a heavy reliance on descriptive data presentation. Generally speaking, the sample sizes are small and subsequently the ability to make definitive extrapolations is very limited. On the other hand, the population that has participated in these supported employment programs historically has never been in competitive employment and has only been in sheltered workshops, day care programs, or on waiting lists. It is reasonable to assume that with such a large number of demonstrations, even with the inability to carefully document replicable procedures and the incumbent subject selection bias, supported employment has made a significant difference in the lives of people who traditionally would not be in an integrated workplace.

Benefits and Costs Associated with Supported Employment Programs

Another question frequently asked about supported employment is, What will it cost? From the beginning of the development of supported employment programs this has been a concern. Although the benefits, monetary and otherwise, have been readily acknowledged by many, the costs involved in developing supported employment programs has varied considerably. However, some studies have looked at costs and benefits.

For example, in one of the early studies, Hill and Wehman (1983) presented an analysis of cost incurred and tax money saved over an approximate four-year period through the implementation of an ongoing supported employment program.

The focus of this analysis was on the amount of money saved rather than on the wages earned by workers with moderate and severe mental retardation. Factors in the cost analysis included the number of months a client had been working, the amount of staff hours expended on the client at the job site, the amount of funds expended proportionally to each client, SSI income saved, and the estimated cost of day programming for the client if no job placement had been made. After almost four years, the public's cumulative savings totaled $620,576 with expenditures being $530,000 and clients' cumulative earnings over half a million dollars.

An extension of this report was completed by Hill, Wehman, Kregel, Banks, and Metzler in 1987 by extending the analysis to eight years. It was found that the positive financial consequence accrued to the public was over one million dollars. Since the study extended over eight years, all figures were corrected for inflation and discounted to 1986 dollars. Individual analysis revealed that all clients benefit financially from the program and that substantial savings to taxpayers resulted from the utilization of a supported employment model.

Echoing the positive benefits associated with supported employment is a telling paper by Noble and Conley (1987). They indicated that evidence of the benefits and costs of supported employment were growing rapidly. Their biggest caveat was that there was a lack of definitive data collected in controlled experimental studies. Heal, McCaughrin, and Tines (1989) also argued about the methodological pitfalls of benefit–cost analysis for supported employment programs. They indicated concern related to logic, omission, and impression of the data. Beale et al. (1989) reported ranges of their data from Illinois indicating similar conclusions to the Hill et al. (1987) paper, but significantly reducing the certainty that taxpayers would definitively benefit from supported employment programming. The group from Illinois also published recently a longer version (over five years) benefit–cost data analysis from supported employment in that state (McCaughrin, Ellis, Rusch, & Heal, 1993).

In related papers associated with cost, Kregel, Hill, and Banks (1988) did an in-depth analysis of employment specialist intervention time for first jobs of fifty-one clients with moderate and severe retardation. This analysis has importance because it focused on the amount of staff intervention time provided as a percentage of the total number of hours worked by the client each week, and compared the amount of intervention time provided to two subsamples. Results from this study indicated that clients previously classified as moderately to severely mentally retarded did not require a significantly greater amount of intervention time than those who were previously classified as borderline or mildly retarded during the first year of employment.

The astute reader will recall that one of the earlier studies reported in this literature review, by Sowers et al., in fact suggested that persons with low IQs would not be able to work competitively or would require tremendous amounts of time to be effective. The Kregel, Hill, and Banks paper cited here provided an eight-year empirical analysis that clearly provided information to the contrary.

Other related papers in the financial and cost analysis area have also been advanced by West, Kregel, and Banks (1990) who studied the likelihood of clients in supported employment receiving fringe benefits. Their study indicated that only 64 percent of supported employees received fringe benefits. Most recently, Sale, Revell, West, and Kregel (1992) reported supported employment fiscal activities from fifty states. Data from a survey of fiscal year 1990 related to supported employment fiscal activity across the United States are presented and sources of different funds are compared to previous years' surveys. Supported employment expenditures grew approximately 19 percent from 1989 to 1990, with nonvocational rehabilitation dollars accounting for over two-thirds of the total state dollars going into supported employment.

It would appear as we move ahead into the 1990s that more and more program-oriented benefit–cost analyses will be necessary on a larger scale in order to determine the cost of intervention, and equally important, the relative importance of benefits and gain versus costs incurred. On a similar level of analysis, it is essential to look within state and across state fiscal aggregates to examine funds expended for supported employment and even more important the source of these funds.

Serving the Underserved and Unserved

A third major area of literature that evolved in supported employment through the 1980s involved isolated and periodic attempts at involving individuals not labeled mentally retarded in supported employment. It is important to remember that in the first six to eight years most supported employment programs involved only those with mild, moderate, and severe mental retardation. However, as it became clear to many that supported employment was an effective alternative to enhancing competitive employment outcomes, people with other disabilities began to try to gain supported employment services for themselves.

Bond (1987) writes that historically vocational rehabilitation for persons with psychiatric disabilities has been ignored and their employment prospects regarded as poor. He identified two models of supported work and transitional employment and summarized vocational research for clients with psychiatric disabilities. In similar fashion, Danley and Anthony (1987) reported what they called the "choose–get–keep" approach to supported employment. This approach attempts to take the place–train model of supported employment and modify it somewhat for people with psychiatric disabilities.

In a recent paper that provided more empirical evidence about supported employment outcomes for people with psychiatric disabilities, McDonald-Wilson, Revell, Nguyen, and Peterson (1991) reported on the outcomes for 212 individuals with psychiatric disability. The findings revealed that the average intervention time for the first fifty-two weeks of placement was ninety-five hours. Food service, custodial jobs, and warehouse work made up over 60 percent of all placements with $4.50 per hour being the average wage for the individual competitive jobs. Job retention was low: only 31 percent remained after twelve months. Bond and McDonel (1991) discussed vocational rehabilitation outcomes for persons with psychiatric disabilities, particularly when a supported employment model was used. To these writers, it was increasingly clear that people with psychiatric impairment can benefit from supported employment.

Supported employment programs have also been utilized with people with severe visual disabilities. Apter (1992) reports that people with severe visual disabilities have had significantly reduced opportunities for obtaining employment or have been employed in jobs that have not matched their abilities. He reported that the Pittsburgh Blind Association established a supported employment program that increased opportunities for competitive employment and that this program had been extremely successful. Griffin and Kendall (1989) also provided a useful discussion on how supported employment can be used and modified for people with visual impairment.

Individuals with physical impairments, particularly those with cerebral palsy, have also received supported employment. West, Callahan, Lewis, Mast, and Meravi (1991) reported positive competitive outcomes of people with severe cerebral palsy after two years. This paper is one of the few data-based reports showing how supported employment can be used to help this group.

Persons with traumatic brain injury have also benefited from supported employment. For example, Wehman, Kreutzer, West, Sherron, Diambra, Fry, Groah, Sale, and Killam (1989) reported on the preinjury/postinjury work histories of twenty persons who had survived severe head injury. All of these persons had a very limited work history postinjury due to the severity of the injury. These problems were reversed once supported employment programs were put into place using an individual placement model. An expanded sample of individuals using a similar model was reported by Wehman et al. (1990). In this paper forty-three persons with severe trau-

matic brain injury were placed into competitive employment with approximately a 70 percent retention rate one year later. This was a group of people who had had extended periods of unconsciousness for up to three months at a time and who faced very debilitating cognitive and physical problems long term.

The results presented in this section provide a small beginning in the right direction for supported employment program development and service delivery models for populations other than people with mental retardation. Many people with other disabilities desire supported employment.

National Survey Data and Policy Analysis

The final area of this literature review involves a brief discussion of a number of the different policy analysis and national survey data papers that have begun to emerge as a result of the national implementation of supported employment programs. One of the earliest papers in this regard, by Kregel, Shafer, Wehman, and West (1989), reported that supported employment for persons with developmental and other severe disabilities has moved rapidly from university-based demonstration projects to the development of comprehensive statewide service delivery systems. In this article was reported a survey of twenty-seven states that receive major systems change grants from the U.S. Department of Education to convert traditional day activity programs to supported employment. This paper reported outcome data from fiscal years 1986 to 1988 in which vocational rehabilitation expenditures approached seventy-five million dollars and obligations from mental health and mental retardation agencies increased by 460 percent. Collectively, over 214 million dollars had been obligated by federal and state agencies for supported employment when this report was published. This amount of money and effort is remarkable indeed considering that less than ten years preceding this time, supported employment was nothing more than a handful of isolated demonstrations scattered around the country.

A follow-up paper by Shafer, Wehman, Kregel, and West (1990) showed that twenty-seven states had received federal supported employment grants. There was an increase of 150 percent (10,000 to 25,000 persons in supported employment demonstration projects) during a three-year period. Furthermore, over 1,400 programs of supported employment were authorized by state agencies during this time. Individual placement options remain prevalent, and the beneficiaries of these services have remained primarily people with mental retardation. Similarly, Shafer, Revell, and Isbister (1991) reported that over a three-year period, 32,000 people were receiving supported employment.

At the same time these studies were occurring, Kiernan, McGaughey, Schalock, Lynch, and McNally (1986; 1991) released a wide-ranging and comprehensive survey of day programs for people with disabilities in the United States. The Kiernan et al. studies looked carefully at the service and closure activity associated with the vocational rehabilitation system for persons with mental retardation and related conditions. They indicated that all by far the largest percentage of people receiving services were labeled as having mild or moderate mental retardation. They further indicated that the addition of supported employment appears to have reduced utilization of sheltered employment as a closure option for those with severe disabilities.

In another paper that looked at national outcome data, West, Revell, and Wehman (1992) showed that from 1986 to 1990 a total of 74,657 supported employment participants were reported by state agencies with over 2,600 provider agencies. While persons with mental retardation continued to be the primary service group, there has been a dramatic increase in the proportion of supported employment participants with mental illness. The availability of extended services funding was found to be limited across a number of disability groups.

CONCLUDING THOUGHTS

Few would argue that in the past decade community integration, supported employment, and self-determination have been the hallmarks of human service rhetoric. Thousands of people with developmental disabilities have returned to their communities from institutions, and thousands more have left sheltered workshops to enter the nations' competitive workforce. Legislation has been crafted such as the Americans with Disabilities Act, the Developmental Disabilities Act, and the Rehabilitation Act Amendments of 1992, for the purpose of promoting community integration, integrated employment, and the opportunity to control one's own destiny.

However, as we enter the middle of this decade, consumers, families, and advocates must ask themselves the following questions: What has actually been accomplished on behalf of adults with developmental disabilities? Have those individuals who want to work in the community been provided sufficient access to supported employment? Are "well-meaning" professionals still keeping adults who would prefer integrated community employment in segregated facilities?

Supported employment has offered many individuals with severe disabilities the opportunities and challenges of a real job in their local communities. In fact, most people who work in the field of rehabilitation would admit that the knowledge available for placing people into competitive employment has greatly increased. Yet there exists a very troubling incongruity between what we know how to do and what actually is occurring. We must examine carefully whether the promises that have been made to consumers with disabilities have been kept.

It is true that all fifty states are participating in supported employment and have shown dramatic increases in the numbers of people who are successfully working. In 1986, the numbers were under 10,000 per year, and, as of 1991, the numbers exceeded 90,000. Although supported employment has expanded as a service, it remains an "add-on" to existing segregated service options. *In fact, there are over a million people, at least, who remain behind in segregated day programs.* Why is this? What impetus will it take for day programs to open their doors and let the consumers who want to leave for work do so?

Day programs must convert to community employment, and consumers must lead the way. If local programs choose not to provide community employment opportunities, then consumers must stand up for themselves. They must demand to choose among a number of different career alternatives that will provide satisfying wages and fringe benefits, suitable working conditions, and opportunities for career advancement.

A reasonable question to ask may be whether consumers would choose to stay in an activity center, sheltered workshop, or at home if given the opportunity to participate in the community. In all likelihood, few people would remain if they were provided the appropriate supports to work competitively. Ask yourself this question: Do you know anyone who wanted to return to an adult activity center after being successfully employed in a real job?

The challenges that face us are many. We must advance a set of national goals and public policy strategies to take supported employment implementation to a higher level. Policies that provide fiscal incentives and agencies that provide supported employment must be developed. And limits must be set on funding levels imposed for day programs that offer primarily segregated services. States will have to set annual goals for including people with severe disabilities in supported employment. Ultimately, we must provide access to community employment for those individuals who want to leave segregated facilities.

REFERENCES

Apter, D. (1992). A successful competitive/supported employment program for people with severe visual disabilities. *Journal of Vocational Rehabilitation, 2*(1), 21–27.

Berg, W. K., Wacker, D. P., & Flynn, T. H. (1990). Teaching generalization and maintenance of work behavior. In F. R. Rusch (Ed.), *Supported employment: Models, methods, and issues.* Baltimore: Paul H. Brookes.

Bond, G. (1987). Supported work as a modification of the transitional employment model for clients with psychiatric disabilities. *Psychosocial Rehabilitation Journal, 11*(2), 55–75.

Bond, G. R., & McDonel, E. C. (1991). Vocational rehabilitation outcomes for persons with psychiatric disabilities: An update. *Journal of Vocational Rehabilitation, 1*(3), 9–20.

Buckley, J., Mank, D., & Sandow, D. (1990). Developing and implementing support strategies. In F. R. Rusch (Ed.), *Supported employment: Models, methods, and issues.* Baltimore: Paul H. Brookes.

Danley, K. S., & Anthony, W. A. (1987). The Choose-Get-Keep approach to supported employment. *American Rehabilitation, 13*(4), 6–9, 27–29.

Griffin, S. L., & Kendall, E. D. (1989). Supported employment for persons with visual impairment or blindness. *Journal of Applied Rehabilitation Counseling, 20*(3), 44–49.

Heal, L. W., McCaughrin, W. B., & Tines, J. J. (1989). Methodological nuances and pitfalls of benefit-cost analysis: A critique. *Research in Developmental Disabilities, 10*, 201–212.

Hill, M., & Wehman, P. (1983). Cost-benefit analysis of placing moderately and severely handicapped individuals into competitive employment. *Journal of the Association for Persons with Severe Handicaps, 8*(1), 30–38.

Hill, M. L., Wehman, P. H., Kregel, J., Banks, P. D., & Metzler, H. M. D. (1987). Employment outcomes for people with moderate and severe disabilities: An eight-year longitudinal analysis of supported competitive employment. *Journal of the Association for Persons with Severe Handicaps, 12*(3), 182–189.

Kiernan, W. E., McGaughey, M. J., Lynch, S. A., Schalock, R. L., & McNally, L. C. (1991, December). *National survey of day and employment programs: Results from state VR agencies.* Boston: Children's Hospital, Training and Research Institute for People with Disabilities.

Kiernan, W. E., McGaughey, M. J., & Schalock, R. C. (1986). *National Employment Survey for Adults with Developmental Disabilities.* Boston: Training and Research Institute for People with Disabilities.

Kregel, J., Hill, M., & Banks, P. D. (1988). Analysis of employment specialist intervention time in supported competitive employment. *American Journal on Mental Retardation, 93*(2), 200–208.

Kregel, J., Shafer, M. S., Wehman, P., & West, M. (1989). Policy development and public expenditures in supported employment: Current strategies to promote statewide systems change. *Journal of the Association for Persons with Severe Handicaps, 14*(4), 283–292.

Kregel, J., & Wehman, P. (1989). Supported employment: Promises deferred for persons with severe disabilities. *Journal of the Association for Persons with Severe Handicaps, 14,* 293–303.

McCaughrin, W. B., Ellis, W. K., Rusch, F. R., & Heal, L. W. (1993). Cost-effectiveness of supported employment. *Mental Retardation, 31,* 41–48.

McNair, J., & Rusch, F. (1992). The Co-worker involvement instrument: A measure of indigenous workplace support. *Career Development for Exceptional Children, 15*(1), 23–26.

MacDonald-Wilson, K. L., Revell, W. G., Nguyen, N., & Peterson, M. E. (1991). Supported employment outcomes for people with psychiatric disability. *Journal of Vocational Rehabilitation, 1*(3), 30–44.

National Association of Developmental Disabilities Council (1990). Forging a new era: The 1990's report on people with developmental disabilities. *Journal of Disability Policy Studies, 1*(4), 15–42.

Nisbet, J., & Hagner, D. (1988). Natural supports in the workplace: A reexamination of supported employment. *Journal of the Association for Persons with Severe Handicaps, 13*(4), 260–267.

Noble, J. H., & Conley, R. W. (1987). Accumulating evidence on the benefits and costs of supported and transitional employment for individuals with severe disabilities. *Journal of the Association for Persons with Severe Disabilities, 12,* 163–174.

Parent, W. S., Kregel, J., & Wehman, P. (1992). *The Vocational Integration Index: A Guide for Rehabilitation Professionals.* Austin, TX: Pro-Ed.

Sale, P., Revell, G., West, M., & Kregel, J. (1992). Achievements and challenges II: An analysis of 1990 supported employment expenditures. *Journal of the Association for Persons with Severe Handicaps, 17*(4), 236–246.

Shafer, M., Revell, G., & Isbister, F. (1991). The national supported employment initiative: A three-year longitudinal analysis of 50 states. *Journal of Vocational Rehabilitation, 1*(1), 9–18.

Shafer, M., Wehman, P., Kregel, J., & West, M. (1990). The national supported employment initiative: A preliminary analysis. *American Journal of Mental Retardation, 95*(3), 316–327.

Sowers, J., Thompson, L. E., & Connis, R. T. (1979). The Food Service Vocational Training Program: A model for training and placement of the mentally retarded. In G. T. Bellamy, G. O'Connor, & O. C. Karan (Eds.), *Vocational Rehabilitation of Severely Handicapped Persons.* Baltimore: University Park Press.

Test, D. W., Grossi, T., & Keul, P. (1988). A functional analysis of the acquisition and maintenance of janitorial skills in a competitive work setting. *Journal of the Association for Persons with Severe Handicaps, 13*(1), 1–7.

Wacker, D. P., Fromm-Steege, G., Berg, W. K., & Flynn, T. H. (1989). Supported employment as an intervention package: A preliminary analysis of functional variables. *Journal of Applied Behavior Analysis, 22,* 429–439.

Wehman, P. (1981). *Competitive employment: New horizons for severely disabled individuals.* Baltimore: Paul H. Brookes.

Wehman, P. (1992). *Achievements and Challenges: A five-year report on the status of the national supported employment initiative, 1986–1990.* Richmond, VA: Virginia Commonwealth University, Rehabilitation Research and Training Center on Supported Employment.

Wehman, P., & Hill, M. (Eds.). (1980). *Vocational Training and Placement of Severely Disabled Persons: Project Employability, Vol. 2, 1980.* Richmond, VA: Virginia Commonwealth University.

Wehman, P., & Kregel, J. (1990). Supported employment for persons with severe and profound mental retardation: A critical analysis. *International Journal of Rehabilitation Research, 13,* 93–107.

Wehman, P., Hill, M., Hill, J., Brooke, V., Ponder, C., Pentecost, J., Pendleton, P., & Britt, C. (1985). Competitive employment for persons with mental retardation: A follow-up six years later. *Mental Retardation, 23*(6), 274–281.

Wehman, P., Hill, M., Goodall, P., Cleveland, P., Brooke, V., & Pentecost, J. (1982). Job placement and follow-up of moderately and severely handicapped individuals after three years. *Journal of the Association for the Severely Handicapped, 7*(2), 5–16.

Wehman, P., Hill, J., Wood, W., & Parent, W. (1987). A report on competitive employment histories of persons labeled severely mentally retarded. *Journal of the Association for Persons with Severe Handicaps, 12*(1), 11–17.

Wehman, P., Hill, J., & Koehler, F. (1979). Placement of developmentally disabled individuals into competitive employment: Three case studies. *Education and Training of the Mentally Retarded, 14*(4), 269–276.

Wehman, P., Kregel, J., & Shafer, M. (Eds.) (1989). *Emerging trends in the national supported employment initiative: A preliminary twenty-seven state analysis.* Richmond, VA: Virginia Commonwealth University, Rehabilitation Research and Training Center on Supported Employment.

Wehman, P., Kreutzer, J., West, M., Sherron, P., Diambra, J., Fry, R., Groah, C., Sale, P., & Killam, S. (1989). Employment outcomes for persons following traumatic brain injury: Preinjury, postinjury, and supported employment. *Brain Injury, 3*(4), 397–412.

Wehman, P., Kreutzer, J., West, M., Sherron, P., Zasler, N., Groah, C., Stonnington, H., Burns, C., & Sale, P. (1990) Return to work for persons with traumatic brain injury: A supported employment approach. *Archives of Physical Medicine and Rehabilitation, 71,* 1047–1052.

Wehman, P., Sale, P., & Parent, W. (1992). *Supported employment: Strategies for integration of workers with disabilities: From research to practice.* Austin, TX: Pro-Ed.

West, M., Callahan, M., Lewis, M. B., Mast, M., & Meravi, A. (1991). Supported employment and assistive technology for individuals with physical impairments. *Journal of Vocational Rehabilitation, 1*(2), 29–39.

West, M., Kregel, J., & Banks, P. D. (1990). Fringe benefits available to supported employment participants. *Rehabilitation Counseling Bulletin, 34*(2), 126–138.

West, M., Revell, W. G., & Wehman, P. (1992). Achievements and challenges I: A five-year report on consumer and system outcomes from the supported employment initiative. *Journal of the Association for Persons with Severe Handicaps, 17*(4), 227–235.

CHAPTER 24

Continuum of Service Options
for Employment

CHOW S. LAM

INTRODUCTION

Offering supported employment options to people with disabilities has been one of the most important developments in rehabilitation (Bellamy, Rhodes, Mank, & Albin, 1988; Rusch, 1990; Wehman & Moon, 1988), and supported employment is now an integral part of rehabilitation service delivery. Many rehabilitation facilities have either added supported employment to their service options or have adopted supported employment as a total program focus (Mank, Buckley, & Rhodes, 1990; Whitehead, Davis, & Fisher, 1989). However, the field still ponders the question, Is supported employment for everybody? This question is similar to that of an infamous one raised by Eysenck (1952): Does psychotherapy work? Some people would say yes and some would say no. Paul (1967) pointed out that the field often asked the wrong question in outcome research. In offering a solution to this problem, Paul suggested that the question should be, "Under what circumstance, with which type of client, using which kind of intervention, would psychotherapy work?" In this chapter, I follow Paul's approach of evaluating program performance to discuss whether supported employment is the choice for all or the extent to which alternatives for employment services may be better for people with disabilities.

My reasons for opposing competitive employment for all (as proposed by Wehman in an earlier chapter) are as follows:

1. Clients with different abilities have different needs and therefore they require a range of employment options to meet the range of their needs.
2. Supported employment alone does not meet all of the needs of all people with disabilities.
3. Clients should have choices and should be allowed to make such choices.

The following paragraphs elaborate my reasons and justify my position.

DIFFERENT ABILITIES AND NEEDS REQUIRE DIFFERENT EMPLOYMENT OPTIONS

Job matching is an integral part of vocational psychology. Parsons (1909), father of the trait-and-factor theory, believed that people have identifiable traits and that occupations demand certain traits. A function of vocational counseling is to facilitate an appropriate job match of the individual with the specific occupation. According to the Minnesota Theory of Work Adjustment, job tenure is contingent on the correspondence between job satisfaction (the job meeting the person's needs) and satisfactoriness (the person meeting the job demands) (Lofquist & Dawis, 1969). A lack of correspondence between either area would cause job termination. A person will quit the job if it does not meet his or her needs. By the same token, a person will get fired if he or she cannot meet the job demands. Based on the above theories, we know that providing only one employment option to people with disabilities would not work. We need a range of employment options to meet different abilities and needs of people with disabilities.

Durand and Neufeldt (1980) and Vash (1977) developed the concept of a continuum of employment options based on the degree of integration with nondisabled persons and job requirements. The highest level of employment is competitive employment followed by supported employment, and then sheltered employment. Lam (1985) defines competitive employment as employment in a community with commensurate remuneration. The worker's performance must conform to the established standards within the business or industry. The requirement of no staff support distinguishes this type of competitive employment from the one proposed by Wehman (Wehman & Kregel, 1984) under the supported employment model.

In defining levels of employment placement for persons with developmental disabilities, Rubinsky (1991) perceives supported employment as consisting of two levels differentiated by the degree of integration with nondisabled persons and with the requirements of the job. The level that provides full integration with nondisabled workers and one-to-one support is known as "individual supported employment," also known as "competitive employment or individualized placement model" (Wehman & Kregel, 1984). Rubinsky (1991) called the other level of supported employment involving minimal integration and close supervision "group supported employment." Within this level, persons with disabilities are provided employment in group situations with full-time supervision. Examples of group supported employment include enclaves, mobile crews, and affirmative industries. According to Rubinsky, sheltered workshops are employment placements that require little interaction with nondisabled individuals and have few job requirements.

Based on the trait-and-factor theory, Rubinsky (1991) hypothesized that different employment levels demand different job requirements. Based on the hierarchy of employment levels, the job requirements of individual supported employment

should be more demanding than those of group supported employment and sheltered employment. Those workers at the individual supported employment level should possess higher vocational aptitudes. To test the first hypothesis, Rubinsky (1991) used the Job Analysis Report Form (JARF), an adapted version of the instrument developed by the Virginia Commonwealth University Rehabilitation Research and Training Center (Moon, Goodall, Barcus, & Brooke, 1986) to identify requirements of sheltered, group supported, and individual supported employment settings.

The JARF identifies requirements of the work environment such as self-initiation of work, strength, endurance, physical mobility, work rate, appearance, communication, degree of social interaction, behavior acceptance range, attention task and perseverance, sequencing of job duties, daily change of routine, reinforcement availability, object discrimination, time, functional reading, and functional math. The sample consisted of seventy-nine jobs held by clients served by eight rehabilitation facilities. Each job was grouped in one of three employment levels according to Rubinsky's definition: (1) sheltered employment (n=30), (2) group supported employment (n=23), and (3) individual supported employment (n=26). Based on rehabilitation staff's ratings on the JARF, a series of one-way ANOVAs were performed in order to evaluate differences in job requirements among the levels of employment. The total score on the JARF was found to differ significantly among the three levels, $F(2,76) = 128.68$, $p < 39.001$, with sheltered employment $M = 20.8$, $SD = 5.2$; group supported employment $M = 33.7$, $SD = 4.6$; and individual supported employment $M = 41.9$, $SD = 5.3$ (the higher the scores, the higher the job demands). Twelve of seventeen items were found significantly different in pairwise comparisons using Tukey's HSD method. The results reveal that job requirements increase as the level of placement becomes more integrated with nondisabled persons.

In testing the second hypothesis that higher employment level requires higher vocational abilities, Rubinsky (1991) studied 108 individuals with developmental disabilities who were evaluated by using the McCarron-Dial Work Evaluation System (MDS) and were placed in one of the three employment levels. Multiple discriminant analysis was used to determine whether three MDS factors (intellectual, sensorimotor, and emotional-coping) could discriminate among the three employment levels. The intellectual factor significantly differentiated among groups, $F (2,104) = 18.44$, $p < .001$. The sensorimotor factor also proved to be a powerful discriminator of employment level, $F (2, 104) = 28.90$, $p < .001$, as was the emotional-coping factor $F (2, 102) = 25.24$, $p < .001$. Thus, persons in sheltered employment groups had less intellectual abilities, lower sensorimotor functioning, and poorer emotional coping than those in group supported employment settings, who in turn were less capable than persons in individual supported employment groups.

Rubinsky (1991) concluded that level of employment was affirmed as a hierarchical construct, based on differing job requirements. The responses to the Job Analysis Report Form clearly support the notion that the requirements of supported employment settings exceed those of sheltered employment. The results further affirmed that persons engaged in different employment levels can be differentiated on the basis of ability measures. In part, this result may explain why more capable individuals tended to be placed in individual supported employment settings, while persons with more severe disabilities remained behind.

In a recent Consensus Validation Conference on "supported employment for people with severe mental retardation," sponsored by the National Institute on Disability and Rehabilitation Research (NIDRR), researchers and practitioners expressed their concerns about the low percentage of individuals with severe mental retardation receiving supported employment services. Over 75,000 individuals with disabilities have gained access to supported employment since 1984, but the primary recipients of supported employment services have been those with mild mental retardation. Data from a 1990 survey show that only 12.2 percent of those served in supported employment are people with severe mental retardation (National Institute, 1993). It seems quite obvious that supported employment, although conceived for individuals with severe mental retardation, is actually more suitable for individuals with mild retardation (see also Lam, 1986). Some persons with severe mental retardation could benefit from supported employment but not all of them. It is going to be a futile effort to force one type of employment on all people with disabilities.

NO ONE PROGRAM CAN MEET ALL THE NEEDS OF ALL PEOPLE WITH DISABILITIES

People, with or without disabilities, have different needs. Work has been one of the most common means to meet human needs. According to Neff (1985), material needs, self-esteem, activity, and respect by others are four universal needs in any kind of work. In a more expanded model, Gay, Weiss, Hendel, Dawis, and Lofquist (1971) identified twenty vocational needs: ability utilization, achievement, activity, advancement, authority, company policies and practices, compensation, co-workers, creativity, independence, moral values, recognition, responsibilities, security, social service, social status, supervision–human relations, supervision–technical, variety, and working conditions. Gay et al. (1971) pointed out that these needs influence individuals' decisions in occupational choice. Given that no one job can meet all needs, it would unreasonable to expect any employment service to do so. However, several needs are particularly salient for supported employment.

The Need for Job Security

Low job retention rate is a major "second generation" concern of supported employment. Jauss, Wacker, Berg, Flynn, and Hurd (1994) asserted that supported employment has proved to be an effective model for placing persons with mental retardation into community-based jobs. Maintaining employment beyond six months, however, continues to be a problem for this population. In a recent review of literature, Fabian (1992) indicated that the job retention rates for people with mental retardation are 66 percent after six months and 33 percent after one year (Kregel, Wehman, Revell, & Hill, 1990). Similar results were reported for persons with chronic mental illness. Based on a survey of 233 supported employment participants with chronic mental illness, Wehman et al. (1990) report a six-month employment retention rate of 66 percent, identical to rates of persons with mental retardation, and a twelve-month retention rate of 59 percent. Fabian and Widefeldt (1989) report a six-month retention rate of 59 percent for a group of individuals with severe mental illness. A lower retention rate was reported by Trotter, Minkhoff, Harrison, and Hoops (1988) who found a four- to six-month retention rate of 35 percent for a smaller supported employment program for people with severe mental illness.

In another longitudinal study, Fabian (1992) studied 249 individuals with severe mental illness. Ninety individuals (36 percent) were placed in supported employment jobs during the time frame under study. In defending the low percentage of referrals in supported employment job placement, Fabian (1992) wrote, "Although 90 job placements represent only 36% of the total number referred to the program, Wehman et al. (1990) also report a 36% job placement rate for all individuals with mental illness referred to supported employment programs in Virginia" (p. 30). Fabian (1992) reported a job retention rate after six months of 59 percent. The largest percentage drop-off rate for the sample occurred in the first month of employment (16 percent) and again at twenty-four months (16 percent), when only 31 percent of the placed group was still working. Fabian (1992) pointed out that such a retention rate is common in supported employment for persons with severe disabilities. She cites a longitudinal supported employment outcome study on 824 individuals characterized as severely disabled, revealing that the twenty-four-month job retention rate is 33.2 percent (Kregel et al., 1990). Based on these results, one can draw the conclusion that only a small fraction (36 percent) of referrals with severe disabilities are placed in supported employment jobs and about 40 percent of them will drop out of employment within a six-month period and only one-third will still be working after twelve months.

Most people often feel that being a nonworker is a sign of "second-class citizenship" and is strongly associated with reduced feelings of personal worth (Neff, 1985). Neff further pointed out that people with disabilities tend to perceive unemployment as a calamity and a disgrace. The low job retention rate among supported employment participants raises the concerns of job security, especially for those who value it. Frequent job turnover also may reduce the participants' self-worth as productive workers. We cannot underestimate the detrimental effects of unemployment or constant fear of unemployment on the individual and his or her family. Persons with disabilities need job security as do we all. For those who want job security, such options should be provided.

The Need for Activity

Feeling productive and keeping busy were essential aspects of work perceived by both persons with disabilities and family members. Often, family members particularly want to see their relative having a work routine and structure. Instead, family members frequently feel frustrated, not knowing what to do with the excessive unsupervised and possibly unsafe free time of their relative. This concern is particularly valid with supported employment because most supported employment placements are part-time jobs (Kiernan, McCaughey, & Schalock, 1986). Thus, many supported employment participants work only two or three days a week, a few hours here and a few hours there. This situation is not a problem when the client prefers shorter working hours and has adequate avocational skills to keep his or her days occupied. However, for clients who need longer working hours with more structure, an alternative employment placement is needed.

One solution for this particular concern is to find employment programs that can provide a longer daily work routine to people with disabilities who value such structure and need it. In a study comparing sheltered and supported employment programs on their effectiveness of providing working hours, Lam (1986) found that sheltered workshop programs provided their clients a more extensive work schedule (more hours) than did the supported employment program, 24.83 hours per week versus 16.17 hours per week. With persons with moderate to severe mental retardation the difference was more profound, 24.67 hours per week versus 15.18 hours per week. Lam recommended that for clients who need this kind of structure, a sheltered workshop program may meet their needs better than a supported employment program.

The Need for Social Interaction with Co-workers

Socialization is a major job outcome and social integration is one of the primary components of supported employment. Studies published during the last five years analyzing outcomes of the national supported employment program initiative revealed that individuals with disabilities were not being successfully integrated into the competitive work environment (Rusch, 1990). Rusch, Chadsey-Rusch, and Johnson (1989) noted that interactions between work trainees and nondisabled personnel are consistently reported far more often with staff trainers than with co-workers. Chadsey-Rusch, Gonzalez, and Tines (1987) found that workers with mental retardation were less likely to engage in non-work-related social interactions than their nondisabled co-workers. Recent evidence suggests that job coaching may, in some instances, actually restrict social integration. Hagner (1989) found that job coaches sometimes brought a human service perspective and a narrow job task focus to work settings and were unaware of, or ignored, the wider culture of workplaces. Further, job coach training can impede the natural social process by which experienced employees teach "the ropes" to new employees and socialize them into the culture of the setting. They can also project the message that some special expertise is required to interact with employees with severe disabilities. Such processes tend to put social distance between supported employees and their fellow employees.

The above concerns lead one to question the true meaning of integration. Merely putting two individuals together is not integration. Integration brings different individuals into free and equal associations in which all are valued. Placing an individual who runs a hundred meters in a hundred seconds with an individual who runs it in ten seconds is not integration because they are not peers. The chasm is so huge that one questions the possibility of forming a valued association. The literature clearly shows that the interaction patterns between nondisabled workers and supported employees generally is not on a free and equal association basis (Chadsey-Rusch, Gonzalez, & Tines, 1987; Rusch, Chadsey-Rusch, & Johnson, 1989). Nondisabled workers seldom invite supported employees for any after work social activities. At times, limited interactions at work are condescending and paternalistic in nature.

Supported employment values social integration and sees it as profitable for persons with severe disabilities to have opportunities to interact with nondisabled people in order to learn or model "normal" behaviors. According to Bandura (1971, 1977), however, for modeling to be effective the modeler and the modelees should be of similar or comparable characteristics. One would question the effectiveness of modeling when the supported employee and the nondisabled worker are extremely dissimilar. Often family members casually mention the difficulty and pain in seeing the lack of societal acceptance of their relative. Also there is concern that persons with disabilities might be socially isolated at work, taken advantage of, or hurt by the comments or actions of co-workers. Although sheltered workshops have been criticized for their segregation, not being accepted is not usually the concern for workers in such settings. On the other hand, the value of integration and mainstreaming in work settings for people with disabilities is still unknown. Some studies showed positive results while others reported otherwise (Bear, Clever, & Proctor, 1991; Szivos-Bach, 1993). People who are interested in this area can refer to other chapters of this book. Once again, for those workers who feel that they are not being accepted or who are socially isolated, other employment service options should be provided.

The Needs of Those Who Are Not Suitable for Supported Employment

Hagner and Murphey (1989) noted that not every client was successful in a supported employment placement. As pointed out previously, only a small proportion of referrals were actually placed in supported employment (Fabian, 1992; Wehman et al., 1990) and more than 60 percent of those placed ended up not keeping the jobs. Thus, it is obvious that other employment service options are needed, especially for people with severe disabilities who are usually excluded from supported employment (Kregel & Wehman, 1989; National Institute, 1993). Rubin and Roessler (1994) suggested that even when the priority is to place people with disabilities in nonsegregated work settings, sheltered workshops must continue to offer stable, structured work opportunities for some individuals with severe disabilities. In a survey of rehabilitation administrators, Whitehead, Davis, and Fisher (1989) found that the majority of facility administrators (83 percent) would like to offer both community placement and extended sheltered work roles. Hence, it would appear that sheltered workshops meet a need for some people with severe disabilities who would not benefit as much from supported employment.

In addition, sheltered workshops are suitable treatment environments for people with severe behavioral problems. Challenging behavior, such as aggression, destruction, severe tantrums, and self-abuse, is a major deterrent to community job success (Hanley-Maxwell, Rusch, & Rappaport, 1989; Shaull & Sabiston, 1990). Theoretically the most effective place in which to change a person's behavior is the problem environment. Locating and securing training sites for people with chal-

lenging behavior in the community, however, is difficult, seemingly because of employers' concerns and rejection (Rubin & Roessler, 1994). Sheltered workshops can circumvent such difficulties. The original intent of sheltered workshops was to provide a protected environment where the person with challenging behavior could experience the stimulation and learning required for work without the competitive factor that would simply add to the psychological trauma previously experienced in normal settings (Rosen, Bussone, Dakunchak, & Cramp, 1993). Disregarding the criticism of sheltered workshops, I personally believe that with changes in operations and philosophy, sheltered workshops can play a major role in serving people with severe disabilities.

CLIENTS SHOULD HAVE CHOICES AND SHOULD BE ALLOWED TO MAKE CHOICES

Brigham (1979) defines choice as "the opportunity to make an uncoerced selection from two or more alternative events, consequences, or responses. By uncoerced, we mean that there are no programmed implicit or explicit consequences for selecting one alternative over the others except for the characteristics of the alternatives themselves" (p.132). Patterson and Curl (1990) express the ethical concerns of choice in supported employment. They point out that although choice has been one of the key components of supported employment services for individuals with psychiatric disabilities (MacDonald-Wilson, Mancuso, Danley, & Anthony, 1989), choice is not always a part of supported employment services for individuals with developmental disabilities. Zirpoli, Hancox, Wieck, and Skarnulis (1989) comment that persons with developmental disabilities and their families have not usually been presented with choices, but with solutions to their problems. The involvement of persons with developmental disabilities in making a vocational choice is often limited to functioning as a token team member in staffing (Hagner & Salomone, 1989). In actual placement choice, O'Brien (1990) indicated that in reality supported employment candidates had a very limited range of options. Supported employment clients were placed in few occupations, mainly in cleaning and custodial (35 percent) and food service (23 percent). These figures suggest that supported employment clients may not be intimately involved in vocational decision making.

Bannerman, Sheldon, Sherman, and Harchik (1990) contend that professionals and treatment staff compromise clients' personal liberties by giving them little or no input into treatment goals, by not acknowledging clients' personal needs and preferences, by not teaching choice making, and by not providing opportunities for choice. Hanley-Maxwell, Szymanski, Parent, and Schriner (1990) commented that current supported employment practices compromise the client's right to self-determination and choice in several subtle forms. They cited restrictions of funding sources, satisfaction of supported employment program goals or accountability needs, and meeting employers' and family members' desires as conflicting factors compromising the client's right to choose. Patterson and Curl (1990), however, cited the arguments in favor of client choice, including the fact that it is guaranteed by legislation (Developmental Disabilities Assistance and Bill of Rights Act, 1979), and that choice better prepares clients to live in the community where individuals are expected to make decisions and choices (Bannerman et al., 1990). Rehabilitation professionals, however, are reluctant to allow clients to choose due mostly to concerns that poor choices on the part of the client could hinder rehabilitation, waste resources, or add to the staff workload.

Several questions can be raised in client choice issues. Who has the right to make a decision that supported employment is the best or only choice for persons with severe disabilities? Do we believe that there should be alternatives in employment services available to persons with disabilities and that these people should be allowed to make their own choices in employment selection? Can clients be allowed to make a choice that they would like to stay in sheltered workshops with their friends? Are they allowed to choose to work in a sheltered

work program with lower hourly wages but longer working hours rather than to work in a supported employment program with higher hourly wages but shorter working hours? If we truly believe the client has the right to choose, then the answers to the above questions should be yes. According to Bannerman et al. (1990), clients at every functional level should be given opportunities to make choices in their residential and work settings. They warned that moral and legal issues arise when the client's right to choose is abridged. If we are truly serving supported employees, then individual choices, desires, and interests should be the primary concern in supported employment practices.

CONCLUSION

As supported employment evolved from a program initiative to a broad-based service option, several issues emerged (Edgar & Levine, 1988; Fabian, 1992; Mank, 1991; Mank, Buckley, & Rhodes, 1990; Nisbet & Callahan, 1987; Olney & Salomone, 1992; Patterson & Curl, 1990). These included job retention rates, social integration and support, client choice, and access to supported employment for persons with severe disabilities. These issues by no means insinuate weaknesses in supported employment, but rather point out concerns and issues in applying supported employment exclusively to every person with a disability. These second generation issues could provide the field a clear picture of future directions of supported employment and serve to "fine tune" the practice.

On the other hand, sheltered workshops, with a long history of serving persons with disabilities, have recently faced scrutiny and criticism. Historically, workshops have been viewed as either transitional or long-term in nature (Wright, 1980). The main purpose of the transitional workshop is to provide a work environment that facilitates an individual's development to a higher level of functioning, with the emphasis on moving the person into the labor market within a specific time frame (Rubin & Roessler, 1994). The long-term workshops intend to provide services for as long as necessary for clients to move on to competitive employment. The original intent of sheltered workshops was to train people with disabilities for competitive employment through remediation of academic deficiency, development of vocational competencies, and treatment of personality maladjustments and behavioral problems. Individuals were expected to progress through a service continuum of prevocational training, vocational training, job placement, and competitive employment. In recent years, sheltered workshops have encountered a considerable degree of criticism, both in terms of their operations and philosophy. The absence of adequate varieties and quantities of work, the predominance of low-paying menial work, and the failure to move clients from workshops into competitive employment are major criticisms (Bellamy, Rhodes, Bourbeau, & Mank, 1986; Greenleigh Associates, 1975; Rusch, Chadsey-Rusch, & Lagomorcino, 1987).

In defending the necessity of sheltered workshops, Rosen, Bussone, Dakunchak, and Cramp (1993) acknowledge the merits of supported employment but point out that "such options (*supported employment,* italics added by this author) do not work equally well for everyone; nor are they generally available. Sheltered workshops

can continue to offer opportunities for a large number of people with disabilities, provided they are able to accommodate to concepts of realistic training and integration" (p. 33). In the same vein, Lam (1986) actually recommended that for clients with severe disabilities who need a more extensive work schedule (more hours), a sheltered workshop program may be better able to meet their needs than a supported employment program. He further pointed out that supported employment may be more appropriate for clients with mild mental retardation. Having both sheltered and supported employment programs available could provide a choice and produce different types of benefits for different individuals. I could not agree more with Shaw's (1987) observation on this controversial topic.

> This vested interest in the supported employment concept tends to encourage an over-zealous approach in attempts to influence the general rehabilitation community. It appears that a more reasonable approach might be to determine ways for supported employment to be integrated into the continuum of available services rather than [to act as] a total replacement. It is not necessary for a new program to be good and to have value, and that the existing programs be bad with no value. (p. 2)

REFERENCES

Bandura, A. (1971). *Psychological modeling: Conflicting theories.* New York: Aldine-Atherton.

Bandura, A. (1977). *Social learning theory.* Englewood Cliffs, NJ: Prentice Hall.

Bannerman, D. J., Sheldon, J. B., Sherman, J. A., & Harchik, A. E. (1990). Balancing the right to habilitation with the right to personal liberties: The rights of people with developmental disabilities to eat too many doughnuts and take a nap. *Journal of Applied Behavior Analysis, 23,* 79–89.

Bear, G. G., Clever, A., & Proctor, W. A. (1991). Self-perception of nonhandicapped children and children with learning disabilities in integrated classes. *Journal of Special Education, 24,* 409–426.

Bellamy, G. T., Rhodes, L. E., Bourbeau, P. E., & Mank, D. M. (1986). Mental retardation services in sheltered workshops and day activity programs:

Consumer benefits and policy alternatives. In F. R. Rusch (Ed.), *Competitive employment: Issues and strategies* (pp. 257–271). Baltimore: Paul H. Brookes.

Bellamy, G. T., Rhodes, L. E., Mank, D. M., & Albin, J. M. (1988). *Supported Employment: A community implementation guide.* Baltimore: Paul H. Brookes.

Brigham, T. A. (1979). Some effects of choice on academic performance. In L. C. Perlmuter & R. A. Monty (Eds.), *Choice and perceived control* (pp.131–142). Hillsdale, NJ: Erlbaum.

Chadsey-Rusch, J., Gonzalez, P., & Tines, J. (1987). *Social ecology of the work place: A study of interactions among employees with and without mental retardation.* Champaign, IL: University of Illinois Transition Institute.

Developmental Disabilities Assistance and Bill of Rights Act, 42 U.S.C. 6001 et seq. (1976 & Supplement III 1979).

Durand, J., & Neufeldt, A. (1980). Comprehensive vocational services. In R. Flynn & K. Wilson (Eds.), *Normalization, socialization and community service.* Baltimore: University Park Press.

Edgar, E., & Levine, P. (1988, January). A longitudinal outcomes study of graduates of special education. *Interchange, 3–5.*

Eysenck, H. J. (1952). The effects of psychotherapy: An evaluation. *Journal of Consulting Psychology, 16,* 319–324.

Fabian, E. S. (1992). Longitudinal outcomes in supported employment: A survival analysis. *Rehabilitation Psychology, 37,* 23–35.

Fabian, E., & Widefeldt, M. S. (1989). Supported employment for individuals with severe psychiatric disabilities: A descriptive study. *Psychosocial Rehabilitation Journal, 13*(2), 53–60.

Gay, E., Weiss, D. J., Hendel, D. D., Dawis, R. V., & Lofquist, L. H. (1971). *Manual for the Minnesota Importance Questionnaire.* Minnesota Studies in Vocational Rehabilitation, No. XXVIII. Minneapolis: University of Minnesota.

Greenleigh Associates, Inc. (1975). *The role of the sheltered workshop in the rehabilitation of the severely handicapped.* New York: Author.

Hagner, D. (1989). *The social integration of supported employees: A qualitative study.* Syracuse, NY: Center on Human Policy.

Hagner, D., & Murphy, S. (1989). Closing the shop on sheltered work: Case studies of organizational changes. *Journal of Rehabilitation, 55*(3), 68–74.

Hagner, D., & Salomone, P. R. (1989). Issues in career decision-making for workers with developmental disabilities. *Career Development Quarterly, 38,* 148–159.

Hanley-Maxwell, C., Rusch, F. R., & Rappaport, J. (1989). A multi-level perspective on community employment problems for adults with mental retardation. *Rehabilitation Counseling Bulletin, 32,* 266–280.

Hanley-Maxwell, C., Szymanski, E. M., Parent, W., & Schriner, K.F. (1990). Supported employment: Revolution, passing fad, or a remake of an old song. *Rehabilitation Education, 4,* 233–246.

Jauss, J. M., Wacker, D. P., Berg, W. K., Flynn, T. H., & Hurd, R. (1994). An evaluation of long-term maintenance in supported employment placements using a hypothesis testing approach. *Journal of Rehabilitation, 60*(1), 52–58.

Kiernan, W. E., McCaughey, M. J., & Schalock, R. C. (1986). *National employment survey for adults with developmental disabilities.* Boston: Children's Hospital, Developmental Evaluation Clinic.

Kregel, J., & Wehman, P. (1989). Supported employment: Promises deferred for persons with severe disabilities. *Journal of the Association for Persons with Severe Handicaps, 14,* 293–303.

Kregel, J., Wehman, P., Revell, W. G., & Hill, M. (1990). Supported employment in Virginia: 1980–1989. In J. Kregel, P. Wehman, & M. S. Shafter (Eds.), *Supported employment for persons with severe disabilities: From research to practice.* Washington, DC: U.S. Department of Education.

Lam, C. S. (1985). *A program evaluation study on employment services for developmentally disabled adults comparing a sheltered workshop program with a supported work program.* Unpublished doctoral dissertation, University of Wisconsin, Madison.

Lam, C. S. (1986). Comparison of sheltered and supported work programs: A pilot study. *Rehabilitation Counseling Bulletin, 30,* 66–82.

Lofquist, L. H., & Dawis, R. V. (1969). *Adjustment to work: A psychological view of man's problem in a work-oriented society.* New York: Appleton-Century-Crofts.

MacDonald-Wilson, Mancuso, L. L., Danley, K. S., & Anthony, W. A. (1989). Supported employment for people with psychiatric disability. *Journal of Applied Rehabilitation Counseling, 20,* 50–57.

Mank, D. (1991). *Natural workplace support approach to transitioning youth with severe disabilities from school to work.* Unpublished manuscript, University of Oregon.

Mank, D., Buckley, J., & Rhodes, L. (1990). National issues for implementation of supported employment. In F. R. Rusch (Ed.), *Supported employment: Models, methods, and issues* (pp. 289–300). Sycamore, IL: Sycamore.

Moon, S., Goodall, P., Barcus, M., & Brooke, V. (1986). *The supported work model of competitive employment for citizens with severe handicaps: A guide for job trainers* (rev. ed.). Richmond, VA: Rehabilitation Research and Training Center, Virginia Commonwealth University.

National Institute on Disability and Rehabilitation Research (1993). *Supported employment for people with severe mental retardation: Consensus statement.* Washington, DC: Author.

Neff, W. S. (1985). *Work and human behavior.* Chicago: Aldine.

Nisbet, J., & Callahan, M. (1988). Achieving success in the integrated workplace: Critical elements in assisting persons with severe disabilities. In S. Taylor, D. Biklen, & J. Knoll (Eds.), *Community integration for people with severe disabilities* (pp. 184–201). New York: Teachers College Press.

O'Brien, J. (1990). Working on: A survey of emerging issues in supported employment for people with severe disabilities. *Perspectives on community building: Discussion report.* Lithonia, GA: Responsive Systems.

Olney, M. F., & Salomone, P. R. (1992). Empowerment and choice in supported employment: Helping people to help themselves. *Journal of Applied Rehabilitation Counseling, 23*(3), 41–44.

Parsons, F. (1909). *Choosing a vocation.* Boston: Houghton Mifflin.

Patterson, J. B., & Curl, R. M. (1990). Ethics education in supported employment preparation. *Rehabilitation Education, 4,* 247–259.

Paul, G. L. (1967). Strategy in outcome research in psychotherapy. *Journal of Consulting Psychology, 31,* 109–118.

Rosen, M., Bussone, A., Dakunchak, P., & Cramp, J. (1993). Sheltered employment and the second generation workshop. *Journal of Rehabilitation, 59*(1), 30–34.

Rubin, S. E., & Roessler, R. T. (1994). *Foundations of the vocational rehabilitation process* (4th ed.). Austin, TX: Pro-Ed.

Rubinsky, S. J. (1991). The use of the McCarron-Dial Work Evaluation System to predict success in sheltered, supported and competitive employment settings. *Vocational Evaluation and Work Adjustment Bulletin, 24,* 129–135.

Rusch, F. (1990). *Supported employment: Models, methods, and issues.* Sycamore, IL: Sycamore.

Rusch, F., Chadsey-Rusch, J., & Johnson, J. (1989). Supported employment: Emerging opportunities for employment integration. In L. Meyer, C. Peck, & L. Brown (Eds.), *Critical issues in the lives of people with severe disabilities.* Baltimore: Paul H. Brookes.

Rusch, F., Chadsey-Rusch, J., & Lagomorcino, T. (1987). Preparing students for employment. In M. E. Snell (Ed.), *Systematic instruction of persons*

with severe handicap. (3rd ed., pp. 471–491). Columbus, OH: Merrill.

Shaull, J. F., & Sabiston, D. (1990). *Supported employment: How to make it work. A professional training seminar.* Los Angeles: Institute for Applied Behavior Analysis.

Shaw, K. J. (1987). Supported employment: The facility perspective. *Commission on Accreditation of Rehabilitation Facilities Newsletter,* p. 2.

Szivos-Bach, S. (1993). Social comparisons, stigma, and mainstreaming: The self esteem of young adults with a mild mental handicap. *Mental Handicap Research, 6,* 217–236.

Trotter, S., Minkoff, K., Harrison, K., & Hoops, J. (1988). Supported work: An innovative approach to vocational rehabilitation of persons who are psychiatrically disabled. *Rehabilitation Psychology, 33,* 27–36.

Vash, C. (1977). *Emerging issues in rehabilitation: Sheltered industrial employment.* Washington, DC: Institute for Research Utilization.

Wehman, P., & Kregel, J. (1984). *A supported work approach to competitive employment of individuals with moderate and severe handicaps.* Richmond: Virginia Commonwealth University, Rehabilitation Research Center.

Wehman, P., & Moon, M. S. (Eds.) (1988). *Vocational rehabilitation and supported employment.* Baltimore: Paul H. Brookes.

Wehman, P., Revell, W. G., Kregel, J., Kreutzer, J., Callahan, M., & Banks, P. D. (1990). Supported employment: An alternative model for vocational rehabilitation of persons with severe neurologic, psychiatric, or physical disabilities. In J. Kregel, P. Wehman, & M. S. Shafter (Eds.), *Supported employment for persons with severe disabilities: From research to practice.* Washington, DC: U.S. Department of Education.

Whitehead, C., Davis, P., & Fisher, M. (1989). The current and future role of rehabilitation facilities in external employment. *Journal of Applied Rehabilitation Counseling, 20*(3), 58–64.

Wright, G. N. (1980). *Total rehabilitation.* Boston: Little, Brown.

Zirpoli, J., Hancox, D., Wieck, C., & Skarnulis, E. R. (1989). Partners in policy-making: Empowering people. *Journal of the Association for Persons with Severe Handicaps, 14,* 163–167.